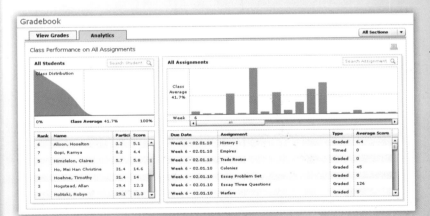

CourseMate

Engaging. Trackable. Affordable.

CourseMate brings course concepts to life with interactive learning, study, and exam preparation tools that support the printed textbook. Watch student comprehension soar as your class works with both the book and the text-specific website. **History CourseMate** goes beyond the page to deliver what you need, with:

Engagement Tracker:

How do you assess your students' engagement in your course? How do you know your students have read the material or viewed the resources you've assigned? How can you tell if your students are struggling with a concept? With **CourseMate**, you can use the included Engagement Tracker to assess student preparation and engagement. Use the tracking tools to see progress for the class as a whole or for individual students. Identify students at risk early in the course. Uncover which concepts are most difficult for your class. Monitor time on task. Keep your students engaged!

Interactive eBook:

In addition to interactive teaching and learning tools, **CourseMate** includes an interactive eBook. Students can take notes, highlight, search and interact with embedded media specific to their book. Use it as a supplement to the printed text, or as a substitute—the choice is your students' with **CourseMate**.

Interactive Teaching and Learning Tools, including:

- Quizzes
- Flashcards
- Videos
- And more!

eAudio *The History Handbook* Podcasts

Carol Berkin and Betty Anderson's **eAudio *The History Handbook* Podcasts** allows students to download podcasts for each chapter of the text! Students will learn both basic and history-specific study skills such as how to read primary sources, research historical topics using print and online sources, and correctly cite sources. In addition to providing a no-nonsense guide to the skills needed in a history course, this handbook also introduces students to the type of questions historians ask and the sources they turn to for answers.

Students can purchase and download the complete eAudio handbook or any of its eighteen individual units to their computer or MP3 player from **CengageBrain.com**. Each 5-15 minute podcast addresses a separate topic designed to develop students' critical thinking and historical analysis skills.

World History Resource Center

This interactive website for World History offers students a wealth of support materials, including:

- **Thousands of live links** to trustworthy online sources
- **Hundreds of primary source materials**, from speeches and letters to legal documents, transcripts, and a variety of digitized original media
- **Online simulations** that actively introduce students to different historical periods and cultural perspectives
- **Interactive timelines** featuring embedded links to pictures of the people, places, and events that shaped particular periods
- **Extensive map resources** from Wadsworth history texts and additional sources—many of which are accompanied by assignable questions and Google Earth™ coordinates

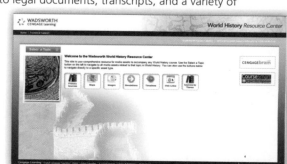

The **World History Resource Center** is the ideal resource for student study, review, and research—and bundled access is free with this text! Ask your sales representative for more information.

The Earth and Its Peoples

A Global History

BRIEF EDITION   FIFTH EDITION

Volume I: To 1550

The Earth and Its Peoples

A Global History

Richard W. Bulliet
Columbia University

Pamela Kyle Crossley
Dartmouth College

Daniel R. Headrick
Roosevelt University

Steven W. Hirsch
Tufts University

Lyman L. Johnson
University of North Carolina–Charlotte

David Northrup
Boston College

WADSWORTH
CENGAGE Learning

Australia • Brazil • Japan • Korea • Mexico • Singapore • Spain • United Kingdom • United States

WADSWORTH
CENGAGE Learning

The Earth and Its Peoples: A Global History, Brief Edition Fifth Edition, Vol. I
Bulliet, Crossley, Headrick, Hirsch, Johnson, Northrup

Senior Publisher: Suzanne Jeans

Senior Sponsoring Editor: Nancy Blaine

Senior Development Editor: Tonya Lobato

Assistant Editor: Lauren Floyd

Editorial Assistant: Emma Goehring

Senior Media Editor: Lisa Ciccolo

Senior Marketing Manager: Katherine Bates

Marketing Coordinator: Lorreen Pelletier

Marketing Communications Manager:
    Caitlin Green

Senior Content Project Manager:
    Carol Newman

Senior Art Director: Cate Rickard Barr

Senior Print Buyer: Judy Inouye

Senior Rights Acquisition Specialist (text):
    Katie Huha

Senior Rights Acquisition Specialist (photos):
    Jennifer Meyer Dare

Production Service: Lachina Publishing Services

Text Designer: Janet Theurer/Theurer Briggs
    Design

Cover Designer: Roycroft Design

Cover Image: Muslim merchants transporting goods by ship, from the so-called Schefer Hariri, 1237 Arabic manuscript, Maqamat, or Assemblies, of al-Hariri, copied and illustrated by al-Wasiti. Arne Hodalic/Corbis Art

Compositor: Lachina Publishing Services

For product information and technology assistance, contact us at
Cengage Learning Customer & Sales Support, 1-800-354-9706

For permission to use material from this text or product,
submit all requests online at **www.cengage.com/permissions**.
Further permissions questions can be emailed to
permissionrequest@cengage.com.

Library of Congress Control Number: 2010932862

Student Edition:
ISBN-13: 978-0-495-91311-5
ISBN-10: 0-495-91311-1

Wadsworth
20 Channel Center Street
Boston, MA 02210
USA

Cengage Learning is a leading provider of customized learning solutions with office locations around the globe, including Singapore, the United Kingdom, Australia, Mexico, Brazil and Japan. Locate your local office at **international.cengage.com/region**.

Cengage Learning products are represented in Canada by Nelson Education, Ltd.

For your course and learning solutions, visit **www.cengage.com**.

Purchase any of our products at your local college store or at our preferred online store **www.cengagebrain.com**.

Printed in Canada
1 2 3 4 5 6 7 14 13 12 11 10

BRIEF CONTENTS

CONTENTS

PART TWO

The Formation of New Cultural Communities, from 1200 B.C.E.   84

GREECE AND IRAN, 1500 B.C.E–500 C.E.   86

INDIA AND SOUTHEAST ASIA, 1500 B.C.E.–1025 C.E.   111

PEOPLES AND CIVILIZATIONS OF THE AMERICAS, 1200 B.C.E.–1500 C.E.   160

NETWORKS OF COMMUNICATION AND EXCHANGE, 300 B.C.E.–600 C.E.   186

PART THREE

Growth and Interaction of Cultural Communities, 600–1200   210

THE RISE OF ISLAM, 600–1200   212

10

CHRISTIAN EUROPE EMERGES, 600–1200   233

11

INNER AND EAST ASIA, 400–1200   259

PART FOUR

Interregional Patterns of Culture and Contact, 1200–1550   284

MONGOL EURASIA AND ITS AFTERMATH, 1200–1500   286

TROPICAL AFRICA AND ASIA, 1200–1500   312

THE LATIN WEST, 1200–1500   332

MAPS

ENVIRONMENT & TECHNOLOGY

ISSUES IN WORLD HISTORY

DIVERSITY & DOMINANCE

MATERIAL CULTURE

When a textbook reaches its fifth edition, the authors feel justified in assessing their work a success. The first edition contained a basic concept. The second used the myriad valuable comments made by teachers and reviewers to make major adjustments in the presentation of that concept. The third and fourth editions incorporated a further round of comments and suggestions aimed at filling lacunae and improving the flow of the exposition. At the same time, pedagogical aids were steadily improved to make the text more accessible to both students and teachers.

Our overall goal in *The Earth and Its Peoples* remains unchanged: to produce a textbook that not only speaks for the past, but speaks to today's students and today's instructors. Students and instructors alike should take away from this text a broad vision of human societies beginning as sparse and disconnected communities reacting creatively to local circumstances; experiencing ever more intensive stages of contact, interpenetration, and cultural expansion and amalgamation; and arriving at a twenty-first-century world situation in which people increasingly visualize a single global community.

Process, not progress, is the keynote of this book: a steady process of change over time, at first differently experienced in various regions, but eventually interconnecting peoples and traditions from all parts of the globe. Students should come away from this book with a sense that the problems and promises of their world are rooted in a past in which people of every sort, in every part of the world, confronted problems of a similar character and coped with them as best they could. We believe our efforts will help students see where their world has come from and learn thereby something useful for their own lives.

Central Themes and Goals of the Text

We have subtitled *The Earth and Its Peoples* "A Global History" because the book explores the common challenges and experiences that unite the human past. Although the dispersal of early humans around the world resulted in many different economic, social, political, and cultural systems, all societies displayed analogous patterns in meeting their needs and exploiting their environments. Our challenge was to select the particular data and episodes that would best illuminate these global patterns of human experience.

To meet this challenge, we adopted two themes to serve as the spinal cord of our history: "Technology and Environment" and "Diversity and Dominance." The first theme represents the commonplace material bases of all human societies at all times. It grants no special favor to any cultural group even as it embraces subjects of the broadest topical, chronological, and geographical range. The second theme expresses the reality that every human society has constructed or inherited structures of domination. We examine practices and institutions of many sorts: military, economic, social, political, religious, and cultural, as well as those based on kinship, gender, and literacy. Simultaneously we recognize that alternative ways of life and visions of societal organization continually manifest themselves both within and in dialogue with every structure of domination.

With respect to the first theme, it is vital for students to understand that technology, in the broad sense of experience-based knowledge of the physical world, underlies all human activity. Writing is a technology, but so is oral transmission from generation to generation of lore about medicinal or poisonous plants. The magnetic compass is a navigational technology, but so is a Polynesian mariner's hard-won knowledge of winds, currents, and tides that made possible the settlement of the Pacific islands.

All technological development has come about in interaction with environments, both physical and human, and has, in turn, affected those environments. The story of how humanity has changed the face of the globe is an integral part of this central theme. Yet technology and the environment do not explain or underlie all important episodes of human experience. The theme of "Diversity and Dominance" informs all our discussions of politics, culture, and society. Thus, when narrating the histories of empires, we describe a range of human experiences within and beyond the imperial frontiers without assuming that the imperial institutions are a more suitable topic for discussion than the economic and social organization of pastoral nomads or the lives of peasant women. When religion and culture occupy our narrative, we focus not only on the dominant tradition but also on the diversity of alternative beliefs and practices.

Changes in the Brief Fifth Edition

We have once again transformed the visual layout of *The Earth and Its Peoples* to keep up with the preferences of today's students. The fifth edition features a bold new two-column design that is more modern and magazine-like in appearance, a reading layout that students have told us they prefer. In addition, every map in the text has been redesigned to be more dynamic and visually engaging. Finally, we have added four more new topics for the feature Material Culture, a student favorite: four-wheeled vehicles, salt, bells, and lamps and candles.

Several changes have been made to the organization of the text to make the narrative more logical and accessible. In **Part Two: The Formation of New Cultural Communities,** we have added a new **Chapter 5: India and Southeast Asia** with material formerly scattered in several places as well as new material from the full edition. Likewise, **Chapter 7: Peoples and Civilizations of the Americas** now contains material on the Olmec and Chavín civilizations, formerly in found Chapter 2. By bringing together the sections on India and Southeast Asia and on the Americas, respectively, we emphasize the continuity of these civilizations.

In **Chapter 15: The Maritime Revolution,** we have brought forward the material on the Columbian Exchange from Chapter 17, on the grounds that the exchange of plants, animals, and diseases began almost immediately after the first maritime contacts between the Eastern and Western Hemispheres.

Finally, we have rewritten **Chapter 29: The Cold War and Decolonization,** bringing the narrative up to 1991 and including new information on the collapse of the Soviet Union. And **Chapter 30: Challenges of the New Century** has been rewritten to reflect long-range trends such as the emergence of China as a great power, new patterns of global migration, the changing environment of the earth, and the nascent global culture and its consequences.

Suggested reading lists have been revised and are available on the textbook website, accessible through cengagebrain.com.

Organization

The brief edition of *The Earth and Its Peoples,* fifth edition, retains the eight broad chronological divisions of previous editions to define its conceptual scheme of global historical development.

In **Part One: The Emergence of Human Communities, to 1500** B.C.E., we examine important patterns of human communal organization. Small, dispersed human communities living by foraging spread to most parts of the world over tens of thousands of years. They responded to enormously diverse environmental conditions, at different times and in different ways discovering how to cultivate plants and utilize the products of domestic animals. On the basis of these new modes of sustenance, populations grew, permanent towns appeared, and political and religious authority, based on collection and control of agricultural surpluses, spread over extensive areas.

Part Two: The Formation of New Cultural Communities, from 1200 B.C.E. introduces the concept of a "cultural community," in the sense of a coherent pattern of activities and symbols pertaining to a specific human community. While all human communities develop distinctive cultures, including those discussed in Part One, historical development in this stage of global history prolonged and magnified the impact of some cultures more than others. In the geographically contiguous African-Eurasian landmass, the cultures that proved to have the most enduring influence traced their roots to the second and first millennia B.C.E.

Part Three: Growth and Interaction of Cultural Communities, 600–1200 deals with early episodes of technological, social, and cultural exchange and interaction on a continental scale both within and beyond the framework of imperial expansion. These are so different from earlier interactions arising from more limited conquests or extensions of political boundaries that they constitute a distinct era in world history, an era that set the world on the path of increasing global interaction and interdependence that it has been following ever since.

In **Part Four: Interregional Patterns of Culture and Contact, 1200–1550,** we take a look at the world during three centuries that saw both intensified cultural and commercial contact and increasingly confident self-definition of cultural communities in Europe, Asia, and Africa. The Mongol conquest of a vast empire extending from the Pacific Ocean to eastern Europe greatly stimulated trade and interaction. In the West, strengthened European kingdoms began maritime expansion in the Atlantic, forging direct ties with sub-Saharan Africa and laying the base for expanded global contacts after 1500.

Part Five: The Globe Encompassed, 1500–1800 treats a period dominated by the global effects of European expansion and continued economic growth. European ships took over, expanded, and extended the maritime trade of the Indian Ocean, coastal Africa, and the Asian rim of the Pacific Ocean. This maritime commercial enterprise had its counterpart in European colonial empires in the Americas and a new Atlantic trading system. The contrasting capacities and fortunes of traditional land empires and new maritime empires, along with the exchange of domestic plants and animals between the hemispheres, underline the technological and environmental dimensions of this first era of complete global interaction.

In **Part Six: Revolutions Reshape the World, 1750–1870,** the word *revolution* is used in several senses: in the political sense of governmental overthrow, as in France and the Americas; in the metaphorical sense of radical transformative change, as in the Industrial Revolution; and in the broadest sense of a perception of a profound change in circumstances and world-view. Technology and environment lie at the core of these developments. With the rapid ascendancy of the Western belief that science and technology could overcome all challenges, technology became not only an instrument of transformation but also an instrument of domination, to the point of threatening the integrity and autonomy of cultural traditions in nonindustrial lands.

Part Seven: Global Diversity and Dominance, 1850–1949 examines the development of a world arena in which people conceived of events on a global scale. Imperialism, world war, international economic connections, and world-encompassing ideological tendencies, like nationalism and socialism, present the picture of a globe becoming increasingly interconnected. European dominance took on a worldwide dimension, seeming at times to threaten the diversity of human cultural experience with permanent subordination to European values and philosophies, while at other times triggering strong political or cultural resistance. The accelerating pace of technological change deepened other sorts of cleavages as well.

For **Part Eight: Perils and Promises of a Global Community, 1945 to the Present,** we decided to divide the last half of the twentieth century into two time periods: 1945 to 1991, and 1991 to the present. Nevertheless, there is a good deal of continuity from chapter to chapter. The challenges of the Cold War, postcolonial nation building, and post–Cold War frictions between different powers and cultures dominate the period and involve global economic, technological, and political forces that become increasingly important factors in all aspects of human life. Technology takes center stage in this part, both because of its integral role in the growth of a global community and because its many benefits in improving the quality of life seem clouded by real and potential negative impacts on the environment.

The brief edition is produced in two formats: A complete edition covers the entire chronology from prehistory to the present, and a two-volume edition can be used for the two-semester survey. Volume I covers the period from prehistory to 1550, and Volume II covers 1500 to the present. There is a brief introduction to Volume II that orients students to the general political and social climate of the world before and up to 1500.

Features and Pedagogical Aids

As with previous editions, the fifth edition offers a number of valuable features and pedagogical aids designed to pique student interest in specific world history topics and help them process and retain key information.

In the fifth edition, as already mentioned, we have included more chapter essays on Material Culture, a feature that calls particular attention to the many ways in which objects and processes of everyday life can help us understand human history on a broad scale. Thus essays like "Wine and Beer in the Ancient World" and "Cotton Clothing" are not only interesting in and of themselves but also suggestive of how today's world historians find meaning in the ordinary dimensions of human life.

The Environment and Technology feature, which has been a valuable resource in all prior editions of *The Earth and Its Peoples,* serves to illuminate the major theme of the text by demonstrating the shared material bases of all human societies across time.

Historical essays for each of the eight parts called Issues in World History were added in the previous edition and were specifically designed to alert students to broad and recurring conceptual issues that are of great interest to contemporary historians; this feature has proved to be an instructor and student favorite.

Finally, Diversity and Dominance, also core to the theme of the text, is the primary source feature that brings a myriad of real historical voices to life in a common struggle for power and autonomy.

Pedagogical aids include the following:

Chapter Opening Focus Questions These questions are keyed to every major subdivision of the chapter through a system of color-coding and serve to help students focus on the core chapter concepts. The unique color-coded system helps students keep track of where they are in the text and easily identify which focus question corresponds to each section of the chapter. The color-coding carries through to the end of each chapter, where the focus questions for each section are answered and summarized.

Section Reviews Short bullet-point reviews appear at the end of each major section in every chapter and remind students of key information.

New Chapter Conclusions Every chapter now ends with a comparative conclusion that will help students synthesize chapter material and understand how it fits into the larger picture.

Key Terms with Definitions Students can handily find definitions for bolded key terms right on the page of the text where the term first appears.

New Icons Throughout each chapter, icons direct students to corresponding online tools, including interactive maps and primary sources.

Chapter Reviews Keyed to the chapter opening focus questions through a system of color-coding, the Chapter Reviews summarize the most important concepts addressed in the chapter, making studying more efficient and effective.

Pronunciation Guide Phonetic spellings for unfamiliar names and terms have been integrated into the text.

Supplements

A wide array of supplements accompanies this text to assist students with different learning needs and to help instructors master today's various classroom challenges.

Instructor Resources

PowerLecture CD-ROM with ExamView® and JoinIn® This dual-platform, all-in-one multimedia resource includes the Instructor's Resource Manual; Test Bank (content developed by Kathleen Addison of California State University, Northridge, and includes key term identification and multiple-choice, short answer, and essay questions); Microsoft® PowerPoint® slides of both lecture outlines and images and maps from the text that can be used as offered or customized by importing personal lecture slides or other material; and JoinIn® PowerPoint® slides with clicker content. Also included is ExamView, an easy-to-use assessment and tutorial system that allows instructors to create, deliver, and customize tests in minutes. Instructors can build tests with as many as 250 questions using up to 12 question types, and using ExamView's complete word-processing capabilities, they can enter an unlimited number of new questions or edit existing ones.

HistoryFinder This searchable online database allows instructors to quickly and easily download thousands of assets, including art, photographs, maps, primary sources, and audio/video clips. Each asset downloads directly into a Microsoft® PowerPoint® slide, allowing instructors to easily create exciting PowerPoint presentations for their classrooms.

eInstructor's Resource Manual Prepared by Sheila Phipps of Appalachian State University. This manual has many features, including instructional objectives, chapter outlines, lecture suggestions, suggested debate and research topics, cooperative learning activities, and suggested online resources. It is available on the instructor's companion website.

WebTutor™ Toolbox on Blackboard® and WebCT® This simplified WebTutor product links directly to the valuable study and assessment tools on the companion website, which includes learning objectives, a glossary, flashcards, crossword puzzles, Internet exercises, interactive quizzing, and web links. Additionally, the WebTutor Toolbox includes the test bank content.

History CourseMate *The Earth and Its Peoples* includes History CourseMate, a complement to your textbook. History CourseMate includes:

- An interactive eBook
- Interactive teaching and learning tools including:
  - Quizzes
  - Flashcards
  - Videos
  - Primary sources
  - Interactive maps
  - and more
- Engagement Tracker, a first-of-its-kind tool that monitors student engagement in the course

Go to login.cengage.com to access these resources, and look for this icon , which denotes a resource available within CourseMate.

Student Resources

The Earth and Its Peoples Website This book-specific website for students features a wide assortment of resources to help them master the textbook subject matter. The website includes a glossary, flashcards, crossword puzzles, learning objectives, interactive quizzing, essay questions, MP3 chapter summaries, an audio pronunciation guide, web links, and more.

Cengagebrain.com This online store saves students time and money by giving them a choice in formats and savings. It is a single destination for more than 10,000 new textbooks, eTextbooks, eChapters, study tools, and audio supplements. Students have the freedom to purchase a-la-carte exactly what they need when they need it. They can save 50 percent on the electronic textbook and can pay as little as $1.99 for an individual eChapter.

Wadsworth World History Resource Center Wadsworth's World History Resource Center gives students access to a "virtual reader" with hundreds of primary sources, including speeches, letters, legal documents and transcripts, poems, maps, simulations, timelines, and additional images that bring history to life, along with interactive assignable exercises. A map feature including Google Earth™ coordinates and exercises will aid in student comprehension of geography and use of maps. Students can compare the traditional textbook map with an aerial view of the location today. It's an ideal resource for study, review, and research. In addition to this map feature, the resource center provides blank maps for student review and testing.

Rand McNally Historical Atlas of the World, 2e This valuable resource features over 70 maps that portray the rich panoply of the world's history from preliterate times to the present. They show how cultures and civilizations were linked and how they interacted. By presenting the dynamics of expansion, cooperation, and conflict, the maps make it clear that history is not static; rather, it is about change and movement across time. This atlas includes maps that display the world from the beginning of civilization; the political development of all major areas of the world; expanded coverage of Africa, Latin America, and the Middle East; the current Islamic world; and the world population change in 1900 and 2000.

Writing for College History, 1e Prepared by Robert M. Frakes, Clarion University. This brief handbook for survey courses in American history, Western civilization/ European history, and world civilization guides students through the various types of writing assignments they encounter in a history class. Providing examples of student writing and candid assessments of student work, this text focuses on the rules and conventions of writing for the college history course.

The History Handbook, 1e Prepared by Carol Berkin of Baruch College, City University of New York, and Betty Anderson of Boston University. This book teaches students both basic and history-specific study skills such as how to take notes, get the most out of lectures and readings, read primary sources, research historical topics, and correctly cite sources. Substantially less expensive than comparable skill-building texts, *The History Handbook* also offers tips for Internet research and evaluating online sources. Additionally, students can purchase and download the *eAudio* version of *The History Handbook* or any of its eighteen individual units at www.cengagebrain.com to listen to on the go.

Doing History: Research and Writing in the Digital Age, 1e Prepared by Michael J. Galgano, J. Chris Arndt, and Raymond M. Hyser of James Madison University. Whether starting down the path as a history major or simply looking for a straightforward and systematic guide to writing a successful paper, students will find this text an indispensable handbook to historical research. Its "soup to nuts" approach to researching and writing about history addresses every step of the process, from locating sources and gathering information to writing clearly and making proper use of various citation styles to avoid plagiarism. Students will also learn how to make the most of every tool available—especially the technology that helps them conduct the process efficiently and effectively.

The Modern Researcher, 6e Prepared by Jacques Barzun and Henry F. Graff of Columbia University. This classic introduction to the techniques of research and the art of expression is used widely in history courses, but it is also appropriate for writing and research methods courses in other departments. Barzun and Graff thoroughly cover every aspect of research, from the selection of a topic through the gathering, analysis, writing, revision, and publication of findings, presenting the process not as a set of rules but through actual cases that put the subtleties of research in a useful context. Part One covers the principles and methods of research; Part Two covers writing, speaking, and getting one's work published.

Reader Program Cengage Learning publishes a number of readers, some containing exclusively primary sources, others a combination of primary and secondary sources, and some designed to guide students through the process of historical inquiry. A complete list of readers is available at Cengage.com/history.

Custom Options Because no one knows students like their teacher, Cengage Learning offers custom solutions for this course—whether it's making a small modification to *The Earth and Its Peoples* to match the syllabus or combining multiple sources to create something truly unique. Instructors can pick and choose chapters, include their own material, and add additional map exercises along with the Rand McNally Atlas to create a text that fits the way they teach. They can ensure that students get the most out of their textbook dollar by giving them exactly what they need. A Cengage Learning representative can help teachers explore custom solutions for this course.

Acknowledgments

We are grateful to the following colleagues who took the time to provide their feedback to help us prepare the fifth edition of *The Earth and Its Peoples*:

Daniel Albert, Salem State College
Steven Berg, Schoolcraft College
Kathryn E. Holland Braund, Auburn University

Ras Michael Brown, Southern Illinois University
Stephen Chappell, James Madison University
Mariana L. R. Dantas, Ohio University
Eric Goldner, California State University, Northridge
Yuxin Ma, University of Louisville
Paul Moore, Tennessee Temple University
Mark R. Munzinger, Radford University
Charles H. Parker, Saint Louis University
Scott Reese, Northern Arizona University
Michael J. Seth, James Madison University
Gregory S. Taylor, Chowan University
Ann Tschetter, University of Nebraska, Lincoln

We also want to extend our thanks to Lynda Schaffer for her early conceptual contributions and to the history departments of Shippensburg University, the United States Air Force Academy, and the State University of New York at New Paltz for arranging reviewer conferences that provided crucial feedback for our revisions.

Our debt to the staff of Cengage Learning remains undiminished in the fifth edition. Nancy Blaine, Senior Sponsoring Editor, has offered us firm but sympathetic guidance throughout the revision process. The authors are grateful for the wonderful work of Tonya Lobato, Senior Development Editor; Carol Newman, Senior Content Project Manager; Nicole Lee Petel, Project Manager; and Catherine Schnurr, Senior Image Research Manager.

Finally, we thank the many students whose questions and concerns, expressed directly or through their instructors, shaped much of this revision. We continue to welcome all our readers' suggestions, queries, and criticisms. Please contact us at our respective institutions.

Richard W. Bulliet Professor of Middle Eastern History at Columbia University, Richard W. Bulliet received his Ph.D. from Harvard University. He has written scholarly works on a number of topics: the social history of medieval Iran (*The Patricians of Nishapur*), the historical competition between pack camels and wheeled transport (*The Camel and the Wheel*), the process of conversion to Islam (*Conversion to Islam in the Medieval Period*), and the overall course of Islamic social history (*Islam: The View from the Edge*). His most recent books include a global history of human-animal relations (*Hunters, Herders, and Hamburgers*) and an affirmation of the historical kinship of Islam and Christianity (*The Case for Islamo-Christian Civilization*). He is the editor of the *Columbia History of the Twentieth Century*. He has published four novels, coedited *The Encyclopedia of the Modern Middle East,* and hosted an educational television series on the Middle East. He was awarded a fellowship by the John Simon Guggenheim Memorial Foundation.

Pamela Kyle Crossley Pamela Kyle Crossley received her Ph.D. in Modern Chinese History from Yale University. She is currently the Robert and Barbara Black Professor of History at Dartmouth College. Her books include *The Wobbling Pivot: An Interpretive History of China Since 1800; What Is Global History?; A Translucent Mirror: History and Identity in Qing Imperial Ideology; The Manchus; Orphan Warriors: Three Manchu Generations and the End of the Qing World;* and (with Lynn Hollen Lees and John W. Servos) *Global Society: The World Since 1900.*

Daniel R. Headrick Daniel R. Headrick received his Ph.D. in History from Princeton University. Professor of History and Social Science at Roosevelt University in Chicago, he is the author of several books on the history of technology, imperialism, and international relations, including *The Tools of Empire: Technology and European Imperialism in the Nineteenth Century; The Tentacles of Progress: Technology Transfer in the Age of Imperialism; The Invisible Weapon: Telecommunications and International Politics; When Information Came of Age: Technologies of Knowledge in the Age of Reason and Revolution, 1700–1850; Technology: A World History;* and *Power over Peoples: Technology, Environments, and Western Imperialism, 1400 to the Present.* His articles have appeared in the *Journal of World History,* the *Journal of Modern History,* and other journals. He has been awarded fellowships by the National Endowment for the Humanities, the John Simon Guggenheim Memorial Foundation, and the Alfred P. Sloan Foundation.

Steven W. Hirsch Steven W. Hirsch holds a Ph.D. in Classics from Stanford University and is currently Associate Professor of Classics and History at Tufts University. He has received grants from the National Endowment for the Humanities and the Massachusetts Foundation for Humanities and Public Policy. His research and publications include *The Friendship of the Barbarians: Xenophon and the Persian Empire,* as well as articles and reviews in the *Classical Journal,* the *American Journal of Philology,* and the *Journal of Interdisciplinary History.* He is currently working on a comparative study of ancient Mediterranean and Chinese civilizations.

Lyman L. Johnson Professor of History at the University of North Carolina at Charlotte, Lyman L. Johnson earned his Ph.D. in Latin American History from the University of Connecticut. A two-time Senior Fulbright-Hays Lecturer, he also has received fellowships from the Tinker Foundation, the Social Science Research Council, the National Endowment for the Humanities, and the American Philosophical Society. His recent books include *Workshop of Revolution: Plebeian Buenos Aires 1776–1810* (forthcoming Duke University Press); *Aftershocks: Earthquakes and*

Popular Politics in Latin America (edited with Jürgen Buchenau); *Death, Dismemberment, and Memory; The Faces of Honor* (edited with Sonya Lipsett-Rivera); and *Colonial Latin America* (with Mark A. Burkholder). He has also published in journals, including the *Hispanic American Historical Review,* the *Journal of Latin American Studies,* the *International Review of Social History,* and *Desarrollo Económico.* He has served as president of the Conference on Latin American History.

David Northrup Professor of History at Boston College, David Northrup earned his Ph.D. in African and European History from the University of California at Los Angeles. He earlier taught in Nigeria with the Peace Corps and at Tuskegee Institute. Research supported by the Fulbright-Hays Commission, the National Endowment for the Humanities, and the Social Science Research Council led to publications concerning precolonial Nigeria; the Congo (1865–1940); the Atlantic slave trade; and Asian, African, and Pacific islander indentured labor in the nineteenth century. His most recent writing has concerned Atlantic history, and his latest book is the second edition of *Africa's Discovery of Europe, 1450–1850.* In 2004 and 2005 he was president of the World History Association.

Where necessary for clarity, dates are followed by the letters C.E. or B.C.E. The abbreviation C.E. stands for "Common Era" and is equivalent to A.D. (*anno Domini,* Latin for "in the year of the Lord"). The abbreviation B.C.E. stands for "before the Common Era" and means the same as B.C. ("before Christ"). In keeping with our goal of approaching world history without special concentration on one culture or another, we chose these neutral abbreviations as appropriate to our enterprise. Because many readers will be more familiar with English than with metric measurements, however, units of measure are generally given in the English system, with metric equivalents following in parentheses.

In general, Chinese has been romanized according to the *pinyin* method. Exceptions include proper names well established in English (e.g., *Canton, Chiang Kai-shek*) and a few English words borrowed from Chinese (e.g., *kowtow*). Spellings of Arabic, Ottoman Turkish, Persian, Mongolian, Manchu, Japanese, and Korean names and terms avoid special diacritical marks for letters that are pronounced only slightly differently in English. An apostrophe is used to indicate when two Chinese syllables are pronounced separately (e.g., *Chang'an*).

For words transliterated from languages that use the Arabic script—Arabic, Ottoman Turkish, Persian, Urdu—the apostrophe indicating separately pronounced syllables may represent either of two special consonants, the *hamza* or the *ain.* Because most English-speakers do not hear the distinction between these two, they have not been distinguished in transliteration and are not indicated when they occur at the beginning or end of a word. As with Chinese, some words and commonly used place-names from these languages are given familiar English spellings (e.g., *Quran* instead of *Qur'an, Cairo* instead of *al-Qahira*). Arabic romanization has normally been used for terms relating to Islam, even where the context justifies slightly different Turkish or Persian forms, again for ease of comprehension.

Before 1492 the inhabitants of the Western Hemisphere had no single name for themselves. They had neither a racial consciousness nor a racial identity. Identity was derived from kin groups, language, cultural practices, and political structures. There was no sense that physical similarities created a shared identity. America's original inhabitants had racial consciousness and racial identity imposed on them by conquest and the occupation of their lands by Europeans after 1492. All of the collective terms for these first American peoples are tainted by this history. *Indians, Native Americans, Amerindians, First Peoples,* and *Indigenous Peoples* are among the terms in common usage. In this book the names of individual cultures and states are used wherever possible. *Amerindian* and other terms that suggest transcultural identity and experience are used most commonly for the period after 1492.

There is an ongoing debate about how best to render Amerindian words in English. It has been common for authors writing in English to follow Mexican usage for Nahuatl and Yucatec Maya words and place-names. In this style, for example, the capital of the Aztec state is spelled *Tenochtitlán,* and the important late Maya city-state is spelled *Chichén Itzá.* Although these forms are still common even in the specialist literature, we have chosen to follow the scholarship that sees these accents as unnecessary. The exceptions are modern place-names, such as *Mérida* and *Yucatán,* which are accented. A similar problem exists for the spelling of Quechua and Ay-mara words from the Andean region of South America. Although there is significant disagreement among scholars, we follow the emerging consensus and use the spellings *khipu* (not *quipu*), *Tiwanaku* (not *Tiahuanaco*), and *Wari* (not *Huari*). However, we keep *Inca* (not *Inka*) and *Cuzco* (not *Cusco*), since these spellings are expected by most of our potential readers and we hope to avoid confusion.

The Earth and Its Peoples

A Global History

Part One

The Emergence of Human Communities, to 1500 B.C.E.

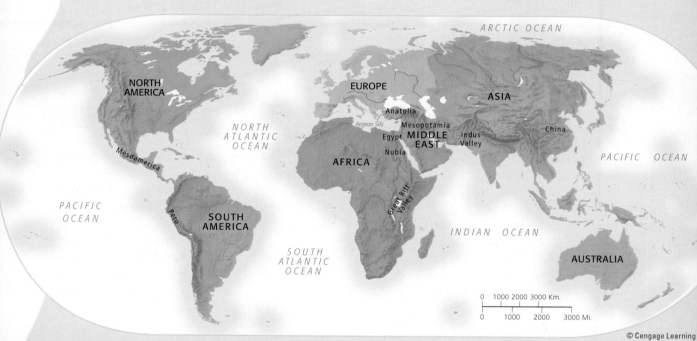

© Cengage Learning

	8000 B.C.E.	7000 B.C.E.	6000 B.C.E.	5000 B.C.E.
AMERICAS		• **7000** Incipient plant domestication in Peru		• **5000** Maize, beans, and squash domestication in Mesoamerica
EUROPE	Spread of Indo-European languages		• **6000** Farming in southern Europe	
AFRICA	• **8000** Farming in eastern Sahara			• **5500** Farming in Egypt
MIDDLE EAST	• **8000** Domestication of plants and animals in Fertile Crescent			• **5000** Irrigation in Mesopotamia
ASIA AND OCEANIA		• **6500** Rice cultivation in China		• **5000** Farming in India

Human beings evolved over several million years from primates in Africa. Able to walk upright and possessing large brains, hands with opposable thumbs, and the capacity for speech, early humans used teamwork and created tools to survive in diverse environments. They spread relatively quickly to almost every habitable area of the world, hunting and gathering wild plant products. Around 10,000 years ago some groups began to cultivate plants, domesticate animals, and make pottery vessels for storage. This led to permanent settlements—at first small villages but eventually larger towns as well.

The earliest complex societies arose in the great river valleys of Iraq, Egypt, Pakistan, and northern China. In these arid regions agriculture depended on river water, and centers of political power arose to organize the labor required to dig and maintain irrigation channels. Kings and priests dominated these early societies from the urban centers, helped by administrators, scribes, soldiers, merchants, craftsmen, and others with specialized skills. Surplus food grown in the countryside by a dependent peasantry sustained the activities of these groups.

Certain centers came to dominate broader expanses of territory, seeking access to raw materials, especially metals. This change also stimulated long-distance trade and diplomatic relations between major powers. Artisans made weapons, tools, and ritual objects from bronze. Culture and technology spread to neighboring regions, such as southern China, Nubia, Syria-Palestine, Anatolia, and the Aegean.

In the Western Hemisphere, different geographical circumstances called forth distinctive patterns of technological and cultural response in the early civilizations in southern Mexico and the Andean region of South America.

4000 B.C.E.	3000 B.C.E.	2000 B.C.E.	1000 B.C.E.
• **4000** Quinoa and potato domestication in Peru	• **3000** Farming in central Mexico	• **2000** Farming in Peru	• **1200** Rise of Olmec civilization in Mesoamerica • **900** Rise of Chavín civilization in Peru
• **4000** Megaliths	**3000–1100** Aegean civilization		• **1000** Iron metallurgy
	• **3100** Unification of Egypt **2575–2134** Old Kingdom Egypt	**2040–1640** Middle Kingdom Egypt • **2000** Rise of Kush in Nubia **1532–1070** New Kingdom Egypt	• **800** Rise of Nubian Kingdom at Napata
	• **3100** Mesopotamian civilization Advent of horses in western Asia **2000** • • **2350** Akkadian kingdom	• **1750** Hammurabi's law code **1700–1200** Hittites dominant in Anatolia	• **911** Rise of Neo-Assyrian Empire
	Bronze metallurgy in China **2000** • **2600–1900** Indus Valley civilization	**1600–1027** Shang kingdom in China	**1027–221** Zhou kingdom in China

From the Origins of Agriculture to the First River-Valley Civilizations

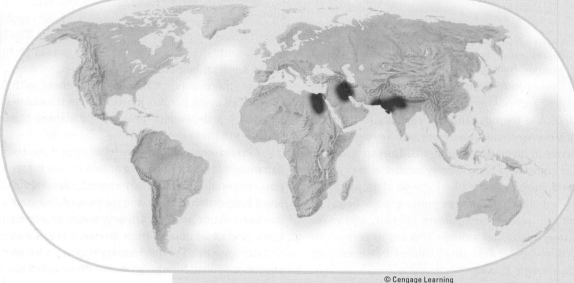

© Cengage Learning

CHAPTER PREVIEW

Before Civilization
How did plant and animal domestication set the scene for the emergence of civilization?

Mesopotamia
How did Mesopotamian civilization emerge?

Egypt
What role did the environment and religion play in Egyptian civilization?

Conclusion

MATERIAL CULTURE: Lamps and Candles

Visit the CourseMate website at **www.cengagebrain.com** for additional study tools and review materials for this chapter.

S ome 5,000 years ago in Mesopotamia (present-day Iraq), people living in Sumer, the world's first urban civilization, cherished the story of Gilgamesh, superhero king of the city of Uruk. The goddess of creation, it recounted, fashioned the wild man Enkidu (EN-kee-doo):

> There was virtue in him of the god of war, of Ninurta himself. His body was rough, he had long hair like a woman's; it waved like the hair of Nisaba, the goddess of corn. His body was covered with matted hair like Samuqan's, the god of cattle. He was innocent of mankind; he knew nothing of the cultivated land. Enkidu ate grass in the hills with the gazelle and jostled with the wild beasts at the water-holes; he had joy of the water with the herds of wild game.

When Gilgamesh learns of Enkidu from a hunter, he sends a temple prostitute to tame him. After her seduction causes the wild beasts to shun him, she says:

> Come with me. I will take you to strong-walled Uruk (OO-rook), to the blessed temple of Ishtar and of Anu, of love and of heaven . . . there all the people are dressed in their gorgeous robes, every day is holiday, the young men and the girls are wonderful to see. How sweet they smell! . . . O Enkidu, you who live life, I will show you Gilgamesh.[1]

The prostitute clothes Enkidu and teaches him to eat cooked food, drink beer, and bathe and oil his body. Her words and actions signal the principal traits of civilized life in Sumer, just as the comparisons of the wild Enkidu to various divinities show Sumer's dependence on grain and livestock.

It has long been said that the first civilizations arose in Mesopotamia and Egypt sometime before 3000 B.C.E. However, since people tend to judge everything by their own viewpoint, it is not safe to accept this assertion without questioning. The Sumerians equated civilization with their own way of life, but other peoples did the same, and lifestyles varied. This, along with the ambiguity of the term *civilization*, makes it difficult to say where civilization began.

Scholars agree that settled agricultural life and certain political, social, economic, and technological traits are indicators of **civilization**, if not of every

civilization. These traits include (1) cities as administrative centers, (2) a political system based on defined territory rather than kinship, (3) many people engaged in specialized, non-food-producing activities, (4) status distinctions based largely on accumulation of wealth, (5) monumental building, (6) a system for keeping permanent records, (7) long-distance trade, and (8) sophisticated interest in science and art.

The earliest societies exhibiting these traits appeared in the floodplains of great rivers: the Tigris (TIE-gris) and Euphrates (you-FRAY-teez) in Iraq, the Indus in Pakistan, the Yellow (Huang He (hwang huh)) in China, and the Nile in Egypt (see Map 1.1). Periodic flooding fertilized the land with silt and provided water for agriculture but also threatened lives and property. To control the floods, the peoples living near the rivers created new technologies and forms of political and social organization.

In this chapter, we describe the origins of domestication among the scattered groups of foragers living at the end of the last Ice Age (a long period when glaciers covered much of North America, Europe, and Asia) and the slow development of farming and herding societies. We then trace the rise of complex societies in Mesopotamia and Egypt from approximately 3500 to 1500 B.C.E. (China, developing slightly later, is discussed in Chapter 2. The Indus Valley civilization will be discussed in Chapter 5.) This story roughly coincides with the origins of writing, allowing us to document aspects of human life not revealed by archaeological evidence alone.

Before Civilization

How did plant and animal domestication set the scene for the emergence of civilization?

Though much remains to be learned, scientists have uncovered a great deal of evidence about life in the earliest periods of human history. Perhaps the most impressive findings are artistic. Evidence of human

---

civilization An ambiguous term often used to denote more complex societies but sometimes used by anthropologists to describe any group of people sharing a set of cultural traits.

creativity first came to light in 1940 near Lascaux in southwestern France with the discovery of a vast underground cavern. The cavern walls were covered with paintings of animals, including many that had been extinct for thousands of years. Similar cave paintings have been found in Spain and elsewhere in southern France.

To even the most skeptical person, these artistic troves reveal rich imaginations and sophisticated skills, qualities also apparent in the stone tools and in the evidence of complex social relations uncovered from prehistoric sites. The production of such artworks and tools over wide areas and long periods of time demonstrates that skills and ideas were not simply individual expressions but were deliberately passed along within societies. These learned patterns of action and expression constitute **culture**. Culture includes material objects, such as dwellings, clothing, tools, and crafts, along with nonmaterial values, beliefs, and languages. Although it is true that some animals also learn new ways, their activities are determined primarily by inherited instincts. Only human communities trace profound cultural developments over time. The development, transmission, and transformation of cultural practices and events are the subject of **history**.

Stone toolmaking, the first recognizable cultural activity, first appeared around 2 million years ago. The **Stone Age**, which lasted from then until around 4,000 years ago, can be a misleading label. Stone tools abound at archaeological sites, but not all tools were of stone. They were made as well of bone, skin, and wood, materials that survive poorly. In addition, this period encompasses many cultures and subperiods. Among the major subdivisions, the **Paleolithic** (pay-lee-oh-LITH-ik) (Old Stone Age) lasted until 10,000 years ago, about 3,000 years after the end of the last Ice Age. The **Neolithic** (nee-oh-LITH-ik) (New Stone Age), which is associated with the origins of agriculture, followed.

Food Gathering and Stone Technology

Fossilized animal bones bearing the marks of butchering tools testify to the scavenging and hunting activities of Stone Age peoples, but anthropologists do not believe that early humans lived primarily on meat. Modern **foragers** (hunting and food-gathering peoples) in the Kalahari Desert of southern Africa and the Ituri Forest of Central Africa derive the bulk of their day-to-day nourishment from wild vegetable foods, eating meat primarily at feasts. Stone Age peoples probably did the same, even though the tools and equipment for gathering and processing vegetable foods have left few archaeological traces.

Like modern foragers, ancient humans would have used skins and baskets woven from plant fibers for collecting fruits, berries, and wild seeds, and they would have dug up edible roots with wooden sticks. Archaeologists suspect that the doughnut-shaped stones often found at Stone Age sites served as weights to make wooden digging sticks more effective.

Cooking makes both meat and vegetables tastier and easier to digest, something early humans may have discovered inadvertently after wildfires. Humans may have begun setting fires deliberately 1 million to 1.5 million years ago, but proof of cooking does not appear until some 12,500 years ago, when clay cooking pots came into use in East Asia.

Studies of present-day foragers also indicate that Ice Age women probably did most of the gathering and cooking, which they could do while caring for small children. Women past childbearing age would have been the most knowledgeable and productive food gatherers. Men, with stronger arms and shoulders, would have been better suited for hunting, particularly

culture Socially transmitted patterns of action and expression. *Material culture* refers to physical objects, such as dwellings, clothing, tools, and crafts. Culture also includes arts, beliefs, knowledge, and technology.
history The study of past events and changes in the development, transmission, and transformation of cultural practices.
Stone Age The historical period characterized by the production of tools from stone and other nonmetallic substances. It was followed in some places by the Bronze Age and more generally by the Iron Age.
Paleolithic The period of the Stone Age associated with the evolution of humans. It predates the Neolithic period.
Neolithic The period of the Stone Age associated with the ancient Agricultural Revolutions. It follows the Paleolithic period.
foragers People who support themselves by hunting wild animals and gathering wild edible plants and insects.

Chronology

	Mesopotamia	Egypt
3500 B.C.E.		
3000 B.C.E.	3000–2350 B.C.E. Early Dynastic (Sumerian)	3100–2575 B.C.E. Early Dynastic
2500 B.C.E.	2350–2230 B.C.E. Akkadian (Semitic)	2575–2134 B.C.E. Old Kingdom 2134–2040 B.C.E. First Intermediate Period
2000 B.C.E.	2112–2004 B.C.E Third Dynasty of Ur (Sumerian) 1900–1600 B.C.E. Old Babylonian (Semitic)	2040–1640 B.C.E. Middle Kingdom 1640–1532 B.C.E Second Intermediate Period
1500 B.C.E.	1500–1150 B.C.E. Kassite	1532–1070 B.C.E. New Kingdom

for hunting large animals. Some early cave art suggests male hunting activities.The same studies, along with archaeological evidence from Ice Age campsites, indicate that early foragers lived in groups that were big enough to defend themselves from predators and divide responsibility for food collection and preparation, but small enough not to exhaust the food resources within walking distance. Even bands of around fifty men, women, and children would have moved regularly to follow migrating animals or collect seasonally ripening plants in different places.

In regions that had severe climates or that lacked natural shelters like caves, people built huts of branches, stones, bones, skins, and leaves as seasonal camps. Animal skins served as clothing, with the earliest evidence of woven cloth appearing about 26,000 years ago. Groups living in the African grasslands and other game-rich areas probably spent only three to five hours a day securing food, clothing, and shelter. This would have left a great deal of time for artistic endeavors, toolmaking, and social life.

The foundations of what later ages called science, art, and religion also date to the Stone Age. Gatherers learned which local plants were edible and when

they ripened, as well as which natural substances were effective for medicine, consciousness altering, dyeing, and other purposes. Hunters learned the habits of game animals. People experimented with techniques of using plant and animal materials for clothing, twine, and construction. Knowledge of the environment included identifying which minerals made good paints and which stones made good tools. All of these aspects of culture were passed orally from generation to generation.

Early music and dance have left no traces, but visual artwork has survived abundantly. Cave paintings appear as early as 32,000 years ago in Europe and North Africa and somewhat later in other parts of the world. Because many feature food animals like wild oxen, reindeer, and horses, some scholars believe that the art recorded hunting scenes or played a magical and religious role in hunting. A newly discovered cave at Vallon Pont-d'Arc (vah-LOH pon-DAHRK) in southern France, however, features rhinoceros, panthers, bears, owls, and a hyena, which probably were not hunted for food. Other drawings include people dressed in animal skins and smeared with paint and stencils of human hands. Some scholars suspect that other marks in cave paintings and on bones may represent efforts at counting or writing. Some cave art suggests that Stone Age people had well-developed religions, but without written texts, it is hard to know what they believed. Some graves from about 100,000 years ago contain stone implements, food, clothing, and red-ochre powder, indicating that early people revered their leaders enough to honor them in death and may have believed in an afterlife.

The Agricultural Revolutions

Around 10,000 years ago, some human groups began to meet their food needs by raising domesticated plants and animals. Gradually over the next millennium, most people became food producers, although hunting and gathering continued in some places.

The term *Neolithic Revolution*, commonly given to the changeover from food gathering to food producing, can be misleading. *Neolithic* means "new stone," but the new tool designs that accompanied the beginnings of agriculture were not the most important feature of this changeover. Nor was the "revolution" a single event. The changeover occurred at different times in different parts of the world. The term **Agricultural Revolutions** is more precise because it emphasizes the central role of food production and signals that the changeover occurred several times. The adoption of agriculture often included the domestication of animals for food.

Food gathering gave way to food production over hundreds of generations. The process may have begun when forager bands, returning year after year to the same seasonal camps, scattered seeds and cleared away weeds to encourage the growth of foods they liked. Such semicultivation could have supplemented food gathering without necessitating permanent settlement. Families choosing to concentrate their energies on food production, however, would have had to settle permanently near their fields.

Specialized stone tools first alerted archaeologists to new food-producing practices: polished or ground stone heads to work the soil, sharp stone chips embedded in bone or wooden handles to cut grasses, and stone mortars to pulverize grain. Early farmers used fire to clear fields of shrubs and trees and discovered that ashes were a natural fertilizer. After the

burn-off, farmers used blades and axes to keep the land clear.

Selection of the highest-yielding strains of wild plants led to the development of domesticated varieties over time. As the principal gatherers of wild plant foods, women probably played a major role in this transition to plant cultivation, but the task of clearing fields probably fell to the men.

In the Middle East, the region with the earliest evidence of agriculture, human selection had transformed certain wild grasses into higher-yielding domesticated grains, now known as emmer wheat and barley, by 8000 B.C.E. Farmers there also discovered that alternating the cultivation of grains and pulses (plants yielding edible seeds such as lentils and peas) helped maintain fertility.

While plants domesticated in the Middle East spread to adjacent lands, agriculture also arose independently in many parts of the world. Exchanges of crops and techniques occurred between regions, but societies that had already settled into farming life borrowed new plants, animals, and farming techniques more readily than foraging groups that were often on the move.

The eastern Sahara, which went through a wet period after 8000 B.C.E., preserves the oldest traces of food production in northern Africa. As in the Middle East, emmer wheat and barley became the principal crops and sheep, goats, and cattle the main domestic animals. When drier conditions set in around 5000 B.C.E., many Saharan farmers moved to the Nile Valley. The river's edge was swampy, but annual flooding provided water for crops farther from the riverbanks.

In Greece, wheat and barley cultivation began as early as 6000 B.C.E. Shortly after 4000 B.C.E., farming developed in the light-soiled plains of central Europe and along the Danube River. As forests receded over the next millennium because of climate changes and human clearing, agriculture spread to other parts of Europe.

Agricultural Revolutions (ancient) The change from food gathering to food production that occurred between ca. 8000 and 2000 B.C.E. Also known as the Neolithic Revolution.

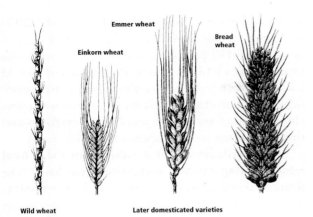

Emmer wheat

Einkorn wheat

Bread wheat

Wild wheat   Later domesticated varieties

Domestication of Wheat   Through selection of the largest seeds of this wild grass, early farmers in the Middle East were able to develop varieties with larger edible kernels. Bread wheat was grown in the Nile Valley by 5000 B.C.E.   From Iris Barn, *Discovering Archaeology* (London: Stonehenge, in association with the American Museum of Natural History, 1981)

Early farmers in Europe and elsewhere practiced shifting cultivation, also known as swidden agriculture. After a few growing seasons, farmers left the fields fallow (abandoned to natural vegetation) and cleared new fields nearby. Between 4000 and 3000 B.C.E., for example, communities of forty to sixty people in the Danube Valley supported themselves on about 500 acres (200 hectares) of farmland, cultivating a third or less each year while leaving the rest fallow to regain its fertility. From around 2600 B.C.E., people in central Europe began using ox-drawn wooden plows instead of hoes to till heavier and richer soils.

Although the lands around the Mediterranean seem to have shared a complex of crops and farming techniques, geographical conditions blocked the spread of wheat and barley elsewhere. Rainfall patterns south of the Sahara favored instead locally domesticated grains—sorghums, millets, and (in Ethiopia) teff. Middle Eastern grains did not grow at all in the humidity of equatorial West Africa; there, yams became an early domestic crop.

Domestic rice originated in southern China, the northern half of Southeast Asia, or northern India, possibly as early as 10,000 B.C.E. but more likely closer to 5000 B.C.E. The warm, wet climate of southern China particularly favored rice. Along with rice, Indian farmers were cultivating hyacinth beans and green and black grams (types of legumes) by about 2000 B.C.E.

In the Americas a decline of game animals in the Tehuacán (teh-wah-KAHN) Valley of Mexico after 8000 B.C.E. increased people's dependence on wild plants. Agriculture based on maize (mayz) (corn) developed there about 3000 B.C.E. and gradually spread. At about the same time, the inhabitants of Peru developed a food production pattern based on potatoes and quinoa (kee-NOH-uh), a protein-rich seed grain. People in the more tropical parts of Mesoamerica cultivated tomatoes, peppers, squash, and potatoes. In South America's tropical forests, the root crop manioc became the staple food after 1500 B.C.E. Manioc and maize then spread to the Caribbean islands.

The domestication of animals expanded rapidly during these same millennia. The first domestic animal, the dog, may have helped hunters well before the Neolithic period and may also have served as a food source. Neolithic period domestic animals initially provided meat but eventually supplied milk, wool, and energy as well.

Refuse dumped outside Middle Eastern villages shows a gradual decline in the number of wild gazelle bones after 7000 B.C.E. This probably reflects the depletion of wild game through overhunting by local farmers. Meat eating, however, did not decline. Sheep and goat bones gradually replaced gazelle bones. Possibly wild sheep and goats learned to graze around agricultural villages to take advantage of the suppression of predators by humans. The tamer animals may gradually have accepted human control and thus became a ready supply of food. The bones of tame animals initially differ so little from those of their wild ancestors that the early stages of domestication are hard to date. However, selective breeding for characteristics like a wooly coat and high milk production eventually yielded distinct breeds of domestic sheep and goats.

Elsewhere, other wild species evolved domestic forms during the centuries before 3000 B.C.E.: cattle in northern Africa and/or the Middle East, donkeys in northern Africa, water buffalo in China, humpedback Zebu (ZEE-boo) cattle in India, horses and two-humped camels in Central Asia, one-humped camels in Arabia, chickens in Southeast Asia, and pigs in several places. Like domestic plant species, varieties of domesticated animals spread from one region to another. The Zebu cattle originally domesticated in India, for example, became important in sub-Saharan Africa about 2,000 years ago.

Zebu cattle and water buffalo became sufficiently tame to be yoked to plows many centuries after domestic stocks first appeared, but once this change occurred, they became essential to the agricultural cycle of grain farmers. In addition, animal droppings provided valuable fertilizer. Wool and milk production also occurred a long time after initial domestication.

In the Americas, domestic llamas provided meat, transport, and wool, while guinea pigs and turkeys provided meat. Dogs assisted hunters and also provided meat. Scholars believe that these were the only domesticated American species. However, despite the geographical isolation of the Americas, domestic chickens first appeared before the coming of the Europeans, presumably by way of Pacific Ocean seafarers.

Pastoralism, a way of life dependent on large herds of grazing livestock, came to predominate in arid regions. As the Sahara approached its maximum dryness around 2500 B.C.E., pastoralists replaced farmers who migrated southward (see Chapter 8). Moving herds to new pastures and watering places throughout the year made pastoralists almost as mobile as foragers and discouraged substantial dwellings and the accumulation of bulky possessions. Like modern pastoralists, early cattle keepers probably relied more heavily on milk than on meat, since killing animals diminished the size of their herds. During wet seasons, they may also have engaged in semicultivation or bartered meat and skins for plant foods from nearby farming communities.

Why did the Agricultural Revolutions occur? Some theories assume that growing crops had obvious advantages. Grain, for example, provided both a dietary staple and the makings of beer. Beer drinking appears frequently in ancient Middle Eastern art and can be dated to as early as 3500 B.C.E. Most researchers today, however, believe that climate change and growing population density drove people to abandon foraging in favor of pastoralism and agriculture. So great was the global warming that ended the last Ice Age that geologists have given the era since about 11,000 B.C.E. a new name: the **Holocene** (HAWL-oh-seen). Scientists have also found evidence that temperate lands were exceptionally warm between 6000 and 2000 B.C.E., when people in many parts of the world adopted agriculture. The precise nature of the climatic crisis probably varied. In the Middle East, shortages of wild food caused by dryness or overhunting may have stimulated food production. Elsewhere, a warmer, wetter climate could have turned grasslands into forest and thereby reduced supplies of game and wild grains.

In many drier parts of the world, where wild food remained abundant, agriculture did not arise. The inhabitants of Australia relied exclusively on foraging until recent centuries, as did some peoples on other continents. Amerindians in the arid grasslands from Alaska to the Gulf of Mexico hunted bison, and salmon fishing sustained groups in the Pacific Northwest. Ample supplies of fish, shellfish, and aquatic animals permitted food gatherers east of the Mississippi River to become increasingly sedentary. In the equatorial rain forest and in the southern part of Africa, conditions also favored retention of older ways.

Whatever the causes, the gradual adoption of food production transformed most parts of the world. A hundred thousand years ago, world population, mostly living in the temperate and tropical regions of Africa and Eurasia, did not exceed 2 million. The population may have fallen still lower during the last glacial epoch, between 32,000 and 13,000 years ago. Agriculture supported a gradual population increase, perhaps to 10 million by 5000 B.C.E., and then a mushrooming to between 50 million and 100 million by 1000 B.C.E.[2]

Life in Neolithic Communities

Evidence that an ecological crisis may have triggered the transition to food production has prompted reexamination of the assumption that farmers enjoyed a better life than foragers. Early farmers probably had to work much harder and for much longer periods than food gatherers. Long days spent clearing and cultivating the land yielded meager harvests. Guarding herds from predators, guiding them

Holocene The geological era since the end of the Great Ice Age about 13,000 years ago.

to fresh pastures, and tending to their needs imposed similar burdens.

There were other problems as well. Although early farmers commanded a more reliable food supply, their diet contained less variety and nutrition than that of foragers. Skeletons show that Neolithic farmers were shorter on average than earlier foragers. Death from contagious diseases ravaged farming settlements, which were contaminated by human waste, infested by disease-bearing vermin and insects, and inhabited by domestic animals—especially pigs and cattle—whose diseases could infect people.

However, a dependable supply of food that could be stored between harvests to see people through nonproductive seasons, droughts, and other calamities proved decisive in the long run. Over several millennia, farmers came to outnumber nonfarmers, permanent settlements generated cultural changes, and specialized crafts appeared in fledgling towns.

Some researchers envision violent struggles between farmers and foragers. Others see a more peaceful transition. Violence may well have accompanied land clearance that constrained the foragers' food supplies. And farmers probably fought for control of the best land. In most cases, however, farmers seem to have displaced foragers by gradual infiltration rather than by conquest.

The archaeologist Colin Renfrew maintains that, over a few centuries, farming populations in Europe could have increased by a factor of fifty to one hundred just on the basis of the dependability of their food supply. In his view, as population densities rose, individuals with fields farthest away from their native village formed new settlements, thus contributing to a steady, nonviolent expansion of agriculture consistent with the archaeological record. An expansion by only 12 to 19 miles (20 to 30 kilometers) in a generation could have brought farming to every corner of Europe between 6500 and 3500 B.C.E.[3] Yet it probably happened gradually enough to minimize sharp conflicts with foragers, who would simply have stayed clear of the agricultural frontier or gradually adopted agriculture themselves. Studies that map genetic changes in the population also suggest a gradual spread of agricultural people across Europe from southeast to northwest.[4]

As they did in forager bands, kinship and marriage bound farming communities together. Nuclear family size (parents and their children) may not have increased, but kinship relations traced back over more generations brought distant cousins into a common kin network. This network encouraged the holding of land by large kinship units known as lineages (LIN-ee-ij) or clans.

Because each person has two parents, four grandparents, eight great-grandparents, and so on, each individual has a bewildering number of ancestors. Some societies trace descent equally through both parents, but most give greater importance to descent through either the mother (matrilineal [mat-ruh-LIN-ee-uhl] societies) or the father (patrilineal [pat-ruh-LIN-ee-uhl] societies). Some scholars believe that descent through women and perhaps rule by women prevailed in early times. The traditions of Kikuyu (ki-KOO-yoo) farmers on Mount Kenya in East Africa, for example, relate that women ruled until the Kikuyu men conspired to get all the women pregnant at once and then overthrew them while they were unable to fight back. No specific evidence can prove or disprove legends such as this, but it is important not to confuse tracing descent through women (matrilineality) with rule by women (matriarchy [MAY-tree-ahr-key]).

Religiously, kinship led to reverence for departed ancestors. Old persons often received elaborate burials. A plastered skull from Jericho (JER-ih-koe) in the Jordan Valley of modern Israel may be evidence of early ancestor reverence or worship at the dawn of agriculture.

The religions of foragers tended to center on sacred groves, springs, and wild animals. In contrast, the rituals of farmers often centered on the Earth Mother, a deity believed to be the source of new life, and divinities representing fire, wind, and rain. Pastoralists tended to worship the all-powerful (and usually male) sky-god.

Assemblages of **megaliths** (meaning "big stones") seem to relate to religious beliefs. One complex built in the Egyptian desert before 5000 B.C.E. includes stone burial chambers, a calendar circle, and pairs of upright stones that frame the rising sun on the

megaliths Structures and complexes of very large stones constructed for ceremonial and religious purposes in Neolithic times.

summer solstice. Stonehenge, a famous megalithic site in England constructed about 2000 B.C.E., marked the position of the sun and other celestial bodies at key points in the year. In Central Asia, the Americas, and other parts of the world, giant earth burial mounds may have served similar ritual and symbolic functions.

In some parts of the world, a few Neolithic villages grew into towns, which served as centers of trade and specialized crafts. Two towns in the Middle East, Jericho on the west bank of the Jordan River and Çatal Hüyük (cha-TAHL hoo-YOOK) in central Anatolia (modern Turkey), have been extensively excavated (Map 1.1 shows their location). Jericho revealed an

elaborate early agricultural settlement. The round mud-brick dwellings characteristic of Jericho around 8000 B.C.E. may have imitated the shape of the tents of foragers who once had camped near Jericho's natural spring. A millennium later, rectangular rooms with finely plastered walls and floors and wide doorways opened onto central courtyards. Surrounding the 10-acre (4-hectare) settlement, a massive stone wall protected against attacks.

The ruins of Çatal Hüyük, an even larger Neolithic town, date to between 7000 and 5000 B.C.E. and cover 32 acres (13 hectares). Its residents lived in plastered mud-brick rooms with elaborate decorations, but Çatal Hüyük had no wall. Instead, the outer

Map 1.1 River-Valley Civilizations, 3500–1500 B.C.E. The earliest complex societies arose in the floodplains of large rivers: in the fourth millennium B.C.E. in the valley of the Tigris and Euphrates Rivers in Mesopotamia and the Nile River in Egypt, in the third millennium B.C.E. in the valley of the Indus River in Pakistan, and in the second millennium B.C.E. in the valley of the Yellow River in China.   © Cengage Learning

 Interactive Map

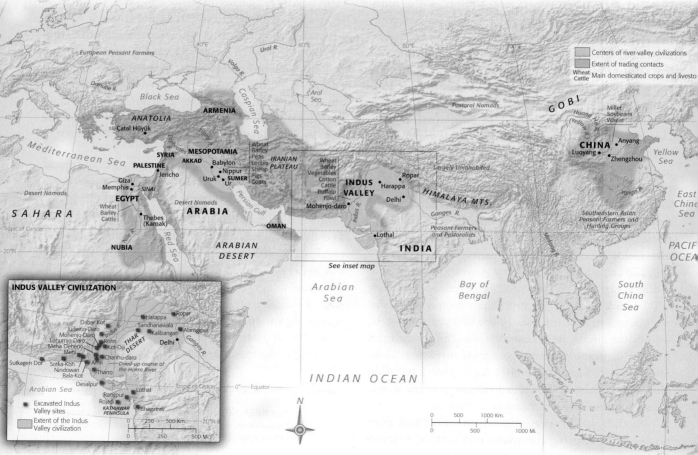

walls of its houses formed a continuous barrier without doors or large windows. Residents entered their houses by climbing down ladders through a hole in the roof. Long-distance trade at Çatal Hüyük featured obsidian, a hard volcanic rock that artisans chipped, ground, and polished into tools, weapons, mirrors, and ornaments. Other residents made fine pottery, wove baskets and woolen cloth, made stone and shell beads, and worked leather and wood. House sizes varied, but nothing indicates that Çatal Hüyük had a dominant class or a centralized political structure.

Representational art at Çatal Hüyük makes it clear that hunting retained a powerful hold on people's minds. Wall paintings of hunting scenes closely resemble earlier cave paintings. Many depict men and women adorned with leopard skins. Men were buried with weapons rather than with farm tools, and bones from rubbish heaps prove that wild game featured prominently in people's diet.

Yet Çatal Hüyük's economy rested on agriculture. The surrounding fields produced barley and emmer wheat, as well as legumes (LEG-yooms) and other vegetables. Pigs were kept along with goats and sheep. Nevertheless, foragers' foods, such as acorns and wild grains, had not yet disappeared.

Çatal Hüyük had one religious shrine for every two houses. At least forty rooms contained shrines with depictions of horned wild bulls, female breasts, goddesses, leopards, and handprints. Rituals involved burning dishes of grain, legumes, and meat but not sacrificing live animals. Statues of plump female deities far outnumber statues of male deities, suggesting that the inhabitants venerated a goddess as their principal deity. The large number of females who were buried elaborately in shrine rooms may have been priestesses of this cult. The site's principal excavator maintains that although male priests existed, "it seems extremely likely that the cult of the goddess was administered mainly by women."[5]

Metalworking became a specialized occupation in the late Neolithic period. At Çatal Hüyük, objects of copper and lead, which occur naturally in fairly pure form, date to about 6400 B.C.E. Silver and gold also appear at early dates in various parts of the world. Because of their rarity and their softness, these metals did not replace stone tools and weapons. The discovery of decorative and ceremonial objects of metal in

SECTION REVIEW

- Paleolithic peoples lived mainly by foraging and hunting; women probably did most of the foraging, and men most of the hunting.

- Stone tools, cave paintings, and evidence of food-gathering techniques suggest that Stone Age peoples laid the foundations of science, art, and religion.

- During the Neolithic period, environmental factors prompted an agricultural revolution through which peoples across the globe shifted from foraging and hunting to settled farming.

- In addition to cultivating crops suited to their environments, Neolithic farmers domesticated animals.

- Neolithic communities tended to cohere around extended kinship ties and religious veneration of ancestors.

- In some parts of the world, Neolithic villages grew into towns in which farm produce supported residents engaged in specialized crafts.

graves indicates that they became symbols of status and power.

Towns, specialized crafts, and religious shrines forced the farmers to produce extra food for non-farmers like priests and artisans. The building of permanent houses, walls, and towers, not to mention megalithic monuments, also called for added labor. Stonehenge, for example, took some 30,000 person-hours to build. Whether these tasks were performed freely or coerced is unknown.

Mesopotamia

How did Mesopotamian civilization emerge?

Mesopotamia means "land between the rivers" in Greek, reflecting the importance of the Euphrates and Tigris Rivers to the way of life in this region. Because of the unpredictable spring floods of these rivers, the peoples of ancient Mesopotamia saw themselves at the mercy of gods who embodied the forces of nature. The

Babylon The largest and most important city in Mesopotamia. It achieved particular eminence as the capital of the Amorite king Hammurabi in the eighteenth century B.C.E. and the Neo-Babylonian king Nebuchadnezzar in the sixth century B.C.E.

Babylonian Creation Myth (**Babylon** was the most important city in southern Mesopotamia in the second and first millennia B.C.E.) climaxes in a cosmic battle between Marduk, the chief god of Babylon, and Tiamat (TIE-ah-mat), a female figure who personifies the salt sea. Marduk cuts up Tiamat and from her body fashions the earth and sky. He then creates the divisions of time, the celestial bodies, rivers, and weather phenomena. From the blood of a defeated rebel god, he creates human beings. Myths of this sort explained to the ancient inhabitants of Mesopotamia the environment in which they were living.

Settled Agriculture in an Unstable Landscape

The plain alongside and between the Tigris and Euphrates Rivers, which originate in the mountains of eastern Anatolia (modern Turkey) and empty into the Persian Gulf, has gained fertility from the silt deposited by river floods over many millennia. Today the plain is mostly in Iraq; it gives way to mountains in the north and east: an arc extending from northern Syria through southeastern Anatolia to the Zagros (ZAG-ruhs) Mountains that separate the plain from the Iranian Plateau. To the west and southwest lie the Syrian and Arabian Deserts, to the southeast the Persian Gulf. Floods in this plain, caused by snow melting in the northern mountains, can be sudden and violent. They come inconveniently in the spring when crops, planted in winter to avoid the torrid summer temperatures, are ripening. Floods can also cause the rivers to change course, abruptly cutting off fields and towns from water and river communication.

Although the first domestication of plants and animals around 8000 B.C.E. occurred nearby, in the "Fertile Crescent" region of northern Syria and southeastern Anatolia, agriculture did not reach Mesopotamia until approximately 5000 B.C.E. "Dry" (unirrigated) farming requires at least 8 inches (20 centimeters) of rain a year. The hot, arid climate of southern Mesopotamia calls for irrigation, the artificial provision of water to crops. Initially, people probably channeled water from smaller streams flowing from the Zagros Mountains. But shortly after 3000 B.C.E. they learned to construct canals from the Tigris and Euphrates to supply water as needed and carry it to more distant fields.

Ox-drawn plows, developed by around 4000 B.C.E., cut a furrow in the earth into which carefully measured amounts of seed dropped from an attached funnel. Farmers favored barley as a cereal crop because it could tolerate the Mesopotamian climate and withstand the toxic effects of salt drawn to the earth's surface by evaporation. Fields stood fallow (unplanted) every other year to replenish the nutrients in the soil. Date palms provided food, fiber, and wood; garden plots produced vegetables; and reeds growing along the rivers and in the marshy southern delta yielded raw material for mats, baskets, huts, and boats. Fish was a dietary staple. Herds of sheep and goats, which grazed on fallow land or the nearby desert, provided wool, milk, and meat. Donkeys, originally domesticated in northeast Africa, joined cattle as beasts of burden in the third millennium B.C.E., as did camels from Arabia and horses from the mountains in the second millennium B.C.E.

The written record begins with the **Sumerians** and marks the division, by some definitions, between prehistory and history. Archaeological evidence places the Sumerians in southern Mesopotamia at least by 5000 B.C.E. and perhaps even earlier. They created the framework of civilization in Mesopotamia during a long period of dominance in the third millennium B.C.E. Other peoples lived in Mesopotamia as well. As early as 2900 B.C.E., personal names recorded in inscriptions from the more northerly cities reveal a non-Sumerian **Semitic** (suh-MIT-ik) language. (*Semitic* refers to a family of languages spoken in parts of western Asia and northern Africa. They include the Aramaic [ar-uh-MAY-ik] and Phoenician [fe-NEE-shuhn] of the ancient world and the Hebrew and Arabic of today.) Possibly the descendants of nomads from the

Sumerians The people who dominated southern Mesopotamia through the end of the third millennium B.C.E. They were responsible for the creation of many fundamental elements of Mesopotamian culture—such as irrigation technology, cuneiform writing, and religious conceptions—later adopted by their Semitic successors.

Semitic Family of related languages long spoken across parts of western Asia and northern Africa. In antiquity these languages included Hebrew, Aramaic, and Phoenician. The most widespread modern members of the Semitic family are Arabic and Hebrew.

desert west of Mesopotamia, these Semites seem to have lived in peace with the Sumerians, adopting their culture and sometimes achieving positions of wealth and power.

By 2000 B.C.E., the Semitic peoples had become politically dominant. From this time on, Akkadian (uh-KAY-dee-uhn), a Semitic language, took precedence over Sumerian, although the Sumerian cultural legacy survived in translation. The Sumerian-Akkadian dictionaries compiled at the time to facilitate translations from Sumerian allow us today to read the language, which has no known relatives. The characteristics and adventures of the Semitic gods also indicate cultural borrowing. This cultural synthesis parallels a biological merging of Sumerians and Semites through intermarriage. Though other ethnic groups, including Kassites (KAS-ite) from the eastern mountains and Elamites (EE-luh-mite) and Persians from farther south in Iran, played roles in Mesopotamian history, the Sumerian/Semitic cultural heritage remained fundamentally unaltered until the arrival of Greeks in the late fourth century B.C.E.

Cities, Kings, and Trade

Mesopotamian farmers usually lived in villages. A group of families, totaling a few hundred persons perhaps, could protect one another, work together at key times in the agricultural cycle, and share tools, barns, and threshing floors. Village society also provided companionship and a pool of potential marriage partners.

Occasionally, as a particularly successful village grew, small satellite villages developed nearby and eventually merged with the main village to form an urban center. Many early Mesopotamian city dwellers went out each day to labor in nearby fields. Other city dwellers, however, depended for food on the surplus food production of the villagers. Some specialized in crafts—for example, pottery, artwork, and weapons, tools, and other objects forged out of metal. Others served the gods or carried out administrative duties. Mesopotamian cities controlled the agricultural land and collected crop surpluses from villages in their vicinity. In return, the city provided rural districts with military protection against bandits and raiders and a market where villagers could acquire manufactured goods produced by urban specialists.

The term **city-state** refers to a self-governing urban center and the agricultural territories it controlled. Stretches of uncultivated land, either desert or swamp, served as buffers between the many small city-states of early Mesopotamia. Nevertheless, disputes over land, water rights, and movable property often sparked hostilities between neighboring cities and the building of protective walls of sun-dried bricks. At other times, cities cooperated, sharing water and allowing traders safe passage through their territories.

Mesopotamians opened new land to agriculture by building and maintaining irrigation networks. Canals brought water from river to field; drainage ditches carried the water back to the river before evaporation could draw harmful salt and minerals to the surface. Weirs (partial dams) raised the water level of the river so that water could flow by gravity into the canals. Dikes along the riverbanks protected against floods. The silt carried by floods clogged the canals, which required frequent dredging. In some places, levers with counterweights lifted buckets of irrigation water out of a river or canal.

Successful operation of such sophisticated irrigation systems depended on leaders compelling or persuading large numbers of people to work together. Other projects called for similar cooperation: harvesting, sheep shearing, building of fortifications and large public buildings, and warfare. Two centers of power, the temple and the palace of the king, have left written records, but details of governmental life remain scanty, as are the hints at some sort of citizens' assembly that may have evolved from traditional village councils.

One or more temples, centrally located, housed each city-state's deity or deities and their associated cults (sets of religious rituals). Temples owned agricultural lands and stored the gifts that worshipers donated. The central location of the temple buildings confirms the importance of cults. Head priests, who

city-state A small independent state consisting of an urban center and the surrounding agricultural territory. A characteristic political form in early Mesopotamia, archaic and classical Greece, Phoenicia, and early Italy.

controlled each shrine and managed its wealth, played prominent political and economic roles.

In the third millennium B.C.E., Sumerian documents show the emergence of a *lugal* (LOO-guhl) or "big man"—what we would call a king. An increase in warfare as ever-larger communities quarreled over land, water, and raw materials may have prompted this development, but details are lacking. According to one theory, communities chose certain men to lead their armies in time of war, and these individuals found ways to prolong their authority in peacetime and assume judicial and ritual functions. Although the lugal's position was not hereditary, it often passed from a father to a capable son.

The location of the temple in the city's heart and the less prominent siting of the king's palace symbolize the later emergence of royalty. The king's power grew at the expense of the priesthood, however, because the army backed him. Although the priests and temples retained influence because of their wealth and religious mystique, they gradually became dependent on the palace. Some Mesopotamian kings claimed divinity, but this concept did not take root. Normally the king portrayed himself as the deity's earthly representative.

By the late third millennium B.C.E., kings assumed responsibility for the upkeep and building of temples and the proper performance of ritual. Other royal responsibilities included maintaining city walls and defenses, extending and repairing irrigation channels, guarding property rights, warding off foreign attacks, and establishing justice.

The *Epic of Gilgamesh* referred to at the beginning of this chapter shows both the ambition of the kings and their value to the community. Gilgamesh, who is probably based on a historical king of Uruk, stirs resentment by demanding sexual favors from new brides, but the community relies on his immense strength, wisdom, and courage. In quest of everlasting glory, Gilgamesh walls the city magnificently, stamping his name on every brick. His journey to the faraway Cedar Mountains reflects the king's role in accessing valuable resources.

A few city-states became powerful enough to dominate their neighbors. Sargon (SAHR-gone), ruler of Akkad (AH-kahd) around 2350 B.C.E., pioneered in uniting many cities under one king and capital. His title, King of Sumer and Akkad, symbolized this claim to universal dominion. Sargon and the four family members who succeeded him over 120 years secured their power in several ways. They razed the walls of conquered cities and installed governors backed by garrisons of Akkadian troops. They gave soldiers land to ensure their loyalty. Being of Semitic stock, they adapted the cuneiform (kyoo-NEE-uh-form) system of writing used for Sumerian (discussed later in the chapter) to express their own language. Their administration featured a uniform system of weights and measures and standardized formats for official documents. These measures facilitated assessment and collection of taxes, recruitment of soldiers, and organization of labor projects.

For reasons that remain obscure, the Akkadian state fell around 2230 B.C.E. The Sumerian language and culture revived in the cities of the southern plain under the Third Dynasty of Ur (2112–2004 B.C.E.), a five-king dynasty that maintained itself for a century through campaigns of conquest and prudent marriage alliances. The Akkadian state had controlled more territory, but tighter government control based on a rapidly expanding bureaucracy and obsessive recordkeeping now secured Ur's dominance. Messengers and well-maintained road stations speeded up communications; and an official calendar, standardized weights and measures, and uniform writing practices improved the central administration. To protect against nomadic Semitic Amorites (AM-uh-rites) from the northwest, the kings erected a wall 125 miles (200 kilometers) long. Eventually, however, nomad incursions combined with an Elamite attack from the southeast toppled the Third Dynasty of Ur.

The Amorites founded a new city at Babylon, not far from Akkad. Toward the end of a long reign, **Hammurabi** (HAM-uh-rah-bee) (r. 1792–1750 B.C.E.) initiated a series of aggressive military campaigns, and Babylon became the capital of what historians have named the "Old Babylonian" state, which eventually stretched beyond Sumer and Akkad into the north

Primary Source: The Epic of Gilgamesh Find out how Gilgamesh's friend Enkidu propels him on a quest for immortality, and whether or not that quest is successful.

and northwest, from 1900 to 1600 B.C.E. Hammurabi's famous Law Code, inscribed on a polished black stone pillar, provided judges with a lengthy set of examples illustrating the principles to be used in deciding cases. Some examples called for severe physical punishments to compensate for crimes. These Amorite notions of justice differed from the monetary penalties prescribed in earlier codes from Ur.

Conquest gave some Mesopotamian city-states access to vital resources. Trade offered an alternative, and long-distance commerce flourished in most periods. Evidence of seagoing vessels appears as early as the fifth millennium B.C.E. Wood, metals, and stone came from foreign lands in exchange for wool, cloth, barley, and vegetable oil. Cedar forests in Lebanon and Syria yielded wood, Anatolia produced silver, Egypt gold, and the eastern Mediterranean and Oman (on the Arabian peninsula) copper. Tin, which in alloy with copper made bronze, came from Afghanistan (in South-Central Asia), and chlorite, a greenish, easily carved stone, from the Iranian plateau. Jewelers and stone-carvers used black diorite from the Persian Gulf,

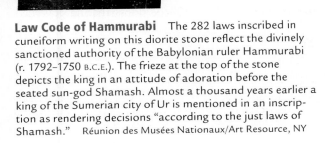

Law Code of Hammurabi   The 282 laws inscribed in cuneiform writing on this diorite stone reflect the divinely sanctioned authority of the Babylonian ruler Hammurabi (r. 1792–1750 B.C.E.). The frieze at the top of the stone depicts the king in an attitude of adoration before the seated sun-god Shamash. Almost a thousand years earlier a king of the Sumerian city of Ur is mentioned in an inscription as rendering decisions "according to the just laws of Shamash."   Réunion des Musées Nationaux/Art Resource, NY

blue lapis lazuli (LAP-is LAZ-uh-lee) from Afghanistan, and reddish carnelian (kahr-NEEL-yuhn) from Pakistan.

Most merchants worked for the palace or the temple in the third millennium B.C.E. Only these institutions commanded the financial resources and organizational skills needed for acquiring, transporting, and protecting valuable commodities. Merchants exchanged surpluses from the royal or temple farmlands for raw materials and luxury goods. In the second millennium B.C.E., independent merchants and merchant guilds gained increasing influence.

Sources do not reveal whether the most important commercial transactions took place in the area just inside the city gates or in the vicinity of the docks. Wherever they occurred, coined money played no role. Coins—stamped metal pieces of state-guaranteed value—first appeared in the sixth century B.C.E. and did not reach Mesopotamia until several centuries later. For most of Mesopotamian history, items that could not be bartered—traded for one another—had their value calculated in relation to fixed weights of precious metal, primarily silver, or measures of grain.

Mesopotamian Society

Urbanized civilizations foster social division, that is, obvious variation in the status and privileges of different groups according to wealth, social function, and legal and political rights. Urbanization, specialization of function, centralization of power, and the use of written records enabled certain groups to amass unprecedented wealth. Temple leaders and the kings controlled large agricultural estates, and the palace administration collected taxes from subjects. How elite individuals acquired large private landholdings is unknown, since land was rarely put up for sale. In some cases, however, debtors lost their land to creditors, or soldiers and priests received land in return for their services.

The Law Code of Hammurabi in the eighteenth century B.C.E. reflects social divisions that may also

Hammurabi   Amorite ruler of Babylon (r. 1792–1750 B.C.E.). He conquered many city-states in southern and northern Mesopotamia and is best known for a code of laws, inscribed on a black stone pillar, illustrating the principles to be used in legal cases.

have been valid for other places and times, despite inevitable fluctuations. It identifies three classes: (1) the free landowning class: royalty, high-ranking officials, warriors, priests, merchants, and some artisans and shopkeepers; (2) the class of dependent farmers and artisans, whose legal attachment to royal, temple, or private estates made them the primary rural work force; and (3) the class of slaves, primarily employed in domestic service.

Penalties prescribed in the Law Code depended on the class of the offender. The lower orders received the most severe punishments. Slaves, many of them prisoners of war from the mountains, and insolvent debtors played a lesser economic role than they would in the later societies of Greece and Rome (see Chapters 4 and 6). Identified by a distinctive hairstyle rather than chains or brands, they would have a barber shave off the telltale mark if they were lucky enough to regain their freedom. Because commodities such as food and oil were distributed to all people in proportion to their age, gender, and task, documents do not always distinguish between slaves or dependent workers and free laborers. In the Old Babylonian period, the class of people who were not dependent on the temple or palace grew, the amount of land and other property in private hands increased, and free laborers became more common.

The daily lives of ordinary Mesopotamians, especially those in villages or on large estates, left few archaeological or literary traces. Peasants built with mud brick and reeds, which quickly disintegrate, and they had few metal possessions. Being illiterate, they left no written record of their lives. It is especially difficult to discover much about the experiences of women. Males dominated the position of **scribe**—an administrator or scholar charged by the temple or palace with reading and writing tasks—and, for the most part, their writings reflect elite male activities. Archaeology only partially fills this gap.

Anthropologists theorize that women lost social standing and freedom with the spread of agriculture.

In hunting and gathering societies, they believe, women's foraging provided most of the community's food. But in Mesopotamia, food production depended on the heavy physical labor of plowing, harvesting, and digging irrigation channels, jobs usually performed by men. Since food surpluses made larger families possible, bearing and raising children became the primary occupation of many women, leaving them little time to acquire the specialized skills of a scribe or artisan.

Women could own property, maintain control of their dowry, and even engage in trade, but men monopolized political life. Some women worked outside the household in textile factories and breweries or as prostitutes, tavern keepers, bakers, or fortunetellers. Home tasks for nonelite women probably included helping with farming, growing vegetables, cooking, cleaning, fetching water, tending the household fire, and weaving baskets and textiles.

The standing of women seems to have declined further in the second millennium B.C.E., perhaps because of the rise of an urbanized middle class and an increase in private wealth. Husbands gained authority in the household and benefited from marriage and divorce laws. A man normally took just one wife, but he could obtain a second if the first gave him no children. In later Mesopotamian history, kings and rich men had several wives. Marriage alliances arranged between families made women instruments for preserving and enhancing family wealth. Alternatively, a family might decide to avoid a daughter's marriage, with the resulting loss of a dowry, by dedicating her to temple service as "god's bride." Constraints on women's lives, such as remaining at home and wearing veils in public, may date back to the second millennium B.C.E. (see Chapter 9).

Gods, Priests, and Temples

The Sumerian gods embodied the forces of nature: Anu the sky, Enlil the air, Enki the water, Utu the sun, and Nanna the moon. The goddess Inanna governed

---

Primary Source: The State Regulates Health Care: Hammurabi's Code and Surgeons Get a glimpse of the various rewards and perilous punishments for surgeons who either succeed or fail at their job in 1800 B.C.E.

scribe In the governments of many ancient societies, a professional position reserved for men who had undergone the lengthy training required to be able to read and write using cuneiforms, hieroglyphics, or other early, cumbersome writing systems.

Mesopotamian Cylinder Seal   Seals indicated the identity of an individual and were impressed into wet clay or wax to "sign" legal documents or mark ownership of an object. This seal, produced in the period of the Akkadian Empire, depicts Ea (second from right), the god of the underground waters, symbolized by the stream with fish emanating from his shoulders; Ishtar, whose attributes of fertility and war are indicated by the date cluster in her hand and the pointed weapons showing above her wings; and the sun-god Shamash, cutting his way out of the mountains with a jagged knife, an evocation of sunrise.   Courtesy of the Trustees of the British Museum

sexual attraction and violence. When the Semitic peoples became dominant, they equated their deities with those of the Sumerians. The Sumerian gods Nanna and Utu, for example, became the Semitic Sin and Shamash, and the goddess Inanna became Ishtar. The Semitic gods took over the myths and many of the rituals of their Sumerian predecessors.

People imagined their gods as anthropomorphic (an-thruh-po-MORE-fik), that is, like humans in form and conduct. The gods had bodies and senses, sought nourishment from sacrifice, enjoyed the worship and obedience of humanity, and experienced the human emotions of lust, love, hate, anger, and envy. Religious beliefs instilled fear of the gods, who could alter the landscape, and a desire to appease them.

Public, state-organized religion stands out in the archaeological record. Cities built temples and showed devotion to the divinity or divinities who protected the community. All the peoples of Sumer regarded Nippur (see Map 1.1) as a religious center because of its temple to the air-god Enlil. As with other temples, they considered it the god's residence and believed the cult statue in its interior shrine embodied his life force. Priests attended this divine image, trying to anticipate and meet its every need

in a daily cycle of waking, bathing, dressing, feeding, moving around, entertaining, soothing, and revering. These rituals reflected the message of the Babylonian Creation Myth that humankind existed only to serve the gods. Several thousand priests may have staffed a large temple like that of the god Marduk at Babylon.

Priests passed their office and sacred lore to their sons, and their families lived on rations of food from the deity's estates. The amount an individual received depended on his rank within a complicated hierarchy of status and specialized function. The high priest performed the central acts in the great rituals. Certain priests pleasured the gods with music, others exorcised evil spirits, and still others interpreted dreams and divined the future by examining the organs of sacrificed animals, reading patterns in rising incense smoke, or casting dice.

A high wall surrounded the temple precinct, which contained the shrine of the chief deity; open plazas; chapels for lesser gods; housing, dining facilities, and offices for priests and other temple staff; and buildings for crafts, storage, and other services. The compound focused on the **ziggurat** (ZIG-uh-rat), a multistory, mud-brick, pyramid-shaped tower approached by ramps and stairs. Scholars are still debating the ziggurat's function and symbolic meaning.

Scholars similarly debate whether common people had much access to temple buildings and how religious practices and beliefs affected their everyday lives. Individuals placed votive statues in the sanctuaries in the belief that these miniature replicas of themselves could continually seek the deity's favor. The survival of many **amulets** (small charms meant to protect the bearer from evil) and representations of a host of demons suggests widespread belief in magic— the use of special words and rituals to manipulate the forces of nature. For example, people believed that a demon caused headaches and could be driven out of the ailing body. Lamashtu, the demon who caused miscarriages, could be frightened off if a pregnant woman wore an amulet with the likeness of the hideous but beneficent demon Pazuzu. A god or goddess might also be persuaded to reveal the future in return for a gift or sacrifice.

Elite and common folk came together in great festivals such as the twelve-day New Year's festival held each spring in Babylon as the new grain was beginning to sprout in the fields. In the early days of the festival, in conjunction with rituals of purification and invocations of Marduk, a priest read to the god's image the text of the Babylonian Creation Epic. Many subsequent activities in the temple courtyard and streets reenacted the events of the myth. Following their belief that time moved in a circular path through a cycle of birth, growth, maturity, and death, people hoped through this ritual to persuade the gods to grant a renewal of time and life at winter's end.

Technology and Science

The term *technology* comes from the Greek word *techne*, meaning "craft" or "specialized knowledge." It normally refers to the tools and processes by which humans manipulate the physical world. However, many scholars also use it more broadly for any specialized knowledge used to transform the natural environment and human society. Ancient Mesopotamian irrigation techniques that expanded agricultural production fit the first definition, priestly belief in their ability to enhance prosperity through prayers and rituals the second.

Writing, which first appeared in Mesopotamia before 3300 B.C.E., partakes more of the second

definition than of the first. The earliest inscribed tablets, found in the chief temple at Uruk, date from a time when the temple was the community's most important economic institution. The most plausible current theory maintains that writing originated from a system of tokens used to keep track of property—sheep, cattle, wagon wheels—as wealth accumulated and the volume and complexity of commerce strained people's memories. The shape and number of tokens inserted in clay "envelopes" (balls of clay) indicated the contents of a shipment or storeroom, and pictures of the tokens incised on the outside of the envelope reminded the reader of what was inside.

Eventually people realized that the incised pictures, the first written symbols, provided an adequate record of the transaction and made the tokens inside the envelope redundant. Each early symbol represented a thing, but it could also stand for the sound of the word for that thing when that sound was a syllable of a longer word. For example, the symbols *shu* for "hand" and *mu* for "water" could be combined to form *shumu*, the word for "name."

The usual method of writing involved pressing the point of a sharpened reed into a moist clay tablet. Because the reed made wedge-shaped impressions, the early pictures, which were more or less realistic, evolved into stylized combinations of strokes and wedges, a system known as **cuneiform** (Latin for "wedge-shaped") writing. Mastering cuneiform, which in any particular period involved several hundred signs, compared to the twenty-five or so in an alphabetic system, required years of practice. In the "tablet-house" attached to a temple or palace,

---

ziggurat A massive pyramidal stepped tower made of mud bricks. It is associated with religious complexes in ancient Mesopotamian cities, but its function is unknown.

amulet Small charm meant to protect the bearer from evil. Found frequently in archaeological excavations in Mesopotamia and Egypt, amulets reflect the religious practices of the common people.

cuneiform a system of writing in which wedge-shaped symbols represented words or syllables. It originated in Mesopotamia and was used initially for Sumerian and Akkadian but later was adapted to represent other languages of western Asia. Because so many symbols had to be learned, literacy was confined to a relatively small group of administrators and scribes.

students learned writing and mathematics under a stern headmaster and endured bullying by older student tutors called "big brothers." The prestige and regular employment that went with their position may have made scribes reluctant to simplify the cuneiform system. Although in the Old Babylonian period the growth of private commerce brought an increase in the number of people who could read and write, literacy remained a rare accomplishment.

Developed originally for the Sumerian language, cuneiform—a system of writing rather than a language—later served to express the Akkadian language of the Mesopotamian Semites as well as other languages of western Asia, such as Hittite, Elamite, and Persian. The remains of the ancient city of Ebla (EH-bluh) in northern Syria illustrate the Mesopotamian influence on other parts of western Asia. Ebla's buildings and artifacts follow Mesopotamian models, and thousands of tablets inscribed with cuneiform symbols bear messages in both Sumerian and the local Semitic dialect. The high point of Ebla's wealth and power occurred from 2400 to 2250 B.C.E., roughly contemporary with the Akkadian Empire. Ebla then controlled extensive territory and derived wealth from agriculture, manufacture of woolen cloth, and trade with Mesopotamia and the Mediterranean coast.

Economic concerns predominate in the earliest Sumerian documents, but cuneiform came to have wide-ranging uses beyond the recordkeeping that apparently inspired its invention. Legal acts that had formerly been validated by the recitation of oral formulas and performance of symbolic acts came to be accompanied by written documents marked with the seals of the participants. Cuneiform similarly served political, literary, religious, and scientific purposes.

Other technologies met the challenges of the physical environment. Irrigation, the basis of Mesopotamian agriculture, required the construction and maintenance of canals, weirs, and dikes. Cattle drew carts and sledges in some locations. In the south, where numerous water channels cut up the landscape, boats and barges predominated. In northern Mesopotamia, donkeys served as pack animals for overland caravans in the centuries before the advent of the camel around 1200 B.C.E.

To improve on stone tools, the Mesopotamians imported ores containing copper, tin, and arsenic. From these they made bronze, a form of copper alloyed with either tin or arsenic. Craftsmen poured molten bronze into molds shaped like weapons or tools. The cooled metal took a sharper edge than stone, was less likely to break, and was more easily repaired. Yet stone implements remained in use among poor people who could not afford bronze.

Clay, Mesopotamia's most abundant resource, went into the making of mud bricks. Whether dried in the sun or baked in an oven for greater durability, these constituted the main building material. Construction of city walls, temples, and palaces required practical knowledge of architecture and engineering. For example, the reed mats that Mesopotamian builders laid between the mud-brick layers of ziggurats served the same stabilizing purpose as girders in modern high-rise construction. The abundance of good clay also made pottery the most common material for dishes, storage vessels, and oil lamps (see Material Culture: Lamps and Candles). By 4000 B.C.E., potters had begun to use a revolving platform called a potter's wheel. Spun by hands or feet, the potter's wheel made possible rapid manufacture in precise and complex shapes.

Military technology changed as armies evolved from the early militias called up for short periods to the well-trained and well-paid full-time soldiers of the late third and second millennia B.C.E. In the early second millennium B.C.E., horses appeared in western Asia, and the horse-drawn chariot, a technically complicated device, came into vogue. Infantry found themselves at the mercy of swift chariots carrying a driver and an archer who could easily overtake them. Using increasingly effective siege machinery, Mesopotamian soldiers learned to climb over, undermine, or knock down the walls protecting the cities of their enemies.

Mesopotamians used a base-60 number system (the origin of the seconds and minutes we use today), in which numbers were expressed as fractions or multiples of 60 (in contrast to our base-10 system). Such advances in mathematics along with careful observation of the skies made the Mesopotamians sophisticated practitioners of astronomy. Mesopotamian priests compiled lists of omens or unusual sightings on earth and in the heavens, together with a record of the events that coincided with them. They consulted these texts at critical times, for they believed that the

Material Culture

Lamps and Candles

It is hard to imagine today how dark the world was after the sun went down throughout most of human history. The glow of a fire did not extend far. Nor were torches easy to make or long-lasting. A stick wrapped with oil-soaked cloth at one end does make an effective torch, but humans were in need of light long before they figured out how to make cloth. As for flammable oil, vegetable oils extracted from the seeds of olive or palm trees, or from plants like flax, lettuce, and corn, became abundant only with the spread of plant domestication in the Neolithic period. Prior to that, animal fat or tallow could be used, though it had the disadvantage of smelling like meat.

The Neolithic revolutions made available not only vegetable oils but also pottery, and later metal, vessels that could be used as lamps. A fireproof vessel would be filled with oil, and a wick would be placed so that one end was immersed in the oil and the other open to the air. The oil would saturate the wick, and a flame touched to the wick would vaporize a small amount of oil and ignite the resultant gas. A poor wick might sputter, smoke, or go out. The pith or inner porous core of plants of the rush family could be used as wicks in rushlamps, or the oil-soaked pith stiffened by part of the outer skin of the rush could be stood upright and lit like slender candles in rushlights.

Aside from the pith of rushes, wicks were usually made of string or a sliver of wood. Since a wick of greater diameter produces a larger flame, braiding was used to make a thicker string. Of all natural fibers, cotton makes the best wicks because of its absorbency. Different varieties of cotton were native to India and pre-Columbian America, but cotton became a major crop in the Middle East only in the early Islamic period of the eighth century C.E.. Christian Europe knew cotton only as an expensive import until the twelfth century, when a cotton industry was founded in northern Italy. Access to superior wicks contributed to an increase in European candle use.

Waxes differ from oils in being solid at room temperature. Molding wax around a wick produces a candle. Beeswax provided an ideal material for odorless candles and was in use for lighting as early as ancient Egyptian times. However, beeswax was scarce and expensive. Some premodern trade routes, such as those going south to the Middle East

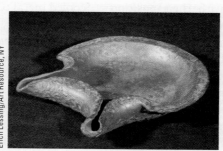

Erich Lessing/Art Resource, NY

Ancient Lamp Vessel This 2,500-year-old oil lamp from Megiddo in Israel has grooves for two wicks. It is made of bronze, a valuable metal. Pottery lamps were much cheaper and show up abundantly in ancient archaeological sites.

along the rivers of Russia, featured beeswax as a major product. Beeswax candles came to play a prominent and often symbolic role in Christian, Jewish, and Buddhist religious rituals. Mosques, on the other hand, were traditionally lit by oil lamps.

Though whaling was practiced in certain coastal regions in prehistoric times, the extraction of whale oil on an industrial scale began in the sixteenth century and grew rapidly over the next three hundred years. Oil extracted from the whale's fat, or blubber, was widely used for lamps. Of even greater value was a wax called spermaceti that was made from an oily substance in the heads of sperm whales. A large whale might yield three tons of spermaceti. It burned without odor in candles and became the standard for candle making until the discovery of paraffin, a wax made from petroleum, in 1830. Paraffin generally replaced spermaceti as the preferred wax for candles.

The small flames of oil lamps and candles did not produce much illumination. Candela is the name of a unit of light intensity that became increasingly precise over the course of the nineteenth and twentieth centuries. It is intended to represent the light produced by a single candle, though many technical specifications, such as the color of the light, make it only an approximation. An even rougher approximation equates 120 candelas with the illumination provided by a 100-watt light bulb. This last approximation suggests how little light a single lamp or candle could provide in premodern times for reading, sewing, or doing any kind of fine work after sundown.

QUESTIONS FOR ANALYSIS

1. How would the provision of artificial light affect patterns of life with the change of seasons?
2. What human activities, such as storytelling, might have been enhanced by a lack of light?
3. How did gradual adoption of gaslight (1792) and the electric light bulb (1879) change people's lives?

SECTION REVIEW

- The first people to develop a complex society that produced written records were the Sumerians.

- Mesopotamian farming villages grew into towns, some of which later expanded into city-states.

- At the expense of the priesthood, kings assumed responsibility for administrative, legal, and military activities.

- The urban civilization of Mesopotamia developed a high degree of social division, a hierarchy in which women steadily lost standing.

- Mesopotamian gods embodied natural forces and were worshiped through public, state-directed, and temple-centered rituals.

- The Mesopotamians developed a wide range of technologies, the most important of which was writing.

recurrence of such phenomena could provide clues to future developments. The underlying premise was that the elements of the material universe, from the microcosmic to the macrocosmic, were interconnected in mysterious but undeniable ways.

Egypt

What role did the environment and religion play in Egyptian civilization?

No place exhibits the impact of the natural environment on the history and culture of a society better than ancient Egypt. Though located at the intersection of Asia and Africa, Egypt was less a crossroads than an isolated land protected by surrounding barriers of desert and a harborless, marshy seacoast. Whereas Mesopotamia was open to migration or invasion and was dependent on imported resources, Egypt's natural isolation and material self-sufficiency fostered a unique culture that for long periods had relatively little to do with other civilizations.

The Land of Egypt: "Gift of the Nile"

The world's longest river, the Nile flows northward from Lake Victoria and draws water from several large tributaries in the highlands of tropical Africa. Carving a narrow valley between a chain of hills on either side, it terminates at the Mediterranean Sea (see Map 1.2). Though bordered mostly

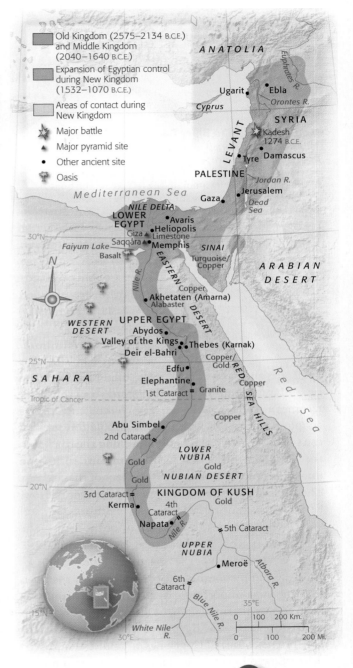

Map 1.2 Ancient Egypt The Nile River, flowing south to north, carved out of the surrounding desert a narrow green valley that became heavily settled in antiquity.
© Cengage Learning

Interactive Map

Model of Egyptian River Boat, ca. 1985 B.C.E.
This model was buried in the tomb of a Middle King-dom official, Meketre, who is shown in the cabin being entertained by musicians. The captain stands in front of the cabin, the helmsman on the left steers the boat with the rudder, while the lookout on the right lets out a weighted line to determine the river's depth. The vessel is being rowed downstream (northward); the white post in the middle would support a mast and sail when traveling upstream. Image copyright © The Metropolitan Museum of Art/Art Resource, NY

History in Focus *Examine the image, paying particular attention to what the figures are doing. What aspects of ancient Egyptian culture and worldview does this model represent? Find the answer online.*

by desert, the banks of the river support lush vegetation. About 100 miles (160 kilometers) from the Mediterranean, the river divides into channels to form a triangular delta. Most of Egypt's population lives on the twisting, green ribbon of land along the river or in the Nile Delta. Bleak deserts of mountains, rocks, and dunes occupy the remaining 90 percent of the country. The ancient Egyptians distinguished between the low-lying, life-sustaining "Black Land" with its dark soil and the elevated, deadly "Red Land" of the desert. The fifth-century B.C.E. Greek traveler Herodotus (he-RA-duh-tuhs) called Egypt the "gift of the Nile."

Travel and communication centered on the river, with the most important cities located upstream away from the Mediterranean. Because the river flows from south to north, the Egyptians called the southern part of the country "Upper Egypt" and the northern delta "Lower Egypt." The First Cataract of the Nile, the northernmost of a series of impassable rocks and rapids below Aswan (AS-wahn) (about 500 miles [800 kilometers] south of the Mediterranean), formed Egypt's southern boundary in most periods, but Egyptian control sometimes extended farther south into what was called "Kush" (later Nubia, today part of southern Egypt and northern Sudan). The Egyptians

also settled certain large oases west of the river, green and habitable "islands" in the midst of the desert.

The hot, sunny climate favored agriculture. Though rain rarely falls south of the delta, the river provided water to irrigation channels that carried water out into the valley and increased the area suitable for planting. In one large depression west of the Nile, drainage techniques reduced the size of Lake Faiyum (fie-YOOM) and allowed land to be reclaimed for agriculture. Each September, the river overflowed its banks, spreading water into the bordering valley. Unlike the Mesopotamians, the Egyptians needed no dams or weirs to raise the level of the river and divert water into channels. Moreover, the Nile, unlike the Tigris and Euphrates, flooded at the best time for grain agriculture. When the flood receded and its waters drained back into the river, the land had a fertile new layer of mineral-rich silt, and farmers could easily plant their crops in the moist soil. The Egyptians' many creation myths commonly featured the emergence of a life-supporting mound of earth from a primeval swamp.

The level of the flood's crest determined the abundance of the following harvest. Too little water left fertile land unirrigated and hence uncultivable, plunging the country into famine. The ebb and flow of successful and failed regimes seems linked to the cycle of floods. Nevertheless, remarkable stability

Primary Source: Hymn for the Nile Discover the degree to which the Nile River is viewed as godlike and the perceived power it has over the survival of the people of Egypt.

characterized most eras, and Egyptians viewed the universe as an orderly and beneficent place.

Egypt had other resources besides the Nile. Papyrus reeds growing in marshes yielded fibers that made good sails, ropes, and a kind of paper. The wild animals and birds and the abundant river fish attracted hunters and fishermen. Building stone could be quarried and floated downstream from southern Egypt. And the state organized armed expeditions and forced labor to exploit nearby resources such as the copper and turquoise deposits in the Sinai desert to the east and gold from Nubia to the south.

The farming villages that appeared in Egypt as early as 5500 B.C.E. relied on domesticated plant and animal species that had emerged several millennia earlier in western Asia. Egypt's emergence as a focal point of civilization, however, stemmed at least partially from a gradual change in climate from the fifth to the third millennium B.C.E. Before that time, the Sahara, today the world's largest desert, had a relatively mild and wet climate. Its lakes and grasslands supported a variety of plant and animal species as well as populations of hunter-gatherers (see Chapter 8). As the climate changed and the Sahara began to dry up, displaced groups migrated into the then marshy Nile Valley, where they developed a sedentary way of life.

Divine Kingship

The increasing population called for greater complexity in political organization, including a form of local kingship. Later generations of Egyptians saw the unification of such smaller units into a single state by Menes (MEH-neez), a ruler from the south, as a pivotal event. Scholars question whether this event, dated to around 3100 B.C.E., took place at the hands of a historical or a mythical figure, but many authorities equate Menes with Narmer, a historical ruler who is shown on a decorated slate palette exulting over defeated enemies. Later kings of Egypt bore the title "Ruler of the Two Lands"—Upper and Lower Egypt—and wore two crowns symbolizing the unification of the country. Unlike Mesopotamia, therefore, Egypt discovered unity early in its history.

Following the practice of Manetho, an Egyptian priest from the fourth century B.C.E., historians divide Egyptian history into thirty dynasties (sequences of kings from the same family). The rise and fall of dynasties often reflect the dominance

of one or another part of the country. Scholars also divide Egyptian history into "Old," "Middle," and "New Kingdoms," each a period of centralized political power and brilliant cultural achievement. "Intermediate Periods" signal political fragmentation and cultural decline. Although experts debate the specific dates, the chronology reflects current opinion.

The Egyptian state centered on the king, often known by the New Kingdom term **pharaoh**, from an Egyptian phrase meaning "palace." From the Old Kingdom on, if not earlier, Egyptians considered the king a god on earth, the incarnation of Horus and the son of the sun-god Re (ray). In this role he maintained **ma'at** (muh-AHT), the divinely authorized order of the universe. As a link between the people and the gods, his benevolent rule ensured the welfare and prosperity of the country. The Egyptians' conception of a divine king, the source of law and justice, may explain the apparent absence in Egypt of an impersonal code of law comparable to Hammurabi's Code in Mesopotamia.

So much depended on the kings that their deaths evoked elaborate efforts to ensure the well-being of their spirits on their journey to rejoin the gods. Carrying out funerary rites, constructing royal tombs, and sustaining the kings' spirits in the afterlife by perpetual offerings in adjoining funerary chapels demanded massive resources. Flat-topped, rectangular tombs made of mud brick sufficed for the earliest rulers, but around 2630 B.C.E., Djoser (JO-sur), a Third Dynasty king, ordered the construction of a stepped **pyramid**—a series of stone platforms laid one on top of the other—at Saqqara (suh-KAHR-uh), near Memphis.

pharaoh The central figure in the ancient Egyptian state. Believed to be an earthly manifestation of the gods, he used his absolute power to maintain the safety and prosperity of Egypt.

ma'at Egyptian term for the concept of divinely created and maintained order in the universe. Reflecting the ancient Egyptians' belief in an essentially beneficent world, the divine ruler was the earthly guarantor of this order.

pyramid A large, triangular stone monument, used in Egypt and Nubia as a burial place for the king. The largest pyramids, erected during the Old Kingdom near Memphis with stone tools and compulsory labor, reflect the Egyptian belief that the proper and spectacular burial of the divine ruler would guarantee the continued prosperity of the land.

Pyramids of Menkaure, Khafre, and Khufu at Giza, ca. 2500 B.C.E. With a width of 755 feet (230 meters) and a height of 480 feet (146 meters), the Great Pyramid of Khufu is the largest stone structure ever built. The construction of these massive edifices depended on relatively simple techniques of stonecutting, transport (the stones were floated downriver on boats and rolled to the site on sledges), and lifting (the stones were dragged up the face of the pyramid on mud-brick ramps). However, the surveying and engineering skills required to level the platform, lay out the measurements, and securely position the blocks were very sophisticated and have withstood the test of time.

Michele Burgess/SuperStock

 History in Focus *These pyramids were built at the very beginning of Egyptian civilization. Why has no one ever built a larger stone structure since then? Find the answer online.*

Rulers of the Fourth Dynasty filled in the steps of Djoser's tomb to create the smooth-sided, limestone pyramids that most often symbolize ancient Egypt. Between 2550 and 2490 B.C.E., the pharaohs Khufu (KOO-foo) and Khefren (KEF-ren) erected huge pyramids at Giza, several miles north of Saqqara, the largest stone structures ever built. Khufu's pyramid originally reached a height of 480 feet (146 meters).

Egyptians accomplished this construction with stone tools (bronze was still expensive and rare) and no machinery other than simple levers, pulleys, and rollers. Calculations of the human muscle power needed to build a pyramid within a ruler's lifetime indicate that large numbers of people must have been pressed into service for part of each year, probably during the flood season, when no agricultural work could be done. The Egyptian masses probably considered this demand for labor a kind of religious service that would help ensure prosperity. Most of Egypt's surplus resources went into constructing these artificial mountains of stone. The age of the great pyramids lasted about a century, though construction of pyramids on a smaller scale continued.

Administration and Communication

Ruling dynasties usually placed their capitals in the area of their original power base. **Memphis**, near today's Cairo at the apex of the Nile Delta, held this central position during the Old Kingdom; but **Thebes**, far to the south, often supplanted it during the Middle and New Kingdoms (see Map 1.2). A complex bureaucracy kept detailed records of the country's resources. At the village, district, and central government levels, bureaucrats kept track of land, labor, products, and people, extracting as taxes as much as 50 percent of the annual revenues of the country. This income supported the palace, bureaucracy,

Memphis The capital of Old Kingdom Egypt, near the head of the Nile Delta. Early rulers were interred in the nearby pyramids.
Thebes Capital city of Egypt and home of the ruling dynasties during the Middle and New Kingdoms. Amon, patron deity of Thebes, became one of the chief gods of Egypt. Monarchs were buried across the river in the Valley of the Kings.

and army, paid for building and maintaining temples, and made possible great monuments celebrating the king's grandeur. The government maintained a monopoly over key sectors of the economy and controlled long-distance trade. The urban middle-class traders who increasingly managed the commerce of Mesopotamia had no parallel in Egypt.

A writing system had been developed before the Early Dynastic period, and literacy was the hallmark of the administrative class. **Hieroglyphics** (high-ruh-GLIF-iks), the earliest form of this system, featured picture symbols standing for words, syllables, or individual sounds. We can read ancient Egyptian writing today only because of the discovery in the early nineteenth century C.E. of the Rosetta stone, an inscription from the second century B.C.E. that gave hieroglyphic and Greek versions of the same text.

Hieroglyphic writing was used on monuments and ornamental inscriptions for a long time. By 2500 B.C.E., however, administrators and copyists had developed a cursive script, in which the original pictorial nature of the symbol was less apparent, for their everyday needs. They wrote with ink on a writing material called **papyrus** (puh-PIE-ruhs), made from the stems of the papyrus reed that grew in the Nile marshes. Papyrus makers laid out the stems in a vertical and horizontal grid pattern, moistened them, and then pounded them with a soft mallet until they adhered into a sheet of writing material. A uniquely Egyptian product, papyrus served scribes throughout the ancient world and was exported in large quantities. The word *paper* comes from Greek and Roman words for papyrus.

Apart from administrative recordkeeping, Egyptian literary compositions included tales of adventure and magic, love poetry, religious hymns, and instruction manuals on technical subjects. Scribes in workshops attached to the temples made copies of traditional texts.

Strong monarchs appointed and promoted officials on the basis of merit and accomplishment, giving them grants of land cultivated by dependent peasants. Low-level officials worked in villages and district capitals; high-ranking officials served in the royal capital. During the Old Kingdom, the tombs of officials lay near the monumental tomb of the king so they could serve him in death as they had in life.

Egyptian history exhibits a recurring tension between the centralizing power of the monarchy and the decentralizing tendencies of the bureaucracy. The shift of officials' tombs from the vicinity of the royal tomb to the home districts where they spent much of their time and exercised power more or less independently signaled the breakdown of centralized power in the late Old Kingdom and First Intermediate Period. Inheritance of administrative posts similarly indicated a decline in centralized power. The early monarchs of the Middle Kingdom restored centralized power by reducing the power and prerogatives of the old elite and creating a new middle class of administrators.

The common observation that Egypt was a land of villages without real cities stems from its capitals being primarily extensions of the palace and central administration. Compared to Mesopotamia, a far larger percentage of the Egyptian population lived in farming villages, and Egypt's wealth derived to a higher degree from cultivating the land. The towns and cities that did exist unfortunately lie buried beneath modern urban sites, since Egypt has too little land in its cultivable region to afford abandonment of a large area.

hieroglyphics A system of writing in which pictorial symbols represented sounds, syllables, or concepts. It was used for official and monumental inscriptions in ancient Egypt. Because of the long period of study required to master this system, literacy in hieroglyphics was confined to a relatively small group of scribes and administrators. Cursive symbol-forms were developed for rapid composition on other media, such as papyrus.

papyrus A reed that grows along the banks of the Nile River in Egypt. From it was produced a paper-like writing medium used by the Egyptians and many other peoples in the ancient Mediterranean and Middle East.

 Primary Source: Advice to Ambitious Young Egyptians: Rise Above the Masses, Become a Scribe! This interesting piece of propaganda serves to convince potential scribes that the job of scribe is the best of all possible occupations.

Egypt largely stuck to itself during the Old and Middle Kingdoms, all foreigners being technically regarded as enemies. When necessary, local militia units backed up a small standing army of professional soldiers. Nomadic groups in the eastern and western deserts and Libyans to the northwest posed a nuisance more than a real danger. The king maintained limited contact with other advanced civilizations in the region, and Egypt's interests abroad focused on maintaining access to resources rather than on acquiring territory. Trade with the coast of the Levant (luh-VANT) (modern Israel, Lebanon, and Syria) brought in cedar wood in return for grain, papyrus, and gold.

Egypt's strongest interests involved goods from the south. Nubia contained gold mines (in Chapter 2 we examine the rise in Nubia of a civilization influenced by Egypt but also vital, original, and long lasting), and the southern course of the Nile offered access to sub-Saharan Africa. In the Old Kingdom, Egyptian noblemen living at Aswan on the southern border led donkey caravans south in search of gold, incense, and products from tropical Africa such as ivory, ebony, and exotic animals. Forts along the border protected Egypt from attack. In the early second millennium B.C.E., Egyptian forces invaded Nubia and extended the Egyptian border as far as the Third Cataract of the Nile, taking possession of the gold fields.

The People of Egypt

The estimated million to a million and a half inhabitants of Egypt included various physical types, ranging from dark-skinned people related to the populations of sub-Saharan Africa to lighter-skinned people akin to the populations of North Africa and western Asia who spoke Berber and Semitic languages, respectively. Though Egypt experienced no migrations or invasions on a scale common in Mesopotamian history, settlers periodically trickled into the Nile Valley and mixed with the local people.

Egypt had less pronounced social divisions than Mesopotamia, where a formal class structure emerged. The king and high-ranking officials enjoyed status, wealth, and power. Below them came lower-level officials, local leaders, priests and other professionals, artisans, and well-to-do farmers. Peasants, at the bottom, constituted the vast majority of the population.

Peasants lived in rural villages and devoted themselves to the seasonally changing tasks of agriculture: plowing, sowing, tending emerging shoots, reaping, threshing, and storing. They maintained irrigation channels, basins, and dikes. Fish and meat from domesticated animals—cattle, sheep, goats, and poultry—supplemented a diet based on wheat or barley, beer, and vegetables. Villages probably shared implements, work animals, and storage facilities and helped one another at peak times in the agricultural cycle and in building projects. Festivals to the local gods and other public celebrations occasionally brought feasting and ceremonies into their lives; labor conscripted for pyramid construction and other state projects brought hardship. If the burden of taxation or compulsory service proved too great, flight into the desert usually offered the only escape.

This account of village life depends on guesswork and bits and pieces of archaeological and literary evidence. Tomb paintings of the elite sometimes depict the lives of common folk. The artists employed conventions to indicate status: obesity for the rich and comfortable, baldness and deformity for the working classes. Egyptian poets frequently employed metaphors of farming and hunting, and papyrus documents preserved in the hot, dry sands tell of property transactions and legal disputes among ordinary people.

Slavery existed on a limited scale and was of little economic significance. Prisoners of war, condemned criminals, and debtors could be found on country estates or in the households of the king and wealthy families. But humane treatment softened the burden of slavery, as did the possibility of being freed.

Scarceness of sources also clouds the experiences of women. What is known about the lives of elite women derives from the possibly distorted impressions of male artists and scribes. Tomb paintings, rendered with dignity and affection, show women of the royal family and elite classes accompanying their husbands and engaging in domestic activities. Subordination to men is evident. The convention of depicting men with a dark red and women with a yellow flesh tone implies that elite women stayed indoors, away from the searing sun. In the beautiful love poetry of the New Kingdom, lovers address each other in terms of apparent equality and express emotions akin to our own ideal of romantic love. Whether this poetry represents the attitudes prevalent in other periods or among nonelite groups remains unknown.

Legal documents show that Egyptian women could own property, inherit from their parents, and will their property to whomever they wished. Marriage, usually monogamous, arose from a couple's decision to establish a household together rather than through legal or religious ceremony. Either party could dissolve the relationship, and the woman retained rights over her dowry in case of divorce. At certain times, queens and queen-mothers played significant behind-the-scenes roles in the politics of the royal court, and priestesses sometimes supervised the cults of female deities. In general, the limited evidence suggests that women in ancient Egypt enjoyed greater respect and more legal rights and social freedom than women in Mesopotamia and other ancient societies.

Belief and Knowledge

Egyptian religion evoked the landscape of the Nile Valley and the vision of cosmic order that this environment fostered. The sun rose every day into a clear and cloudless sky, and the river flooded on schedule every year, ensuring a bounteous harvest. Recurrent cycles and periodic renewal seemed a part of the natural world. Egyptians imagined the sky to be a great ocean surrounding the inhabited world. The sun-god Re traversed its waters in a boat by day, then returned through the Underworld at night, fighting off the attacks of demonic serpents so that he could be born anew each morning. In one especially popular story, Osiris (oh-SIGH-ris), a god who once ruled the land of Egypt, dies at the hand of his jealous brother Seth, who scatters his dismembered remains. Isis, Osiris's sister and wife, finds and reassembles the pieces, while Horus, his son, takes revenge on Seth. Restored to life and installed as king of the Underworld, Osiris represented hope for a new life in a world beyond this one.

The king, represented as Horus and as the son of Re, fit into the pattern of the dead returning to life and the sun-god renewing life. As Egypt's chief priest, he intervened with the gods on behalf of his land and people. When a particular town became the capital of a ruling dynasty, the chief god of that town gained prominence throughout the land. Thus did Ptah (puh-TAH) of Memphis, Re of Heliopolis (he-lee-OP-uh-lis), and Amon (AH-muhn) of Thebes become gods of all Egypt, serving to unify the country and strengthen the monarchy.

Egyptian rulers zealously built new temples, refurbished old ones, and made lavish gifts to the gods, at the same time overseeing construction of their own tombs. Thus, much of the country's wealth went for religious purposes in the ceaseless effort to win the gods' favor, maintain the continuity of divine kingship, and ensure the renewal of life-giving forces.

Some deities normally appear with animal heads; others always take human form. Few myths about the origins and adventures of the gods have survived, but there must have been a rich oral tradition. Many towns had temples in which locally prominent deities were thought to reside. Such local deities could be viewed as manifestations of the great gods, and gods could merge to form hybrids, such as Amon-Re. Ordinary believers were excluded from cult activities in the inner reaches of the temples, where priests served the daily needs of the deity by attending to his or her statue. Food offered to the image was later distributed to temple staff. As in Mesopotamia, some temples possessed extensive landholdings worked by dependent peasants, and the priests who administered the deity's wealth played an influential role locally and sometimes throughout the land.

During great festivals, the priests paraded a boat-shaped litter carrying the shrouded statue and cult items of the deity around the town. This brought large numbers of people into contact with the deity in an outpouring of devotion and celebration. Little is known about the day-to-day beliefs and practices of the common people, however. At home, family members revered and made small offerings to Bes, the

Primary Source: The Egyptian Book of the Dead's Declaration of Innocence Read the number of potential sins that would likely tarnish a journeying spirit and prevent entrance into the realm of the blessed.

grotesque god of marriage and domestic happiness, to local deities, and to the family's ancestors. They relied on amulets and depictions of demonic figures to ward off evil forces. In later times, Greeks and Romans commented on the Egyptian devotion to magic.

Egyptians believed in the afterlife and prepared extensively for a safe passage and a comfortable existence once they arrived. Hazards abounded on the soul's journey after death. The Egyptian Book of the Dead, present in many excavated tombs, contained rituals and spells to protect the journeying spirit. The weighing of the deceased's heart (believed to be the source of personality, intellect, and emotion) in the presence of the judges of the Underworld presented the ultimate challenge—the one that determined whether the deceased had led a good life and deserved to reach the blessed destination.

The Egyptians' obsession with the afterlife caused concerns about the physical condition of the dead body and led them to perfect techniques of mummification for preserving it. The idea probably derived from the slow decomposition of bodies buried in hot, dry sand on the edge of the desert, an early practice. The elite classes spent the most on mummification. Specialists removed vital organs for preservation and storage in stone jars laid out around the corpse and filled the body cavities with various packing materials. After immersing the cadaver for long periods in dehydrating and preserving chemicals, they wrapped it in linen. They then placed the **mummy** in one or more decorated wooden caskets within a tomb.

Building tombs at the edge of the desert left the lowlands free for farming. Pictures and samples of food and objects from everyday life accompanied the mummy to provide whatever he or she might need in the next life. Much of what is now known about ancient Egyptian life comes from examining utilitarian and luxury household objects found in tombs. Small figurines called shawabtis (shuh-WAB-tees) represented the servants whom the deceased might need or the laborers he might send as substitutes if asked to provide compulsory labor. The elite classes ordered chapels attached to their tombs and left endowments to subsidize the daily attendance of a priest and offerings of foodstuffs to sustain their spirits for eternity.

The form of the tomb also reflected wealth and status. Simple pit graves or small mud-brick chambers sufficed for the common people. Members of the privileged classes built larger tombs and covered the walls with pictures and inscriptions. Kings erected pyramids and other grand edifices, employing trickery to hide the sealed chamber containing the body and treasures, as well as curses and other magical precautions to deter tomb robbers. Rarely did they succeed, however. Archaeologists have seldom discovered an undisturbed royal tomb.

The ancient Egyptians explored many areas of knowledge and developed advantageous technologies. They learned about chemistry through developing the mummification process, which also provided opportunities to learn about human anatomy. Egyptian doctors served in royal courts throughout western Asia because of their relatively advanced medical knowledge and techniques.

The endless cycle of flooding and irrigation spurred the development of mathematics to determine the dimensions of fields and calculate the quantity of agricultural produce owed to the state. Through careful observation of the stars, Egyptians constructed the most accurate calendar in the world. They knew that when the star Sirius appeared on the horizon shortly before sunrise, the Nile flood surge was imminent.

For pyramids, temple complexes, and other monumental building projects, vast quantities of earth had to be moved and the construction site made level. Large stones had to be quarried, dragged on rollers, floated downstream on barges, lifted into place along ramps of packed earth, carved to the exact size needed, and then made smooth. Long underground passageways connected mortuary temples by the river

mummy A body preserved by chemical processes or special natural circumstances, often in the belief that the deceased will need it again in the afterlife. In ancient Egypt the bodies of people who could afford mummification underwent a complex process of removing organs, filling body cavities, dehydrating the corpse, and then wrapping the body with linen bandages and enclosing it in a wooden sarcophagus.

with tombs near the desert's edge. More practically, several Egyptian kings dredged a canal more than 50 miles (80 kilometers) long to connect the Nile Valley to the Red Sea and expedite the transport of goods.

Besides river barges for transporting building stones, the Nile carried lightweight ships equipped with sails and oars. These sometimes ventured into the Mediterranean and Red Seas. Canals and flooded basins limited the use of carts and sledges, but archaeologists have discovered an 8-mile (13-kilometer) road made of slabs of sandstone and limestone connecting a rock quarry with Faiyum Lake. The oldest known paved road in the world, it dates to the second half of the third millennium B.C.E.

Conclusion

It is surely no accident that the first civilizations to develop high levels of political centralization, urbanization, and technology were situated in river valleys where rainfall was insufficient for reliable agriculture. Mesopotamian and Egyptian rulers channeled significant human resources into the construction and maintenance of canals, dams, and dikes. This effort required the formation of political centers that could organize the necessary labor force.

In both Egypt and Mesopotamia, kingship emerged as the dominant political form. The Egyptian king's divine origins and symbolic association with the forces of renewal made him central to the welfare of the entire country and gave him a religious monopoly superseding the authority of the temples and priests. Egyptian monarchs lavished much of the country's wealth on their tombs, believing that a proper burial would ensure the continuity of kingship and the attendant blessings that it brought to the land and people. Mesopotamian rulers, who were not normally regarded as divine, built new cities, towering walls, splendid palaces, and religious edifices as lasting testaments to their power.

The unpredictable floods in the Tigris-Euphrates Basin were a constant source of alarm for the people of Mesopotamia. In contrast, the predictable, opportune, and gradual Nile floods were eagerly anticipated events in Egypt. The relationship with nature stamped the worldview of both peoples. Mesopotamians tried to appease their harsh deities so as to survive in a dangerous world. Egyptians largely trusted in and nurtured the supernatural powers they believed guaranteed orderliness and prosperity. The Egyptians also believed that, although the journey to the next world was beset with hazards, the righteous spirit that overcame them could look forward to a blessed existence. In contrast, terrifying visions of the afterlife torment Gilgamesh, the Mesopotamian hero king: disembodied spirits stumbling around in the darkness of the Underworld for all eternity, eating dust and clay and slaving for the heartless gods of that realm.

Although the populations of Egypt and Mesopotamia were ethnically diverse, both regions experienced a remarkable degree of cultural continuity. New immigrants assimilated to the dominant language, belief system, and lifestyles of the civilization. Mesopotamian women's apparent loss of freedom and legal privilege in the second millennium B.C.E. may have been related to the higher degree of urbanization and class stratification in this society. In contrast, Egyptian pictorial documents, love poems, and legal records indicate respect and greater equality for women in the valley of the Nile.

CHAPTER REVIEW

 Download the MP3 audio file of the Chapter Review to listen to on the go.

How did plant and animal domestication set the scene for the emergence of civilization? (page 5)

Domestic plants and animals made it possible for sizeable populations to live even in regions that offered little support for foraging groups. As farming became the main source of food, settlement in villages became a normal way of life. In time, this led to complex political structures and the division of labor characteristic of civilized life.

How did Mesopotamian civilization emerge? (page 13)

The first Mesopotamian people to keep written records were the Sumerians. Some Sumerian towns grew into city-states composed of an urban center that ruled surrounding agricultural land. Priests originally dominated these states, but they gave way to kings who assumed religious, administrative, legal, and military responsibilities. Sharp social divisions were reflected in the class-based penalties of the Law Code of Hammurabi. Mesopotamian gods embodied the uncertain forces of the environment. The people strove to appease them through state-organized rites focused on temples maintained by priests. Mesopotamian cultures pioneered cuneiform writing, canal irrigation, bronze casting, and monumental architecture.

What role did the environment and religion play in Egyptian civilization? (page 23)

Protected by deserts and coastal marshes and nurtured by the predictable flooding of the Nile River, Egyptian civilization was relatively self-sufficient and secure. As the Sahara Desert dried and the population in the Nile Valley increased, political organization became more complex, eventually unifying into a single kingdom under a divine king, the pharaoh. Less urban and socially stratified than Mesopotamian society, Egypt relied on peasant farmers with few slaves and a comparatively free female population. Egyptian religion embodied the orderly and benign qualities of the Nile and involved a complex vision of the afterlife. Much wealth went for religious purposes: preparing for the afterlife and glorifying the pharaoh. To this end the Egyptians constructed monumental tombs and temples and applied their knowledge of chemistry and anatomy to mummification.

Key Terms

civilization (p. 5)

culture (p. 6)

history (p. 6)

Stone Age (p. 6)

Paleolithic (p. 6)

Neolithic (p. 6)

foragers (p. 6)

Agricultural Revolutions (p. 8)

Holocene (p. 10)

megalith (p. 11)

Babylon (p. 13)

Sumerians (p. 14)

Semitic (p. 14)

city-state (p. 15)

Hammurabi (p. 17)

scribe (p. 18)

ziggurat (p. 20)

amulet (p. 20)

cuneiform (p. 20)

pharaoh (p. 25)

ma'at (p. 25)

pyramid (p. 25)

Memphis (p. 26)

Thebes (p. 26)

hieroglyphics (p. 27)

papyrus (p. 27)

mummy (p. 30)

Web Resources

Pronunciation Guide

Interactive Maps

- MAP 1.1 River-Valley Civilizations, 3500–1500 B.C.E.
- MAP 1.2 Ancient Egypt

Primary Sources

- The Epic of Gilgamesh
- The State Regulates Health Care: Hammurabi's Code and Surgeons
- Hymn for the Nile
- Advice to Ambitious Young Egyptians: Rise Above the Masses, Become a Scribe!
- The Egyptian Book of the Dead's Declaration of Innocence

Answers to the History in Focus Questions

See photos on page 24, "Model of Egyptian River Boat, ca. 1985 B.C.E." and page 26 "Pyramids of Menkaure, Khafre, and Khufu at Giza, ca. 2500 B.C.E."

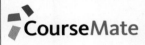
CourseMate

Visit the CourseMate website at www.cengagebrain.com for additional study tools and review materials for this chapter.

CHAPTER 2

4500 B.C.E.–350 C.E.

New Civilizations in the Eastern Hemisphere

© Cengage Learning

CHAPTER PREVIEW

Early China, 2000–221 B.C.E.
How did early Chinese rulers use religion to justify and strengthen their power?

Nubia, 3100 B.C.E.–350 C.E.
How did the technological and cultural influences of Egypt affect the formation of Nubia?

The Origins of Indo-European Languages, 4500–1800 B.C.E.
How did most Europeans come to speak Indo-European languages?

Celtic Europe, 1000–50 B.C.E.
What is known about the Celts, and how did their religious beliefs help to shape their society?

Conclusion

DIVERSITY AND DOMINANCE: Human Nature and Good Government in the *Analects* of Confucius and the Legalist Writings of Han Fei

 Visit the CourseMate website at **www.cengagebrain.com** for additional study tools and review materials for this chapter.

Around 2200 B.C.E. an Egyptian official named Harkhuf (HAHR-koof), who lived at Aswan (AS-wahn) on the southern boundary of Egypt, set out on his fourth trek to a place called Yam, far to the south in the land that later came to be called Nubia. He brought gifts from the Egyptian pharaoh for the ruler of Yam, and he returned home with three hundred donkeyloads of incense, ebony, ivory, and other exotic products. Despite the diplomatic fiction of exchanging gifts, we should probably consider Harkhuf a trader; and the prize of this trip was so special that the eight-year-old boy pharaoh Pepi II could not contain his excitement. He wrote:

> Come north to the residence at once! Hurry and bring with you this pygmy whom you brought from the land of the horizon-dwellers live, hale, and healthy, for the dances of the god, to gladden the heart, to delight the heart of king Neferkare [Pepi] who lives forever! When he goes down with you into the ship, get worthy men to be around him on deck, lest he fall into the water! When he lies down at night, get worthy men to lie around him in his tent. Inspect ten times at night! My majesty desires to see this pygmy more than the gifts of the mine-land and of Punt![1]

Some scholars identify Yam with Kerma, later the capital of the kingdom of Nubia, on the upper Nile in modern Sudan. For Egyptians, Nubia was a wild and dangerous place—though pygmies came from farther south. But it was developing a more complex political organization that fostered trade with Egypt and tropical regions farther south.

The civilizations we saw in Chapter 1 (as well as the first civilizations in South Asia, East Asia, and the Americas that we will see in later chapters) originated in river valleys surrounded by dry lands where farming was difficult or impossible without irrigation. Peasants dissatisfied with their situation had nowhere else to go and were therefore forced to pay rent, taxes, and tithes and provide free labor when the leaders of the society demanded it.

On rain-watered lands, however—that is, in areas that received at least 8 inches (20 centimeters) of rain a year during the growing season—the situation was very different. If Neolithic farmers did not form

complex societies with cities and governments until much later, it was not because they did not think to, but because, with ample land available, those dissatisfied with their fields or their neighbors could find new arable land elsewhere. It was therefore difficult for some members of a community to demand labor or a share of the crops of others in exchange for political protection or religious services. Not until the population grew enough to occupy most of the arable land could the most powerful members of society turn their weaker neighbors into civilized peasants. Only then did civilization spread to areas in contact with the original civilizations, where a growing population began to fully occupy the arable land.

Some of the complex societies examined in this chapter developed in river valleys; others did not. Whereas the Egyptian and Mesopotamian civilizations discussed in the last chapter were originally largely self-sufficient, the civilizations discussed in this chapter and the next were partially shaped by networks of long-distance trade.

In the second millennium B.C.E. a civilization based on irrigation agriculture arose along the valley of the Yellow River and its tributaries in northern China. In the same epoch, in Nubia (southern Egypt and northern Sudan), the first complex society in tropical Africa continued to develop from the roots observed earlier by Harkhuf. Earlier, the first millennium B.C.E. witnessed the spread of Celtic peoples across much of continental Europe. These societies had no contact with one another and represent a variety of responses to environmental and historical circumstances. However, as we shall see, they have certain features in common and collectively point to a distinct stage in the development of human societies.

Early China, 2000–221 B.C.E.

How did early Chinese rulers use religion to justify and strengthen their power?

On the eastern edge of the great Eurasian landmass, Neolithic cultures developed as early as 8000 B.C.E., and a more complex civilization evolved in the second millennium B.C.E. Under the Shang and Zhou monarchs, many of the institutions and values of classical Chinese civilization emerged and spread south and west. As elsewhere, the rise of cities, specialization of labor, bureaucratic government, writing, and other advanced technologies depended on intensive agriculture along a great river system—the Yellow River (Huang He [hwong HUH]) and its tributaries. Although archaeological finds indicate some movement of goods and ideas from western to eastern Asia, developments in China were largely independent of the complex societies in the Middle East and the Indus Valley.

Geography and Resources

With mountains and deserts to the west and north making overland travel difficult and slow (see Map 2.1), the great river systems of eastern China—the Yellow and the Yangzi (yang-zuh) Rivers and their tributaries—provide the main axes of east-west movement. In the eastern river valleys dense populations practiced intensive agriculture; on the steppe lands of Mongolia, the deserts and oases of Xinjiang (shin-jyahng), and the high plateau of Tibet, sparser populations lived largely

Map 2.1 China in the Shang and Zhou Periods, 1750–221 B.C.E. The Shang dynasty arose in the second millennium B.C.E. in the floodplain of the Yellow River. Whereas southern China benefits from the monsoon rains, northern China depends on irrigation. As population increased, the Han Chinese migrated from their eastern homeland to other parts of China, carrying with them their technologies and cultural practices. Other ethnic groups predominated in more outlying regions, and the nomadic peoples of the northwest constantly challenged Chinese authority.   © Cengage Learning

Interactive Map

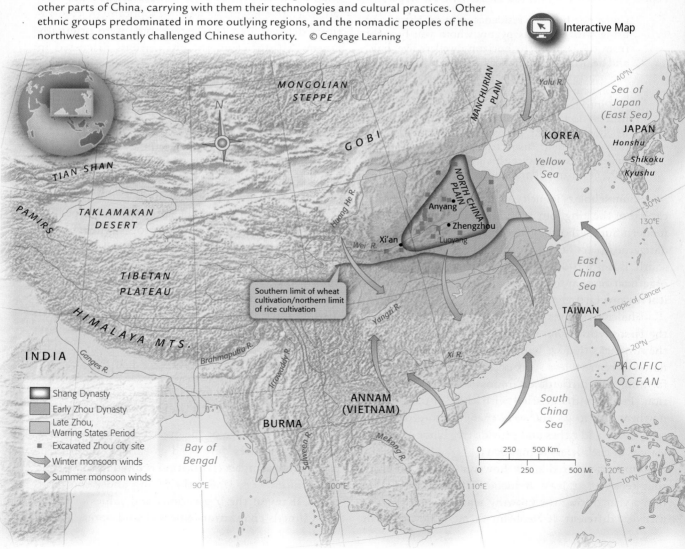

Chronology

	China	Nubia	Celtic Europe
	8000–2000 B.C.E. Neolithic cultures	**4500 B.C.E.** Early agriculture in Nubia	
2500 B.C.E.		**2200 B.C.E.** Harkhuf's expeditions to Yam	
2000 B.C.E.	**2000 B.C.E.** Bronze metallurgy **1750–1027 B.C.E.** Shang dynasty	**1750 B.C.E.** Rise of kingdom of Kush based on Kerma	
1500 B.C.E		**1500 B.C.E.** Egyptian conquest of Nubia	
	1027–221 B.C.E. Zhou dynasty		
1000 B.C.E		**1000 B.C.E.** Decline of Egyptian control in Nubia **750 B.C.E.** Rise of kingdom based on Napata **712–660 B.C.E.** Nubian kings rule Egypt	**1000 B.C.E.** Origin of Celtic culture in central Europe
500 B.C.E.	**551–479 B.C.E.** Confucius		**500 B.C.E.** Celtic elites trade for Mediterranean goods **500–300 B.C.E.** Migrations across Europe
		300 B.C.E.–350 C.E. Kingdom of Meroë	

by herding. Within the eastern agricultural zone, the north and the south have strikingly different environments. The monsoons that affect South and Southeast Asia also drench southern China with heavy rainfall in the summer, the most beneficial time for agriculture. Rainfall is more erratic and sparse in northern China. As in Mesopotamia, where civilizations developed in relatively unfriendly environments, China's early history unfolded in the demanding environment of the northern plains. By the third century C.E., however, the gradual flow of population toward the warmer southern lands caused the political and intellectual center to move south.

Since prehistoric times, winds blowing from Central Asia had deposited a yellowish-brown dust called **loess** (less) on the North China Plain, creating an abundance of potentially productive land (this dust suspended in the water gives the Yellow River its distinctive hue and name). The thick soil was extremely fertile and soft enough to be worked with wooden digging sticks. However, in some areas forests had to be cleared; more importantly, recurrent floods on the Yellow River necessitated earthen dikes and overflow channels. In this landscape, agriculture demanded the coordinated efforts of large groups of people. To cope with the periodic droughts, catch basins (reservoirs) were dug to store river water and rainfall. As the population grew, people built retaining walls to partition the hillsides into tiers of flat arable terraces.

loess A fine, light silt deposited by wind and water. It constitutes the fertile soil of the Yellow River Valley in northern China. Because loess soil is not compacted, it can be worked with a simple digging stick, but it leaves the region vulnerable to devastating floods.

The staple crops were millet, a grain indigenous to China, and wheat, originally from the Middle East. Rice required a warmer climate and prospered in the south. The cultivation of rice in the Yangzi River Valley and the south required a great outlay of labor. Rice paddies—the fields where rice is grown—must be absolutely flat and surrounded by irrigation channels to bring or drain water according to precise schedules. Seedlings sprout in a nursery and are transplanted one by one to the paddy, which is then flooded. Flooding eliminates weeds and rival plants and supports microscopic organisms that keep the soil fertile. When the crop is ripe, the paddy is drained, the rice stalks are harvested with a sickle, and the edible kernels are separated out. The reward for this effort is a harvest that can feed more people per cultivated acre than any other grain, which explains why the south eventually became more populous than the north.

Archaeological evidence shows that the Neolithic populations grew millet, raised pigs and chickens, and used stone tools. They made pottery on a wheel and fired it in high-temperature kilns. They also pioneered silk production, first raising silkworms on mulberry trees, then unraveling their cocoon filament to spin into thread. Lacking stone, they built walls by hammering soil inside temporary wooden frames until it became hard as cement. By 2000 B.C.E. they had begun casting bronze (roughly a thousand years after the Middle East Bronze Age).

Legends say that the ancient dynasty of the Xia ruled the core region of the Yellow River Valley. Some archaeologists identify the Xia with the Neolithic Longshan cultural complex in the centuries before and after 2000 B.C.E. However, history proper begins with the rise of the Shang clans, which coincides with the earliest Chinese written records.

The Shang Period, 1750–1027 B.C.E.

The **Shang** (shahng) originated in the part of the Yellow River Valley that lies in the present-day province of Henan (heh-nahn). After 1750 B.C.E. they extended their control north into Mongolia, west as far as Gansu (gahn-soo), and south to the Yangzi River Valley. The warrior aristocracy that dominated Shang society reveled in warfare, hunting (for recreation and to fine-tune battle skills), exchanging gifts, and feasting. The king ruled the core area of the Shang state directly. Aristocrats served as generals, ambassadors, and supervisors of public projects. Other members of the royal family and high-ranking nobility governed outlying provinces. The most distant regions were governed by native rulers who swore allegiance to the Shang king.

The king was often on the road, traveling to the courts of his subordinates to reinforce their loyalty. Frequent military campaigns, often against the nomadic peoples who occupied the steppe and desert regions to the north and west, occupied the warrior elite and yielded considerable plunder. Prisoners of war taken in these campaigns served as slaves in the Shang capital.

The Shang kingdom had several capitals. The last and most important was near modern Anyang (ahn-yahng) (see Map 2.1). Shang cities were centers of political control and religion. Surrounded by massive walls of pounded earth, they contained palaces, administrative buildings, storehouses, royal tombs, shrines of gods and ancestors, and housing for aristocrats. Commoners lived in agricultural villages outside these centers. Urban street grids aligned with the north star and gates opening to the cardinal directions demonstrate an ongoing Chinese concern with feng shui (fung shway), the spatial orientation of buildings according to a sense of cosmic order.

Writing was the key to effective administration. Pictograms (pictures representing objects and concepts) and phonetic symbols representing the sounds of syllables were combined to form a complex system of hundreds of signs. Only a small educated elite had the time to master this system. Despite substantial changes through the ages, the fundamental principles of the Chinese system still endure. As a result, people speaking languages that sound quite different, such as Mandarin and Cantonese, can read and understand the same text.

Shang ideology glorified the king as the intermediary between the people and Heaven. Shang

Shang The dominant people in the earliest Chinese dynasty for which we have written records (ca. 1750–1027 B.C.E.). Ancestor worship, divination by means of oracle bones, and the use of bronze vessels for ritual purposes were major elements of Shang culture.

Women Beating Chimes
This scene, from a bronze vessel of the
Zhou era, illustrates the important role of music in
festivals, religious rituals, and court ceremonials. During the politically fragmented later (Eastern) Zhou era, many small
states marked their independence by having their own musical scales and distinctive arrangements of orchestral instruments.　Drawn from a bronze vessel in the Sichuan Museum, China

religion also revered and made sacrifices to male ancestors, who were believed to be intensely interested in the fortunes of their descendants. Burials of kings also entailed sacrifices, not only of animals but also of humans, including noble officials of the court, women, servants, soldiers, and prisoners of war. Before taking any action, the Shang rulers used divination to determine the will of Heaven.

Bronze weapons and ritual vessels symbolized authority and nobility. Shang tombs contain many such objects. The relatively modest tomb of one queen yielded 450 bronze articles (ritual vessels, bells, weapons, and mirrors)—remarkable because copper and tin, the principal ingredients of bronze, were not plentiful in northern China. (Also found in the same tomb were numerous objects of jade, bone, ivory, and stone, seven thousand cowrie shells, sixteen sacrificed men, women, and children, and six dogs!)

Finding and mining deposits of copper and tin, transporting the refined metal to the capital, and crafting these beautifully wrought weapons and vessels constituted a major Shang enterprise. Bronzesmiths working in foundries outside the main cities also made chariot fittings and musical instruments. Stylized depictions of real and imaginary animals were a favorite decorative theme.

Far-reaching networks of trade brought jade, ivory, and mother of pearl (a hard, shiny substance from the interior of mollusk shells) used for jewelry, carved figurines, and decorative inlays to the Shang. Some evidence suggests that Shang China may have exchanged goods and ideas with distant Mesopotamia. The horse-drawn chariot, which the Shang adopted from the nomads of the northwest, became a formidable instrument of war.

The Zhou Period, 1027–221 B.C.E.

Shang domination of central and northern China lasted more than six centuries. In the eleventh century B.C.E. the last Shang king was defeated by Wu, the ruler of **Zhou** (joe), a dependent state in the Wei (way) River Valley. The Zhou line of kings (ca. 1027–221 B.C.E.) was the longest-lasting and most revered of all dynasties in Chinese history. Just as the Semitic peoples in Mesopotamia had adopted and adapted the Sumerian legacy (see Chapter 1), the Zhou preserved the essentials of Shang culture and added new elements of ideology and technology.

To justify their seizure of power to the restive remnants of the Shang clans, the early Zhou monarchs styled themselves "Son of Heaven." Their rule

Zhou The people and dynasty that took over the dominant position in north China from the Shang and created the concept of the Mandate of Heaven to justify their rule. The Zhou era, particularly the vigorous early period (1027–771 B.C.E.), was remembered in Chinese tradition as a time of prosperity and benevolent rule. In the later Zhou period (771–221 B.C.E.), centralized control broke down, and warfare among many small states became frequent.

Warring States Period Bronze Figurine The figurine of a youth, made of bronze, was produced in the Warring States Period, but the jade birds perched atop the staffs were originally carved in the Shang era. The youth has braided hair and is wearing boots and an elaborately decorated robe. The chain may indicate that these were live birds rather than images.   Museum of Fine Arts, Boston, Maria Antoinette Evans Fund. Photograph © 2008 Museum of Fine Arts, Boston 31.976

was called the **Mandate of Heaven**. According to the new theory advanced by their propagandists, the ruler had been chosen by the supreme deity, known as "Heaven," and would retain his backing as long as he served as a wise, principled, and energetic guardian of his people. Prosperity and stability proved divine favor, but royal misbehavior, a fault attributed to the last Shang ruler, could forfeit Heaven's mandate. Corruption, violence, and insurrection were signs of divine displeasure.

The Zhou kings continued some of the Shang rituals, but there was a marked decline in the practice of divination and in extravagant sacrifices and burials. The priestly power of the ruling class, the only ones who had been able to make contact with the spirits of ancestors during the Shang period, faded away. The resulting separation of religion and government made way for the development of important philosophical and mystical systems. The bronze vessels that had been sacred implements in the Shang period now became family treasures.

The early period of Zhou rule, the eleventh through ninth centuries B.C.E., is sometimes called the Western Zhou era because of the location of the capitals in the western part of the kingdom. These centuries saw the development of a sophisticated administrative apparatus. The Zhou built a series of capital cities with pounded-earth foundations and walls. The major buildings all faced south, in keeping with the feng shui principles of harmonious relationship with the terrain, the forces of wind, water, and sunlight, and the invisible energy perceived to be flowing through the natural world. All government officials, including the king, were supposed to be models of morality, fairness, and concern for the welfare of the people.

Like the Shang, the Zhou regime was decentralized. Members and allies of the royal family ruled more than a hundred largely autonomous territories. Elaborate court ceremonials, embellished by music and dance, impressed on observers the glory of Zhou rule and reinforced the bonds of obligation between rulers and ruled.

Around 800 B.C.E. Zhou power began to wane. Ambitious local rulers operated ever more independently and waged war on one another, while nomadic peoples attacked the northwest frontiers (see Map 2.1). In 771 B.C.E. members of the Zhou lineage relocated to a new, more secure, eastern capital near Luoyang (LWOE-yahng), initiating the five-hundred-year Eastern Zhou era. There they continued to hold the royal title and receive at least nominal homage from local rulers, the real power brokers of the age. Historians conventionally divide this period of political fragmentation, shifting centers of power, and fierce competition among numerous small states into the "Spring and Autumn Period," from 771 to 481 B.C.E., after a collection of chronicles that give annual entries for those

Mandate of Heaven Chinese religious and political ideology developed by the Zhou, according to which it was the prerogative of Heaven, the chief deity, to grant power to the ruler of China and to take away that power if the ruler failed to conduct himself justly and in the best interests of his subjects.

two seasons, and the "Warring States Period," from 480 to the unification of China in 221 B.C.E.

Numerous competing kingdoms meant numerous capital cities, some of which became quite large. To the north, long walls of pounded earth were constructed, the ancestors of the Great Wall of China, to protect the kingdoms from each other and from nomads. Chinese armies adopted the nomad practice of putting fighters on horseback. The northwest nomads were probably also the source of the iron-working skills that led to iron replacing bronze as the primary metal for tools and weapons around 600 B.C.E. Bureaucracies in many states expanded their functions, composing law codes, collecting taxes directly, imposing monetary standards, and managing large-scale public works projects. Eventually this activity led to a philosophy called **Legalism**, which argued that maintaining the wealth and power of the state justified authoritarian political control. Legalists maintained that human nature is essentially wicked and that people behave properly only if compelled by strict laws and harsh punishments. They believed that every aspect of human society ought to be controlled and personal freedom sacrificed for the good of the state.

Confucianism, Daoism, and Chinese Society

Bureaucratic government superseded aristocratic rule in some of the major Zhou states. To maintain their influence, aristocrats sought a new role as advisers to the rulers. Kongzi (551–479 B.C.E.)—known in the West by the Latin form of his name, **Confucius**—lived through the political flux and social change of this anxious time. Coming from one of the smaller states, he had not been particularly successful in obtaining administrative posts. However, his doctrine of duty and public service, initially aimed at fellow aristocrats, was to become a central influence in Chinese thought.

Many elements in Confucius's teaching had roots in earlier Chinese belief, including folk religion and the rites of the Zhou royal family, such as the veneration of ancestors and elders and worship of the deity Heaven. Confucius drew a parallel between the family and the state. Just as the family is a hierarchy, with the father at its top, sons next, then wives and daughters in order of age, so too the state is a hierarchy, with the ruler at the top, the public officials as the sons, and the common people as the women.

Confucius took a traditional term for the feelings between family members (*ren*) and expanded it into a universal ideal of benevolence toward all humanity, which he believed was the foundation of moral government. Government exists, he said, to serve the people, and the administrator or ruler gains respect and authority by displaying fairness and integrity. Confucian teachings emphasized benevolence, avoidance of violence, justice, rationalism, loyalty, and dignity.

Though Confucius had little influence in his own time, his later follower Mencius (Mengzi, 371–289 B.C.E.), who opposed despotism and argued against the authoritarian ideology of the Legalists, made the master's teachings much better known (see Diversity and Dominance: Human Nature and Good Government in the *Analects* of Confucius and the Legalist Writings of Han Fei). Confucianism eventually became the dominant political philosophy and the core of the educational system for government officials (see Chapter 6).

The Warring States Period also saw the rise of the school of thought known as **Daoism** (DOW-izm). According to tradition, Laozi (low-zuh), the originator of Daoism (believed to have lived in the sixth century B.C.E., though some scholars doubt his existence), sought to stop the warfare of the age by urging humanity to follow the *Dao*, or "path." Daoists

Legalism In China, a political philosophy that emphasized the unruliness of human nature and justified state coercion and control. The ruling class invoked it to validate the authoritarian nature of the regime and its profligate expenditure of subjects' lives and labor. It was later superseded by a more benevolent Confucian doctrine of governmental moderation.

Confucius Western name for the Chinese philosopher Kongzi (551–479 B.C.E.). His doctrine of duty and public service had a great influence on subsequent Chinese thought and served as a code of conduct for government officials.

Daoism Chinese school of thought, originating in the Warring States Period with Laozi (604–531 B.C.E.). Daoism offered an alternative to the Confucian emphasis on hierarchy and duty. Daoists believe that the world is always changing and is devoid of absolute morality or meaning. They accept the world as they find it, avoid futile struggles, and deviate as little as possible from the Dao, or "path" of nature.

Human Nature and Good Government
in the *Analects* of Confucius and the Legalist Writings of Han Fei

Although monarchy (the rule of one man) was the standard form of government in ancient China and was rarely challenged, political theorists and philosophers thought a great deal about the qualities of the ideal ruler, his relationship to his subjects, and the means by which he controlled them. These considerations about how to govern people were inevitably molded by fundamental assumptions about the nature of human beings. In the Warring States Period, as the major states struggled desperately with one another for survival and expansion, such discussions took on a special urgency, and the Confucians and Legalists came to represent two powerful, and largely contradictory, points of view.

The Analects are a collection of sayings of Confucius, probably compiled and written down several generations after he lived, though some elements may have been added even later. They cover a wide range of matters, including ethics, government, education, music, and rituals. Taken as a whole, they are a guide to living an honorable, virtuous, useful, and satisfying life. While subject to reinterpretation according to the circumstances of the times, Confucian principles have had a great influence on Chinese values and behavior ever since.

Han Fei (280–233 B.C.E.), who was, ironically, at one time the student of a Confucian teacher, became a Legalist writer and political adviser to the ruler of the ambitious state of Qin. Eventually he lost out in a power struggle at court and was forced to kill himself.

The following selections illuminate the profound disagreements between Confucians and Legalists over the essential nature of human beings and how the ruler should conduct himself in order to most effectively govern his subjects and protect his kingdom.

Confucius

4:5 Confucius said: "Riches and honors are what all men desire. But if they cannot be attained in accordance with the *dao* [the way] they should not be kept. Poverty and low status are what all men hate. But if they cannot be avoided while staying in accordance with the *dao*, you should not avoid them. If a Superior Man departs from *ren* [humaneness], how can he be worthy of that name? A Superior Man never leaves *ren* for even the time of a single meal. In moments of haste he acts according to it. In times of difficulty or confusion he acts according to it."

16:8 Confucius said: "The Superior Man stands in awe of three things: (1) He is in awe of the decree of Heaven. (2) He is in awe of great men. (3) He is in awe of the words of the sages. The inferior man does not know the decree of Heaven; takes great men lightly and laughs at the words of the sages."

4:14 Confucius said: "I don't worry about not having a good position; I worry about the means I use to gain position. I don't worry about being unknown; I seek to be known in the right way."

7:15 Confucius said: "I can live with coarse rice to eat, water for drink and my arm as a pillow and still be happy. Wealth and honors that one possesses in the midst of injustice are like floating clouds."

13:6 Confucius said: "When you have gotten your own life straightened out, things will go well without your giving orders. But if your own life isn't straightened out, even if you give orders, no one will follow them."

12:2 Zhonggong asked about the meaning of *ren*. The Master said: "Go out of your home as if you were receiving an important guest. Employ the people as if you were assisting at a great ceremony. What you don't want done to yourself, don't do to others. Live in your town without stirring up resentments, and live in your household without stirring up resentments."

1:5 Confucius said: "If you would govern a state of a thousand chariots (a small-to-middle-size state), you must pay strict attention to business, be true to your word, be economical in expenditure and love the people. You should use them according to the seasons."

2:3 Confucius said: "If you govern the people legalistically and control them by punishment, they will avoid crime, but have no personal sense of shame. If you govern them by means of virtue and control them with propriety, they will gain their own sense of shame, and thus correct themselves."

12:7 Zigong asked about government. The Master said, "Enough food, enough weapons and the confidence of the people." Zigong said, "Suppose you had no alternative but to give up one of these three, which one would be let go of first?" The Master said, "Weapons." Zigong said, "What if you had to give up one of the remaining two, which one would it be?" The Master said, "Food. From ancient times, death has come to all men, but a people without confidence in its rulers will not stand."

12:19 Ji Kang Zi asked Confucius about government saying: "Suppose I were to kill the unjust, in order to advance the just. Would that be all right?"

Confucius replied: "In doing government, what is the need of killing? If you desire good, the people will be good. The nature of the Superior Man is like the wind, the nature of the inferior man is like the grass. When the wind blows over the grass, it always bends."

2:19 The Duke of Ai asked: "How can I make the people follow me?" Confucius replied: "Advance the upright and set aside the crooked, and the people will follow you. Advance the crooked and set aside the upright, and the people will not follow you."

2:20 Ji Kang Zi asked: "How can I make the people reverent and loyal, so they will work positively for me?" Confucius said, "Approach them with dignity, and they will be reverent. Be filial and compassionate and they will be loyal. Promote the able and teach the incompetent, and they will work positively for you."

Han Fei

Past and present have different customs; new and old adopt different measures. To try to use the ways of a generous and lenient government to rule the people of a critical age is like trying to drive a runaway horse without using reins or whips. This is the misfortune that ignorance invites. . . .

Humaneness [ren] may make one shed tears and be reluctant to apply penalties, but law makes it clear that such penalties must be applied. The ancient kings allowed law to be supreme and did not give in to their tearful longings. Hence it is obvious that humaneness cannot be used to achieve order in the state. . . .

The best rewards are those that are generous and predictable, so that the people may profit by them. The best penalties are those that are severe and inescapable, so that the people will fear them. The best laws are those that are uniform and inflexible, so that the people can understand them. . . .

Hardly ten men of true integrity and good faith can be found today, and yet the offices of the state number in the hundreds. . . . Therefore the way of the enlightened ruler is to unify the laws instead of seeking for wise men, to lay down firm policies instead of longing for men of good faith. . . .

When a sage rules the state, he does not depend on people's doing good of themselves; he sees to it that they are not allowed to do what is bad. If he depends on people's doing good of themselves, then within his borders he can count fewer than ten instances of success. But if he sees to it that they are not allowed to do what is bad, then the whole state can be brought to a uniform level of order. Those who rule must employ measures that will be effective with the majority and discard those that will be effective with only a few. Therefore they devote themselves not to virtue but to law. . . .

When the Confucians of the present time counsel rulers, they do not praise those measures that will bring order today, but talk only of the achievements of the men who brought order in the past. . . . No ruler with proper standards will tolerate them. Therefore the enlightened ruler works with facts and discards useless theories. He does not talk about deeds of humaneness and rightness, and he does not listen to the words of scholars. . . .

Nowadays, those who do not understand how to govern invariably say, "You must win the hearts of the people!" . . . The reason you cannot rely on the wisdom of the people is that they have the minds of little children. If the child's head is not shaved, its sores will spread; and if its boil is not lanced, it will become sicker than ever . . . for it does not understand that the little pain it suffers now will bring great benefit later. . . .

Now, the ruler presses the people to till the land and open up new pastures so as to increase their means of livelihood, and yet they consider him harsh; he draws up a penal code and makes the punishments more severe in order to put a stop to evil, and yet the people consider him stern. . . . He makes certain that everyone within his borders understands warfare and sees to it that there are no private exemptions from military service; he unites the strength of the state and fights fiercely in order to take its enemies captive, and yet the people consider him violent. . . . [These] types of undertaking all ensure order and safety to the state, and yet the people do not have sense enough to rejoice in them.

QUESTIONS FOR ANALYSIS

1. What do Confucius and Han Fei believe about the nature of human beings? Are they intrinsically good and well-behaved, or bad and prone to misbehave?
2. What are the qualities of an ideal ruler for Confucius and Han Fei?
3. By what means can the ruler influence his subjects in Confucian thought? How should the ruler compel obedience in the people in Legalist thought?
4. What do Confucians and Legalists think about the value of the past as a model for the present?
5. Why might Confucius's passionate concern for ethical behavior on the part of officials and rulers arise at a time when the size and power of governments were growing?

Source: Confucius excerpts from *The Analects of Confucius*, translated by A. Charles Muller at http://www.acmuller.net/con-dao/analects.html. Copyright © Charles Muller 2010. Reprinted by permission of the author. Han Fei selections from *Sources of Chinese Tradition*, vol. 1, 2nd ed., by Wm. Theodore de Bary and Irene Bloom. Copyright © 2000 Columbia University Press. Reprinted with permission of the publisher.

accepted the world as they found it, adhering to the "path" of nature and avoiding useless struggles. They avoided violence if at all possible and took the minimal action necessary for a task; rather than fight the current of a stream, a wise man allows the onrushing waters to pass around him. This passivity arose from the Daoist's sense that the world was always changing and lacked any absolute morality or meaning. In the end, Daoists believed, all that matters is the individual's fundamental understanding of the "path."

The original Daoist philosophy was greatly expanded in subsequent centuries to incorporate popular beliefs, magic, and mysticism. Daoism represented an important stream of thought throughout Chinese history. By idealizing individuals who find their own "path" to right conduct, it offered an alternative to the Confucian emphasis on hierarchy and duty and to the Legalists' approval of force.

Social organization also changed in this period. The kinship structures of the Shang and early Zhou periods, based on the clan (a relatively large group of related families), gave way to the three-generation family of grandparents, parents, and children as the fundamental social unit. A related development was the emergence of the concept of private property. Land was considered to belong to the men of the family and was divided equally among the sons when the father died.

Little is known about the conditions of life for women in early China. Some scholars believe that women may have acted as shamans, entering into trances to communicate with supernatural forces, making requests on behalf of their communities, and receiving predictions of the future. By the time written records begin to illuminate our knowledge of women's experiences, however, they show women in a subordinate position in the strongly patriarchal family.

Confucian thought codified this male-female hierarchy. Only men could conduct rituals and make offerings to the ancestors, though women could help

SECTION REVIEW

- Neolithic farming communities grew in the Yellow and Yangzi River Valleys and adapted to the very different environments of each.

- The Shang dynasty emerged in the Yellow River Valley and grew to encompass parts of the Yangzi River Valley.

- Shang technologies included pictographic writing, bronze work, and artifacts related to royal divination, male ancestor worship, and the power of the warrior aristocracy.

- The first king of the Zhou dynasty defeated the Shang, claiming the Mandate of Heaven as justification for this victory.

- Like the Shang, the Zhou state was decentralized, and it devolved into a collection of independent and hostile states.

- Legalism became the major political philosophy, but Confucianism and Daoism also emerged and established most of the basic principles of Chinese culture.

maintain the household's ancestral shrines. Fathers held authority over the women and children, arranged marriages for their offspring, and could sell the labor of family members. A man was limited to one wife but was permitted additional sexual partners, who had the lower status of concubines. The elite classes used marriage to create political alliances, and it was common for the groom's family to offer a substantial "bride-gift," a proof of the wealth and standing of his family, to the family of the prospective bride. A man whose wife died had a duty to remarry in order to produce male heirs to keep alive the cult of the ancestors.

These differences in male and female activities were explained by the concept of **yin** and **yang**, the complementary nature of female and male roles in the natural order. The male principle (yang) was equated with the sun—active, bright, and shining; the female principle (yin) corresponded to the moon—passive, shaded, and reflective. Female gentleness balanced male toughness, female endurance and need for completion balanced male action and initiative, and

 Primary Source: The Book of Documents Read along as a new king receives advice and warnings about the careful path he must tread to keep his kingdom safe from ruin.

yin/yang In Chinese belief, complementary factors that help to maintain the equilibrium of the world. Yin is associated with feminine, dark, and passive qualities; yang with masculine, light, and active qualities.

female supportiveness balanced male leadership. In its earliest form, the theory considered yin and yang as equal and alternately dominant, like night and day, creating balance in the world. However, as a result of the changing role of women in the Zhou period and the pervasive influence of Confucian ideology, the male principle came to be seen as superior to the female.

Nubia, 3100 B.C.E.–350 C.E.

How did the technological and cultural influences of Egypt affect the formation of Nubia?

Since the first century the name *Nubia* has been applied to a 1,000-mile (1,600-kilometer) stretch of the Nile Valley lying between Aswan and Khartoum (kahr-TOOM) and straddling the southern part of the modern nation of Egypt and the northern part of Sudan (see Map 1.2). The ancient Egyptians called it Tasety, meaning "Land of the Bow," after the favorite weapon of its warriors. Nubia is the only trade corridor and continuously inhabited stretch of territory connecting sub-Saharan Africa (the lands south of the Sahara Desert) with North Africa. It was richly endowed with natural resources such as gold, copper, and semiprecious stones.

Egypt's quest for Nubian gold helps explain the early rise of a civilization with a complex political organization, social stratification, metallurgy, monumental building, and writing. However, most scholars today have moved away from the traditional view that Nubian civilization derived from Egypt and emphasize the mutually beneficial interactions between the two lands and the growing evidence that Nubian culture drew on influences from sub-Saharan Africa.

Early Cultures and Egyptian Domination, 2300–100 B.C.E

The central geographical feature of Nubia, as of Egypt, is the Nile River. The Nubian segment of the Nile River flows through a landscape of rocky desert, grassland, and fertile plain. In a torrid climate with minimal rainfall, agriculture depended on river irrigation. Six cataracts, barriers formed by large boulders and rapids, obstructed boat traffic. Boats operating between the cataracts and caravans skirting the river made travel possible.

In the fifth millennium B.C.E. bands of people in northern Nubia made the transition from seminomadic hunting and gathering to a settled life based on grain agriculture and cattle herding. The majority of the population came to live in agricultural villages alongside the river. Even before 3000 B.C.E. Egyptian craftsmen were working in ivory and ebony that must have come from tropical Africa by way of Nubia.

As we saw with the journey of Harkhuf at the beginning of this chapter, Nubia enters the Egyptian historical record around 2200 B.C.E. in accounts of trade missions. At that time Aswan, just north of the First Cataract, was the southern limit of Egyptian control. Egyptian noblemen stationed there led donkey caravans south in search of gold, incense, ebony, ivory, slaves, and exotic animals. This was dangerous work, requiring delicate negotiations with local Nubian chiefs to secure protection, but it brought substantial rewards to those who succeeded.

During the Middle Kingdom (ca. 2040–1640 B.C.E.), Egypt adopted a more aggressive stance toward Nubia. Egyptian rulers sought to control the gold mines in the desert east of the Nile and to cut out the Nubian middlemen who drove up the cost of luxury goods from the tropics. A string of mud-brick forts on islands and riverbanks south of the Second Cataract were built to protect Egypt's southern frontier and regulate the flow of commerce. These Egyptian garrisons were sufficiently intimidating that relations with the indigenous population of northern Nubia, while intermittent, were generally peaceful.

Farther south, where the Nile makes a great U-shaped turn in a fertile plain (see Map 1.2), a more complex political entity evolved from the chiefdoms of the third millennium B.C.E. The Egyptians gave the name **Kush** to the kingdom whose capital was located

Kush An Egyptian name for Nubia, the region alongside the Nile River south of Egypt, where an indigenous kingdom with its own distinctive institutions and cultural traditions arose in the early second millennium B.C.E. It was deeply influenced by Egyptian culture and at times under the control of Egypt, which coveted its rich deposits of gold and luxury products from sub-Saharan Africa carried up the Nile corridor.

Gebel Barkal This model of Gebel Barkal, the "Holy Mountain" of Nubia, made of sandstone and with traces of the original paint, was deposited in the Temple of Amon at Gebel Barkal by a Nubian king. The original door is missing, as well as the seated figurine inside, possibly an image of Amon. Resting on a band representing a swamp with papyrus reeds, the doorway is flanked on either side by relief images of a winged goddess and a king wearing a short kilt.   Museum of Fine Arts, Boston. Harvard University, Boston Museum of Fine Arts Expedition, Maria Antoinette Evans Fund. Photograph © Museum of Fine Arts, Boston 21.3234

at Kerma, one of the earliest urbanized centers in tropical Africa. Beginning around 1750 B.C.E. the kings of Kush marshaled a labor force to build monumental walls and structures of mud brick. Royal burials containing dozens and even hundreds of sacrificed servants and wives, along with sumptuous objects, testify to the wealth and power of the rulers of Kush and suggest a belief in some sort of afterlife in which attendants and possessions would be useful. Kushite craftsmen showed skill in metalworking, whether for weapons or jewelry, and their pottery surpassed anything produced in Egypt.

During the expansionist New Kingdom (ca. 1532–1070 B.C.E.) the Egyptians penetrated more deeply into Nubia (see Chapter 3). They destroyed Kush and its capital and extended their frontier to the Fourth Cataract. A high-ranking Egyptian official called "Overseer of Southern Lands" or "King's Son of Kush" ruled Nubia from a new administrative center at Napata (nah-PAH-tuh), near Gebel Barkal (JEB-uhl BAHR-kahl), the "Holy Mountain," believed to be the home of a local god. Egypt exploited the gold mines of Nubia to help buttress its commerce with other lands. Fatalities were high among native workers in the brutal desert climate, and the army had to ward off attacks from desert nomads.

Five hundred years of Egyptian domination in Nubia left many traces. The Egyptian government imposed Egyptian culture on the native population. Children from elite families who were brought to the Egyptian royal court to guarantee the good behavior of their fathers absorbed Egyptian language, culture,

 History in Focus *In what ways do the carvings on this object reflect Egyptian influences? What is distinctively Nubian about it? Find the answer online.*

and religion, which they later carried home with them. Other Nubians served the Egyptians as archers. The manufactured goods that they brought back to Nubia have been found in their graves. The Nubians built Egyptian-style towns and erected stone temples to Egyptian gods, particularly Amon. The frequent depiction of Amon with the head of a ram may reflect a blending of the chief Egyptian god with a Nubian ram deity.

The Kingdom of Meroë, 800 B.C.E.–350 C.E.

Egypt's weakness after 1200 B.C.E. led to the collapse of its authority in Nubia. In the eighth century B.C.E. a powerful new native kingdom emerged in southern Nubia. Its history can be divided into two parts. During the early

Andrew McConnell / Robert Harding

Temple of the Lion-Headed God Apedemaq at Naqa in Nubia, First Century C.E. The carved reliefs on this temple wall depict King Natakamani in the company of gods Horus and Apedemak. The architectural form and artistic style are Egyptian, but the gods are part-Nubian, part-Egyptian. The costume of the monarch also reflects the trend in the Meroitic era to draw upon sub-Saharan examples.

period, between the eighth and fourth centuries B.C.E., Napata, the former Egyptian headquarters, was the primary center. During the later period, from the fourth century B.C.E. to the fourth century C.E., the center was farther south, at **Meroë** (MER-oh-ee), near the Sixth Cataract.

For half a century, from around 712 to 660 B.C.E., the kings of Nubia ruled all of Egypt as the Twenty-fifth Dynasty. They conducted themselves in the age-old manner of Egyptian rulers, using Egyptian titles, costumes, and burial customs. However, they kept their Nubian names and were depicted with physical features suggesting peoples of sub-Saharan Africa. Building on a monumental scale for the first time in centuries and reinvigorating Egyptian art, architecture, and religion, they inaugurated an artistic and cultural renaissance. The Nubian kings resided at Memphis, the Old Kingdom capital, while Thebes, the New Kingdom capital, was the residence of a celibate female member of the king's family who was titled "God's Wife of Amon."

The Nubian dynasty made a disastrous mistake in 701 B.C.E. when it offered help to local rulers in Syria-Palestine who were struggling against the Assyrian Empire. The Assyrians retaliated by invading Egypt and driving the Nubian monarchs back to their southern domain by 660 B.C.E. Napata again became the chief royal residence and religious center of the kingdom. However, Egyptian cultural influences remained strong. Court documents continued to be written in Egyptian hieroglyphs, and the mummified remains of the rulers were buried in modestly sized sandstone pyramids along with hundreds of shawabti (shuh-WAB-tee) figurines.

By the end of the fourth century B.C.E. the center of gravity had shifted south to Meroë, perhaps because Meroë was better situated for agriculture and trade, the economic mainstays of the Nubian kingdom. As a result, sub-Saharan cultural patterns gradually replaced Egyptian ones. Egyptian hieroglyphs gave way to a new set of symbols, still essentially undeciphered, for writing the Meroitic language. People continued to worship Amon as well as Isis, an Egyptian goddess connected to fertility and sexuality, but those deities had to share the stage with Nubian deities like the lion-god Apedemak. Meroitic art combined Egyptian, Greco-Roman, and indigenous traditions.

Meroë Capital of a flourishing kingdom in southern Nubia from the fourth century B.C.E. to the fourth century C.E. In this period Nubian culture shows more independence from Egypt and the influence of sub-Saharan Africa.

Women of the royal family played an important role in Meroitic politics, another reflection of the influence of sub-Saharan Africa. The Nubians employed a matrilineal system in which the king was succeeded by the son of his sister. Nubian queens sometimes ruled by themselves and sometimes in partnership with their husbands. Greek, Roman, and biblical sources refer to a queen of Nubia named Candace. Since these sources relate to different times, Candace was probably a title rather than a proper name. At least seven queens ruled between 284 B.C.E. and 115 C.E. They are depicted in scenes reserved for male rulers in Egyptian imagery, smiting enemies in battle and being suckled by the mother-goddess Isis. Roman sources marvel at the fierce resistance put up by a one-eyed warrior-queen.

Meroë was a huge city for its time, more than a square mile in area, and it overlooked fertile grasslands and dominated converging trade routes. Great reservoirs were dug to catch precious rainfall. The city was a major center for iron smelting (after 1000 B.C.E. iron had replaced bronze as the primary metal for tools and weapons). The Temple of Amon was approached by an avenue of stone rams, and the enclosed "Royal City" was filled with palaces, temples, and administrative buildings. In 2002 archaeologists using a magnetometer to detect structures buried in the sand discovered a large palace, which they plan to excavate.

Meroë collapsed in the early fourth century C.E. It may have been overrun by nomads from the western desert who had become more mobile because of the arrival of the camel in North Africa. However, Meroë had already been weakened when profitable commerce with the Roman Empire was diverted to the Red Sea and to the rising kingdom of Aksum (AHK-soom) in present-day Ethiopia (see Chapter 6).

The Origins of Indo-European Languages, 4500–1800 B.C.E.

How did most Europeans come to speak Indo-European languages?

Before about 3000 B.C.E., Europe was populated in part by hunter-gatherers and in part by Neolithic farmers. The lower Danube Valley was the most populated part

SECTION REVIEW

- Fertile and rich in natural resources, Nubia became an important source of raw materials for Egypt.
- Egyptian cultural influence moved deeper into Nubia as the Middle and New Kingdoms extended Egyptian authority farther south.
- The rich Nubian kingdom of Kush fell to the New Kingdom, but after five hundred years a Nubian dynasty rose and took control of Egypt itself for a short time.
- After the fall of this dynasty, Meroë assumed control of southern Nubia, which was dominated by sub-Saharan cultural practices.
- Royal women played important roles throughout Meroë's history.
- Meroë was a large and powerful city in its prime, but it was already weak by the time it fell, perhaps to nomadic invaders.

of Europe, with many large farming villages. These people, ancestors of present-day Europeans, spoke languages that have long since disappeared.

Meanwhile, on the steppes of southern Russia north of the Black Sea and the Capsian Sea, there were no farmers; instead, some of the people who lived there hunted and gathered, while others herded sheep, goats, and cattle in the river valleys. Among the herders were people who spoke a language that linguists have reconstructed and named Proto-Indo-European. Between 4800 and 4600 B.C.E., these people domesticated the horse. Because they could herd far more animals on horseback than on foot, they became the wealthiest people in the region. Around 3500–3100 B.C.E., when they invented wagons with solid wheels that could be pulled by teams of oxen, they were able to leave the river valleys and spread out over the grasslands year-round, carrying tents, equipment, and water for weeks at a time.

With these innovations and their large herds, nomadic herdsmen were able to migrate long distances. Some made their way to Iran and eventually to India, while others migrated westward to central and western Europe. (It is because of the affinities between the oldest written language of India, Sanskrit, and the oldest written languages of Europe, Greek and Latin, that linguists call them Indo-European languages.)

Others moved into the lower Danube Valley after 3100 B.C.E. and from there spread out over the rest of Europe. With their horseback-riding skills and their impressive wealth in livestock, they attracted followers among the indigenous peoples or defeated those who resisted. As they divided into migrating groups, their original mother-tongue changed into several daughter languages, the ancestors of Greek, Latin, Romance languages, and Germanic languages. The language group that settled in the westernmost part of Europe, along the Atlantic coast and the British Isles, became known as the Celts.

Celtic Europe, 1000–50 B.C.E.

What is known about the Celts, and how did their religious beliefs help to shape their society?

The southern peninsulas of Europe—present-day Spain, Italy, and Greece—share in the relatively mild climate of all the Mediterranean lands and are separated from "continental" Europe to the north by high mountains (the Pyrenees and Alps). Consequently, the history of southern Europe in antiquity is primarily connected to that of the Middle East, at least until the Roman conquests north of the Alps (see Chapters 3, 4, and 6).

Continental Europe (including the modern nations of France, Germany, Switzerland, Austria, the Czech Republic, Slovakia, Hungary, Poland, and Romania) was more forested but was well suited to agriculture and herding. It contained broad plains with good soil and had a temperate climate with cold winters, warm summers, and ample rainfall. Large, navigable rivers (the Rhone, Rhine, and Danube) facilitated travel and the exploitation of natural resources like timber and metals.

Humans had lived in this part of Europe for many thousands of years, but their lack of a writing system limits our knowledge of the earliest inhabitants. Around 500 B.C.E. Celtic peoples spread across a substantial portion of Europe and, by coming into contact with the literate societies of the Mediterranean, entered the historical record. Information about the early **Celts** (kelts) comes from the archaeological record, Greek and Roman authors, and the Celtic oral traditions of Wales and Ireland that were written down during the European Middle Ages.

The Spread of the Celts

The term *Celtic* refers to a branch of the Indo-European family of languages found throughout Europe and in western and southern Asia. Scholars link the Celtic language group to archaeological remains first appearing in parts of present-day Germany, Austria, and the Czech Republic after 1000 B.C.E. Many early Celts lived in or near hill-forts—lofty natural locations made more defensible by earthwork fortifications. By 500 B.C.E. Celtic elites were trading with Mediterranean societies for craft goods and wine. This contact may have stimulated the new styles of Celtic manufacture and art that appeared at this time.

These new cultural features coincided with Celtic migrations to many parts of Europe. The motives behind these population movements, their precise timing, and the manner in which they were carried out are not well understood. Celts occupied nearly all of France and much of Britain and Ireland, and they merged with indigenous peoples to create the Celtiberian culture of northern Spain. Other Celtic groups overran northern Italy in the fifth century B.C.E., raided into central Greece, and settled in central Anatolia (modern Turkey). By 300 B.C.E. Celtic peoples were spread across Europe north of the Alps, from present-day Hungary to Spain and Ireland.

Although these widely diffused Celtic groups shared language and culture, there was no Celtic "state." Instead they were divided into hundreds of small, loosely organized chiefdoms. Traditional depictions of Celtic society come largely from the observations of Greek and Roman writers. However, current scholarship focuses on the differences as much as the similarities among Celtic peoples. It is unlikely that the ancient Celts ever identified themselves as

Celts Peoples sharing a common language and culture that originated in central Europe in the first half of the first millennium B.C.E. After 500 B.C.E., they spread as far as Anatolia in the east and Spain and the British Isles in the west. They were later overtaken by Roman conquest and Germanic invasions. Their descendants survive on the western fringe of Europe (Brittany, Wales, Scotland, and Ireland).

belonging to anything akin to our modern conception of "Celtic civilization."

The Greeks and Romans remarked particularly on the appearance of male Celts—their burly size, long red hair (which they often made stiff and upright by applying a cement-like solution of lime), shaggy mustaches, and loud, deep voices. Trousers (usually an indication of horse-riding peoples) and twisted gold neck collars were similarly distinctive, but not as unusual as the terrifying warriors who fought naked and collected the skulls of defeated enemies. The surviving accounts describe the Celts as wildly fond of war, courageous, childishly impulsive and emotional, and fond of boasting and exaggeration, yet quick-witted and eager to learn.

Celtic Society

The Roman general Julius Caesar, who conquered Gaul (present-day France) between 58 and 51 B.C.E., penned the greatest source of information about Celtic society. Many Celtic groups in Gaul had once been ruled by kings, but by about 60 B.C.E. they periodically chose public officials, perhaps under Greek and Roman influence. Their society was divided into an elite class of warriors, professional groups of priests and bards (singers of poems about glorious deeds), and commoners. The warriors owned land and flocks of cattle and sheep and monopolized both wealth and power. The common people labored on their land. The Celts built houses (usually round in Britain, rectangular in France) out of wattle and daub—a wooden framework filled in with clay and straw—with thatched straw roofs. Several such houses belonging to related families might be surrounded by a wooden fence for protection.

The warriors of Welsh and Irish legend reflect a stage of political and social development less complex than that of the Celts in Gaul. They raided one another's flocks, reveled in drunken feasts, and engaged in contests of strength and wit. At banquets warriors would fight to the death just to claim the choicest cut of the meat, the "hero's portion."

Druids, the Celtic priests in Gaul and Britain, formed a well-organized fraternity that performed religious, judicial, and educational functions. Trainees spent years memorizing prayers, secret rituals, legal precedents, and other traditions. The priesthood was the one Celtic institution that crossed tribal lines. The Druids sometimes headed off warfare between feuding groups and served as judges in cases involving Celts from different groups. In the first century C.E. the Roman government attempted to stamp out the Druids, probably because of concern that they might

The Gundestrup Cauldron This silver vessel was found in a peat bog in Denmark, but it must have come from elsewhere. It is usually dated to the second or first century B.C.E. On the inside left are Celtic warriors on horse and on foot, with lozenge-shaped shields and long battle-horns. On the inside right is a horned deity, possibly Cernunnos. The National Museum of Denmark

Druids The class of religious experts who conducted rituals and preserved sacred lore among some ancient Celtic peoples. They provided education and mediated disputes between kinship groups.

serve as a rallying point for Celtic opposition to Roman rule, and also because of their involvement in human sacrifices.

The Celts supported large populations by tilling the heavy but fertile soils of continental Europe, and their metallurgical skills probably surpassed those of the Mediterranean peoples. Celts living on the Atlantic shore of France built sturdy oceangoing boats, and they developed extensive trade networks along Europe's large, navigable rivers. One lucrative commodity was tin, which Celtic traders from southwest England brought to Greek buyers in southern France. By the first century B.C.E. some hill-forts were evolving into urban centers.

Women's lives were focused on child rearing, food production, and some crafts. Their situation was superior to that of women in the Middle East and in the Greek and Roman Mediterranean. Greek and Roman sources depict Celtic women as strong and proud. Welsh and Irish tales portray self-assured women who sit at banquets with their husbands, engage in witty conversation, and provide ingenious solutions to vexing problems. Marriage was a partnership to which both parties contributed property, and each party had the right to inherit the estate if the other died. Celtic women also had greater freedom in their sexual relations than did their southern counterparts.

Tombs of elite women have yielded rich collections of clothing, jewelry, and furniture for use in the next world. Daughters of the elite were married to leading members of other tribes to create alliances. When the Romans invaded Celtic Britain in the first century C.E., they sometimes were opposed by Celtic tribes headed by queens, although some experts see this as an abnormal circumstance created by the Roman invasion itself.

Belief and Knowledge

Historians know the names of more than four hundred Celtic gods and goddesses, mostly associated with particular localities or kinship groups. More widely revered deities included Lug (loog), the god of light, crafts, and inventions; the horse-goddess Epona (eh-POh-nuh); and the horned god Cernunnos (KURN-you-nuhs). "The Mothers," three goddesses depicted together holding symbols of abundance, probably played a part in a fertility cult. Halloween and May

SECTION REVIEW

- From central and eastern Europe, Celtic peoples spread across the continent.
- These peoples shared language and culture but no single state.
- Although Celtic societies varied in complexity, they all shared the institution of the Druid priesthood, practiced agriculture, and developed sophisticated technologies.
- Celtic women enjoyed relatively high status, and some even led warriors against Roman invaders.
- Celtic religion involved a vast array of deities and some sort of afterlife.
- Celtic culture declined under Roman rule, and the Germanic migrations pushed it to the western margin of Europe.

Day preserve the ancient Celtic holidays of Samhain (SAH-win) and Beltaine (BEHL-tayn), respectively, which took place at key moments in the agricultural cycle.

The early Celts did not build temples, but instead worshiped wherever they felt the presence of divinity—at springs, groves, and hilltops. At the sources of the Seine and Marne Rivers in France, archaeologists have found huge caches of Celtic wooden statues thrown into the water by worshipers.

Wagons filled with extensive grave goods show up in elite burials, suggesting a belief in some sort of afterlife. In Irish and Welsh legends, heroes and gods pass back and forth between the natural and supernatural worlds much more readily than in the mythology of other cultures, and magical occurrences are commonplace. Celtic priests set forth a doctrine of reincarnation—the rebirth of the soul in a new body.

The evolution of Celtic society in Spain, southern Britain, France, and parts of central Europe slowed after the Roman conquests from the second century B.C.E. to the first century C.E. The peoples in these lands largely assimilated Roman ways (see Chapter 6). From the third century C.E. on, Germanic invaders from the east diminished the Celts still further. Only on the western fringes of the European continent—in Brittany (northwest France), Wales, Scotland, and Ireland—did Celtic peoples maintain their language, art, and culture into modern times.

Conclusion

The civilizations of early China, Nubia, and Celtic Europe emerged in very different ecological contexts in widely separated parts of the globe. The patterns of organization, technology, behavior, and belief that they developed were, in large part, responses to the challenges and opportunities of those environments.

In the North China Plain, as in the river-valley civilizations of Mesopotamia and Egypt, the presence of great, flood-prone rivers and the lack of dependable rainfall led to the formation of powerful institutions capable of organizing large numbers of people to dig and maintain irrigation channels and build dikes. An authoritarian central government has been a recurring feature of Chinese history, beginning with the Shang monarchy and warrior elite.

In Nubia, the initial impetus for the formation of a strong state was the need for protection from desert nomads and from the Egyptian rulers who coveted Nubian gold and other resources. Control of these resources and of the trade route between sub-Saharan Africa and the north, as well as the agricultural surplus to feed administrators and specialists in the urban centers, made the rulers of Kush, Napata, and Meroë wealthy and formidable.

The Celtic peoples of continental Europe never developed a strong state. They occupied fertile lands with adequate rainfall for agriculture, grazing territory for flocks, and timber for fuel and construction. Kinship groups dominated by warrior elites and controlling compact territories were the usual form of organization.

CHAPTER REVIEW

Download the MP3 audio file of the Chapter Review to listen to on the go.

How did early Chinese rulers use religion to justify and strengthen their power? (page 35)

Throughout history, elites have used religion to bolster their position. The Shang rulers of China were indispensable intermediaries between their kingdom and powerful and protective ancestors and gods. Bronze vessels were used to make offerings to ancestral spirits, and royal and elite families were buried in elaborate tombs that were intended to serve the occupant in the afterlife. Their Zhou successors developed the concept of the ruler as divine Son of Heaven who ruled in accord with the Mandate of Heaven.

How did the technological and cultural influences of Egypt affect the formation of Nubia? (page 45)

The civilization that developed in Nubia was powerfully influenced by its interactions with the more complex and technologically advanced neighboring society in Egypt. Nubia was engaged in trade with Egypt for most of its history, and Egyptians often sought to control and dominate the gold trade. In the New Kingdom period, the Egyptian government imposed Egyptian culture, language, and religion on the native population, and Nubian architecture came to be based on Egyptian models. In the eighth century B.C.E. the kingdom of Meroë emerged and Nubia controlled all of Egypt for half a century. While they kept their Nubian names, the rulers imitated the style of Egyptian rulers and kept many Egyptian traditions. By the fourth century, power shifted south to Meroë and sub-Saharan African cultural influences replaced Egyptian ones.

How did most Europeans come to speak Indo-European languages? (page 48)

Most of the languages of Europe, Iran, and India originated with nomadic herdsmen who domesticated horses and invented ox-drawn wagons. Those who migrated to Europe after 3100 B.C.E. induced the indigenous inhabitants to adopt their languages, including the ancestor of the language of the Celts.

What is known about the Celts, and how did their religious beliefs help to shape their society? (page 49)

The Celtic elites of central Europe initially traded for luxury goods with the Mediterranean, and when they began to expand into lands to the west and south after 500 B.C.E. they came into even closer contact with Mediterranean peoples. Eventually many Celtic groups were incorporated into the Roman Empire. Druids, the Celtic priests in Gaul and Britain, performed religious and other functions. Rather than constructing temples, the Celts worshiped hundreds of gods and goddesses in natural surroundings, where they felt the presence of divinity. By the first century C.E., the Romans had conquered parts of Europe and assimilated many Celts to their ways.

Key Terms

loess *(p. 37)*

Shang *(p. 38)*

Zhou *(p. 39)*

Mandate of Heaven *(p. 40)*

Legalism *(p. 41)*

Confucius *(p. 41)*

Daoism *(p. 41)*

yin/yang *(p. 44)*

Kush *(p. 45)*

Meroë *(p. 47)*

Celts *(p. 49)*

Druids *(p. 50)*

Web Resources

Pronunciation Guide

Interactive Map

• MAP 2.1 China in the Shang and Zhou Periods, 1750–221 B.C.E.

Primary Source

• The Book of Documents

Answer to the History in Focus Question

See photo on page 46, "Gebel Barkal."

CourseMate

Visit the CourseMate website at www.cengagebrain.com for additional study tools and review materials for this chapter.

The Mediterranean and Middle East

© Cengage Learning

CHAPTER PREVIEW

The Cosmopolitan Middle East, 1700–1100 B.C.E.
How did a cosmopolitan civilization develop in the Middle East during the Late Bronze Age, and what forms did it take?

The Aegean World, 2000–1100 B.C.E.
What civilizations emerged in the Aegean world, and what relationship did they have to the older civilizations to the east?

The Assyrian Empire, 911–612 B.C.E.
How did the Assyrian Empire rise to power and eventually dominate most of the ancient Middle East?

Israel, 2000–500 B.C.E.
How did the civilization of Israel develop, following both familiar cultural patterns and a unique course of its own?

Phoenicia and the Mediterranean, 1200–500 B.C.E.
How did the Phoenicians rise to commercial dominance over much of the Mediterranean world?

Failure and Transformation, 750–550 B.C.E.
What factors prompted the transformation of the ancient Middle East between 750 and 550 B.C.E.?

Conclusion

ENVIRONMENT AND TECHNOLOGY: Ancient Textiles and Dyes

Visit the CourseMate website at **www.cengagebrain.com** for additional study tools and review materials for this chapter.

Ancient stories—even those that are not historically accurate—provide valuable insights into how people thought about their origins and identity. One story concerned the city of Carthage (KAHR-thuhj) in present-day Tunisia, which for centuries dominated the commerce of the western Mediterranean. Tradition held that Dido, a member of the royal family of the Phoenician city-state of Tyre (tire) in southern Lebanon, fled with her supporters to the western Mediterranean after her brother, the king of Tyre, murdered her husband. On the North African coast the refugees made friendly contact with local people, who agreed to give them as much land as a cow's hide could cover. By cleverly cutting the hide into narrow strips, they were able to mark out a substantial piece of territory for Kart Khadasht, the "New City" (called Carthago by their Roman enemies). Later, faithful to the memory of her dead husband, Dido committed suicide rather than marry a local chieftain.

This story highlights the spread of cultural patterns from older centers to new regions in the Mediterranean lands and western Asia. Just as Egyptian cultural influences helped transform Nubian society, influences from the older centers in Mesopotamia and Egypt penetrated throughout western Asia and the Mediterranean. Far-flung trade, diplomatic contacts, military conquests, and the relocation of large numbers of people spread knowledge, beliefs, practices, and technologies.

By the end of the second millennium B.C.E. many of the societies of the region had entered the **Iron Age**. Iron offered advantages over bronze. It was a single metal rather than an alloy and thus was simpler to obtain, and iron ore was plentiful. Once the technology of iron making had been mastered—high-temperature heating to turn the ore into a soft "bloom" followed by pounding to remove impurities and quenching for hardness—iron tools were found to have sharper and longer-lasting edges than bronze tools.

The Hittites of iron-rich Anatolia had learned to make iron implements by 1500 B.C.E. but did not share their knowledge. Some scholars believe that, in the disrupted period after 1200 B.C.E., blacksmiths from the Hittite core area migrated and spread the technology. Others speculate that metalworkers who could not obtain copper and tin turned to dumps of slag (the byproduct of bronze production) containing iron residue and found that they could create useful objects from it.

The first part of this chapter picks up the story of Mesopotamia and Egypt in the Late Bronze Age, the second millennium B.C.E.: their complex relations with neighboring peoples, the development of a prosperous, "cosmopolitan" network of states in the Middle East, and the destruction and decline that set in around 1200 B.C.E. We also look at how the Minoan and Mycenaean civilizations of the Aegean Sea adopted the technologies and cultural patterns of the older Middle Eastern centers and prospered through long-distance trading.

Turning to the Early Iron Age, from 1000 to 500 B.C.E., the focus will be on three societies: the Assyrians of northern Mesopotamia; the Israelites; and the Phoenicians of Lebanon, Syria, and their Carthaginian colonies in the western Mediterranean.

The Cosmopolitan Middle East, 1700–1100 B.C.E.

How did a cosmopolitan civilization develop in the Middle East during the Late Bronze Age, and what forms did it take?

Although outside invaders overwhelmed Mesopotamia and Egypt in the seventeenth century B.C.E. (see Chapter 1), the outsiders were eventually either ejected or assimilated, and conditions of stability and prosperity returned. Between 1500 and 1200 B.C.E. large territorial states dominated the Middle East (see Map 3.1). Smaller city-states, kingdoms, and kinship groups fell under their control as they competed for access to commodities and trade routes.

Historians have called the Late Bronze Age a "cosmopolitan" era, meaning a time of widely shared cultures and lifestyles. Diplomatic relations and

Iron Age Historians' term for the period during which iron was the primary metal for tools and weapons. The advent of iron technology began at different times in different parts of the world.

commercial contacts between states fostered flows of goods and ideas, and elite groups shared similar values and high living standards. The peasants who constituted the majority of the population may have seen some improvement in their standard of living, but they reaped far fewer benefits from the increasing contacts and trade.

Western Asia

By 1500 B.C.E. Mesopotamia was divided into two distinct political zones: Babylonia in the south and Assyria in the north (see Map 3.1). The city of Babylon had first gained ascendancy under the dynasty of Hammurabi in the eighteenth and seventeenth centuries B.C.E., but Kassite (KAS-ite) peoples from the Zagros (ZAH-groes) Mountains to the east had seized power by 1500 B.C.E. Though

Kassite names derive from their native, non-Semitic language, the Kassites otherwise embraced Babylonian language and culture and intermarried with the native population. For 350 years, the Kassite lords of Babylonia defended their core area and traded for raw materials, but they did not pursue territorial conquest.

The Assyrians of the north proved more ambitious. As early as the twentieth century B.C.E. the city of Ashur (AH-shoor), the leading urban center on the northern Tigris, anchored a busy trade route across the northern Mesopotamian plain and onto the Anatolian Plateau. Assyrian merchants established settlements outside the walls of important Anatolian cities. They imported textiles and tin, used to make bronze, in exchange for Anatolian silver. In the eighteenth century B.C.E. an Assyrian dynasty briefly controlled

Map 3.1   The Middle East in the Second Millennium B.C.E.   Although warfare was not uncommon, treaties, diplomatic missions, and correspondence in Akkadian cuneiform fostered cooperative relationships between states. All were tied together by extensive networks of exchange centering on the trade in metals. Peripheral regions, such as Nubia and the Aegean Sea, were drawn into the web of commerce.   © Cengage Learning

Interactive Map

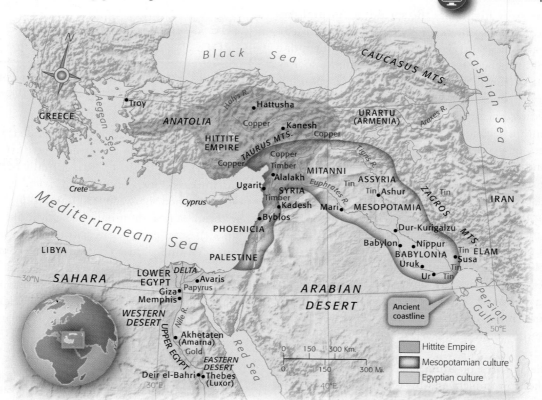

Chronology

	Western Asia	Egypt	Syria-Palestine	Mediterranean
2000 B.C.E.	**2000** B.C.E. Horses in use	**2040–1640** B.C.E. Middle Kingdom		**2000** B.C.E. Rise of Minoan civilization; early Greeks arrive
			1800 B.C.E. Abraham migrates to Canaan	
	1700–1200 B.C.E. Hittites dominate Anatolia	**1640–1532** B.C.E. Hyksos in northern Egypt **1532** B.C.E. New Kingdom begins		**1600** B.C.E. Rise of Mycenaean civilization
1500 B.C.E.	**1500** B.C.E. Hittites pioneer iron	**1490** B.C.E. Hatshepsut's Punt expedition	**1500** B.C.E. "Alphabetic" script at Ugarit	
	1500 B.C.E. Kassites in Mesopotamia			**1450** B.C.E. Destruction of Minoan palaces in Crete
		1290–1224 B.C.E. Ramesses the Great	**1250–1200** B.C.E. Israelites in Canaan	**1200–1150** B.C.E. Destruction of Mycenaean centers in Greece
1000 B.C.E.	**1200** B.C.E. Hittite kingdom ends	**1200–1150** B.C.E. Sea Peoples attack Egypt **1070** B.C.E. New Kingdom ends	**1150** B.C.E. Philistines settle Israel's coast **1000** B.C.E. Jerusalem made Israelite capital	
	911 B.C.E. Neo-Assyrian Empire **744–727** B.C.E. Tiglathpileser	**750** B.C.E. Kush controls Egypt **671** B.C.E. Assyrians conquer Egypt	**969** B.C.E. Hiram of Tyre comes to power **721** B.C.E. Assyrian conquest of northern kingdom	**814** B.C.E. Foundation of Carthage
600 B.C.E.	**668–627** B.C.E. Ashurbanipal **612** B.C.E. Fall of Assyria			
			587 B.C.E. Capture of Jerusalem	**550–330** B.C.E. Rivalry of Carthaginians and Greeks in western Mediterranean
			515 B.C.E. Deportees from Babylon return to Jerusalem	

the upper Euphrates River near the present-day Syria-Iraq border. The trade routes connecting Mesopotamia to Anatolia and the Syria-Palestine coast were key to the power of this "Old Assyrian" kingdom. After 1400 B.C.E. a resurgent "Middle Assyrian" kingdom again engaged in campaigns of conquest and economic expansion.

Other ambitious states developed around the Mesopotamian heartland, including Elam in southwest Iran. Most formidable were the **Hittites** (HIT-ites), who

Hittites A people from central Anatolia who established an empire in Anatolia and Syria in the Late Bronze Age. With wealth from the trade in metals and military power based on chariot forces, the Hittites vied with New Kingdom Egypt for control of Syria-Palestine before falling to unidentified attackers ca. 1200 B.C.E.

The Mortuary Temple of Queen Hatshepsut at Deir el-Bahri, Egypt, ca. 1460 B.C.E. This beautiful complex of terraces, ramps, and colonnades featured relief sculptures and texts commemorating the famous expedition to Punt.

 History In Focus *What does the structure and placement of the building in the landscape tell you about the role Hatshepsut played in the Egypt of her day? Find the answer online.*

became the foremost power in Anatolia from around 1700 to 1200 B.C.E. From their capital at Hattusha (haht-tush-SHAH), near present-day Ankara (ANG-kur-ruh) in central Turkey, they deployed the fearsome new technology of horse-drawn war chariots. Iron was the Hittites' specialty, and Anatolia's rich deposits of copper, silver, and iron played a major role in Hittite commerce.

During the second millennium B.C.E. Meso-potamian political and cultural concepts spread across much of western Asia. Akkadian (uh-KAY-dee-uhn) became the language of diplomacy and correspondence between governments. The Elamites (EE-luh-mites) and Hittites, among others, adapted the cuneiform system to write their own languages. In the Syrian coastal city of Ugarit (OO-guh-reet) thirty cuneiform symbols were used to write consonant sounds, an early example of the alphabetic principle and a considerable advance over the hundreds of signs required in conventional cuneiform writing.

New Kingdom Egypt

After flourishing for nearly four hundred years (see Chapter 1), the Egyptian Middle Kingdom lost strength in the seventeenth century B.C.E. Egypt entered a period of political fragmentation and economic decline. Around 1640 B.C.E. it came under foreign rule for the first time, at the hands of the Hyksos (HICK-soes), or "Princes of Foreign Lands."

Historians are uncertain who the Hyksos were. Semitic peoples had been migrating from the Levant (present-day Syria, Lebanon, Jordan, Israel, and the Palestinian territories) into the eastern Nile Delta for centuries. In the chaotic conditions of this time, other peoples may have joined them, establishing control first in the delta and then in the middle of the country. The Hyksos had war chariots and composite bows made of wood and horn for greater range, which gave them an advantage over the Egyptians. The Hyksos intermarried with Egyptians and assimilated to native ways. They spoke Egyptian and maintained

Egyptian institutions and culture. Nevertheless, unlike in Mesopotamia, the Egyptians continued to regard the Hyksos as "foreigners."

As with the formation of the Middle Kingdom five hundred years earlier, the reunification of Egypt under a native dynasty was accomplished by princes from Thebes. After three decades of warfare, Kamose (KAH-mose) and Ahmose (AH-mose) expelled the Hyksos from Egypt and inaugurated the New Kingdom, which lasted from about 1532 to 1070 B.C.E.

New Kingdom Egypt saw a shift from traditional Egyptian isolationism to aggressive expansionism northward into the Levant and southward into Nubia. Timber, gold, and copper in taxes and tribute (payments from conquered territories) were the prizes of this expansion. The occupied lands also provided a buffer against foreign attack. In Nubia, Egypt imposed direct control and pressed the native population to adopt Egyptian language and culture (see Chapter 2). In the Levant, the Egyptians stationed garrisons at strategically placed forts and supported local rulers willing to collaborate.

The New Kingdom was a period of innovation. Egyptian soldiers, administrators, diplomats, and merchants traveled widely and learned about exotic fruits and vegetables, as well as new technologies, such as new musical instruments and improved potter's wheels and weaver's looms.

At least one woman held the throne of New Kingdom Egypt. When Pharaoh Tuthmosis (tuth-MOE-sis) II died, his queen, **Hatshepsut** (hat-SHEP-soot), served as regent for her young stepson and soon claimed the royal title for herself (r. 1473–1458 B.C.E.). In inscriptions she often used the male pronoun to refer to herself, and drawings and sculptures show her wearing the long beard of the ruler of Egypt.

Around 1490 B.C.E. Hatshepsut sent a naval expedition down the Red Sea to Punt (poont), an exotic land that historians believe may have been near the coast of eastern Sudan or Eritrea. Hatshepsut was in quest of myrrh (murr), a reddish-brown resin that the Egyptians burned in religious rites and used in medicines and cosmetics. She hoped to bypass the middlemen who drove up the price exorbitantly and establish direct trade between Punt and Egypt. When the expedition returned with myrrh and various sub-Saharan luxuries—ebony and other rare woods, ivory,

live monkeys, panther skins—Hatshepsut celebrated the achievement in words and pictures on the walls of a mortuary temple she built for herself. She may have used the success of this expedition to bolster her claim to the throne. After her death, in a reaction that reflected some official opposition to a woman ruler, her image was defaced and her name blotted out wherever it appeared.

Another ruler who departed from traditional ways ascended the throne as Amenhotep (ah-muhn-HOE-tep) IV. He soon began to refer to himself as **Akhenaten** (ah-ken-AHT-n) (r. 1353–1335 B.C.E.), meaning "beneficial to the Aten (AHT-n)" (the disk of the sun). He thus publicized his belief in Aten as the supreme deity. He closed the temples of other gods, challenging the age-old supremacy of the chief god Amon (AH-muhn) and the power and influence of Amon's priests.

Some scholars maintain that Akhenaten pioneered monotheism—the belief in one exclusive god. Akhenaten's goal, however, was more likely a reassertion of the king's superiority over the priests and a renewal of belief in the king's divinity. Worship of Aten was confined to the royal family: the people of Egypt were pressed to revere the divine ruler.

Akhenaten built a new capital at modern-day Amarna (ah-MAHR-nuh), halfway between Memphis and Thebes (see Map 3.1). He relocated thousands of Egyptians to construct the site and serve the ruling elite. His artists created a new style that broke with the conventions of earlier art: the king, his wife Nefertiti (nef-uhr-TEE-tee), and their daughters were depicted in fluid, natural poses with strangely elongated heads and limbs and swelling abdomens.

Hatshepsut Queen of Egypt (r. 1473–1458 B.C.E.). She dispatched a naval expedition down the Red Sea to Punt (possibly northeast Sudan or Eritria), the faraway source of myrrh. There is evidence of opposition to a woman as ruler, and after her death her name and image were frequently defaced.

Akhenaten Egyptian pharaoh (r. 1353–1335 B.C.E.). He built a new capital at Amarna, fostered a new style of naturalistic art, and created a religious revolution by imposing worship of the sun-disk. The Amarna letters, largely from his reign, preserve official correspondence with subjects and neighbors.

Colossal Statues of Ramesses II at Abu Simbel Strategically placed at a bend in the Nile River so as to face the southern frontier, this monument was an advertisement of Egyptian power. A temple was carved into the cliff behind the gigantic statues of the pharaoh. In a modern marvel of engineering, the monument was moved to higher ground in 1960 C.E. to protect it from rising waters when a dam was constructed.

Government officials, priests, and others whose privileges and wealth were linked to the traditional system strongly resented these reforms. After Akhenaten's death the temples were reopened, Amon was reinstated as chief god, the capital returned to Thebes, and the priests regained their influence. The boy-king Tutankhamun (tuht-uhnk-AH-muhn) (r. 1333–1323 B.C.E.), one of the immediate successors of Akhenaten and famous solely because his tomb had not been pillaged by tomb robbers when it was found, reveals both in his name (meaning "beautiful in life is Amon") and in his insignificant reign the ultimate failure of Akhenaten's revolution.

In 1323 B.C.E. the general Haremhab seized the throne and established a new dynasty, the Ramessides (RAM-ih-side). The rulers of this line renewed the policy of conquest and expansion that Akhenaten had neglected. **Ramesses** (RAM-ih-seez) **II**—sometimes called Ramesses the Great—ruled for sixty-six years (r. 1290–1224 B.C.E.) and dominated his age. Living into

his nineties, he may have fathered more than a hundred children. Since 1990 archaeologists have been excavating a network of more than a hundred corridors and chambers carved deep into a hillside in the Valley of the Kings where many sons of Ramesses were buried.

Commerce and Communication

Early in his reign Ramesses II fought a major battle against the Hittites at Kadesh in northern Syria (1285 B.C.E.). Although Egyptian propaganda boasted of a great victory, the lack of territorial gains suggests that it was essentially a draw. In subsequent years Egyptian and Hittite diplomats negotiated a

Ramesses II A long-lived ruler of New Kingdom Egypt (r. 1290–1224 B.C.E.). He reached an accommodation with the Hittites of Anatolia after a standoff in battle at Kadesh in Syria. He built on a grand scale throughout Egypt.

- The Late Bronze Age saw the rise of a cosmopolitan culture in the ancient Middle East.
- Mesopotamia was divided between Babylonia and the increasingly powerful Assyrians.
- In Anatolia, the technologically advanced Hittites became the major political force, and both they and other outlying peoples absorbed Mesopotamian cultural and political concepts.
- After a century of foreign domination, the New Kingdom in Egypt ushered in a period of expansion abroad and innovation at home.
- During the Late Bronze Age, long-distance trade in metals expanded, and the arrival of the horse made possible larger states and empires.

treaty, which was strengthened by Ramesses's marriage to a Hittite princess. At issue was control of Syria-Palestine. The inland cities of Syria-Palestine—such as Mari (MAR-ree) on the upper Euphrates and Alalakh (UH-luh-luhk) in western Syria—were hubs of international trade. The coastal towns—particularly Ugarit and the Phoenician towns of the Lebanese seaboard—served as transshipment points for trade to and from the lands ringing the Mediterranean Sea.

Commerce in metals energized the long-distance trade. We have seen the Assyrian traffic in silver from Anatolia and the Egyptian passion for Nubian gold (see Chapter 2). Copper came from Anatolia and Cyprus, tin from Afghanistan and possibly the British Isles. Both commodities traveled long distances and passed through many hands before reaching their final destinations.

New modes of transportation expedited communications and commerce across great distances and inhospitable landscapes. Horses arrived in western Asia around 2000 B.C.E. First used by nomads in Central Asia, they were brought into Mesopotamia through the Zagros Mountains and reached Egypt by 1600 B.C.E. The speed of the horse contributed to the creation of large states and empires. Soldiers and government agents could cover great distances quickly, and swift, maneuverable horse-drawn chariots became the premier instrument of war.

Sometime after 1500 B.C.E. in western Asia, but not for another thousand years in Egypt, people began to

make common use of camels, though the animal was domesticated much earlier in southern Arabia. Their strength made them ideal pack animals, and their ability to go without water made travel across barren terrain possible.

The Aegean World, 2000–1100 B.C.E.

What civilizations emerged in the Aegean world, and what relationship did they have to the older civilizations to the east?

In this era of far-flung trade and communication, the emergence of the Minoan (mih-NO-uhn) civilization on the island of Crete and the Mycenaean (my-suh-NEE-uhn) civilization of Greece demonstrates the fertilizing influence of older centers on outlying lands and peoples. The landscape of southern Greece and the Aegean islands is rocky and arid, with small plains lying between ranges of hills. The limited arable land was suitable for grains, grapevines, and olive trees. Flocks of sheep and goats grazed the slopes. Sharply indented coastlines, natural harbors, and small islands within sight of one another made the sea the fastest and least costly mode of travel. Lacking metals and timber, Aegean peoples had to import these commodities from abroad. As a result, the rise, success, and eventual fall of the Minoan and Mycenaean societies were closely tied to their relations with other peoples in the region.

Minoan Crete

The **Minoan** civilization that had come into being on the island of Crete by 2000 B.C.E. (see Map 3.1) featured centralized government, monumental building, bronze metallurgy, writing, and recordkeeping. Archaeologists named this civilization after the legendary King Minos, who was said to have ruled a vast naval empire, including southern Greece, and to have kept the monstrous

Minoan Prosperous civilization on the Aegean island of Crete in the second millennium B.C.E. The Minoans engaged in far-flung commerce around the Mediterranean and exerted powerful cultural influences on the early Greeks.

Minotaur (MIN-uh-tor) (half-man, half-bull) beneath his palace in a mazelike labyrinth built by the ingenious inventor Daedalus (DED-ih-luhs).

The ethnicity of the Minoans is uncertain, and their writing has not been deciphered. But their sprawling palace complexes at Cnossus (NOSS-suhs), Phaistos (FIE-stuhs), and Mallia (mahl-YAH) and the distribution of Cretan pottery and other artifacts around the Mediterranean and Middle East testify to widespread trading connections. Egyptian, Syrian, and Mesopotamian influences can be seen in the design of the Minoan palaces, but the absence of identifiable representations of Cretan rulers contrasts sharply with the grandiose depictions of kings in the Middle East and suggests a different conception of authority. Also noteworthy are the absence of fortifications at the palace sites and the presence of high-quality indoor plumbing.

Statuettes of women with elaborate headdresses and serpents coiling around their limbs may represent fertility goddesses. Colorful frescoes (paintings done on a moist plaster surface) on palace walls portray groups of women in frilly, layered skirts engaged in conversation or watching rituals or entertainment, as well as young acrobats vaulting over the horns of an onrushing bull, either for sport or as a religious activity. Servants carrying jars and fishermen throwing nets and hooks from their boats suggest a joyful attitude toward work, but this may say more about elite ideals than about the reality of daily toil. Stylized vase paintings depicting plants with swaying leaves and playful octopuses with undulating tentacles reflect a delight in nature's beauty.

All the Cretan palaces except Cnossus, along with the houses of the elite and peasants in the countryside, were deliberately destroyed around 1450 B.C.E. Because Mycenaean Greeks took over at Cnossus, most historians regard them as the likely culprits.

Mycenaean Greece

Most historians believe that speakers of an Indo-European language ancestral to Greek migrated into the Greek peninsula around 2000 B.C.E. Through intermarriage, blending of languages, and melding of cultural practices, the indigenous population and the newcomers created the first Greek culture. For centuries this society remained simple and static. Farmers and shepherds lived in Stone Age conditions, wringing a bare living from the land. Then, sometime around 1600 B.C.E., life changed relatively suddenly.

More than a century ago a German businessman, Heinrich Schliemann (SHLEE-muhn), set out to prove that the *Iliad* and the *Odyssey* were true. These epics attributed to the poet Homer, who probably lived shortly before 700 B.C.E., spoke of Agamemnon (ag-uh-MEM-non), the king of **Mycenae** (my-SEE-nee) in southern Greece. In 1876 Schliemann stunned the scholarly world by discovering at Mycenae a circle of graves at the base of deep, rectangular shafts. These **shaft graves** contained the bodies of men, women, and children and were filled with gold jewelry and ornaments, weapons, and utensils. Clearly, some people in this society had acquired wealth, authority, and the capacity to mobilize human labor. Subsequent excavation uncovered a large palace complex, massive walls, more shaft graves, and other evidence of a rich and technologically advanced civilization that lasted from around 1600 to 1150 B.C.E.

The sudden appearance of Mycenaean culture in mainland Greece is puzzling. There is no archaeological evidence of Cretan political control of the mainland, but Crete exerted an undeniable cultural influence. The Mycenaeans borrowed the Minoan ideas of the palace, centralized economy, and administrative bureaucracy, as well as the Minoan writing system. They adopted Minoan styles and techniques of architecture, pottery making, and fresco and vase painting. But how did they suddenly accumulate power and wealth? Most historians look to the profits from trade and piracy and perhaps also to the pay and booty brought back by mercenaries (soldiers who served for pay in foreign lands).

Mycenae Site of a fortified palace complex in southern Greece that controlled a Late Bronze Age kingdom. In Homer's epic poems, Mycenae was the base of King Agamemnon, who commanded the Greeks besieging Troy. Contemporary archaeologists call the complex Greek society of the second millennium B.C.E. "Mycenaean."

shaft graves A term used for the burial sites of elite members of Mycenaean Greek society in the mid-second millennium B.C.E. At the bottom of deep shafts lined with stone slabs, the bodies were laid out along with gold and bronze jewelry, implements, weapons, and masks.

Gate of Mycenae This gate topped with a relief sculpture of lions, symbols of the city of Mycenae, protected the entrance to the city. The massive stones show the dangers and insecurity of life in Greece in the second millennium B.C.E.

Excavations at other centers have revealed that Mycenae exemplifies the common pattern: a citadel built on a hilltop and surrounded by high, thick fortifications made of stones so large that later Greeks believed that the legendary giant, one-eyed Cyclopes (SIGH-kloe-pees), had lifted them into place. The fortified enclosure provided refuge for the community in time of danger and contained the palace and administrative complex. The large central hall with an open hearth and columned porch was surrounded by courtyards, living quarters for the royal family and their retainers, and offices, storerooms, and workshops. Brightly painted scenes of war, the hunt, and daily life, as well as natural motifs, covered the palace walls.

Over four thousand baked clay tablets written in a script called **Linear B** provide additional information. Like its predecessor, the undeciphered Minoan script called Linear A, Linear B uses pictorial signs to represent syllables, but the language is an early form of Greek. The palace bureaucracy kept track of people, animals, and objects in exhaustive detail. The tablets list everything from the number of chariot wheels in palace storerooms and the rations paid to textile workers to the gifts dedicated to various gods and the ships stationed along the coasts. The government organized and coordinated grain production and controlled the wool industry. Scribes kept track of flocks in the field, the sheared wool and its allocation to spinners and weavers, and the production, storage, and distribution of textiles. However, individual people—even kings—receive no mention, leaving us largely in the dark about the political and legal systems, social structures, gender relations, and religious beliefs, not to mention particular historical events.

In Homer's *Iliad*, Agamemnon, the king of Mycenae, leads a great expedition of Greeks from different regions against the city of Troy in northwest Anatolia. In addition, the Mycenaean centers reflect a remarkable similarity in buildings, tombs, utensils, tools, clothing, and works of art. Some scholars argue that political unity must have lain behind this cultural uniformity. The *Iliad*, however, revolves around the difficulties Agamemnon has in asserting control over other leaders. Moreover, the archaeological remains and the Linear B tablets suggest that Mycenae, Pylos (PIE-lohs), and other centers wielded power independently.

The seafaring skills of the Minoans and Mycenaeans encouraged long-distance trade. Commercial vessels depended primarily on sails, and their crews navigated during daylight hours to keep the land in sight and then went ashore at night to eat and sleep.

Linear B A set of syllabic symbols, derived from the writing system of Minoan Crete, used in the Mycenaean palaces of the Late Bronze Age to write an early form of Greek. It was used primarily for palace records, and the surviving Linear B tablets provide substantial information about the economic organization of Mycenaean society and tantalizing clues about political, social, and religious institutions.

The ships' shallow keels enabled the crews to pull them up onto the beach.

Cretan and Greek pottery and crafted goods are found not only around the Aegean but also in other parts of the Mediterranean and Middle East, sometimes in enough quantity and variety to suggest settlements of Aegean peoples. The oldest artifacts are Minoan, but eventually Greek wares predominated. This indicates that Cretan merchants pioneered trade routes and then admitted Mycenaean traders, who eventually supplanted them in the fifteenth century B.C.E.

The many Aegean pots found throughout the region must once have contained such products as wine and olive oil. Weapons and other crafted goods may also have been exported, along with slaves and mercenary soldiers. As for imports, amber from northern Europe and ivory carved in Syria have been discovered at Aegean sites, and the large population of southwest Greece probably relied on imported grain. Above all, the Aegean lands needed metals, both the gold prized by rulers and the copper and tin needed to make bronze. Sunken ships carrying copper ingots, probably from Cyprus, have been found at the bottom of the Mediterranean (see Map 3.1). As in early China, metal goods belonged mostly to the elite and may have been symbols of their superior status. Homer's description of bronze tripods piled up in the storerooms of heroes brings to mind the bronze vessels buried in Shang tombs (see Chapter 2).

Mycenaeans were tough, warlike, and acquisitive. They traded with those who were strong and took from those who were weak. This may have provoked conflict with the Hittite kings of Anatolia in the fourteenth and thirteenth centuries B.C.E. Documents found in the archives at Hattusha, the Hittite capital, refer to the king and land of Ahhijawa (uh-key-YAW-wuh), most likely a Hittite rendering of Achaeans (uh-KEY-uhns), the term used most frequently by Homer for the Greeks. The documents indicate that relations were sometimes friendly, sometimes strained, and that the people of Ahhijawa were aggressive and tried to take advantage of Hittite preoccupation or weakness. The *Iliad*, Homer's tale of the Achaeans' ten-year siege and eventual destruction of Troy, a city on the fringes of Hittite territory that controlled the sea route between the Mediterranean and Black Seas, should

be seen against this backdrop. Archaeology has confirmed a destruction at Troy around 1200 B.C.E.

The Fall of Late Bronze Age Civilizations

For reasons that remain obscure, large numbers of people were on the move around 1200 B.C.E. As migrants swarmed into one region, they displaced other peoples, who then joined the tide of refugees. This process culminated in the destruction of many of the old Middle Eastern and Mediterranean centers. Around 1200 B.C.E. unidentified invaders destroyed Hattusha and the Hittite kingdom. Moving south into Syria, the tide of destruction swept away the great coastal city of Ugarit. Around 1220 B.C.E., Merneptah (mehr-NEH-ptuh), the son and successor of Ramesses II, repulsed an assault on the Nile Delta by people he described as "Libyans and Northerners coming from all lands." About thirty years later Ramesses III checked a major invasion of southern Syria-Palestine by "Sea Peoples," who became known as Philistines (FIH-luh-steens) (the origin of the name *Palestine*, sometimes used for this region). Although he claimed a great victory, the Philistines occupied the coast, and Egypt soon withdrew. The Egyptians also lost their foothold in Nubia, opening the way for the emergence of the native kingdom centered in Napata (see Chapter 2).

Among the invaders listed in the Egyptian inscriptions are the Ekwesh (ECK-wesh), who could be Achaeans—that is, Greeks. Whether or not the Mycenaeans participated in these or other invasions, their own centers collapsed in the first half of the twelfth century B.C.E. The rulers apparently saw trouble coming; at some sites they undertook more extensive fortifications and measures to ensure water supplies. But their efforts were in vain. Nearly all the palaces were destroyed. The Linear B tablets survive only because they were baked hard in the resulting fires.

Curiously, archaeology reveals no trace of foreign invaders. Yet it is unlikely to be coincidental that Mycenaean civilization collapsed at roughly the same time as the fall of other regional civilizations. The position of the Mycenaean ruling class may have depended on imports of vital commodities and profits from trade, and they may have suffered from the destruction of trading partners and disruption of routes. Competition for limited resources may have led to internal unrest and, ultimately, political collapse.

SECTION REVIEW

- Influenced by contact with older cultures, Minoan Crete was the first European civilization to develop a complex government and advanced technologies.

- The Minoans participated in extensive long-distance trade, which prompted a blending of foreign and indigenous cultural forms and practices.

- Minoan civilization was deliberately destroyed, perhaps by Mycenaean Greeks.

- In Greece, Mycenaean civilization rose suddenly and developed common patterns of settlement, organization, and technology.

- The Mycenaeans participated in long-distance trade and piracy activities, which likely became the basis of later heroic legends.

- Large migrations precipitated the collapse of many Late Bronze Age civilizations, including the Mycenaean, after which Greece entered a Dark Age.

The destruction of the palaces ended the domination of the ruling class. The administrative apparatus revealed in the Linear B tablets disappeared, and writing passed out of use along with the palace officials who had utilized it. Archaeological studies indicate the depopulation of some regions of Greece and a flow of people to other regions that escaped destruction. The Greek language persisted, and a thousand years later people were still worshiping gods mentioned in the Linear B tablets. People also continued to make the vessels and implements that they were familiar with, although there was a marked decline in artistic and technical skill in the now impoverished society. Mycenaean cultural uniformity gave way to regional variations in shapes, styles, and techniques, reflecting the increased isolation of different Greek areas. The peoples of the region entered a centuries-long "Dark Age" of poverty, isolation, and loss of knowledge.

The Assyrian Empire, 911–612 B.C.E.

How did the Assyrian Empire rise to power and eventually dominate most of the ancient Middle East?

New centers emerged in the centuries after 1000 B.C.E. The chief force for change was the powerful and aggressive **Neo-Assyrian Empire** (911–612 B.C.E.). Although historians sometimes apply the term *empire* to earlier regional powers, the Assyrians of this era were the first to rule over far-flung lands and diverse peoples.

The Assyrian homeland in northern Mesopotamia differs substantially from the flat expanse of Sumer and Akkad to the south. It is hillier, has a more temperate and rainier climate, and is exposed to raiders from the mountains to the east and north and the arid plain to the west. Peasant farmers, accustomed to defending themselves against marauders, provided the foot-soldiers for the ceaseless campaigns of the Neo-Assyrian Empire: westward across the steppe and desert as far as the Mediterranean, north into mountainous Urartu (ur-RAHR-too) (modern Armenia), east across the Zagros range onto the Iranian Plateau, and south along the Tigris River to Babylonia.

These campaigns followed important trade routes and provided immediate booty and the prospect of tribute and taxes. They also secured access to iron and silver and brought the Assyrians control of international commerce. As noted earlier, Assyria had a long tradition of commercial and political interests in Syria and Anatolia. However, what started out as an aggressive program of self-defense and reassertion of old claims soon became more ambitious. Driven by pride, greed, and religious conviction, the Assyrians defeated the great kingdoms of the day—Elam (southwest Iran), Urartu, Babylon, and Egypt. Larger in extent than its predecessors, the Assyrian Empire was founded on the principle of enriching the imperial center at the expense of the subjugated periphery.

The king was literally and symbolically the center of the Assyrian universe. The land belonged to him, and all the people, even the highest-ranking officials, were his servants. Assyrians believed that the gods chose the king as their earthly representative. Normally the king chose a son as successor, and his choice

---

Neo-Assyrian Empire An empire extending from western Iran to Syria-Palestine, conquered by the Assyrians of northern Mesopotamia between the tenth and seventh centuries B.C.E. They used force and terror and exploited the wealth and labor of their subjects. They also preserved and continued the cultural and scientific developments of Mesopotamian civilization.

Section of Balawat Gates Bronze bands with images of military campaigns and court life were affixed to the cedar-wood gates of a palace built by the Assyrian king Shalmaneser III (r. 858–824 B.C.E.).

British Museum/Michael Holford

was confirmed by divine oracles and the Assyrian elite. In the revered ancient city of Ashur the high priest anointed the new king by sprinkling his head with oil and gave him the insignia of kingship: a crown and scepter. The kings were buried in Ashur.

Every day messengers and spies brought the king information from every corner of the empire. He made decisions, appointed officials, and heard complaints. He dictated his correspondence to an army of scribes and received and entertained foreign envoys and high-ranking government figures. As the country's military leader, the king was responsible for planning campaigns, and he often was away from the capital commanding operations in the field.

Among other responsibilities, the king supervised the state religion, devoting much time to public and private rituals and to temple maintenance. He consulted the gods through elaborate rituals, and all state actions were carried out in the name of Ashur, the chief god. Military victories gave proof of Ashur's superiority over the gods of the conquered peoples.

Relentless government propaganda secured popular support for military campaigns that mostly

benefited the king and the nobility. Royal inscriptions posted throughout the empire catalogued military victories, extolled the king, and promised ruthless punishments for those who resisted. Relief sculptures depicting hunts, battles, sieges, executions, and deportations covered the walls of the royal palaces at Kalhu (KAL-oo) and Nineveh (NIN-uh-vuh). The king loomed over most scenes, larger than anyone else, muscular and fierce, with the appearance of a god. Visitors to the Assyrian court were undoubtedly awed—and intimidated.

Conquest and Control

Superior military organization and technology made the Assyrians' unprecedented conquests possible. At first, armies consisted of soldiers who served in return for grants of land and peasants and slaves contributed by large landowners. Later, King Tiglathpileser (TIG-lath-pih-LEE-zuhr) (r. 744–727 B.C.E.) maintained a core of professional soldiers made up of Assyrians and the most warlike subject peoples. At its peak the Assyrian state could mobilize half a million troops, including lightly armed bowmen and

Primary Source: An Assyrian Emperor's Résumé: Ferocious Conquests a Specialty Destruction, devastation, and severed heads: find out what happens when the Assyrian emperor is slighted.

slingers, armored spearmen, cavalry equipped with bows or spears, and four-man chariots.

Iron weapons and cavalry gave the Assyrians their edge. However, Assyrian engineers also developed ways of attacking fortified towns. They tunneled under the walls, built movable towers for their archers, and applied battering rams to weak points. Some of the best-fortified cities of the Middle East—Babylon, Thebes in Egypt, Tyre in Phoenicia, and Susa in Elam—yielded to these tactics. Couriers and signal fires provided long-distance communication, while a network of spies gathered intelligence.

Terror tactics discouraged resistance and rebellion. Civilians were thrown into fires, prisoners were skinned alive, and the severed heads of defeated rulers were hung on city walls, all of which was well publicized. **Mass deportation**—the forcible uprooting and resettling of entire communities—broke the spirit of rebellious peoples. Sumer, Babylon, Urartu, Egypt, and the Hittites had done this before, but the Neo-Assyrian monarchs used deportation on an unprecedented scale. Surviving documents record the relocation of over one million people, and historians estimate that the true figure exceeds four million. Deportation also shifted human resources from the periphery to the center, where the deportees worked on royal and noble estates, opened new lands for agriculture, and built palaces and cities. Deportees who were craftsmen and soldiers could be assigned to the Assyrian army.

Faced with an array of peoples with different languages, customs, religions, and political organization, the Assyrians never found a single, enduring method of governing. Control tended to be tight and effective at the center and in lands closest to the core area, and less so farther away. The Assyrian kings waged many campaigns to reimpose control on territories subdued in previous wars.

Assyrian provincial officials oversaw the payment of tribute and taxes, maintained law and order, raised troops, undertook public works, and provisioned armies and administrators passing through their territory. Provincial governors were subject to frequent inspections by royal overseers. The elite class was bound to the monarch by oaths of obedience, fear of punishment, and the expectation of land grants or shares of booty and taxes. Skilled

professionals—priests, diviners, scribes, doctors, and artisans—were similarly bound.

The Assyrians ruthlessly exploited the wealth and resources of their subjects to fund their military campaigns and administration. Wealth from the periphery flowed to the center, where the king and nobility grew rich. Proud kings expanded the ancestral capital and religious center at Ashur and built magnificent new royal cities encircled by high walls and containing ornate palaces and temples. Dur Sharrukin (DOOR SHAH-roo-keen), the "Fortress of Sargon," was completed in a mere ten years, thanks to a massive labor force composed of prisoners of war and Assyrian citizens who owed periodic service to the state.

Yet the Assyrian Empire was not simply parasitic. There is some evidence of royal investment in provincial infrastructure. The cities and merchant classes thrived on expanded long-distance commerce, and some subject populations were surprisingly loyal to their Assyrian rulers.

Assyrian Society and Culture

In the core area people belonged to the same three classes that had existed in Hammurabi's Babylon a millennium before (see Chapter 1): (1) free, landowning citizens, (2) farmers and artisans attached to the estates of the king or other rich landholders, and (3) slaves. Slaves—debtors and prisoners of war—had legal rights and, if sufficiently talented, could rise to positions of influence.

The government normally did not distinguish between native Assyrians and the increasingly large number of immigrants and deportees residing in the Assyrian homeland. All were referred to as "human beings," entitled to the same legal protections and liable for the same labor and military service. Over time the inflow of outsiders changed the ethnic makeup of the core area.

The vast majority of subjects worked on the land. The agricultural surpluses they produced allowed

---

mass deportation The forcible removal and relocation of large numbers of people or entire populations. The mass deportations practiced by the Assyrian and Persian Empires were meant as a terrifying warning of the consequences of rebellion. They also brought labor to the imperial center.

- One of the most important civilizations to emerge after the upheavals of the Late Bronze Age was the Neo-Assyrian Empire.

- Led by all-powerful kings, the Assyrians waged campaigns of aggressive expansion.

- The Assyrians' military success rested on superior organization and technology, such as iron weapons, cavalry, and the ability to attack fortifications.

- The Assyrians controlled subject peoples through terror tactics and mass deportations.

- The Assyrian state exploited subject territories, transporting wealth from the periphery to the center of the empire.

- The Assyrians built upon the social structures and technologies of earlier Mesopotamian civilizations and left important records of Mesopotamian life.

substantial numbers of people—the standing army, government officials, religious experts, merchants, and artisans—to engage in specialized activities.

Most trade took place at the local level, with individual artisans and small workshops producing pottery, tools, and clothing. The state fostered long-distance trade, since imported luxury goods—metals, fine textiles, dyes, gems, and ivory—pleased the elite and brought in substantial customs revenues. Silver was the basic medium of exchange, weighed out for each transaction in a time before the invention of coinage.

Building on earlier Mesopotamian traditions, Assyrian scholars recorded lists of plant and animal names, geographic terms, and astronomical occurrences, and they made original contributions in mathematics and astronomy. Exorcists sought to expel the demons they believed caused disease, but more rational physicians experimented with medicines and surgical treatments.

Some Assyrian temples may have had libraries. At Nineveh the palace of **Ashurbanipal** (ah-shur-BAH-nee-pahl) (r. 668–627 B.C.E.), one of the last Assyrian kings, yielded more than twenty-five thousand tablets or fragments of tablets, including official documents as well as literary and scientific texts. Some were originals that had been brought to the capital; others were copies made at the king's request. Ashurbanipal avidly collected the literary and scientific heritage of

Mesopotamia, and the "House of Knowledge" referred to in some of the documents may have been an academy of learned men in the imperial center. Much of what we know about Mesopotamian art, literature, and science and earlier Mesopotamian history comes from discoveries at Assyrian sites.

Israel, 2000–500 B.C.E.

How did the civilization of Israel develop, following both familiar cultural patterns and a unique course of its own?

On the western edge of the Assyrian Empire lived a people who were destined to play an important role in world history. The history of ancient Israel is marked by two interconnected dramas that played out from around 2000 to 500 B.C.E. First, a loose collection of nomadic kinship groups engaged in herding and caravan traffic became a sedentary, agricultural people, developed complex political and social institutions, and became integrated into the commercial and diplomatic networks of the Middle East. Second, these people transformed the austere cult of a desert god into the concept of a single, all-powerful, and all-knowing deity, in the process creating the ethical and intellectual traditions that underlie the beliefs and values of Judaism, Christianity, and Islam.

The land at the heart of this story has borne various names—Canaan, Israel, Syria-Palestine—as have the people—Hebrews, Israelites, Jews. For the sake of consistency, the people are referred to here as Israelites, the land they occupied in antiquity as **Israel**.

Being at a crossroads between Syria, Egypt, Arabia, and Mesopotamia has given Israel an importance in history out of all proportion to its size. Its

Ashurbanipal The seventh century B.C.E. Assyrian ruler who assembled a large collection of writings drawn from the ancient literary, religious, and scientific traditions of Mesopotamia. The many tablets unearthed by archaeologists constitute one of the most important sources of present-day knowledge of the long literary tradition of Mesopotamia.
Israel In antiquity, the land between the eastern shore of the Mediterranean and the Jordan River, occupied by the Israelites from the early second millennium B.C.E.

natural resources are few. The Negev Desert and the vast wasteland of the Sinai (SIE-nie) lay to the south. The Mediterranean coastal plain was occupied throughout much of this period by Philistines, who were of uncertain ethnic origin. The center of Israel featured rock-strewn hills. Galilee to the north, with its sea of the same name, was a relatively fertile land of grassy hills and small plains from which the narrow ribbon of the Jordan River flowed down into the Dead Sea, so named because its high salt content is toxic to life.

Origins, Exodus, and Settlement

The fundamental source of information about ancient Israel is the collection of writings preserved in the **Hebrew Bible** (called the Old Testament by Christians). The Hebrew Bible brings together several collections of materials that originated with different groups, employed distinctive vocabularies, and gave particular interpretations of past events. Traditions about the Israelites' early days were long transmitted orally. Not until the tenth century B.C.E. were they written down in a script borrowed from the Phoenicians. The text that we have today dates from the fifth century B.C.E., with a few later additions, and reflects the point of view of the priests who controlled the Temple in Jerusalem. Historians disagree about how accurately this document represents Israelite history. In the absence of other written sources, however, it provides a foundation to be used critically and modified in light of archaeological discoveries.

The Hebrew language of the Bible reflects the speech of the Israelites until about 500 B.C.E. It is a Semitic language, most closely related to Phoenician and Aramaic (which later supplanted Hebrew in Israel), more distantly related to Arabic and the Akkadian language of the Assyrians. This linguistic affinity probably parallels the Israelites' ethnic relationship to the neighboring peoples.

The early history of Israel embodies a familiar story of nomadic pastoralists who occupied marginal land between the arid desert and settled agricultural areas. Early on, these nomads raided the farms and villages of settled peoples, but eventually they settled down to an agricultural way of life and later developed a unified state.

The Hebrew Bible focuses on the family of Abraham. Born in the city of Ur in southern Mesopotamia, Abraham rejected the idol worship of his homeland and migrated with his family and livestock across the Syrian Desert. Eventually he arrived in the land of Israel, which, according to the biblical account, had been promised to him and his descendants as part of a "covenant," or pact, with the Israelite god, Yahweh.

These "recollections" of the journey of Abraham (who, if he was a real person, probably lived in the twentieth century B.C.E.) may compress the experiences of generations of pastoralists who migrated from the grazing lands between the upper reaches of the Tigris and Euphrates Rivers to the Mediterranean coastal plain. Following the usual pattern in the region, Abraham, his family, and his companions camped by a permanent water source in the dry season and then drove herds of sheep, cattle, and donkeys to traditional grazing areas during the rest of the year. The animals provided them with milk, cheese, meat, and cloth.

The early Israelites and the settled peoples of the region were suspicious of one another. This friction between nomadic herders and settled farmers, as well as the Israelites' view of their ancestors as having been nomads, comes through in the story of the innocent shepherd Abel, who was killed by his farmer brother Cain.

Abraham's son Isaac and then his grandson Jacob became the leaders of this wandering group of herders. In the next generation the squabbling sons of Jacob's several wives sold their brother Joseph as a slave to passing merchants heading for Egypt. The Bible relates that through luck and ability Joseph became a high official at Pharaoh's court. Thus he was able to help his people when drought struck and

Primary Source: Moses Descends Mount Sinai with the Ten Commandments Discover what happens when God speaks to Moses.

Hebrew Bible A collection of sacred books containing diverse materials concerning the origins, experiences, beliefs, and practices of the Israelites. Most of the extant text was compiled by members of the priestly class in the fifth century B.C.E. and reflects the concerns and views of this group.

forced the Israelites to migrate to Egypt. The sophisticated Egyptians feared and looked down on these rough herders and eventually reduced the Israelites to slaves, putting them to work on the building projects of the pharaoh.

Several points need to be made about this version of events. First, the biblical account glosses over the period from 1700 to 1500 B.C.E., when Egypt was dominated by the Hyksos. Since the Hyksos are thought to have been Semitic groups that infiltrated the Nile Delta from the northeast, the Israelite migration to Egypt and later enslavement could have been connected to the Hyksos' rise and fall. Second, although the surviving Egyptian sources do not refer to Israelite slaves, they do complain about *Apiru* (uh-PEE-roo), a derogatory term applied to caravan drivers, outcasts, bandits, and other marginal groups. The word seems to designate a class of people rather than a particular ethnic group, but some scholars believe there may be a connection between the similar-sounding terms *Apiru* and *Hebrew*. Third, the period of alleged Israelite slavery coincided with the era of ambitious building programs launched by several New Kingdom pharaohs.

The Bible further relates that Moses, an Israelite with connections to the Egyptian royal family, led the Israelites out of captivity. The narrative of their departure, the Exodus, is overlaid with folktale motifs, including the ten plagues that Yahweh inflicted on Egypt to persuade the pharaoh to release the Israelites and the miraculous parting of the Red Sea that enabled the refugees to escape. It is possible that oral tradition may have preserved memories of a real emigration from Egypt followed by years of wandering in the wilderness of Sinai.

During their reported forty years in the desert, the Israelites became devoted to a stern and warlike god. According to the Hebrew Bible, Yahweh made a covenant with the Israelites: they would be his "Chosen People" if they promised to worship him exclusively. This pact was confirmed by tablets that Moses brought down from the top of Mount Sinai. Written on the tablets were the Ten Commandments, which set out the basic tenets of Jewish belief and practice. The Commandments prohibited murder, adultery, theft, lying, and envy and demanded respect for parents and rest from work on the Sabbath, the seventh day of the week.

Joshua, Moses's successor, is named as leading the Israelites from the east side of the Jordan River into the land of Canaan (KAY-nuhn) (modern Israel and the Palestinian territories). They attacked and destroyed Jericho (JEI-rih-koe) and other Canaanite (KAY-nuh-nite) cities. Archaeological evidence confirms the destruction of some Canaanite towns between 1250 and 1200 B.C.E., though not precisely the towns mentioned in the biblical account. Shortly thereafter, lowland sites were resettled and new sites were established in the hills, thanks to the development of cisterns carved into rock to hold rainwater and the construction of terraces for farming. The material culture of the new settlers was cruder but continued Canaanite patterns.

Most scholars doubt that Canaan was conquered by a unified Israelite army. In a time of widespread disruption, movements of peoples, and decline and destruction of cities throughout this region, it is more likely that Israelite migrants took advantage of the disorder and were joined by other loosely organized groups and even refugees from the Canaanite cities.

In a pattern common throughout history, the new coalition of peoples invented a common ancestry. The "Children of Israel," as they called themselves, were divided into twelve tribes supposedly descended from the sons of Jacob and Joseph. Each tribe installed itself in a different part of the country. Its chief was primarily responsible for mediating disputes and safeguarding the group. Charismatic figures called "Judges" famed for their bravery or diplomacy enjoyed a special standing that transcended tribal boundaries. The tribes also shared a shrine in the hill country at Shiloh (SHIE-loe), which housed the Ark of the Covenant, a sacred chest containing the tablets that Yahweh had given Moses.

Rise of the Monarchy

The time of troubles that struck the eastern Mediterranean around 1200 B.C.E. brought the Philistines to the coastal plain, where they fought frequently with the Israelites in the hills. The long-haired strongman Samson, who toppled a Philistine temple, and the shepherd boy David, whose slingshot felled the towering Philistine warrior Goliath, became biblical heroes. A religious leader named Samuel recognized the need for a stronger central authority to lead the Israelites

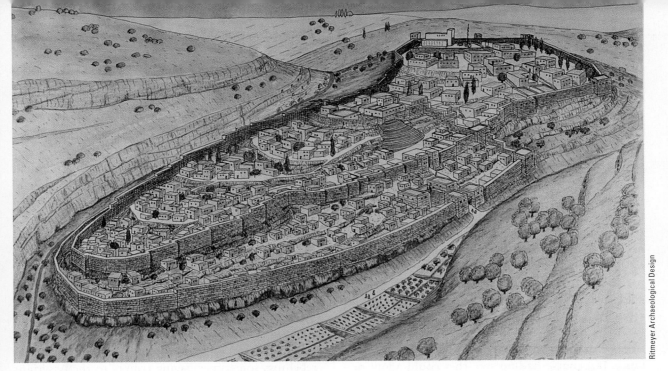

Artist's Rendering of Solomon's Jerusalem Strategically located in the middle of lands occupied by the Israelite tribes and on a high plateau overlooking the central hills and the Judaean desert, Jerusalem was captured around 1000 B.C.E. by King David, who made it his capital (the City of David is at left, the citadel and palace complex at center). The next king, Solomon, built the First Temple to serve as the center of worship of the Israelite god, Yahweh. Solomon's Temple (at upper right) was destroyed during the Neo-Babylonian sack of the city in 587 B.C.E. The modest structure soon built to take its place was replaced by the magnificent Second Temple, erected by King Herod in the last decades of the first century B.C.E. and destroyed by the Romans in 70 C.E.

against the Philistine city-states, and he anointed Saul as the first king of Israel around 1020 B.C.E. When Saul perished in battle, the throne passed to David (r. ca. 1000–960 B.C.E.), who oversaw Israel's transition from a tribal confederacy to a unified monarchy. He strengthened royal authority by making the captured hill city of Jerusalem, which lay outside tribal boundaries, his capital. Soon after, David brought the Ark to Jerusalem, making the city the religious as well as the political center of the kingdom.

The reign of David's son Solomon (r. ca. 960–920 B.C.E.) marked the high point of the Israelite monarchy. Alliances and trade linked Israel with near and distant lands. Solomon and Hiram, the king of Phoenician Tyre, together commissioned a fleet that sailed into the Red Sea and brought back gold, ivory, jewels, sandalwood, and exotic animals. The story of the visit to Solomon by the queen of Sheba, who brought gold, precious stones, and spices, may be mythical, but it reflects the reality of trade with Saba (SUH-buh) in south Arabia (present-day Yemen) or the Horn of

Africa (present-day Somalia). Such wealth supported a lavish court life, a sizeable bureaucracy, and an intimidating chariot army that made Israel a regional power. Solomon undertook an ambitious building program employing slaves and the compulsory labor of citizens. To strengthen the link between religious and secular authority, he built the **First Temple** in Jerusalem.

The Temple priests became a powerful and wealthy class, receiving a share of the annual harvest

First Temple A monumental sanctuary built in Jerusalem by King Solomon in the tenth century B.C.E. to be the religious center for the Israelite god Yahweh. The Temple priesthood conducted sacrifices, received a tithe or percentage of agricultural revenues, and became economically and politically powerful. The First Temple was destroyed by the Babylonians in 587 B.C.E. and was rebuilt on a modest scale in the late sixth century B.C.E. It was replaced by King Herod's Second Temple in the late first century B.C.E. and destroyed by the Romans in 70 C.E.

in return for making animal sacrifices to Yahweh. The expansion of Jerusalem, new commercial opportunities, and the increasing prestige of the Temple hierarchy contributed to a growing gap between urban and rural, rich and poor. Fiery prophets, claiming revelation from Yahweh, accused the monarchs and aristocracy of corruption, impiety, and neglect of the poor.

The Israelites lived in extended families, several generations residing together under the authority of the eldest male. Arranged marriages were an important economic as well as social institution. To prove his financial worthiness, the groom gave a substantial gift to the father of the bride. Her entire family participated in the ceremonial weighing of silver or gold. The wife's dowry often included a slave girl who attended her for life.

Male heirs were of paramount importance, and firstborn sons received a double share of the inheritance. If a couple had no son, they could adopt one, or the husband could have a child by the wife's slave attendant. If a man died childless, his brother was expected to marry his widow and father an heir.

Women provided the family with important goods and services but could not inherit property or initiate divorce. An unfaithful woman could be put to death. Working-class women shared in farming and herding chores in addition to caring for the house and children. Some urban women worked outside the home as cooks, bakers, perfumers, wet nurses (a recent mother hired to suckle another person's child), prostitutes, and singers of laments at funerals. A few women reached positions of influence, such as Deborah the Judge, who led troops in battle against the Canaanites. Women known collectively as "wise women" appear to have composed sacred texts in poetry and prose. This reality has been obscured, in part by the male bias of the Hebrew Bible, in part because the status of women declined as Israelite society became more urbanized.

Fragmentation and Dispersal

After Solomon's death around 920 B.C.E., resentment over royal demands and the neglect of tribal rights split the monarchy into two kingdoms: Israel in the north, with its capital at Samaria (suh-MAH-ree-yuh), and Judah (JOO-duh) in the southern territory around Jerusalem. The two were sometimes at war, sometimes allied.

This period saw the final formulation of **monotheism**, the absolute belief in Yahweh as the one and only god. Nevertheless, religious leaders still had to contend with cults professing polytheism (the belief in multiple gods). The rituals of the Canaanite storm-god Baal (BAHL) and the fertility goddess Astarte (uh-STAHR-tee) attracted many Israelites. Prophets condemned the adoption of foreign rituals and threatened that Yahweh would punish Israel severely.

The small states of Syria and the two Israelite kingdoms laid aside their rivalries to mount a joint resistance to the Neo-Assyrian Empire, but to no avail. In 721 B.C.E. the Assyrians destroyed the northern kingdom of Israel and deported much of its population to the east. New settlers were brought in from Syria, Babylon, and Iran, changing the area's ethnic, cultural, and religious character. The kingdom of Judah survived for more than a century, sometimes rebelling, sometimes paying tribute to the Assyrians or the Neo-Babylonian kings (626–539 B.C.E.) that succeeded them.

When the Neo-Babylonian monarch Nebuchadnezzar (NAB-oo-kuhd-nez-uhr) captured Jerusalem in 587 B.C.E., he destroyed the Temple and deported to Babylon the royal family, the aristocracy, and many skilled workers. The deportees prospered so well in their new home "by the waters of Babylon" that half a century later most of their descendants refused the offer of the Persian monarch Cyrus (see Chapter 4) to return to their homeland. This was the origin of the **Diaspora** (die-ASS-peh-rah)—a Greek word meaning "dispersion" or "scattering." This dispersion outside the homeland of many Jews—as we may now call these people, since an independent Israel no

monotheism Belief in the existence of a single divine entity. Some scholars cite the devotion of the Egyptian pharaoh Akhenaten to Aten (sun-disk) and his suppression of traditional gods as the earliest instance. The Israelite worship of Yahweh developed into an exclusive belief in one god, and this concept passed into Christianity and Islam.

Diaspora A Greek word meaning "dispersal," used to describe the communities of a given ethnic group living outside their homeland. Jews, for example, spread from Israel to western Asia and Mediterranean lands in antiquity and today can be found throughout the world.

SECTION REVIEW

- As the Hebrew Bible suggests, the Israelites began as nomadic pastoralists who, after a period of enslavement, settled permanently in Canaan.
- Pressure from hostile Philistines forced the Israelites to adopt a more complex government.
- The resulting monarchy unified the Israelites into the kingdom of Israel, which reached its height under Solomon.
- During the monarchy, the temple priests became a powerful class, and Israelite society became more urban and economically divided.
- Patrilineal extended families became the basic social unit, and the status of women steadily declined.
- After the breakup of Israel, Jewish monotheism reached its final form, successive conquests created the Diaspora, and a distinct Jewish identity emerged.

Phoenicia and the Mediterranean, 1200–500 B.C.E.

How did the Phoenicians rise to commercial dominance over much of the Mediterranean world?

The people who occupied the coast of Lebanon developed their own **Phoenician** (fuh-NEE-shun) civilization. Ancient writers generally used this Greek word instead of "Can'ani"—Canaanites—the word they used for themselves.

The Phoenician City-States

Many Canaanite settlements were destroyed during the violent upheavals and mass migrations around 1200 B.C.E. discussed earlier. Aramaeans (ah-ruh-MAY-uhns)—nomadic pastoralists like the early Israelites—migrated into the interior portions of Syria while Israelites and Philistines gained dominance farther south.

By 1100 B.C.E. Canaanite territory had shrunk to a narrow strip of Lebanon between the mountains and the sea. New political forms and seaborne commerce provided the keys to Canaanite survival. Sometime after 1000 B.C.E. the Canaanites encountered the Greeks, who referred to them as *Phoinikes*, or Phoenicians. The term may mean "red men" and refer to the color of their skin, or it may refer to the precious purple dye they extracted from the murex snail (see Environment and Technology: Ancient Textiles and Dyes).

Rivers and rocky spurs sliced the Lebanese coastal plain into a series of small city-states, notably Byblos (BIB-loss), Sidon (SIE-duhn), and Tyre. Exchange of raw materials (cedar and pine, metals, incense, papyrus), foodstuffs (wine, spices, salted fish), and crafted luxury goods (textiles, carved ivory, glass) brought wealth and influence to the Phoenician city-states.

longer existed—continues to this day. To maintain their religion and culture, the Diaspora communities developed institutions like the synagogue (Greek for "bringing together"), a communal meeting place that served religious, educational, and social functions.

The Babylonian Jews that did make the long trek back to Judah met with a cold reception from the local population. Persevering, they rebuilt the Temple in modest form and drafted the Deuteronomic (doo-tuhr-uh-NAHM-ik) Code of law and conduct (*deuteronomic* is Greek for "second set of laws"). The fifth century B.C.E. also saw the compilation of much of the Hebrew Bible in roughly its present form.

Exile and loss of political autonomy sharpened Jewish identity. Jews lived by a rigid set of rules. Dietary restrictions forbade the eating of pork and shellfish and mandated that meat and dairy products not be consumed together. Ritual baths were used to achieve spiritual purity, and women were required to take ritual baths after menstruation. The Jews venerated the Sabbath (Saturday, the seventh day of the week) by refraining from work and from fighting, following the example of Yahweh, who, according to the Bible, rested on the seventh day after creating the world. These strictures and others, including a ban on marrying non-Jews, tended to isolate the Jews from other peoples, but they also fostered a powerful sense of community.

Phoenicians Semitic-speaking Canaanites living on the coast of Lebanon and Syria in the first millennium B.C.E. From major cities such as Tyre and Sidon, Phoenician merchants and sailors explored the Mediterranean, engaged in widespread commerce, and founded Carthage and other colonies in the western Mediterranean.

Ancient Textiles and Dyes

Throughout human history the production of textiles—cloth for clothing, blankets, carpets, and coverings of various sorts—required an expenditure of human labor second only to the work necessary to provide food. Nevertheless, textile production in antiquity has left few archaeological traces. The plant fibers and animal hair used for cloth quickly decompose except in rare circumstances. Some textile remains have been found in the hot, dry conditions of Egypt, the cool, arid Andes of South America, and the peat bogs of northern Europe. But most of our knowledge of ancient textiles depends on the discovery of equipment used in textile production—such as spindles, loom weights, and dyeing vats—and on pictorial representations and descriptions in texts.

Cloth production usually has been the work of women for a simple but important reason. Responsibility for child rearing limits women's ability to participate in other activities but does not consume all their time and energy. In many societies textile production has been complementary to child-rearing activities, for it can be done in the home, is relatively safe, does not require great concentration, and can be interrupted without consequence. The growing and harvesting of plants such as cotton or flax (from which linen is made) and the shearing of wool from sheep and, in the Andes, llamas are outdoor activities, but the subsequent stages of production can be carried out inside the home. The basic methods of textile production did not change much from early antiquity until the late eighteenth century C.E., when the fabrication of textiles was transferred to mills and mass production began.

When textile production has been considered "women's work," most of the output has been for household consumption. However, women weavers in Peru developed new raw materials, new techniques, and new decorative motifs around three thousand years ago. They began to use the wool of llamas and alpacas in addition to cotton. Three women worked side by side and passed the weft from hand to hand to produce a fabric of greater width. Women weavers also introduced embroidery and decorated garments with new religious motifs, such as the jaguar-god. Their high-quality textiles were given as tribute to the elite and were used to trade for luxury goods.

More typically, men dominated commercial production. In ancient Phoenicia, fine textiles with bright, permanent colors became a major export product. Most prized was the red-purple known as Tyrian purple because Tyre was the major source. Persian and Hellenistic kings wore robes dyed this color, and a white toga with a purple border was the sign of a Roman senator.

The production of Tyrian purple was an exceedingly laborious process. The spiny dye-murex snail lives on the sandy Mediterranean bottom at depths ranging from 30 to 500 feet (10 to 150 meters). Nine thousand snails were needed to produce 1 gram (0.035 ounce) of dye. The dye was made from a colorless liquid in the snail's hypobranchial gland. The gland sacs were removed, crushed, soaked with salt, and exposed to sunlight and air for some days; then they were subject to controlled boiling and heating.

Huge mounds of broken shells on the Phoenician coast are testimony to the ancient industry. The snail may have been rendered nearly extinct at many locations, and some scholars speculate that Phoenician colonization in the Mediterranean was motivated in part by the search for new sources of snails.

Ancient Peruvian Textiles The weaving of Chavín was famous for its color and symbolic imagery. Artisans both wove designs into the fabric and used paint or dyes to decorate plain fabric. This early Chavín painted fabric was used in a burial. Notice how the face suggests a jaguar and the headdress includes the image of a serpent. Private collection.

Expansion to the Mediterranean

Before 1000 B.C.E. Byblos was the most important Phoenician city-state. The English word *bible* comes from the Greek *biblion*, meaning "book written on papyrus from Byblos." The Greeks recognized the Phoenicians as the inventors of the alphabet, which used about two dozen symbols, each of which represented a consonant or long vowel. (The Greeks added symbols for short vowel sounds—see Chapter 4.) Little Phoenician writing survives, probably because scribes used perishable papyrus. As a result, little is known about the internal affairs of the Phoenician cities beyond the names of some kings.

After 1000 B.C.E. Tyre surpassed Byblos. Located on an offshore island, Tyre was practically impregnable. It had two harbors—one facing north, the other south—that were connected by a canal. The city boasted a large marketplace, a magnificent palace complex with treasury and archives, and temples to the gods Melqart (MEL-kahrt) and Astarte. Some of its thirty thousand or more inhabitants lived in suburbs on the mainland. Its one weakness was its dependence on the mainland for food and fresh water.

In the century following Tyre turned its attention westward, establishing colonies on Cyprus, a copper-rich island 100 miles (161 kilometers) from the coast (see Map 3.2). In the ninth century B.C.E., the Phoenicians of Lebanon began to explore and colonize parts of the western Mediterranean, including the coasts of North Africa and Spain, and the islands of Sicily and Sardinia. The Phoenicians were primarily interested in access to valuable raw materials and trading opportunities.

By 700 B.C.E., when Homer mentions Phoenician seafarers in the Aegean Sea, a string of settlements in the western Mediterranean formed a "Phoenician

Map 3.2 Colonization of the Mediterranean In the ninth century B.C.E., the Phoenecians of Lebanon began to explore and colonize parts of the western Mediterranean, including the coast of North Africa, southern and eastern Spain, and the islands of Sicily and Sardinia. The Phoenecians were primarily interested in access to valuable raw materials and trading opportunities.
© Cengage Learning

Interactive Map

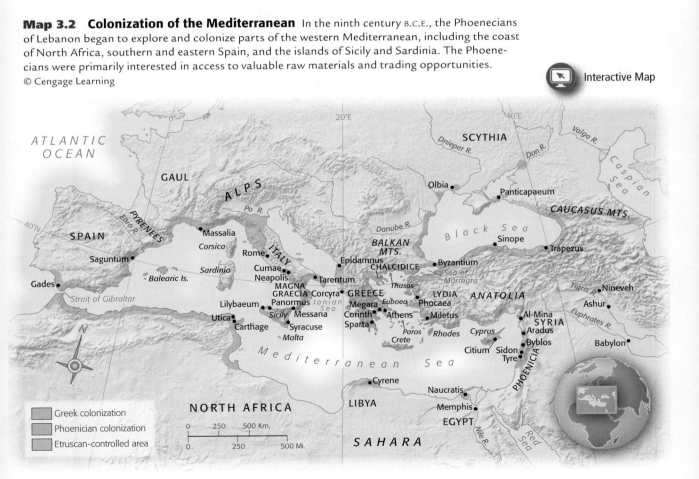

triangle": the North African coast from western Libya to Morocco; the south and southeast coast of Spain, including Gades (GAH-days) (modern Cadiz [kuh-DEEZ]) on the Strait of Gibraltar; and the islands of Sardinia, Sicily, and Malta off the coast of Italy (see Map 3.2). The colonists situated many of these new settlements on promontories or offshore islands in imitation of Tyre.

Overseas settlement provided new sources of trade goods and new trading partners as well as an outlet for excess population. Tyre tried to stave off the Assyrian kings by paying tribute, but in 701 B.C.E. it finally fell to an Assyrian army. Sidon then became the leading city in Phoenicia.

Phoenician activities in the west often involved conflict with the Greeks, who were also expanding trade and establishing colonies. This rivalry centered on Sicily. Phoenicians occupied the western end of the island, Greeks its eastern and central parts. Centuries of warfare for control of Sicily left written accounts of atrocities, massacres, wholesale enslavements, and mass deportations. The high level of brutality suggests that each side believed its survival to be at stake. By the mid-third century B.C.E., the Tyrian colony of Carthage in Tunisia commanded the Phoenician colonial forces and controlled all of Sicily.

Carthage's Commercial Empire

Thanks to Greek and Roman reports about their wars, historians know more about **Carthage** and the other Phoenician colonies than they do about the Phoenician homeland. For example, the account of the origins of Carthage that began this chapter comes from Roman sources (most famously Virgil's epic poem *The Aeneid*) but is probably based on a Carthaginian original. Archaeological excavation has roughly confirmed the city's traditional foundation date of 814 B.C.E. Situated just outside the present-day city of Tunis, Carthage controlled the middle portion of the Mediterranean where Europe comes closest to Africa. The new settlement grew rapidly and soon dominated other Phoenician colonies in the west.

Occupying a narrow promontory, Carthage stretched between Byrsa (BURR-suh), the original hilltop citadel of the community, and a double harbor.

The inner harbor could accommodate 220 warships. A watchtower allowed surveillance of the surrounding area, and high walls made it impossible to see in from the outside. The outer commercial harbor was filled with docks for merchant ships and shipyards. In case of attack, a huge iron chain could close off the harbor.

Government offices ringed a large central square where magistrates heard legal cases outdoors. The inner city was a maze of narrow, winding streets, multistory apartment buildings, and sacred enclosures. Farther out lay a sprawling suburban district where the wealthy built spacious villas amid fields and vegetable gardens. This entire urban complex was enclosed by a wall 22 miles (35 kilometers) in length. At the most critical point—the 2.5-mile-wide (4-kilometer-wide) isthmus connecting the promontory to the mainland—the wall was over 40 feet (13 meters) high and 30 feet (10 meters) thick and had high watchtowers.

With a population of roughly 400,000, Carthage was one of the largest cities in the world by 500 B.C.E. The population was ethnically diverse, including people of Phoenician stock, indigenous peoples likely to have been the ancestors of modern-day Berbers, and immigrants from other Mediterranean lands and sub-Saharan Africa. Contrary to the story of Dido's reluctance to remarry, Phoenicians intermarried quite readily with other peoples.

Each year two "judges" were elected from upper-class families to serve as heads of state and carry out administrative and judicial functions. The real seat of power was the Senate, where members of the leading merchant families, who sat for life, formulated policy and directed the affairs of the state. An inner circle of thirty or so senators made the crucial decisions. From time to time the leadership convened an Assembly of the citizens to elect public officials or vote on important issues, particularly when the leaders were divided or wanted to stir up popular enthusiasm for some venture.

Carthage City located in present-day Tunisia, founded by Phoenicians ca. 800 B.C.E. It became a major commercial center and naval power in the western Mediterranean until defeated by Rome in the third century B.C.E.

There is little evidence at Carthage of the kind of social and political unrest that later plagued Greece and Rome (see Chapters 4 and 6). This perception may be due in part to the limited information in existing sources about internal affairs at Carthage. However, a merchant aristocracy (unlike an aristocracy of birth) was not a closed circle, and a climate of economic and social mobility allowed newly successful families and individuals to push their way into the circle of politically influential citizens. The ruling class also made sure that everyone benefited from the riches of empire.

Carthaginian power rested on its navy, which dominated the western Mediterranean for centuries. Phoenician towns provided a chain of friendly ports. The Carthaginian fleet consisted of fast, maneuverable galleys—oared warships. A galley had a sturdy, pointed ram in front that could pierce the hull of an enemy vessel below the water line, while marines (soldiers aboard a ship) fired weapons. Innovations in the placement of benches and oars made room for 30, 50, and eventually as many as 170 rowers.

Carthaginian foreign policy reflected Carthage's economic interests. Protecting the sea-lanes, gaining access to raw materials, and fostering trade mattered most to the dominant merchant class. Foreign merchants were free to sail to Carthage to market their goods, but if they tried to operate on their own, they risked having their ships sunk by the Carthaginian navy. Treaties between Carthage and other states included formal recognition of this maritime commercial monopoly.

The archaeological record provides few clues about the commodities traded. Commerce may have included perishable goods—foodstuffs, textiles, animal skins, slaves—and raw metals such as silver, lead, iron, and tin, whose Carthaginian origin would not be evident. We know that Carthaginian ships carried goods manufactured elsewhere and that products brought to Carthage by foreign traders were re-exported.

There is also evidence for trade with sub-Saharan Africa. Hanno (HA-noe), a Carthaginian captain of the fifth century B.C.E., claimed to have sailed through the Strait of Gibraltar into the Atlantic Ocean and to have explored the West African coast (see Map 3.2). His report includes vivid descriptions of ferocious savages, drums in the night, and rivers of fire. Scholars

SECTION REVIEW

- After the Late Bronze Age migrations, the Phoenician city-states rose on the coast of Lebanon.
- Under pressure from the east, the Phoenicians steadily expanded westward through the Mediterranean, establishing colonies that often clashed with those of the Greeks.
- This expansion resulted in a powerful maritime commercial network, through which goods and technologies spread throughout the Mediterranean world.
- Carthage became the leading Phoenician city and the major power of the western Mediterranean.
- Carthaginian seafarers traveled into the Atlantic, exploring the coasts of Africa and Europe.
- Carthage ruled most of its commercial empire indirectly, did not emphasize warfare, and practiced child sacrifice.

have had difficulty matching Hanno's topographic descriptions and distances to the geography of West Africa, and some regard his account as outright fiction. Others believe that he misstated distances and exaggerated dangers to keep others from following his route. Other Carthaginians explored the Atlantic coast of Spain and France and secured control of an important source of tin in the "Tin Islands," probably Cornwall in southwestern England.

War and Religion

Carthage did not directly rule a large amount of territory. A belt of fertile land in northeastern Tunisia, owned by Carthaginians but worked by native peasants and imported slaves, provided a secure food supply. Beyond this core area the Carthaginians ruled most of their "empire" indirectly and allowed other Phoenician communities in the western Mediterranean to remain independent. These communities looked to Carthage for military protection and followed its lead in foreign policy. Only Sardinia and southern Spain came under the control of a Carthaginian governor and garrison, presumably to safeguard their resources.

Trade may explain the unusual fact that citizens were not required to serve in the army: they were of more value as traders and sailors. Since the indigenous North African population was not politically or militarily well organized, Carthage had little to fear from

The Tophet of Carthage Here, from the seventh to second centuries B.C.E., the cremated bodies of sacrificed children were buried. Archaeological excavation has confirmed the claim in ancient sources that the Carthaginians sacrificed children to their gods at times of crisis. Stone markers, decorated with magical signs and symbols of divinities as well as family names, were placed over ceramic urns containing the ashes and charred bones of one or more infants or, occasionally, older children.

enemies close to home. When Carthage was drawn into wars with the Greeks and Romans from the sixth through third centuries B.C.E., it relied on mercenaries from the most warlike peoples in its dominions or from neighboring areas—Numidians from North Africa, Iberians from Spain, Gauls from France, and various Italian peoples. These well-paid mercenaries served under the command of Carthaginian officers.

Another sign that war was not the primary business of the state was the separation of military command from civilian government. Generals were chosen by the Senate and kept in office for as long as they were needed. In contrast, the kings of Assyria and the other major states of the ancient Middle East normally led military campaigns.

Like the deities of Mesopotamia (see Chapter 1), the Carthaginian gods—chiefly Baal Hammon (BAHL ha-MOHN), a male storm-god, and Tanit (TAH-nit), a female fertility-goddess—were powerful and capricious entities. Roman sources report that members of the Carthaginian elite would sacrifice their own male children to appease the gods in times of crisis.

Excavations at Carthage and elsewhere have turned up tophets (TOE-fets)—walled enclosures with thousands of small, sealed urns containing the burned bones of children. Although some scholars argue that these were infants born prematurely or taken by childhood illnesses, most maintain that the western Phoenicians practiced child sacrifice on a more or less regular basis. Originally practiced by the upper classes, child sacrifice seems to have become more common and to have involved broader elements of the population after 400 B.C.E.

Plutarch (PLOO-tark), a Greek who lived around 100 C.E., long after the demise of Carthage, wrote the following on the basis of earlier sources:

> The Carthaginians are a hard and gloomy people, submissive to their rulers and harsh to their subjects, running to extremes of cowardice in times of fear and of cruelty in times of anger; they keep obstinately to their decisions, are austere, and care little for amusement or the graces of life.[1]

We should not take the hostile opinions of Greek and Roman sources at face value. Still, it is clear that

JTB Photo/Photolibrary

the Carthaginians were perceived as different and that cultural barriers, leading to misunderstanding and prejudice, played a significant role in ongoing conflicts. The struggle between Carthage and Rome for control of the western Mediterranean was especially protracted and bloody (see Chapter 6).

Failure and Transformation, 750–550 B.C.E.

What factors prompted the transformation of the ancient Middle East between 750 and 550 B.C.E.?

The extension of Assyrian power over the entire Middle East had enormous consequences for all the peoples of this region and caused the stories of Mesopotamia, Israel, and Phoenicia to converge. In 721 B.C.E. the Assyrians destroyed the northern kingdom of Israel, and for over a century the southern kingdom of Judah was exposed to relentless pressure. Assyrian threats spurred the Phoenicians to colonize and exploit the western Mediterranean. Even Egypt, for so long impregnable behind its desert barriers, fell to Assyrian invaders in the mid-seventh century B.C.E. Thebes, its ancient capital, never recovered.

Closer to the Assyrian homeland, the southern plains of Sumer and Akkad, the birthplace of Mesopotamian civilization, were reduced to a protectorate, while Babylon was alternately razed and rebuilt by Assyrian kings. Urartu and Elam, Assyria's great power rivals, were destroyed. By 650 B.C.E. Assyria stood unchallenged in western Asia. But the arms race with Urartu, war expenditures, and ever-lengthening borders sapped Assyrian resources. Brutality and exploitation aroused the hatred of conquered peoples. At the same time, changes in the ethnic composition of the army and the population of the homeland reduced popular support for the Assyrian state.

Two new political entities spearheaded resistance to Assyria. First, Babylonia had been revived by the Neo-Babylonian, or Chaldaean (chal-DEE-uhn), dynasty (the Chaldaeans had infiltrated southern Mesopotamia around 1000 B.C.E.). Second, the Medes (MEEDS), an Iranian people, were extending

SECTION REVIEW

- The Assyrians transformed the Middle East, conquering Egypt, Israel, Urartu, and Elam.

- Yet the Assyrian empire was overextended and their conquests weakened them. With the help of the Medes, the Chaldaeans overthrew the Assyrians and established a Neo-Babylonian kingdom.

- Babylon, rebuilt by the Chaldaeans, became the greatest city in the world in the sixth century B.C.E.

their kingdom in the Zagros Mountains and Iranian Plateau in the seventh century B.C.E. The two powers launched a series of attacks on the Assyrian homeland that destroyed its chief cities by 612 B.C.E.

The rapidity of the Assyrian fall is stunning. The destruction systematically carried out by the victors led to the depopulation of northern Mesopotamia. Two centuries later, when a corps of Greek mercenaries passed by mounds that concealed the ruins of the Assyrian capitals, the Athenian chronicler Xenophon (ZEN-uh-fahn) had no inkling that their empire had ever existed.

Conclusion

Beside the already ancient river-valley kingdoms, the period from 2000 to 500 B.C.E. saw two kinds of societies emerge in the Middle East and the Mediterranean world. One kind was a great and powerful empire, that of the Assyrians, which used advanced military tactics and weapons, and sheer brutality, to conquer and exploit a large area with many diverse peoples. The other was small kingdoms like Israel and Minoan Crete or even city-states like those of Phoenicia and Carthage that lived from trade rather than tribute. Small states and societies were always vulnerable to attack by larger, more powerful neighbors, and sometimes they succumbed, like Israel and the Phoenician cities. Yet just as often, they survived or reappeared. And sometimes, as we shall see in the next chapter, they turned the tables on their bigger adversaries.

CHAPTER REVIEW

 Download the MP3 audio file of the Chapter Review to listen to on the go.

How did a cosmopolitan civilization develop in the Middle East during the Late Bronze Age, and what forms did it take? (page 55)

Historians refer to the Late Bronze Age in the Middle East as a "cosmopolitan" era because it was a time of shared cultures and lifestyles. The patterns of culture that originated in the river-valley civilizations of Egypt and Mesopotamia persisted into this era. Peoples such as the Amorites, Kassites, and Chaldaeans, who migrated into the Tigris-Euphrates plain, were largely assimilated into the Sumerian-Semitic cultural tradition, adopting its language, religious beliefs, political and social institutions, and forms of artistic expression. Similarly, the Hyksos, who migrated into the Nile Delta and controlled much of Egypt for a time, adopted the ancient ways of Egypt. When the founders of the New Kingdom finally ended Hyksos domination, they reinstituted the united monarchy and the religious and cultural traditions of earlier eras.

What civilizations emerged in the Aegean world, and what relationship did they have to the older civilizations to the east? (page 61)

The Late Bronze Age expansion of commerce and communication stimulated the emergence of new civilizations, including the Minoan and Mycenaean peoples in the Aegean Sea. These new civilizations often borrowed heavily from the technologies and cultural practices of Mesopotamia and Egypt, creating dynamic syntheses of imported and indigenous elements. Cretan art and architecture display the wide range of cultural influences from the Minoans' extensive trading contacts, as well as the unique forms of Minoan civilization. The Mycenaean Greeks built their own civilization under the influence of Minoan Crete, and their palaces served as centers for crafts, trade, and administrative recordkeeping. Trade brought the Mycenaeans, like the Minoans, into steady contact with older eastern civilizations.

How did the Assyrian Empire rise to power and eventually dominate most of the ancient Middle East? (page 65)

Ultimately, the very interdependence of the societies of the Middle East and eastern Mediterranean made them vulnerable to the destructions and disorder of the decades around 1200 B.C.E. The entire region slipped into a "Dark Age" of isolation, stagnation, and decline that lasted several centuries. The early centuries after 1000 B.C.E. saw a resurgence of political organization and international commerce, as well as the spread of technologies and ideas. The Neo-Assyrian Empire, the great power of the time, represented a continuation of the Mesopotamian tradition, though the center of empire moved to the north. The king wielded supreme authority in all areas, and state propaganda presented him as all-powerful and victorious. The Assyrians won control of their empire through superior organization and military technology and maintained it through terror and mass deportation of subject peoples. Assyrian social structure mirrored that of earlier Mesopotamian cultures, with most people working the land. Assyrian scholarship built on earlier traditions, and Ashurbanipal's library collected the literary and scientific heritage of Mesopotamia.

How did the civilization of Israel develop, following both familiar cultural patterns and a unique course of its own? (page 68)

Our main textual source of information about the Israelites, the Hebrew Bible, must be reconciled with archaeological findings. It recounts that the Israelites began as nomadic pastoralists who wandered from Mesopotamia to the Mediterranean coastal plain and then to Egypt, where they suffered enslavement. During the Exodus, Yahweh and the Israelites entered into the covenant. The Israelites then settled permanently in Canaan, where they coalesced into a political federation, the "Children of Israel." Conflict with the Philistines forced them to adopt a more complex political structure. The resulting monarchy reached its height under Solomon, during whose reign the Temple priests rose to prominence and Israelite society grew more urban and economically stratified. After Solomon's death the kingdom divided into Samaria and Judah, and the monotheism that Judaism would bequeath to the world reached its final form. While the long, slow evolution of the Israelites from a society of nomadic pastoralists to an agriculturally based monarchy followed a common pattern in ancient western Asia, the religious and ethical concepts that they formulated were unique and have had a powerful impact on world history.

How did the Phoenicians rise to commercial dominance over much of the Mediterranean world? (page 73)

After the upheavals of the Late Bronze Age, the Phoenician city-states along the coast of Lebanon flourished. Under pressure from the Neo-Assyrian Empire, the Phoenicians, with Tyre in the lead, began spreading westward into the Mediterranean. Overseas expansion increased trade and often brought Phoenician colonists into conflict with the Greeks. In addition to pursuing international trade, the Phoenicians developed an alphabetic writing system that many other cultures borrowed and adapted to their languages. Carthage became the most important city outside the Phoenician homeland. Ruled by leading merchant families, it extended its commercial empire throughout the western Mediterranean, maintaining power through naval superiority.

What factors prompted the transformation of the ancient Middle East between 750 and 550 B.C.E.? (page 79)

The far-reaching expansion and subsequent rapid fall of the Assyrian Empire was the most important factor in the transformation of the ancient Middle East. The Assyrians destroyed many older states and, directly or indirectly, displaced large numbers of people. Their brutality, as well as the population shifts that resulted from their mass deportations, undercut support for their state. The Chaldaeans and Medes led resistance to Assyrian rule, and the empire swiftly collapsed.

Key Terms

Iron Age *(p. 55)*

Hittites *(p. 57)*

Hatshepsut *(p. 59)*

Akhenaten *(p. 59)*

Ramesses II *(p. 60)*

Minoan *(p. 61)*

Mycenae *(p. 62)*

shaft graves *(p. 62)*

Linear B *(p. 63)*

Neo-Assyrian Empire *(p. 65)*

mass deportation *(p. 67)*

Ashurbanipal *(p. 68)*

Israel *(p. 68)*

Hebrew Bible *(p. 69)*

First Temple *(p. 71)*

monotheism *(p. 72)*

Diaspora *(p. 72)*

Phoenicians *(p. 73)*

Carthage *(p. 76)*

Web Resources

Pronunciation Guide

Interactive Maps

- MAP 3.1 The Middle East in the Second Millennium B.C.E.
- MAP 3.2 Colonization of the Mediterranean

Visit the CourseMate website at www.cengagebrain.com for additional study tools and review materials for this chapter.

Primary Sources

- An Assyrian Emperor's Résumé: Ferocious Conquests a Specialty
- Moses Descends Mount Sinai with the Ten Commandments

Answer to the History in Focus Question

See photo on page 58, "The Mortuary Temple of Queen Hatshepsut at Deir el-Bahri, Egypt, ca. 1460 B.C.E."

Animal Domestication

Because the earliest domestication of plants and animals took place long before the existence of written records, we cannot be sure how and when humans first learned to plant crops and make use of tamed animals. Historians usually link the two processes as part of a Neolithic Revolution, but they were not necessarily connected.

The domestication of plants is much better understood than the domestication of animals. Foraging bands of humans primarily lived on wild seeds, fruits, and tubers. Eventually some humans tried planting seeds and tubers, favoring varieties that they particularly liked, and a variety that may have been rare in the wild became more common. When such a variety suited human needs, usually by having more food value or being easier to grow or process, people stopped collecting the wild types and relied on farming and further developing their new domestic type.

In the case of animals, the basis of selection to suit human needs is less apparent. Experts looking at ancient bones and images interpret changes in hair color, horn shape, and other visible features as indicators of domestication. But these visible changes did not generally serve human purposes. It is usually assumed that animals were domesticated for their meat, but even this is questionable. Dogs, which may have become domestic tens of thousands of years before any other species, were not eaten in most cultures, and cats, which became domestic much later, were eaten even less often. As for the uses most commonly associated with domestic animals, some of the most important, such as milking cows, shearing sheep, and harnessing oxen and horses to pull plows and vehicles, first appeared hundreds and even thousands of years after domestication.

Cattle, sheep, and goats became domestic around ten thousand years ago in the Middle East and North Africa. Coincidentally, wheat and barley were being domesticated at roughly the same time in the same general area. This is the main reason historians generally conclude that plant and animal domestication are closely related. Yet other major meat animals, such as chickens, which originated as jungle fowl in Southeast Asia, and pigs, which probably became domestic separately in several parts of North Africa, Europe, and Asia, have no agreed-upon association with early plant domestication. Nor is plant domestication connected with the horses and camels that became domestic in western Asia and the donkeys that became domestic in the Sahara region around six thousand years ago. Moreover, though the wild forebears of these species were probably eaten, the domestic forms were usually not used for meat.

In the Middle East humans may have originally kept wild sheep, goats, and cattle for food, though wild cattle were large and dangerous and must have been hard to control. It is questionable whether, in the earliest stages, keeping these animals captive for food would have been more productive than hunting. It is even more questionable whether the humans who kept animals for this purpose had any reason to anticipate that life in captivity would cause them to become domestic.

Human motivations for domesticating animals can be better assessed after a consideration of the physical changes involved in going from wild to domestic. Genetically transmitted tameness, defined as the ability to live with and accept handling by humans, lies at the core of the domestication process. In separate experiments with wild rats and foxes in the twentieth century, scientists found that wild individuals with strong fight-or-flight tendencies reproduce poorly in captivity, whereas individuals with the lowest adrenaline levels have the most offspring in captivity. In the wild, the same low level of excitability would have made these individuals vulnerable to predators and kept their reproduction rate down. However, early humans probably preferred the animals that seemed the tamest and destroyed those that were most wild. In the rat and fox experiments, after twenty generations or so, the surviving animals were born with much smaller adrenal glands and greatly reduced fight-or-flight reactions. Since adrenaline production normally increases in the transition to adulthood, many of the low-adrenaline animals also retained juvenile characteristics, such as floppy ears and pushed-in snouts, both indicators of domestication.

Historians disagree about whether animal domestication was a deliberate process or the unanticipated outcome of keeping animals for other purposes. Some assume that domestication was an understood and reproducible process. Others argue that, since a twenty-generation time span for wild cattle and other large quadrupeds would have amounted to several human lifetimes, it is unlikely that the people who ended up with domestic cows had any recollection of how the process started. This would also rule out the possibility that people who had unwittingly domesticated one species would have attempted to repeat the process with other species, since they did not know what they and their ancestors had done to produce genetically transmitted tameness.

Historians who assume that domestication was an understood and reproducible process tend to conclude that humans domesticated every species that could be domesticated. This is unlikely. Twentieth-century efforts to domesticate bison, eland, and elk have not fully succeeded, but they have generally not been maintained for as long as twenty generations. Rats and foxes have more rapid reproduction rates, and the experiments with them succeeded.

Animal domestication is probably best studied on a case-by-case basis as an unintended result of other processes. In some instances, sacrifice probably played a key role. Religious traditions of animal sacrifice rarely utilize, and sometimes prohibit, the ritual killing of wild animals. It is reasonable to suppose that the practice of capturing wild animals and holding them for sacrifice eventually led to the appearance of genetically transmitted tameness as an unplanned result.

Horses and camels were domesticated relatively late, and most likely not for meat consumption. The societies within which these animals first appeared as domestic species already had domestic sheep, goats, and cattle for meat, and they used oxen to carry loads and pull plows and carts. Horses, camels, and later reindeer may represent successful experiments with substituting one draft animal for another, with genetically transmitted tameness an unexpected consequence of separating animals trained for riding or pulling carts from their wilder kin.

Once human societies had developed the full range of uses of domestic animals—meat, eggs, milk, fiber, labor, transport—the likelihood of domesticating more species diminished. In the absence of concrete knowledge of how domestication had occurred, it was usually easier for people to move domestic livestock to new locations than to attempt to develop new domestic species. Domestic animals accompanied human groups wherever they ventured, and this practice triggered enormous environmental changes as domestic animals, and their human keepers, competed with wild species for food and living space.

Part Two

The Formation of New Cultural Communities, from 1200 B.C.E.

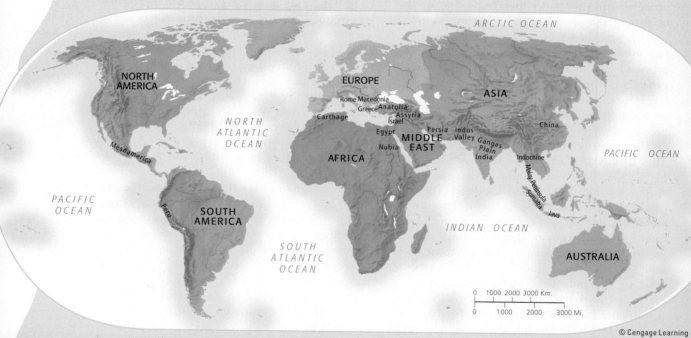

© Cengage Learning

	1000 B.C.E.	800 B.C.E.	600 B.C.E.
AMERICAS	1200–400 Olmec civilization in Mesoamerica	900–250 Chavín civilization in Peru	Gold metallurgy in Chavín **500** •
EUROPE	• 1000 Iron metallurgy	800–500 Archaic period in Greece	Celts spread across Europe **500** • **477–404** Athenian Empire and democracy Roman Republic **507** •
AFRICA	Rise of Nubian kingdom at Napata **800** •	• **814** Carthage founded 712–660 Nubian domination of Egypt	Hanno of Carthage explores West African coast **465** •
MIDDLE EAST	• **1000** David establishes Jerusalem as capital of Israel **911–612** Neo-Assyrian Empire	Babylonian conquest of Jerusalem **587** •	**522–486** Darius I rules Persian Empire
ASIA AND OCEANIA	• **1000** Aryans settle Ganges Plain 1027–221 Zhou kingdom in China	Iron metallurgy in China **600** •	**563–483** Life of the Buddha **551–479** Life of Confucius

CHAPTER 4
Greece and Iran, 1500 B.C.E.–500 C.E.
CHAPTER 5
India and Southeast Asia, 1500 B.C.E.–1025 C.E.
CHAPTER 6
An Age of Empires: Rome and Han China, 753 B.C.E.–330 C.E.

CHAPTER 7
Peoples and Civilizations of the Americas, 1200 B.C.E.–1500 C.E.
CHAPTER 8
Networks of Communication and Exchange, 300 B.C.E.–600 C.E.

From 1000 B.C.E. to 600 C.E. important changes in the ways of life established in the river-valley civilizations in the two previous millennia occurred, and the scale of human institutions and activities increased. On the shores of the Mediterranean and in Iran, India, and Southeast Asia, new centers arose in lands watered by rainfall and worked by a free peasantry. These societies developed new patterns of political and social organization and economic activity, and they moved in new intellectual, artistic, and spiritual directions.

The rulers of the empires of this era constructed extensive networks of roads and promoted urbanization. These measures brought more rapid communication, trade over greater distances, and the broad diffusion of religious ideas, artistic styles, and technologies. Large cultural zones unified by common traditions emerged—Iranian, Hellenistic, Roman, Hindu, and Chinese—and exercised substantial influence on subsequent ages.

The expansion of agriculture and trade and improvements in technology led to population increases, the spread of cities, and the growth of a comfortable middle class. In many places iron replaced bronze as the preferred metal for weapons, tools, and utensils, and metals were available to more people than in the preceding age. People using iron tools cleared extensive forests around the Mediterranean, in India, and in eastern China. Iron weapons gave an advantage to the armies of Greece, Rome, and imperial China.

New systems of writing, more easily and rapidly learned, moved the preservation and transmission of knowledge out of the control of specialists and gave birth to new ways of thinking, new genres of literature, and new types of scientific endeavor.

In the Western Hemisphere, the development of urban, agricultural civilizations in the Andes, the Yucatán lowlands, and the central plateau of Mexico, first noted among the Olmec of Mesoamerica and the Chavín culture of Peru, climaxed in the Maya, Aztec, and Andean cultures. The cultural exchanges and interactions that mark this era in Eurasia and Africa have counterparts in the Western Hemisphere.

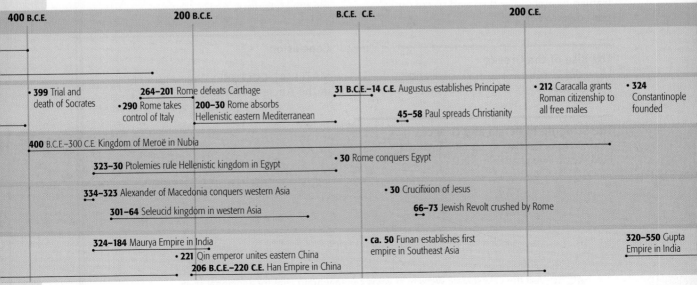

400 B.C.E.   200 B.C.E.   B.C.E. C.E.   200 C.E.

- **399** Trial and death of Socrates
- **264–201** Rome defeats Carthage
- **290** Rome takes control of Italy
- **200–30** Rome absorbs Hellenistic eastern Mediterranean
- **31 B.C.E.–14 C.E.** Augustus establishes Principate
- **45–58** Paul spreads Christianity
- **212** Caracalla grants Roman citizenship to all free males
- **324** Constantinople founded

- **400** B.C.E.–300 C.E. Kingdom of Meroë in Nubia
- **323–30** Ptolemies rule Hellenistic kingdom in Egypt
- **30** Rome conquers Egypt

- **334–323** Alexander of Macedonia conquers western Asia
- **301–64** Seleucid kingdom in western Asia
- **30** Crucifixion of Jesus
- **66–73** Jewish Revolt crushed by Rome

- **324–184** Maurya Empire in India
- **221** Qin emperor unites eastern China
- **206 B.C.E.–220 C.E.** Han Empire in China
- **ca. 50** Funan establishes first empire in Southeast Asia
- **320–550** Gupta Empire in India

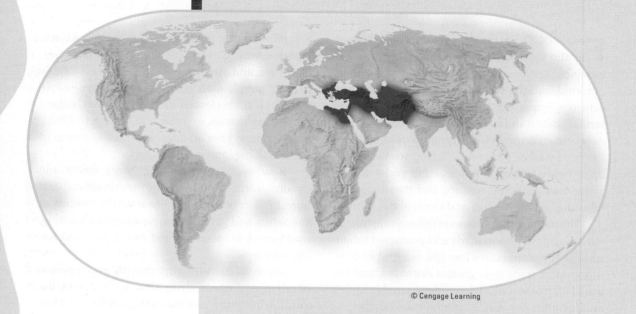

© Cengage Learning

CHAPTER PREVIEW

Ancient Iran
How did the Persian Empire rise from its Iranian homeland and spread to encompass diverse cultures?

The Rise of the Greeks
How did Greek civilization evolve and spread beyond its original territories?

The Struggle of Persia and Greece
How did the Persian Wars lead into the Hellenistic Age that followed?

The Hellenistic Synthesis
How did a cultural synthesis develop during the Hellenistic Age?

Conclusion

MATERIAL CULTURE: Wine and Beer in the Ancient World

 Visit the CourseMate website at **www.cengagebrain.com** for additional study tools and review materials for this chapter.

The Greek historian Herodotus (heh-ROD-uh-tuss) (ca. 485–425 B.C.E.) relates that the Persian king Darius (duh-RIE-us) I, whose empire stretched from eastern Europe to northwest India, questioned some Greek and Indian sages. Under what circumstances, he asked the Greeks, would they eat their deceased fathers' bodies? The Greeks, who practiced cremation, recoiled in revulsion. Darius then asked the Indians whether they would ever burn the bodies of their dead parents. This similarly repelled them because they practiced ritual eating of the bodies of the dead. Herodotus argues from this that every group of people regards its own practices as "natural" and superior. This story reminds us that ancient sources such as Herodotus's writings are sometimes accurate, as Herodotus is about Greek funerary customs, and sometimes wildly inaccurate, as are his views on Indian rituals.

The story also reminds us that the Persian Empire and the Hellenistic Greek kingdoms that succeeded it brought together peoples and cultural systems from Europe, Africa, and Asia that previously had had little direct contact with one another. This cross-cultural interaction both alarmed and stimulated the peoples involved, in some instances giving rise to new cultural syntheses.

This chapter recounts the experiences of the Persians and Greeks in the first millennium B.C.E. Historians traditionally consider the rivalry of Greeks and Persians the first act of an age-long drama: the clash of East and West, of fundamentally different ways of life destined to collide. Ironically, Greeks and Persians had more in common than they realized. They spoke related languages belonging to the Indo-European family, and they inherited similar cultural traits, forms of social organization, and religious outlooks from their shared past.

Ancient Iran

How did the Persian Empire rise from its Iranian homeland and spread to encompass diverse cultures?

Iran, the "land of the Aryans," links western Asia and southern and Central Asia. In the sixth century B.C.E., the Persians of southwest Iran created the largest empire the world had yet seen. Heirs to the Assyrian and Babylonian imperial tradition, they introduced distinctly Iranian elements and developed new forms of political and economic organization.

Scant written evidence from within the Persian Empire forces us to rely on works by Greeks—ignorant outsiders at best, usually hostile, and interested primarily in events affecting themselves. This leaves us largely uninformed about developments in the central and eastern portions of the Persian Empire, though archaeology and close analysis of the few writings from within the empire can supplement and help correct the Greek perspective.

Geography and Resources

The Zagros Mountains bound Iran on the west, the Caucasus (KAW-kuh-suhs) Mountains and Caspian Sea on the northwest and north, and the mountains of Afghanistan (ancient Arachosia) and the desert of Baluchistan (buh-loo-chi-STAN) (ancient Gedrosia) on the east and southeast. The southern limit is a barren seacoast on the Persian Gulf and Indian Ocean. The northeast lies open to attacks or population movements from Central Asia.

Winter precipitation in the mountains feeds streams that either flow away from the central plateau into rivers that drain into seas or flow into the plateau and terminate in salt lakes and deserts. Husbanding water is the key to survival in Iran's arid interior. Lacking a great river like the Nile, Indus, or Tigris-Euphrates, ancient Iran had a sparse population, most numerous in the moister north and west and decreasing toward the arid south and east. The Great Salt Desert, covering much of eastern Iran and Baluchistan, did not support life. Mountain barriers separated scattered settlements on the southern coastal plains from the interior plateau.

Wheat and barley grown during the comparatively wet winter season were the most common crops. However, by 800 B.C.E., Iranian farmers had worked out techniques for digging underground irrigation channels that prevented evaporation and used gravity to deliver water from the subsurface water table in the foothills of the mountains to fields in otherwise uncultivable desert. Constructing these channels and the vertical shafts that gave access to them demanded labor cooperation, but since each village had its own channel, the large-scale, government-sponsored irrigation projects typical of Mesopotamia were probably not required. This favored the rise of local aristocracies capable of defending their lands.

The mountains yielded copper, tin, iron, gold, and silver, all exploited on a limited scale in antiquity, as well as wood for fuel, construction, and crafts, the hillsides being more heavily wooded than they are now. Export goods consisted largely of metals and products from farther east carried across Iran by traders.

The Rise of the Persian Empire

The term *Iranian* as used for premodern history describes a group or peoples speaking related languages and sharing certain cultural characteristics. They lived in a broad swath of territory between the Zagros Mountains and Central Asia, with some groups as far east as northwest China. One group, the Medes (Mada in Iranian),* gained political dominance in northwestern Iran in the late second millennium B.C.E., influenced in part by the ancient centers in Mesopotamia and Urartu (modern Armenia and northeast Turkey). The Medes played a major role in destroying the Assyrian Empire in the late seventh century B.C.E. and extended their control westward across Assyria into Anatolia (modern Turkey). They also projected power southeastward into the land of the Elamites, which was increasingly identified with an immigrant Iranian people known as the Persians (Parsa).

The Persian rulers, called Achaemenids (a-KEY-muh-nids) because of an ancestor named Achaemenes, cemented relations with the Median court through marriage. **Cyrus** (Kurush), the son of a Persian chieftain and a Median princess, united the Persian tribes and overthrew the Median monarch around 550 B.C.E. The differences between these two peoples being slight—notably in dialect and costume—Cyrus placed both Medes and Persians in positions of responsibility and retained the framework of Median rule. The

Greeks could not readily tell the two apart and may not have recorded their history accurately.

Patriarchal family organization among the Medes and Persians, like that of the Greeks, Romans, and most other Indo-European peoples, gave the male head of the household authority over family members. The warrior class dominated the other two social and occupational classes, the priests and peasants. Noble warriors, the king the most illustrious among them, owned land and took pleasure in hunting, fighting, and feasting. The priests, or magi (*magush*), supervised sacrifices and other rituals. Village-based farmers and shepherds made up the third class.

Over the course of two decades, Cyrus (r. 550–530 B.C.E.) redrew the map of western Asia. In 546 B.C.E., he won a cavalry battle outside Sardis, the capital of Lydia in western Anatolia, reportedly because the smell of his camels caused a panic among his opponents' horses. All Anatolia, including the Greek city-states on the western coast, came under Persian control. In 539 B.C.E., he swept into southern Mesopotamia, where the Neo-Babylonian dynasty had ruled since the collapse of Assyrian power (see Chapter 3). Disaffected elements within Babylon surrendered the city to Cyrus. Cyrus respected the Babylonian priesthood and had his son crowned king in accordance with local tradition.

Cyrus died in 530 B.C.E. while campaigning against nomadic Iranians in the northeast. His son Cambyses (kam-BIE-sees) (Kambujiya, r. 530–522 B.C.E.) set his sights on Egypt. Defeating the Egyptians in bloody battle, the Persians sent exploratory expeditions south to Nubia and west to Libya. Greek sources depict Cambyses as a cruel and impious madman, but contemporary Egyptian documents reflect a practical outlook. Like his father, he cultivated local priests and notables and respected their traditions.

Cyrus (600–530 B.C.E.) Founder of the Achaemenid Persian Empire. Between 550 and 530 B.C.E. he conquered Media, Lydia, and Babylon. Revered in the traditions of both Iran and the subject peoples, he employed Persians and Medes in his administration and respected the institutions and beliefs of subject peoples.

---

* Familiar Greek names of Iranian groups and individuals are followed by the original Iranian names in parentheses.

Chronology

Greece and the Hellenistic World	Persian Empire
1500 B.C.E. 1000 B.C.E. 1150–800 B.C.E. Greece's "Dark Age" 800 B.C.E. ca. 800 B.C.E. Greek seafaring resumes 600 B.C.E. 500 B.C.E. 400 B.C.E. 431–404 B.C.E. Peloponnesian War 300 B.C.E. 100 B.C.E. 30 B.C.E. Rome annexes Egypt	ca. 1000 B.C.E. Persians settle in southwest Iran 550–530 B.C.E Reign of Cyrus 480–470 B.C.E. Xerxes invades Greece 334–323 B.C.E. Alexander the Great defeats Persia

When Cambyses died in 522 B.C.E., **Darius I** (Darayavaush) seized the throne, crushing challengers with skill, energy, and ruthlessness. The Medes now played lesser roles; most important posts went to leading Persian nobles. Darius (r. 522–486 B.C.E.) extended Persian control eastward to the Indus Valley and westward into Europe, bridging the Danube River and chasing the nomadic Scythians (SITH-ee-uhns) north of the Black Sea. In maritime matters, Darius dispatched a fleet to explore the route from the Indus Delta to the Red Sea and completed a canal linking the Red Sea with the Nile.

Imperial Organization and Ideology

Each of the empire's twenty provinces, stretching from eastern Europe to Pakistan, was placed under a Persian **satrap** (SAY-trap), or governor, usually a relative or connection by marriage. The satrap's court mirrored the royal court on a smaller scale. Governorships frequently became hereditary, so that satraps' families lived in the province governed by their head, acquired knowledge about local conditions, and formed connections with the local elite. The farther a province was from the empire's center, the more autonomy the satrap had, since slow communications made contact with the royal center difficult.

Darius prescribed how much precious metal each province owed annually; the satrap collected and sent it. Some went for necessary expenditures, but most was hoarded. This increasingly took precious metal out of circulation, forcing up the price of gold and silver and making it hard for provinces to meet their quotas. Evidence from Babylonia shows increasing taxes and official corruption and a corresponding economic decline by the fourth century B.C.E.

Royal roads, well maintained and patrolled, connected outlying provinces to the imperial center. Way stations sheltered important travelers and couriers. Garrisons controlled movements at strategic points: mountain passes, river crossings, and important urban centers. The ancient Elamite capital of Susa, in southwest Iran, served as the imperial administrative center. Greeks and others went there with requests and messages for the king. It took at least three months to make the journey to Susa. For Greek ambassadors, the time spent traveling, waiting for an audience, and returning home could take a year or more.

The king lived and traveled with numerous wives and children. Information about the royal women comes from foreign sources and is thus suspect. The Book of Esther in the Hebrew Bible tells how King Ahasuerus (uh-HAZZ-yoo-ear-uhs) (Xerxes [ZERK-sees] to the Greeks) picked the Jewish woman Esther as a wife, putting her in a position to save the Jewish

Darius I (ca. 558–486 B.C.E.) Third ruler of the Persian Empire (r. 522–486 B.C.E.). He crushed the widespread initial resistance to his rule and gave all major government posts to Persians rather than to Medes. He established a system of provinces and tribute, began construction of Persepolis, and expanded Persian control in the east (Pakistan) and west (northern Greece).
satrap The governor of a province in the Achaemenid Persian Empire, often a relative of the king. He was responsible for protection of the province and for forwarding tribute to the central administration. Satraps in outlying provinces enjoyed considerable autonomy.

Courtesy of the Oriental Institute of the University of Chicago

View of the East Front of the Apadana (Audience Hall) at Persepolis, ca. 500 B.C.E. To the right lies the Gateway of Xerxes. Persepolis, in the Persian homeland, was built by Darius I and his son Xerxes, and it was used for ceremonies of special importance to the Persian king and people—coronations, royal weddings, funerals, and the New Year's festival. The stone foundations, walls, and stairways of Persepolis are filled with sculpted images of members of the court and embassies bringing gifts, offering a vision of the grandeur and harmony of the Persian Empire.

people from a plot to massacre them. Greek sources depict royal women as pawns in power struggles and as intriguers, poisoning rival wives and plotting their sons' paths to the throne.

The king's entourage also included (1) sons of Persian aristocrats, who were educated at court and also served as hostages for their parents' loyalty; (2) noblemen who attended the king when not on other assignments; (3) administrative officers; (4) the royal bodyguard; and (5) courtiers and slaves. Long gone were the simple days when the king hunted and caroused with his warrior companions. Inspired by Mesopotamian conceptions of monarchy, the Persian king became an aloof figure of majesty and splendor: "The Great King, King of Kings, King in Persia, King of countries." He referred to everyone, even the Persian nobility, as "my slaves," and anyone who approached him had to bow down before him.

The king owned vast tracts of land throughout the empire, some of which he gave to his supporters. Donations called "bow land," "horse land," and "chariot land" in Babylonian documents obliged the recipient to provide military service. The *paradayadam* (meaning "walled enclosure"—the term has come into English as *paradise*), consisting of gardens or orchards belonging to the king or high nobility, symbolized the prosperity of the king and his servants.

Tradition remembered Darius as issuing the "laws of the King," appointing royal judges throughout the empire, and encouraging the codification of the laws of subject peoples. As master of a decentralized empire, he allowed each people its own traditions and ordinances.

Sometimes the kings returned to **Persepolis** (Parsa), a ceremonial capital in the Persian homeland

Persepolis A complex of palaces, reception halls, and treasury buildings erected by the Persian kings Darius I and Xerxes in the Persian homeland. It is believed that the New Year's festival was celebrated here, as well as the coronations, weddings, and funerals of the Persian kings, who were buried in cliff-tombs nearby.

in southwest Iran that had been founded by Darius and completed by his son Xerxes (Ahasueras). The palaces, audience halls, treasury buildings, and barracks built on an artificial platform extending from a mountainside took inspiration from Mesopotamia, where the Assyrian kings had created fortress-cities to advertise their power.

Texts found in Persepolis and inscribed in Elamite cuneiform on baked clay tablets show government officials distributing food and other goods to workers of various nationalities, some of them prisoners of war working on construction projects, irrigation networks, or royal estates. Women received less than men of equivalent status, but pregnant women and new mothers received more. Skilled workers of either sex received more than the unskilled.

The relief sculptures on the foundations, walls, and stairwells at Persepolis feature representatives of the peoples of the empire—recognizable by distinctive hairstyles, beards, dress, hats, and footwear—bringing gifts to the king. These images did not depict a real ceremony but rather advertised the vast extent, abundant resources, and cooperative spirit of the empire. One scene shows erect subjects effortlessly shouldering a giant platform bearing Darius's throne. Similar scenes from the Assyrian Empire show the subjects staggering under the weight. Persepolis probably served as a setting for New Year's festivals, coronations, marriages, and funerals. Tombs cut into the cliffs at nearby Naqsh-i Rustam (NUHK-shee ROOS-tuhm) sheltered the remains of Darius and his successors.

Several dozen inscriptions cut into cliff faces provide perspectives on the imperial ideology. At Naqsh-i Rustam, for example, Darius claims:

> Ahuramazda (ah-HOOR-uh-MAZZ-duh) [the chief Persian deity], when he saw this earth in commotion, thereafter bestowed it upon me, made me king. . . . By the favor of Ahuramazda I put it down in its place. . . . I am of such a sort that I am a friend to right, I am not a friend to wrong. It is not my desire that the weak man should have wrong done to him by the mighty; nor is that my desire, that the mighty man should have wrong done to him by the weak.[1]

Since the religion of **Zoroastrianism** (zo-ro-ASS-tree-uh-niz-um) recognized Ahuramazda as god, it seems certain that Darius and his successors were Zoroastrians. Questions surround the origins of this religion. Worshipers believe that Zarathustra (Zoroaster in Greek) wrote hymns called Gathas, the dialect and physical setting of which indicate an origin in northern Afghanistan. Scholarly guesses place Zarathustra's life sometime between 1700 and 500 B.C.E. According to Zarathustra, Ahuramazda, "the wise lord," created the world. Angra Mainyu (ANG-ruh MINE-yoo), "the hostile spirit," and a host of demons threaten it. In this dualist universe, the struggle between good and evil plays out over 12,000 years. At the end of time, good will prevail, and the world will return to the pure state of creation. In the meantime, humanity participates in this cosmic struggle, and individuals reap rewards or torments in the afterlife according to their actions.

The Persians also drew on pre-Zoroastrian moral and metaphysical concepts. Alive to the beauties of nature, they venerated water, which they kept pure, and fire, which burned continuously at altars. Bodily purity, a matter of intense concern, ceased with death. Zoroastrians exposed corpses to carrion-eating birds and the elements to avoid sullying the earth through burial or fire through cremation. Some earlier gods, such as Mithra, a sun-deity and defender of oaths and compacts, retained divine status despite Zarathustra's focus on one god. The Persians honored promises and

Primary Source: Gathas Listen in as Zarathustra ponders the fate of the righteous and the liars.

Zoroastrianism A religion originating in ancient Iran with the prophet Zoroaster. It centered on a single benevolent deity—Ahuramazda—who engaged in a twelve-thousand-year struggle with demonic forces before prevailing and restoring a pristine world. Emphasizing truth-telling, purity, and reverence for nature, the religion demanded that humans choose sides in the struggle between good and evil. Those whose good conduct indicated their support for Ahuramazda would be rewarded in the afterlife. Others would be punished. The religion of the Achaemenid Persians, Zoroastrianism may have spread within their realms and influenced Judaism, Christianity, and other faiths.

telling the truth. Darius's inscriptions castigate evildoers as followers of "the Lie."

Zoroastrianism preached belief in one supreme deity, maintained high ethical standards, and promised salvation. Expanding with the advance of the Persian Empire, it may have influenced Judaism and thus, indirectly, Christianity. God and the Devil, Heaven and Hell, reward and punishment, the Messiah and the end of time: all appear in this belief system. Yet the Islamic conquest of Iran in the seventh century C.E. (see Chapter 9) triggered the faith's decline. Only tiny communities survive in Iran now. Larger communities, called Parsees, live in South Asia.

The Rise of the Greeks

How did Greek civilization evolve and spread beyond its original territories?

The cultural features that emerged in resource-poor Greece in the first millennium B.C.E. depended on access to foreign markets and sources of raw materials. Greek merchants and mercenaries brought home not only raw materials and crafted goods but also ideas. Population pressure, poverty, war, and political crises prompted Greeks to venture throughout the Mediterranean and western Asia, carrying with them their language and culture and exerting influence on other societies. Greek identity and interest in geography, ethnography, and history grew from experience with non-Greek practices and beliefs, as well as from a two-century-long rivalry with the Persian Empire.

Geography and Resources

Bounded by the Atlantic, the Alps, the Syrian Desert, and the Sahara, the lands of the Mediterranean climatic zone share seasonal weather patterns and many plants and animals. In summer, a stalled weather front near the entrance of the Mediterranean holds up storms from the Atlantic and allows winds from the Sahara to flow over the region. In winter, the front dissolves, and ocean storms roll in, bringing waves, wind, and cold. Such similarities facilitated migration within the zone, since people did not have to change familiar practices and occupations.

Greek civilization arose on the Greek mainland, the Aegean islands, and Anatolia's western coast. As we saw in Chapter 3, small plains between low mountain ranges characterize southern Greece, a land with no navigable rivers. The islands dotting the Aegean, inhabited from early times, made sailing from Greece to Ionia (western Anatolia) comparatively easy. From about 1000 B.C.E., Greeks began to settle Ionia, where rivers with broad, fertile plains made for a comfortable life. These coastal Greeks maintained closer contact with Greeks across the Aegean than with the peoples of Anatolia's rugged interior. The sea served as a connector, not a barrier.

Mainland farmers depended on rainfall to water their crops. In the south, limited land, thin topsoil, and sparse rainfall supported only small populations. Farmers planted the plains with barley, which is hardier than wheat, and the edges of the plains with olive trees. Grapevines grew on the terraced lower slopes of the foothills. Sheep and goats grazed the hillsides. Northern Greece, with more rainfall and broader plains, supported herds of cattle and horses. Resources included abundant building stone and fine marble, but few metal deposits or forests.

The difficulty and expense of overland transport, the availability of good anchorages, and the need to import metals, timber, and grain drew the Greeks to the sea. They obtained timber from the northern Aegean, gold and iron from Anatolia, copper from Cyprus, tin from the western Mediterranean, and grain from the Black Sea, Egypt, and Sicily. Though never comfortable with "the wine-dark sea," as Homer called it, the Greeks relied on it, their small, frail ships hugging the coastline or island hopping where possible.

The Emergence of the Polis

After the destruction of the Mycenaean palace-states (see Chapter 3), Greece lapsed into a "Dark Age" (ca. 1150–800 B.C.E.), a time of depopulation, poverty, and backwardness that has left few archaeological traces. Decline of trade and lack of access to resources lay behind the poverty of the Dark Age. Within Greece, regional distinctiveness in pottery and crafts indicates declining interconnections.

By reestablishing contact between the Aegean and the Middle East, Phoenician traders (see Chapter 3) gave Greek civilization a push that inaugurated the Archaic period of Greek history (ca. 800–480 B.C.E.). Greek seafarers reappeared in Mediterranean waters looking for raw materials, trade opportunities, and fertile farmland.

Lifelike human and animal figures and imaginative mythical beasts on painted Greek pottery signal new ideas from the east, as does the adoption of an alphabetic writing system of Phoenician inspiration. Cuneiform or hieroglyphics, systems in which several hundred symbols stood for syllables rather than letters, took years of training and remained the preserve of an elite scribal class. By contrast, the alphabetic symbols made literacy easier to acquire.

First used for economic purposes or for preserving oral poetry, the Greek alphabet facilitated new forms of literature, law codes, religious dedications, and epitaphs. Yet Greek culture continued to center on storytelling, rituals, and performances. Theatrical drama, philosophical dialogues, and political and courtroom oratory demonstrate the dynamic interaction of speaking and writing.

Population grew rapidly during the Archaic period. Cemeteries around Athens show a five- to sevenfold increase during the eighth century B.C.E. Herding gave way to intensive farming on the previously uncultivated margins of the plains. Increasing population and prosperity stimulated the importation of food and raw materials, a merging of villages into urban centers, and specialization of labor. Freed from farming by rising surpluses, some people developed skills in crafts, commerce, and religion.

The Greek **polis** (POE-lis), or city-state, ranging in size from a few thousand souls to several hundred thousand in the case of Athens, consisted of an urban center and the surrounding countryside. Typically, a fortified hilltop, the *acropolis* ("top of the city"), offered refuge in emergencies. The town spread around its base. In the open area around government buildings and markets, called an *agora* ("gathering place"), citizens debated the decisions of leaders and organized for war. Walls surrounded the urban center, but population growth prompted construction beyond them. Food came from surrounding farms, though many who lived within the walls worked nearby fields. Unlike the dependent rural workers of Mesopotamia, Greek farmers enjoyed full citizenship.

Frequent city-state conflicts led, by the early seventh century B.C.E., to a kind of warfare based on **hoplites**—heavily armored infantrymen who fought in close formation. Protected by helmet, breastplate, and leg guards, each hoplite brandished a thrusting spear while guarding his left side and the right side of the hoplite beside him with a round shield, keeping a sword in reserve. Victory depended on maintaining one's battle line while breaking open the enemy's. The losers suffered most of their casualties while fleeing.

Private citizens, mostly farmers called up for brief periods rather than professional soldiers, served as hoplites. Courage to stand one's ground counted for more than strength for bearing weapons and armor. When an army approached, the farmers of the polis under attack mustered to defend their land and

polis The Greek term for a city-state, an urban center and the agricultural territory under its control. It was the characteristic form of political organization in southern and central Greece in the Archaic and Classical periods. Of the hundreds of city-states in the Mediterranean and Black Sea regions settled by Greeks, some were oligarchic, others democratic, depending on the powers delegated to the Council and the Assembly.

hoplite A heavily armored Greek infantryman of the Archaic and Classical periods who fought in the close-packed phalanx formation. Hoplite armies—militias composed of middle- and upper-class citizens supplying their own equipment—were for centuries superior to all other military forces.

buildings. The clash of hoplite lines resulted in quick decisions. Battles rarely lasted more than a few hours, with the survivors promptly returning home to their farms.

As population growth strained the agricultural resources of the small plains, many city-states sent excess population abroad to establish independent colonies. Sometimes people were chosen by lot to be colonists and forbidden to return on pain of death. At other times people in search of adventure or an escape from poverty volunteered. Colonists sought the approval of the god Apollo at his sanctuary at Delphi and then departed by sea carrying a fire from the communal hearth of the mother city, a symbol of the kinship and religious ties that would connect the two communities. The "founder," a prominent member of the mother city, chose a hill or other natural refuge, assigned parcels of land, and drafted laws. Sometimes colonists intermarried with local inhabitants; alternatively, they drove them away or reduced them to semiservility.

From the mid-eighth through the mid-sixth centuries B.C.E., colonists spread Greek culture to the northern Aegean area, the Libyan coast of North Africa, and around the Black Sea, with southern Italy and Sicily becoming heavily Greek. Establishing new homes, farms, and communities posed many challenges, but the similarity in climate and ecology helped the Greek settlers transplant their way of life.

Greeks called themselves *Hellenes* (HELL-leans) (the Romans later used *Graeci*) to distinguish themselves from *barbaroi* (literally "non-Greek speakers," whence the English word *barbarian*). Interaction with new peoples and exposure to their cultures made the Greeks aware of their unity of language, religion, and lifestyle. It also introduced them to new ideas and technologies. Developments in the colonial world traveled back to the Greek homeland: urban planning, forms of political organization, and new intellectual currents.

Coinage, invented in the early sixth century B.C.E. in Lydia (western Anatolia), spread throughout the Greek world and beyond. Scarcity, durability, divisibility, and ease of use made silver, gold, and copper appropriate for minting into metal pieces of state-guaranteed weight and purity. (Societies in other parts of the world used items with similar qualities,

including beads, hard-shelled beans, and cowrie shells.) Coinage made weighing quantities of metal obsolete and fostered quicker trading transactions, better recordkeeping, and easier wealth storage. Trade grew, as did the total wealth of communities, but different weight standards used by different states often confused exchanges of currencies.

Colonization relieved pressures within the Archaic Greek world but did not eliminate political instability. At some point, councils representing the noble families superseded the Dark Age kings depicted in Homer's *Iliad* and *Odyssey*. This aristocracy derived wealth and power from landownership. The peasants who farmed these lands kept only a portion of their harvest. Debt slaves, people who lost their freedom when they could not repay money or seed borrowed from the lord, also worked the land. Free peasants owned small farms and joined urban-based craftsmen and merchants as part of a "middle class."

Tyrants—individuals who seized power in violation of normal political institutions—gained control of many city-states in the mid-seventh and sixth centuries B.C.E. Often disgruntled aristocrats with middle-class backing, such tyrants appealed to hoplite soldiers, whose numbers increased with growing prosperity and lower prices for weaponry. The tyrants granted these supporters political rights.

Some tyrants passed their positions on to sons, but communities eventually expelled the tyrant families and opted for oligarchy (OLL-ih-gahr-key), in which a group of the wealthiest men held power, or **democracy**, in which all free adult males shared power. The absence of a professional military class made this broadening of the political system possible.

tyrant The term the Greeks used to describe someone who seized and held power in violation of the normal procedures and traditions of the community. Tyrants appeared in many Greek city-states in the seventh and sixth centuries B.C.E., often taking advantage of the disaffection of the emerging middle class and, by weakening the old elite, unwittingly contributing to the evolution of democracy.

democracy A system of government in which all "citizens" (however defined) have equal political and legal rights, privileges, and protections, as in the Greek city-state of Athens in the fifth and fourth centuries B.C.E.

Vase Painting Depicting a Sacrifice to the God Apollo, ca. 440 B.C.E. For the Greeks, who believed in a multitude of gods who looked and behaved like humans, the central act of worship was the sacrifice, the ritualized offering of a gift. Sacrifice created a relationship between the human worshiper and the deity and raised expectations that the god would bestow favors in return. Here we see a number of male devotees, wearing their finest clothing and garlands in their hair, near a sacred outdoor altar and statue of Apollo. The god is shown at the far right, standing on a pedestal and holding his characteristic bow and laurel branch. The first worshiper offers the god bones wrapped in fat. All of the worshipers will feast on the meat carried by the boy. Bildarchiv Preussischer Kultburbesitz/Art Resource, NY

Even before they invaded the Greek peninsula at the end of the third millennium B.C.E., the Greeks worshiped several sky-gods, such as Zeus, who sent storms and lightning, and Poseidon, who controlled the sea and earthquakes. Homer's *Iliad* and *Odyssey*, which schoolboys memorized and performers recited, gave personalities to these deities. He portrayed them as anthropomorphic (an-thruh-puh-MORE-fik), or humanlike in appearance (though taller, more beautiful, and more powerful, with a supernatural radiance), with humanlike emotions of love, anger, and jealousy. More than anything else, immortality distinguished gods from humans.

State religious ceremonies conferred civic identity. **Sacrifice**, the central ritual, took place at altars in front of temples where the gods were thought to reside. Gifts as humble as a small cake or a cup of wine poured on the ground accompanied prayers for favor and protection. In grander sacrifices, people would kill one or more animals, smear the altar with its blood, and burn parts of its body so that the aroma would ascend to the gods.

Oracles situated at sacred sites responded to human pleas for information, advice, or prediction. At Delphi in central Greece, the most honored site, the god Apollo spoke through his priestess, the Pythia (PITH-ee-uh). The male priests who administered the sanctuary interpreted her obscure utterances. Our dependence on literary texts that express the values of an educated urban elite limits our knowledge of fertility cults, which were usually based on female deities and appealed to the agricultural majority of the population.

sacrifice A gift given to a deity, often with the aim of creating a relationship, gaining favor, and obligating the god to provide some benefit to the sacrificer, sometimes in order to sustain the deity and thereby guarantee the continuing vitality of the natural world. The object devoted to the deity could be as simple as a cup of wine poured on the ground, a live animal slain on the altar, or, in the most extreme case, the ritual killing of a human being.

New Intellectual Currents

Prosperity, new technologies, and social and political development led to innovations in intellectual and artistic outlook, including a growing emphasis on the individual. In early Greek communities, the family enveloped the individual, and land belonged collectively to the family, including ancestors and descendants. Ripped from this communal network and forced to resettle elsewhere, colonists became models of individualism, as did the tyrant who seized power for himself alone. The concept of humanism—a valuing of the uniqueness, talents, and rights of the individual—remains a central tenet of Western civilization.

In the new lyric poetry, short verses deal with personal subjects drawn from the poet's experience. Archilochus (ahr-KIL-uh-kuhs), a soldier and poet living in the first half of the seventh century B.C.E., wrote:

> Some barbarian is waving my shield, since I was obliged to leave that perfectly good piece of equipment behind under a bush. But I got away, so what does it matter? Let the shield go; I can buy another one equally good.[2]

Here Archilochus pokes fun at the heroic ideal that scorned soldiers who ran from the enemy. In challenging traditional values and expressing personal feelings, lyric poets pointed toward the modern Western conception of poetry.

In religion, thinkers now known as pre-Socratic philosophers called into question Homer's representations of the gods. Xenophanes (zeh-NOFF-eh-nees), living in the sixth century B.C.E., protested:

> But if cattle and horses or lions had hands, or were able to draw with their hands and do the works that men can do, horses would draw the forms of the gods like horses, and cattle like cattle, and they would make their bodies such as they each had themselves.[3]

The term *pre-Socratic* refers to philosophers before Plato, a student of Socrates, who in the later fifth century B.C.E. shifted the focus of philosophy to ethical questions. They rejected traditional explanations of the origins and nature of the world and sought more rational answers: How was the world created? What is it made of? Why does it change? Some postulated that earth, air, fire, and water, the primal elements, combine or dissolve to form the substances found in nature. One taught that microscopic atoms (from a Greek word meaning "indivisible") move through the void of space, colliding randomly and combining in various ways to form the natural world. This intuition coincidentally resembles modern atomic theory. Most pre-Socratics came from Ionia and southern Italy, where Greeks lived close to non-Greeks. Encountering peoples with different ideas may have stimulated some of their thoughts.

Also in Ionia in the sixth century B.C.E., men later referred to as logographers ("writers of prose accounts") gathered information on ethnography (the physical characteristics and cultural practices of a people), Mediterranean geography, the foundation of cities, and the origins of famous families. They called their accumulation of information *historia*, "investigation/research." **Herodotus** (ca. 485–425 B.C.E.), from Halicarnassus in southwest Anatolia, published his *Histories*. Its early parts contain geographic and ethnographic reports, legends, folktales, and marvels. Later parts focus on the Persian-Greek wars of the previous generation. He opens his work as follows:

> I, Herodotus of Halicarnassus, am here setting forth my history, that time may not draw the color from what man has brought into being, nor those great and wonderful deeds, manifested by both Greeks and barbarians, fail of their report, and, together with all this, the reason why they fought one another.[4]

His search for causes reveals the thinking of a true historian. Thus did *historia* begin to narrow and acquire the modern meaning of *history*, with Herodotus gaining the nickname *Father of History*.

Herodotus (ca. 485–425 B.C.E.) Heir to the technique of historia—"investigation"—developed by Greeks in the late Archaic period. He came from a Greek community in Anatolia and traveled extensively collecting information in western Asia and the Mediterranean lands. He traced the antecedents of and chronicled the Persian Wars between the Greek city-states and the Persian Empire, thus originating the Western tradition of historical writing.

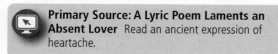

Primary Source: A Lyric Poem Laments an Absent Lover Read an ancient expression of heartache.

The Acropolis at Athens This steep, defensible plateau jutting out from the Attic Plain served as a Mycenaean fortress in the second millennium B.C.E. The site of Athens has been continuously occupied since that time. In the mid-sixth century B.C.E. the tyrant Pisistratus built a temple to Athena, the patron goddess of the community. It was destroyed by the Persians when they invaded Greece in 480 B.C.E. In the 440s, Pericles instituted a building program using funds from the naval empire that Athens headed. These construction projects, including a new temple to Athena—the Parthenon—brought glory to the city and popularity to Pericles and to the new democracy that he championed.

Robert Harding World Imagery

 History in Focus *Why did the Athenians build their temple on top of a hill rather than in the city below? What does this tell you about their views on the relationship between gods and humans? Find the answer online.*

Athens and Sparta

Athens and Sparta, the preeminent city-states of the late Archaic and Classical periods, differed in character despite environmental and cultural similarities. The Spartans' ancestors migrated into the Peloponnese (PELL-eh-puh-neze), the southernmost part of Greece, around 1000 B.C.E. Their community resembled others until the seventh century B.C.E., when the population increases and shortage of farmland that affected all communities prompted them to react differently. Instead of sending out colonies, the Spartans invaded the fertile plain of Messenia to the west. The resulting takeover, aided perhaps by hoplite tactics, saw the Messenians reduced to the status of helots (HELL-uts), the most abused and exploited population on the Greek mainland.

The Spartan state quickly turned into a military camp, always prepared for a helot uprising. The state divided Messenia and Laconia, the Spartan homeland, into several thousand lots, each assigned to a Spartan citizen. Helots worked the land and turned over part of their harvest to their Spartan masters. Freed from farming, the Spartans devoted their lives to military affairs.

The Spartan army outclassed all others because it did not rely on militias summoned only during crises. The Spartans paid a price, however. Taken from their families and put into barracks at age seven, boys underwent a severe regimen of discipline, beatings, and deprivation. The demands of the state consumed a Spartan male's whole life.

The economic, political, and cultural revival of the Archaic Greek world passed Sparta by: no poets or artists, no precious metals or coinage, no commerce or other activities that could introduce inequality. The fifth-century B.C.E. historian Thucydides (thoo-SID-ih-dees), a native of Athens, remarked that in his day Sparta looked like a large village and that no future observer of the site would be able to guess its power.

Other Greeks admired Spartan courage, commitment, and martial skills but abhorred their arrogance, ignorance, and cruelty. The Spartan Council of Elders and two kings, who commanded in battle, practiced a cautious and isolationist foreign policy. Reluctant to venture far for fear of a helot uprising, they worked for peace through the Peloponnesian League, a system of alliances with their neighbors.

Athens, by comparison, possessed an unusually large and populous territory: the fertile plains of Attica with their groves of olive trees. By the fifth century B.C.E., Athens numbered approximately 300,000 people. Villages and a few larger towns dotted the peninsula where the urban center stood beside the sheer-sided Acropolis some 5 miles (8 kilometers) from the sea.

In 594 B.C.E., to avoid civil war, the Athenians conferred lawgiving powers on Solon, an aristocrat with ties to the merchant community. He divided the citizens into four classes based on the yield of their farms. The top three classes could hold state offices. The lowest class, with little or no property, held no offices but could participate in meetings of the Assembly. Although a far cry from democracy, this linkage between rights, privileges, and wealth broke the power of a dominant cluster of aristocratic families and favored social and political mobility. By abolishing debt slavery, Solon also guaranteed the freedom of Athenian citizens.

Despite Solon's efforts, in 546 B.C.E. an aristocrat named Pisistratus (pie-SIS-truh-tuhs) seized power. Most Athenians still lived in villages, identified primarily with their district, and accepted the leadership of landlords who lived in sturdy manor houses. So the tyrant Pisistratus turned to the urban population as opposed to the villagers loyal to the landlords. He undertook building projects, including a Temple of Athena on the Acropolis, and instituted or expanded popular urban festivals: the City Dionysia (die-ul-NIZ-eeuh), later famous for dramatic performances, and the Panathenaea (pan-ath-uh-NEE-uh), a religious procession combined with athletic and poetic competitions.

With Spartan assistance, the Athenians expelled Pisistratus's sons, who had inherited his position. In the 460s and 450s B.C.E., **Pericles** (PER-eh-kleez) led a democratic movement to transfer all power to popular organs of government: the Assembly, the Council of 500, and the People's Courts. Henceforward, Athenians of moderate or slender means could hold office and participate in politics. Selected by lot for even the highest positions, officials now received pay for their services so they could afford to leave their other occupations. Some key offices—managing public money, commanding military forces—were filled by elections that took into account the candidates' abilities.

The Assembly of all citizens held open debates several times a month; anyone could speak to the

SECTION REVIEW

- Geographical and environmental barriers turned Greeks to the sea.
- Under Phoenician influence, the Greeks built a new civilization centered on the polis.
- Overseas colonization extended Greek culture, but it did not relieve political instability.
- State religious ceremonies solidified civic identity.
- New forms of intellectual inquiry and artistic production emerged.
- Evolving along divergent paths, Athens and Sparta became the preeminent city-states.

issues of the day. Members of the Council of 500 took turns presiding and representing the Athenian state. Through effective political organizing, Pericles dominated Athenian politics from 461 B.C.E. until his death in 429 B.C.E.

Athens's economic position paralleled its political evolution. From the time of Pisistratus, Athenian pottery becomes increasingly prominent at archaeological sites around the Mediterranean. These pots often contained olive oil, Athens's chief export, but elegant painted vases were themselves luxury commodities. Trade-related increases in the size and prosperity of the middle class help explain the growth of Athenian democracy.

The Struggle of Persia and Greece

How did the Persian Wars lead into the Hellenistic Age that followed?

The Persian-Greek wars dominated Greek life in the fifth and fourth centuries B.C.E. Persians probably

Pericles (ca. 495–429 B.C.E.) Aristocratic leader who guided the Athenian state through the transformation to full participatory democracy for all male citizens, supervised construction of the Acropolis, and pursued a policy of imperial expansion that led to the Peloponnesian War. He formulated a strategy of attrition but died from the plague early in the war.

considered developments farther east more important. Nevertheless, in the end, the encounters profoundly affected the history of the eastern Mediterranean and western Asia.

Early Encounters

Cyrus's conquest of Lydia in 546 B.C.E. led to the subjugation of the Ionian Greek cities. Some groups and individuals collaborated with the Persian government, but in 499 B.C.E. Greeks and other subject peoples on the western frontier staged the Ionian Revolt. The Persians needed five years and massive infusions of troops and resources to stamp out the insurrection.

This failed revolt led to the **Persian Wars**: two Persian attacks on Greece in the early fifth century B.C.E. In 490 B.C.E., Darius dispatched a naval fleet to punish Eretria (er-EH-tree-uh) and Athens, two mainland Greek states allied with the Ionian rebels. Disloyal citizens betrayed Eretria to the Persians, who marched the survivors off to exile. In this, as in many other things, the Persians copied their Assyrian predecessors, although they did not boast of mass deportations. Athens would probably have suffered a similar fate if its hoplites had not defeated the lighter-armed Persian troops in a sharp engagement at Marathon, 26 miles (42 kilometers) from Athens.

Xerxes (Khshayarsha, r. 486–465 B.C.E.) succeeded his father in 486 B.C.E. and soon turned his attention to the troublesome Greeks. In 480 B.C.E., he gathered a huge invasion force, including contingents from all over the Persian Empire and a large fleet. Crossing the Hellespont (the narrow strait separating Europe and Asia) and traversing Thrace, the Persian throng descended into central and southern Greece. Xerxes sent messengers ahead demanding of the city-states "earth and water"—tokens of submission.

Many city-states complied. But in southern Greece the Spartans formed an alliance that historians call the Hellenic League. At the pass of Thermopylae (thuhr-MOP-uh-lee) in central Greece, three hundred Spartans and their king fought to the last man to buy time for their fellows to escape. The Persians sacked Athens, but the outnumbered Athenians lured the Persian navy into narrow waters at nearby Salamis (SAH-lah-miss), where, despite their numbers, they could not maneuver. The Persians lost their advantage, and the Athenians administered a devastating defeat. A rout of the Persian army at Plataea the following spring relieved the immediate threat.

Athens's stubborn refusal to submit and the effectiveness of the Athenian navy earned the city great respect. Naval strategies dominated the next phase of the war, which was designed to liberate Greek states still under Persian control. This gave Athens priority over land-based, isolationist Sparta. The Delian League, formed in 477 B.C.E., brought the Greek states together. In less than twenty years, League forces led by Athenian generals swept the Persians from the eastern Mediterranean and freed all Greek communities except those in distant Cyprus.

The Height of Athenian Power

Scholars date the Classical period of Greek history (480–323 B.C.E.) to this defense of the Greek homeland. Ironically, Athens exploited its crucial role in these events to become an imperial power. Some Greek allies contributed money instead of troops, and the Athenians used the money to strengthen their navy. They treated other members of the Delian League as subjects and demanded annual contributions. States attempting to leave the League were brought back by force, stripped of their defenses, and subordinated to Athens.

Athenian naval technology transformed Greek warfare and brought power and wealth to Athens itself. Unlike commercial sailing ships, which over time had developed a stabler and more capacious round-bodied design, military vessels relied on large numbers of rowers. Having little deck room or storage space, these ships hugged the coastline and put ashore nightly to replenish food supplies and let the crew sleep. Fifty-oared ships had dominated naval warfare

---

Persian Wars Conflicts between Greek city-states and the Persian Empire, ranging from the Ionian Revolt (499–494 B.C.E.) through Darius's punitive expedition that failed at Marathon (490 B.C.E.) and the defeat of Xerxes' massive invasion of Greece by the Spartan-led Hellenic League (480–479 B.C.E.). This first major setback for Persian arms launched the Greeks into their period of greatest cultural productivity. Herodotus chronicled these events in the first "history" in the Western tradition.

Replica of Ancient Greek Trireme Greek warships had a metal-tipped ram in front to pierce the hulls of enemy vessels and a pair of steering rudders in the rear. Though equipped with masts and sails, in battle these warships were propelled by 170 rowers. This modern, full-sized replica, manned by international volunteer crews, is helping scholars to determine attainable speeds and maneuvering techniques.

until the late sixth century B.C.E., when sleek, fast **triremes** (TRY-reems) powered by 170 rowers brought an end to crude engagements in which warriors cleared the enemy's decks with spears and arrows before boarding and fighting hand to hand. Approximately 115 by 18 feet (35 by 6 meters) in size, the trireme positioned rowers on three levels with oars of different lengths to avoid interference. The fragile vessels could achieve up to 7 knots in short bursts. Athenian crews, by constant practice, became the best in the eastern Mediterranean. They disabled enemy vessels by sheering off their oars, smashing their hulls below the water line with an iron-tipped prow, or forcing collisions by running around them in ever-tighter circles.

The primacy of the fleet contributed to a democratic system in which each male citizen had, at least in principle, an equal voice. The middle or upper class produced hoplites, who bought their own armor and weapons. Rowers came from the lower classes, but they insisted on full rights as protectors of the community.

Athenian maritime power reached farther than any citizen militia. Victors in Greek wars seldom occupied enemy lands permanently (the exception being Sparta's takeover of Messenia). Booty with minor adjustments to boundary lines sufficed. But Athens could exert continual domination and readily did so to promote its commerce. Athens's port, Piraeus

(pih-RAY-uhs), became the most important commercial center in the eastern Mediterranean.

Annual dues from subject states subsidized the increasingly expensive Athenian democracy and paid the construction costs of the Parthenon, a majestic temple to Athena on the Acropolis. The Athenian leader Pericles gained extraordinary popularity by hiring many Athenians to construct and decorate this and other monuments. When political enemies protested Pericles' use of Delian League funds for construction, he replied: "They [Athens's subjects] do not give us a single horse, nor a soldier, nor a ship. All they supply is money. . . . It is no more than fair that after Athens has been equipped with all she needs to carry on the war, she should apply the surplus to public works, which, once completed, will bring her glory for all time."[5]

The proceeds of empire indirectly subsidized the festivals at which the dramatic tragedies of Aeschylus, Sophocles, and Euripides and the comedies of Aristophanes (ar-uh-STOFF-uh-neze) were performed.

trireme Greek and Phoenician warship of the fifth and fourth centuries B.C.E. It was sleek and light, powered by 170 oars arranged in three vertical tiers. Manned by skilled sailors, it was capable of short bursts of speed and complex maneuvers.

The brightest and most creative artists and thinkers flocked to Athens. Traveling teachers called Sophists ("wise men") provided instruction in logic and public speaking to fee-paying pupils. The new discipline of rhetoric—the crafting of attractive and persuasive arguments—gave those with training and quick wits a great advantage in politics and the courts. Greeks became connoisseurs of oratory, eagerly listening for each innovation yet so aware of the power of words that *sophist* came to mean one who uses cleverness to manipulate reality.

These intellectual currents came together in 399 B.C.E. when the philosopher **Socrates** (ca. 470–399 B.C.E.) went on trial charged with corrupting the youth of Athens and not believing in the city's gods. A sculptor by trade, Socrates spent his time conversing with young men who enjoyed hearing him deflate the pretensions of those who thought themselves wise. He wryly commented that he knew one more thing than everyone else: that he knew nothing.

At his trial, Socrates easily disposed of the actual charges: he was a deeply religious man, and the families of the young men he associated with supported him. He argued that the real basis of the prosecution was twofold: (1) blame for attempts by several of his aristocratic students to overthrow the Athenian democracy and (2) blame for the controversial teachings of the Sophists, which many believed undermined morality and religious tradition. In Athenian trials, juries of hundreds of citizens decided guilt and punishment, often spurred by emotion more than legal principles. Convicted by a close vote, Socrates maintained his innocence and said he should be rewarded for his services instead. This led the jury to condemn him to death by drinking hemlock. Socrates' disciples considered him a martyr, and smart young men like Plato withdrew from public life and dedicated themselves to philosophical pursuits.

Socrates himself wrote nothing, preferring to converse with people he met in the street. His disciple Plato (ca. 428–347 B.C.E.) may represent the first truly literate generation. He learned from books and habitually wrote down his thoughts. On the outskirts of Athens, Plato founded the Academy, a school where young men could pursue higher education. Yet even Plato reflected the oral culture of his upbringing by writing dialogues—an oral form—in which his protagonist, Socrates, uses the "Socratic method" of question and answer to reach a deeper understanding of values like justice, excellence, and wisdom. Plato refused to write down the most advanced teachings of the Academy. Higher reality, he believed, appeared only in pale reflection in the sensible world and could be grasped only by "initiates" who had completed the earlier stages.

Inequality in Classical Greece

The Athenian democracy that historically underlies modern traditions of democracy included only a small percentage of Attica's population: true citizens—free adult males of pure Athenian ancestry. Excluding women, children, slaves, and foreigners, this group amounted to 30,000 or 40,000 people out of approximately 300,000. Equally exclusive practices probably existed in less well-known Greek democracies.

Slaves, mostly foreigners, constituted perhaps one-third of the population of Attica in the fifth and fourth centuries B.C.E. The average Athenian family owned one or more. Slaves ran the shop or worked the farm while the master attended meetings of the Assembly or served on a board overseeing the day-to-day activities of the state. As "living pieces of property," slaves did any work, submitted to any sexual acts, and suffered any punishments their owners ordained, though some communities prohibited arbitrarily killing slaves. Overall, Greece saw few of the extremes of cruelty and abuse inflicted on slaves in other places and times.

Farms being small, most slaves performed domestic service rather than field labor, often working with the master or mistress on the same tasks. Daily contact fostered relationships between owners and slaves that made it hard for owners to act inhumanely. Still, Greek thinkers justified slavery by arguing that *barbaroi* (non-Greeks) lacked the capacity to reason and

Socrates Athenian philosopher (ca. 470–399 B.C.E.) who shifted the emphasis of philosophical investigation from questions of natural science to ethics and human behavior. He attracted young disciples from elite families but made enemies by revealing the ignorance and pretensions of others, culminating in his trial and execution by the Athenian state.

thus were better off under Greek owners. The stigma attached to slavery was so great that most Athenians refused to work as wage laborers because following an employer's orders resembled being his slave.

The position of women varied. Spartan women, who were expected to bear and raise strong children, exercised regularly and enjoyed a level of public visibility and outspokenness that shocked other Greeks. At the opposite extreme, Athenians confined and oppressed women. Ironically, the exploitation of women in Athens reflects the high degree of freedom that Athenian men enjoyed in the democratic state.

Inequality marked Athenian marriages. A man of thirty—reasonably educated, a war veteran, and experienced in business and politics—commonly married, after negotiating with her parents, a teenage girl with no formal education and minimal training in weaving, cooking, and household management. Coming into the home of a husband she hardly knew, the wife had no political rights and limited legal protection. Given the differences in age, social experience, and authority, the relationship between husband and wife resembled that of father and daughter. The function of marriage was to produce children, preferably male. The ancients were sufficiently ashamed of infanticide—the killing through exposure of unwanted children—to say little about it. But it is likely that more girls than boys were abandoned.

The husband spent his day outdoors attending to work or political responsibilities; he dined with male friends at night (see Material Culture: Wine and Beer in the Ancient World). The wife stayed home to cook, clean, raise the children, and supervise the servants. The closest relationship in the family was likely to be between the wife and her slave attendant, a woman of roughly the same age. The servant could be sent on errands. The wife stayed home, except to attend funerals and certain festivals or make discreet visits to female relatives. Greek men claimed that confinement to the home stifled female promiscuity and prevented illegitimate births that could threaten family property and erode regulation of citizenship rights. Athenian law allowed a husband to kill an adulterer caught in the act with his wife.

Without documents written by women, we cannot tell how Athenian women felt about their situation. Women's festivals, such as the Thesmophoria

(thes-moe-FOE-ree-uh), provided a rare opportunity for women to get out. During this three-day festival, the women of Athens lived together and managed their own affairs in a great encampment, carrying out mysterious rituals meant to enhance the fertility of the land. Bold and self-assertive women appeared on the Athenian stage: the defiant Antigone (an-TIG-uh-nee) of Sophocles' play, who buried her brother despite the king's prohibition; and the wives in Aristophanes' comedy *Lysistrata* (lis-us-STRAH-tuh), who withheld sex from their husbands until the men ended a war. Although imagined by men and probably reflecting a fear of strong women, these characters must partly reflect the playwrights' mothers, sisters, and wives.

To find their intellectual and emotional "equal," men often looked to other men. Bisexuality arose as much from the social structure as from biological inclinations. An older man commonly admired, pursued, and mentored a youth, thus making bisexuality part of the youth's education and initiation into the adult male community. Though commonplace among the intellectual groups that loom large in the written sources, the frequency of bisexuality and the confinement of women among the Athenian masses remain uncertain.

Failure of the City-State and Triumph of the Macedonians

Athens's rise to empire led in 431 B.C.E. to the outbreak of the **Peloponnesian War**, a struggle for survival between Athenian and Spartan alliances that encompassed most of the Greek world. To insulate themselves from attack by land, in midcentury the Athenians had built three long walls connecting the city with the port of Piraeus and the adjacent shoreline. As long as Athens controlled the sea-lanes and could provision itself, a land-based siege could not starve it into submission.

Peloponnesian War A protracted (431–404 B.C.E.) and costly conflict between the Athenian and Spartan alliance systems that convulsed most of the Greek world. The war was largely a consequence of Athenian imperialism. Possession of a naval empire allowed Athens to fight a war of attrition. Ultimately Sparta prevailed because of Athenian errors and Persian financial support.

Material Culture

Wine and Beer in the Ancient World

The most prized beverages of ancient peoples were wine and beer. Sediments found in jars excavated at a site in northwest Iran prove that techniques for the manufacture of wine were known as early as the sixth millennium B.C.E. Beer dates back at least as far as the fourth millennium B.C.E. Archaeological excavations have brought to light the equipment used in preparing, transporting, serving, and imbibing these beverages.

In Egypt and Mesopotamia, beer, which was made from wheat or barley by a rather elaborate process, was the staple drink of both the elite and the common people. Women prepared beer for the family in their homes, and breweries produced large quantities for sale. Because the production process left some chaff floating on the surface of the liquid, various means were employed to filter out this unwelcome byproduct. Sculptures on Mesopotamian stone reliefs and seals show a number of drinkers drawing on straws immersed in a single large bowl. Archaeologists have found examples of the perforated metal cones that fit over the submerged ends of the straws and filtered the liquid beer drawn through them. It is likely that the sharing of beer from a common vessel by several people had social implications, creating a bond of friendship among the participants. Archaeologists have also found individual beer "mugs" resembling a modern watering can: closed bowls with a perforated spout to filter the chaff and a semicircular channel carrying the liquid into the drinker's mouth.

In Greece, Rome, and other Mediterranean lands, where the climate was suitable for cultivating grape vines, wine was the preferred beverage. Vines were prepared in February and periodically pinched and pruned. The full-grown grapes were picked in September, then crushed (with a winepress or by people trampling on them) to produce a liquid that was sealed in casks for fermentation. The new vintage was sampled the following February. Exuberant religious festivals marked the key moments in the cycle. Initially expensive and therefore confined to the wealthy and for religious ceremonies, in later antiquity wine became available to a wider spectrum of people. Unlike beer, which requires refrigeration, wine can be stored for a long time in sealed containers and thus could be transported and traded across the ancient Mediterranean lands, continental Europe, and western Asia. The usual containers for wine were long, conical pottery jars, which the Greeks called amphoras.

The Greeks normally mixed wine with water, and they developed an elaborate array of vessels, made of pottery, metal, and glass, to facilitate mixing, serving, and drinking the precious liquid. Kraters were large mixing bowls into which the wine and water were poured. The hydria was used to carry water, and a heater could be used to warm the water when that was desired. Another special vessel could be used to chill the wine by immersion in cold water. Ladles (long-handled spoons) and elegantly narrow vessels with spouts were used to pour the concoction into the drinkers' cups. The most popular shapes for individual drinking vessels were a shallow bowl with two handles, called a kylix, and the

Royal Guard Drinking Beer Through a Straw Early forms of beer were nutritious foods but contained unappetizing residue from the fermentation process. Straws up to 40 centimeters in length had one end closed but with tiny perforations to filter the liquid. Common people used straws of clay or reed, but the elite might use silver or gold. As with fermented drinks in some parts of Africa today, beer drinking was often a social occasion with more than one person sipping from a large beer container at the same time. Bildarchiv Preussischer Kulturbesitz/Art Resource, NY

kantharos, a large, deep, two-handled cup. Another popular implement in Greece and western Asia was the rhyton, a horn-shaped vessel that tapered into the head and forepaws of an animal with a small hole at the base. The drinker would fill the horn, holding his thumb over the hole until he was ready to drink or pour, then move his thumb and release a thin stream of wine that appeared to be coming out of the animal's mouth.

The drinking equipment belonging to wealthy Greeks was often decorated with representations of the god of wine, Dionysus, holding a kantharos and surrounded by a dense tangle of vines and grape clusters. His entourage included the half-human, half-horse centaurs and the maenads, literally "crazy women." These were female worshipers who drank wine and engaged in frenzied dancing until they achieved an ecstatic state and sensed the presence of the god.

Greeks, Romans, and other Mediterranean peoples used wine for more conventional religious ceremonies, pouring libations on the ground or on the altar as an offering to the gods. It was also used on occasion for medical purposes, as a disinfectant and painkiller, or as an ingredient in various medicines. Above all, wine was featured at the banquets and drinking parties that forged and deepened social bonds. In the Greek world, the symposion (meaning "drinking together") was held after the meal. Someone, usually the host, presided over the affair, making the crucial decision about the proportion of water to wine, suggesting topics of conversation, and trying to keep some semblance of order. There might be entertainment in the form of musicians, dancers, and acrobats.

In Shang China, magnificent bronze vessels whose surfaces were covered with abstract designs and representations of otherworldly animals were fashioned for use in elaborate ceremonies at ancestral shrines. The vessels contained offerings of wine and food for the spirits of the family's ancestors, who were imagined to still need sustenance in the afterlife. The treasured bronze vessels were often buried with their owners so that they could continue to employ them after death. In later periods, as the ancestral sacrifices became less important, beautiful bronze vessels, as well as their ceramic counterparts, became part of the equipment at the banquets of the well-to-do.

At the start of the war, Pericles broke precedent by refusing to engage the Spartan-led armies that invaded Attica each year. He knew that the enemy hoplites must soon return to their farms. Thus, instead of culminating in a short, decisive battle, the Peloponnesian War dragged on for nearly three decades, with great loss of life and resources. It sapped the morale of all Greece and ended only with the defeat of Athens in a naval battle in 404 B.C.E. The Persian Empire had bankrolled the construction of ships by the Spartan alliance, so Sparta was able to take the conflict into Athens's own element, the sea.

The victorious Spartans, who had entered the war championing "the freedom of the Greeks," took over Athens's overseas empire until their increasingly high-handed behavior aroused the opposition of other city-states. Indeed, the fourth century B.C.E. was a time of nearly continuous skirmishing among Greek states. The independent polis that lent glory to Greek culture also fostered rivalries and fears among neighbors.

The Persians recouped old losses. By the King's Peace of 387 B.C.E., encompassing most of the war-weary Greek states, all of western Asia, including the Ionian Greek communities, went to Persia. The Persian king guaranteed a status quo that kept the Greeks divided and weak until rebellions in Egypt, Cyprus, and Phoenicia, combined with trouble from some western satraps, diverted his attention from thoughts of another Greek invasion.

Meanwhile, in northern Greece Philip II (r. 359–336 B.C.E.) was transforming his previously backward kingdom of Macedonia into a premier military power. (Although southern Greeks long doubted the "Greekness" of the rough and rowdy Macedonians, modern scholarship considers their language and culture Greek at base, though influenced by non-Greek neighbors.) Philip improved the traditional hoplite formation. He increased its striking power and mobility by equipping his soldiers with longer thrusting spears and lighter armor. Using horses bred on Macedonia's broad grassy plains, he experimented with coordinating infantry and cavalry. Finally, his engineers developed new siege weapons, including the first catapults—machines using the power of twisted cords that, when relaxed, hurled arrows or stones great distances.

In 338 B.C.E., Philip defeated a southern coalition and established the Confederacy of Corinth to control the Greek city-states. Appointed military commander of all the Greeks, he planned a campaign against Persia and established a bridgehead on the Asiatic side of the Hellespont. These plans may have reflected the advice of Greek thinkers who urged an anti-Persian crusade to unify their quarrelsome countrymen.

An assassin cut short Philip's ambitions in 336 [ ]6–323 B.C.E.), his son, crossed into [ ]wing revenge for Xerxes' invasion [ ]arlier. He defeated the Persians in [ ]s—against the western satraps at [ ]n northwest Anatolia and against [ ]36–330 B.C.E.) himself at Issus in [ ] and at Gaugamela (GAW-guh- [ ]abylon.

[ ]reat, as he came to be called, main- [ ]dministrative system but replaced [ ]th Macedonians and Greeks. To [ ]ints, he settled wounded and aged [ ]es of Greek-style cities, beginning

with Alexandria in Egypt. After his victory at Gaugamela (331 B.C.E.), he experimented with leaving cooperative Persian officials in place, also admitting some Persians and other Iranians into his army and court circle. Adopting elements of Persian dress and court ceremonials, he married several Iranian women who had royal or aristocratic connections and pressed his leading comrades to do the same.

In opting for unexpected policies that the Macedonian nobility fiercely resented, Alexander probably acted from both pragmatic and idealistic motives. His Asian campaign began with visions of glory, booty, and revenge. But the farther east he traveled, the more he saw himself as the legitimate successor of the Persian king (a claim facilitated by the death of Darius III). Alexander may have recognized that he had responsibilities to all the peoples who fell under his control and that controlling so vast an empire would require the cooperation of local leaders. In this, he followed the example of the Achaemenids.

The Hellenistic Synthesis

How did a cultural synthesis develop during the Hellenistic Age?

Historians call the epoch following Alexander's conquests the **Hellenistic Age** (323–30 B.C.E.) because large parts of northeastern Africa and western Asia became "Hellenized"—that is, influenced by Greek culture. Greeks migrated in large numbers from their overcrowded homeland to serve as a privileged class of soldiers and administrators on the new frontiers, where they replicated the lifestyle of the city-state. This

Alexander (356–323 B.C.E.) King of Macedonia in northern Greece. Between 334 and 323 B.C.E. he conquered the Persian Empire, reached the Indus Valley, founded many Greek-style cities, and spread Greek culture across the Middle East. Later known as Alexander the Great.

Hellenistic Age Historians' term for the era, usually dated 323–30 B.C.E., in which Greek culture spread across western Asia and northeastern Africa after the conquests of Alexander the Great. The period ended with the fall of the last major Hellenistic kingdom to Rome, but Greek cultural influence persisted until the seventh century C.E.

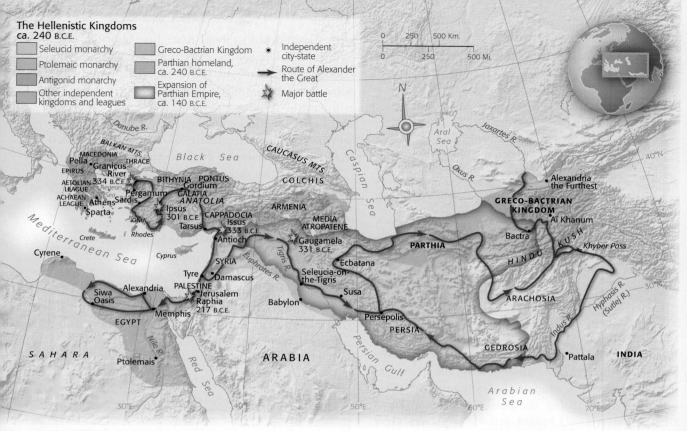

Map 4.1 Hellenistic Civilization After the death of Alexander the Great in 323 B.C.E., his vast empire split apart into a number of large and small political entities. A Macedonian dynasty was established on each continent: the Antigonids ruled the Macedonian homeland and tried to extend their control over southern Greece; the Ptolemies ruled Egypt; and the Seleucids inherited most of Alexander's conquests in Asia, but lost control of the eastern portions to the Parthians in the second century B.C.E. This period saw Greeks emigrating in large numbers from their overcrowded homeland to serve as a privileged class of soldiers and administrators in the new territories, where they replicated the lifestyle of the city-state. © Cengage Learning

Interactive Map

era of large kingdoms containing ethnically mixed populations, great cities, powerful rulers, pervasive bureaucracies, and vast disparities in wealth differed profoundly from the Archaic and Classical ages with their small, homogeneous, independent city-states. The Hellenistic world more closely resembled our own in its long-distance trade and communications, new institutions like libraries and universities, new kinds of scholarship and science, and sophisticated tastes in art and literature.

When he died suddenly in 323 B.C.E. at the age of thirty-two, Alexander had no plans for the succession. A half-century of chaos followed as the most ambitious and ruthless of his generals struggled to

succeed him. When the dust cleared, they had broken the empire into three major kingdoms, each ruled by a Macedonian dynasty: the Seleucid (sih-LOO-sid), Ptolemaic (tawl-uh-MAY-ik), and Antigonid (an-TIG-uh-nid) kingdoms (see Map 4.1). The Antigonids ruled the Macedonian homeland and tried with varying success to extend their control over southern Greece; the Ptolemies ruled Egypt; and the Seleucids inherited the majority of Alexander's conquests in Asia. A rough balance of power prevented any of the three from gaining the upper hand and enabled smaller states to survive by playing off the great powers.

The Seleucids, who ruled the bulk of Alexander's empire, faced the greatest challenges. The Indus Valley and Afghanistan soon split off, and over the course of the third and second centuries B.C.E., Iran fell to the Parthians (see Chapter 8). Thereafter Mesopotamia, Syria, and parts of Anatolia constituted the Seleucid core; the kings ruled from Antioch in Syria. Like the Persians before them, they governed many different ethnic groups organized under various political and social forms. In the farming villages, where most of the population resided, the Seleucids maintained an administration modeled on the Persian system. They also continued Alexander's policy of founding Greek-style cities to serve as administrative centers and attract colonists from Greece. The Seleucids desperately needed Greek soldiers, engineers, and administrators.

In Europe, the Antigonid dynasty ruled the Macedonian homeland and parts of northern Greece. Compact and ethnically homogeneous, the Antigonid kingdom experienced little of the hostility that the Seleucid and Ptolemaic rulers faced. Macedonian garrisons gave the Antigonids a toehold in central and southern Greece, and the shadow of Macedonian intervention always threatened the south. The southern states responded by joining confederations, such as the Achaean (uh-KEY-uhn) League in the Peloponnese, in which the member states maintained local autonomy but pooled resources and military power.

Athens and Sparta stood apart from these confederations. Never abandoning their myth of invincibility, the Spartans made a number of heroic but futile stands against Macedonian armies. Athens, now cherished for the artistic and literary accomplishments of the fifth century B.C.E., pursued a policy of neutrality. The city became a large museum, filled with the relics and memories of a glorious past, as well as a university town that attracted the children of the well-to-do from all over the Mediterranean and western Asia.

Egypt under the Ptolemies

The dynasty of the **Ptolemies** (TAWL-uh-meze) ruled Egypt and sometimes laid claim to Palestine. Since most Egyptians belonged to one ethnic group and lived in villages alongside the Nile, the Ptolemies took over much of the administrative structure of the pharaohs. The Ptolemies ruled from **Alexandria**. Memphis and Thebes, the capitals of ancient

Egypt, had been located upriver. Alexandria, situated near the mouth of the westernmost branch of the Nile, linked Egypt with the Mediterranean world. In the language of the Ptolemaic bureaucracy, Alexandria was technically "beside Egypt" rather than in it, as if to emphasize the gulf between rulers and subjects and the fact that it was not on the Nile River.

Like the Seleucids, the Ptolemies encouraged Greek immigration. In return for collaboration in the military or civil administration, the immigrants received land and a privileged position in the new society. But the Ptolemies did not plant Greek-style cities throughout the Egyptian countryside and made no effort to force the Greek language or customs on the Egyptian population. So separate was the ruling class from the subject population that only the last Ptolemy, Queen Cleopatra (r. 51–30 B.C.E.), bothered to learn the Egyptian language. The advent of new masters brought few changes to the Egyptian peasants. Vast revenues poured into the royal treasury from rents (the king owned most of the land), taxes, and royal monopolies on olive oil, salt, papyrus, and other key commodities. Nevertheless, from the early second century B.C.E., native insurrections in the countryside, though quickly stamped out by government forces and Greek and Hellenized settlers, indicate growing resentment of Greek exploitation and arrogance.

Alexandria, the greatest Hellenistic city with a population of nearly half a million, had at its heart the royal compound, containing the palace and administrative buildings. The magnificent Mausoleum of

Ptolemies The Macedonian dynasty descended from one of Alexander the Great's officers that ruled Egypt for three centuries (323–30 B.C.E.). From their magnificent capital at Alexandria on the Mediterranean coast, the Ptolemies largely took over the system created by Egyptian pharaohs to extract the wealth of the land, rewarding Greeks and Hellenized non-Greeks serving in the military and administration.

Alexandria City on the Mediterranean coast of Egypt founded by Alexander. It became the capital of the Hellenistic kingdom of the Ptolemies. It contained the famous Library and the Museum—a center for leading scientific and literary figures. Its merchants engaged in trade with areas bordering the Mediterranean and the Indian Ocean.

SECTION REVIEW

- The death of Alexander the Great and the breakup of his empire inaugurated the Hellenistic Age.

- Large kingdoms were ruled by Macedonian dynasties in which Greek culture was fused with local traditions.

- Most Greek city-states retained autonomy through alliances, but Sparta and Athens stood apart and lost power.

- Egypt under the Ptolemies was the most successful Hellenistic state, and its capital Alexandria became the greatest Hellenistic city.

Alexander enshrined Alexander's body, which the first Ptolemy had stolen during its return to Macedonia for burial. He had hoped that the luster of the great conqueror, who was declared to be a god, would give him legitimacy as a ruler.

The famed Library of Alexandria had several hundred thousand volumes. The Museum, or "House of the Muses" (divinities who presided over the arts and sciences), supported the work of the greatest poets, philosophers, doctors, and scientists. A great lighthouse—a multistory tower with a fiery beacon visible at a distance of 30 miles (48 kilometers)—guided seafarers to two harbors serving the commerce of the Mediterranean, the Red Sea, and the Indian Ocean.

Alexandrian Greeks enjoyed citizenship in a polis, complete with Assembly, Council, and officials overseeing local affairs. They took advantage of Greek-style amenities and institutions: public baths and shaded arcades, theaters featuring revivals of ancient plays, and concert halls for musical performances and demonstrations of oratory. Young men of the privileged elite took classes at gymnasiums where athletics and fitness combined with music and literature in the curriculum. Jews had their own civic corporation, officials, and courts and predominated in two of the five main residential districts. The sights, sounds, and smells of Syria, Anatolia, and the Egyptian countryside lent distinctiveness to other quarters.

Hellenistic Societies

In all the Hellenistic states, ambitious members of the indigenous populations learned the Greek language and adopted elements of the Greek lifestyle, because doing so helped them become part of a privileged and wealthy ruling class. Language and customs more than physical traits made a person a Greek. The Hellenistic Age saw a spontaneous synthesis of Greek and indigenous ways. Egyptians migrated to Alexandria, and Greeks and Egyptians intermarried in the villages. Greeks living amid the monuments and descendants of the ancient civilizations of Egypt and western Asia learned the mathematical and astronomical wisdom of Mesopotamia, the mortuary rituals of Egypt, and the attractions of foreign religions. With little official planning or blessing and stemming for the most part from the day-to-day experiences of ordinary people, a great multicultural experiment unfolded as Greek and Middle Eastern cultural traits clashed and merged.

Conclusion

Greece and Iran represent two ways in which societies with shared Indo-European linguistic and religious roots adapted to different geographical environments and indigenous cultures. Although scholars can easily trace resemblances among gods, customs, and philosophical outlooks in these areas, the peoples themselves had no sense of kinship with one another. Only briefly, under Alexander the Great, did they come into direct contact in meaningful ways, and the resulting Hellenistic culture touched all three regions.

While some technologies, such as coinage, took hold in all areas and trade flourished, both overland and across the Mediterranean Sea, local circumstances dictated political and social formations. The ancient cultural centers of Egypt and Mesopotamia influenced the Greeks and the Persians.

In comparing the histories of these regions, the question arises of the degree to which different states and societies follow similar paths because of shared heritages, as opposed to responding similarly but independently to analogous challenges. We will explore this subject in the next chapter through a comparison of Rome and China under the Han dynasty.

CHAPTER REVIEW

 Download the MP3 audio file of the Chapter Review to listen to on the go.

How did the Persian Empire rise from its Iranian homeland and spread to encompass diverse cultures? (page 87)

The Medes, who were the first Iranians to build a complex political order, helped destroy the Assyrian Empire. Cyrus then united the Persians and overthrew the Medes, prompting the two similar cultures to blend. Expansion into Mesopotamia, Syria, and Anatolia connected the Persian Empire with older cultural and commercial networks. Under Darius I, the empire reached its fullest extent and basic governmental structure: provinces governed by satraps, tribute money funneled to the center, and a decentralized legal system. An extensive road and post system connected the imperial center with the periphery.

How did Greek civilization evolve and spread beyond its original territories? (page 92)

A rugged geography inhibiting overland travel turned the Greeks to the sea. The focus of this Greek civilization was the polis, whose citizens participated in government and defended it as hoplites. Population pressures spurred overseas colonization, which spread Greek culture throughout the Mediterranean world. This period saw the emergence of new forms of literary and intellectual endeavor, such as history and philosophical inquiry.

How did the Persian Wars lead into the Hellenistic Age that followed? (page 98)

Athens, Sparta, and their allies repulsed Persian invasions on land and at sea. Victory left Athens a naval power with an overseas empire and sufficient wealth from tribute and trade to finance temples on the Acropolis and other cultural achievements in drama and philosophy. Rivalry between Sparta and Athens exploded into the Peloponnesian War, which shattered Athens and weakened the other city-states. Exploiting this weakness, Persia recovered old losses but encountered Macedonian expansion and ultimate defeat by Alexander the Great.

How did a cultural synthesis develop during the Hellenistic Age? (page 105)

The death of Alexander the Great ushered in the Hellenistic Age. From his empire his generals carved kingdoms for themselves, founding Macedonian dynasties that presided over an international Greek culture. The Seleucids ruled the largest kingdom, founding Greek-style cities but ruling in the Persian manner. Both they and the Ptolemies encouraged Greek immigration, but in Egypt Greeks remained a class apart and had little to do with native Egyptians. The Antigonids ruled Macedonia, but the southern and central Greek cities resisted them through alliances. Sparta and Athens remained apart, both losing power in the region. Alexandria became the major Hellenistic city, a showcase of the cultural synthesis that marked the age.

Key Terms

Cyrus (p. 88)
Darius I (p. 89)
satrap (p. 89)
Persepolis (p. 90)
Zoroastrianism (p. 91)
polis (p. 93)
hoplite (p. 93)
tyrant (p. 94)
democracy (p. 94)
sacrifice (p. 95)
Herodotus (p. 96)
Pericles (p. 98)
Persian Wars (p. 99)
trireme (p. 100)
Socrates (p. 101)
Peloponnesian War (p. 102)
Alexander (p. 105)
Hellenistic Age (p. 105)
Ptolemies (p. 107)
Alexandria (p. 107)

Web Resources

Pronunciation Guide

Interactive Map

• MAP 4.1 Hellenistic Civilization

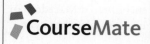 Visit the CourseMate website at www.cengagebrain.com for additional study tools and review materials for this chapter.

Primary Sources

• Gathas

• A Lyric Poem Laments an AbsentLover

Answer to the History in Focus Question

See photo on page 97, "The Acropolis at Athens."

India and Southeast Asia

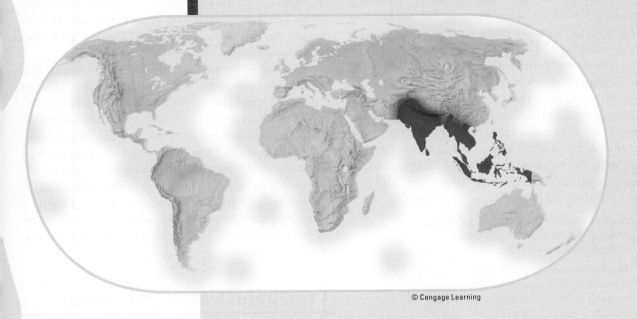

© Cengage Learning

CHAPTER PREVIEW

The Indus Valley Civilization
What does material evidence tell us about the Indus Valley civilization and the most likely reason for its collapse?

Foundations of Indian Civilization
What historical forces led to the development of complex social groupings in ancient India?

Indian Imperial Expansion and Collapse
In the face of powerful forces that tended to keep India fragmented, how did the Mauryan Empire of the fourth to second centuries B.C.E. and the Gupta Empire of the fourth to sixth centuries C.E. succeed in unifying much of India?

Southeast Asia, 50–1025 C.E.
How did the geography of Southeast Asia contribute to its commerce and to the influence of Hinduism and Buddhism?

Conclusion

ENVIRONMENT AND TECHNOLOGY:
Indian Mathematics

Visit the CourseMate website at **www.cengagebrain.com** for additional study tools and review materials for this chapter.

In the Bhagavad-Gita (BUH-guh-vahd GEE-tuh), the most renowned Indian sacred text, the legendary warrior Arjuna (AHR-joo-nuh) rides out in his chariot to the open space between two armies preparing for battle. Torn between his social duty to fight for his family's claim to the throne and his conscience, which balks at the prospect of killing relatives, friends, and former teachers in the enemy camp, Arjuna slumps down in his chariot and refuses to fight. But his driver, the god Krishna (KRISH-nuh) in disguise, persuades him, in a carefully structured dialogue, both of the necessity to fulfill his duty as a warrior and of the proper frame of mind for performing these acts. In the climactic moment of the dialogue Krishna endows Arjuna with a "divine eye" and permits him to see the true appearance of God:

It was a multiform, wondrous vision,
with countless mouths and eyes
and celestial ornaments,

Everywhere was boundless divinity
containing all astonishing things,
wearing divine garlands and garments,
anointed with divine perfume.

If the light of a thousand suns
were to rise in the sky at once,
it would be like the light
of that great spirit.

Arjuna saw all the universe
in its many ways and parts,
standing as one in the body
of the god of gods.[1]

In all of world literature, this is one of the most compelling attempts to depict the nature of deity. Graphic images emphasize the vastness, diversity, and multiplicity of the god, but in the end we learn that Krishna is the organizing principle behind all creation, that behind diversity and multiplicity lies a higher unity.

This is an apt metaphor for Indian civilization. The enormous variety of the Indian landscape is mirrored in the patchwork of ethnic and linguistic groups that occupy it, the political fragmentation that has marked most of Indian history, the elaborate hierarchy of social groups into which the Indian population is divided, and the thousands of deities who are worshiped at innumerable holy places that dot the subcontinent. Yet, in the end, one can speak of an Indian civilization united by shared views and values.

This chapter surveys the history of South and Southeast Asia from approximately 1500 B.C.E. to 1025 C.E., highlighting the evolution of defining features of Indian civilization. Considerable attention is given to Indian religious conceptions, due both to religion's profound role in shaping Indian society and the sources of information available to historians. For reasons that will be explained below, writing came late to India, and ancient Indians did not develop a historical consciousness like other peoples of antiquity and took little interest in recording specific historical events.

The Indus Valley Civilization

What does material evidence tell us about the Indus Valley civilization and the most likely reason for its collapse?

Civilization developed almost as early in South Asia as in Mesopotamia and Egypt. Just as each Middle Eastern civilization centered on a great river valley, so civilization in the Indian subcontinent originated on the fertile floodplain of the Indus River, where settled farming created the agricultural surplus essential to urbanized society.

Natural Environment A plain of more than 1 million acres (400,000 hectares) stretches between the mountains of western Pakistan and the Thar Desert to the east in Sind, the central portion of the Indus Valley (see Map 5.1). Silt carried downstream and deposited on the land by the Indus River over many centuries has elevated the riverbed and its banks above the level of the plain. Twice a year, the river overflows and inundates surrounding land as far as 10 miles (16 kilometers) distant. Snow-

---

1. From Bhagavad-Gita, translated by Barbara Stoler Miller, translation copyright © 1986 by Barbara Stoler Miller. Used by permission of Bantam Books, a division of Random House, Inc.

Chronology

India		Southeast Asia
2500 B.C.E.	2600 B.C.E. Beginnings of Indus Valley civilization	
2000 B.C.E.	1900 B.C.E. End of Indus Valley civilization	
1500 B.C.E.	ca. 1500 B.C.E. Indo-Europeans in northwest India	ca. 1600 B.C.E. Beginnings of migrations from mainland Southeast Asia to islands in the Indian and Pacific Oceans
1000 B.C.E.	ca. 1000 B.C.E. Indo-Europeans settle the Ganges Plain	
500 B.C.E.	ca. 500 B.C.E. Beginning of Buddhism and Jainism	
300 B.C.E.	300 B.C.E. Tamil kingdoms	
	324 B.C.E. Maurya Empire founded	
1 C.E.		ca. 50–560 C.E. Funan dominates southern Indochina and the Isthmus of Kra
300 C.E.	320 C.E. Gupta Empire begins	
500 C.E.		ca. 500 C.E. Trade route develops through the Straits of Malacca
600 C.E.	606–647 C.E. Reign of Harsha Vardhana	683 C.E. Rise of Srivijaya in Sumatra
700 C.E.		770–825 C.E. Construction of Borobodur in Java
1000 C.E.		1025 C.E. Decline of Srivijaya

melt from the Pamir (pah-MEER) and Himalaya Mountains feeds the flood in March and April. In August, the monsoons bring rains from the southwest that feed a second flood. Though extremely dry for the rest of the year, Sind's floods make two crops a year possible. In ancient times, the Hakra (HAK-ruh) River (sometimes referred to as the Saraswati), which has since dried up, ran parallel to the Indus about 25 miles (40 kilometers) to the east and supplied water to a second cultivable area.

Adjacent regions shared distinctive cultural traits with this core area. In Punjab (literally "five waters"), to the northeast, five rivers converge to feed the main stream of the Indus. Closer to the northern mountains, the Punjab receives more rainfall but less floodwater than Sind. Culturally similar settlements extend from the Punjab as far east as Delhi (DEL-ee) in northwest India. Settlement also extended through the Indus delta in southern Sind down into India's hook-shaped Kathiawar (kah-tee-h-WAHR) Peninsula, an area of alluvial plains and coastal marshes. The Indus Valley civilization, as scholars labeled this area of cultural homogeneity when they first discovered it eighty years ago, covered an area roughly equivalent to modern France.

Material Culture

Although archaeologists have located several hundred communities that flourished from approximately 2600 to 1900 B.C.E., the remains of two urban sites, known by the modern names **Harappa** and **Mohenjo-Daro** (moe-hen-joe-DAHR-oh), best typify the Indus Valley civilization. Unfortunately, the high water table at these sites makes excavation of the earliest levels of settlement nearly impossible.

Scholars once believed that the people who created this civilization spoke Dravidian (druh-VID-ee-uhn) languages related to those spoken today in

Harappa Site of one of the great cities of the Indus Valley civilization of the third millennium B.C.E. It was located on the northwest frontier of the zone of cultivation (in modern Pakistan) and may have been a center for the acquisition of raw materials, such as metals and precious stones, from Afghanistan and Iran.

Mohenjo-Daro Largest of the cities of the Indus Valley civilization. It was centrally located in the extensive floodplain of the Indus River in contemporary Pakistan. Little is known about the political institutions of Indus Valley communities, but the large scale of construction at Mohenjo-Daro, the orderly grid of streets, and the standardization of building materials are evidence of central planning.

southern India. Invaders from the northwest speaking Indo-European languages, they thought, conquered these people around 1500 B.C.E., causing some of them to migrate to the southeast. Skeletal evidence, however, indicates that the population of the Indus Valley has remained stable from ancient times to the present. Settled agriculture in this region seems to date back to at least 5000 B.C.E.

The writing system of the Indus Valley people contained more than four hundred signs to represent syllables and words. Archaeologists have recovered thousands of inscribed seal stones and copper tablets. The inscriptions are so brief, however, that no one has yet deciphered them, though some scholars believe they represent an early Dravidian language.

Harappa, 3.5 miles (5.6 kilometers) in circumference, may have housed a population of 35,000, and Mohenjo-Daro several times that. These cities show marked similarities in planning and construction: high, thick, encircling walls of brick; streets laid out in a rectangular grid; and covered drainpipes to carry away waste. The consistent width of streets and length of city blocks, and the uniformity of the mud bricks used in construction, suggest a strong central authority, located possibly in the citadel—an elevated, enclosed compound containing large buildings. Scholars think the well-ventilated structures near the citadel stored grain for local use and for export. The presence of barracks may point to some regimentation of skilled artisans.

Though it is presumed that these urban centers controlled the surrounding farmlands, different centers may have served different functions, which might account for their locations. Mohenjo-Daro seems to dominate the great floodplain of the Indus. Harappa, which is nearly 500 miles (800 kilometers) to the north, sits in the zone where farmlands give way to pasturelands. No settlements have been found west of Harappa, which may have served as a gateway for copper, tin, precious stones, and other resources coming from the northwest. Coastal towns to the south engaged in seaborne trade with Sumer and lands around the Persian Gulf, as well as in fishing and gathering highly prized seashells. Although published accounts of the Indus Valley civilization tend to treat Mohenjo-Daro and Harappa, the most extensively excavated sites, as the norm, most people surely

Man from Mohenjo-Daro, ca. 2600–1900 B.C.E. This statue of a seated man wearing a cloak and headband was carved from a soft stone called steatite. It is often called the "Priest-King" because some scholars believe it may represent someone with religious and secular authority, but the true identity and status of this person are unknown.   Scala/ Art Resource, NY

 History in Focus *Besides the cloak and headband, do you see any other clues to this person's status? What does his facial expression tell you? Find the answer online.*

lived in smaller settlements, which exhibit the same artifacts and the same standardization of styles and shapes as the large cities.

Metal appears more frequently in Indus Valley sites than in Mesopotamia or Egypt. Tools and other useful objects outweigh in importance the decorative objects—jewelry and the like—so often found in those other regions. Whereas metal goods were largely the possessions of elite groups in the Middle East, in the Indus Valley they belonged to a broad cross-section of the population.

Technologically, the Indus Valley people showed skill in irrigation, used the potter's wheel, and fired

- As in Mesopotamia and Egypt, and roughly in the same time period, the wide, fertile Indus Valley supported a large urban civilization.
- Cities like Harappa and Mohenjo-Daro and their artifacts display uniformity of planning and construction and standardization of styles and shapes.
- The Indus Valley civilization developed sophisticated technologies, including a still-undeciphered writing system.
- Cities exchanged goods with each other and maintained extensive trade contacts with other ancient civilizations.
- The Indus Valley civilization collapsed when the cities were abandoned, most likely because of "systems failure."

bricks in kilns for use in the foundations of large public buildings (sun-dried bricks exposed to floodwaters would have dissolved quickly). Smiths worked with various metals—gold, silver, copper, and tin. The varying ratios of tin to copper in their bronze objects suggest awareness of the hardness of different mixtures. They used less tin, a relatively scarce metal, in objects that did not require maximum hardness, like knives, and more tin in things like axes that had to be harder.

Archaeological finds point to widespread trading contacts. Mountain passes through the northwest granted access to the valuable resources of eastern Iran and Afghanistan, as well as to ore deposits in western India. These resources included metals (such as copper and tin), precious stones (lapis lazuli, jade, and turquoise), building stone, and timber. Rivers provided thoroughfares for transporting goods within the zone of Indus Valley culture.

Inhabitants of the Indus Valley and of Mesopotamia obtained raw materials from some of the same sources. The discovery of Indus Valley seal stones in the Tigris-Euphrates Valley indicates that merchants from the former region may have acted as middlemen in long-distance trade, obtaining raw materials from the northwest and shipping them to the Persian Gulf.

We know little about the political, social, economic, and religious structures of Indus Valley society. Efforts to link artifacts and images to cultural features characteristic of later periods of Indian history, including sociopolitical institutions (a system of hereditary occupational groups, the predominant role of priests), architectural forms (bathing tanks like those later found in Hindu temples, private interior courtyards in houses), and religious beliefs and practices (depictions of gods and sacred animals on the seal stones, a cult of the mother-goddess), remain speculative. Further knowledge on these matters awaits additional archaeological finds and deciphering of the Indus Valley script.

Transformation of the Indus Valley Civilization

The Indus Valley cities were abandoned sometime after 1900 B.C.E. Archaeologists once thought that invaders destroyed them, but they now believe this civilization suffered "systems failure"—a breakdown of the fragile interrelationship of political, social, and economic systems that sustained order and prosperity. The precipitating cause may have been one or more natural disasters, such as an earthquake or massive flooding. Gradual ecological changes may also have played a role as the Hakra river system dried up and salinization (an increase in the amount of plant-inhibiting salt in the soil) and erosion increased.

Towns left dry by a change of riverbed, seaports removed from the coast by silt deposited in deltas, and regions suffering loss of fertile soil would have necessitated the relocation of populations and a change in the livelihood of those who remained. The causes, patterns, and pace of change probably varied, with urbanization persisting longer in some regions than in others. The urban centers eventually succumbed, however, and village-based farming and herding took their place. As the interaction between regions lessened, regional variation replaced the standardization of technology and style of the previous era.

Historians can do little more than speculate about the causes behind the changes and the experiences of the people who lived in the Indus Valley around 1900 B.C.E. Two tendencies bear remembering, however. In most cases like this, the majority of the population adjusts to the new circumstances. But members of the political and social elite, who depend on urban centers and complex political and economic structures, lose the source of their authority and merge with the population as a whole.

Foundations of Indian Civilization

What historical forces led to the development of complex social groupings in ancient India?

India is called a *subcontinent* because it is a large—roughly 2,000 miles (3,200 kilometers) in both length and breadth—and physically isolated landmass within the continent of Asia. The Himalayas (him-uh-LAY-uhs), the world's highest mountains, form a barrier to the north; the Indian Ocean bounds it on the east, south, and west (see Map 5.1). The one frontier easily accessible to invaders and migrating peoples lies to the northwest. But people using this corridor must cross over the mountain barrier of the Hindu Kush in Afghanistan and the Thar (tahr) Desert east of the Indus River.

The Indian Subcontinent

This region divides into three topographical zones. The mountainous northern zone takes in the heavily forested foothills and high meadows on the edge of the Hindu Kush and Himalaya ranges. Next come the great basins of the Indus and Ganges Rivers. Originating in the Himalayas, these rivers flood annually, leaving layers of silt that over time have created large fertile plains. The Vindhya range and the Deccan (de-KAN), an arid, rocky plateau reminiscent of the American Southwest, separate northern India from the third zone, the peninsula proper. The Malabar Coast in the west, the Coromandel Coast in the east with its web of rivers descending from the Deccan, the flatlands of Tamil Nadu on the southern tip of the peninsula, and the island of Sri Lanka often have followed paths of political and cultural development separate from those of northern India.

The mountainous northern rim shelters the subcontinent from cold Arctic winds and gives it a subtropical climate. The **monsoon** (seasonal wind) comes annually when the Indian Ocean lags behind the Asian landmass in heating and cooling with the changing seasons. The temperature difference between water and land acts like a bellows, producing a great wind over the ocean. The southwest monsoon begins in June off the coast of East Africa, picks up

moisture from the Indian Ocean, and delivers heavy precipitation to the Ganges Basin and the rain-forest belt on India's western coast. The moist, flat Ganges Delta (modern Bengal) favors rice production. Elsewhere, wheat, barley, and millet predominate. Indus Valley farmers, in contrast, see little precipitation and therefore rely on extensive irrigation.

Indian Ocean mariners learned to ride the monsoon winds across open waters from northeast to southwest in January and to make the return voyage in July. Ships ventured across the Arabian Sea to the Persian Gulf, the southern coast of Arabia, and East Africa, and east across the Bay of Bengal to Indochina and Indonesia (see Chapter 8).

The Vedic Age, 1500–500 B.C.E.

Many features of later Indian civilization surely date back to the Indus Valley civilization of the third and early second millennia B.C.E. Since the writing from that period remains undeciphered, the earliest textual knowledge about Indian roots comes from the period 1500 to 500 B.C.E., called the "Vedic Age" after religious texts known as the **Vedas**. While most historians believe that Indo-European speaking nomads migrated into northwest India at the beginning of the period, others argue for a much earlier Indo-European presence in this region deriving from the spread of agriculture (see Chapter 2).

After the collapse of the Indus Valley civilization, the central authority presumed to have organized large-scale irrigation disappeared. The region became home to bands of Vedic-speaking cattle herders who

monsoon Seasonal winds in the Indian Ocean caused by the differences in temperature between the rapidly heating and cooling landmasses of Africa and Asia and the slowly changing ocean waters. These strong and predictable winds have long been ridden across the open sea by sailors, and the large amounts of rainfall that they deposit on parts of India, Southeast Asia, and China allow for the cultivation of several crops a year.

Vedas Early Indian sacred "knowledge"—the literal meaning of the term—long preserved and communicated orally by Brahmin priests and eventually written down. These religious texts, including the thousand poetic hymns to various deities contained in the Rig Veda, are our main source of information about the Vedic period (ca. 1500–500 B.C.E.).

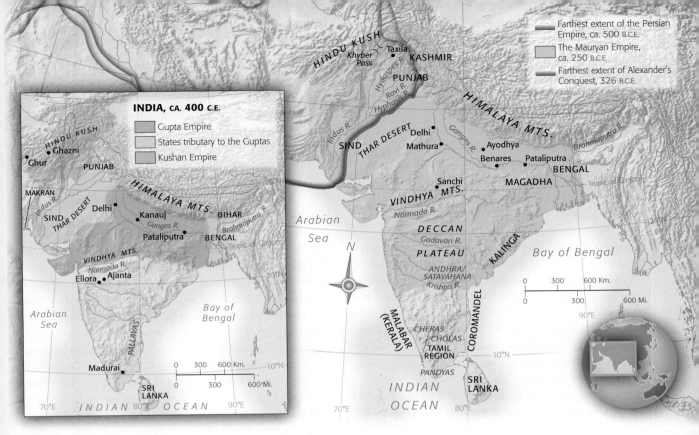

Map 5.1 **Ancient India** Mountains and ocean largely separate the Indian subcontinent from the rest of Asia. Migrations and invasions usually came through the Khyber Pass in the northwest. Peoples speaking Indo-European languages migrated into the broad valleys of the Indus and Ganges Rivers in the north. Dravidian-speaking peoples remained the dominant population in the south. The diversity of the Indian landscape, the multiplicity of ethnic groups, and the primary identification of people with their class and caste lie behind the division into many small states that has characterized much of Indian political history. © Cengage Learning

 Interactive Map

also engaged in farming. As with other Indo-European peoples—Celts, Greeks, Iranians, Romans—patriarchal traditions made the father dominant in the family just as the king ruled the group as a whole. Warriors boasted of their martial skill and courage, relished combat, feasted on beef, and filled their leisure time with chariot racing and gambling.

After 1000 B.C.E., some groups pushed eastward into the Ganges Plain. Iron tools—harder than bronze and able to hold a sharper edge—allowed settlers to fell trees and work the newly cleared land with ox-drawn plows. The fertile plain, watered by the annual monsoon, sustained two or three crops a year. As in Greece at roughly the same time, the use of iron tools must have led to a population increase.

Stories about this era, written down much later but preserved by oral recitation, speak of rivalry and warfare between two peoples: the Aryas, speakers of Vedic Sanskrit and practitioners of the sacrificial religion prescribed in the Vedas, and the Dasas, indigenous speakers of Dravidian languages, whose religion, it is pointedly noted in the Vedas, did not involve sacrifice to or worship of the Vedic gods. Some scholars argue that the real process by which Arya groups became dominant in the north involved the absorption of some Dasas into Arya populations and a merging of elites from both groups. For the most part, however, Aryas pushed the Dasas south into central and southern India, where their descendants still live. Indo-European languages descended from those of the Aryas predominate in northern India today, while Dravidian languages prevail in the south.

The cultural and religious differences between the Aryas and the indigenous peoples contributed to sharp social divisions. A system of *varnas*, literally "colors" but usually translated as "castes," indicated something akin to classes. Individuals belonged by birth to one of four varnas: *Brahmins*, the group comprising priests and scholars; *Kshatriyas* (kshuh-TREE-yuhs), warriors and the king; *Vaishyas* (VIESH-yuhs), all other Aryas; and *Shudras* (SHOOD-ras), non-Aryas who were servants and slaves of the other three varnas. The designation *Shudra* originally may have signified Dasa. Indeed, the term *dasa* came to mean "slave." Eventually a fifth group emerged: the Untouchables. Excluded from the caste system and shunned by the other castes, they worked in demeaning or polluting trades such as tanning, which involved touching dead animals, and sweeping away ashes after cremations.

According to one creation myth, a primordial man named Purusha allowed himself to be sacrificed. From his mouth sprang the varna of Brahmin priests. From his arms came the Kshatriya warriors; from his thighs the Vaishya merchants, artisans, and peasants; and from his feet the Shudra workers.

Within the broad varna divisions, the population further divided into numerous smaller groups, called *jatis*, or castes. Each jati had its proper occupation, duties, and rituals. Members of a given jati lived and married within the group and ate only with fellow jati members. Elaborate rules governed interactions between groups. Members of higher-status groups feared pollution from contacting lower-caste individuals and had to undergo rituals of purification to remove any taint.

The caste system became connected to a belief in reincarnation. Brahmin priests taught that every living creature had an immortal essence: the *atman*, or "self." Separated from the body at death, the atman returned in the body of an insect, an animal, or a human depending on the **karma**, or deeds, of the atman in its previous incarnations. People of exemplary goodness returned in a higher caste. Those who misbehaved fell to a lower caste or even a lower life form. The underlying message ran: You are where you deserve to be, and the only way to improve your lot in the next incarnation is to accept your current station and its attendant duties.

Many of the Vedic deities, mostly male, were associated with the heavens. Indra, like Zeus a god of war and master of the thunderbolt, commanded the greatest devotion and represented the chieftains who led their warriors into battle. Agni, the fire-god, consumed the sacrifice and bridged the spheres of gods and humans. Vedic religion centered on sacrifice, the dedication to a god of a valued possession, often a living creature. The offerings invigorated the gods and thereby sustained their creative powers and promoted stability in the world.

Brahmin priests alone knew the rituals and prayers. The Rig Veda, a collection of more than a thousand poetic hymns to various deities, and the Brahmanas, detailed prose descriptions and explanations of ritual procedures, all in the Sanskrit language of the Arya upper classes, passed orally from one generation of priests to the next. The Brahmins may have opposed the introduction of writing. This would explain why this technology did not spread in India until the Gupta period (320–550 C.E.). The priests' "knowledge" (the term *veda* means just that) earned them rewards for officiating at sacrifices and gave them social and political power as the intermediaries between gods and humans.

Primary Source: The Rig Veda Read how Indra, "the thunder-wielder," slew Vritra, "firstborn of dragons," and how Purusha created the universe through an act of ritual sacrifice.

varna/jati Two categories of social identity of great importance in Indian history. *Varna* are the four major social divisions: the *Brahmin* priest class, the *Kshatriya* warrior/administrator class, the *Vaishya* merchant/farmer class, and the *Shudra* laborer class. Within the system *varna* are many jati, regional groups of people who have a common occupational sphere, and who marry, eat, and generally interact with other members of their group.

karma In Indian tradition, the residue of deeds performed in past and present lives that adheres to a "spirit" and determines what form it will assume in its next life cycle. The doctrines of karma and reincarnation were used by the elite in ancient India to encourage people to accept their social position and do their duty.

As elsewhere in the ancient world, the lives of Indian women left few traces. Limited evidence indicates that in the Vedic period women studied sacred lore, composed religious hymns, and participated in sacrifices. They could own property and usually did not marry until their middle or late teens. A number of strong and resourceful women appear in the Mahabharata epic (explained below). In the Ramayana epic, on the other hand, we see the familiar motif of the hero Rama rescuing his wife Sita after she has been abducted.

The internal divisions of Indian society, the complex hierarchy of groups, and the claims of some to superior virtue and purity provided each individual with a clear identity and role and offered the benefits of group solidarity and support. Sometimes groups even upgraded their status within the system, which was not entirely static and provided mechanisms for releasing social tensions. Many of these features persisted into modern times.

Challenges to the Old Order: Jainism and Buddhism

After 700 B.C.E., reactions against Brahmin power and privilege emerged. People who objected to the rigid social hierarchy could always retreat to the forest that covered much of ancient India. Never far away, these wild places symbolized freedom from societal constraints. Individuals who wandered in the forest sometimes attracted followers. Questioning priestly power and the necessity of sacrifices, they offered alternate paths to salvation: individual pursuit of insight into the nature of the self and the universe through physical and mental discipline (*yoga*), which included dietary restrictions and meditation. They taught that by distancing oneself from desire for the things of this world, one could achieve *moksha*, or liberation, "a deep, dreamless sleep" that released one from endless reincarnations through union with the divine force of the universe. The Upanishads, which continue the explanations of ritual begun in the Brahmanas, also reflect this questioning of Vedic ritualism.

Jainism (JINE-iz-uhm) and Buddhism challenged not only Vedic ritualism but also the authority of the Vedic priests themselves. Jainism took its name from the teacher Mahavira (540–468 B.C.E.), known to his followers as Jina, "the Conqueror." Mahavira respected

the life force so much that he commanded strict nonviolence. Jains wore masks to avoid inadvertently inhaling small insects and brushed off the seat before sitting down. Some practiced extreme asceticism by practicing nudity and eventually starving themselves to death. Less zealous Jains engaged in commerce in cities, since agricultural work inevitably involved killing.

Buddhism, a far more successful movement, stemmed from the life of Siddhartha Gautama (563–483 B.C.E.), known as the **Buddha**, "the Enlightened One," about whom myriad legends have arisen. From a Kshatriya family in what is now Nepal, he enjoyed the princely lifestyle that was his birthright until he experienced a change of heart and gave up family and privilege to become a wandering ascetic. After six years, he decided that asceticism was no more likely to produce spiritual insight than his earlier luxurious life, so he opted for a "Middle Path." Sitting under a tree in a deer park near Benares on the Ganges River, he gained a sudden and profound insight, which he set forth as "Four Noble Truths": (1) life is suffering, (2) suffering arises from desire, (3) the solution to suffering lies in curbing desire, and (4) desire can be curbed if a person follows the "Eightfold Path" of right views, aspirations, speech, conduct, livelihood, effort, mindfulness, and meditation. Rising up, the Buddha preached his First Sermon, a central text of Buddhism, and set into motion the "Wheel of the Law." He soon attracted followers, some of whom took vows of celibacy, nonviolence, and poverty.

At first, Buddhism centered on the individual. It denied the usefulness of the gods to a person seeking enlightenment. What mattered was living moderately to minimize desire and suffering, and searching for

moksha The Hindu concept of the spirit's "liberation" from the endless cycle of rebirths. There are various avenues—such as physical discipline, meditation, and acts of devotion to the gods—by which the spirit can distance itself from desire for the things of this world and be merged with the divine force that animates the universe.

Buddha (563–483 B.C.E.) An Indian prince named Siddhartha Gautama, who renounced his wealth and social position. After becoming "enlightened" (the meaning of *Buddha*) he enunciated the principles of Buddhism. This doctrine evolved and spread throughout India and to Southeast, East, and Central Asia.

Carved Stone Gateway Leading to the Great Stupa at Sanchi Pilgrims traveled long distances to visit stupas, mounds containing relics of the Buddha. The complex at Sanchi, in central India, was begun by Ashoka in the third century B.C.E., though the gates probably date to the first century C.E. This relief shows a royal procession bringing the remains of the Buddha to the city of Kushina-gara.

Dinodia Photo Library

spiritual truth through self-discipline and meditation. One should seek *nirvana*, literally "snuffing out the flame," a release from the cycle of reincarnations and enjoyment of perpetual tranquility. Whereas the Upanishadic tradition emphasized the eternal survival of the atman, the "self" or nonmaterial essence of the individual, Buddhism regarded the individual as a composite of features such as breath and wind, but without a soul.

At his death, Buddha left no final instructions, urging his disciples to "be their own lamp." His followers spread his philosophy throughout India and into Central, Southeast, and East Asia. Its wide appeal subverted its individualistic and atheistic underpinnings. Buddhist monasteries with hierarchies of monks and nuns came into being. Worshipers erected *stupas* (large earthen mounds symbolizing the universe) over relics of the cremated founder and other holy men and walked around them in a clockwise direction. Believers began to worship the Buddha himself as a god. Many Buddhists also revered *bodhisattvas* (boe-dih-SUT-vuhs), men and women who had achieved enlightenment and were on the threshold of

nirvana but chose rebirth into mortal bodies to help others along the path to salvation.

Early representations show the Buddha only indirectly, through symbols such as his footprints, begging bowl, or the tree under which he achieved enlightenment, as if to emphasize his achievement of a state of nonexistence. From the second century C.E., however, statues of the Buddha and bodhisattvas proliferated, sculpted in styles that showed the influence of the Greek settlements established in Bactria (northern Afghanistan) by Alexander the Great. A schism emerged within Buddhism. Devotees of **Mahayana** (mah-huh-YAH-nuh) ("Great Vehicle") **Buddhism** embraced the popular new features. Practitioners of **Theravada** (there-eh-VAH-duh) ("Teachings of the Elders") **Buddhism** followed most of the original teachings of the founder.

Primary Source: Setting in Motion the Wheels of Law Siddartha's first sermon contains the core teaching of Buddhism: to escape, by following the Middle Path, the suffering caused by desire.

Mahayana Buddhism "Great Vehicle" branch of Buddhism followed in China, Japan, and Central Asia. The focus is on reverence for Buddha and for bodhisattvas, enlightened persons who have postponed nirvana to help others attain enlightenment.

Theravada Buddhism "Way of the Elders" branch of Buddhism followed in Sri Lanka and much of Southeast Asia. Theravada remains close to the original principles set forth by the Buddha; it downplays the importance of gods and emphasizes austerity and the individual's search for enlightenment.

The Rise of Hinduism

Challenged by the new religious movements, Vedic religion evolved by the fourth century C.E. into **Hinduism**, the dominant religion in South Asia today. (The term *Hinduism* originated with Islamic invaders in the eleventh century C.E. as a label for the diverse practices they encountered: "what the Indians do.") Though based on the Vedic religion of northern India, Hinduism incorporated Dravidian cultural elements from the south, such as intense devotion to a deity and the prominence of goddesses.

Brahmin priests survived the transition with their social status and influence intact, but sacrifice lost its central place. Opportunities for individual worshipers to have direct contact with deities increased. Hinduism emphasized the worshiper's personal devotion to a particular deity, usually Vishnu or Shiva, or Devi ("the Goddess"). The goddess is of Dravidian origin, and her incorporation into the cult shows how Arya and indigenous cultures fused to form Hindu civilization. Vishnu, who has a clear Aryan pedigree, remains more popular in northern India, and Shiva is dominant in the south. These deities appear in many guises, bear various cult names, and give rise to a complex symbolism of stories, companion animals, birds, and objects.

Vishnu, the preserver, benevolently helps his devotees in time of need. Hindus believe that whenever demonic forces threaten the cosmic order, an *avatara*, or incarnation of Vishnu, appears on earth. His avatars include the legendary hero Rama, the cowherd god Krishna, and the Buddha (a clear attempt to co-opt the rival religion's founder). Shiva, who lives in ascetic isolation on Mount Kailasa in the Himalayas, represents a cyclical process of creation and destruction that is symbolized in statues showing him dancing. Devi can manifest herself as a full-bodied mother goddess representing fertility and procreation, as Shiva's loving wife, Parvati, or as the frightening deity who, under the name Kali or Durga, lets loose violence and destruction.

The multiplicity of gods (330 million according to one tradition), sects, and local practices within Hinduism reflects the ethnic, linguistic, and cultural diversity of India. Yet within this variety, there is unity. A worshiper's devotion to one god or goddess does not entail denial of the other main deities or the

host of lesser divinities and spirits. Ultimately, all are manifestations of a single divine force pervading the universe. This underlying unity appears in the way various manifestations of Devi represent different female potentials, in composite statues—half Shiva, half Vishnu—signifying complementary aspects of one cosmic principle.

Hindus may approach god and obtain divine favor through special knowledge of sacred truths, mental and physical discipline, or extraordinary devotion to the deity. Worship centers on temples, which range from humble shrines to richly decorated stone edifices built under royal patronage. Statues beckon the deity to take up temporary residence within the image and be available to eager worshipers. *Puja*, or service to the deity, can include bathing, clothing, or feeding the statue. Glimpsing the divine image conveys potent blessings.

Sacred places where a worshiper can directly sense and benefit from divine power dot the Indian subcontinent. Mystery and sanctity surround certain mountains, caves, trees, plants, and rocks. *Tirthayatra*, the term for a pilgrimage site, means "journey to a river crossing," illustrating the association of Hindu sacred

Hinduism A general term for a wide variety of beliefs and ritual practices that have developed in the Indian subcontinent since antiquity. Hinduism has roots in ancient Vedic, Buddhist, and south Indian religious concepts and practices. It spread along the trade routes to Southeast Asia.

Meenakshi Temple, Madurai, India
Some 15,000 pilgrims a day visit the large Hindu temple of Meenakshi (the fish-eyed goddess) in the ancient holy city of Madurai in India's southeastern province of Tamil Nadu. The temple complex dates from at least 1000 c.e., although the elaborately painted statues of these gopuram (gate towers) have been rebuilt and restored many times. The largest gopura rises 150 feet (46 meters) above the ground.

Jean Louis Nou/akg-images

places with flowing water. The Ganges River is especially sacred. Millions of worshipers travel each year to bathe and receive the restorative and purifying power of its waters. Pilgrimage to shrines fosters contact and exchange of ideas among people from different parts of India, helping to create a broad Hindu identity and the concept of India as a single civilization.

Religious duties depend on social standing and gender as well as stage of life. Young men from the three highest classes (Brahmin, Kshatriya, and Vaishya) undergo ritual rebirth through the ceremony of the sacred thread, marking attainment of manhood and readiness to receive religious knowledge. The life cycle then passes through four stages: (1) student of the sacred texts, (2) married householder with children and material goods, (3) forest dweller meditating on the meaning of existence after the birth of his grandchildren, and (4) wandering ascetic awaiting death. The person living such a life fulfills first his duties to society and then his duties to himself, leaving him disconnected from the world and prepared for moksha (liberation).

Hinduism responded to the needs of people for personal deities with whom they could establish direct connections. The austerity of early Buddhism, its denial of the importance of gods, and its demand that individuals find their own path to enlightenment may have required too much of ordinary people.

What eventually made Mahayana Buddhism popular—gods, saints, and myths—also made it more easily absorbed into the social and cultural fabric of Hinduism.

Indian Imperial Expansion and Collapse

In the face of powerful forces that tended to keep India fragmented, how did the Mauryan Empire of the fourth to second centuries B.C.E. and the Gupta Empire of the fourth to sixth centuries C.E. succeed in unifying much of India?

Political unity has rarely lasted in India. The varied terrain—mountains, foothills, plains, forests, steppes, deserts—favors different forms of organization and economic activity. Peoples occupying topographically diverse zones may also differ in language and cultural practices. Caste and family have generated the strongest feeling of personal identity, allegiance to a higher political authority being a secondary concern. Nevertheless, two empires arose in the Ganges Plain: the Mauryan Empire of the fourth to second centuries B.C.E. and the Gupta Empire of the fourth to sixth centuries C.E.

The Mauryan Empire, 324–184 B.C.E.

Among the many kinship groups and independent states that dotted the north Indian landscape, the kingdom of Magadha, in the modern Indian state of Bihar, began to play an influential role around 600 B.C.E. thanks to wealth based on agriculture, iron mines, and strategic location astride the trade routes of the eastern Ganges Basin. In the late fourth century B.C.E., Chandragupta Maurya (MORE-yuh), a man of Vaishya or Shudra origins, took control of Magadha and founded the **Mauryan Empire**. Greek tradition claimed that Alexander the Great met an Indian native named "Sandracottus," an apparent corruption of "Chandragupta," when his armies reached the Punjab (northern Pakistan) in 326 B.C.E., implying that he might have served as a role model for the new ruler.

Greek rule in the Punjab collapsed after Alexander's death, allowing Chandragupta (r. 324–301 B.C.E.) and his successors Bindusara (r. 301–269 B.C.E.) and Ashoka (r. 269–232 B.C.E.) to extend Mauryan control over the entire subcontinent except for its southern tip.

Tradition holds that Kautilya, a crafty elderly Brahmin, guided Chandragupta and wrote a treatise on government, the *Arthashastra*. Although recent studies have shown that the existing form of the Arthashastra dates only to the third century C.E., its core may well go back to Kautilya. This pragmatic guide to political success advocates the so-called *mandata* (circle) theory of foreign policy: "My enemy's enemy is my friend." It also lists schemes for enforcing and increasing tax collection and prescribes the use of spies to keep watch on one's subjects.

A quarter of all agricultural output went in taxes to support the Mauryan government. Relatives and associates of the king governed districts based on ethnic boundaries. The imperial army—with infantry, cavalry, chariot, and elephant divisions—secured central authority, which also controlled mining,

shipbuilding, and arms making. Standard coinage fostered support for the government and promoted trade.

The Mauryan kings ruled from Pataliputra (modern Patna), where five tributaries join the Ganges. Descriptions by foreign visitors testify to the international connections of the Indian monarchs. Surrounded by a timber wall and moat, the city extended along the river for 8 miles (13 kilometers). Six governing committees oversaw manufacturing, trade, sales, taxes, the welfare of foreigners, and the registration of births and deaths.

Ashoka, Chandragupta's grandson, began his reign by extending the boundaries of the empire. After killing, wounding, or deporting thousands of people during his conquest of Kalinga (modern Orissa, a coastal region southeast of Magadha), remorse overcame him and he converted to Buddhism, thereafter preaching nonviolence, morality, moderation, and religious tolerance in both government and private life.

Ashoka publicized this program through edicts inscribed on great rocks and polished sandstone, the earliest decipherable Indian texts:

> For . . . many hundreds of years the sacrificial slaughter of animals, violence toward creatures, unfilial conduct toward kinsmen, improper conduct toward Brahmins and ascetics [have increased]. Now with the practice of morality by King [Ashoka], the sound of war drums has become the call to morality. . . . You [government officials] are appointed to rule over thousands of human beings in the expectation that you will win the affection of all men. All men are my children. Just as I desire that my children will fare well and be happy in this world and the next, I desire the same for all men. . . . King [Ashoka] . . . desires that there should be the growth of the essential spirit of morality or holiness among all sects. . . .

Mauryan Empire The first state to unify most of the Indian subcontinent. It was founded by Chandragupta Maurya in 324 B.C.E. and survived until 184 B.C.E. From its capital at Pataliputra in the Ganges Valley it grew wealthy from taxes on agriculture, iron mining, and control of trade routes.

Ashoka Third ruler of the Mauryan Empire in India (r. 269–232 B.C.E.). He converted to Buddhism and broadcast his precepts on inscribed stones and pillars, the earliest surviving Indian writing.

There should not be glorification of one's own sect and denunciation of the sect of others for little or no reason. For all the sects are worthy of reverence for one reason or another.[2]

Despite his commitment to employ peaceful means whenever possible, Ashoka reminded potential transgressors that "the king, remorseful as he is, has the strength to punish the wrongdoers who do not repent."

Commerce and Culture in an Era of Political Fragmentation

The Mauryan Empire prospered for a time after Ashoka's death in 232 B.C.E. Then, weakened by dynastic disputes, it collapsed under attacks from the northwest in 184 B.C.E. Five hundred years passed before another state succeeded in extending control over northern India. Despite the political fragmentation, however, economic, cultural, and intellectual development continued. The roads and towns of the Mauryans fostered commerce within the subcontinent, while land and sea routes linked India to China, Southeast Asia, Central Asia, the Middle East, East Africa, and the lands of the Mediterranean. Guilds of merchants and artisans regulated the lives of their members and had an important voice in local affairs. They patronized culture and endowed religious sects, particularly Buddhism and Jainism, with temples and monuments.

During the last centuries B.C.E. and the first centuries C.E., the greatest Indian epics, the Ramayana and the Mahabharata, based on centuries-old oral predecessors, achieved their final form. They place the events they describe in the distant past, but their proud kings, beautiful queens, family wars, heroic conduct, and chivalric values seem to reflect the late Vedic period, when Aryan warrior societies moved onto the Ganges Plain.

The Ramayana relates the exploits of Rama, a heroic prince who came to be considered an incarnation of Vishnu. When the chief of the demons kidnaps his wife, Sita, he destroys the demons with the help of his brother and a troop of monkeys. The vast **Mahabharata**—eight times the length of the *Iliad* and *Odyssey* combined—tells how two sets of cousins, the Pandavas and Kauravas, quarreled over succession to the throne and fought a cataclysmic battle at Kurukshetra. The battle is so destructive on both sides that

Yudhishthira, the eldest of the Pandava brothers and their leader, accepts the fruits of victory only reluctantly because the battle losses were so great.

The **Bhagavad-Gita** is a self-contained (and perhaps originally separate) episode set in the battle. The hero Arjuna shrinks from fighting his kinsmen until his charioteer, the god Krishna, tutors him on the necessity of fulfilling his duty as a warrior. Death means nothing in a universe of endless reincarnation. The Bhagavad-Gita resolves the tension in Indian civilization between duty to society and duty to one's soul. Dutiful action taken without regard for personal benefit serves society and may earn release from the cycle of rebirths.

Science and technology flourished in this era as well. Indian doctors applied herbal remedies and served in the courts of western and southern Asia. In linguistics, Panini (late fourth century B.C.E.) undertook a detailed analysis of Sanskrit word forms and grammar. This led to the standardization of Sanskrit, which arrested its natural development and turned it into a formal, literary language. Prakrits—popular dialects—emerged to become the ancestors of the modern languages of northern and central India.

Historians of southern India consider the period from the third century B.C.E. to the third century C.E., dominated by three often feuding **Tamil kingdoms**—the Cholas, Pandyas, and Cheras—a "classical" period for Tamil art and literature. Patronized by the Pandya kings and guided by an academy of five hundred authors, Tamil writers composed grammatical treatises, collections of ethical proverbs, epics, and short poems about love, war, wealth, and the beauty of nature while performers excelled in music, dance, and drama.

Mahabharata A vast epic chronicling the events leading up to a cataclysmic battle between related kinship groups in early India. It includes the Bhagavad-Gita, the most important work of Indian sacred literature.
Bhagavad-Gita The most important work of Indian sacred literature, a dialogue between the great warrior Arjuna and the god Krishna on duty and the fate of the spirit.
Tamil kingdoms The kingdoms of southern India, inhabited primarily by speakers of Dravidian languages, which developed in partial isolation, and somewhat differently, from the Aryan north. They produced epics, poetry, and performance arts. Elements of Tamil religious beliefs were merged into the Hindu synthesis.

Indian Mathematics

The so-called Arabic numerals used in most parts of the world today were developed in India. The Indian system of place-value notation was far more efficient than the unwieldy numerical systems of Egyptians, Greeks, and Romans, and the invention of zero was a profound intellectual achievement. This system is used even more widely than the alphabet derived from the Phoenicians (see Chapter 4) and is, in one sense, the only truly global language.

In its fully developed form the Indian method of arithmetic notation employed a base-10 system. It had separate columns for ones, tens, hundreds, and so forth, as well as a zero sign to indicate the absence of units in a given column. This system makes possible the economical expression of even very large numbers. And it allows for the performance of calculations not possible in a system like the numerals of the Romans, where any real calculation had to be done mentally or on a counting board.

A series of early Indian inscriptions using the numerals from 1 to 9 are deeds of property given to religious institutions by kings or other wealthy individuals. They were incised in the Sanskrit language on copper plates. The earliest known example has a date equivalent to 595 C.E. A sign for zero is attested by the eighth century, but textual evidence leads to the inference that a place-value system and the zero concept were already known in the fifth century.

This Indian system spread to the Middle East, Southeast Asia, and East Asia by the seventh century. Other

Copper Plate with Indian Numerals This property deed from western India shows an early form of the symbol system for numbers that spread to the Middle East and Europe and today is used all over the world. Facsimile by Georges Ifrah. Reproduced by permission of Georges Ifrah.

peoples quickly recognized its capabilities and adopted it, sometimes using indigenous symbols. Europe received the new technology somewhat later. Gerbert of Aurillac, a French Christian monk, spent time in Spain between 967 and 970, where he was exposed to the mathematics of the Arabs. A great scholar and teacher who eventually became Pope Sylvester II (r. 999–1003), he spread word of the "Arabic" system in the Christian West.

Knowledge of the Indian system of mathematical notation eventually spread throughout Europe, partly through the use of a mechanical calculating device—an improved version of the Roman counting board, with counters inscribed with variants of the Indian numeral forms. Because the counters could be turned sideways or upside down, at first there was considerable variation in the forms. But by the twelfth century they had become standardized into forms close to those in use today. As the capabilities of the place-value system for calculations became clear, the counting board fell into disuse. This led to the adoption of the zero sign— not necessary on the counting board, where a column could be left empty—by the twelfth century. Leonardo Fibonacci, a thirteenth-century C.E. Italian who learned algebra in Muslim North Africa and employed the Arabic numeral system in his mathematical treatise, gave additional impetus to the movement to discard the traditional system of Roman numerals.

Why was this marvelous system of mathematical notation invented in ancient India? The answer may lie in the way its range and versatility correspond to elements of Indian cosmology. The Indians conceived of immense spans of time—trillions of years (far exceeding current scientific estimates of the age of the universe as approximately 14 billion years)—during which innumerable universes like our own were created, existed for a finite time, then were destroyed. In one popular creation myth, Vishnu is slumbering on the coils of a giant serpent at the bottom of the ocean, and worlds are being created and destroyed as he exhales and inhales. In Indian thought our world, like others, has existed for a series of epochs lasting more than 4 million years, yet the period of its existence is but a brief and insignificant moment in the vast sweep of time. The Indians developed a number system that allowed them to express concepts of this magnitude.

The Gupta Empire, 320–550 C.E.

Like its Mauryan predecessor, the **Gupta Empire** grew from the kingdom of Magadha and had its capital at Pataliputra. Its founder called himself Chandra Gupta (r. 320–335 C.E.), borrowing the name of the Mauryan founder. Though they never controlled as much land as the Mauryans, the Gupta monarchs took the title "Great King of Kings."

Trade, agriculture, and iron mining brought prosperity to the Guptas as they had to the Mauryans, and the kings followed similar methods of taxation and administration. In addition to a 25 percent tax on agriculture, users of the irrigation network paid fees, and some commodities were subject to special taxes. The state maintained monopolies over mining and salt production, exploited state-owned farmlands, and required subjects to work a specified number of days on maintaining roads, wells, and irrigation works.

The Gupta administration and intelligence network were smaller and less pervasive than those of the Mauryans. A powerful army maintained tight control of the empire's core, but provincial governors had a freer hand, which they sometimes used to exploit the populace. Governorships often passed from father to son within high-ranking military or administrative families. The most distant areas, controlled by kinship groups or subordinate kings, made annual donations of tribute. Garrisons stationed at frontier points kept trade routes open and ensured the collection of customs duties.

A constant round of solemn rituals, dramatic ceremonies, and cultural events in Pataliputra demonstrated to visitors from remote areas the benefits of belonging to the empire. Modern historians call such a regime a **theater-state**. Ruler and subjects in the Gupta theater-state had an economic relationship. The former accumulated luxury goods and profits from trade and redistributed them to dependents through gifts and other means. Subordinate princes gained prestige by emulating the center and maintained close ties through visits, gifts, and marriages with the Gupta family. Gupta patronage also supported the Indian mathematicians, who invented the concept of zero and developed the so-called Arabic numerals and place-value notation (see Environment and Technology: Indian Mathematics).

The moist climate of the Ganges Plain does not favor the preservation of buildings and artifacts, so archaeology has little to say about the Gupta era. However, a Chinese Buddhist monk named Faxian (fah-shee-en), who made a pilgrimage to the homeland of his faith around 400 C.E., penned a description of the Gupta kingdom:

> The cities and towns of this country are the greatest of all in the Middle Kingdom. The inhabitants are rich and prosperous, and vie with one another in the practice of benevolence and righteousness. . . . The heads of the Vaishya families in them establish in the cities houses for dispensing charity and medicines. All the poor and destitute in the country, orphans, widowers, and childless men, maimed people and cripples, and all who are diseased, go to those houses, and are provided with every kind of help.[3]

At this time, the civil disabilities of women, which had always existed as custom, hardened into law with the emergence of law books like *The Laws of Manu*. Indian women lost the right to own or inherit property, and girls married at increasingly early ages, sometimes at six or seven. The husband could thus ensure his wife's virginity, and, by bringing her up in his own household, he could train her to suit his purposes. As in Confucian China, a woman owed obedience to her father, then her husband, and finally her sons (see Chapter 2). In certain parts of India, a practice called *sati* (suh-TEE) required a widow to cremate

Primary Source: The Laws of Manu See how the principle of Dharma justifies the traditional roles of men and women, and of priests, warriors, merchants, and servants in Hindu society.

Gupta Empire A powerful Indian state based, like its Mauryan predecessor, on a capital at Pataliputra in the Ganges Valley. It controlled most of the Indian subcontinent through a combination of military force and its prestige as a center of sophisticated culture.

theater-state Historians' term for a state that acquires prestige and power by developing attractive cultural forms and staging elaborate public ceremonies (as well as redistributing valuable resources) to attract and bind subjects to the center. The Gupta Empire is an example of such a state.

herself on her husband's funeral pyre. Widows who refused to follow this custom could not remarry and suffered social rejection.

Entry into a Jainist or Buddhist religious community offered some women an escape from male control. Women from powerful families and courtesans trained in poetry and music, as well as sexual technique, sometimes enjoyed high social standing and gave money for Buddhist stupas and other shrines.

The Gupta monarchs sought sanctity through reviving Vedic practices. The influence of Brahmin priests gained renewed prominence. Yet the kings also patronized Buddhist and Jain endeavors. Buddhist monasteries with hundreds, even thousands, of monks and nuns flourished in the cities. Northern India drew Buddhist pilgrims from Southeast and East Asia to the birthplace of their faith.

The classic form of the Hindu temple, evolved during the Gupta era, symbolizes the sacred mountain or palace where the gods reside. Sitting atop a raised platform surmounted by high towers, it mirrored the order of the universe. From an exterior courtyard, worshipers approached the central shrine containing the statue of the deity. In rich temples, painted or sculpted gods and mythical events covered the walls. Frescoes and statues also adorned cave temples carved into cliffs.

The vibrant commerce of the period of fragmentation continued under the Guptas. Coins served as the medium of exchange, and artisan guilds influenced the economic, political, and religious life of towns. The Guptas sought control of the ports on the Arabian Sea but saw trade with the weakening Roman Empire decline. Trade with Southeast and East Asia increased, however. Merchants from eastern and southern India voyaged to the Malay (muh-LAY) Peninsula and the islands of Indonesia to exchange cotton cloth, ivory, metalwork, and exotic animals for Chinese silk or Indonesian spices. The overland Silk Road from China brought further trade but was vulnerable to disruption by Central Asian nomads (see Chapter 6).

The Gupta Empire collapsed around 550 C.E. under the pressure of nomadic invaders from the northwest. In the early seventh century, Harsha Vardhana (r. 606–647 C.E.), the ruler of the region around Delhi, briefly restored imperial power. An account of his reign by a courtier named Bana shows him to be a

SECTION REVIEW

- Chandragupta Maurya took control of the kingdom of Magadha and established the Mauryan Empire.
- The collapse of Greek rule in the Punjab enabled Chandragupta and his successors to expand the empire.
- The empire reached its fullest extent under Ashoka, after whose death the empire disintegrated.
- Economic and cultural activity continued during an era of fragmentation; to the south, Tamil culture entered its classical period.
- Also centered in Magadha, the Gupta Empire was less centralized than the Mauryan, but it thrived on the same economies.
- The Guptas revived Vedic practices and presided over both the legal hardening of gender discrimination and the expansion of overseas trade.

fervent Buddhist, poet, patron of artists, and dynamic warrior. After Harsha's death, northern India reverted to political fragmentation and remained divided until the Muslim invasions of the eleventh and twelfth centuries (see Chapter 12).

Southeast Asia, 50–1025 C.E.

How did the geography of Southeast Asia contribute to its commerce and to the influence of Hinduism and Buddhism?

Southeast Asia consists of three geographical zones: the Indochina mainland, the Malay Peninsula, and thousands of islands extending on an east-west axis far out into the Pacific Ocean (see Map 5.2). Encompassing a vast area of land and water, this region is now occupied by the countries of Myanmar (myahn-MAH) (Burma), Thailand, Laos, Cambodia, Vietnam, Malaysia, Singapore, Indonesia, Brunei (broo-NIE), and the Philippines. Poised between the ancient centers of China and India, Southeast Asia has been influenced by the cultures of both civilizations. The region first rose to prominence and prosperity because of its intermediate role in the trade exchanges between southern and eastern Asia.

The strategic importance of Southeast Asia is enhanced by the region's natural resources. This is a geologically active zone; the islands are the tops of a chain of volcanoes. Lying along the equator, Southeast Asia has a tropical climate. The temperature hovers around 80 degrees Fahrenheit (30 degrees Celsius), and the monsoon winds provide dependable rainfall throughout the year. Thanks to several growing cycles each year, the region is capable of supporting a large human population. The most fertile agricultural lands lie along the floodplains of the largest silt-bearing rivers or contain rich volcanic soil deposited by ancient eruptions.

Early Civilization

Rain forest covers much of Southeast Asia. As early as 2000 B.C.E. people in this region were clearing land for farming by cutting and burning the vegetation. The cleared land was farmed for several growing seasons. When the soil was exhausted, the farmers abandoned the patch, allowing the forest to reclaim it, while they cleared and cultivated other nearby fields in similar fashion. Rice was the staple food—labor-intensive, but able to support a large population. A number of plant and animal species spread from Southeast Asia to other regions, including rice, soybeans, sugar cane, yams, bananas, coconuts, chickens, and pigs.

The Malay peoples who became the dominant population in this region were the product of several waves of migration from southern China beginning around 3000 B.C.E. Some indigenous peoples merged with the Malay newcomers; others retreated to remote mountain and forest zones. Subsequently, rising population and disputes within communities prompted streams of people to leave the Southeast Asian mainland for the islands. By the first millennium B.C.E. Southeast Asians had developed impressive navigational skills. They knew how to ride the monsoon winds and interpret the patterns of swells, winds, clouds, and bird and sea life. Over a period of several thousand years groups of Malay peoples in large, double outrigger canoes spread out across the Pacific and Indian Oceans—half the circumference of the earth—to settle thousands of islands.

The inhabitants of Southeast Asia clustered along riverbanks or in fertile volcanic plains. Their fields and villages were never far from the rain forest, with its wild animals and numerous plant species. Forest trees provided fruit, wood, and spices. The shallow waters surrounding the islands teemed with fish. This region was also an early center of metallurgy. Metalsmiths heated copper and tin ore to the right temperature for producing and shaping bronze implements by using hollow bamboo tubes to funnel oxygen to the furnace.

Northern Indochina, by its geographic proximity, was vulnerable to Chinese pressure and cultural influences, and it was under Chinese political control for a thousand years (111 B.C.E.–939 C.E.). Farther south, larger states emerged in the early centuries C.E. in response to two powerful forces: commerce and Hindu-Buddhist culture. Southeast Asia was situated along the trade routes that merchants used to carry Chinese silk westward to India and the Mediterranean. The movements of nomadic peoples had disrupted the old land route across Central Asia. But in India demand for silk was increasing—both for domestic use and for transshipment to satisfy the fast-growing luxury market in the Roman Empire. Gradually merchants extended this exchange network to include goods from Southeast Asia, such as aromatic woods, resins, and cinnamon, pepper, cloves, nutmeg, and other spices. By serving this trade network and controlling key points, Southeast Asian centers rose to prominence.

The other force leading to the rise of larger political entities was the influence of Hindu-Buddhist culture imported from India. Commerce brought Indian merchants and sailors into the ports of Southeast Asia. As Buddhism spread, Southeast Asia became a way station for Indian missionaries and East Asian pilgrims going to and coming from the birthplace of their faith. Shrewd Malay rulers looked to Indian traditions as a rich source of ideas and prestige. They borrowed Sanskrit terms such as *maharaja* (mah-huh-RAH-juh) (great king), utilized Indian models of bureaucracy, ceremonial practices, and forms of artistic representation, and employed priests, administrators, and scribes skilled in Sanskrit writing to expedite government business Their special connection to powerful gods and higher knowledge raised them above their rivals.

The Southeast Asian kingdoms, however, were not just passive recipients of Indian culture. They took what was useful to them and synthesized it with indigenous beliefs, values, and institutions—for example, local concepts of chiefship, ancestor worship, and

Map 5.2 Southeast Asia Southeast Asia's position between the ancient centers of civilization in India and China had a major impact on its history. In the first millennium C.E. a series of powerful and wealthy states arose in the region by gaining control of major trade routes: first Funan, based in southern Vietnam, Cambodia, and the Malay Peninsula, then Srivijaya on the island of Sumatra, then smaller states on the island of Java. Shifting trade routes led to the demise of one and the rise of others. © Cengage Learning

Interactive Map

forms of oaths. Moreover, they trained their own people in the new ways, so that the bureaucracy contained both foreign experts and native disciples. The whole process amounted to a cultural dialogue between India and Southeast Asia, in which both were active participants.

The first major Southeast Asian center, called "**Funan**" (FOO-nahn) by Chinese visitors, flourished between the first and sixth centuries C.E., (see Map 5.2). Its capital was at the modern site of Oc-Eo in southern Vietnam. Funan occupied the delta of the Mekong (MAY-kawng) River, a "rice bowl" capable of supporting a large population. The rulers mobilized large numbers of laborers to dig irrigation channels and prevent destructive floods. By extending its control over most of southern Indochina and the Malay Peninsula, Funan was able to dominate the trade route from India to China. The route began in the ports of northeast India, crossed the Bay of Bengal, continued by land over the Isthmus of Kra on the

Malay Peninsula, then across the South China Sea (see Map 5.2). Indian merchants found that offloading their goods from ships and carrying them across the narrow strip of land was safer than making the 1,000-mile (1,600-kilometer) voyage around the Malay Peninsula—a dangerous trip marked by treacherous currents, rocky shoals, and pirates. Once the portage across the isthmus was finished, the merchants needed food and lodging while waiting for the monsoon winds to shift so they could make the last leg of the voyage to China by sea. Funan stockpiled food and provided security for those engaged in this trade—in return for customs duties and other fees.

Funan An early complex society in Southeast Asia between the first and sixth centuries C.E. It was centered in the rich rice-growing region of southern Vietnam, and it controlled the passage of trade across the Malaysian isthmus.

Chinese observers have left reports of the prosperity and sophistication of Funan, emphasizing the presence of walled cities, palaces, archives, systems of taxation, and state-organized agriculture. Nevertheless, Funan declined in the sixth century. The most likely explanation is that international trade routes changed and Funan no longer held a strategic position.

The Srivijayan Kingdom

By the sixth century a new, all-sea route had developed. Merchants and travelers from south India and Sri Lanka sailed through the Strait of Malacca (between the west side of the Malay Peninsula and the northeast coast of the island of Sumatra) and into the South China Sea. This route presented both human and navigational hazards, but it significantly shortened the journey.

A new center of power, **Srivijaya** (sree-vih-JUH-yuh)—Sanskrit for "Great Conquest"—dominated the new southerly route by 683 C.E.. The capital of the Srivijayan kingdom was at modern-day Palembang in southeastern Sumatra, 50 miles (80 kilometers) up the broad and navigable Musi River, with a good natural harbor. The kingdom was well situated to control the southern part of the Malay Peninsula, Sumatra, parts of Java and Borneo, and the Malacca (muh-LAH-kuh) and Sunda straits—vital passageways for shipping (see Map 5.2).

The Srivijayan capital gained ascendancy over its rivals and assumed control of the international trade route by fusing four distinct ecological zones into an interdependent network. The core area was the productive agricultural plain along the Musi River. The king and his clerks, judges, and tax collectors controlled this zone directly. Control was less direct over the second zone, the upland regions of Sumatra's interior, with its commercially valuable forest products. Local rulers there were bound to the center by oaths of loyalty, elaborate court ceremonies, and the sharing of profits from trade. The third zone consisted of river ports that had been Srivijaya's main rivals. They were conquered and controlled thanks to an alliance between Srivijaya and neighboring sea nomads, pirates who served as a Srivijayan navy in return for a steady income.

The fourth zone was a fertile "rice bowl" on the central plain of the nearby island of Java—a region

SECTION REVIEW

- Climate and resources enabled Southeast Asia to support large human populations.
- Located on the trade and pilgrimage routes between China and India, Southeast Asia came under strong Hindu and Buddhist influence.
- Shrewd rulers used Indian knowledge and personnel to enhance their power and prestige.
- Funan rose to prominence between the first and sixth centuries C.E. by controlling the trade route across the Malay Peninsula.
- The Srivijayan kingdom flourished between the seventh and eleventh centuries C.E. and dominated the new international trade route through the Straits of Malacca.

so productive, because of its volcanic soil, that it houses and feeds the majority of the population of present-day Indonesia. Srivijayan monarchs maintained alliances, cemented by intermarriage, with several ruling dynasties in this region, and the Srivijayan kings claimed descent from the main Javanese dynasty. These arrangements gave Srivijaya access to large quantities of foodstuffs that people living in the capital and merchants and sailors visiting the various ports needed.

The kings of Srivijaya who constructed and maintained this complex network of social, political, and economic relationships were men of energy and skill. Although their authority depended in part on force, it owed more to diplomatic and even theatrical talents. Like the Gupta monarchy, Srivijaya was a theater-state, securing its preeminence and binding dependents by its sheer splendor and its ability to attract labor, talent, and luxury products. The court was the scene of ceremonies designed to dazzle observers and reinforce an image of wealth, power, and sanctity. Subordinate rulers took oaths of loyalty carrying

Srivijaya A state based on the Indonesian island of Sumatra, between the seventh and eleventh centuries C.E. It amassed wealth and power by a combination of selective adaptation of Indian technologies and concepts, control of the lucrative trade routes between India and China, and skillful showmanship and diplomacy in holding together a disparate realm of inland and coastal territories.

Aerial View of the Buddhist Monument at Borobodur, Java The great monument of volcanic stone was more than 300 feet (90 meters) in length and over 100 feet (30 meters) high. Pilgrims made a 3-mile-long (nearly 5-kilometer-long) winding ascent through ten levels intended to represent the ideal Buddhist journey from ignorance to enlightenment. Numerous sculptured reliefs depicting Buddhist legends provide glimpses of daily life in early Java.

Luca Tettoni/Robert Harding World Imagery

dire threats of punishment for violations, and in their home locales they imitated the splendid ceremonials of the capital.

The Srivijayan king, drawing upon Buddhist conceptions, presented himself as a bodhisattva, one who had achieved enlightenment and utilized his precious insights for the betterment of his subjects. The king was believed to have magical powers, controlling powerful forces of fertility associated with the rivers in flood and mediating between the spiritually potent realms of the mountains and the sea. He was also said to be so wealthy that he deposited bricks of gold in the river estuary to appease the local gods, and a hillside near town was covered with silver and gold images of the Buddha. The gold originated in East or West Africa and came to Southeast Asia through trade with the Muslim world (see Chapter 8).

The kings built and patronized Buddhist monasteries and schools. In central Java local dynasties allied with Srivijaya built magnificent temple complexes to advertise their glory. The most famous of these, **Borobodur** (booh-roe-boe-DOOR), built between 770 and 825 C.E., was the largest human construction in the Southern Hemisphere.

The kings of Srivijaya carried out this marvelous balancing act for centuries. But the system was

vulnerable to shifts in the pattern of international trade. Some such change must have contributed to the decline of Srivijaya in the eleventh century, even though the immediate cause was a destructive raid on the capital by forces of the Chola kingdom of southeast India in 1025 C.E.

After the decline of Srivijaya, leadership passed to new, vigorous kingdoms on the eastern end of Java, and the maritime realm of Southeast Asia remained prosperous and connected to international trade networks. Through the ages Europeans remained dimly aware of this region as a source of spices and other luxury items. Some four centuries after the decline of Srivijaya, an Italian navigator serving under the flag of Spain—Christopher Columbus—sailed westward across the Atlantic Ocean, seeking to establish a direct route to the fabled "Indies" from which the spices came.

Borobodur A massive stone monument on the Indonesian island of Java, erected by the Sailendra kings around 800 C.E. The winding ascent through ten levels, decorated with rich relief carving, is a Buddhist allegory for the progressive stages of enlightenment.

Conclusion

This chapter traces the emergence of complex societies in India and Southeast Asia between the second millennium B.C.E. and the first millennium C.E. Because of migrations, trade, and the spread of belief systems, an Indian style of civilization spread throughout the subcontinent and adjoining regions and eventually made its way to Southeast Asia. In this period were laid cultural foundations that in large measure still endure.

The development and spread of belief systems—Vedism, Buddhism, Jainism, and Hinduism—have a central place in this chapter because nearly all the sources are religious. Ancient Indians did not develop a historical consciousness like their Israelite, Greek, and Chinese contemporaries because they held a strikingly different view of time. The distinctive Indian conception—of vast epochs in which universes are created and destroyed again and again and the essential spirit of living creatures is reincarnated repeatedly—made the particulars of any brief moment seem relatively unimportant.

Political and social division has been the norm throughout much of the history of India, a consequence of the diversity of the subcontinent and the complex mix of ethnic and linguistic groups inhabiting it. The elaborate structure of classes and castes was a response to this diversity. Strong central governments, such as those of the Mauryan and Gupta kings,

rose to dominance by gaining control of resources and important trade routes and developing effective military and administrative institutions. However, the periods of fragmentation and multiple centers of power were as dynamic as the periods of unity.

Many distinctive social and intellectual features of Indian civilization—the class and caste system, models of kingship and statecraft, and Vedic, Jainist, and Buddhist belief systems—originated in the north, where descendants of Indo-European immigrants predominated. Hinduism embraced elements drawn from the Dravidian cultures of the south as well as from Buddhism. The capacity of the Hindu tradition to assimilate a wide range of popular beliefs facilitated the spread of a common Indian civilization across the subcontinent, although there was considerable variation from one region to another.

Southeast Asia, as a crossroads of trade, received influences from China and India. Commerce brought migrants and merchants from both regions to Southeast Asia. As Buddhism spread, Southeast Asia became a way station for Indian missionaries and Chinese pilgrims. Malay rulers looked to Indian traditions as a rich source of ideas and prestige, and used Indian models of bureaucracy, ceremonial practices, and forms of artistic representation. Thus the Southeast Asian kingdoms synthesized foreign cultural influences with indigenous beliefs, values, and institutions.

CHAPTER REVIEW

Download the MP3 audio file of the Chapter Review to listen to on the go.

What does material evidence tell us about the Indus Valley civilization and the most likely reason for its collapse? (page 112)

The cities of Harappa and Mohenjo-Daro provide evidence of early civilization in the fertile Indus Valley. Both display a striking uniformity of planning and construction, including high brick walls and a rectangular grid of streets. Excavated artifacts exhibit standard shapes and styles, with some evidence indicating trade with resource-rich regions to the north and Mesopotamia to the west. Unfortunately, the writing system of this civilization remains undeciphered. The abandonment of the cities signaled the end of this civilization. The probable cause was "systems failure" resulting from ecological changes in the river valley and along the coast.

What historical forces led to the development of complex social groupings in ancient India? (page 116)

Arya kinship groups moving into northwest India after 1500 B.C.E. established a religiously sanctioned class (varna) system of priests, warriors, landowners and merchants, and peasants and laborers. With further subdivisions into castes (jati), this system ordered the relations among ethnically, linguistically, and culturally diverse populations. Various forms of resistance to the secular and religious domination of the Brahmins arose, including the more egalitarian Buddhist and Jainist belief systems. Traditionalists responded to this through Hinduism, which provided people with a number of ways to make personal connections with the gods.

In the face of powerful forces that tended to keep India fragmented, how did the Mauryan Empire of the fourth to second centuries B.C.E. and the Gupta Empire of the fourth to sixth centuries C.E. succeed in unifying much of India? (page 122)

Despite geographical obstacles, religious diversity, and social orientation toward the caste system, the Mauryan (fourth to second centuries B.C.E.) and Gupta (fourth to sixth centuries C.E.) rulers brought most of the subcontinent under their control. Both dynasties exploited the agricultural productivity of the Ganges Plain, monopolized mining and weapons production, built standing armies, and developed complex bureaucracies and networks of spies. These centralizing factors encouraged urban growth, long-distance trade, and new forms of art and literature.

How did the geography of Southeast Asia contribute to its commerce and to the influence of Hinduism and Buddhism? (page 127)

Southeast Asia, a region rich in resources with a tropical climate favorable for agriculture, generated a lively trade, both locally and with South and East Asia. South Asian sailors, merchants, and pilgrims brought Hinduism and Buddhism to the region. Kingdoms in southern Indochina, the Malay Peninsula, and Java found their ideas appealing. Malay rulers blended Indian religions with local traditions to produce a distinctive civilization.

Key Terms

Harappa *(p. 113)*	Hinduism *(p. 121)*
Mohenjo-Daro *(p. 113)*	Mauryan Empire *(p. 123)*
monsoon *(p. 116)*	Ashoka *(p. 123)*
Vedas *(p. 116)*	Mahabharata *(p. 124)*
varnas/jati *(p. 118)*	Bhagavad-Gita *(p. 124)*
karma *(p. 118)*	Tamil kingdoms *(p. 124)*
moksha *(p. 119)*	Gupta Empire *(p. 126)*
Buddha *(p. 119)*	theater-state *(p. 126)*
Mahayana Buddhism (p. 120)	Funan *(p. 129)*
Theravada Buddhism (p. 120)	Srivijaya *(p. 130)*
	Borobodur *(p. 131)*

Web Resources

Pronunciation Guide

Interactive Maps

- MAP 5.1 Ancient India
- MAP 5.2 Southeast Asia

Visit the CourseMate website at www.cengagebrain.com for additional study tools and review materials for this chapter.

Primary Sources

- The Rig Veda
- Setting in Motion the Wheels of Law
- The Laws of Manu

Answer to the History in Focus Question

See photo on page 114, "Man from Mohenjo-Daro, ca. 2600–1900 B.C.E."

An Age of Empires: Rome and Han China

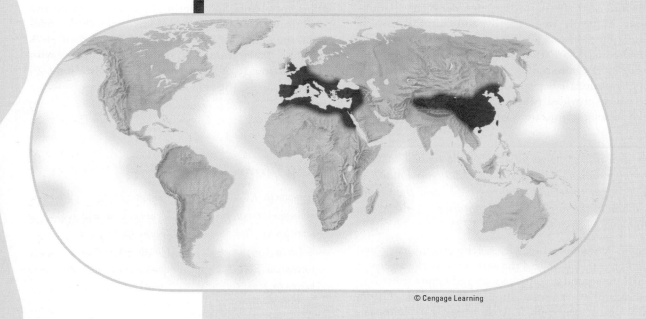

© Cengage Learning

CHAPTER PREVIEW

Rome's Creation of a Mediterranean Empire, 753 B.C.E.–330 C.E.
How did Rome create and maintain its vast Mediterranean empire?

The Origins of Imperial China, 221 B.C.E.–220 C.E.
How did imperial China evolve from its beginnings into the Han state?

Conclusion

DIVERSITY AND DOMINANCE: The Treatment of Slaves in Rome and China

Visit the CourseMate website at **www.cengagebrain.com** for additional study tools and review materials for this chapter.

According to Chinese sources, in the year 166 C.E., a group of travelers identifying themselves as delegates from Andun, the king of distant Da Qin, arrived at the court of the Chinese emperor Huan, one of the Han rulers. Andun was Marcus Aurelius Antoninus, the emperor of Rome.

These first known "Romans" to reach China probably hailed from one of Rome's eastern provinces, perhaps Egypt or Syria, and may have stretched the truth in claiming to be representatives of the Roman emperor. The Chinese officials had had no direct contact with the Roman Empire, however, and so the travelers, probably merchants hoping to trade for highly prized Chinese silk, easily got away with the imposture.

Direct or regular contact between the empires never developed, but the episode reveals that in the early centuries C.E. Rome and China dimly recognized each other's existence across the far-flung trading networks that spanned the Eastern Hemisphere. Both states, moreover, emerged from the last centuries B.C.E. and the first centuries C.E. as a new kind of empire, both qualitatively and quantitatively.

Since neither empire influenced the other, what caused them to arise and flourish at the same time? Some stress supposedly common factors, such as climate change or challenges from Central Asian nomads, but no theory has won the general support of scholars. The Roman Empire encompassed the lands surrounding the Mediterranean Sea and substantial portions of inland Europe and the Middle East. The Han Empire, named for China's ruling family, stretched from the Pacific Ocean to the oases of Central Asia. The largest empires the world had yet seen, they nevertheless managed to centralize control, achieve unprecedented stability and longevity, and assert dominance over the many cultures and peoples within their borders.

Rome's Creation of a Mediterranean Empire, 753 B.C.E.–330 C.E.

How did Rome create and maintain its vast Mediterranean empire?

The boot-shaped Italian peninsula, with the large island of Sicily, constitutes a bridge almost linking Europe and Africa (see Map 6.1). Rome too lay at a crossroads, being situated at the midpoint of the peninsula, about 15 miles (24 kilometers) from its western coast, where a north-south road intersected an east-west river route. The Tiber River on one side and a double ring of seven hills on the other afforded natural protection to the site.

The Apennine Mountains form Italy's spine, separating the eastern and western coastal plains, and the arc of the Alps shields it on the north. Navigable rivers and passes through the Apennines, and even through the snowcapped Alps, eased travel by merchants and armies. The Mediterranean climate afforded a long growing season and favorable conditions for a wide variety of crops. Hillside forests, today largely gone, provided timber for construction and fuel. Iron and other metals came from the region of Etruria in the northwest.

Although hills account for 75 percent of Italy's land area, the coastal plains and river valleys provide arable land, with fertile volcanic soil capable of supporting a much larger population than Greece. As it expanded within Italy, the Roman state tapped these human resources.

A Republic of Farmers

According to legend, Romulus, cast adrift on the Tiber River as a baby and nursed by a she-wolf, founded Rome in 753 B.C.E. Archaeological research, however, has revealed occupation on the Palatine Hill, one of the city's seven hills, dating to 1000 B.C.E. Several hilltop communities merged shortly before 600 B.C.E., forming an urban nucleus made possible by the draining of a swamp on the site of the future Roman Forum (civic center).

The Latin speech and cultural patterns of the inhabitants of the site resembled those of most of the other peoples of the peninsula. However, tradition remembered Etruscan immigrants arriving in the seventh century B.C.E. and being taken in; Rome came to pride itself on offering hospitality to exiles and outcasts.

Agriculture anchored the economy of early Rome, and land constituted wealth. Landownership brought social status and political privilege while buttressing fundamental values. Most early Romans cultivated their own small plots of land, but a few families managed to acquire large tracts of land. The heads of these wealthy families served in the Senate, a "Council of

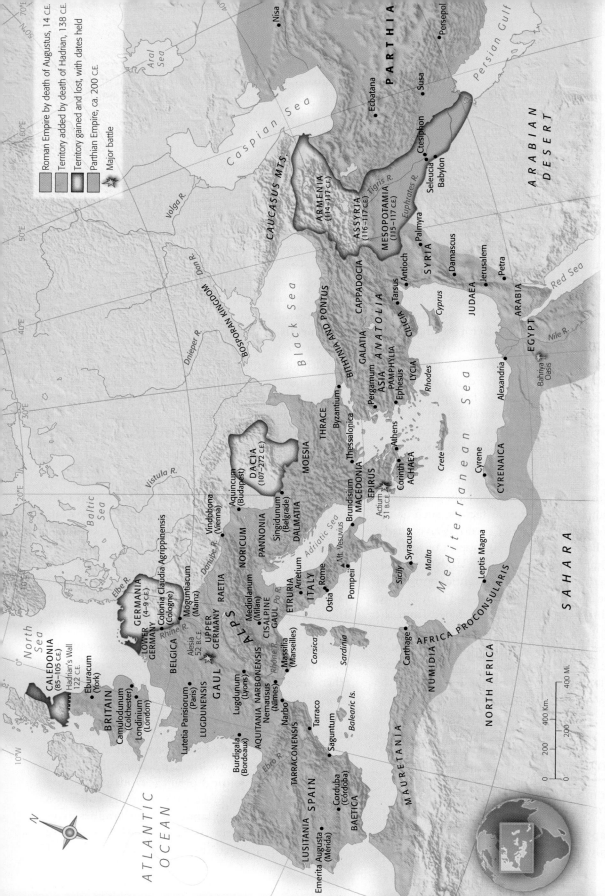

Map 6.1 The Roman Empire The Roman Empire came to encompass all the lands surrounding the Mediterranean Sea, as well as parts of continental Europe. When the emperor Augustus died in 14 C.E., he left instructions to his successors not to expand beyond the limits he had set, but his successor Claudius invaded southern Britain in the mid-first century and the soldier-emperor Trajan added Romania early in the second century. Deserts and seas provided solid natural boundaries, but the long and vulnerable river border in central and eastern Europe would eventually prove expensive to defend and vulnerable to invasion by Germanic and Central Asian peoples.   © Cengage Learning

Interactive Map

Roman Empire by death of Augustus, 14 C.E.

Territory added by death of Hadrian, 138 C.E.

Territory gained and lost, with dates held

Parthian Empire, ca. 200 C.E.

★ Major battle

North Sea

ATLANTIC OCEAN

CALEDONIA
(85–105 C.E.)

Hadrian's Wall
122 C.E.

BRITAIN
Camulodunum
(Colchester)
Londinium
(London)

Eburacum
(York)

Baltic Sea

GERMANIA
(4–9 C.E.)

LOWER
GERMANY

Colonia Claudia Agrippinensis
(Cologne)

Moguntiacum
(Mainz)

UPPER
GERMANY

BELGICA

Alesia
52 B.C.E.

Elbe R.

Rhine R.

Vistula R.

Vindobona
(Vienna)

Aquincum
(Budapest)

NORICUM

RAETIA

ALPS

Mediolanum
(Milan)

CISALPINE
GAUL

Danube R.

PANNONIA

Singidunum
(Belgrade)

DACIA
(107–272 C.E.)

DALMATIA

Adriatic Sea

MOESIA

THRACE

Byzantium

BITHYNIA AND PONTUS

GALATIA

CAPPADOCIA

GAUL

Lugdunum
(Lyons)

Lutetia Parisiorum
(Paris)

LUGDUNENSIS

Nemausus
(Nîmes)

AQUITANIA NARBONENSIS

Narbo

Burdigala
(Bordeaux)

Rhône R.

Massilia
(Marseilles)

Po R.

ETRURIA

Arretium

ITALY

Rome

Ostia

Pompeii

Mt. Vesuvius

Corsica

Sardinia

Brundisium

MACEDONIA

Thessalonica

EPIRUS

Actium
31 B.C.E.

Corinth

Athens

ACHAEA

Mediterranean Sea

Crete

Rhodes

Cyprus

ASIA

Pergamum

Ephesus

ANATOLIA

LYCIA

PAMPHYLIA

CILICIA

Tarsus

Antioch

SYRIA

Damascus

Palmyra

ARMENIA
(114–117 C.E.)

ASSYRIA
(116–117 C.E.)

MESOPOTAMIA
(115–117 C.E.)

Tigris R.

Euphrates R.

Seleucia

Ctesiphon

Babylon

Susa

Ecbatana

Persepol

Persian Gulf

PARTHIA

Nisa

Aral Sea

Caspian Sea

Volga R.

Don R.

Dnieper R.

BOSPORAN KINGDOM

Black Sea

CAUCASUS MTS.

JUDAEA

Jerusalem

Petra

ARABIA

Red Sea

Nile R.

EGYPT

Alexandria

Bahriya
Oasis

ARABIAN DESERT

Syracuse

Sicily

Malta

Carthage

AFRICA PROCONSULARIS

Leptis Magna

Cyrene

CYRENAICA

NUMIDIA

NORTH AFRICA

MAURETANIA

SAHARA

SPAIN

TARRACONENSIS

Tarraco

Saguntum

Balearic Is.

Ebro R.

LUSITANIA

Emerita Augusta
(Mérida)

Corduba
(Córdoba)

BAETICA

0   200   400 Km.

0   200   400 Mi.

N

Chronology

	Rome	China
500 B.C.E. **300 B.C.E.**	**1000 B.C.E.** First settlement on site of Rome **507 B.C.E.** Establishment of the Republic **264–202 B.C.E.** Wars against Carthage guarantee Roman control of western Mediterranean	**480–221 B.C.E.** Warring States Period **221 B.C.E.** Qin emperor unites eastern China **206 B.C.E.** Han dynasty succeeds Qin
200 B.C.E. **100 B.C.E.**	**200–146 B.C.E.** Wars against Hellenistic kingdoms lead to control of eastern Mediterranean **88–31 B.C.E.** Civil wars and failure of the Republic **31 B.C.E.–14 C.E.** Augustus establishes the Principate	**187–40 B.C.E.** Emperor Wu expands the Han Empire
50 C.E. **200 C.E.**		**23 C.E.** Han capital transferred from Chang'an to Luoyang
300 C.E.	**235–284 C.E.** Third-century crisis **324 C.E.** Constantine moves capital to Constantinople	**220 C.E.** Fall of Han Empire

Elders" that dominated the politics of the Roman state. Their families constituted the senatorial class. Tradition maintains that seven kings ruled Rome between 753 and 507 B.C.E., Romulus being the first and the tyrannical Tarquinius Superbus the last. In 507 B.C.E., members of the senatorial class, led by Brutus "the Liberator," deposed Tarquinius Superbus and instituted a *res publica*, a "public possession," or republic.

Far from being a democracy, the **Roman Republic**, which lasted from 507 to 31 B.C.E., vested power in several assemblies. Male citizens could attend their sessions, but the votes of the wealthy counted for more than the votes of the poor. The hierarchy of state officials, elected for one year, culminated in two consuls, who presided over the Senate and other assemblies and commanded the army on campaigns.

Technically an advisory council, first to the kings and later to the annually changing Republican officials, the **Roman Senate** increasingly made policy and governed. Senators nominated their sons for public offices and filled senatorial vacancies with former officials. This self-perpetuating body, whose members served for life, brought together wealth, influence, and political and military experience.

Roman families consisted of several generations as well as domestic slaves. The oldest living male, the

paterfamilias, exercised absolute authority over every family member. This *auctoritas*, enjoyed by important male members of the society as a whole, enabled a man to inspire and demand obedience from his inferiors.

Complex ties of obligation, such as the **patron/client relationship**, bound together individuals and families. *Clients* sought the help and protection of *patrons*, men of wealth and influence. A senator might

Roman Republic The period from 507 to 31 B.C.E., during which Rome was largely governed by the aristocratic Roman Senate.

Roman Senate A council whose members were the heads of wealthy, landowning families. Originally an advisory body to the early kings, in the era of the Roman Republic the Senate effectively governed the Roman state and the growing empire. Under Senate leadership, Rome conquered an empire of unprecedented extent in the lands surrounding the Mediterranean Sea. In the first century B.C.E. quarrels among powerful and ambitious senators and failure to address social and economic problems led to civil wars and the emergence of the rule of the emperors.

patron/client relationship In ancient Rome, a fundamental social relationship in which the patron—a wealthy and powerful individual—provided legal and economic protection and assistance to clients, men of lesser status and means, and in return the clients supported the political careers and economic interests of their patron.

have dozens or even hundreds of clients to whom he provided legal advice and representation, physical protection, and monetary loans in tough times. In turn, the client followed his patron out to battle, supported him in the political arena, worked on his land, and even contributed to his daughter's dowry. Throngs of clients awaited their patrons in the morning and accompanied them to the Forum for the day's business. Especially large retinues brought great prestige. Middle-class clients of the aristocracy might be patrons to poorer men. Rome thus accepted and institutionalized inequality and made of it a system of mutual benefits and obligations.

Roman women played no public role and hence appear infrequently in sources. Nearly all information pertains to those in the upper classes. In early Rome, a woman never ceased to be a child in the eyes of the law. She started out under the absolute authority of her paterfamilias. When she married, she came under the jurisdiction of the paterfamilias of her husband's family. Unable to own property or represent herself in legal proceedings, she had to depend on a male guardian to advocate her interests.

Despite the limitations, Roman women seem less constrained than their Greek counterparts (see Chapter 4). Over time, they gained greater personal protection and economic freedom. Some took advantage of a form of marriage that left a woman under the jurisdiction of her father and independent after his death. Many stories involve strong women who greatly influenced their husbands or sons and thereby helped shape Roman history. Roman poets expressed love for women who appeared educated and outspoken, and the careers of the early emperors abound with tales of self-assured and assertive queen-mothers and consorts.

Like other Italian peoples, Romans believed in invisible, shapeless forces known as *numina*. Vesta, the living, pulsating energy of fire, dwelled in the hearth. Janus guarded the door. The Penates watched over food stored in the cupboard. Other deities resided in hills, caves, grottoes, and springs. Small offerings of cakes and liquids supplicated the favor of these spirits. Certain gods operated in larger spheres—for example, Jupiter, the god of the sky, and Mars, initially a god of agriculture as well as war.

The Romans strove to maintain the *pax deorum* ("peace of the gods"), a covenant between the gods and the Roman state. Boards of priests drawn from the aristocracy performed sacrifices and other rituals to win the gods' favor. In return, the Roman state counted on the gods for success in its undertakings. When the Romans encountered the Greeks of southern Italy, they equated their major deities with gods from the Greek pantheon, such as Zeus (Jupiter) and Ares (Mars), and took over the myths attached to them.

Expansion in Italy and the Mediterranean

The fledgling Roman Republic of 500 B.C.E. did not stand out among the city-states of Latium, a region of central Italy. Three and a half centuries later, Rome commanded a huge empire encompassing virtually all the Mediterranean lands. Expansion began slowly but picked up momentum, peaking in the third and second centuries B.C.E.

Some scholars ascribe Rome's success to the greed and aggressiveness of a people fond of war. Others observe that the structure of the Roman state encouraged

Statue of a Roman Carrying Busts of His Ancestors, First Century B.C.E. Roman society was extremely conscious of status, and the status of an elite Roman family was determined in large part by the public achievements of ancestors and living members. A visitor to a Roman home found portraits of distinguished ancestors in the entry hall, along with labels listing the offices they held. Portrait heads were carried in funeral processions. Alinari/Art Resource, NY

recourse to war, because the two consuls had only one year in office in which to gain military glory. The Romans invariably claimed they were only defending themselves. Possibly fear drove the Romans to expand their territory: each new conquest became vulnerable, necessitating ever more buffers against attack.

Ongoing friction between the pastoral hill peoples of the Apennines, who depended on herding, and the farmers of the coastal plains sparked Rome's conquest of Italy. In the fifth century B.C.E., Rome achieved leadership within a league of central Italian cities organized for defense against the hill peoples. In the fourth century B.C.E., the Romans occasionally defended the wealthy and sophisticated cities of Campania, the region on the Bay of Naples possessing the richest farmland in the peninsula. By 290 B.C.E., after three wars with the peoples of Samnium in central Italy, the Romans had extended their "protection" over nearly the entire peninsula.

The Romans consolidated their hold over Italy by granting the political, legal, and economic privileges of citizenship to conquered populations. In this, they contrasted with the Greeks, who did not share citizenship with outsiders (see Chapter 4). The Romans co-opted the most influential elements within the conquered communities and made Rome's interests their interests. Rome also demanded that its Italian subjects provide soldiers; this seemingly inexhaustible reservoir of manpower bolstered military success. Rome could endure higher casualties than the enemy and prevail by sheer numbers.

Between 264 and 202 B.C.E., Rome fought two protracted wars against the Carthaginians, those energetic descendants of the Phoenicians who had settled in Tunisia and dominated the commerce of the western Mediterranean (see Chapter 3). The Roman state emerged as the master of the western Mediterranean and acquired its first overseas provinces in Sicily, Sardinia, and Spain (see Map 6.1). Between 200 and 146 B.C.E., a series of wars pitted the Roman state against the major Hellenistic kingdoms in the eastern Mediterranean. Reluctant to occupy such distant territories, the Romans withdrew their troops. But when the settlements they imposed failed to take root, a frustrated Roman government took over direct administration of these turbulent lands. The conquest of the Celtic peoples of Gaul (modern France; see Chapter

2) by Rome's most brilliant general, Gaius Julius Caesar, between 59 and 51 B.C.E. led to the first territorial acquisitions in Europe's heartland.

The Romans resisted extending to distant provinces the governing system and privileges of citizenship they employed in Italy. Indigenous elite groups willing to collaborate with Rome enjoyed considerable autonomy, including responsibility for local administration and tax collection. Every year a senator, usually someone who had held high office, served as governor in each province. Accompanied by a surprisingly small retinue of friends and relations who served as advisers and deputies, the governor defended the province against outside attack and internal disruption, oversaw the collection of taxes, and judged legal cases.

Over time, this system proved inadequate. Officials chosen through political connections often lacked competence, and the one-year period of service gave them little time to gain experience. A few governors extorted huge sums of money from the provincial populace. Rome still depended on the institutions and attitudes of a city-state to govern an ever-growing empire.

The Failure of the Republic

The frequent wars and territorial expansion of the third and second centuries B.C.E. set off changes in the Italian landscape. Peasant farmers spent long periods of time away from home on military service, while most of the wealth generated by conquest and empire ended up helping the upper classes purchase Italian land. Investors easily acquired the property of absent soldier-farmers by purchase, deception, or intimidation. The small self-sufficient farms of the Italian countryside, whose peasant owners provided the backbone of the Roman legions (units of 6,000 soldiers), gave way to *latifundia*, literally "broad estates," or ranches.

The new owners had ample space to graze herds of cattle or grow grapes for wine in the place of less profitable wheat. Thus, much of Italy, especially in the cities, became dependent on expensive imported grain. Meanwhile, cheap slave labor provided by war prisoners made it hard for peasants who had lost their farms to find work in the countryside (see Diversity and Dominance: The Treatment of Slaves in Rome and China). They moved to Rome and other cities, but found no work

Diversity & Dominance

The Treatment of Slaves in Rome and China

Although slaves were found in most ancient societies, Rome was one of the few in which slave labor became the indispensable foundation of the economy. In the course of the frequent wars of the second century B.C.E., large numbers of prisoners were carried into slavery. The prices of such slaves were low, and landowners and manufacturers found they could compel slaves to work longer and harder than hired laborers. Periodically, the harsh working and living conditions resulted in slave revolts.

The following excerpt, from one of several surviving manuals on agriculture, gives advice about controlling and efficiently exploiting slaves.

When the head of a household arrives at his estate, after he has prayed to the family god, he must go round his farm on a tour of inspection on the very same day, if that is possible, if not, then on the next day. When he has found out how his farm has been cultivated and which jobs have been done and which have not been done, then on the next day after that he must call in his manager and ask him which are the jobs that have been done and which remain, and whether they were done on time, and whether what still has to be done can be done, and how much wine and grain and anything else has been produced. When he has found this out, he must make a calculation of the labor and the time taken. If the work doesn't seem to him to be sufficient, and the manager starts to say how hard he tried, but the slaves weren't any good, and the weather was awful, and the slaves ran away, and he was required to carry out some public works, then when he has finished mentioning these and all sorts of other excuses, you must draw his attention to your calculation of the labor employed and time taken. If he claims that it rained all the time, there are all sorts of jobs that can be done in rainy weather—washing wine-jars, coating them with pitch, cleaning the house, storing grain, shifting muck, digging a manure pit, cleaning seed, mending ropes or making new ones; the slaves ought to have been mending their patchwork cloaks and their hoods.

On festival days they would have been able to clean out old ditches, work on the public highway, prune back brambles, dig up the garden, clear a meadow, tie up bundles of sticks, remove thorns, grind barley and get on with cleaning. If he claims that the slaves have been ill, they needn't have been given such large rations. When you have found out about all these things to your satisfaction, make sure that all the work that remains to be done will be carried out. . . . The head of the household [on his tour of inspection] should examine his herds and arrange a sale; he should sell the oil if the price makes it worthwhile, and any wine and grain that is surplus to needs; he should sell any old oxen, cattle or sheep that are not up to standard, wool and hides, an old cart or old tools, an old slave, a sick slave—anything else that is surplus to requirements. The head of a household ought to sell, and not to buy. (Cato the Elder, *Concerning Agriculture*, bk. 2, second century B.C.E.)

Cato, the Roman author of that excerpt, was notorious for his stern manner and hard-edged traditionalism, and while he does not represent the approach of all Roman masters—in reality, the treatment of slaves varied widely—he expresses a point of view that Roman society found acceptable.

Slavery was far less prominent in ancient China. During the Warring States Period, dependent peasants as well as slaves worked the large holdings of the landowning aristocracy. The Qin government sought to abolish slavery, but the institution persisted into the Han period, although it involved only a small fraction of the population and was not a central component of the economy. The relatives of criminals could be seized and enslaved, and poor families sometimes sold unwanted children into slavery. In China, slaves, whether they belonged to the state or to individuals, generally performed domestic tasks, as can be seen in the following text.

Wang Ziyuan of Shu Commandery went to the Jian River on business, and went up to the home of the widow Yang Hui, who had a male slave named Bianliao. Wang Ziyuan requested him to go and buy some wine. Picking up a big stick, Bianliao climbed to the top of the grave mound and said: "When my master bought me, Bianliao, he only contracted for me to care for the grave and did not contract for me to buy wine for some other gentleman."

Wang Ziyuan was furious and said to the widow: "Wouldn't you prefer to sell this slave?"

Yang Hui said: "The slave's father offered him to people, but no one wanted him." Wang Ziyuan immediately settled on the sale contract.

The slave again said: "Enter in the contract everything you wish to order me to do. I, Bianliao, will not do anything not in the contract."

Wang Ziyuan said: "Agreed."

The text of the contract said:

Third year of Shenjiao, the first month, the fifteenth day, the gentleman Wang Ziyuan, of Zizhong, purchases from the lady Yang Hui of Anzhi village in Zhengdu, the bearded male slave, Bianliao, of her husband's household. The fixed sale [price] is 15,000 [cash]. The slave shall obey orders about all kinds of work and may not argue.

He shall rise at dawn and do an early sweeping. After eating he shall wash up. Ordinarily he should pound the grain mortar, tie up broom straws, carve bowls and bore wells, scoop out ditches, tie up fallen fences, hoe the garden, trim up paths and dike up plots of land, cut big flails, bend bamboos to make rakes, and scrape and fix the well pulley. In going and coming he may not ride horseback or in the cart, [nor may he] sit crosslegged or make a hubbub. When he gets out of bed he shall shake his head [to wake up], fish, cut forage, plait reeds and card hemp, draw water for gruel, and help in making zumo [drink]. He shall weave shoes and make [other] coarse things. . . .

In the second month at the vernal equinox he shall bank the dikes and repair the boundary walls [of the fields]; prune the mulberry trees, skin the palm trees, plant melons to make gourd [utensils], select eggplant [seeds for planting], and transplant onion sets; burn plant remains to generate the fields, pile up refuse and break up lumps [in the soil]. At midday he shall dry out things in the sun. At cockcrow he shall rise and pound grain in the mortar, exercise and curry the horses, the donkeys, and likewise the mules. . . . [The list of tasks continues for two-and-a-half pages.]

He shall be industrious and quick-working, and he may not idle and loaf. When the slave is old and his strength spent, he shall plant marsh grass and weave mats. When his work is over and he wishes to rest he should pound a picul [of grain]. Late at night when there is no work he shall wash clothes really white. If he has private savings they shall be the master's gift, or from

guests. The slave may not have evil secrets; affairs should be open and reported. If the slave does not heed instructions, he shall be whipped a hundred strokes.

The reading of the text of the contract came to an end. The slave was speechless and his lips were tied. Wildly he beat his head on the ground, and beat himself with his hands; from his eyes the tears streamed down, and the drivel from his nose hung a foot long.

He said: "If it is to be exactly as master Wang says, I would rather return soon along the yellow-soil road, with the grave worms boring through my head. Had I known before I would have bought the wine for master Wang, I would not have dared to do that wrong." (Wang Bao, first century B.C.E.)

This story was meant to be humorous and no doubt exaggerates the amount of work that could be demanded from a slave, but it shows that Chinese slaves could be forced to work hard and engaged in many of the same menial tasks as their Roman counterparts. It is hard to imagine a Roman slave daring to refuse a request and arguing publicly with a nobleman without being severely punished. It also appears that slaves in China were legally protected by contracts that specified and limited what could be demanded of them.

QUESTIONS FOR ANALYSIS

1. Why might slavery have been less important in Han China than in the Roman Empire? Why would the treatment of slaves have been less harsh in China than in Rome?

2. In what ways were slaves treated like other forms of property, such as animals and tools? In what ways was a slave's "humanity" taken into account?

3. What are some of the passive-resistance tactics that slaves resorted to, and what did they achieve by these actions?

Source: First selection from Thomas Wiedemann, *Greek and Roman Slavery* (Baltimore: Johns Hopkins University Press, 1981), 183–184. © 1981 by Johns Hopkins University Press. Reproduced by permission of Taylor & Francis Books UK. Second selection from C. Martin Wilbur, *Slavery in China During the Former Han Dynasty, 206 B.C.–A.D. 25* (New York: Russell & Russell, 1967). Reprinted with permission of Scribner, a division of Simon & Schuster, Inc. from *Slavery in China During the Former Han Dynasty* by Clarence Martin Wilbur (Russell & Russell, New York, 1967).

there either and ended up living in poverty. The grow-ing urban masses, idle and prone to riot, would play a major role in the political struggles of the late Republic.

The decline of peasant farmers in Italy produced a shortage of men who owned the minimum amount of property required for military service. During a war that the Romans fought in North Africa at the end of the second century B.C.E., Gaius Marius—a "new man" as the Romans labeled politically active individuals from outside the traditional ruling class—achieved political prominence by enlisting in the legions poor propertyless men to whom he promised farms upon retirement from military service. These grateful troops helped Marius get elected to an unprecedented (and illegal) six consulships.

Between 88 and 31 B.C.E., several ambitious indi-viduals—Sulla, Pompey, Julius Caesar, Mark Antony, and Octavian—commanded armies that were more loyal to them than to the state. Their use of Roman troops to increase their personal power led to civil wars between military factions. The generals who seized Rome on several occasions executed their polit-ical opponents and exercised dictatorial control.

Julius Caesar's grandnephew and heir, Octavian (63 B.C.E.–14 C.E.), eliminated all rivals by 31 B.C.E. and set about refashioning the Roman system of govern-ment while retaining the offices, honors, and social prerogatives of the senatorial class. A dictator in fact, he never called himself king or emperor, claiming merely to be *princeps*, "first among equals"; hence the term **Roman Principate** for the period following the Roman Republic. **Augustus**, a title Octavian received from the Senate, implied prosperity and piety and became the name by which he is known to posterity. Augustus's ruthlessness, patience, and intuitive grasp of psychology enabled him to manipulate each group in society. When he died in 14 C.E., after forty-five years of carefully veiled rule, scarcely anyone could remember the Republic. During his reign, the empire expanded into Egypt and parts of the Middle East and central Europe, leaving only the southern half of Brit-ain and modern Romania to be added later.

Primary Source: A Man of Unlimited Ambition: Julius Caesar Read about the plots and intrigues of the Roman court.

Peter Rockwell, Rome

Scene from Trajan's Column, Rome, ca. 113 C.E. The Roman emperor Trajan erected a marble column 125 feet (38 meters) in height to commemorate his triumphant campaign in Dacia (modern Romania). The relief carving, which snakes around the column for 656 feet (200 meters), illustrates numerous episodes of the conquest and provided a detailed pictorial record of the equipment and practices of the Roman army in the field. This panel depicts soldiers building a fort.

Roman Principate A term used to characterize Roman government in the first three centuries C.E., based on the ambiguous title *princeps* ("first citi-zen") adopted by Augustus to conceal his military dictatorship.

Augustus (63 B.C.E.–14 C.E.) Honorific name of Octa-vian, founder of the Roman Principate, the military dictatorship that replaced the failing rule of the Roman Senate. After defeating all rivals, between 31 B.C.E. and 14 C.E. he laid the groundwork for several centuries of stability and prosperity in the Roman Empire.

Roman Aqueduct near Tarragona The growth of towns and cities challenged Roman officials to provide an adequate supply of water. Aqueducts channeled water from a source, sometimes many miles away, to an urban complex using only the force of gravity. To bring water from high ground into the city, Roman engineers designed long, continuous rows of arches that maintained a steady downhill slope. Scholars can sometimes estimate the population of an ancient city by calculating the amount of water that was available to it.

So popular was Augustus that four members of his family succeeded to the position of "emperor" (as we call it) despite serious personal and political shortcomings. After the mid-first century C.E., other families obtained the post. In theory, the Senate affirmed the early emperors; in reality, the armies chose them. By the second century C.E., the so-called Good Emperors instituted a new mechanism of succession: each designated as his successor a mature man of proven ability whom he adopted as his son and with whom he shared offices and privileges.

Augustus had allied himself with the *equites*, the class of well-to-do Italian merchants and landowners second in wealth and social status only to the senatorial class. These competent and self-assured individuals became the core of a new civil service. At last Rome had an administrative bureaucracy capable of managing a large empire with considerable honesty, consistency, and efficiency.

An Urban Empire

Calling the Roman Empire of the first three centuries C.E. an "urban" empire does not mean that most people lived in cities and towns. Perhaps 80 percent of the empire's 50 to 60 million people lived in agricultural villages or on isolated farms. The network of towns and cities served as administrative centers, however, with corresponding benefits for the urban populace.

Numerous towns had several thousand inhabitants. A handful of major cities—Alexandria in Egypt, Antioch in Syria, and Carthage—had populations of several hundred thousand. Rome itself had approximately a million residents. The largest cities put huge strains on the government's technical ability to provide food and water and remove sewage.

At Rome, the upper classes lived in elegant hillside townhouses. The house centered around an *atrium*, a rectangular courtyard with an open skylight to let in light and rainwater for drinking and washing. A dining room for dinner and drinking parties, an interior garden, a kitchen, and perhaps a private bath surrounded the atrium with bedrooms on an upper level. Pebble mosaics on the floors and frescoes of mythological

equites In ancient Italy, prosperous landowners second in wealth and status to the senatorial aristocracy. The Roman emperors allied with this group to counterbalance the influence of the old aristocracy and used the *equites* to staff the imperial civil service.

143

Roman Shop Selling Food and Drink The bustling town of Pompeii on the Bay of Naples was buried in ash by the eruption of Mt. Vesuvius in 79 C.E. Archaeologists have unearthed the streets, stores, and houses of this typical Roman town. Shops such as this sold hot food and drink served from clay vessels set into the counter. Shelves and niches behind the counter contained other items. In the background can be seen a well-paved street and a public fountain where the inhabitants could fetch water.

scenes or outdoor vistas on the walls and ceilings gave a sense of openness in the absence of windows. Many aristocrats owned a number of villas in the countryside as retreats from the pressures of city life.

The poor inhabited crowded slums in the low-lying parts of the city. Damp, dark, and smelly, with few furnishings, their wooden tenements suffered from frequent fires. Fortunately, Romans could spend the day outdoors for much of the year.

Other cities and towns, including the ramshackle settlements that sprang up beside frontier forts, mirrored the capital city in political organization, physical layout, and appearance. A town council and two annually elected officials drawn from prosperous members of the community maintained law and order and collected both urban and rural taxes. In return for the privilege of running local affairs and in appreciation of the state's protection of their wealth and position, this "municipal aristocracy" served Rome loyally. In striving to imitate Roman senators, they lavishly endowed their cities and towns, which had little revenue of their own, with attractive elements of Roman urban life: a forum, government buildings, temples, gardens, baths, theaters, amphitheaters, and games and public entertainments of all sorts. These amenities made the situation of the urban poor superior to that of the rural poor. Poor people in a city could pass time at the baths, seek refuge from the elements under the colonnades, and attend the games.

Hard work and drudgery marked life in the countryside, relieved only by occasional festive days and the everyday pleasures of sex, family, and social exchange. Rural people had to fend for themselves in dealing with bandits, wild animals, and other hazards. People outside urban centers had little direct contact with the government beyond an occasional run-in with bullying soldiers and the dreaded arrival of the tax collector.

The concentration of ownership reversed temporarily during the civil wars that ended the Republic; it resumed under the emperors. But the end of new conquests reduced the number of slaves and forced landowners to find new labor. Landlords turned to tenant farmers, whom they allowed to live on and cultivate plots of land in return for a portion of their crop. The landowners themselves still lived in cities and hired foremen to manage their estates. Thus, wealth based on rural productivity became concentrated in the cities.

Some urban dwellers became rich from manufacture and trade. The *pax romana* ("Roman peace"),

pax romana Literally, "Roman peace," it connoted the stability and prosperity that Roman rule brought to the lands of the Roman Empire in the first two centuries C.E. The movement of people and trade goods along Roman roads and safe seas allowed for the spread of cultural practices, technologies, and religious ideas.

the safety and stability guaranteed by Roman might, favored commerce. Meat and vegetables usually could be exchanged only locally because transportation was costly and many products spoiled quickly. The city of Rome, however, depended on grain shipments from Sicily and Egypt to feed its huge population. Special naval squadrons performed this task.

Some exporters dealt in glass, metalwork, delicate pottery, and other fine manufactures. The centers of production, first located in Italy, moved into the provinces as knowledge of the necessary skills spread. Roman armies on the frontiers provided a large market, and their presence promoted the prosperity of border provinces. Other merchants traded in luxury items from beyond the empire's boundaries, especially Chinese silks, Indian spices, and Arabian incense. The tax revenues of rich provinces like Gaul (France) and Egypt flowed to Rome to support the emperor and the central government, and to the frontier provinces to subsidize the armies.

Romanization, the spread of the Latin language and Roman way of life, proved an enduring consequence of empire among the diverse peoples in the western provinces. Hellenism dominated the eastern Mediterranean (see Chapter 4). Portuguese, Spanish, French, Italian, and Romanian evolved from the Latin language, proving that the language of the conquerors spread among the common people as well as the elite. However, in frontier areas along the Rhine and Danube Rivers, where Roman control was tenuous and migrations by Germanic peoples were changing the ethnic balance by the third century C.E., Latin made only limited headway.

The Roman government did not force Romanization. The inhabitants of the provinces themselves chose Latin and adopted cultural practices like wearing the *toga* (the traditional cloak worn by Roman male citizens). Making this choice brought advantages, as do learning English and wearing a suit and tie today in some developing nations. Latin facilitated dealings with the administration and helped merchants get contracts to supply the military. Many also must have been drawn by the aura of success surrounding the language and culture of a people who had created so vast an empire.

As towns sprang up and acquired the Roman urban amenities, they attracted ambitious members of the indigenous populations. The empire gradually and reluctantly extended Roman citizenship, with its attendant privileges, legal protections, and certain tax exemptions, to people living outside Italy. Completing a twenty-six-year term of service in the native military units that backed up the Roman legions earned soldiers citizenship that could pass to their descendants. Emperors granted citizenship to individuals or entire communities as rewards for service. Then in 212 C.E. the emperor Caracalla granted citizenship to all free, adult, male inhabitants of the empire.

The gradual extension of citizenship mirrored the empire's transformation from an Italian dominion over the Mediterranean lands into a commonwealth of peoples. As early as the first century C.E., some of the leading literary and intellectual figures came from the provinces. By the second century, even the emperors hailed from Spain, Gaul, and North Africa.

The Rise of Christianity

The Jewish homeland of Judaea (see Chapter 3), roughly equivalent to present-day Israel, came under direct Roman rule in 6 C.E. Over the next half-century, the insensitivity of the Roman governors to the Jewish belief in one god increased tensions with the inhabitants. Various kinds of opposition to Roman rule sprang up. Many Jews anticipated the arrival of the Messiah, the "Anointed One," presumed to be a military leader who would liberate the Jewish people and drive the Romans out.

It is in this context that we must see the career of **Jesus**, a young carpenter from the Galilee region in northern Israel. In place of what he considered

---

Romanization The process by which the Latin language and Roman culture became dominant in the western provinces of the Roman Empire. The Roman government did not actively seek to Romanize the subject peoples, but indigenous peoples in the provinces often chose to Romanize because of the political and economic advantages that it brought, as well as the allure of Roman success.

Jesus (ca. 5 B.C.E.–34 C.E.) A Jew from Galilee in northern Israel who sought to reform Jewish beliefs and practices. He was executed as a revolutionary by the Romans. Hailed as the Messiah and son of God by his followers, he became the central figure in Christianity, a belief system that developed in the centuries after his death.

excessive concern with money and power among Jewish leaders and perfunctory religious observance by mainstream Jews, Jesus prescribed a return to the personal faith and spirituality of an earlier age. He eventually attracted the attention of the Jewish authorities in Jerusalem, who regarded popular reformers as potential troublemakers. They turned him over to the Roman governor, Pontius Pilate. Jesus was imprisoned, condemned, and executed by crucifixion, a punishment usually reserved for common criminals. His followers, the Apostles, subsequently sought to spread his teachings and their belief that he had been resurrected (returned from death to life) among their fellow Jews.

Paul, a Jew from the Greek city of Tarsus in southern Anatolia, converted to the new creed and between 45 and 58 C.E. devoted himself to spreading the word. Traveling throughout Syria-Palestine, Anatolia, and Greece, he found most Jews unwilling to accept his claim that Jesus was the Messiah and had ushered in a new age. Frustrated, Paul redirected his efforts toward non-Jews (sometimes called "gentiles") who were also experiencing a spiritual hunger. He set up a string of Christian (from the Greek term *christos*, meaning "anointed one," given to Jesus by his followers) communities in the eastern Mediterranean.

Paul's career exemplifies the cosmopolitan nature of the Roman Empire in this era. Speaking both Greek and Aramaic, he moved comfortably between the Greco-Roman and Jewish worlds. He used Roman roads, depended on the peace guaranteed by Roman arms, called on his Roman citizenship to protect him from local authorities, and moved from city to city in his quest for converts.

In 66 C.E., tensions in Roman Judaea erupted in a revolt that lasted until 73. The Jerusalem-based Christian community, which focused on converting Jews, fell victim to the Roman reconquest. This cleared the field for Paul's non-Jewish converts, and Christianity began to diverge more and more from its Jewish roots. The sect grew slowly but steadily. Many early converts came from disenfranchised groups: women, slaves, and the urban poor. They hoped to receive the respect not accorded them in the larger society and to obtain positions of responsibility when the early Christian communities elected their leaders. However, as the religious movement grew and prospered, it developed a hierarchy of priests and bishops and engaged in bitter disputes over theological doctrine (see Chapter 10).

As monotheists forbidden to worship other gods, early Christians met persecution from Roman officials, who often took their refusal to worship the emperor as a sign of disloyalty. Nevertheless, despite mob attacks and occasional government attempts at suppression (or perhaps because of them), the Christian movement continued to attract converts. By the late third century C.E., adherents to Christianity were a sizeable minority within the empire and included many educated and prosperous people holding local and imperial posts.

During the Greek Classical period, a number of "mystery" cults had gained popularity by claiming to provide secret information about the nature of life and death and promising a blessed afterlife to their adherents. In the Hellenistic and Roman periods, belief systems making similar promises arose in the eastern Mediterranean and spread throughout the Greco-Roman lands, responding to a spiritual and intellectual hunger not satisfied by paganism. These included the cults of the mother-goddess Cybele in Anatolia, the Egyptian goddess Isis, and the Iranian sun-god Mithra. As we shall see, the ultimate victory of Christianity over these rivals arose from historical circumstances as much as from spiritual appeal.

Technology and Transformation

The ease and safety of travel brought by Roman arms and engineering helped the early Christians spread their faith. Surviving remnants of roads, fortification walls, aqueducts, and buildings testify to the Romans' engineering expertise. Some of the best engineers served with the army, building bridges, siege works, and siege weapons. In peacetime,

Paul (ca. 5–65 C.E.) A Jew from the Greek city of Tarsus in Anatolia, he initially persecuted the followers of Jesus but became a Christian after receiving a revelation on the road to Syrian Damascus. Taking advantage of his Hellenized background and Roman citizenship, he traveled throughout Syria-Palestine, Anatolia, and Greece, preaching the new religion and establishing churches. Finding his greatest success among pagans ("gentiles"), he began the process by which Christianity separated from Judaism.

soldiers often worked on construction projects. **Aqueducts**—long elevated or underground conduits—used gravity to carry water from a source to an urban center. The Romans pioneered the use of arches, which allowed the even distribution of great weights without thick supporting walls. The invention of concrete—a mixture of lime powder, sand, and water that could be poured into molds—enabled the construction of vast vaulted and domed interior spaces, in contrast to the rectilinear post-and-lintel designs employed by the Greeks and Egyptians.

Defending borders that stretched for thousands of miles posed a great administrative challenge. In a document released after his death, Augustus advised against expanding the empire because the costs of administration and defense would exceed any increase in revenues. His successors' reorganization and redeployment of the Roman army reflect the shift from an offensive to a defensive strategy. Mountains, deserts, and seas protected the empire at most points. But the lengthy Rhine/Danube frontier in Germany and central Europe was vulnerable and thus was guarded by forts whose relatively small garrisons were not always up to the task of repelling raiders. On more desolate frontiers in Britain and North Africa, the Romans built long walls to keep out the peoples who lived beyond.

Most of Rome's neighbors lacked sufficient technology and military organization to pose a serious threat. The one exception lay on the eastern frontier, where the Parthian kingdom controlled the lands that are today Iran and Iraq. Rome and Parthia fought exhaustingly for centuries, with neither side gaining significant territory.

The Roman state prospered for two and a half centuries after Augustus stabilized the political situation and instituted a program of reforms. In the third century C.E., cracks in the edifice became visible. Historians call the period from 235 to 284 C.E. the **third-century crisis**, a time when political, military, and economic problems nearly destroyed the empire. A frequent change of rulers marked the crisis, as twenty or more men claimed the office of emperor during this period. Most reigned for only a few months or years before being overthrown by a rival or killed by their own troops. Germanic peoples on the Rhine/Danube frontier took advantage of the disorders to raid

deep into the empire. For the first time in centuries, Roman cities built protective walls. Some regions, feeling a lack of imperial protection, turned to anyone who promised to put their interests first.

Political and military emergencies devastated the empire's economy. Buying the loyalty of the army and paying to defend the increasingly permeable frontiers drained the treasury. The resultant demands for more tax revenues from the provinces, as well as the interruption of commerce by fighting, eroded urban prosperity. Shortsighted emperors, desperate for cash, secretly reduced the amount of precious metal in Roman coins and pocketed the excess. But the public quickly caught on, and the devalued coinage became less and less acceptable in the marketplace. Indeed, the empire reverted to a barter economy, which curtailed large-scale and long-distance commerce even more.

The municipal aristocracy, once the empire's most vital and public-spirited class, suffered heavily. As town councilors, its members had to make up any shortfall in taxes owed to the state. As the decline in trade eroded their wealth, which often derived from manufacture and commerce, many evaded their civic duties and even went into hiding.

Population shifted out of the cities and into the countryside. Many people sought employment and protection from raiders and government officials on the estates of wealthy and powerful country landowners. Just when things looked bleakest, one man pulled the empire back from the brink. Diocletian, like several other emperors, hailed from one of the eastern European provinces most vulnerable to invasion. Of humble origins, he rose through the ranks of the army

---

aqueduct A conduit, either elevated or underground, that used gravity to carry water from a source to a location—usually a city—that needed it. The Romans built many aqueducts in a period of substantial urbanization.

third-century crisis Historians' term for the political, military, and economic turmoil that beset the Roman Empire during much of the third century C.E.: frequent changes of ruler, civil wars, barbarian invasions, decline of urban centers, and near-destruction of long-distance commerce and the monetary economy. After 284 C.E. Diocletian restored order by making fundamental changes.

and gained power in 284. He was so successful that he ruled for over twenty years and died in bed.

To halt inflation (the process by which prices rise as the value of money declines), Diocletian issued an edict specifying the maximum prices for various commodities and services. To ensure an adequate labor supply in vital services, he froze people in their professions and made them train their sons to succeed them. This unprecedented regulation of prices and vocations had unforeseen consequences. A "black market" arose among buyers and sellers who chose to ignore the price controls. More broadly, many imperial citizens began to see the government as an oppressive entity that no longer deserved their loyalty.

When Diocletian resigned in 305, the old divisiveness reemerged as various claimants battled for the throne. By 324, a general named **Constantine** (r. 306–337) had reunited the empire under his sole rule. In 312, Constantine won a key battle at the Milvian Bridge over the Tiber River near Rome. He later claimed that before this battle, he had seen in the sky a cross (the sign of the Christian God) superimposed on the sun. Believing that the Christian God had helped him achieve the victory, Constantine converted to Christianity. Throughout his reign, he supported the Christian church, although he tolerated other beliefs as well. Historians disagree about whether Constantine's conversion resulted from spiritual motives or from a pragmatic desire to unify the empire under a single religion. Regardless of the reason, large numbers of people now converted because they saw that Christians had advantages over non-Christians in seeking offices and favors.

Constantine also transferred the capital in 324 from Rome to Byzantium, an ancient Greek city on the Bosporus (BAHS-puhr-uhs) strait connecting the Mediterranean and the Black Sea. Renamed Constantinople (cahn-stan-tih-NO-pul) ("City of Constantine"), it represented a concentration of attention on the threatened imperial borders in eastern Europe (see Map 6.1). The cities and middle classes of the eastern provinces had better withstood the third-century crisis than those in the west. In addition, more educated people and more Christians lived in the east (see Chapter 10).

Some see the conversion of Constantine and the transfer of the imperial capital as events marking the

SECTION REVIEW

- From a collection of farming communities, Rome evolved into a republic dominated by wealthy land-owning families who controlled the Senate.
- Through a series of wars, the Republic grew into an overseas empire.
- Political crises destroyed the Republic, and under Augustus and his successors, Rome expanded as a prosperous urban empire.
- Christianity emerged from tensions between Jewish and Roman culture and spread through the preaching of Paul of Tarsus.
- The third-century crisis nearly destroyed the empire until Diocletian's reforms stabilized the state briefly.
- Constantine reunited the empire, granted tolerance to Christianity, and moved the capital to Byzantium.

end of Roman history. But many of the important changes that culminated during Constantine's reign had their roots in the previous two centuries, and the Roman Empire as a whole survived for at least another century. Moreover, the eastern, or Byzantine, portion of it (discussed in Chapter 10) survived Constantine by more than a thousand years. Nevertheless, the Roman Empire of the fourth century differed fundamentally from what had existed before, a fact that justifies seeing Constantine's reign as the beginning of a new epoch in the West.

The Origins of Imperial China, 221 B.C.E.–220 C.E.

How did imperial China evolve from its beginnings into the Han state?

A fragmentation seemingly dictated by geography characterized the early history of China (see Chapter 2). The Shang (ca. 1750–1027 B.C.E.) and Zhou (1027–221 B.C.E.) wielded authority over a relatively compact zone in northeastern China. The last few centuries of

Constantine (285–337 C.E.) Roman emperor (r. 306–337). After reuniting the Roman Empire, he moved the capital to Constantinople and made Christianity a favored religion.

nominal Zhou rule—the Warring States Period—saw rivalry among a group of small states, a situation reminiscent of the contemporary Greek city-states (see Chapter 4). As in Greece, competition and conflict fostered many elements of a national culture.

In the second half of the third century B.C.E. the Qin (chin) state in the Wei (way) Valley conquered its rivals and created China's first empire (221–206 B.C.E.). But it barely survived the death of its founder, Shi Huangdi. Power passed to a new dynasty, the Han,

which ruled China from 206 B.C.E. to 220 C.E. (see Map 6.2). The imperial tradition of political and cultural unity thus begun lasted into the twentieth century and still has meaning for China today.

Resources and Population

An imperial state controlling lands of great diversity in topography, climate, plant and animal life, and human population faced greater obstacles to long-distance communications and a uniform way of

Map 6.2 Han China The Qin and Han rulers of northeast China extended their control over all of eastern China and extensive territories to the west. A series of walls in the north and northwest, built to check the incursions of nomadic peoples from the steppes, were joined together to form the ancestor of the present-day Great Wall of China. An extensive network of roads connecting towns, cities, and frontier forts promoted rapid communication and facilitated trade. The Silk Road carried China's most treasured product to Central, South, and West Asia and the Mediterranean lands.
© Cengage Learning

Interactive Map

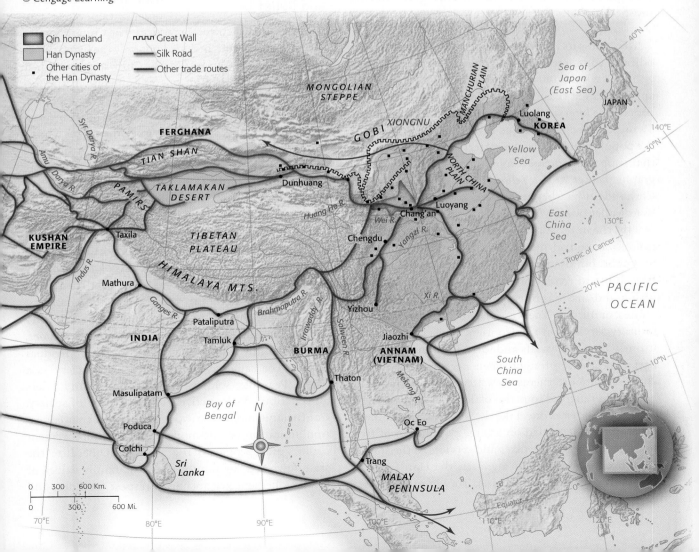

life than did the Roman Empire. Rome's territories were roughly similar in climate and agriculture, and Rome benefited from an internal sea—the Mediterranean—that facilitated rapid and inexpensive transport. What resources, technologies, institutions, and values made the Chinese empire possible? Agriculture produced the wealth and taxes that supported the institutions of imperial China. The main tax, a percentage of the annual harvest, funded government activities ranging from the luxurious lifestyle of the royal court to the military garrisons on the frontiers. The imperial capitals, first Chang'an (chahng-ahn) and later Luoyang (LWOE-yahng), housed large populations that had to be fed. As intensive agriculture spread in the Yangzi River Valley, the need to transport southern crops to the north spurred the construction of canals to connect the Yangzi with the Yellow River. The government also stored surplus grain during prosperous times for sale at reasonable prices during shortages.

To assess its labor resources, the government periodically conducted a census. Results survive for the years 2 C.E. and 140 C.E. The earlier survey indicates approximately 12 million households and 60 million people; the later, not quite 10 million households and 49 million people. Then as now, the vast majority of the population lived in the eastern river-valley regions that supported intensive agriculture. The early demographic center in the Yellow River Valley and North China Plain had begun to shift south to the Yangzi River Valley by early Han times.

In the intervals between seasonal agricultural tasks, able-bodied men donated one month of labor to public building projects—palaces, temples, fortifications, and roads—or to transporting goods, excavating and maintaining canals, cultivating imperial estates, or mining. The state also required two years of military service. On the frontiers, conscripted young Chinese men built walls and forts, kept an eye on barbarian neighbors, fought when necessary, and grew crops to support themselves. Registers of land and households enabled imperial officials to keep track of money and services due. Like the Romans, the Chinese governments depended on a large population of free peasants to contribute taxes and services to the state.

Throughout the Han dynasty, the Han Chinese gradually expanded into the territory of other ethnic

groups. Population growth in the core regions and a shortage of good land spurred the pioneers onward. Sometimes the government organized new settlements—at strategic sites, for example, and on the frontiers. Neighboring kingdoms also invited Chinese settlers so they could exploit their skills and learn their technologies.

Han people preferred regions suitable to the agriculture they had practiced in the eastern river valleys. On the northern frontier, they pushed back nomadic populations. They also expanded into the tropical forests of southern China and settled in the western oases. Places not suitable for their preferred kind of agriculture, particularly the steppe and deserts, did not attract them.

Hierarchy, Obedience, and Belief

The Han Chinese brought with them their social organization, values, language, and other cultural practices. The Chinese family, the basic social unit, included not only the living generations but also the ancestors. The Chinese believed their ancestors maintained an ongoing interest in the fortunes of the family and therefore consulted, appeased, and venerated their ancestors to maintain their favor. Viewed as a living, self-renewing organism, the family required sons to perpetuate itself and ensure the immortality offered by the ancestor cult.

The doctrine of Confucius (Kongzi), which had its origins in the sixth century B.C.E. (see Chapter 2), became a fundamental source of values in the imperial period. Confucianism considered hierarchy a natural social phenomenon and assigned tasks and rules of conduct to each person. Absolute authority rested with the father, who presided over the rituals that linked living family members to the ancestors. People saw themselves as having responsibilities within the domestic hierarchy according to gender, age, and family relationship rather than as individual agents. The same concepts operated in society as a whole. Peasants, soldiers, administrators, and rulers all contributed distinctively to the welfare of society. Confucianism optimistically maintained that education, imitation of role models, and self-improvement could guide people to the right path. Because the state mirrored the family, the basic family values of loyalty, obedience to authority, respect for elders and ancestors, and concern for honor and appropriate conduct carried over into relations between individuals and the state.

Contemporary written sources say little about the experiences of women. Confucian ethics stressed the impropriety of women participating in public life. Traditional wisdom about the appropriate female conduct appears in a story of the mother of the Confucian philosopher Mencius (Mengzi):

> A woman's duties are to cook the five grains, heat the wine, look after her parents-in-law, make clothes, and that is all! ... [She] has no ambition to manage affairs outside the house. .... She must follow the "three submissions." When she is young, she must submit to her parents. After her marriage, she must submit to her husband. When she is widowed, she must submit to her son.[1]

This ideal, perpetuated by males of the upper classes who composed most of the surviving texts, placed women under considerable pressure to conform. Women of the lower classes, less affected by Confucian ways of thinking, may have been less constrained than their more "privileged" counterparts.

After her parents arranged her marriage, a young bride went to live with her husband's family, who saw her as a stranger until she proved herself. Ability and force of personality (as well as the capacity to produce sons) could make a difference, but dissension between the wife and her mother-in-law and sisters-in-law grew out of their competition for influence with husbands, sons, and brothers and for a larger share of the economic resources held in common by the family.

Like the early Romans, the Chinese believed that divinity resided within nature rather than outside and above it. They worshiped and tried to appease the forces of nature. The state maintained shrines to the lords of rain and winds, as well as to certain great rivers and high mountains. Gathering at mounds or altars dedicated to local earth spirits, people sacrificed sheep and pigs and beat drums to promote fertility. Unusual natural phenomena like eclipses or heavy rains prompted them to tie a red cord around

the sacred spot, symbolically restraining the deity. A belief that supernatural forces, bringing good and evil fortune, flowed through the landscape led experts in *feng shui*, "earth divination," to determine the most favorable location and orientation for buildings and graves. The faithful adapted their lives to the complex rhythms of nature.

Some people sought to cheat death by taking life-enhancing drugs or building ostentatious tombs, flanked by towers or covered by mounds of earth, and filling them with what they believed they would need for a blessed afterlife. The objects in these tombs provide a wealth of knowledge about Han society.

The First Chinese Empire

As mentioned, in the second half of the third century B.C.E., the state of the **Qin** suddenly burst forth and took over the other "warring states" one by one. By 221 B.C.E., the first emperor had united the northern plain and the Yangzi River Valley under one rule, marking the creation of China and the inauguration of the imperial age. The name *China* may derive from *Qin*.

The Qin ruler, entitled **Shi Huangdi** ("First Emperor"), and his adviser Li Si were able and ruthless men who exploited the exhaustion resulting from centuries of interstate rivalry. The Qin homeland in the valley of the Wei, a tributary of the Yellow River, provided a large pool of sturdy peasants to serve in the army but was less urbanized and commercialized than the kingdoms farther east. Mobilizing manpower for irrigation and flood control works had

Primary Source: Lessons for Women Get a taste of what life was like for women of the Han state.

Qin A people and state in the Wei Valley of eastern China that conquered rival states and created the first Chinese empire (221–206 B.C.E.). The Qin ruler, Shi Huangdi, standardized many features of Chinese society and ruthlessly marshaled subjects for military and construction projects, engendering hostility that led to the fall of his dynasty shortly after his death. The Qin framework was largely taken over by the succeeding Han Empire.

Shi Huangdi Founder of the short-lived Qin dynasty and creator of the first Chinese Empire (r. 221–210 B.C.E.). He is remembered for his ruthless conquests of rival states, standardization of practices, and forcible organization of labor for military and engineering tasks. His tomb, with its army of life-size terracotta soldiers, has been partially excavated.

Terracotta Soldiers from the Tomb of Shi Huangdi, "First Emperor" of China Thousands of these life-size, baked-clay figures, each with distinctive features, have been unearthed. This buried model army reflects the power and totalitarian rule of the Qin Empire.

History in Focus *What does this image suggest about the political situation in which Shi Huangdi came to imperial power? Find the answer online.*

strengthened the authority of the Qin king at the expense of the nobles and taught his administrators organizational skills.

Shi Huangdi and Li Si created a totalitarian structure that subordinated the individual to the needs of the state. They cracked down on Confucianism, regarding its demands for benevolent and non-violent conduct from rulers as a check on the absolute power they sought. They favored instead a philosophy known as Legalism (see Chapter 2). Its major proponent, Li Si himself, considered the will of the ruler supreme. Discipline and obedience maintained through the rigid application of rewards and punishments defined the lives of his subjects.

The new regime sought to eliminate the landowning aristocracy of the conquered states and the system supporting their wealth and power. It abolished primogeniture—the eldest son's inheritance of a family's lands—because it allowed a few individuals to accumulate vast estates. Estates now had to be broken up and passed on to several heirs.

Slaves and peasant serfs, who owed the landlord a substantial portion of their harvest, worked the lands of the aristocracy. The Qin abolished slavery and established a free peasantry who owed taxes and labor, as well as military service, to the state.

During the Warring States Period, the small states had emphasized their independence through differing symbolic practices. For example, each state had its own forms of music, with different scales, systems of notation, and instruments. The Qin imposed standard weights, measures, and coinage, a uniform law code, a common system of writing, and even regulations governing the axle length of carts so as to standardize road and street widths.

Thousands of miles of roads, comparable in scale to the roads of the Roman Empire, connected the parts of the empire and helped move Qin armies quickly. The Qin also built canals to connect the northern and southern river systems. The 20-mile-long (32.2-kilometer-long) Magic Canal, which ingeniously linked two rivers that flowed in opposite directions with strong currents, is still in use. The frontier walls of the old states were gradually combined into a continuous barricade, the precursor of the Great Wall, to protect cultivated lands from raids by northern nomads. But

Shi Huangdi's financial exploitation and demands for forced labor led, after his death in 210 B.C.E., to rebellions that ended the dynasty.

The Long Reign of the Han

When the dust cleared, Liu Bang, possibly a peasant by background, established a new dynasty, the **Han** (206 B.C.E.–220 C.E.). Rejecting the excesses and mistakes of the Qin, he restored the institutions of a venerable past. Yet the Han administration retained much of the structure and Legalist ideology put in place by the Qin, though with less fanatical zeal. A form of Confucianism revised to address the circumstances of a large, centralized political entity tempered the Legalist methods. This Confucianism emphasized the benevolence of government and the appropriateness of particular rituals and behaviors in a manifestly hierarchical society. The Han administration became the standard for later ages, and the Chinese people today refer to themselves ethnically as Han.

After eighty years of imperial consolidation, Emperor Wu (r. 140–87 B.C.E.) launched a period of military expansion, south into Fujian, Guangdong, and present-day North Vietnam and north into Manchuria and present-day North Korea. Han armies went west, to inner Mongolia and Xinjiang (SHIN-jyahng), to secure the lucrative Silk Road (see Chapter 8). However, controlling the newly acquired territories proved expensive, so Wu's successors curtailed further expansion.

The Han Empire endured, with a brief interruption, for more than four hundred years. **Chang'an**, in the Wei Valley, an ancient seat of power from which the Zhou and Qin dynasties had emerged, served as the capital from 202 B.C.E. to 8 C.E.—the period of the Early, or Western, Han. From 23 to 220 C.E., the Later, or Eastern, Han established its base in the more centrally located Luoyang.

A wall of pounded earth and brick 15 miles (24 kilometers) in circumference surrounded Chang'an, which had a population of 246,000 in 2 C.E. Contemporaries described it as a bustling place, filled with courtiers, officials, soldiers, merchants, craftsmen, and foreign visitors. Broad thoroughfares running north and south intersected others running east and west. High walls protected and restricted access to the imperial palaces, administrative offices, barracks, and storehouses. Temples and marketplaces were scattered about the civic center. Chang'an became a model of urban planning, its main features being imitated throughout the Han Empire.

Living in multistory houses, wearing fine silks, and traveling about the capital in ornate horse-drawn carriages, well-to-do officials and merchants devoted their leisure time to art and literature, occult religious practices, elegant banquets, and various entertainments: music and dance, juggling and acrobatics, dog and horse races, cock and tiger fights. Common people inhabited a sprawling warren of alleys, living in dwellings packed "as closely as the teeth of a comb," as one poet put it.

As in the Zhou monarchy (see Chapter 2), people thought that the emperor, the "Son of Heaven," enjoyed the Mandate of Heaven, standing at the center of government and society like a father wielding authority in a family and linking the living generations with the ancestors. The emperor brought the support of powerful imperial ancestors and guaranteed the harmonious interaction of Heaven and earth. More than his Roman counterpart, he was regarded as a divinity on earth. His word was law. Failure to govern well, however, could lose him the backing of Heaven. Given their belief that events in Heaven, the natural world, and human society corresponded, his subjects might regard floods, droughts, and earthquakes as both the consequences and symptoms of ethical failure and mismanagement. Successful revolutions thus proved to many that Heaven had withdrawn its support from an unworthy ruler.

Secluded within the palace compound, surrounded by his many wives and children, servants, courtiers, and officials, the emperor presided over an unceasing round of pomp and ritual emphasizing

Han A term used to designate the ethnic Chinese people who originated in the Yellow River Valley and spread throughout regions of China suitable for agriculture, as well as the dynasty of emperors who ruled from 206 B.C.E. to 220 C.E.

Chang'an City in the Wei Valley in eastern China. It became the capital of the Qin and early Han Empires. Its main features were imitated in the cities and towns that sprang up throughout the Han Empire.

the worship of Heaven and imperial ancestors, as well as the practical business of government. When the emperor died, his chief widow chose his heir from the male members of the ruling clan, thus making the royal compound a hive of intrigue.

A prime minister, a civil service director, and nine ministers charged with military, economic, legal, and religious responsibilities ran the central government. As in imperial Rome, the Han depended on local officials for the day-to-day administration of the vast empire. Local people collected taxes and dispatched revenues to the central government, oversaw conscription for the army and labor projects, provided local protection, and settled disputes. The remote central government rarely impinged on the lives of most citizens, who normally contacted only local officials. Who, then, were these local officials?

The Han period saw the rise of a class that scholars call the **gentry**. To weaken the rural aristocrats, the Qin and Han emperors allied themselves with the class next in wealth below them. These moderately prosperous landowners, usually men with education and valued expertise, resembled the Roman *equites* favored by Augustus and his successors. The local officials who came from this class became a privileged and respected group within Chinese society and made the government more efficient and responsive.

The new gentry class, with imperial support, adopted a version of Confucianism that provided a system for training officials to be intellectually capable and morally worthy of their roles and set forth a code of conduct for measuring their performance. Chinese tradition speaks of an imperial university, located outside Chang'an and said to have thirty thousand students, as well as provincial centers of learning. From these centers, students entered government service, receiving distinctive emblems and privileges, including preferential legal treatment and exemption from military service, as they advanced in rank. In theory, young men from any class could rise in the state hierarchy. In practice, sons of the gentry had an advantage because they received better training in the Confucian classics. Gradually, the gentry became a new aristocracy of sorts, banding together in cliques and family alliances that worked to advance the careers of group members.

Daoism, which originated in the Warring States Period (see Chapter 2), took deeper root among the common people in the Han period. With its emphasis on the *Dao*, or "path," of nature, its valuing of harmony with the cycles and patterns of the natural world, and its search for enlightenment through solitary contemplation and physical and mental discipline rather than education, Daoism called into question age-old beliefs and values and rejected the hierarchy, rules, and rituals of Confucianism. It urged passive acceptance of the disorder of the world, denial of ambition, contentment with simple pleasures, and trust in one's own instincts.

Technology and Trade

Chinese tradition, which seems to recognize the importance of technology for the success and spread of Chinese civilization, credits the legendary first five emperors with the introduction of major new technologies.

The advent of bronze tools around 1500 B.C.E. helped open land for agriculture on the North China Plain. A millennium later, iron arrived, and the Qin took full advantage of this technology. Chinese metalworkers used more advanced techniques than metalworkers elsewhere in the world. Whereas Roman blacksmiths produced wrought-iron tools and weapons by hammering heated iron, the Chinese mastered the technique of liquefying iron and pouring it into molds. The resulting cast-iron and steel tools and weapons had a higher carbon content and were harder and more durable.

In the succeeding centuries, crossbows and cavalry helped the Chinese military to beat off the attacks of nomads. The watermill, which harnessed the power of running water to turn a grindstone, appeared in China long before it did in Europe. Horse collar and breast strap harnessing that did not constrict the animal's neck allowed horses in China to pull heavier loads than European horses could.

gentry In China, the class of prosperous families, next in wealth below the rural aristocrats, from which the emperors drew their administrative personnel. Respected for their education and expertise, these officials became a privileged group and made the government more efficient and responsive than in the past.

Han-Era (First Century B.C.E.) Stone Rubbing of a Horse-Drawn Carriage The "trace harness," a strap running across the horse's chest, was a Chinese invention that allowed horses to pull far heavier loads than were possible with the constricting throat harness used in Europe. In the Han period, officials, professionals, and soldiers who served the regime enjoyed a lifestyle made pleasant by fine clothing, comfortable transportation, servants, and delightful pastimes, but at the same time they were guided by a Confucian emphasis on duty, honesty, and appropriate behavior. From Wu family shrine, Jiaxiang, Shantung. From *Chin-shih-so* [Jinshisuo]

The Han rulers continued the Qin road-building program. Besides using the roads to move troops and supplies, the government created a network of official couriers using horses, boats, and even footpaths, with food and shelter provided at relay stations. Canal construction also continued, and river navigation improved.

The population growth and increasing trade that resulted gave rise to local market centers. Some of these became county seats from which imperial officials operated. Estimates of the proportion of the population living in Han towns and cities range from 10 percent, a number roughly comparable to Europe, to 30 percent.

Silk dominated China's export trade. Silk cocoons are secreted onto the leaves of mulberry trees by silkworms. The Chinese understood this and kept it a closely guarded secret, which gave them a monopoly on the manufacture of silk. Carried through the Central Asian oases to the Middle East, India, and the Mediterranean, and passing through the hands of middlemen who added their own fees to the price, this beautiful textile may have increased in value a hundred-fold by the end of its journey. Controlling the Silk Road and its profits justified periodic military campaigns into Central Asia and the installation there of garrisons and Chinese colonies.

The Decline of the Han Empire

For the Han, as for the Romans, maintaining frontier security, particularly in the north and northwest, posed a serious challenge. In the end, non-Chinese peoples raiding across the frontier or moving into imperial territory proved a major factor in bringing the empire down.

The different ways of life of farmers, who usually accepted Han rule, and herders, who preferred their own kings, gave rise to insulting stereotypes on both sides. The settled Chinese thought of nomads as "barbarians"—rough, uncivilized people—a viewpoint much like that of the Romans, who looked down on the Germanic peoples on their frontiers.

Often, the closeness of herding and farming populations led to commercial exchange. The nomads sought agricultural products and crafted goods, while the settled peoples bought horses and other herd animals and animal products. Sometimes, however, nomad raiders seized what they wanted from farming

Gold Belt Buckle, Xiongnu, Second Century B.C.E.
The Xiongnu, herders in the lands north of China, shared the artistic conventions of nomadic peoples across the steppes of Eurasia, such as this fluid, twisting representation of the animals on which they depended for their livelihood. Shi Huangdi's military incursions into their pasturelands in the late third century B.C.E. catalyzed the formation of the Xiongnu Confederacy, whose horse-riding warriors challenged the Chinese for centuries.   Image copyright © The Metropolitan Museum of Art/Art Resource, NY

settlements. Tough and warlike because of their way of life, mounted nomads struck swiftly and as swiftly disappeared.

Although nomadic groups tended to be small and inclined to fight one another, circumstances and a charismatic leader could bring them together from time to time. In the Han period, the **Xiongnu** (SHE-OONG-noo), a great confederacy of Turkic peoples, threatened the empire, though they were usually contained on the frontier by cavalry forces created to match the nomads' mobility. This strategy made access to good horses and pastureland a state priority. Other strategies included maintaining garrisons and colonies of soldier-farmers on the frontier, settling compliant nomads within the borders to serve as a buffer, bribing nomad chiefs to promote disunity, and paying protection money. The "tributary system," in which nomad rulers accepted Chinese supremacy and exchanged tribute payments for marriages to Chinese princesses, receptions at court, and imperial gifts worth more than the tribute, often worked well.

Yet military vigilance burdened Han finances and made the economic troubles of later Han times worse. Despite measures to suppress the aristocracy and turn land over to a free peasantry, by the end of the first century B.C.E. nobles and successful merchants again acquired control of huge estates, and many peasants

sought their protection against the exactions of the imperial government. This trend spread over the next two centuries. As strongmen largely independent of imperial control emerged, the central government lost tax revenues and manpower. Military conscription broke down, forcing the government to hire more and more foreign soldiers and officers. These served for pay, but their loyalty was weak.

The Han regime fell in 220 C.E. for several reasons: factional intrigues within the ruling clan, official corruption and inefficiency, uprisings of desperate and hungry peasants, the spread of banditry, unsuccessful reform movements, attacks by nomads, and the ambitions of rural warlords. China entered a period of political fragmentation and economic and cultural regression that lasted until the rise of the Sui (sway) and Tang (tahng) dynasties in the late sixth and early seventh centuries C.E., a story that we take up in Chapter 11.

Xiongnu A confederation of nomadic peoples living beyond the northwest frontier of ancient China. Chinese rulers tried a variety of defenses and stratagems to ward off these "barbarians," as they called them, and finally succeeded in dispersing the Xiongnu in the first century C.E.

SECTION REVIEW

- Imperial China rested on a foundation of agriculture, and periodic censuses ensured a ready supply of labor for public works.

- The extended family was the basic social unit, and Confucianism provided the value system.

- The Qin established the first empire, in which all individuality was subordinate to the state.

- Under the Han dynasty, the empire grew, the Confucian scholar-official rose to prominence, and Daoism gained more popularity with the common people.

- The Qin and Han periods saw technological advancement, steady urbanization, and expansion of the silk trade.

- The burden of defense against nomadic invaders weakened the empire, which collapsed because of several factors, ushering in a period of fragmentation.

Conclusion

Agriculture was the fundamental economic activity and source of government revenues in both Roman and Chinese civilizations. Both empires depended initially on free peasantry—sturdy farmers who could be pressed into military service or other forms of compulsory labor. Conflicts over who owned the land and how it was to be used caused political and social turmoil in both places. Roman and Chinese autocratic rulers secured their positions by breaking the power of old aristocratic families, seizing their excess land, and giving it to small farmers and to themselves. Later, when wealthy noblemen again gained control of vast estates worked by dependent tenant farmers, the authority of the state eroded.

From ethnically homogeneous cores, both empires spread into territories with diverse ecosystems, populations, and ways of life. The cultural unity that resulted has persisted, at least in part, to the present day. Military conquest paved the way, but Italian and Han settlers, outstripping the resources of their core areas, moved into new regions, bringing along their languages, beliefs, customs, and technologies. Conquered peoples were also attracted to the culture and success of the ruler nation. To administer far-flung territories and large populations, both empires delegated considerable autonomy to local officials. Administrators were drawn from educated and capable members of a prosperous middle class.

Roads built to expedite the movement of troops became the highways of commerce and culture. Urban networks provided local administrative bases, furthering commerce and radiating imperial culture to the countryside. While a large majority of the population lived in the country, city-dwellers enjoyed most of the advantages of empire. Rome and Chang'an provided models for outlying cities. Travelers could find in outlying regions the same types and styles of buildings and public spaces that they knew from the capital.

Similar problems of defense—long borders located far from the capital and aggressive neighbors—prompted both empires to build walls and chains of forts to protect against incursions. Frontier defense was so costly that it eventually eroded both empires' prosperity. As governments demanded more taxes and services from the civilian population, they lost the loyalty of the people, many of whom sought protection on the estates of powerful landowners. The Roman and Han governments eventually came to rely on soldiers hired from the same "barbarian" peoples confronting them on the frontiers. As the empires became weaker, the borders were overrun and the central governments collapsed. Ironically, the triumphant immigrant groups respected the imperial culture so deeply that they strove to maintain it once they were in power.

Though the empires failed in similar fashion, the long-term consequences differed. In China the imperial model revived in subsequent eras, but the lands of the Roman Empire never reunified. One reason is that the two cultures had different attitudes toward the individual and the state. In China individuals were deeply embedded in families with precisely defined hierarchies, unquestioning obedience, and solemn rituals of deference to elders and ancestors. Respect for authority was deep-seated. Confucianism, which sanctified family hierarchy and provided a code of conduct for public officials, preceded the imperial system. This cultural base could adapt with little change to diverse political circumstances. The Roman family also respected hierarchy and obedience, but it was not the organizational model of the Roman state.

Confucianism had no Roman equivalent to orient society when the state collapsed.

Moreover, opportunities for economic and social mobility were greater in the Roman Empire than in ancient China. Whereas the merchant class in China was frequently disparaged and constrained by the government, the absence of government interference in the Roman Empire resulted in greater economic mobility and a thriving and influential middle class in the towns and cities. The Roman army also differed from the Chinese, the former being composed of professional soldiers who increasingly gained privileges and took part in political conflict, and the latter relying on draftees who served for two years and remained on the margins of power struggles.

Although Roman emperors tried to create an ideology to bolster their position, Republican traditions and ambiguities about the imperial role stemming from the time of Augustus presented obstacles. Thus Roman rulers were likely to be chosen by the army or by the Senate. The dynastic principle never took root, and the cult of the emperor had little spiritual content. In contrast, the Chinese believed that the emperor was the divine Son of Heaven and drew authority from the power of the royal ancestors.

Finally, Christianity's insistence on monotheism negated the Roman emperor's pretensions to divinity, which had evolved from Hellenistic polytheism. The spread of Christianity during the Late Roman Empire and the decline of the western half of the empire in the fifth century C.E. (see Chapter 10) constituted an irreversible break with the past. By contrast, Buddhism, which came to China in the early centuries C.E. and flourished in the post-Han era (see Chapter 11), was more easily reconciled with traditional Chinese values and beliefs.

CHAPTER REVIEW

 Download the MP3 audio file of the Chapter Review to listen to on the go.

How did Rome create and maintain its vast Mediterranean empire? (page 135)

The Romans were successful empire-builders because of their superior military organization and training, and a series of very capable generals. They co-opted the ruling elites and brought peace and prosperity to the peoples of the lands they annexed. Yet Rome's military success led to social and economic disruption and acute political struggles. Out of this crisis emerged the Principate, which persevered for several centuries. The emperors developed more effective administrative techniques, and local elites embraced Roman culture.

How did imperial China evolve from its beginnings into the Han state? (page 148)

In China, the "First Emperor" established the Qin Empire with key elements for unification already in place. The preceding Shang and Zhou states, though not empires, had controlled the North China Plain and developed the concept of the Mandate of Heaven, a claim to divine backing for the ruler as the Son of Heaven. Furthermore, the Legalist political philosophy justified authoritarian measures. But the harshness of the new order generated resistance that soon brought down the Qin, and its Han successors built a durable imperial regime on a moderated version of Qin structures that incorporated Confucian principles.

Key Terms

Roman Republic (p. 137)
Roman Senate (p. 137)
patron/client relationship (p. 137)
Roman Principate (p. 142)
Augustus (p. 142)
equites (p. 143)
pax romana (p. 144)
Romanization (p. 145)
Jesus (p. 145)

Paul (p. 146)
aqueduct (p. 147)
third-century crisis (p. 147)
Constantine (p. 148)
Qin (p. 151)
Shi Huangdi (p. 151)
Han (p. 153)
Chang'an (p. 153)
gentry (p. 154)
Xiongnu (p. 156)

Web Resources

Pronunciation Guide

Interactive Maps

- MAP 5.1 The Roman Empire
- MAP 5.2 Han China

 **CourseMate** Visit the CourseMate website at www.cengagebrain.com for additional study tools and review materials for this chapter.

Primary Sources

- A Man of Unlimited Ambition: Julius Caesar
- Lessons for Women

Answer to the History in Focus Question

See photo on page 152, "Terracotta Soldiers from the Tomb of Shi Huangdi, 'First Emperor' of China."

CHAPTER 7

1200 B.C.E.–1500 C.E.

Peoples and Civilizations of the Americas

© Cengage Learning

CHAPTER PREVIEW

First Civilizations of the Americas: The Olmec and Chavín, 1200–250 B.C.E.
What role did nature and the environment play in the early civilizations of the Americas?

Classic-Era Culture and Society in Mesoamerica, 200–900
What were the most important shared characteristics of Mesoamerican cultures in the classic period?

The Postclassic Period in Mesoamerica, 900–1500
What role did warfare play in the postclassic period of Mesoamerica?

Northern Peoples
In what ways did Mesoamerica influence the cultural centers in North America?

Andean Civilizations, 200–1500
How did the Amerindian peoples of the Andean area adapt to their environment and produce socially complex and politically advanced societies?

Conclusion

DIVERSITY & DOMINANCE:
Burials as Historic Texts

 Visit the CourseMate website at **www.cengagebrain.com** for additional study tools and review materials for this chapter.

Humans reached the Western Hemisphere through a series of migrations from Asia. Some scholars believe that the first migrations occurred as early as 35,000 to 25,000 B.C.E., but most accept a later date of 20,000 to 13,000 B.C.E. Although some limited contacts with other cultures—for example, with Polynesians—may have occurred later, the peoples in the Western Hemisphere were virtually isolated from the rest of the world for at least 15,000 years. Thus, while technological innovations passed back and forth among the civilizations of Asia, Africa, and Europe, the peoples of the Americas faced the challenges of the natural environment on their own.

As people spread throughout the hemisphere, they encountered environments that ranged from polar extremes to tropical rain forests to towering mountain ranges. Mesoamerica (Mexico and northern Central America) and the mountainous Andean region of South America proved conducive to the emergence of complex societies. Well before 1000 B.C.E., plant domestication, technological innovation, and a limited trade led to greater social stratification and the beginnings of urbanization in both regions. Cultural elites used their increasing political and religious authority to organize great numbers of laborers for projects such as large-scale irrigation and drainage works, cleared forests, and hillside terracing, thus providing the economic platform for the construction of urban centers.

The Amerindian[1] hereditary elites organized their societies to meet these challenges, even as their ambitions ignited new conflicts. No single set of political institutions or technologies worked in every environment, and American cultures varied widely. Productive and diversified agriculture and cities that rivaled the Chinese and Roman capitals in size and beauty developed in Mesoamerica and the Andean region of South America. In the rest of the hemisphere, indigenous peoples maintained a wide variety of settlement patterns, political forms, and cultural traditions based on combinations of hunting and agriculture.

First Civilizations of the Americas: The Olmec and Chavín, 1200–250 B.C.E.

What role did nature and the environment play in the early civilizations of the Americas?

By 1000 B.C.E. the major urban centers of Mesoamerica and the Andes, dominated by monumental structures devoted to religions and the elite, had begun to project their political and cultural power over broad territories: they had become civilizations. The cultural legacies of the two most important of these early civilizations, the Olmec of Mesoamerica and the Chavín of the Andes, would persist for more than a thousand years.

The Mesoamerican Olmec, 1200–400 B.C.E.

Mesoamerica is extremely active geologically, experiencing both earthquakes and volcanic eruptions. Mountain ranges break the region into microenvironments, including the temperate climates of the Valley of Mexico and the Guatemalan highlands, the tropical forests of the Peten and Gulf of Mexico coast, the rain forest of the southern Yucatán and Belize, and the drier scrub forest of the northern Yucatán (see Map 7.1).

Within these ecological niches, craftsmen made use of a wide variety of indigenous plants, as well as minerals like obsidian, quartz, and jade. But no animals were domesticated. Eventually, contacts across these environmental boundaries led to trade and cultural exchange. Enhanced trade, increasing agricultural productivity, and rising population led, in turn, to urbanization and the appearance of powerful political and religious elites. Yet even though all Mesoamerican civilizations shared fundamental elements of material culture, technology, religious belief and ritual, political organization, art, architecture, and sports, the region was never unified politically.

The most influential early Mesoamerican civilization was the Olmec, flourishing between 1200 and 400 B.C.E. (see Map 7.1). The center of Olmec civilization was located near the tropical Atlantic coast of what are now the Mexican states of Veracruz and Tabasco. Olmec cultural influence reached as far as

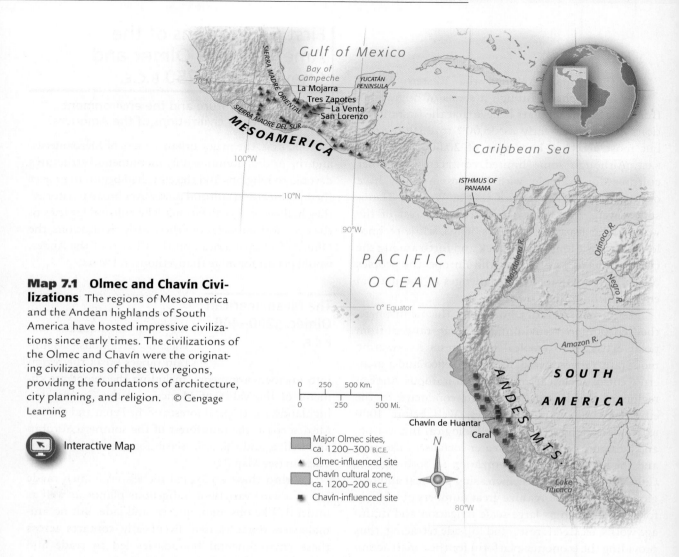

Map 7.1 Olmec and Chavín Civilizations The regions of Mesoamerica and the Andean highlands of South America have hosted impressive civilizations since early times. The civilizations of the Olmec and Chavín were the originating civilizations of these two regions, providing the foundations of architecture, city planning, and religion. © Cengage Learning

Interactive Map

Major Olmec sites, ca. 1200–300 B.C.E.

Olmec-influenced site

Chavín cultural zone, ca. 1200–200 B.C.E.

Chavín-influenced site

the Pacific coast of Central America and the Central Plateau of Mexico.

The earliest settlements in the region depended on rich plant diversity and fishing, but by 3500 B.C.E. the staples of the Mesoamerican diet—maize, beans, and squash—had been domesticated. Manioc, a calorie-rich root crop, was also grown in the floodplains of the region. The ability of farmers to produce dependable surpluses of these products permitted the first stages of craft specialization and social stratification. As religious and political elites emerged, they used their prestige and authority to organize the population to dig irrigation and drainage canals, develop raised fields in wetlands that could be farmed more

intensively, and construct the large-scale religious and civic buildings that became the cultural signature of Olmec civilization.

San Lorenzo and some smaller centers nearby formed the cultural core of the early **Olmec** civilization (1200–900 B.C.E.). La Venta (la-BEN-tah), which

Olmec The first Mesoamerican civilization. Between ca. 1200 and 400 B.C.E., the Olmec people of central Mexico created a vibrant civilization that included intensive agriculture, wide-ranging trade, ceremonial centers, and monumental construction. The Olmec had great cultural influence on later Mesoamerican societies.

Chronology

	Mesoamerica	Northern Peoples	Andes
3500 B.C.E.	**3500 B.C.E.** Early agriculture		**3500 B.C.E.** Early agriculture
			2600 B.C.E. Rise of Caral
1200 B.C.E.	**1200–900 B.C.E.** Rise of Olmec civilization centered on San Lorenzo		
900 B.C.E.	**900–600 B.C.E.** La Venta, the dominant Olmec center		**900–250 B.C.E.** Chavín civilization
500 B.C.E.			**500 B.C.E.** Early metallurgy
100 B.C.E.	**100 B.C.E.** Teotihuacan founded		
100 C.E.		**100–400** Hopewell culture in Ohio River Valley	
200			**200–700** Moche culture of Peruvian coast
	250 Maya early classic period begins		
500			**500–1000** Tiwanaku and Wari control Peruvian highlands
700		**700** Anasazi and Mississippian cultures begin	
800	**CA. 750** Teotihuacan destroyed **800–900** Maya centers abandoned, end of classic period		
900	**968** Toltec capital of Tula founded		
1000		**1050–1250** Cahokia reaches peak power	
1100	**1156** Tula destroyed	**1150** Collapse of Anasazi centers begins	
1200		**1200** Anasazi culture declines	**1200** Chimú begins military expansion
1300	**1325** Aztec capital Tenochtitlan founded		
1400			**1438** Inca expansion begins **1465** Inca conquer Chimú
1500		**1500** Mississippian culture declines	**1500–1525** Inca conquer Ecuador
	1502 Moctezuma II crowned Aztec ruler		

developed at about the same time, became the most important Olmec center after 900 B.C.E. when San Lorenzo was abandoned or destroyed. Très Zapotes (TRACE zah-POE-tess) was the last dominant center, rising to prominence after La Venta collapsed or was destroyed around 600 B.C.E. (see Map 7.1). Relationships among these centers are unclear. Scholars have found little evidence to suggest that they were either rival city-states or dependent units of a centralized political authority. It appears that each center developed independently to exploit and exchange specialized products like salt, cacao (chocolate beans), potters' clay, and limestone. Each major Olmec center was eventually abandoned, its monuments defaced and buried and its buildings destroyed. Archaeologists interpret these events differently;

some see them as evidence of internal upheavals or military defeat by neighboring peoples, and others suggest that they were associated with the death of a ruler.

Large artificial platforms and mounds of packed earth dominated Olmec urban centers and framed the collective ritual and political activities that brought the rural population to the cities at special times in the year. Some of the platforms also served as foundations for elite residences. The Olmec laid out their cities in alignment with the paths of certain stars, reflecting concern for astronomical events. Since these centers had small permanent populations, the scale of construction suggests that the Olmec elite could command the labor of thousands of men and women from the surrounding area for low-skill tasks like moving dirt and stone. Skilled artisans who lived in or near the urban core decorated the buildings with carvings and sculptures. They also produced the exquisite carved jade figurines, necklaces, and ceremonial knives and axes that distinguish Olmec culture. Archaeological evidence points to merchants trading with distant peoples for obsidian, jade, and pottery.

It seems likely that the rise of major urban centers coincided with the appearance of a form of kingship that combined religious and secular roles. Finely crafted objects decorated the households of the elite and distinguished their dress from that of the commoners, who lived in dispersed small structures constructed of sticks and mud. Colossal carved stone heads, some as large as 11 feet (3.4 meters) high, seem to reflect the authority of the

rulers and their families. Since each head is unique and suggestive of an individual personality, most archaeologists believe they were carved to memorialize individual rulers. This theory is reinforced by the location of the heads close to the major urban centers, especially San Lorenzo. These remarkable stone sculptures are the best-known monuments of Olmec culture.

The organization of collective labor by the Olmec elites benefited the commoners by increasing food production and making it more diverse and reliable. Ceramic products such as utilitarian pots and small figurines as well as small stone carvings associated with religious belief have been found in commoner households. This suggests that at least some advantages gained from urbanization and growing elite power were shared broadly in the society.

The Olmec elite used elaborate religious rituals to control this complex society. Thousands of commoners were drawn from the countryside to attend awe-inspiring ceremonies at the centers. The elevated platforms and mounds with carved stone veneers served as potent backdrops for these rituals. Rulers

Olmec Head Giant heads sculpted from basalt are a widely recognized legacy of Olmec culture. Sixteen heads have been found, the largest approximately 11 feet (3.4 meters) tall. Experts in Olmec archaeology believe the heads are portraits of individual rulers, warriors, or ballplayers.

Georg Gerster/Photo Researchers, Inc.

and their close kin associated themselves with the gods through bloodletting and human sacrifice, evidence of which is found in all the urban centers. The Olmec were polytheistic, and most of their deities had dual (male and female) natures. Human and animal characteristics were also blended. Surviving representations of jaguars, crocodiles, snakes, and sharks suggest that these powerful animals provided the most enduring images used in Olmec religious representation. Humans transforming themselves into these animals constitute a common decorative motif. Rulers were especially associated with the jaguar.

Practical advice about the periodic rains essential to agricultural life came from a class of shamans and healers. They directed the planning of urban centers to reflect astronomical observations and were responsible for developing a form of writing that may have influenced later innovations among the Maya. From their close observation of the stars, they produced a calendar that was used to organize ritual life and agriculture. The Olmec were also the likely originators of a ritual ball game that became an enduring part of Mesoamerican ceremonial life.

The discovery of Olmec products and images, such as jade carvings decorated with the jaguar-god, as far away as central Mexico provides evidence that the Olmec exercised cultural influence over a wide area even though they never created an empire. This influence would endure for centuries.

Early South American Civilization: Chavín, 900–250 B.C.E.

Geography played an important role in the development of human society in the Andes. The region's diverse environment—a mountainous core, arid coastal plain, and dense interior jungles—challenged human populations, encouraging the development of specialized regional production as well as complex social institutions and cultural values that facilitated interregional exchanges and shared labor responsibilities. These adaptations to environmental challenge became enduring features of Andean civilization.

The earliest urban centers in the Andean region were villages of a few hundred people built along the coastal plain or in the foothills near the coast. The abundance of fish and mollusks along the coast

of Peru provided a dependable supply of food that helped make the development of early cities possible. The coastal populations traded these products along with decorative shells for maize, other foods, and textiles produced in the foothills. The two regions also exchanged ceremonial practices, religious motifs, and aesthetic ideas. Recent discoveries demonstrate that as early as 2600 B.C.E. the vast site called Caral had developed many of the characteristics now viewed as the hallmarks of later Andean civilization, including ceremonial plazas, pyramids, elevated platforms and mounds, and extensive irrigation works. The scale of the public works in Caral suggests a population of thousands and a political structure capable of organizing the production and distribution of maritime and agricultural products over a broad area.

Chavín, one of the most impressive of South America's early urban civilizations (see Map 7.1), inherited many of the cultural and economic characteristics of Caral. Its capital, Chavín de Huantar (cha-BEAN day WAHN-tar), was located at 10,300 feet (3,139 meters) in the eastern range of the Andes north of the modern city of Lima. Between 900 and 250 B.C.E., a period roughly coinciding with Olmec civilization in Mesoamerica, Chavín dominated a densely populated region that included large areas of the Peruvian coastal plain and Andean foothills. Chavín de Huantar's location at the intersection of trade routes connecting the coast with populous mountain valleys and the tropical lowlands on the eastern flank of the Andes allowed the city's rulers to control trade among these distinct ecological zones and gain an important economic advantage over regional rivals.

Chavín's dominance as a ceremonial and commercial center depended on earlier developments in agriculture and trade, including the introduction of maize cultivation from Mesoamerica. Maize increased the food supplies of the coast and interior foothills,

Chavín The first major urban civilization in South America (900–250 B.C.E.). Its capital, Chavín de Huántar, was located high in the Andes Mountains of Peru. Chavín became politically and economically dominant in a densely populated region that included two distinct ecological zones, the Peruvian coastal plain and the Andean foothills.

allowing greater levels of urbanization. As Chavín grew, its trade linked the coastal economy with the producers of quinoa (a local grain), potatoes, and llamas in the high mountain valleys and, to a lesser extent, with Amazonian producers of coca and fruits.

Reciprocal labor obligations that permitted the construction and maintenance of roads, bridges, temples, palaces, and large irrigation and drainage projects, as well as textile production, developed as well. In later times groups of related families who held land communally and claimed descent from a common ancestor organized these labor obligations. Group members thought of each other as brothers and sisters and were obligated to aid each other, providing a model for the organization of labor and the distribution of goods at every level of Andean society.

Llamas, the only domesticated beasts of burden in the Americas, played an important role in the integration of the Andean region. They were first domesticated in the mountainous interior of Peru and were crucial to Chavín's development. Llamas provided meat and wool and helped transport goods. A single driver could control ten to thirty animals, each carrying up to 70 pounds (32 kilograms); a human porter could carry only about 50 pounds (22.5 kilograms). The increased use of llamas to move goods from one ecological zone to another promoted specialization of production and increased trade.

The enormous scale of the capital and the dispersal of Chavín's pottery styles, religious motifs, and architectural forms over a wide area suggest that Chavín imposed some form of political integration and trade dependency on its neighbors that may have relied in part on military force. However, most modern scholars believe that, as in the case of the Olmec civilization, Chavín's influence depended more on the development of an attractive and convincing religious belief system and related rituals. Chavín's most potent religious symbol, a jaguar deity, was dispersed over a broad area, and archaeological evidence suggests that Chavín de Huantar served as a pilgrimage site.

The architectural signature of Chavín was a large complex of multilevel platforms made of packed earth or rubble and faced with cut stone or adobe (sun-dried brick made of clay and straw). Small buildings used for ritual purposes or as elite residences were built on these platforms. Nearly all the buildings were decorated with relief carvings of serpents, condors,

jaguars, or humans. The largest building at Chavín de Huantar measured 250 feet (76 meters) on each side and rose to a height of 50 feet (15 meters). About one-third of its interior is hollow, containing narrow galleries and small rooms that may have housed the remains of royal ancestors.

American metallurgy was first developed in the Andean region. The later introduction of metallurgy in Mesoamerica, like the appearance of maize agriculture in the Andes, suggests sustained contacts between the two regions. Archaeological investigations of Chavín de Huantar and smaller centers have revealed remarkable three-dimensional silver, gold, and gold alloy ornaments that represent a clear advance over earlier technologies. Bronze and iron, however, were unknown.

Improvements in both the manufacture and the decoration of textiles are also associated with the rise of Chavín. The quality of these products, which were probably used only by the elite or in religious rituals, added to the reputation and prestige of the culture and aided in the projection of its power and influence. The most common decorative motif in sculpture, pottery, and textiles was a jaguar-man similar in conception to the Olmec symbol. In both civilizations and in many other cultures in the Americas, this powerful predator provided an enduring image of religious authority and a vehicle through which the gods could act in the world of men and women.

Class distinctions also appear to have increased in Chavín. Priests directed religious life, and there is evidence that both local chiefs and a more powerful chief or king dominated Chavín's politics. Excavations of graves reveal that superior-quality textiles as well as gold crowns, breastplates, and jewelry distinguished rulers from commoners.

There is no convincing evidence, like defaced buildings or broken images, that the eclipse of Chavín (unlike the Olmec centers) was associated with conquest or rebellion. However, recent investigations

llama A hoofed animal indigenous to the Andes Mountains. It was the only domesticated beast of burden in the Americas before the arrival of Europeans. The use of llamas to transport goods made possible specialized production and trade among people living in different ecological zones and fostered the integration of these zones by Chavín and later Andean states.

SECTION REVIEW

- From farming communities of Mesoamerica emerged the urban civilization of the Olmec.

- Olmec cities were centers of specialized crafts, long-distance trade, royal authority, and mass religious observance.

- Shamans and healers directed urban planning, issued practical advice, and devised many of the technologies and rituals inherited by later civilizations of the region.

- In the ecologically diverse Andes, a wide range of settled communities developed, from which emerged the Chavín civilization.

- Chavín de Huantar dominated a large territory as a ceremonial and commercial center, and its rulers organized extensive construction projects.

- The Chavín people used domesticated llamas, developed important technologies, and devised a unifying religious system, all of which influenced later Andean civilizations.

statecraft, architecture, and urban planning associated with Chavín influenced the Andean region for centuries.

Classic-Era Culture and Society in Mesoamerica, 200–900

What were the most important shared characteristics of Mesoamerican cultures in the classic period?

Between 200 and 900, the peoples of Mesoamerica created a civilization based on similarities in material culture, religious beliefs and practices, and social structures, despite differences in language and the absence of regional political integration. Building on the achievements of the Olmec and others, the peoples then living in Mesoamerica developed new political institutions, made great strides in astronomy and mathematics, and improved agricultural productivity.

Archaeologists call this mix of achievements the classic period. Population grew, a greater variety of products were traded over longer distances, social hierarchies became more complex, and great cities

have suggested that increased warfare throughout the region around 200 B.C.E. disrupted Chavín's trade and undermined the authority of the governing elite. Regardless of what caused the collapse of this powerful culture, the technologies, material culture,

Chrysler Museum of Art/Justin Kerr

The Mesoamerican Ball Game From Guatemala to Arizona, archaeologists have found evidence of an ancient ball game played with a solid rubber ball on slope-sided courts shaped like a capital T. Among the Maya the game was associated with a creation myth and thus had deep religious meaning. There is evidence that some players were sacrificed. In this scene from a ceramic jar, players wearing elaborate ritual clothing—which includes heavy, protective pads around the chest and waist—play with a ball much larger than the ball actually used in such games. Some representations show balls drawn to suggest a human head.

VALLEY OF MEXICO, 1519

Map 7.2 Major Mesoamerican Civilizations, 1000 B.C.E.–1519 C.E. The Maya civilization, with its many rival cities, covered the highlands of Guatemala and the Yucatán Peninsula. From their island capital of Tenochtitlan, the Aztecs militarily and commercially dominated southern Mexico. Aztec achievements were built on the legacy of earlier civilizations such as the Olmec and Maya.
© Cengage Learning

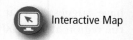 Interactive Map

served as governing and religious centers. Impressive platforms and pyramids were devoted to religious functions. Large urban populations, divided into classes, served hereditary political and religious elites who also controlled the nearby towns and countryside.

The agricultural foundation of Mesoamerican civilization had been developed centuries earlier. The major agricultural technologies—irrigation, wetland drainage, and hillside terracing—preceded the cities built after 200 C.E. by more than a thousand years. What made the achievements of the classic era possible was the extended reach and power of religious and political leaders. The impressive architecture and great size of Teotihuacan (teh-o-tee-WAH-kahn) and the great Maya cities such as Tikal illustrate both Mesoamerican aesthetic achievements and the development of powerful political institutions.

northeast of modern Mexico City (see Map 7.2), housed between 125,000 and 200,000 inhabitants. The largest city in the Americas, it outshone all but a few contemporary European and Asian cities.

The religious architecture of Teotihuacan included enormous pyramids dedicated to the sun and moon and more than twenty smaller temples devoted to other gods, all of which flanked a central avenue. The god Quetzalcoatl (kate-zahl CO-ah-tal), the feathered serpent, was considered the originator of agriculture and the arts. Like the Olmec, the people of Teotihuacan practiced human sacrifice as a sacred duty toward the gods and as a necessity for the well-being of human society. The excavation of the temple of Quetzalcoatl uncovered scores of sacrificial victims.

Teotihuacan's urban population had grown rapidly from the forced relocation of villagers following

Teotihuacan

At the height of its power, from 450 to 600 C.E., **Teotihuacan** (100 B.C.E.–750 C.E.), located about 30 miles (48 kilometers)

Teotihuacan A powerful city-state in central Mexico (100 B.C.E.–750 C.E.). Its population was about 150,000 at its peak in 600.

The Pyramid of the Sun The Pyramid of the Sun is the largest pyramid in Teotihuacan. The smaller Temple of Quetzacoatl displays the serpent images associated with this culture god common to most Mesoamerican civilizations.

volcanic eruptions. Nevertheless, more than two-thirds of the city's residents continued to farm, walking from their city homes to the fields. The elite used the city's growing labor resources to expand agriculture by draining swamps, building irrigation works, and cutting terraces into hillsides. They also expanded **chinampas** (chee-NAM-pahs), misleadingly called "floating gardens." These narrow artificial islands, anchored by trees and created by heaping lake muck and waste material on beds of reeds, were crucial in sustaining the growing population because the sub-surface irrigation resisted frost and thus permitted year-round agriculture.

The housing of commoners changed as the population grew. Apartment-like stone buildings housed, among other people, the craftsmen who produced goods for export. Teotihuacan pottery has turned up throughout central Mexico and even in the Maya region of Guatemala. More than 2 percent of the urban population crafted similarly widespread obsidian tools and weapons.

The city's role as a religious center signified divine approval of the increasingly prosperous elite. Members of this elite controlled the state bureaucracy, tax collection, and commerce. Their diet and style of dress reflected their prestige, and they lived in separate aristocratic compounds. Temple and palace murals confirm the central position and great prestige of the priestly class. Pilgrims came to Teotihuacan from far away, and some became permanent residents.

Unlike other classic-period societies, the people of Teotihuacan did not have a single ruler. The deeds of the rulers do not feature in public art, nor were rulers represented by statues as in other Mesoamerican civilizations. Thus historians debate the role of the military at Teotihuacan. Unlike later postclassic civilizations, Teotihuacan was not an imperial state controlled by a military elite, and the absence of walls or

chinampas Raised fields constructed along lakeshores in Mesoamerica to increase agricultural yields.

169

The Great Plaza at Tikal Still visible in the ruins of Tikal, in modern Guatemala, are the impressive architectural and artistic achievements of the classic-era Maya. Maya centers provided a dramatic setting for the rituals that dominated public life. Construction of Tikal began before 150 B.C.E.; the city was abandoned about 900 C.E. A ball court and residences for the elite were part of the Great Plaza.

other defensive structures before 500 suggests relative peace. However, archaeology points to a powerful military protecting long-distance trade and compelling peasants to hand over their surplus production. Representations of soldiers in typical Teotihuacan dress in the Maya region of Guatemala may indicate that the military were used to expand trade.

The forces that brought about the end of Teotihuacan about 750 remain a mystery, but evidence of weakness appears as early as 500, when the urban population declined to about 40,000 and the city began to build defensive walls. Fortifications and pictorial evidence from murals suggest that the city's final decades were violent. Indications of conflict within the ruling elite and of mismanagement of resources have challenged earlier theories of conquest by a rival city nearby or by nomadic peoples from the north. Class conflict and the breakdown of public order may explain the destruction of the most important temples in the city center, the defacing of religious images, and the burning of elite palaces. The eclipse of Teotihuacan reverberated throughout Mexico and into Central America.

The Maya

Contemporary with Teotihuacan, the **Maya** developed a civilization in the region that today includes Guatemala, Honduras, Belize, and southern Mexico (see Map 7.2). The

History in Focus *Examine the image "The Great Plaza at Tikal." Try to imagine the scale of these religious structures, and keep in mind that the mass of common people stood below on the flat ground. What do you think they would see during the frequent public rituals? What do you think they would not see? What does that suggest to you about the nature of Maya ritual and its role in public life? Find the answer online.*

difficulties of a tropical climate and fragile soils make the cultural and architectural achievements of the Maya all the more remarkable. Although they shared a single culture, they never unified politically. Instead, rival kingdoms led by hereditary rulers competed for dominance.

Today, Maya farmers cut down small trees and brush and burn the dead vegetation to fertilize the land. This swidden agriculture produces high yields for a few years, but it exhausts the soil's nutrients, eventually forcing a move to fresh land. The high population levels of the Maya classic period (250–900 C.E.) required more intensive forms of agriculture.

Maya Mesoamerican civilization concentrated in Mexico's Yucatán Peninsula and in Guatemala and Honduras but never unified into a single empire. Major contributions were in mathematics, astronomy, and development of the calendar.

Maya living near the major urban centers achieved high yields by draining swamps and building elevated fields. They used irrigation in areas with long dry seasons and built terraced hillsides in the cooler highlands. Nearly every household planted a garden to provide condiments and fruits. The Maya also practiced forest management, favoring the growth of useful trees and shrubs and promoting the conservation of deer and other animals hunted for food.

During the classic period, city-states proliferated, the most powerful controlling groups of smaller dependent cities. Religious temples and rituals linked the power of kings to the gods. Unlike earlier sites, these cities had dense central precincts dominated by buildings that were commonly aligned with the movements of the sun and Venus. High pyramids and elaborately decorated palaces, often built on high ground or constructed mounds, surrounded open plazas, an awesome prospect for the masses drawn in for religious and political rituals.

Bas-reliefs and bright paint covered nearly all public buildings. Common motifs included religious allegories, the genealogies of rulers, and important historical events. Carved altars and stone monoliths arose near major temples. Masses of men and women aided only by levers and stone tools cut and carried construction materials and lifted them into place.

The Maya cosmos consisted of three layers connected along a vertical axis that traced the course of the sun. The earthly arena of human existence came between the heavens, conceptualized as a sky-monster, and a dark underworld. A sacred tree rose through the layers, its roots in the underworld and its branches in the heavens. The temple precincts of Maya cities physically represented this cosmology: the pyramids as sacred mountains reaching to the heavens, their doorways as portals to the underworld.

Rulers and other members of the elite decorated their bodies with paint and tattoos and wore elaborate costumes of textiles, animal skins, and feathers to project both secular power and divine sanction. Kings communicated directly with the supernatural residents of the other worlds and with deified royal ancestors through bloodletting rituals and hallucinogenic trances. Scenes of rulers drawing blood from lips, ears, and penises are common in frescoes and on painted pottery.

Warfare in particular was infused with religious meaning and elaborate rituals. Scenes of battle and the torture and sacrifice of captives appear frequently. Days of fasting, sacred ritual, and purification rites preceded battle. The king, his kinsmen, and other ranking nobles fought personally, with the goal of taking captives. Elite captives nearly always became sacrificial victims; commoners usually became slaves.

Few women directly ruled Maya kingdoms, though women from ruling lineages did play important political and religious roles. The consorts of male rulers participated in bloodletting rituals and in other public ceremonies. Their noble blood helped legitimate their husbands' rule. Though generally patrilineal (tracing descent in the male line), some male rulers traced their lineages from both the male and the female lines. Some rulers emphasized the female line if it held higher status. As for women of the lower classes, scholars believe that they played a central role in religious ritual, household economy, gardening, and weaving.

Building on Olmec precedents, the Maya developed the calendar, mathematics, and writing. The complexity of their calendric system, with each day marked by three separate dating systems, reflects their interest in time and the cosmos. Like other Mesoamerican peoples, the Maya had a calendar that tracked the ritual cycle (260 days divided into 13 months of 20 days) as well as a solar calendar (365 days divided into 18 months of 20 days, plus 5 "unfavorable days" at the end of the year). The concurrence of these two calendars every 52 years was considered especially ominous. Alone among Mesoamerican peoples, the Maya also maintained a continuous "long count" calendar, which began at a fixed date in the past that scholars have identified as 3114 B.C.E., a date probably associated with creation.

The Maya system of mathematics, which underlay the calendar, incorporated the concept of the zero and place value, but it had limited notational signs. Maya writing used hieroglyphs that signified whole words or concepts as well as phonetic cues or syllables. Aspects of public life, religious belief, and the biographies of rulers and their ancestors were recorded in deerskin and bark-paper books, on pottery, and on the stone columns and monumental buildings of the urban centers.

- Between 200 and 900 C.E., Mesoamerican peoples built civilizations with characteristics derived from Olmec culture.

- Their achievements were made possible by the increased power of political and religious leaders.

- Both Teotihuacan and the Maya city-states were supported by intensive agriculture and contained monumental religious architecture.

- Teotihuacan grew into a powerful economic and religious center without a single ruler or powerful military elite.

- The Maya city-states were ruled by kings and elites that practiced ritualized warfare.

- Maya women appear to have enjoyed high status, and both civilizations adopted practices and technologies from their Olmec predecessors.

Abandonment or destruction befell many of the major urban centers between 800 and 900, although a small number survived for centuries. In some areas, decades of urban population decline and increased warfare preceded the collapse. Some experts maintain that the destruction of Teotihuacan after 650 disrupted trade, thus undermining the legitimacy of

Maya rulers who used trade goods in rituals. Others suggest that population pressure led to environmental degradation and declining agricultural productivity. This, in turn, might have caused social conflict and warfare as desperate elites sought additional agricultural land through conquest.

The Postclassic Period in Mesoamerica, 900–1500

What role did warfare play in the postclassic period of Mesoamerica?

The collapse of Teotihuacan and many of the major Maya centers occurred over more than a century and a half, making the division between classic and postclassic periods somewhat arbitrary. In fact, some important classic-period civilizations survived unscathed, and essential cultural characteristics in religious belief and practice, architecture, urban planning, and social organization carried over to the postclassic period.

Nevertheless, important differences exist. The population of Mesoamerica apparently expanded

Maya Scribe Maya scribes used a complex writing system to record religious concepts and memorialize the actions of their kings. An artisan painted this picture of a scribe on a ceramic plate.

© Justin Kerr

during the postclassic period, causing an intensification of agricultural practices and increased warfare. The governing elites of the major postclassic states—the Toltecs and the Aztecs—increased the size of their armies and developed political institutions that facilitated control of large territories gained through conquest.

The Toltecs

Scholars speculate that the **Toltecs** (TOLL-teks) originated as a satellite population protecting the northern frontier of Teotihuacan from nomad raids. After migrating south, they created an important postclassic civilization on the legacy of Teotihuacan. Memories of their military achievements and the violent imagery of their political and religious rituals dominated the Mesoamerican imagination in the late postclassic period. In the fourteenth century, the Aztecs and their contemporaries erroneously believed that the Toltecs created nearly all of Mesoamerica's cultural monuments. One Aztec source declared:

> In truth [the Toltecs] invented all the precious and marvelous things. . . . All that now exists was their discovery. . . . And these Toltecs were very wise; they were thinkers, for they originated the year count, the day count. All their discoveries formed the book for interpreting dreams. . . . And so wise were they [that] they understood the stars which were in the heavens.[2]

Actually, the most important Toltec innovations came in politics and war. The Toltecs created the first conquest state as they extended their political influence from north of modern Mexico City to Central America. Established about 968, Tula (TOO-la), the Toltec capital, followed the grand style (see Map 7.2), with public architecture that featured colonnaded patios and numerous temples. Though smaller than Teotihuacan, Tula dominated central Mexico. Nearly all its public buildings and temples carried scenes of human sacrifice, and representations of warriors on public buildings reflect an increasingly warlike and violent world-view.

Two chieftains or kings apparently ruled the Toltec state together, a system that may eventually have sapped Toltec power and opened Tula to destruction. Sometime after 1000, a struggle between elite groups from rival religious cults undermined the state. According to later Aztec legends, Topiltzin (tow-PEELT-zeen)—one of the two rulers and a priest of the cult of Quetzalcoatl—and his followers bitterly accepted exile in the east. One text relates the following:

> Thereupon he [Topiltzin] looked toward Tula, and then wept. . . . And when he had done these things . . . he went to reach the seacoast. Then he fashioned a raft of serpents. When he had arranged the raft, he placed himself as if it were his boat. Then he set off across the sea.[3]

Toltec decline set in after 1150. By 1175 internal conflict and northern invaders had wreaked destruction upon Tula, triggering a centuries-long process of cultural and political assimilation to produce a new political order based on the Toltec heritage. The Aztecs became the most important of these late postclassic peoples.

The Aztecs

The Mexica (meh-SHE-ca), more commonly known as the **Aztecs**, pushed into central Mexico from the north after Tula's fall. As their power grew through political alliances and military conquest, they created a regional power called the Aztec Empire. When they arrived, the Mexica were organized as an **altepetl** (al-TEH-pe-tel), an ethnic state led by a tlatoani (tlah-toh-AHN-ee) or ruler. A group of **calpolli** (cal-POH-yee), each with up to a hundred families, served as the foundation of the altepetl, controlling land allocation, tax collection, and local religious life.

Adapting to the political and social practices that they found among the urbanized agriculturalists of the Valley of Mexico, the Mexica first worked as serfs and mercenaries for more powerful neighbors. Once

Toltecs Powerful postclassic empire in central Mexico (900–1156) that influenced much of Mesoamerica. Aztecs claimed ties to this earlier civilization.

Aztecs Also known as Mexica, the Aztecs created a powerful empire in central Mexico (1325–1521). They forced defeated peoples to provide goods and labor.

altepetl An ethnic state in ancient Mesoamerica, the common political building block of that region.

calpolli A group of up to a hundred families that served as a social building block of an altepetl in ancient Mesoamerica.

they gained strength around 1325, they relocated to some small islands near the shore of Lake Texcoco, where they founded their twin capitals, **Tenochtitlan** (teh-noch-TIT-lan) and Tlatelolco (tla-TEH-lol-co) (together the foundation for modern Mexico City).

The increased economic independence and political security gained by seizing control of farmland along the lakeshore eased the introduction of a monarchical system similar to that of more powerful neighboring states. Power increasingly flowed to hereditary aristocrats and monarchs, though the latter did not wield absolute power. A council of powerful aristocrats selected new rulers from males of the ruling lineage. The ruler demonstrated his divine mandate by making new conquests and renegotiating tribute payments from dependencies. War acquired religious meaning, providing the ruler with legitimacy and increasing the prestige of successful warriors.

One Spaniard who witnessed the conquest of the Aztec Empire remembered his first meeting with the Aztec ruler Moctezuma (mock-teh-ZU-ma) II (r. 1502–1520): "Many great lords walked before the great Montezuma [Moctezuma II], sweeping the ground on which he was to tread and laying down cloaks so that his feet should not touch the earth. Not one of these chieftains dared look him in the face."[4]Although warfare increased male privilege, women held substantial power and influence. Following the birth of a boy, his umbilical cord was buried on the battlefield and he was given implements to signal his occupation or his role as a warrior. In the case of a girl, her umbilical cord was buried near the hearth and she was given weaving implements and female clothing. Death rituals also marked gender identities as distinct but complementary. Women dominated the household and the markets and served as teachers and priestesses. They also founded lineages, including the royal line.

As kinship-based clans lost influence, social divisions sharpened. Conquest allowed the warrior elite to seize land and peasant labor as spoils of war. The elite owned extensive estates cultivated by slaves and landless commoners. The lower classes received some benefits from imperial expansion but lost most of their influence over decisions. Hereditary nobles monopolized the highest social ranks, although some commoners gained status through success on

the battlefield or by entering the priesthood. Calpolli members fought together as military units.

Small dwellings and a limited diet of staples marked the life of commoners. Nobles enjoyed more luxuries: well-built two-story houses, rich dress and jewelry, meat, and expensive imports like chocolate brought from Maya country to the south. Polygamy was a noble privilege.

The Aztec state fed an urban population of approximately 150,000 by efficiently organizing the clans and additional laborers sent by defeated peoples to expand agricultural land. Land reclamation centered on a dike more than 5 miles (9 kilometers) long by 23 feet (7 meters) wide that separated the freshwater and saltwater parts of Lake Texcoco. The dike, whose construction consumed 4 million person-days, supported greater irrigation and more chinampas, which contributed maize, fruits, and vegetables to the Tenochtitlan markets. A **tribute system** imposed on conquered peoples helped relieve the capital's population pressure. Nearby political dependencies supplied one-quarter of Tenochtitlan's maize, beans, and other crops. The Aztecs also demanded cotton cloth, military equipment, luxury goods like jade and feathers, and sacrificial victims.

A specialized class of merchants controlled long-distance trade. Lacking draft animals and wheeled vehicles, they mostly traded lightweight and valuable products like gold, jewels, feathered garments, cacao, and animal skins. Merchants also provided political and military intelligence. Operating beyond the reach of Aztec military power, merchant expeditions carried arms and often used them. Although some merchants became wealthy and powerful, none could enter the ranks of the high nobility.

Tenochtitlan Capital of the Aztec Empire, located on an island in Lake Texcoco. Its population was about 150,000 on the eve of Spanish conquest. Mexico City was constructed on its ruins.

tribute system A system in which defeated peoples were forced to pay a tax in the form of goods and labor. This forced transfer of food, cloth, and other goods subsidized the development of large cities. An important component of the Aztec and Inca economies.

SECTION REVIEW

- Postclassic civilizations carried on the basic forms of religious belief and ritual, architecture, city planning, and social organization of their predecessors.

- Mesoamerican populations increased, causing intensified agriculture and warfare.

- The Toltecs built upon Teotihuacan's legacy, achieving notable innovations in politics and war.

- Adopting Toltec practices, the Aztecs built an urban, imperial state ruled by kings and aristocrats who practiced ritualized warfare.

- Clan ties gave way to class-based distinctions reinforced by ceremony, and a tribute system evolved to support urban populations.

- Merchants controlled long-distance trade, and religious ritual involving human sacrifice dominated public life.

Mesoamerican commerce took place without money or credit, but cacao, quills filled with gold, and cotton cloth provided standard units of value in barter transactions. Aztec expansion integrated producers and consumers in the central Mexican economy so that the markets of Tenochtitlan and Tlatelolco offered goods from as far away as Central America and what is now the southwestern border of the United States. Hernán Cortés (1485–1547), the Spanish adventurer who conquered the Aztecs, admired the abundance of the Aztec marketplace:

> One square in particular is twice as big as that of Salamanca and completely surrounded by arcades where there are daily more than sixty thousand folk buying and selling. . . . There is nothing to be found in all the land which is not sold in these markets, for over and above what I have mentioned there are so many and such various things that on account of their very number . . . I cannot detail them.[5]

The combined population of Tenochtitlan and Tlatelolco and the cities and hamlets of the surrounding lakeshore totaled approximately 500,000 by 1500. In the island capital, canals and streets intersected at right angles. Three causeways connected the city to the lakeshore.

Religious rituals dominated public life. The Aztecs worshiped numerous gods, most of them having both male and female natures. As the Aztec state grew in power and wealth, the cult of Huitzilopochtli (wheat-zeel-oh-POSHT-lee), the southern hummingbird, grew in importance. Although originally associated with war, Huitzilopochtli eventually symbolized the sun, which was worshiped as a divinity throughout Mesoamerica. To bring the sun's warmth to the world, Huitzilopochtli required a daily diet of human hearts. Twin temples devoted to Huitzilopochtli and Tlaloc, the rain-god—the two symbolizing war and agriculture as the bases of the Aztec system—dominated Tenochtitlan.

Sacrificial victims—preferably war captives but also criminals, slaves, and people provided as tribute—transformed the Mesoamerican tradition of human sacrifice by increasing its scale. Thousands of lives were taken every year. Some scholars have emphasized the politically intimidating nature of this rising tide, noting that sacrifices took place before large crowds that included leaders from enemy and subject states, as well as the masses of Aztec society.

Northern Peoples

In what ways did Mesoamerica influence the cultural centers in North America?

Mesoamerica's classic period ended around 900 C.E. By then, settled life and complex social and political structures based on improved agriculture and population growth had appeared in the southwestern desert of today's United States and in eastern river valleys. Along the Ohio River, Amerindian peoples living in large villages with monumental earthworks practiced hunting and gathering and harvested locally domesticated seed crops.

Cultivating maize introduced from Mesoamerica required large-scale irrigation projects in the southwestern desert and the eastern river valleys. However, the two regions evolved different political traditions. The Anasazi (ah-nah-SAH-zee) and their neighbors in the southwest maintained a relatively egalitarian social structure and a political organization based on kinship and age. The mound builders of the east had hereditary chiefs who wielded both secular and religious authority over the political center and subordinate small towns.

Mesa Verde Cliff Dwelling Located in southern Colorado, the Anasazi cliff dwellings of the Mesa Verde region hosted a population of about 7,000 in 1250 C.E. The construction of housing complexes and religious buildings in the area's large caves was prompted by increased warfare in the region.

Southwestern Desert Cultures

Immigrants from Mexico brought irrigation agriculture to Arizona around 300 B.C.E. With two harvests per year, population grew and villages appeared. The Hohokam of the Salt and Gila River Valleys show strong Mexican influence, with platform mounds and ball courts similar to those of Mesoamerica. Hohokam pottery, clay figurines, cast copper bells, and turquoise mosaics also reflect Mexican influence. By 1000 C.E., the Hohokam had constructed an elaborate irrigation system that included one canal more than 18 miles (30 kilometers) in length. Hohokam agricultural and ceramic technology gradually spread, but it was the Anasazi to the north who left the most vivid legacy.

Archaeologists use **Anasazi**, a Navajo word meaning "ancient ones," to identify a number of dispersed desert cultures in the Four Corners region of Arizona, New Mexico, Colorado, and Utah. Between 500 and 750 C.E. the early Anasazi lived in large villages and grew maize, beans, and squash. Their cultural life centered on underground buildings called kivas, which they may have used for weaving cotton and making pottery with geometric patterns. After 900, they began to construct large multistory residential and ritual centers.

Chaco Canyon sheltered one of the largest communities: eight large towns in the canyon itself and four more on surrounding mesas, suggesting a regional population of approximately 15,000. Each town contained hundreds of rooms arranged in tiers around a central plaza. At Pueblo Bonito, the largest town, a four-story block of residences and storage spaces contained more than 650 rooms. Pueblo Bonito had thirty-eight kivas, including a great kiva more than 65 feet (19 meters) in diameter. Social life and craft activities took place in small, open plazas or common rooms. Hunting, trade, and irrigation work often drew men away from the village. Besides preparing food and caring for children, women shared

Anasazi Important culture of what is now the southwest United States (700–1200). Centered on Chaco Canyon in New Mexico and Mesa Verde in Colorado, the Anasazi culture built multistory residences and worshiped in subterranean buildings called kivas.

in agricultural tasks and many crafts. Among modern Pueblos, the cultural descendants of the Anasazi, houses and furnishings belong to women formed into extended families with their mothers and sisters.

Late in Chaco's development, traders provided turquoise to Toltec-period peoples in northern Mexico in exchange for shell jewelry, copper bells, macaws, and trumpets. More important signs of Mesoamerican influence, such as pyramid-shaped mounds, ball courts, and class distinctions signaled by burials or residences, do not appear at Chaco. It appears more likely that the Chaco Canyon culture developed from earlier societies in the region.

Drought probably forced the abandonment of Chaco Canyon in the twelfth century. Nevertheless, the Anasazi continued in the Four Corners region for more than a century. Anasazi settlements on the Colorado Plateau and in Arizona used large natural caves high above valley floors. Such hard-to-reach locations suggest increased warfare, probably provoked by population pressure on limited arable land. The Pueblo peoples of the Rio Grande Valley and Arizona still live in multistory villages and worship in kivas.

Mound Builders: The Hopewell and Mississippian Cultures

From around 100 C.E. the Hopewell culture spread through the Ohio River Valley. Hopewell people constructed large villages characterized by monumental earthworks. Once established, Hopewell influence spread west to Illinois, Michigan, and Wisconsin, east to New York and Ontario, and south to Alabama, Louisiana, Mississippi, and even Florida. For sustenance the Hopewell people depended on hunting and gathering and a limited agriculture based on domesticated seed crops. Hopewell is an early example of a North American **chiefdom**—a territory with a population as large as 10,000 ruled by a hereditary leader with both religious and secular responsibilities. Chiefs organized periodic rituals of feasting and gift giving that established bonds among diverse kinship groups and guaranteed access to specialized crops and craft goods. They also managed long-distance trade that provided luxury goods and additional food supplies.

The largest Hopewell towns in the Ohio River Valley served as ceremonial and political centers and had several thousand inhabitants. Large mounds housing elite burials and serving as platforms for temples and the chief's residence dominated these centers. Elite burial vaults containing valuable goods like river pearls and copper jewelry sometimes entomb women and retainers apparently sacrificed to accompany a dead chief into the afterlife. The abandonment of major Hopewell sites around 400 C.E. has no clear environmental or political explanation.

Hopewell technology and mound building were linked to the development of Mississippian culture (700–1500 C.E.). Maize, beans, and squash suggest an indirect link to Mesoamerica. The urbanized Mississippian chiefdoms resulted from the accumulated effects of small increases in agricultural productivity, the adoption of the bow and arrow, and the expansion of trade networks. The largest towns shared a common urban plan based on a central plaza surrounded by large platform mounds. There, people bartered essential commodities, such as flint used for weapons and tools.

SECTION REVIEW

- In parts of North America, agricultural improvements and population growth stimulated the development of complex societies.

- In Chaco Canyon, the Anasazi practiced irrigated agriculture and produced architecture that suggests an egalitarian society.

- Some Chaco Canyon settlements exerted broad territorial influence until changing conditions forced relocation to less accessible sites.

- The Hopewell peoples built large villages with monumental earthworks and organized themselves into hierarchical chiefdoms.

- The Mississippian culture built on these patterns, with great sites such as Cahokia revealing stratified societies.

chiefdom Form of political organization with rule by a hereditary leader who held power over a collection of villages and towns. Less powerful than kingdoms and empires, chiefdoms were based on gift giving and commercial links.

The Mississippian culture culminated in the urban site of Cahokia, located near East St. Louis, Illinois. North America's largest mound, a terraced structure 100 feet (30 meters) high and 1,037 by 790 feet (316 by 241 meters) at the base, stands at its center, an area of elite housing and temples ringed by areas where commoners lived. At its height in about 1200, Cahokia had a population of some 30,000—as large as the great Maya city of Tikal.

Cahokia controlled surrounding agricultural lands and a number of secondary towns ruled by subchiefs. One tomb containing more than fifty young women and retainers sacrificed to accompany a ruler after death suggests the exalted position of Cahokia's chiefs. Nothing links the decline and eventual abandonment of Cahokia (1250) to military defeat or civil war, although climate changes and population pressures may have undermined its vitality. Smaller Mississippian centers flourished in the southeastern United States until the arrival of Europeans.

Andean Civilizations, 200–1500

How did the Amerindian peoples of the Andean area adapt to their environment and produce socially complex and politically advanced societies?

Much of the Andean region's mountainous zone seems too high for agriculture and human habitation, and the arid plain of its Pacific coastland poses difficult challenges to cultivation. To the east of the Andes Mountains, the hot, humid Amazon headwaters also discouraged the organization of complex societies. Yet the Amerindian peoples of the region developed some of the most socially complex and politically advanced societies of the Western Hemisphere (see Map 7.3).

Cultural Response to Environmental Challenge

People living in the high mountain valleys and on the dry coastal plain overcame their environmental challenges through effective organization of labor using a record-keeping system more limited than those of Mesoamerica. A system of knotted colored cords, **khipus** (KEY-pooz), helped administrators record population counts and tribute obligations. Large-scale drainage

Map 7.3 Andean Civilizations, 200 B.C.E.–1532 C.E.
In response to environmental challenges posed by an arid coastal plain and high interior mountain ranges, Andean peoples made complex social and technological adaptations. Irrigation systems, the domestication of the llama, metallurgy, and shared labor obligations helped provide a firm economic foundation for powerful, centralized states. In 1532 the Inca Empire's vast territory stretched from modern Chile in the south to Colombia in the north.
© Cengage Learning

Interactive Map

and irrigation works and the terracing of hillsides to control erosion and provide additional farmland increased agricultural production. People worked collectively on road building, urban construction, and even textile production.

khipus System of knotted colored cords used by pre-literate Andean peoples to transmit information.

The clan, or **ayllu** (aye-YOU), provided the foundation for Andean achievement. Members of an ayllu claiming descent from a common ancestor, though not necessarily related in fact, held land communally. Ayllu members thought of each other as brothers and sisters with obligations to help each other in tasks beyond the ability of a single household.

When territorial states ruled by hereditary aristocracies and kings developed after 1000 B.C.E., these obligations grew in scale. The **mit'a** (MEET-ah) system required ayllu members to work the fields and care for the herds of llamas and alpacas owned by religious establishments, the royal court, and the aristocracy. Each allyu met a yearly quota of workers for specific tasks. Mit'a laborers built and maintained roads, bridges, temples, palaces, and large irrigation and drainage projects. They produced textiles and goods essential to ritual life, such as coca and beer made from maize.

Jobs divided along gender lines, but the work of men and women was interdependent. Men hunted and served as soldiers and administrators, while women had responsibilities in textile production, agriculture, and the home. One early Spanish commentator remarked:

> [Women] did not just perform domestic tasks, but also [labored] in the fields, in the cultivation of their lands, in building houses, and carrying burdens. . . . And more than once I heard that while women were carrying these burdens, they would feel labor pains, and giving birth, they would go to a place where there was water and wash the baby and themselves. Putting the baby on top of the load they were carrying, they would then continue walking as before they gave birth.[6]

The unique environmental challenges of the Andean region led to distinctive highland and coastal cultures. Here, more than in Mesoamerica, geography influenced regional cultural integration and state formation. Because the region's mountain ranges created a multitude of small ecological areas with specialized resources, each community sought to control a variety of environments to gain access to essential goods. Coastal regions produced maize, fish, and cotton, and mountain valleys contributed quinoa, potatoes, and other tubers. Higher elevations contributed the wool and meat of llamas and alpacas. The Amazonian region provided coca and fruits. Colonists sent to exploit these ecological niches remained linked to their original region and ayllu by marriage and ritual. Historians commonly refer to this system of controlled exchange across ecological boundaries as vertical integration, or verticality.

Moche and Chimú

Around 200 C.E., some four centuries after the collapse of Chavín, the **Moche** (MO-che) achieved dominance of the north coastal region of Peru. They did not establish a centralized state, but they did deploy military forces, and major urban centers like Cerro Blanco (see Map 7.3) established hegemony over smaller towns and villages.

The Moche cultivated maize, quinoa, beans, manioc, and sweet potatoes with the aid of massive irrigation works. At higher elevations, they produced coca, which was used ritually. Complex networks of canals and aqueducts connecting fields with water sources as far away as 75 miles (121 kilometers) depended on mit'a labor imposed on Moche commoners and subject peoples. Large herds of llamas transported goods across difficult terrain. Their wool, along with cotton, provided raw material for textile production, and their meat was an important dietary element.

Murals and decorated ceramics show Moche society to be stratified and theocratic. Labor organization helped to promote class divisions. Wealth and power, along with political control, lay with the priests and military leaders, a situation reinforced by military conquest of neighboring regions. The elite lived above the commoners on large platforms at Moche ceremonial centers. Their rich clothing, including tall headdresses, confirmed their divine status and set them further apart from commoners. Gold and gold alloy jewelry signified social position: gold plates suspended from the noses concealed the lower portion of the faces, and large gold plugs decorated the ears.

ayllu Andean lineage group or kin-based community.
mit'a Andean labor system based on shared obligations to help kinsmen and work on behalf of the ruler and religious organizations.
Moche Civilization of north coast of Peru (200–700 C.E.). An important Andean civilization that built extensive irrigation networks as well as impressive urban centers dominated by brick temples.

One tomb of a warrior-priest buried from the Lambeyeque Valley contained a treasure that included gold, silver, and copper jewelry, textiles, feather ornaments, and shells. Two women and three men accompanied him in death. Each retainer had one foot amputated to ensure continued subservience and dependence in the afterlife (see Diversity and Dominance: Burials as Historic Texts).

Commoners lived by subsistence farming and labored for their ayllu and the elite. Agriculture, the care of llama herds, and the household economy involved both men and women. Commoners lived in one-room buildings clustered in the outlying areas of cities and in surrounding agricultural zones.

Moche textiles, ceramics, and metallurgy give evidence of numerous skilled artisans. As in Chavín, women played a major role in textile production; even elite women devoted time to weaving. Moche craftsmen produced highly individualized portrait vases, ceramics decorated with line drawings representing myths and rituals, and vessels depicting explicit sexual acts. Their metalwork included gold and silver objects devoted to religious and decorative functions or to elite adornment, as well as heavy copper and copper alloy tools for agricultural and military purposes.

The archaeological record shows that the rapid decline of the major centers coincided with a succession of natural disasters in the sixth century and the rise of a new military power in the Andean highlands. When an earthquake altered the course of the Moche River, major flooding caused serious damage, and a thirty-year period of drought expanded the area of coastal sand dunes, which then blew over cultivated fields, overwhelming the irrigation system. As the land dried, periodic heavy rains caused erosion, which further damaged the economy. Religious and political leaders whose privileges stemmed from a claimed ability to control natural forces through rituals lost credibility. Despite massive efforts to maintain irrigation and the construction of new urban centers in less vulnerable valleys to the north, Moche civilization never recovered. In the eighth century, a new military power, the **Wari** (WAH-ree), put pressure on trade routes linking the coastal region with the highlands and thus contributed to the disappearance of the Moche.

At the end of the Moche period, the **Chimú** (chee-MOO) developed a more powerful coastal civilization centered on Chan Chan, a capital built around 800 C.E. near the earlier Moche cultural center. Chimú expanded aggressively after 1200 and at the apex of its power controlled 625 miles (1,000 kilometers) of the Peruvian coast.

Within Chan Chan was a series of walled compounds, each one containing a burial pyramid. Scholars believe that each Chimú ruler built his own walled compound in Chan Chan and was buried there beneath a pyramid. Sacrifices and rich grave goods accompanied each royal burial. As with the Moche, Chimú's rulers separated themselves from the masses and demonstrated divine favor by consuming rare and beautiful textiles, ceramics, and precious metals. The Chimú dynasty may have practiced split inheritance, the goods and lands of the deceased ruler going to secondary heirs or for religious sacrifices. The heir who inherited the throne therefore had to construct his own residence compound and undertake new conquests to fund his household. After the Inca conquered the northern coast in 1465, they borrowed from the rituals and court customs of Chimú.

Tiwanaku and Wari

After 500 C.E., two powerful civilizations developed in the Andean highlands. At nearly 13,000 feet (3,962 meters) on the high, treeless plain near Lake Titicaca in modern Bolivia stand the ruins of **Tiwanaku** (tee-wah-NA-coo) (see Map 7.3). Initial occupation may have occurred as early as 400 B.C.E., but significant urbanization began only after 200 C.E. Modern excavations provide the outline of vast drainage projects that reclaimed nearly 200,000 acres (8,000 hectares) of rich lakeside marshes for agriculture. This system of raised fields and ditches permitted intensive cultivation similar to that achieved through chinampas in Mesoamerica. Fish and llamas added protein to a diet largely dependent on potatoes and grains. Llamas

Wari Andean civilization culturally linked to Tiwanaku, perhaps beginning as a colony of Tiwanaku.
Chimú Powerful Peruvian civilization based on conquest. Located in the region earlier dominated by Moche. Conquered by Inca in 1465.
Tiwanaku Name of capital city and empire centered on the region near Lake Titicaca in modern Bolivia (500–1000 C.E.).

Diversity & Dominance

Burials as Historic Texts

Efforts to reveal the history of the Americas before the arrival of Europeans depend on the work of archaeologists. The burials of rulers and other members of elites can be viewed as historical texts that describe how textiles, precious metals, beautifully decorated ceramics, and other commodities were used to reinforce the political and cultural power of ruling lineages. In public, members of the elite were always surrounded by the most desirable goods and rarest products as well as by elaborate rituals and ceremonies. The effect was to create an aura of godlike power. The material elements of political and cultural power were also integrated into the experience of death and burial as members of the elite were sent into the afterlife.

The first photograph is of an excavated Moche tomb in Sipán, Peru. The Moche (200 C.E.–ca. 700 C.E.), one of the most important of the pre-Inca civilizations of the Andean region, were masters of metallurgy, ceramics, and textiles. The excavations at Sipán revealed a "warrior-priest" buried with an amazing array of gold ornaments, jewels, textiles, and ceramics. Also buried with him were five human sacrifices: two women, perhaps wives or concubines, two male servants, and a warrior. Three of these victims—the warrior, one woman, and a male servant—are each missing a foot, as if to guarantee their continued faithfulness to the deceased ruler in the afterlife.

The second photograph shows the excavation of a classic-era (250 C.E.–ca. 900 C.E.) Maya burial at Río Azul in Guatemala. After death this elite male was laid out on a carved wooden platform and cotton mattress and his body painted with decorations. Mourners covered his body in rich textiles and surrounded him with valuable goods. These included a necklace of individual stones carved in the shape of heads, perhaps a symbol of his prowess in battle, and high-quality ceramics, some filled with foods consumed by the elite like cacao. The careful preparation of the burial chamber had required the work of numerous artisans and laborers, as was the case in the burial of the Moche warrior-priest. In death, as in life, these early American civilizations acknowledged the high status, political power, and religious authority of their elites.

QUESTIONS FOR ANALYSIS

1. If these burials are texts, what are stories?
2. Are there any visible differences in the two burials?
3. What questions might historians ask of these burials that cannot be answered?
4. Can modern burials be read as texts in similar ways to these ancient burials?

Heinze Plenge/National Geographic Stock

George Mobley/National Geographic Stock

Burials Reveal Ancient Civilizations *(Left)* Around 300 C.E. this Moche warrior-priest was buried amid rich tribute at Sipán in Peru. Also buried were the bodies of retainers or kinsmen probably sacrificed to accompany this powerful man. The body lies with the head on the right and the feet on the left. *(Right)* Similarly, the burial of a member of the Maya elite at Río Azul in northern Guatemala indicates the care taken to surround the powerful with fine ceramics, jewelry, and other valuable goods.

also serviced long-distance trade that brought in maize, coca, tropical fruits, and medicinal plants.

Tiwanaku's construction featured high-quality stone masonry. An organized work force—probably thousands of laborers over a period of years—moved large stones and quarried blocks many miles to construct a terraced pyramid, walled enclosures, and a reservoir. With copper alloy tools their only metallic resource, Tiwanaku's artisans cut stone so precisely that little mortar was needed to fit the blocks. They also produced gigantic human statuary; the largest example, a stern figure with a military bearing, was cut from a single stone 24 feet (7 meters) high.

Evidence of daily life is scarce, but Tiwanaku clearly had a stratified society ruled by a hereditary elite. Most women and men devoted their time to agriculture and the care of llamas, though construction and pottery required specialized artisans. Tiwanaku ceramics found in distant places suggest a specialized merchant class as well.

Many scholars portray Tiwanaku as the capital of a vast empire, a precursor to the later Inca state. The elite certainly controlled a large, disciplined labor force in the surrounding region, and conquests and the establishment of colonies provided the highland capital with products from ecologically distinct zones. Tiwanaku influence also extended eastward to the Amazon rain forest and southward to the coastal oases of the Atacama Desert in Chile. But archaeological evidence suggests that, in comparison with contemporary Teotihuacan in central Mexico, Tiwanaku had a relatively small full-time population of around 30,000 and served as a ceremonial and political center for a large regional population more than as a metropolis.

The contemporary site of Wari, about 450 miles (751 kilometers) to the northwest, had cultural and technological links to Tiwanaku, but the exact relationship remains unclear. Each had a unique cultural signature. Wari exceeded Tiwanaku in size, measuring nearly 4 square miles (10 square kilometers). A massive wall surrounded the city center, which included a large temple and numerous multifamily housing blocks. Housing for commoners sprawled across a suburban zone. Unlike most other urban centers in the Andes, Wari had no central planning.

The small scale of its monumental architecture and the near absence of cut stone masonry in public and private buildings distinguish Wari from Tiwanaku.

Wari ceramic style also differs, the difference enabling experts to trace Wari's expansion, at a time of increasing warfare throughout the Andes, to the coastal area earlier controlled by the Moche and to the northern highlands. Wari roads maintained communications with remote fortified dependencies. Perhaps as a consequence of military conflict, both Tiwanaku and Wari declined to insignificance by about 1000 C.E.

The Inca

In little more than one hundred years, the **Inca** developed a vast imperial state, which they called "Land of Four Corners." By 1525, this empire had a population of more than 6 million inhabitants and stretched from the Maule River in Chile to northern Ecuador and from the Pacific coast across the Andes to the upper Amazon and, in the south, into Argentina (see Map 7.3). In the early fifteenth century, the Inca competed for power locally in the southern highlands, an area of limited significance after the collapse of Wari. Centered in the valley of Cuzco, the Inca were initially organized as a chiefdom based on reciprocal gift giving and the redistribution of food and textiles. In the 1430s strong leaders consolidated political authority and undertook a campaign of military expansion.

The Inca state incorporated traditional Andean social customs and economic practices. Tiwanaku had used colonists to provide resources from ecologically distinct zones. The Inca built on this practice by using their large, professional military to conquer distant territories and by increasing the scale of forced exchanges.

Like earlier highland civilizations, the Inca were pastoralists, their prosperity and military strength depending on vast herds of llamas and alpacas. Both men and women cared for these herds—the women weaving woolen cloth, the men driving animals in long-distance trade. This pastoral background led the Inca to believe that the gods and their ruler shared the obligations of the shepherd to his flock, an idea reminiscent of the Old Testament image conveyed by the lines "The Lord is my Shepherd."

Cuzco, the imperial capital, and the provincial cities, the royal court, the imperial armies, and the

Inca Largest and most powerful Andean empire. Controlled the Pacific coast of South America from Ecuador to Chile from its capital of Cuzco.

state's religious cults all rested on the efforts of mit'a laborers. The mit'a system also provided the bare necessities for the old, weak, and ill of Inca society. Each ayllu contributed approximately one-seventh of its adult male population to meet these collective obligations. These draft laborers served as soldiers, construction workers, craftsmen, and runners to carry messages along post roads. They also drained swamps, terraced mountainsides, filled in valley floors, built and maintained irrigation works, and built storage facilities and roads. Inca laborers constructed 13,000 miles (20,930 kilometers) of road, which facilitated military troop movements, administration, and trade.

Imperial administration incorporated existing political structures and established elite groups. The hereditary chiefs of ayllus carried out administrative and judicial functions. As the Inca expanded, they generally left local rulers in place. Rebellion was possible, but the Inca controlled this risk by taking hostages and building military garrisons. Rulers of defeated regions sent their heirs to live at the Inca court in Cuzco, and representations of important local gods were brought to Cuzco to join the imperial pantheon.

Conquests magnified the authority of the Inca ruler and led to the creation of an imperial bureaucracy drawn from his kinsmen. The royal family claimed descent from the sun, the primary Inca god. Members of the royal family lived in palaces maintained by armies of servants. Political and religious rituals dominated the lives of the ruler and his family and helped legitimize their authority. Because extending imperial boundaries by warfare constituted an imperial duty, each new ruler began his reign with conquest.

At the height of Inca power in 1530, Cuzco had a population of fewer than 30,000, a fifth that of Tenochtitlan at the same time. Nevertheless, Cuzco contains impressive buildings constructed of carefully cut stones fitted together without mortar. Laid out in the shape of a giant puma (a mountain lion), the city's center contained the palaces each ruler built on ascending the throne, as well as the major temples. The Temple of the Sun had an interior lined with sheets of gold and a patio decorated with golden representations of llamas and maize. The ruler made every effort to awe and intimidate visitors and residents with a nearly continuous series of rituals, feasts, and sacrifices. Sacrifices of textiles, animals,

SECTION REVIEW

- Andean peoples overcame the challenges of their environment through superior organization.
- The Moche used these technologies to maintain a decentralized, socially stratified state.
- The Chimú built a centralized monarchy based on split inheritance and conquest.
- Tiwanaku and Wari exploited highland resources; the latter city was larger but had no central planning.
- The Inca extended traditional Andean practices to build the largest empire in the region.
- The Inca developed no new technologies but increased agricultural yield to support ever-growing populations.

and other goods sent as tribute dominated the city's calendar. The destruction of these valuable commodities and a small number of human sacrifices conveyed an impression of splendor and sumptuous abundance that appeared to validate the ruler's descent from the sun.

We know that astronomical observation occupied the priestly class, as in Mesoamerica, but the Inca calendar is unknown. Nonoral communication involved the khipus borrowed from earlier Andean civilizations. Inca weaving and metallurgy, building on earlier regional developments, excelled that of Mesoamerica. Inca craftsmen produced tools and weapons of copper and bronze along with decorative objects of gold and silver. Inca women produced textiles of extraordinary beauty from cotton and llama and alpaca wool.

The Inca did not introduce new technologies, but they increased economic output and added to the region's prosperity. Ruling large populations in environmentally distinct regions allowed the Inca to multiply exchanges between ecological niches. But imperial economic and political expansion reduced equality and diminished local autonomy. The imperial elite lived in richly decorated palaces in Cuzco and other urban centers, increasingly cut off from common people. The royal court held members of the provincial nobility at arm's length, and commoners faced execution if they looked directly at the ruler's face.

After only a century of regional dominance, the Inca Empire faced a crisis in 1526. The death of the Inca ruler Huayna Capac at the conclusion of the conquest of Ecuador initiated a bloody struggle for the throne. Powerful factions coalesced around two sons whose rivalry compelled both the military and the Inca elite to choose sides. The resulting civil war weakened imperial institutions and ignited the resentments of conquered peoples spread over more than 3,000 miles (4,830 kilometers) of mountainous terrain. On the eve of the arrival of Europeans, this violent conflict undermined the institutions and economy of Andean civilization.

Conclusion

The Aztec and Inca Empires culminate long historical developments in Mesoamerica and the Andes. Each empire was created militarily and depended as much on strong armies as on wise rulers or economic productivity. Both adopted and adapted political institutions, economic forms and technologies, and religious practices from their predecessors. Their rulers legitimized their authority by serving as intermediaries with the gods, and major cities were religious political centers with dominating religious architecture. Both regions depended on mobilizing ever-larger work forces to meet growing needs rather than on technological innovation.

Elementary markets developed in Mesoamerica to distribute specialized regional production, although the forced payment of goods as tribute helped sustain cities like Tenochtitlan and Cuzco. In the Andes reciprocal labor obligations and managed exchange relationships were used to allocate goods. The Aztecs forced defeated peoples to provide food, textiles, and even sacrificial victims, but they left local hereditary elites in place. The Inca, in contrast, created a centralized imperial administrative structure managed by a trained bureaucracy and used reciprocal labor obligations to produce and distribute goods.

Agricultural technology centering on maize, beans, and squash diffused from Mesoamerica to influence the major cultures of North America. In the southwestern desert of the United States, the Anasazi and other peoples utilized irrigated agriculture, a technology crucial also to Mesoamerican and Andean cultures.

As the Western Hemisphere's long isolation drew to a close in the late fifteenth century, both Aztec and Inca Empires were challenged by powerful neighbors or internal revolts. Similar challenges had contributed to the earlier decline of great civilizations in both regions. In previous cases, a long period of adjustment and development of new institutions followed the collapse of powers such as the Toltecs in Mesoamerica and Tiwanaku in the Andes. The arrival of Europeans was to change this pattern.

CHAPTER REVIEW

 Download the MP3 audio file of the Chapter Review to listen to on the go.

What role did nature and the environment play in the early civilizations of the Americas? (page 161)

The people of the Americas lived in virtual isolation from the rest of the world for at least 15,000 years. During this period, they learned to adapt to their natural environment on their own. The Olmec organized their population to dig irrigation and drainage canals and to cultivate the land. Chavín agriculture depended on the introduction of maize cultivation as well as trade with other regions. Llamas were used to transport goods along newly constructed roads and bridges. Artificial platforms and mounds of packed earth dominated both civilizations' urban centers. Olmec shamans planned urban centers to be aligned with the stars.

What were the most important shared characteristics of Mesoamerican cultures in the classic period? (page 167)

Mesoamerican civilization was based largely on a relationship with the gods and the environment. At Teotihuacan, people worshiped many gods and constructed pyramids devoted to the sun, the moon, and Quetzalcoatl. Human sacrifice was deemed essential to the well-being of society. Maya city-states also featured impressive temples, often built on high ground and reflecting the Maya cosmos.

As both political leaders and priests, rulers participated in bloodletting rituals and hallucinogenic trances. The people of Teotihuacan brought marginal lands into production and expanded the use of chinampas. The Maya contended with a tropical climate and fragile soils. People living near cities manipulated their environment by draining swamps and building elevated fields.

What role did warfare play in the postclassic period of Mesoamerica? (page 172)

The Toltecs were known for their military achievements. Images of war and violence appear on nearly all their public buildings and temples. The Mexica created a regional power called the Aztec Empire. Aztec rulers demonstrated their divine mandates by undertaking military conquests. Their chief deity was Huitzilopochtli, who was originally associated with war and came to be identified as the sun. The Aztecs offered up human sacrifices to the gods, usually consisting of war captives, criminals, and slaves.

In what ways did Mesoamerica influence the cultural centers in North America? (page 175)

Cultural centers in the southwest United States exhibit strong Mexican influence. Hohokam sites have platform mounds and ball courts, as well as pottery, clay figurines, and turquoise mosaics. To the north lived the Anasazi, who left the most vivid legacy of desert culture. One of the largest communities of the Anasazi was located in Chaco Canyon. Though Chaco trade goods show up in Toltec-period sites in northern Mexico, the Chaco culture seems to have developed independently. Beginning around 100 C.E., the Hopewell culture spread through the Ohio River Valley. Hopewell earthen mounds housed elite burials and served as platforms for temples and homes for chiefs. Similar mound building occurred in the Mississippian culture. Evidence of a Mesoamerican influence on either culture is rare.

How did the Amerindian peoples of the Andean area adapt to their environment and produce socially complex and politically advanced societies? (page 178)

Both the Andes Mountains and the bordering coastal plain posed great environmental challenges. The Amerindian response was effective organization of human labor for digging irrigation works, terracing hillsides, and building roads. Andean societies functioned through clans called ayllus that provided labor and goods to their hereditary chiefs. They also exchanged goods across ecological boundaries. Each community's production suited its ecological niche: coastal regions produced maize, fish, and cotton; mountain valleys contributed quinoa and potatoes; higher elevations contributed the wool and meat of animals; and the Amazonian region provided coca and fruits. The institutions of the ayllu and the state managed exchanges that fostered integration and growth.

Key Terms

Olmec (p. 162)	tribute system (p. 174)
Chavín (p. 165)	Anasazi (p. 176)
llama (p. 166)	chiefdom (p. 177)
Teotihuacan (p. 168)	khipus (p. 178)
Chinampas (p. 169)	ayllu (p. 179)
Maya (p. 170)	mit'a (p. 179)
Toltecs (p. 173)	Moche (p. 179)
Aztecs (p. 173)	Wari (p. 180)
altepetl (p. 173)	Chimú (p. 180)
calpolli (p. 173)	Tiwanaku (p. 180)
Tenochtitlan (p. 174)	Inca (p. 182)

Web Resources

Interactive Maps
- MAP 7.1 Olmec and Chavín Civilizations
- MAP 7.2 Major Mesoamerican Civilizations, 1000 B.C.E.–1519 C.E.
- MAP 7.3 Andean Civilizations, 200 B.C.E.–1532 C.E.

Answer to the History in Focus Question
See photo on page 170, "The Great Plaza at Tikal."

 Visit the CourseMate website at www.cengagebrain.com for additional study tools and review materials for this chapter.

CHAPTER 8

300 B.C.E.–600 C.E.

Networks of Communication and Exchange

© Cengage Learning

Visit the CourseMate website at **www.cengagebrain.com** for additional study tools and review materials for this chapter.

Inspired by the tradition of the Silk Road, a Chinese poet named Po Zhuyi (boh joo-yee) nostalgically wrote:

> Iranian whirling girl, Iranian whirling girl—
> Her heart answers to the strings,
> Her hands answer to the drums.
> At the sound of the strings and drums, she raises her arms,
> Like whirling snowflakes tossed about, she turns in her twirling dance.
> Iranian whirling girl,
> You came from Sogdiana (sog-dee-A-nuh).
> In vain did you labor to come east more than ten thousand tricents.
> For in the central plains there were already some who could do the Iranian whirl,
> And in a contest of wonderful abilities, you would not be their equal.[1]

The western part of Central Asia, the region around Samarkand (SAM-mar-kand) and Bukhara (boo-CAR-ruh) known in the eighth century C.E. as Sogdiana, was 2,500 miles (4,000 kilometers) from the Chinese capital of Chang'an (chahng-ahn). The route between these points was called in modern times the **Silk Road**, after one of the major products that were traded. Caravans took more than four months to trek across the mostly unsettled deserts, mountains, and grasslands, carrying with them agricultural goods, manufactured products, and ideas. Musicians and dancing girls traveled, too—as did camel pullers, merchants, monks, and pilgrims. The Silk Road was a means of connecting peoples and parts of the world as well as a social system.

With every expansion of territory, the growing wealth of temples, kings, and emperors enticed traders to venture ever farther afield for precious goods. For the most part, the customers were wealthy elites. But the new products, agricultural and industrial processes, and foreign ideas and customs these long-distance traders brought with them sometimes affected an entire society.

1. From *The Columbia Anthology of Traditional Chinese Literature*, edited and translated by Victor H. Mair. Copyright © 1994 Columbia University Press. Reprinted with permission of the publisher.

Travelers and traders seldom owned much land or wielded political power. Socially isolated (sometimes by law) and secretive because any talk about markets, products, routes, and travel conditions could help their competitors, they nevertheless contributed more to drawing the world together than did all but a few kings and emperors.

This chapter examines the social systems and historical impact of exchange networks that developed between 300 B.C.E. and 600 C.E. in Europe, Asia, and Africa. The Silk Road and the Indian Ocean Maritime System illustrate long-distance trade in this era. At the same time that shorter trade routes developed across the Sahara, the Bantu-speaking peoples within sub-Saharan Africa began a folk migration throughout Africa, carrying with them technologies, language, and ideas. A third pattern of cultural contact and exchange is illustrated by the spread of Buddhism in Asia and Christianity in Africa and Asia; Chapter 6 discussed the spread of Christian missionary activity in the Roman Empire.

The Silk Road

What factors contributed to the growth of trade along the Silk Road?

Archaeology and linguistic studies show that the peoples of Central Asia engaged in long-distance movement and exchange from at least 1500 B.C.E. In Roman times Europeans became captivated by the idea of a trade route linking the lands of the Mediterranean with China by way of Mesopotamia, Iran, and Central Asia. This Silk Road experienced several periods of heavy use (see Map 8.1), the first beginning around 100 B.C.E.

Origins and Operations   The Seleucid kings who succeeded to the eastern parts of Alexander the Great's empire in the third century B.C.E. focused their energies on Mesopotamia and Syria. This allowed an Iranian nomadic leader to establish an independent kingdom in northeastern Iran. The

Silk Road Caravan routes connecting China and the Middle East across Central Asia and Iran.

Interactive Map

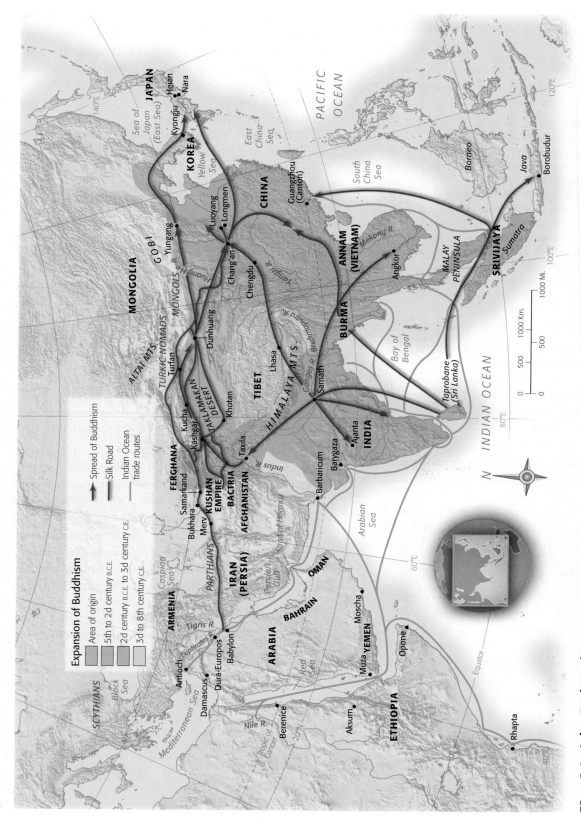

Map 8.1 Asian Trade and Communication Routes The overland Silk Road was vulnerable to political disruption, but it was much shorter than the maritime route from the South China Sea to the Red Sea, and ships were more expensive than pack animals. Moreover, China's political centers were in the north. © Cengage Learning

Chronology

	Silk Road	Indian Ocean Trade	Saharan Trade
500 B.C.E.			500 B.C.E. –CA. 1000 C.E. Bantu migrations
	247 B.C.E. Parthian rule begins in Iran		
	128 B.C.E. General Zhang Jian reaches Ferghana		CA. 200 B.C.E. Camel nomads in southern Sahara
	100 B.C.E.–300 C.E. Kushans rule northern Afghanistan and Sogdiana		46 B.C.E. First mention of camels in northern Sahara
1 C.E.	1st century C.E. First evidence of the stirrup	1st century C.E. Indonesian migration to Madagascar	
300 C.E.			CA. 300 Beginning of camel nomadism in northern Sahara
	CA. 400 Buddhist pilgrim Faxian travels Silk Road		
		CA. 900 Arab and Persian merchants in Canton	

Parthians, a people originally from east of the Caspian Sea, had become a major force by 247 B.C.E. They left few written sources, and recurring wars with Greeks and Romans to the west prevented travelers from the Mediterranean region from gaining firm knowledge of their kingdom. It seems likely, however, that they helped foster the Silk Road by being located on the threshold of Central Asia and sharing customs with steppe nomads farther to the east. In 128 B.C.E. a Chinese general named Zhang Jian (jahng jee-en) made his first exploratory journey across the deserts and mountains of Inner Asia on behalf of Emperor Wu of the Han dynasty. After crossing the broad and desolate Tarim Basin north of Tibet, he reached the fertile valley of Ferghana (fer-GAH-nuh) and for the first time encountered westward-flowing rivers. There he found horse breeders whose animals far outclassed any horses he had seen. Later Chinese historians looked on General Zhang, who ultimately led eighteen expeditions, as the originator of overland trade with the western lands, and they credited him with personally introducing a whole garden of new plants and trees to China.

Long-distance travel suited the people of the steppes more than the Chinese. The populations of Ferghana and neighboring regions included many nomads who followed their herds. Their migrations had little to do with trade, but they provided pack animals and controlled transit across their lands. The trading demands that brought the Silk Road into being were Chinese eagerness for western products, especially horses, and, on the western end, the organized Parthian state, which had captured

Iranian Musicians from Silk Road This three-color glazed pottery figurine, 23 inches (58.4 centimeters) high, comes from a northern Chinese tomb of the Tang era (sixth to ninth centuries C.E.). The musicians playing Iranian instruments confirm the migration of Iranian culture across the Silk Road. At the same time, dishes decorated by the Chinese three-color glaze technique were in vogue in northern Iran. The National Museum of Chinese History

Parthians Iranian ruling dynasty between ca. 247 B.C.E. and 224 C.E.

Lee Boltin/The Bridgeman Art Library

Scythian Breastplate This superbly crafted gold ornament from the fourth century B.C.E. features animal combat in the lower tier, flower motifs in the center, and scenes from Scythian pastoral life in the upper. Two men prepare a fleece garment in the middle of the upper tier while on either side young animals are suckling and a ewe is being milked. Note the contrast between the simplicity of nomadic life and the luxury represented by the gold ornament itself.

SECTION REVIEW

- The rise of the Parthian kingdom helped foster the Silk Road to meet Middle Eastern and European demand for Chinese silk.
- General Zhang led expeditions that established the route from China through Central Asia.
- Central Asian nomads facilitated the movement of goods through their lands.
- Central Asian cities grew as a result of Silk Road trade.
- In addition to silk, agricultural products traveled both ways along the Silk Road.

In addition to silk, traders going west from China carried new fruits such as peaches and apricots, which the Romans mistakenly attributed to other eastern lands, calling them Persian plums and Armenian plums, respectively. They also carried cinnamon, ginger, and other spices that could not be grown in the West.

the flourishing markets of Mesopotamia from the Seleucids.

By 100 B.C.E., Greeks, and later the Romans, could buy Chinese silk from Parthian traders in Mesopotamian border entrepôts. Yet caravans also bought and sold goods along the way in prosperous Central Asian cities like Samarkand and Bukhara. These cities grew and flourished, often under the rule of local princes.

General Zhang definitely seems to have brought two plants to China: alfalfa and wine grapes. The former provided the best fodder for horses. In addition, Chinese farmers adopted pistachios, walnuts, pomegranates, sesame, coriander, spinach, and other new crops. Chinese artisans and physicians made good use of other trade products, such as jasmine oil, oak galls (used in tanning animal hides, dyeing, and making ink), sal ammoniac (for medicines), copper oxides, zinc, and precious stones.

Nomadism in Central and Inner Asia

The Silk Road could not have functioned without pastoral nomads to provide animals, animal handlers, and protection. Descriptions of steppe nomads known as Scythians appear in the history of the Greek writer Herodotus in the sixth century B.C.E., who portrays them as superb riders, herdsmen, and hunters living in the steppes north of the Black and Caspian Seas. The Scythians moved regularly and efficiently with flocks and herds of enormous size to prevent overgrazing. They were also fearsome horse archers. Their homes, which were made of felt spread over a lightweight framework, were transported on four-wheeled wagons drawn by oxen. This custom continued for another two thousand years in the grasslands and deserts extending eastward to the borders of China.

Nomads were familiar with agriculture and willing to use products grown by farmers, but their ideal was self-sufficiency. Since their wanderings with their herds normally took them far from any farming region, self-sufficiency dictated foods they could provide for themselves—primarily meat and milk—and clothing made from felt, leather, and furs. Women oversaw the breeding and birthing of livestock and the preparation of furs.

Sasanid Silver Plate with Gold Decoration The Sasanid aristocracy, based in the countryside, invested part of its wealth in silver plates and vessels. This image of a Sasanid king hunting on horseback also reflects a favorite aristocratic pastime.   Erich Lessing/Art Resource, NY

who originated as nomads in northeastern Iran, the Sasanids came from the southwest, the same region that earlier gave rise to the Achaemenids (see Chapter 4).

In contrast to the sparse material remains of the Parthian period, Sasanid silver work and silk fabrics testify to the sumptuous and sedentary lifestyle of the warrior elite. Cities in Iran were small walled communities that served more as military strongpoints protecting long-distance trade than as centers of population and production.

The Silk Road now brought many new crops to Mesopotamia. Sasanid farmers pioneered in planting cotton, sugar cane, rice, citrus trees, eggplants, and other crops adopted from India and China. Although the acreage devoted to new crops increased slowly, these products became important consumption and trade items in later centuries.

Nomads were most dependent on settled regions for the bronze or iron used in bridles, stirrups, cart fittings, and weapons. They acquired metal implements in trade and reworked them to suit their purposes. Scythians in the Ukraine worked extensively with iron as early as the fourth century B.C.E., and Turkish-speaking peoples had large ironworks in western Mongolia in the 600s C.E. Steppe nomads situated near settled areas also traded wool, leather, and horses for wood, silk, vegetables, and grain.

The Sasanid Empire and the Silk Road, 224–600

How did the Sasanid Empire evolve under the influence of east-west trade?

The rise of the **Sasanid Empire** in Iran brought a continuation of the rivalry between Rome and the Parthians along the Euphrates frontier and an intensification of trade along the Silk Road; but otherwise this empire differed greatly from its Parthian predecessor. Ardashir, a descendant of an ancestor named Sasan, defeated the Parthians around 224 and became sole ruler of Iran two years later. Unlike the Parthians,

Religions and the Sasanid Empire

The Sasanids established their Zoroastrian faith (see Chapter 4) as a state religion similar to Christianity in the Byzantine Empire (see Chapter 6). The proclamation of Christianity and Zoroastrianism as official faiths marked the fresh emergence of religion as an instrument of politics both within and between the empires. This politicization of religion greatly affected the culture of the Silk Road.

Both Zoroastrianism and Christianity practiced intolerance. A late-third-century inscription in Iran boasts of the persecutions of Christians, Jews, and Buddhists carried out by the Zoroastrian high priest. Yet sizeable Christian and Jewish communities

Sasanid Empire Iranian empire, established ca. 224, with a capital in Ctesiphon, Mesopotamia. The Sasanid emperors established Zoroastrianism as the state religion. Islamic Arab armies overthrew the empire ca. 640.

remained, especially in Mesopotamia. Similarly, from the fourth century onward, councils of Christian bishops declared many theological beliefs heretical—so unacceptable that they were un-Christian.

Christians became pawns in the political rivalry with the Byzantines and were sometimes persecuted, sometimes patronized, by the Sasanid kings. In 431 a council of bishops called by the Byzantine emperor declared the Nestorian Christians heretics for overemphasizing the humanness of Christ. The Nestorians believed that a human nature and a divine nature coexisted in Jesus and that Mary was not the mother of God, as many other Christians maintained, but the mother of the human Jesus. After the bishops' ruling, the Nestorians sought refuge under the Sasanid shah and engaged in missionary activities along the Silk Road.

A parallel episode within Zoroastrianism transpired in the third century. A preacher named Mani founded a new religion in Mesopotamia: Manichaeism. He preached a dualist faith—a struggle between Good and Evil—theologically derived from Zoroastrianism. Although at first Mani enjoyed the favor of the shah, he and many of his followers were martyred in 276. His religion survived and spread widely, particularly along the Silk Road. Nestorian missionaries thus competed with Manichaean missionaries for converts in Central Asia.

The Impact of the Silk Road

As trade became a more important part of Central Asian life, Iranian-speaking peoples increasingly settled in trading cities and surrounding farm villages. By the sixth century C.E., nomads originally from the Altai Mountains farther east had spread across the steppes and become the dominant pastoral group. These peoples spoke Turkic languages unrelated to the Iranian tongues. The nomads continued to live in the round, portable felt huts called yurts that can still occasionally be seen in Central Asia, but prosperous individuals, both Turks and Iranians, built stately homes decorated with brightly colored wall paintings. The paintings show people wearing Chinese silks and Iranian brocades and riding on richly outfitted horses and camels. They also indicate an avid interest in Buddhism (see below), which competed with Nestorian Christianity, Manichaeism, and Zoroastrianism in a lively and inquiring intellectual milieu.

SECTION REVIEW

- Originating in southern Iran, the Sasanids overthrew the Parthians and continued their predecessors' rivalry with Rome.
- Sasanid farmers pioneered the cultivation of Silk Road crops.
- Sasanid kings made Zoroastrianism the state religion, and other religions, particularly Christianity, experienced both toleration and persecution.
- Silk Road trade encouraged movements of peoples in Iran and Central Asia, as well as the exchange of religious ideas and military technology.

Missionary influences exemplify the impact of foreign customs and beliefs on the peoples along the Silk Road. Military technology affords an example of the opposite phenomenon, steppe customs radiating into foreign lands. Chariot warfare and the use of mounted bowmen originated in Central Asia and spread eastward and westward through military campaigns and folk migrations that began in the second millennium B.C.E. and recurred throughout the period of the Silk Road.

Evidence of the **stirrup**, one of the most important inventions, comes first from the Kushan people who ruled northern Afghanistan in approximately the first century C.E. At first a solid bar, then a loop of leather to support the rider's big toe, and finally a device of leather and metal or wood supporting the instep, the stirrup gave riders far greater stability in the saddle—which itself was in all likelihood an earlier Central Asian invention. Using stirrups, a mounted warrior could supplement his bow and arrow with a long lance and charge his enemy at a gallop without fear that the impact of his attack would push him off his mount. Far to the west, the stirrup made possible the armored knights who dominated the battlefields of Europe (see Chapter 10), and it contributed to the superiority of the Tang cavalry in China (see Chapter 11).

stirrup Device for securing a horseman's feet, enabling him to wield weapons more effectively. First evidence of the use of stirrups was among the Kushan people of northern Afghanistan in approximately the first century C.E.

Indian Ocean Sailing Vessel Ships like this one, in a rock carving on the Buddhist temple of Borobodur in Java, probably carried colonists from Indonesia to Madagascar.

The Indian Ocean Maritime System

How did geography affect Indian Ocean trade routes?

A multilingual, multiethnic society of seafarers established the **Indian Ocean Maritime System**, a trade network across the Indian Ocean and the South China Sea. These people left few records and seldom played a visible part in the rise and fall of kingdoms and empires, but they forged increasingly strong economic and social ties between the coastal lands of East Africa, southern Arabia, the Persian Gulf, India, Southeast Asia, and southern China.

This trade took place in three distinct regions: (1) In the South China Sea, Chinese and Malays (including Indonesians) dominated trade. (2) From the east coast of India to the islands of Southeast Asia, Indians and Malays were the main traders. (3) From the west coast of India to the Persian Gulf and the east coast of Africa, merchants and sailors were predominantly Persians and Arabs. However, Chinese and Malay sailors could and did voyage to East Africa, and by 900 C.E. Arab and Persian traders reached Canton in southern China.

From the time of Herodotus in the fifth century B.C.E., Greek writers regaled their readers with stories of marvelous voyages down the Red Sea into the Indian Ocean and around Africa from the west. Most often, they attributed such trips to the Phoenicians, the most fearless of Mediterranean seafarers. Occasionally a Greek appears. One such was Hippalus, a Greek ship's pilot who was said to have discovered the seasonal monsoon winds that facilitate sailing across the Indian Ocean (see Diversity and Dominance: Travel Accounts of Africa and India).

Of course, the regular seasonal alternation of steady winds could not have remained unnoticed for thousands of years, waiting for an alert Greek to happen along. The great voyages and discoveries made before written records became common should surely be attributed to the peoples who lived around the Indian Ocean rather than to interlopers from the Mediterranean Sea. The story of Hippalus resembles the Chinese story of General Zhang Jian, whose role in opening trade with Central Asia overshadows the anonymous contributions made by the indigenous peoples. The Chinese may indeed have learned from

Indian Ocean Maritime System In premodern times, a network of seaports, trade routes, and maritime culture linking countries on the rim of the Indian Ocean from Africa to Indonesia.

Travel Accounts of Africa and India

The most revealing description of ancient trade in the Indian Ocean and of the diversity and economic forces shaping the Indian Ocean trading system, "The Periplus of the Erythraean Sea," a sailing itinerary (periplus in Greek), was composed in the first century C.E. *by an unknown Greco-Egyptian merchant. It highlights the diversity of peoples and products from the Red Sea to the Bay of Bengal. Historians believe that the descriptions of market towns were based on firsthand experience. The following passages deal with East Africa and the coastal lands of the Indian subcontinent (see Map 8.1).*

Of the designated ports on the Erythraean Sea [Indian Ocean], and the market-towns around it, the first is the Egyptian port of Mussel Harbor. To those sailing down from that place, on the right hand . . . there is Berenice. The harbors of both are at the boundary of Egypt. . . .

On the right-hand coast next below Berenice is the country of the Berbers. Along the shore are the Fish-Eaters, living in scattered caves in the narrow valleys. Further inland are the Berbers, and beyond them the Wild-flesh-Eaters and Calf-Eaters, each tribe governed by its chief; and behind them, further inland, in the country towards the west, there lies a city called Meroe.

Below the Calf-Eaters there is a little market-town on the shore . . . called Ptolemais of the Hunts, from which the hunters started for the interior under the dynasty of the Ptolemies. . . . But the place has no harbor and is reached only by small boats. . . .

Beyond this place, the coast trending toward the south, there is the Market and Cape of Spices, an abrupt promontory, at the very end of the Berber coast toward the east. . . . A sign of an approaching storm . . . is that the deep water becomes more turbid and changes its color. When this happens they all run to a large promontory called Tabae, which offers safe shelter. . . .

Beyond Tabae [lies] . . . another market-town called Opone. . . . [I]n it the greatest quantity of cinnamon is produced . . . and slaves of the better sort, which are brought to Egypt in increasing numbers. . . .

[Ships also come] from the places across this sea, from . . . Barygaza, bringing to these . . . market-towns the products of their own places; wheat, rice, clarified butter, sesame oil, cotton cloth . . . and honey from the reed called sacchari [sugar cane]. Some make the voyage especially to these market-towns, and others exchange their cargoes while sailing along the coast. This country is not subject to a King, but each market-town is ruled by its separate chief.

Beyond Opone, the shore trending more toward the south . . . this coast [the Somali region of Azania, or East Africa] is destitute of harbors . . . until the Pyralax islands [Zanzibar]. . . . [A] little to the south of south-west . . . is the island Menuthias [Madagascar], about three hundred stadia from the mainland, low and wooded, in which there are rivers and many kinds of birds and the mountain-tortoise. There are no wild beasts except the crocodiles; but there they do not attack men. In this place there are sewed boats, and canoes hollowed from single logs. . . .

Two days' sail beyond, there lies the very last market-town of the continent of Azania, which is called Rhapta [Dar es-Salaam]; which has its name from the sewed boats (rhapton ploiarion) . . . ; in which there is ivory in great quantity, and tortoise-shell. Along this coast live men of piratical habits, very great in stature, and under separate chiefs for each place. . . .

And these markets of Azania are the very last of the continent that stretches down on the right hand from Berenice; for beyond these places the unexplored ocean curves around toward the west, and running along by the regions to the south of Aethiopia and Libya and Africa, it mingles with the western sea. . . .

Now the whole country of India has very many rivers, and very great ebb and flow of the tides. . . . But about Barygaza [Broach] it is much greater, so that the bottom is suddenly seen, and now parts of the dry land are sea, and now it is dry where ships were sailing just before; and the rivers, under the inrush of the flood tide, when the whole force of the sea is directed against them, are driven upwards more strongly against their natural current. . . .

The country inland from Barygaza is inhabited by numerous tribes. . . . Above these is the very warlike nation of the Bactrians, who are under their own king. And Alexander, setting out from these parts, penetrated to the Ganges. . . . [T]o the present day ancient drachmae are current in Barygaza, coming from this country, bearing inscriptions in Greek letters, and the devices of those who reigned after Alexander. . . .

Inland from this place and to the east, is the city called Ozene [Ujjain]. . . . [F]rom this place are brought down all things needed for the welfare of the country about Barygaza, and many things for our trade: agate and carnelian, Indian muslins. . . .

There are imported into this market-town, wine, Italian preferred, also Laodicean and Arabian; copper, tin, and lead; coral and topaz; thin clothing and inferior sorts of all kinds . . . gold and silver coin, on which there is a profit when exchanged for the money of the country. . . . And for the King there are brought into those places very costly vessels of silver, singing boys, beautiful maidens for the harem, fine wines, thin clothing of the finest weaves, and the choicest ointments. There are exported from these places [spices], ivory, agate and carnelian . . . cotton cloth of all kinds, silk cloth. . . .

Beyond Barygaza the adjoining coast extends in a straight line from north to south. . . . The inland country back from the coast toward the east comprises many desert regions and great mountains; and all kinds of wild beasts—leopards, tigers, elephants, enormous serpents, hyenas, and baboons of many sorts; and many populous nations, as far as the Ganges. . . .

This whole voyage as above described . . . they used to make in small vessels, sailing close around the shores of the gulfs; and Hippalus was the pilot who by observing the location of the ports and the conditions of the sea, first discovered how to lay his course straight across the ocean. . . .

About the following region, the course trending toward the east, lying out at sea toward the west is the island Palaesimundu, called by the ancients Taprobane [Sri Lanka]. . . . It produces pearls, transparent stones, muslins, and tortoiseshell. . . .

Beyond this, the course trending toward the north, there are many barbarous tribes, among whom are the Cirrhadae, a race of men with flattened noses, very savage; another tribe, the Bargysi; and the Horse-faces and the Long-faces, who are said to be cannibals.

After these, the course turns toward the east again, and sailing with the ocean to the right and the shore remaining beyond to the left, Ganges comes into view. . . . And just opposite this river there is an island in the ocean, the last part of the inhabited world toward the east, under the rising sun itself; it is called Chryse; and it has the best tortoise-shell of all the places on the Erythraean Sea.

After this region under the very north, the sea outside ending in a land called This, there is a very great inland city called Thinae, from which raw silk and silk yarn and silk cloth are brought on foot. . . . But the land of This is not easy of access; few men come from there, and seldom.

The Chinese traveler Xuanzang (600–664) journeyed across Inner Asia to India, making pilgrimage to Buddhist holy places and searching for Sanskrit scriptures to take back to China with him. His descriptions of the places he visited reflect his interests. The following passages come from his description of India.

Towns and Buildings

The towns and villages have inner gates; the walls are wide and high; the streets and lanes are tortuous, and the roads winding. The thoroughfares are dirty and the stalls arranged on both sides of the road with appropriate signs. Butchers, fishers, dancers, executioners, and scavengers, and so on, have their abodes without the city. In coming and going these persons are bound to keep on the left side of the road till they arrive at their homes. Their houses are surrounded by low walls, and form the suburbs. The earth being soft and muddy, the walls of the town are mostly built of brick or tiles. The towers on the walls are constructed of wood or bamboo; the houses have balconies and belvederes, which are made of wood, with a coating of lime or mortar, and covered with tiles. The different buildings have the same form as those in China: rushes, or dry branches, or tiles, or boards are used for covering them. The walls are covered with lime and mud, mixed with cow's dung for purity. At different seasons they scatter flowers about. Such are some of their different customs.

Dress and Appearance

Their clothing is not cut or fashioned; they mostly affect fresh-white garments; they esteem little those of mixed color or ornamented. The men wind their garments round their middle, then gather them under the armpits, and let them fall down across the body, hanging to the right. The robes of the women fall down to the ground; they completely cover their shoulders.

195

They wear a little knot of hair on their crowns, and let the rest of their hair fall loose. Some of the men cut off their moustaches, and have other odd customs.... In North India, where the air is cold, they wear short and close-fitting garments.... The dress and ornaments worn by the nonbelievers are varied and mixed. Some wear peacocks' feathers; some wear as ornaments necklaces made of skull bones; some have no clothing, but go naked; some wear leaf or bark garments; some pull out their hair and cut off their moustaches; others have bushy whiskers and their hair braided on the top of their heads. The costume is not uniform, and the color, whether red or white, not constant.

QUESTIONS FOR ANALYSIS

1. How do the differing interests of a trader and a religious pilgrim show up in what they report?
2. How do these narratives show the influence of the countries the authors are coming from?
3. Given the different viewpoints of travelers, what is the value of travel accounts as sources for history?

Source: Samuel Beal, *Buddhist Records of the Western World*, translated from the Chinese of Hiuen Tsiang (A.D. 629) (London: Trubner and Company, 1884; reprint Delhi: Oriental Books Reprint Corporation, 1969), 73–76.

General Zhang and the Greeks from Hippalus, but other people played important roles anonymously.

Indian Ocean voyages differed in several ways from Mediterranean voyages. Mediterranean sailors of the time of Alexander used square sails and long banks of oars to maneuver among the sea's many islands and small harbors. In contrast, Indian Ocean vessels relied on roughly triangular lateen sails in running before the wind on long ocean stretches. Whereas Mediterranean shipbuilders nailed their vessels together, the planks of Indian Ocean ships were pierced, tied together with palm fiber, and caulked with bitumen. Mediterranean sailors rarely ventured out of sight of land. Indian Ocean sailors, thanks to the monsoon winds, could cover long reaches entirely at sea.

These technological differences prove that the world of the Indian Ocean developed differently than the world of the Mediterranean Sea, where the Phoenicians and Greeks established colonies that maintained contact with their home cities (see Chapters 3 and 4). The traders of the Indian Ocean, where distances were greater and contacts less frequent, seldom retained political ties with their homelands. The colonies they established were sometimes socially distinctive but rarely independent of the local political powers.

Origins of Contact

By 2000 B.C.E. Sumerian records indicate regular trade between Mesopotamia, the islands of the Persian Gulf, Oman, and the Indus Valley. However, this early trading contact broke off, and later Mesopotamian trade references mention East Africa more often than India.

A similarly early chapter in Indian Ocean history concerns migrations from Southeast Asia to Madagascar, the world's fourth largest island, situated off the southeastern coast of Africa. About two thousand years ago, people from one of the many Indonesian islands of Southeast Asia established themselves in that forested, mountainous land 6,000 miles (9,500 kilometers) from home. They could not possibly have carried enough supplies for a direct voyage across the Indian Ocean, so their route must have touched the coasts of India and southern Arabia. No physical remains of their journeys have been discovered, however.

Apparently, the sailing canoes of these people plied the seas along the increasingly familiar route for several hundred years. Settlers farmed the new land and entered into relations with Africans who found their way across the 250-mile-wide (400-kilometer-wide) Mozambique (moe-zam-BEEK) Channel around the fifth century C.E. Descendants of the seafarers preserved the language of their homeland and some of its culture, such as the cultivation of bananas, yams, and other native Southeast Asian plants. These food crops spread to mainland Africa. But the memory of their distant origins gradually faded, not to be recovered until modern times, when scholars established the linguistic link between the two lands.

The Impact of Indian Ocean Trade

The demand for products from the coastal lands inspired mariners to persist in their long ocean voyages. Africa produced exotic animals, wood, and ivory. Since ivory also came from India, Mesopotamia, and North Africa, the extent of

African ivory exports cannot be determined. The highlands of northern Somalia and southern Arabia grew the scrubby trees whose aromatic resins were valued as frankincense and myrrh. Pearls abounded in the Persian Gulf, and evidence of ancient copper mines has been found in Oman in southeastern Arabia. India shipped spices and manufactured goods, and more spices came from Southeast Asia, along with manufactured items, particularly pottery, obtained in trade with China. In sum, the Indian Ocean trading region had a great variety of highly valued products. Given the long distances and the comparative lack of islands, however, the volume of trade there was undoubtedly much lower than in the Mediterranean Sea.

The culture of the Indian Ocean ports was often isolated from the hinterlands, particularly in the west. The coasts of the Arabian peninsula, the African side of the Red Sea, southern Iran, and northern India (today's Pakistan) were mostly barren desert. Ports in all these areas tended to be small, and many suffered from meager supplies of fresh water. Farther south in India, the monsoon provided ample water, but steep mountains cut off the coastal plain from the interior of the country. Thus few ports between Zanzibar and Sri Lanka had substantial inland populations within easy reach. The head of the Persian Gulf was one exception: ship-borne trade was possible from the port of Apologus (the precursor of modern Basra) as far north as Babylon.

By contrast, eastern India, the Malay Peninsula, and Indonesia afforded more hospitable and densely populated shores with easier access to inland populations. Though the fishers, sailors, and traders of the western Indian Ocean system supplied a long series of kingdoms and empires, none of these consumer societies became primarily maritime in orientation, as the Greeks and Phoenicians did in the Mediterranean. In contrast, seaborne trade and influence seem to have been important even to the earliest states of Southeast Asia (see Chapter 5).

In coastal areas throughout the Indian Ocean system, small groups of seafarers sometimes had a significant social impact despite their lack of political power. Women seldom accompanied the men on long sea voyages, so sailors and merchants often married local women in port cities. The families thus established were bilingual and bicultural. As in many

SECTION REVIEW

- The Indian Ocean Maritime System grew from the voyages of a collection of diverse seafaring traders.
- Unlike the Mediterranean, the Indian Ocean developed no network of colonies with home ties.
- The system originated in early Mesopotamian trade routes and the migrations of Southeast Asian peoples to Madagascar.
- Trade in a broad range of goods flourished in ports where distinct cultures evolved.

other situations in world history, women played a crucial though not well-documented role as mediators between cultures. Not only did they raise their children to be more cosmopolitan than children from inland regions, but they also introduced the men to customs and attitudes that they carried with them when they returned to sea. As a consequence, the designation of specific seafarers as Persian, Arab, Indian, or Malay often conceals mixed heritages and a rich cultural diversity.

Routes Across the Sahara

Why did trade begin across the Sahara Desert?

The windswept Sahara, a desert stretching from the Red Sea to the Atlantic Ocean and broken only by the Nile River, isolates sub-Saharan Africa from the Mediterranean world (see Map 8.2). The current dryness of the Sahara dates only to about 2500 B.C.E. The period of drying out that preceded that date lasted twenty-five centuries and encompassed several cultural changes. During that time, travel between a slowly shrinking number of grassy areas was comparatively easy. However, by 300 B.C.E., scarcity of water was restricting travel to a few difficult routes initially known only to desert nomads. Trade over **trans-Saharan caravan routes**, at first only a trickle, eventually expanded into a significant stream.

trans-Saharan caravan routes Trading network linking North Africa with sub-Saharan Africa across the Sahara.

Cattle Herders in Saharan Rock Art These paintings represent the most artistically accomplished type of Saharan art. Herding societies of modern times living in the Sahel region south of the Sahara strongly resemble the society depicted here.

Courtesy, Mrs. Irene Lhote. Photo: Henri Lhote

 History in Focus *Examine the paintings. What clues does the depiction of people, animals, and objects give us about early Saharan society and culture? Find the answer online.*

Early Saharan Cultures

Sprawling sand dunes, sandy plains, and vast expanses of exposed rock make up most of the great desert. Stark and rugged mountain and highland areas separate its northern and southern portions. The cliffs and caves of these highlands, the last spots where water and grassland could be found as the climate changed, preserve rock paintings and engravings that constitute the primary evidence for early Saharan history.

Though dating is difficult, what appear to be the earliest images, left by hunters in much wetter times, include elephants, giraffes, rhinoceros, crocodiles, and other animals that have long been extinct in the region. Overlaps in the artwork indicate that the hunting societies were gradually joined by new cultures based on cattle breeding and well adapted to the sparse grazing that remained. Domestic cattle may have originated in western Asia or in North Africa. They certainly reached the Sahara before it became completely dry. The beautiful paintings of cattle and scenes of daily life seen in the Saharan rock art depict pastoral societies that bear little similarity to any

in western Asia. The people seem physically akin to today's West Africans, and the customs depicted, such as dancing and wearing masks, as well as the breeds of cattle, particularly those with piebald coloring (splotches of black and white), strongly suggest later societies to the south of the Sahara. These factors support the hypothesis that some southern cultural patterns originated in the Sahara.

Overlaps in artwork also show that horse herders succeeded the cattle herders. The rock art changes dramatically in style, from the superb realism of the cattle pictures to sketchier images that are often strongly geometric. Moreover, the horses are frequently shown drawing light chariots. According to the most common theory, intrepid charioteers from the Mediterranean shore drove their flimsy vehicles across the desert and established societies in the few remaining grassy areas of the central Saharan highlands. Some scholars suggest possible chariot routes that refugees from the collapse of the Mycenaean and Minoan civilizations of Greece and Crete (see Chapter 3) might have followed deep into the desert around the twelfth century B.C.E. However, no archaeological evidence of actual chariot use in the Sahara has been discovered, and it is difficult to imagine large numbers of refugees from the politically chaotic Mediterranean region driving chariots into a waterless, trackless desert in search of a new homeland

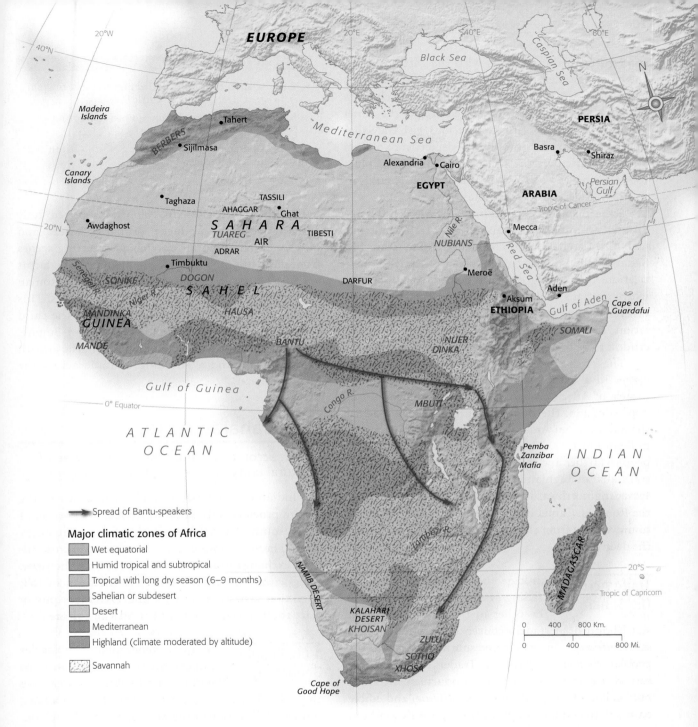

Map 8.2 Africa and the Trans-Saharan Trade Routes The Sahara and the surrounding oceans isolated most of Africa from foreign contact before 1000 C.E. The Nile Valley, a few trading points on the east coast, and limited transdesert trade provided exceptions to this rule, but the dominant forms of sub-Saharan African culture originated far to the west, north of the Gulf of Guinea.
© Cengage Learning

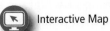
Interactive Map

somewhere to the south. As with the cattle herders, therefore, the identity of the Saharan horse breeders and the source of their passion for drawing chariots remain a mystery. Only with the coming of the camel is it possible to make firm connections with the Saharan nomads of today through the depiction of objects and geometric patterns still used by the veiled, blue-robed Tuareg (TWAH-reg) people of the highlands in southern Algeria, Niger, and Mali.

Some historians maintain that the Romans inaugurated an important trans-Saharan trade, but they lack firm archaeological evidence. More plausibly, Saharan trade relates to the spread of camel domestication. Supporting evidence comes from rock art, where overlaps of images imply that camel riders in desert costume constitute the latest Saharan population. The camel-oriented images are decidedly the crudest to be found in the region.

The first mention of camels in North Africa comes in a Latin text of 46 B.C.E. Since the native camels of Africa probably died out before the era of domestication, the domestic animals likely reached the Sahara from Arabia by way of Egypt in the first millennium B.C.E. They could have been adopted by peoples farther and farther to the west, from one central Saharan highland to the next, only much later spreading northward and coming to the attention of the Romans. Camel herding made it easier for people to move away from the Saharan highlands and roam the deep desert.

Trade Across the Sahara

Linkage between two different trading systems, one in the south, the other in the north, developed slowly. Southern traders concentrated on supplying salt from large deposits in the southern desert to the peoples of sub-Saharan Africa. Traders from the equatorial forest zone brought forest products, such as kola nuts (a condiment and source of caffeine) and edible palm oil, to trading centers near the desert's southern fringe. Each group received the products they needed in their homelands from the other, or from the farming peoples of the **Sahel** (SAH-hel)—literally "the coast" in Arabic, the southern borderlands of the Sahara (see Map 8.2). Middlemen who were native to the Sahel played an important role in this trade, but precise historical details are lacking.

SECTION REVIEW

- Early Saharan cultures included hunting societies and, in isolated areas, groups of cattle breeders.
- Later, horse and camel herders joined these groups.
- Camel-riding nomads most likely pioneered the trans-Saharan trade routes, linking North African and sub-Saharan trade networks.

In the north, Roman colonists supplied Italy with agricultural products, primarily wheat and olives. Surviving mosaic pavements depicting scenes from daily life show that people living on the farms and in the towns of the interior consumed Roman manufactured goods and shared Roman styles. This northern pattern began to change only in the third century C.E. with the decline of the Roman Empire, the abandonment of many Roman farms, the growth of nomadism, and a lessening of trade across the Mediterranean.

Sub-Saharan Africa

What accounts for the substantial degree of cultural unity in Africa south of the Sahara?

The Indian Ocean network and later trade across the Sahara provided **sub-Saharan Africa**, the portion of Africa south of the Sahara, with a few external contacts. The most important African network of cultural exchange from 500 B.C.E. to 1000 C.E., however, arose within the region and took the form of folk migration. These migrations and exchanges put in place enduring characteristics of African culture.

A Challenging Geography

Many geographic obstacles impede access to and movement within sub-Saharan Africa (see Map 8.2). The Sahara, the Atlantic and Indian Oceans, and the Red Sea form the boundaries of the region. With the exception of the Nile, a ribbon of green

Sahel Belt south of the Sahara; literally "the coast" in Arabic.
sub-Saharan Africa Portion of the African continent lying south of the Sahara.

traversing the Sahara from south to north, the major river systems empty into oceans: the Senegal, Niger, and Zaire (zah-EER) Rivers empty into the Atlantic, and the Zambezi River empties into the Mozambique Channel of the Indian Ocean. Rapids limit the use of these rivers for navigation.

Stretching over 50 degrees of latitude, sub-Saharan Africa encompasses dramatically different environments. A 4,000-mile (6,500-kilometer) trek from the southern edge of the Sahara to the Cape of Good Hope would take a traveler from the flat, semiarid plains of the Sahel region to tropical **savanna** covered by long grasses and scattered forest, and then to **tropical rain forest** on the lower Niger and in the Zaire Basin. The rain forest gives way to another broad expanse of savanna, followed by more steppe and desert, and finally by a region of temperate highlands at the southern extremity, located as far south of the equator as Greece and Sicily are to its north. East-west travel is comparatively easy in the steppe and savanna regions—a caravan from Senegal to the Red Sea would have traversed a distance comparable to that of the Silk Road—but difficult in the equatorial rain-forest belt and across the mountains and deep rift valleys that abut the rain forest to the east and separate East from West Africa.

The Development of Cultural Unity

Cultural heritages shared by the educated elites within each region of the world—heritages that some anthropologists call **"great traditions"**—typically include a written language, common legal and belief systems, ethical codes, and other intellectual attitudes. They loom large in written records as traditions that rise above the diversity of local customs and beliefs commonly distinguished as **"small traditions."**

By the year 1 C.E. sub-Saharan Africa had become a distinct cultural region, though one not shaped by imperial conquest or characterized by a shared elite culture, a "great tradition." The cultural unity of sub-Saharan Africa rested on similar characteristics shared to varying degrees by many popular cultures, or "small traditions." These had developed during the region's long period of isolation from the rest of the world and had been refined, renewed, and interwoven by repeated episodes of migration and social

interaction. Historians know little about this complex prehistory. Thus, to a greater degree than in other regions, they call on anthropological descriptions, oral history, and comparatively late records of various "small traditions" to reconstruct the broad outlines of cultural formation.

Sub-Saharan Africa's cultural unity is less immediately apparent than its diversity. By one estimate, Africa is home to two thousand distinct languages, many corresponding to social and belief systems endowed with distinctive rituals and cosmologies. There are likewise numerous food production systems, ranging from hunting and gathering—very differently carried out by the Mbuti (m-BOO-tee) Pygmies of the equatorial rain forest and the Khoisan (KOI-sahn) peoples of the southwestern deserts—to the cultivation of bananas, yams, and other root crops in forest clearings and of sorghum and other grains in the savanna lands. Pastoral societies, particularly those depending on cattle, display somewhat less diversity across the Sahel and savanna belt from Senegal to Kenya.

Sub-Saharan Africa covered a larger and more diverse area than any other cultural region in the first millennium C.E. and had a lower overall population density. Thus societies and polities had ample room to form and reform, and a substantial amount of space separated different groups. The contacts that did occur did not last long enough to produce rigid cultural uniformity.

In addition, for centuries external conquerors could not penetrate the region's natural barriers and impose a uniform culture. The Egyptians occupied

savanna Tropical or subtropical grassland, either treeless or with occasional clumps of trees. Most extensive in sub-Saharan Africa but also present in South America.

tropical rain forest High-precipitation forest zones of the Americas, Africa, and Asia lying between the Tropic of Cancer and the Tropic of Capricorn.

"great traditions" Anthropologists' term for a literate, well-institutionalized complex of religious and social beliefs and practices adhered to by diverse societies over a broad geographical area.

"small traditions" Anthropologists' term for a localized, usually nonliterate, set of customs and beliefs adhered to by a single society, often in conjunction with a "great tradition."

Nubia, and some traces of Egyptian influence appear in Saharan rock art farther west, but the Nile cataracts and the vast swampland in the Nile's upper reaches blocked movement farther south. The Romans sent expeditions against pastoral peoples living in the Libyan Sahara but could not incorporate them into the Roman world.

African Cultural Characteristics

European travelers who got to know the sub-Saharan region well in the nineteenth and twentieth centuries observed broad commonalities underlying African life and culture. In agriculture, the common technique was cultivation by hoe and digging stick. Musically, different groups of Africans played many instruments, especially types of drums, but common features, particularly in rhythm, gave African music as a whole a distinctive character. Music played an important role in social rituals, as did dancing and wearing masks, which often showed great artistry in their design.

African kingdoms varied, but kingship displayed common features, most notably the ritual isolation of the king himself. Fixed social categories—age groupings, kinship divisions, distinct gender roles and relations, and occupational groupings—also show resemblances from one region to another, even in societies too small to organize themselves into kingdoms. Though not hierarchical, these categories played a role similar to the divisions between noble, commoner, and slave prevalent where kings ruled. Such indications of underlying cultural unity have led modern observers to identify a common African quality throughout most of the region, even though most sub-Saharan Africans themselves did not perceive it. An eminent Belgian anthropologist, Jacques Maquet, has called this quality "Africanity."

Some historians hypothesize that this cultural unity emanated from the peoples who once occupied the southern Sahara. In Paleolithic times, periods of dryness alternated with periods of wetness as the Ice Age that locked up much of the world's fresh water in glaciers and icecaps came and went. When European glaciers receded with the waning of the Ice Age, a storm belt brought increased wetness to the Saharan region. Rushing rivers scoured deep canyons. Now filled with fine sand, those canyons are easily visible on flights over the southern parts of the desert. As the glaciers receded farther, the storm belt moved northward to Europe, and dryness set in after 5000 B.C.E. As a consequence, runs the hypothesis, the region's population migrated southward, becoming increasingly concentrated in the Sahel, which may have been the initial incubation center for Pan-African cultural patterns.

Increasing dryness and the resulting difficulty in supporting the population would have driven some people out of this core into more sparsely settled lands to the east, west, and south. In a parallel development farther to the east, migration away from the growing aridity of the desert seems to have contributed to the settling of the Nile Valley and the emergence of the Old Kingdom of Egypt (see Chapter 1).

The Advent of Iron and the Bantu

Archaeology confirms that agriculture had become common between the equator and the Sahara by the early second millennium B.C.E. It then spread southward, displacing hunting and gathering as a way of life. Moreover, botanical evidence indicates that banana trees, probably introduced to southeastern Africa from Southeast Asia, made their way north and west, retracing in the opposite direction the presumed migration routes of the first agriculturists.

Archaeology has also uncovered traces of copper mining in the Sahara from the early first millennium B.C.E. Copper appears in the Niger Valley somewhat later and in the Central African copper belt after 400 C.E. Most important of all, iron smelting began in northern sub-Saharan Africa in the early first millennium C.E. and spread southward from there.

Many historians believe that the secret of smelting iron, which requires very high temperatures, was discovered only once, by the Hittites of Anatolia (modern Turkey) around 1500 B.C.E. (see Chapter 3). If that is the case, it is hard to explain how iron smelting reached sub-Saharan Africa. The earliest evidence of ironworking from the kingdom of Meroë, situated on the upper Nile and in cultural contact with Egypt, is no earlier than the evidence from West Africa (northern Nigeria). Even less plausible than the Nile Valley as a route of technological diffusion is the idea of a spread southward from Phoenician settlements in

North Africa, since archaeological evidence has failed to substantiate the vague Greek and Latin accounts of Phoenician excursions to the south. A more plausible scenario focuses on Africans' discovering for themselves how to smelt iron. Some historians suggest that they might have done so while firing pottery in kilns. No firm evidence exists to prove or disprove this theory.

Linguistic analysis provides the strongest evidence of extensive contacts among sub-Saharan Africans in the first millennium C.E.—and offers suggestions about the spread of iron. More than three hundred languages spoken south of the equator belong to the branch of the Niger-Congo family known as **Bantu**, after the word meaning "people" in most of the languages.

The distribution of the Bantu languages both north and south of the equator is consistent with a divergence beginning in the first millennium B.C.E. By comparing core words common to most of the languages, linguists have drawn some conclusions about the original Bantu-speakers, whom they call "proto-Bantu." These people engaged in fishing, using canoes, nets, lines, and hooks. They lived in permanent villages on the edge of the rain forest, where they grew yams and grains and harvested wild palm nuts from which they pressed oil. They possessed domesticated goats, dogs, and perhaps other animals. They made pottery and cloth. Linguists surmise that the proto-Bantu homeland was near the modern boundary of Nigeria and Cameroon.

Because the presumed home of the proto-Bantu lies near the known sites of early iron smelting, migration by Bantu-speakers seems a likely mechanism for

the southward spread of iron. The migrants probably used iron axes and hoes to hack out forest clearings and plant crops. According to this scenario, their actions would have established an economic basis for new societies capable of sustaining much denser populations than could earlier societies dependent on hunting and gathering alone. Thus the period from 500 B.C.E. to 1000 C.E. saw a massive transfer of Bantu traditions and practices southward, eastward, and westward and their transformation, through intermingling with preexisting societies, into Pan-African traditions and practices.

The Spread of Ideas

Why do some goods and ideas travel more easily than others?

Ideas, like social customs, religious attitudes, and artistic styles, can spread along trade routes and through folk migrations. In both cases, documenting the dissemination of ideas, particularly in preliterate societies, poses a difficult historical problem.

Ideas and Material Evidence

Historians know about some ideas only through the survival of written sources. Other ideas do not depend on writing but are inherent in material objects studied by archaeologists and anthropologists. Customs surrounding the eating of pork are a case in point. Scholars disagree about whether pigs became domestic in only one place, from which the practice of pig keeping spread elsewhere, or whether several peoples hit on the same idea at different times and in different places.

Southeast Asia was an important early center of pig domestication. Anthropological studies tell us that the eating of pork became highly ritualized in this area and that it was sometimes allowed only on ceremonial occasions. On the other side of the Indian Ocean, wild swine were common in the Nile swamps of ancient Egypt. There, too, pigs took on a sacred role,

Bantu Collective name of a large group of sub-Saharan African languages and of the peoples speaking these languages.

being associated with the evil god Set, and eating them was prohibited. The biblical prohibition on the Israelites' eating pork, echoed later by the Muslims, probably came from Egypt in the second millennium B.C.E.

In a third locale in eastern Iran, an archaeological site dating from the third millennium B.C.E. provides evidence of another religious taboo relating to pork. Although the area around the site was swampy and home to many wild pigs, not a single pig bone has been found. Yet small pig figurines seem to have been used as symbolic religious offerings, and the later Iranian religion associates the boar with an important god.

What accounts for the apparent connection between domestic pigs and religion in these far-flung areas? There is no way of knowing. It has been hypothesized that pigs were first domesticated in Southeast Asia by people who had no herd animals—sheep, goats, cattle, or horses—and who relied on fish for most of their animal protein. The pig therefore became a special animal to them. The practice of pig raising, along with religious beliefs and rituals associated with the consumption of pork, could conceivably have spread from Southeast Asia along the maritime routes of the Indian Ocean, eventually reaching Iran and Egypt. But no evidence survives to support this hypothesis. In this case, therefore, material evidence can only hint at the spread of religious ideas, leaving the door open for other explanations.

A more certain example of objects' indicating the spread of an idea is the practice of hammering a carved die onto a piece of precious metal and using the resulting coin as a medium of exchange. From its origin in the Lydian kingdom in Anatolia in the first millennium B.C.E. (see Chapter 4), the idea of trading by means of struck coinage spread rapidly to Europe, North Africa, and India. Was the low-value copper coinage of China, made by pouring molten metal into a mold, also inspired by this practice from far away? It may have been, but it might also derive from indigenous Chinese metalworking.

Primary Source: Setting in Motion the Wheel of the Law Find out which two extremes the Buddha advised his followers to avoid.

The Spread of Buddhism

While material objects associated with religious beliefs and rituals are important indicators of the spread of spiritual ideas, written sources deal with the spread of today's major religions. Buddhism grew to become, with Christianity and Islam (see Chapter 9), one of the most popular and widespread religions in the world. In all three cases, the religious ideas spread without dependency on a single ethnic or kinship group.

King Ashoka, the Mauryan ruler of India, and Kanishka, the greatest king of the Kushans of northern Afghanistan, promoted Buddhism between the third century B.C.E. and the second century C.E. However, monks, missionaries, and pilgrims who crisscrossed India, followed the Silk Road, or took ships on the Indian Ocean brought the Buddha's teachings to Southeast Asia, China, Korea, and ultimately Japan (see Map 8.1).

One such traveler was the Chinese pilgrim Faxian (fah-shee-en) (died between 418 and 423 C.E.), who left a written account of his travels. Faxian began his trip in the company of a Chinese envoy to an unspecified ruler or people in Central Asia. After traveling from one Buddhist site to another across Afghanistan and India, he reached Sri Lanka, a Buddhist land, where he lived for two years. He then embarked for China on a merchant ship with two hundred men aboard. A storm drove the ship to Java, which he chose not to describe since it was Hindu rather than Buddhist. After five months ashore, Faxian finally reached China on another ship.

Less reliable accounts make reference to missionaries traveling to Syria, Egypt, and Macedonia, as well as to Southeast Asia. One of Ashoka's sons allegedly led a band of missionaries to Sri Lanka. Later, his sister brought a company of nuns there, along with a branch of the sacred Bo tree under which the Buddha had received enlightenment. At the same time, there are reports of other monks traveling to Burma, Thailand, and Sumatra. Ashoka's missionaries may also have reached Tibet by way of trade routes across the Himalayas.

The different lands that received the story and teachings of the Buddha preserved or adapted them in different ways. Theravada Buddhism, "Teachings of the Elder," was centered in Sri Lanka. Holding closely to the Buddha's earliest teachings, it maintained

Stele of Aksum This 70-foot (21-meter) stone is the tallest remnant of a field of stelae, or standing stones, marking the tombs of Aksumite kings. The carvings of doors, windows, and beam ends imitate common features of Aksumite architecture, suggesting that each stele symbolized a multistory royal palace. The largest stelae date from the fourth century C.E.

(Photo credit: Werner Forman/Art Resource, NY)

that the goal of religion, available only to monks, is *nirvana*, the total absence of suffering and the end of the cycle of rebirth (see Chapter 5). This teaching contrasted with Mahayana, or "Great Vehicle" Buddhism, which stressed the goal of becoming a *bodhisattva*, a person who attains nirvana but chooses to remain in human company to help and guide others.

The Spread of Christianity

The post-Roman development of Christianity in Europe is discussed in Chapter 10. The Christian faith enjoyed an earlier spread in Asia and Africa before its confrontation with Islam (described in Chapter 9). Jerusalem in Palestine, Antioch in Syria, and Alexandria in Egypt became centers of Christian authority soon after the crucifixion, but the spread of Christianity to Armenia and Ethiopia illustrates the connections between religion, trade, and imperial politics.

Situated in eastern Anatolia (modern Turkey), **Armenia** served recurrently as a battleground between Iranian states to the south and east and Mediterranean states to the west. Each imperial power wanted to control this region so close to the frontier where Silk Road traders met their Mediterranean counterparts. In Parthian times, Armenia's kings favored Zoroastrianism. The invention of an Armenian alphabet in the early fifth century opened the way to a wider spread of Christianity. The Iranians did not give up domination easily, but within a century the Armenian Apostolic Church had become the center of Armenian cultural life.

Far to the south Christians similarly sought to outflank Iran. The Christian emperors in Constantinople (see Chapter 6) sent missionaries along the Red Sea trade route to seek converts in Yemen and **Ethiopia**. In the fourth century C.E. a Syrian philosopher traveling with two young relatives sailed to India. On the way back the ship docked at a Red Sea port occupied by Ethiopians from the prosperous kingdom of Aksum. Being then at odds with the Romans, the Ethiopians killed everyone on board except the two boys, Aedisius—who later narrated this story—and Frumentius. Impressed by their learning, the king made the former his cupbearer and the latter his treasurer and secretary.

When the king died, his wife urged Frumentius to govern Aksum on her behalf and that of her infant son, Ezana. As regent, Frumentius sought out Roman Christians among the merchants who visited the country and helped them establish Christian communities. When he became king, Ezana, who may have become a Christian, permitted Aedisius and Frumentius to return to Syria. The patriarch of Alexandria, on learning about the progress of Christianity in Aksum, elevated Frumentius to the rank of bishop, though he had not previously been a clergyman, and sent him back to Ethiopia as the first leader of its church.

Armenia One of the earliest Christian kingdoms, situated in eastern Anatolia and the western Caucasus and occupied by speakers of the Armenian language.
Ethiopia East African highland nation lying east of the Nile River.

SECTION REVIEW

- Material evidence can offer hints about the spread of ideas.

- Material and documentary evidence show the spread of Buddhism from India along the land and sea trade routes to elsewhere in Asia.

- Lands in which Buddhism took hold adapted its teachings in different ways, a process that resulted in the split between Mahayana and Theravada.

- Christianity spread through a combination of trade and imperial politics, with significant Christian societies emerging in Armenia and Ethiopia.

The spread of Christianity into Nubia, the land south of Egypt along the Nile River, proceeded from Ethiopia rather than Egypt. Politically and economically, Ethiopia became a power at the western end of the Indian Ocean trading system, occasionally even extending its influence across the Red Sea and asserting itself in Yemen (see Map 8.2).

Conclusion

The growing networks of transportation and trade that developed in the third century B.C.E. linked societies and cultures throughout the Eastern Hemisphere.

Merchants and pilgrims were the first to pioneer connections across long distances and often forbidding terrains, such as across Central Asia, the Himalayas, or the Sahara Desert. Due to the cost of travel, merchants could only carry items of great value and small bulk, such as silk and precious metals. But they also brought animals, such as camels, that could withstand the trip. Seeds of useful plants, such as cotton and fruits, were also spread by traders. New technologies, such as stirrups for horseback riders, made their way across Eurasia, while iron-making spread throughout Africa.

Along with physical objects came ideas. Missionaries spread religions far from their origins. Zoroastrians from Iran and Christians from the Middle East penetrated into Central Asia. Shipping across the Indian Ocean helped Hinduism spread to Southeast Asia. Most successful was Buddhism, which spread from India to Southeast Asia, Tibet, China, and Japan. Languages and other cultural forms also migrated with people; the diffusion of Bantu languages into East and Central Africa is a case in point. In short, in the last centuries before the Common Era, travel and commerce was increasingly bringing together the various parts of Eurasia and Africa and the once-separate cultures and civilizations.

CHAPTER REVIEW

 Download the MP3 audio file of the Chapter Review to listen to on the go.

What factors contributed to the growth of trade along the Silk Road? (page 187)

Occasional contacts across the heart of Asia undoubtedly occurred for many centuries before the Silk Road regularized communication. Cooperative relations between caravan traders and pastoral nomads in the Central Asian grasslands were the key to this regularization. The fact that the Parthian rulers of Iran were themselves of nomadic origin played an important role. In later centuries, trans-Asian trade fared best when pastoral peoples dominated either China or Iran or both.

How did the Sasanid Empire evolve under the influence of east-west trade? (page 191)

Originating in southwest Iran, the Sasanids overthrew the Parthians and took on their predecessors' conflicts with Rome. Benefiting from Silk Road trade, Sasanid farmers introduced the cultivation of many new crops from India and China. Sasanid kings supported Zoroastrianism as the state religion, continuing a larger trend toward the politicization of religion. Other religions often suffered persecution, but the Sasanid king welcomed Nestorian Christians fleeing official persecution in Byzantium. Nestorians traveled the Silk Road as missionaries, but they were only one of many religious groups that used the route to spread their ideas. Silk Road trade prompted many Iranians to move into cities and drew the Turks into the steppes north of Iran. In addition to goods and ideas, military technology moved along the Silk Road, particularly the stirrup, which revolutionized mounted warfare.

How did geography affect Indian Ocean trade routes? (page 193)

Maritime trade in general is strongly affected by such things as wind patterns, the presence of islands, and good seaports. The monsoon system in particular determined the seasons of trade across the Indian Ocean. In addition, coastal areas that had ample water supplies and easy communications with inland markets and population centers developed different relations with sea traders than did regions where coastal deserts were cut off from the interior by mountains.

Why did trade begin across the Sahara Desert? (page 197)

The beginnings of trade across the barren wastes of the Sahara bear comparison with the Silk Road and Indian Ocean trade. Political and economic contacts between pastoral nomads who supply caravan animals played an important role, but trade was also influenced by the location of markets on both the northern and southern sides, as well as the connections those markets had with suppliers and consumers farther away from the desert.

What accounts for the substantial degree of cultural unity in Africa south of the Sahara? (page 200)

The Sahara changed over time from a verdant state to one of exceptional dryness. This change forced cattle-herding peoples who lived in the areas that were drying up to move southward. This movement, in turn, contributed to the widespread migrations of Bantu-speaking peoples. Their shared linguistic and cultural characteristics led to a high degree of cultural similarity despite the fact that the various migrating groups settled in places that were not so close together as to encourage complex political development stretching over large parts of the continent.

Why do some goods and ideas travel more easily than others? (page 203)

The Bantu migrations contrast with contacts made along trade routes in terms of the sorts of cultural characteristics that enjoy wide geographic spread. Migrating in groups, the Bantu were able to maintain their social structures and rituals along with their techniques of agriculture and metal using. Along overland and seaborne trade routes where the number of travelers was comparatively small, on the other hand, the social practices of the merchants had less influence than the goods they carried, which were often highly prized. To be sure, religious missionaries often traveled by caravan or ship, but the doctrines they preached seldom fully replaced earlier religions.

Key Terms

Silk Road (p. 187)	sub-Saharan Africa (p. 200)
Parthians (p. 189)	savanna (p. 201)
Sasanid Empire (p. 191)	tropical rain forest (p. 201)
stirrup (p. 192)	"great traditions" (p. 201)
Indian Ocean Maritime System (p. 193)	"small traditions" (p. 201)
trans-Saharan caravan routes (p. 197)	Bantu (p. 203)
Sahel (p. 200)	Armenia (p. 205)
	Ethiopia (p. 205)

Web Resources

Pronunciation Guide

Interactive Maps
- MAP 8.1 Asian Trade and Communication Routes
- MAP 8.2 Africa and the Trans-Saharan Trade Routes

Primary Source
- Setting in Motion the Wheel of the Law

Answer to the History in Focus Question
See photo on page 198, "Cattle Herders in Saharan Rock Art."

 Visit the CourseMate website at www.cengagebrain.com for additional study tools and review materials for this chapter.

Oral Societies and the Consequences of Literacy

The availability of written documents is one of the key factors historians use to divide human prehistory from history. When we can read what the people of the past thought and said about their lives, we can begin to understand their cultures, institutions, values, and beliefs in ways that are not possible based only on the material remains unearthed by archaeologists.

There are profound differences between nonliterate and literate societies. However, literacy and nonliteracy are not absolute alternatives. Personal literacy ranges from illiteracy through many shades of partial literacy (the ability to write one's name or to read simple texts with difficulty) to the fluent ability to read that is possessed by anyone reading this textbook. And there are degrees of societal literacy, ranging from nonliteracy through so-called craft literacy—in which a small specialized elite uses writing for limited purposes, such as administrative recordkeeping—and a spectrum of conditions in which more and more people use writing for more and more purposes, up to the near-universal literacy and the use of writing for innumerable purposes that is the norm in the developed world in our times.

The vast majority of human beings of the last five to six thousand years living in societies that possessed the technology of writing were not themselves literate. If most people in a society rely on the spoken word and memory, that culture is essentially "oral" even if some members know how to write. The differences between oral and literate cultures are immense, affecting not only the kinds of knowledge that are valued and the forms in which information is preserved, but also the very use of language, the categories for conceptualizing the world, and ultimately the hard-wiring of the individual human brain (now recognized by neuroscientists to be strongly influenced by individual experience and mental activity).

Ancient Greece of the Archaic and Classical periods (ca. 800–323 B.C.E.) offers a particularly instructive case study because we can observe the process by which writing was introduced into an oral society as well as the far-reaching consequences. The Greeks of the Dark Age and early Archaic period lived in a purely oral society; all knowledge was preserved in human memory and passed on by telling it to others. The Iliad and the Odyssey (ca. 700 B.C.E.), Homer's epic poems, reflect this state of affairs. Scholars recognize that the creator of these poems was an oral poet, almost certainly not literate, who had heard and memorized the poems of predecessors and retold them his own way. The poems are treasuries of information that this society regarded as useful—events of the past; the conduct expected of warriors, kings, noblewomen, and servants; how to perform a sacrifice, build a raft, put on armor, and entertain guests; and much more.

Embedding this information in a story and using the colorful language, fixed phrases, and predictable rhythm of poetry made it easier for poet and audience to remember vast amounts of material. The early Greek poets, drawing on their strong memories, skill with words, and talent for dramatic performance, developed highly specialized techniques to assist them in memorizing and presenting their tales. They played a vital role in the preservation and transmission of information and thus enjoyed a relatively high social standing and comfortable standard of living. Analogous groups can be found in many other oral cultures of the past, including the bards of medieval Celtic lands, Norse skalds, west African griots, and the tribal historians of Native American peoples.

Nevertheless, human memory, however cleverly trained and well practiced, can only do so much. Oral societies must be extremely selective about what information to preserve in the limited storage medium of human memory, and they are slow to give up old information to make way for new.

Sometime in the eighth century B.C.E. the Greeks borrowed the system of writing used by the

Phoenicians of Lebanon and, in adapting it to their language, created the first purely alphabetic writing, employing several dozen symbols to express the sounds of speech. The Greek alphabet, although relatively simple to learn as compared to the large and cumbersome sets of symbols in such craft-literacy systems as cuneiform, hieroglyphics, or Linear B, was probably known at first only to a small number of people and used for restricted purposes. Scholars believe that it may have taken three or four centuries for knowledge of reading and writing to spread to large numbers of Greeks and for the written word to became the primary storage medium for the accumulated knowledge of Greek civilization. Throughout that time Greece was still primarily an oral society, even though some Greeks, mostly highly educated members of the upper classes, were beginning to write down poems, scientific speculations, stories about the past, philosophic musings, and the laws of their communities.

It is no accident that some of the most important intellectual and artistic achievements of the Greeks, including early science, history, drama, and rhetoric, developed in the period when oral and literate ways existed side-by-side. Scholars have persuasively argued that writing, by opening up a virtually limitless capacity to store information, released the human mind from the hard discipline of memorization and ended the need to be so painfully selective about what was preserved. This made previously unimaginable innovation and experimentation possible. We can observe changes in the Greek language as it developed a vocabulary full of abstract nouns, accompanied by increasing complex sentence structure now that the reader had time to go back over the text.

Nevertheless, all the developments associated with literacy were shaped by the deeply rooted oral habits of Greek culture. It is often said that Plato (ca. 429–347 B.C.E.) and his contemporaries of the later Classical period may have been the first generation of Greeks who learned much of what they knew from books. Even so, Plato was a disciple of the philosopher Socrates, who wrote nothing, and Plato employed the oral form of the dialogue, a dramatized sequence of questions and answers, to convey his ideas in written form.

The transition from orality to literacy met stiff resistance in some quarters. Groups whose position in the oral culture was based on the special knowledge only they possessed—members of the elite who judged disputes, priests who knew the time-honored formulas and rituals for appeasing the gods, oral poets who preserved and performed the stories of a heroic past—resented the consequences of literacy. They did what they could to inflame the common people's suspicions of the impiety of literate men who sought scientific explanations for phenomena, such as lightning and eclipses, that had traditionally been attributed to the will and action of the gods. They attacked the so-called Sophists, or "wise men," who charged fees to teach what they claimed were the skills necessary for success, accusing them of subverting traditional morals and corrupting the young.

Other societies, ancient and modern, offer parallel examples of these processes. Oral "specialists" in antiquity, including the Brahmin priests of India and the Celtic Druids, preserved in memory valuable religious information about how to win the favor of the gods. These groups jealously guarded their knowledge because it was the basis of their livelihood and social standing. Determined to select and maintain control over those who received this knowledge, they resisted committing it to writing even after that technology was available. The ways in which oral authorities feel threatened by writing and resist it can be seen in the following quotation from a twentieth-century C.E. "griot," an oral rememberer and teller of the past in Mali in West Africa:

> We griots are depositories of the knowledge of the past. . . . Other peoples use writing to record the past, but this invention has killed the faculty of memory among them. They do not feel the past anymore, for writing lacks the warmth of the human voice. With them everybody thinks he knows, whereas Learning should be a secret. . . . What paltry learning is that which is congealed in dumb books! . . . For generations we have passed on the history of kings from father to son. The narrative was passed on to me without alteration, for I received it free from all untruth.[2]

This point of view is hard for us to grasp, living as we do in an intensely literate society in which the written word is often felt to be more authoritative and objective than the spoken word. It is important, in striving to understand societies of the past, not to superimpose our assumptions on them and to appreciate the complex interplay of oral and literate patterns in many of them.

Part Three

Growth and Interaction of Cultural Communities, 600–1200

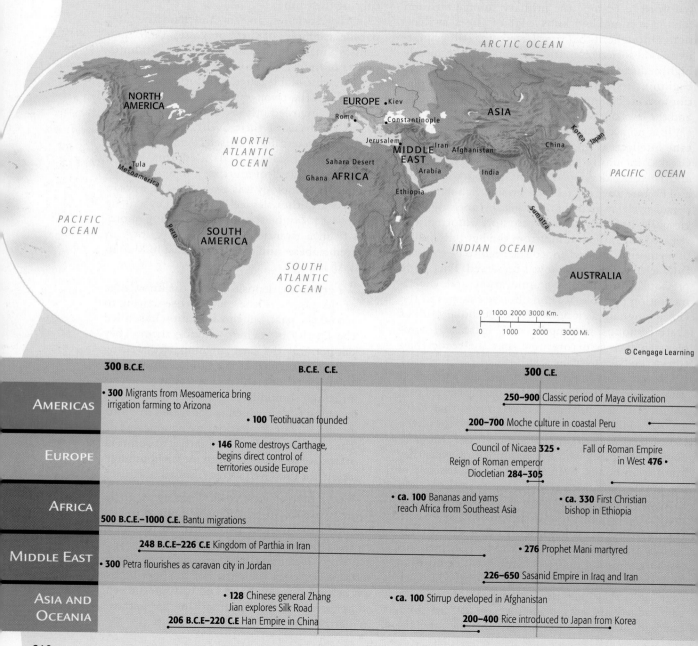

© Cengage Learning

	300 B.C.E.	B.C.E. C.E.	300 C.E.
AMERICAS	• **300** Migrants from Mesoamerica bring irrigation farming to Arizona		**250–900** Classic period of Maya civilization
	• **100** Teotihuacan founded		**200–700** Moche culture in coastal Peru
EUROPE	• **146** Rome destroys Carthage, begins direct control of territories ouside Europe		Council of Nicaea **325** • Fall of Roman Empire in West **476** • Reign of Roman emperor Diocletian **284–305**
AFRICA	**500 B.C.E.–1000 C.E.** Bantu migrations	• **ca. 100** Bananas and yams reach Africa from Southeast Asia	• **ca. 330** First Christian bishop in Ethiopia
MIDDLE EAST	**248 B.C.E–226 C.E** Kingdom of Parthia in Iran • **300** Petra flourishes as caravan city in Jordan		• **276** Prophet Mani martyred **226–650** Sasanid Empire in Iraq and Iran
ASIA AND OCEANIA	• **128** Chinese general Zhang Jian explores Silk Road **206 B.C.E–220 C.E** Han Empire in China	• **ca. 100** Stirrup developed in Afghanistan	**200–400** Rice introduced to Japan from Korea

In 300 B.C.E., societies had only limited contacts beyond their frontiers. By 1200 C.E., this situation had changed. Traders, migrating peoples, and missionaries brought peoples together. Products and technologies moved along long-distance trade networks: the Silk Road across Asia, Saharan caravan routes, and sea-lanes connecting the Indian Ocean coastlands.

Migrating Bantu peoples from West Africa spread iron and new farming techniques through much of sub-Saharan Africa and helped foster a distinctive African culture. Conquering Arabs from the Arabian peninsula, inspired by the Prophet Muhammad, established Muslim rule from Spain to India, laying the foundation of a new culture.

In Asia, missionaries and pilgrims helped Buddhism spread from India to Sri Lanka, Tibet, Southeast Asia, and East Asia. The new faith interacted with older philosophies and religions to produce distinctive cultural patterns. Simultaneously, the Tang Empire in China disseminated Chinese culture and technologies throughout Inner and East Asia.

In Europe, monks and missionaries spread Christian beliefs that became enmeshed with new political and social structures: a struggle between royal and church authority in western Europe; a union of religious and imperial authority in the Byzantine east; and a similar but distinctive society in Kievan Russia. The Crusades reconnected western Europe with the lands of the east.

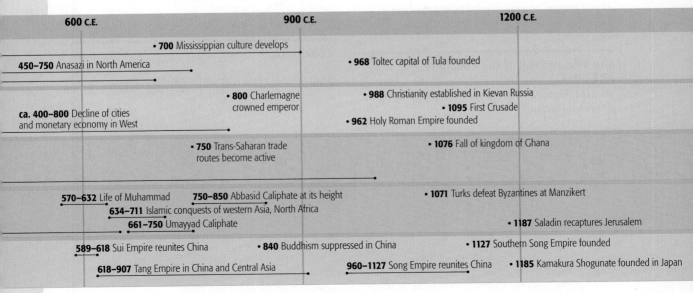

600 C.E.   900 C.E.   1200 C.E.

• **700** Mississippian culture develops

450–750 Anasazi in North America

• **968** Toltec capital of Tula founded

• **800** Charlemagne crowned emperor

• **988** Christianity established in Kievan Russia

• **1095** First Crusade

ca. 400–800 Decline of cities and monetary economy in West

• **962** Holy Roman Empire founded

• **750** Trans-Saharan trade routes become active

• **1076** Fall of kingdom of Ghana

570–632 Life of Muhammad   **750–850** Abbasid Caliphate at its height

• **1071** Turks defeat Byzantines at Manzikert

634–711 Islamic conquests of western Asia, North Africa

661–750 Umayyad Caliphate

• **1187** Saladin recaptures Jerusalem

589–618 Sui Empire reunites China   • **840** Buddhism suppressed in China

• **1127** Southern Song Empire founded

618–907 Tang Empire in China and Central Asia

960–1127 Song Empire reunites China   • **1185** Kamakura Shogunate founded in Japan

211

The Rise of Islam

© Cengage Learning

212

Visit the CourseMate website at **www.cengagebrain.com** for additional study tools and review materials for this chapter.

Knowledge of papermaking, which spread from China to the Middle East after Arab conquests in the seventh century C.E. established an Islamic caliphate stretching from Spain to Central Asia, provided a medium that was superior to papyrus and parchment and well suited to a variety of purposes. Maps, miniature paintings, and, of course, books became increasingly common and inexpensive. With cheaper books came bookstores, and one of the most informative manuscripts of the period of the Islamic caliphate is a *Fihrist*, or descriptive catalog, of the books sold at one bookstore in Baghdad.

Abu al-Faraj Muhammad al-Nadim, a man with good connections at the caliph's court, compiled the catalog, though his father probably founded the bookstore. Its latest entry dates to ca. 990, al-Nadim's death date. Superbly educated, al-Nadim wrote such well-informed comments on books and authors that his catalog presents a detailed survey of the intellectual world of Baghdad.

The first of the *Fihrist*'s ten books deals with Arabic language and sacred scriptures: the Quran, the Torah, and the Gospel. The second covers Arabic grammar, and the third writings from people connected with the caliph's court: historians, government officials, singers, jesters, and the ruler's boon companions. *Al-Nadim* means "book companion," so it is assumed that he knew this milieu well. After dealing with Arabic poetry, Muslim sects, and Islamic law in Books 3 through 6, he comes to Greek philosophy, science, and medicine in Book 7.

Most things we would find today in a bookstore are relegated to the final three chapters. Book 8 divides into three sections, the first being "Story Tellers and Stories." Here he lists a Persian book called *A Thousand Stories*, which in translation became *The Arabian Nights*. Al-Nadim's version no longer survives. The collection we have today comes from a manuscript written five hundred years later.

Then come books about "Exorcists, Jugglers, and Magicians," followed by "Miscellaneous Subjects and Fables." These include books on "Freckles, Twitching, Moles, and Shoulders," "Horsemanship, Bearing of Arms, the Implements of War," "Veterinary Surgery,"

History in Focus *Pay special attention to the placement of the figures in relation to each other in this image. What does this suggest about social distinctions within the world of Islamic scholarship? Find the answer online.*

Bibliothèque nationale de France

Scholarly Life in Medieval Islam Books being scarce and expensive, teachers dictated to their students, as shown on the right. Notice that the student is writing on a single sheet of paper while the scholar in the center holds an entire book. On the left, an author presents his work to a wealthy patron.

"Birds of Prey, Sport with Them and Medical Care of Them," "Interpretation of Dreams," "Perfume," "Cooked Food," "Poisons," and "Amulets and Charms."

Non-Muslim sects and foreign lands—India, Indochina, and China—fill Book 9, leaving Book 10 for a few final notes on philosophers not mentioned previously.

All together, the thousands of titles and authors commented on by al-Nadim provide both a panorama of what interested book buyers in tenth-century Baghdad and a saddening picture of how profound the loss of knowledge has been since that glorious era.

The Origins of Islam

How did the traditions and religious views of pre-Islamic peoples become integrated into the culture shaped by Islam?

The Arabs of 600 C.E. lived exclusively in the Arabian peninsula and on the desert fringes of Syria, Jordan, and Iraq. Along their Euphrates frontier, the Sasanids subsidized nomadic Arab chieftains to protect their empire from invasion. The Byzantines did the same with Arabs on their Jordanian frontier. Arab pastoralists farther to the south remained isolated and independent, seldom engaging the attention of the shahs and emperors. It was in these interior Arabian lands that the religion of Islam took form.

The Arabian Peninsula Before Muhammad

Throughout history people living on the Arabian peninsula have subsisted more as farmers than as pastoral nomads. Farming villages have supported the comparatively dense population of Yemen, where abundant rainfall waters the highlands during the spring monsoon, and small inlets along the southern coast have favored fishing and trading communities. But the enormous sea of sand known as the "Empty Quarter" isolated many southern regions from the Arabian interior. In the seventh century, most people in southern Arabia knew more about Africa, India, and the Persian Gulf than about the forbidding interior and the scattered camel- and sheep-herding nomads who lived there.

Caravan trading provided a rare link among peoples. Nomads derived income from providing camels, guides, and safe passage to merchants bringing the primary product of the south, the aromatic resins frankincense and myrrh, to northern customers. Return caravans brought manufactured products from Mesopotamia and Syria.

Nomad dominance of the caravan trade received a boost from the invention of militarily efficient camel saddles. This invention contributed to the rise of Arab-dominated caravan cities and to Arab pastoralists becoming the primary suppliers of animal power throughout the region. By 600 C.E., wheeled vehicles—mostly ox carts and horse-drawn chariots—had all but disappeared from the Middle East, replaced by pack camels and donkeys.

Arabs who accompanied the caravans became familiar with the cultures and lifestyles of the Sasanid and Byzantine Empires, and many of those who pastured their herds on the imperial frontiers adopted one form or another of Christianity. Even in the interior deserts, Semitic polytheism, with its worship of natural forces and celestial bodies, began to encounter more sophisticated religions.

Mecca, a late-blooming caravan city, occupies a barren mountain valley halfway between Yemen and Syria and somewhat inland from the Red Sea coast. A nomadic kin group known as the Quraysh (koo-RYYSH) settled in Mecca in the fifth century and assumed control of trade. Mecca rapidly achieved a measure of prosperity, partly because it was too far from Byzantine Syria, Sasanid Iraq, and Ethiopian-controlled Yemen for them to attack it.

A cubical shrine with idols inside called the Ka'ba (KAH-buh), a holy well called Zamzam, and a sacred precinct surrounding the two wherein killing was prohibited contributed to the emergence of Mecca as a pilgrimage site. Some Meccans associated the shrine with stories known to Jews and Christians. They regarded Abraham (Ibrahim in Arabic) as the builder of the Ka'ba, and they identified a site outside Mecca as the location where God asked Abraham to sacrifice his son. The son was not Isaac (Ishaq in Arabic), the son of Sarah, but Ishmael (Isma'il in Arabic), the

---

Mecca City in Arabia; birthplace of Muhammad; location of the Ka'ba, the holiest shrine in Islam.

Chronology

	The Arab Lands	Iran and Central Asia
600	570–632 Life of the Prophet Muhammad 634 Conquests of Iraq and Syria commence 639–642 Conquest of Egypt by Arabs 656–661 Ali caliph; first civil war 661–750 Umayyad Caliphate rules from Damascus	
700	711 Berbers and Arabs invade Spain from North Africa 750 Beginning of Abbasid Caliphate 755 Umayyad state established in Spain	711 Arabs capture Sind in India
800	776–809 Caliphate of Harun al-Rashid 835–892 Abbasid capital moved from Baghdad to Samarra	
900		875 Independent Samanid state founded in Bukhara
	909 Fatimids seize North Africa, found Shi'ite caliphate 929 Abd al-Rahman III declares himself caliph in Cordoba 945 Shi'ite Buyids take control in Baghdad	945 Buyids from northern Iran take control of Abbasid Caliphate
1000	969 Fatimids conquer Egypt	1036 Beginning of Turkish Seljuk rule in Khurasan
1100	1055 Seljuk Turks take control in Baghdad 1099 First Crusade captures Jerusalem 1171 Fall of Fatimid Egypt 1187 Saladin recaptures Jerusalem	
1220	1250 Mamluks control Egypt 1258 Mongols sack Baghdad and end Abbasid Caliphate 1260 Mamluks defeat Mongols at Ain Jalut	

son of Hagar, cited in the Bible as the forefather of the Arabs.

Muhammad in Mecca

Born in Mecca in 570, **Muhammad** grew up an orphan in the house of his uncle. He engaged in trade and married a Quraysh widow named Khadija (kah-DEE-juh), whose caravan interests he superintended. Their son died in childhood, but several daughters survived. Around 610 Muhammad began meditating at night in the mountainous terrain around Mecca. During one night vigil, known to later tradition as the "Night of Power and Excellence," a being whom Muhammad later understood to be the angel Gabriel (Jibra'il in Arabic) spoke to him:

Proclaim! In the name of your Lord who created. Created man from a clot of congealed blood. Proclaim! And your Lord is the Most Bountiful. He who has taught by the pen. Taught man that which he knew not.[1]

For three years Muhammad shared this and subsequent revelations only with close friends and family members. This period culminated in his conviction that he was hearing the words of God (Allah [AH-luh] in Arabic). Khadija, his uncle's son Ali, his friend Abu Bakr (ah-boo BAK-uhr), and others close to him

Muhammad (570–632 C.E.) Arab prophet; founder of religion of Islam.

shared this conviction. The revelations continued until Muhammad's death in 632.

Like most people of the time, including Christians and Jews, the Arabs believed in unseen spirits: gods, demonic *shaitans*, and desert spirits called *jinns* who were thought to possess seers and poets. Therefore, when Muhammad recited his rhymed revelations in public, many people believed he was inspired by an unseen spirit, even if it was not, as Muhammad asserted, the one true god.

Muhammad's earliest revelations called on people to witness that one god had created the universe and everything in it, including themselves. At the end of time, their souls would be judged, their sins balanced against their good deeds. The blameless would go to paradise; the sinful would taste hellfire:

> By the night as it conceals the light;
> By the day as it appears in glory;
> By the mystery of the creation of male and female;
> Verily, the ends ye strive for are diverse.
> So he who gives in charity and fears God,
> And in all sincerity testifies to the best,
> We will indeed make smooth for him the path to Bliss.
> But he who is a greedy miser and thinks himself self-sufficient,
> And gives the lie to the best,
> We will indeed make smooth for him the path to misery.[2]

The revelation called all people to submit to God and accept Muhammad as the last of his messengers. Doing so made one a **Muslim**, meaning one who makes "submission," **Islam**, to the will of God.

Because earlier messengers mentioned in the revelations included Noah, Moses, and Jesus, Muhammad's hearers connected his message with Judaism and Christianity, religions they were already familiar with. Yet his revelations charged the Jews and Christians with being negligent in preserving God's revealed word. Thus, even though they identified Abraham/Ibrahim, whom Muslims consider the first Muslim, as the builder of the Ka'ba, which superseded Jerusalem as the focus of Muslim prayer in 624, Muhammad's followers considered his revelation more perfect than the Bible because it had not gone through an editing process.

Some scholars maintain that Muhammad appealed especially to people distressed over wealth replacing kinship as the most important aspect of social relations and over neglect of orphans and other powerless people. Most Muslims, however, put less emphasis on a social message than on the power and beauty of Muhammad's recitations.

Formation of the Umma

Mecca's leaders feared that accepting Muhammad as the sole agent of the one true God would threaten their power and prosperity. They pressured his kin to disavow him and persecuted the weakest of his followers. Stymied by this hostility, Muhammad and his followers fled Mecca in 622 to take up residence in the agricultural community of **Medina** 215 miles (346 kilometers) to the north. This hijra (HIJ-ruh) marks the beginning of the Muslim calendar.

Prior to the hijra, Medinan representatives had met with Muhammad and agreed to accept and protect him and his followers because they saw him as an inspired leader who could calm their perpetual feuding. Together, the Meccan migrants and major groups in Medina bound themselves into a single **umma** (UM-muh), a community defined by acceptance of Islam and of Muhammad as the "Messenger of God," his most common title. Partly because three Jewish kin groups chose to retain their own faith, the direction of prayer was changed from Jerusalem toward the Ka'ba in Mecca, now thought of as the "House of God."

Having left their Meccan kin groups, the immigrants in Medina felt vulnerable. During the last decade of his life, Muhammad took active

Muslim An adherent of the Islamic religion; a person who "submits" (in Arabic, *Islam* means "submission") to the will of God.

Islam Religion expounded by the Prophet Muhammad (570–632 C.E.) on the basis of his reception of divine revelations, which were collected after his death into the Quran. In the tradition of Judaism and Christianity, and sharing much of their lore, Islam calls on all people to recognize one creator god—Allah—who rewards or punishes believers after death according to how they led their lives.

Medina City in western Arabia to which the Prophet Muhammad and his followers emigrated in 622 to escape persecution in Mecca.

umma The community of all Muslims. A major innovation against the background of seventh-century Arabia, where traditionally kinship rather than faith had determined membership in a community.

responsibility for his umma. Fresh revelations provided a framework for regulating social and legal affairs and stirred the Muslims to fight against the still-unbelieving city of Mecca. At various points during the war, Muhammad charged the Jewish kin groups, whom he had initially hoped would recognize him as God's messenger, with disloyalty, and he finally expelled or eliminated them. The sporadic war, largely conducted by raiding and negotiating with desert nomads, sapped Mecca's strength and convinced many Meccans that God favored Muhammad. In 630 Mecca surrendered, and Muhammad and his followers made the pilgrimage to the Ka'ba unhindered.

Muhammad stayed in Medina, which had grown into a bustling city-state. Delegations came to him from all over Arabia and returned home with believers who could teach them about Islam and collect their alms. Muhammad's mission to bring God's message to humanity had brought him unchallenged control of a state that was coming to dominate the Arabian peninsula.

In 632, after a brief illness, Muhammad died. Within twenty-four hours a group of Medinan leaders, along with three of Muhammad's close friends, determined that Abu Bakr, one of the earliest believers and the father of Muhammad's favorite wife A'isha (AH-ee-shah), should succeed him. They called him the *khalifa* (kah-LEE-fuh), or "successor," the English version of which is *caliph*. But calling Abu Bakr a successor did not clarify his powers. Everyone knew that neither Abu Bakr nor anyone else could receive revelations, and they likewise knew that Muhammad's revelations made no provision for succession or for any government purpose beyond maintaining the umma.

Abu Bakr continued and confirmed Muhammad's religious practices, notably the so-called Five Pillars of Islam: (1) avowal that there is only one god and Muhammad is his messenger, (2) prayer five times a day, (3) fasting during the lunar month of Ramadan, (4) paying alms, and (5) making the pilgrimage to Mecca at least once during one's lifetime. He also

reestablished and expanded Muslim authority over Arabia's communities, some of which had abandoned their allegiance to Medina or followed various would-be prophets. Muslim armies fought hard to confirm the authority of the newborn **caliphate**. In the process, some fighting spilled over into non-Arab areas in Iraq.

Reportedly, Abu Bakr ordered the men who had written down Muhammad's revelations to collect them in a book. Hitherto written haphazardly on pieces of leather or bone, these now became a single document gathered into chapters. Muslims believe the **Quran** (kuh-RAHN), or the Recitation, acquired its final form around the year 650. They see it not as the words of Muhammad but as the unalterable word of God. Theologically, it compares not so much to the Bible, a book written by many hands over many centuries, as to the person of Jesus Christ, whom Christians consider an earthly manifestation of God.

Though united in accepting God's will, the umma soon disagreed over the succession to the caliphate. When rebels assassinated the third caliph, Uthman (ooth-MAHN), in 656, and the assassins nominated Ali, Muhammad's first cousin and the husband of his daughter Fatima, to succeed him, civil war broke out. Ali had been passed over three times previously, even though many people considered him to be the Prophet's natural heir. Those who believed Ali was the Prophet's heir came to be known as **Shi'ites**, after the Arabic term *Shi'at Ali* ("Party of Ali").

When Ali accepted the nomination to be caliph, two of Muhammad's close companions and his favorite wife A'isha challenged him. Ali defeated them in the Battle of the Camel (656), so called because the fighting raged around the camel on which A'isha was seated in an enclosed woman's saddle.

After the battle, the governor of Syria, Mu'awiya (moo-AH-we-yuh), a kinsman of the slain Uthman

---

caliphate   Office established in succession to the Prophet Muhammad, to rule the Islamic empire; also the name of that empire.

Quran   Book composed of divine revelations made to the Prophet Muhammad between ca. 610 and his death in 632; the sacred text of the religion of Islam.

Shi'ites   Muslims belonging to the branch of Islam that believes that God vests leadership of the community in a descendant of Muhammad's son-in-law Ali. Shi'ism is the state religion of Iran.

Primary Source: The Constitution of Medina: Muslims and Jews at the Dawn of Islam Learn about the contract Muhammad sets forth between the Muslims and Jews of his time.

SECTION REVIEW

- Islam emerged among the nomadic pastoralists and caravan traders of the Arabian peninsula.
- Mecca grew as a caravan city and pilgrimage site identified with Jewish and Christian stories.
- Muhammad experienced revelations that called people to submit to God's will.
- Facing hostility in Mecca, Muhammad and his followers fled to Medina, where they formed the umma.
- As caliph succeeding Muhammad, Abu Bakr confirmed the Five Pillars of Islam and ordered the composition of the Quran.
- Civil war within the umma resulted in the Sunni/Shi'ite division and the foundation of the Umayyad Caliphate.

from the Umayya clan of the Quraysh, renewed the challenge. Inconclusive battle gave way to arbitration. The arbitrators decided that Uthman, whom his assassins considered corrupt, had not deserved death and that Ali had erred in accepting the caliphate. Ali rejected these findings, but before fighting could resume, one of his own supporters killed him for agreeing to the arbitration. Mu'awiya offered Ali's son Hasan a dignified retirement and thus emerged as caliph in 661.

Mu'awiya chose his own son, Yazid, to succeed him, thereby instituting the **Umayyad** (oo-MY-ad) **Caliphate**. When Hasan's brother Husayn revolted in 680 to reestablish the right of Ali's family to rule, Yazid ordered Husayn and his family killed. Sympathy for Husayn's martyrdom helped transform Shi'ism from a political movement into a religious sect.

Several variations in Shi'ite belief developed, but Shi'ites all agree that Ali was the rightful successor to Muhammad and that God's choice as Imam, leader of the Muslim community, has always been one or another of Ali's descendants. They see the caliphal office as more secular than religious. Because the Shi'ites seldom held power, their religious feelings came to focus on outpourings of sympathy for Husayn and other martyrs and on messianic dreams that one of their Imams would someday triumph.

Those Muslims who supported the first three caliphs gradually came to be called "People of Tradition and Community"—in Arabic, *Ahl al-Sunna wa'l-Jama'a*, **Sunnis** for short. Sunnis consider the caliphs

to be Imams. As for Ali's followers who had abhorred his acceptance of arbitration, they evolved into small and rebellious Kharijite sects (from *kharaja*, meaning "to secede or rebel") claiming righteousness for themselves alone. These three divisions of Islam, the last now quite minor, still survive.

The Rise and Fall of the Caliphate, 632–1258

Was the Baghdad caliphate really the high point of Muslim civilization?

The Islamic caliphate built on the conquests the Arabs carried out after Muhammad's death gave birth to a dynamic and creative religious society. By the late 800s, however, one piece after another of this huge realm broke away. Yet the idea of a caliphate, however unrealistic, remains today a touchstone of Sunni belief in the unity of the umma.

Sunni Islam never gave a single person the power to define true belief, expel heretics, and discipline clergy. Thus, unlike Christian popes and patriarchs, the caliphs had little basis for reestablishing their universal authority once they lost political and military power.

The Islamic Conquests, 634–711

Arab conquests outside Arabia began under the second caliph, Umar (r. 634–644). Arab armies wrenched Syria (636) and Egypt (639–642) away from the Byzantine Empire and defeated the last Sasanid shah, Yazdigird III (r. 632–651). After a decade-long lull, expansion began again. Tunisia fell and became the governing center from which was organized, in 711, the conquest of Spain by an Arab-led army mostly composed of Berbers from North Africa. In the same year, Sind—the southern

Umayyad Caliphate First hereditary dynasty of Muslim caliphs (661 to 750). From their capital at Damascus, the Umayyads ruled an empire that extended from Spain to India. Overthrown by the Abbasid Caliphate.
Sunnis Muslims belonging to the branch of Islam that believes that the community should select its own leadership. The majority religion in most Islamic countries.

Indus Valley in today's Pakistan—succumbed to invaders from Iraq. The Muslim dominion remained roughly stable in size for three centuries until conquest began anew in the eleventh century. India and Anatolia experienced invasions; sub-Saharan Africa and other regions saw Islam expand peacefully by trade and conversion.

Muhammad's close companions, men of political and economic sophistication inspired by his charisma, guided the conquests. The social structure and hardy nature of Arab society lent itself to flexible military operations; and the authority of Medina, reconfirmed during the caliphate of Abu Bakr, ensured obedience.

The decision made during Umar's caliphate to prohibit Arabs from assuming ownership of conquered territory proved important. Umar tied army service, with its regular pay and windfalls of booty, to residence in military camps—two in Iraq (Kufa and Basra), one in Egypt (Fustat), and one in Tunisia (Qairawan). East of Iraq, Arabs settled around small garrison towns at strategic locations and in one large garrison at Marv in present-day Turkmenistan. This policy kept the armies together and ready for action and preserved normal life in the countryside, where some three-fourths of the population lived. Only a tiny proportion of the Syrian, Egyptian, Iranian, and Iraqi populations understood the Arabic language.

The million or so Arabs who participated in the conquests over several generations constituted a small, self-isolated ruling minority living on the taxes paid by a vastly larger non-Arab, non-Muslim subject population. The Arabs had little material incentive to encourage conversion, and there is no evidence of coherent missionary efforts to spread Islam during the conquest period.

The Umayyad and Early Abbasid Caliphates, 661–850

The Umayyad caliphs presided over an Arab realm rather than a religious empire. Ruling from Damascus, their armies consisted almost entirely of Muslim Arabs. Sasanid and Byzantine administrative practices continued in force. Only gradually did the caliphs replace non-Muslim secretaries and tax officials with Muslims and introduce Arabic as the language of government. Distinctively

Muslim silver and gold coins introduced early in the eighth century symbolized the new order. Henceforward, silver dirhams and gold dinars bearing Arabic religious phrases circulated in monetary exchanges from Morocco to the frontiers of China.

The Umayyad dynasty fell in 750 after a decade of growing unrest. Converts to Islam numbered no more than 10 percent of the indigenous population, but they were still important because of the comparatively small number of Arab warriors. These converts resented Arab social domination. In addition, non-Syrian Arabs envied the Syrian domination of caliphal affairs, and pious Muslims looked askance at the secular and even irreligious behavior of the caliphs. Finally, Shi'ites and Kharijites attacked the Umayyad family's legitimacy as rulers, launching a number of rebellions.

In 747 a rebellion began in Khurasan (kor-uh-SAHN) in what is today northeastern Iran, and overthrew the last Umayyad caliph three years later, though one family member escaped to Spain to found an Umayyad principality there in 755. Many Shi'ites supported the rebellion, thinking they were fighting for the family of Ali. As it turned out, the family of Abbas, one of Muhammad's uncles, controlled the secret organization that coordinated the revolt. Upon victory they established the **Abbasid** (ah-BASS-id) **Caliphate**. Some of the Abbasid caliphs who ruled after 750 befriended their relatives in Ali's family, and one even flirted with transferring the caliphate to them. The Abbasid family, however, held on to the caliphate until 1258, when Mongol invaders killed the last of them in Baghdad (see Chapter 11).

Initially, the Abbasid dynasty made a fine show of leadership and piety. Theology and religious law became preoccupations at court and among a growing community of scholars devoted to interpreting the Quran, collecting the sayings of the Prophet, and compiling Arabic grammar. (In recent years, some Western scholars have maintained that the Quran,

Abbasid Caliphate Descendants of the Prophet Muhammad's uncle, al-Abbas, the Abbasids overthrew the Umayyad Caliphate and ruled an Islamic empire from their capital in Baghdad (founded 762) from 750 to 1258.

the sayings of the Prophet, and the biography of the Prophet were all composed around this time to provide a legendary base for the regime. This reinterpretation of Islamic origins has not been generally accepted either in the scholarly community or among Muslims.) Some caliphs sponsored ambitious projects to translate great works of Greek, Persian, and Indian thought into Arabic.

With its roots among the semi-Persianized Arabs of Khurasan, the new dynasty gradually adopted the ceremonies and customs of the Sasanid shahs. Government grew increasingly complex in Baghdad, the newly built capital city on the Tigris River. As more non-Arabs converted to Islam, the ruling elite became more cosmopolitan. Greek, Iranian, Central Asian, and African cultural currents met in the capital and gave rise to an abundance of literary works, a process facilitated by the introduction of papermaking from China. Arab poets neglected the traditional odes extolling life in the desert and wrote instead wine songs (despite Islam's prohibition of alcohol) or poems in praise of their patrons.

The translation of Aristotle into Arabic, the founding of the main currents of theology and law, and the splendor of the Abbasid court—reflected in stories of *The Arabian Nights* set in the time of the caliph Harun al-Rashid (hah-ROON al-rah-SHEED) (r. 776–809)—in some respects warrant calling the early Abbasid period a "golden age." Yet the refinement of Baghdad culture only slowly made its way into the provinces. Egypt remained predominantly Christian and Coptic-speaking in the early Abbasid period. Iran never adopted Arabic as a spoken tongue. Most of Berber-speaking North Africa rebelled and freed itself of direct caliphal rule after 740.

Gradual conversion to Islam among the conquered population accelerated in the second quarter of the ninth century. Social discrimination against non-Arab converts gradually faded, and the Arabs themselves—at least those living in cosmopolitan urban settings—lost their previously strong attachment to kinship and ethnic identity.

Political Fragmentation, 850–1050

Abbasid decline became evident in the second half of the ninth century as conversion to Islam accelerated (see Map 9.1). No government

ruling so vast an empire could hold power easily. Caravans traveled only 20 miles (32 kilometers) a day, and the couriers of the caliphal post system usually did not exceed 100 miles (160 kilometers) a day. News of frontier revolts took weeks to reach Baghdad. Military responses might take months.

During the first two Islamic centuries, revolts against Muslim rule had been a concern. The Muslim umma had therefore clung together, despite the long distances. But with the growing conversion of the population to Islam, fears that Islamic dominion might be overthrown faded. Once they became the overwhelming majority, Muslims realized that a highly centralized empire did not necessarily serve the interests of all the people.

By the middle of the ninth century, revolts targeting Arab or Muslim domination gave way to movements within the Islamic community concentrating on seizure of territory and formation of principalities. None of the states carved out of the Abbasid Caliphate after that time repudiated or even threatened Islam. They did, however, cut the flow of tax revenues to Baghdad, thereby increasing local prosperity. Increasingly starved for funds by breakaway provinces and by an unexplained fall in revenues from Iraq itself, the caliphate experienced a crisis in the late ninth century. Distrusting generals and troops from outlying areas, the caliphs purchased Turkic slaves, **mamluks** (MAM-luke), from Central Asia and established them as a standing army. Well trained and hardy, the Turks proved an effective but expensive military force. When the government could not pay them, the mamluks took it on themselves to seat and unseat caliphs, a process made easier by the construction of a new capital at Samarra, north of Baghdad on the Tigris River.

The Turks dominated Samarra without interference from an unruly Baghdad populace that regarded them as rude and highhanded. However, the money and effort that went into the huge city, which was occupied only from 835 to 892, further sapped the

mamluks Under the Islamic system of military slavery, Turkic military slaves who formed an important part of the armed forces of the Abbasid Caliphate of the ninth and tenth centuries. Mamluks eventually founded their own state, ruling Egypt and Syria (1250–1517).

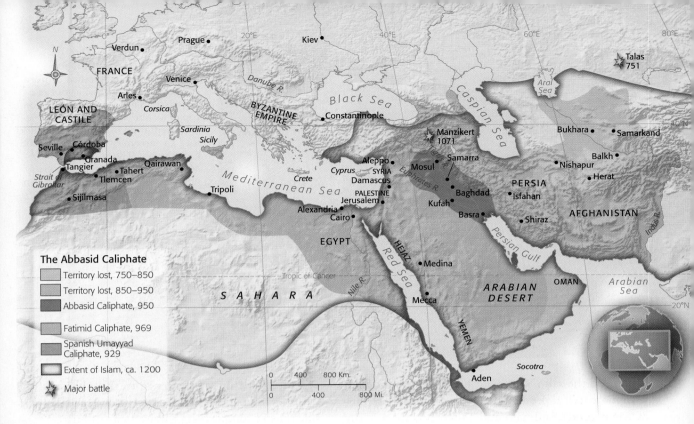

Map 9.1 **Rise and Fall of the Abbasid Caliphate** Though Abbasid rulers occupied the caliphal seat in Iraq from 750 to 1258, when Mongol armies destroyed Baghdad, real political power waned sharply and steadily after 850. The rival caliphates of the Fatimids (909–1171) and Spanish Umayyads (929–976) were comparatively short-lived. © Cengage Learning

Interactive Map

caliphs' financial strength and deflected labor from more productive pursuits.

In 945, after several attempts to find a strongman to save it, the Abbasid Caliphate fell under the control of rude mountain warriors from Daylam in northern Iran. Led by the Shi'ite Buyid (BOO-yid) family, they conquered western Iran as well as Iraq. Each Buyid commander ruled his own principality. After two centuries of glory, the sun began to set on Baghdad. The Abbasid caliph remained, but the Buyid princes controlled him. Being Shi'ites, the Buyids had no special reverence for the Sunni caliph. The Shi'ite teachings they followed held that the twelfth and last Imam had disappeared around 873 and would return as a messiah only at the end of time. Thus they had no Shi'ite Imam to defer to and retained the caliph only to help control their predominantly Sunni subjects.

Dynamic growth in outlying provinces paralleled the caliphate's gradual loss of temporal power. In the east in 875, the dynasty of the Samanids (sah-MAN-id), one of several Iranian families to achieve independence, established a glittering court in Bukhara, a major city on the Silk Road (see Map 9.1). Samanid princes patronized literature and learning, but the language they favored was Persian written in Arabic letters. For the first time, a non-Arabic literature rose to challenge the eminence of Arabic within the Islamic world.

In the west, the Berber revolts against Arab rule led to the appearance after 740 of the city-states of Sijilmasa (sih-jil-MAS-suh) and Tahert (TAH-hert) on the northern fringe of the Sahara. The Kharijite beliefs of these states' rulers interfered with their east-west overland trade and led them to develop the first regular trade across the Sahara desert. Once traders looked to the desert, they discovered that Berber speakers in the southern Sahara were already carrying salt from the desert into the Sahel region. The northern traders discovered that they could trade salt for gold by providing the southern nomads, who

Tomb of the Samanids in Bukhara This early-tenth-century structure has the basic layout of a Zoroastrian fire temple: a dome on top of a cube. However, geometric ornamentation in baked brick marks it as an early masterpiece of Islamic architecture. The Samanid family achieved independence as rulers of northeastern Iran and western Central Asia in the tenth century.

Bridgeman-Ciraudon/Art Resource, NY

controlled the salt sources but had little use for gold, with more useful products, such as copper and manufactured goods. Sijilmasa and Tahert became wealthy cities, the former minting gold coins that circulated as far away as Egypt and Syria.

The earliest known sub-Saharan beneficiary of the new exchange system was the kingdom of **Ghana** (GAH-nuh). It first appears in an Arabic text of the late eighth century as the "land of gold." Few details survive about the early years of this realm, which was established by the Soninke (soh-NIN-kay) people and covered parts of Mali, Mauritania, and Senegal, but it prospered until 1076, when it was conquered by nomads from the desert. It was one of the first lands outside the orbit of the caliphate to experience a gradual and peaceful conversion to Islam.

The North African city-states lost their independence after the Fatimid (FAT-uh-mid) dynasty, whose members claimed (perhaps falsely) to be Shi'ite Imams descended from Ali, established itself in Tunisia in 909. After consolidating their hold on northwest Africa, the Fatimids culminated their rise to power by conquering Egypt in 969. Claiming the title of caliph in a direct challenge to the Abbasids, the Fatimid rulers governed from a palace complex outside the old conquest-era garrison city of Fustat (fuss-THAT). They named the complex Cairo. For the first time Egypt became a major cultural, intellectual, and political center of Islam. The abundance of Fatimid gold coinage, now channeled to Egypt from West Africa, made the Fatimids an economic power in the Mediterranean.

Cut off from the rest of the Islamic world by the Strait of Gibraltar and, from 740 onward, by independent city-states in Morocco and Algeria, Umayyad Spain developed a distinctive Islamic culture blending Roman, Germanic, and Jewish traditions with those of the Arabs and Berbers. Historians disagree on how rapidly and completely the Spanish population converted to Islam. If we assume a process similar to that in the eastern regions, it seems likely that the most rapid surge in Islamization occurred in the middle of the tenth century.

As in the east, governing cities symbolized the Islamic presence in al-Andalus, as the Muslims called

Primary Source: The Book of Routes and Realms Find out about the ruler who became king when he was eighty-five years old.

Ghana First known kingdom in sub-Saharan West Africa between the sixth and thirteenth centuries C.E. Also the modern West African country once known as the Gold Coast.

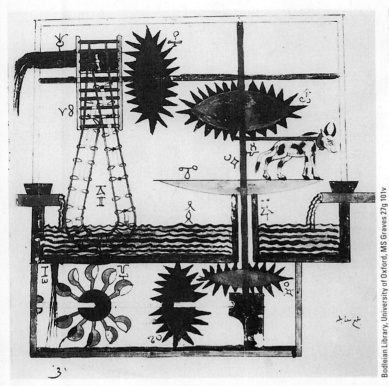

Model of a Water-Lifting Device The artist's effort to render a three-dimensional construction in two dimensions shows a talent for schematic drawing.

their Iberian territories. Cordoba, Seville, Toledo, and other cities grew substantially, becoming much larger and richer than contemporary cities in neighboring France. Converts to Islam and their descendants, unconverted Arabic-speaking Christians, and Jews joined with the comparatively few descendants of Arab settlers to create new architectural and literary styles. In the countryside, where the Berbers preferred to settle, a fusion of preexisting agricultural technologies with new crops, notably citrus fruits, and irrigation techniques from the east gave Spain the most diverse and sophisticated agricultural economy in Europe.

The rulers of al-Andalus took the title *caliph* only in 929, when Abd al-Rahman (AHB-d al-ruh-MAHN) III (r. 912–961) did so in response to a similar declaration by the newly established (909) Fatimid ruler in Tunisia. By the century's end, however, this caliphate encountered challenges from breakaway movements that eventually splintered al-Andalus into a number of small states. Political decay did not impede cultural growth. Some of the greatest writers and thinkers in Jewish history worked in Muslim Spain in the eleventh and twelfth centuries, sometimes

writing in Arabic, sometimes in Hebrew. Judah Halevi (1075–1141) composed exquisite poetry and explored questions of religious philosophy. Maimonides (1135–1204) made a major compilation of Judaic law and expounded on Aristotelian philosophy. At the same time, Islamic thought in Spain attained its loftiest peaks in Ibn Hazm's (994–1064) treatises on love and other subjects, the Aristotelian philosophical writings of Ibn Rushd (IB-uhn RUSHED) (1126–1198, known in Latin as Averroës [uh-VERR-oh-eez]) and Ibn Tufayl (IB-uhn too-FILE) (d. 1185), and the mystic speculations of Ibn al-Arabi (IB-uhn ahl-AH-rah-bee) (1165–1240). Christians, too, shared in the intellectual and cultural dynamism of al-Andalus. Translations from Arabic to Latin made during this period had a profound effect on the later intellectual development of western Europe (see Chapter 10).

The Samanids, Fatimids, and Spanish Umayyads, three of many regional principalities, represent the political diversity and awakening of local awareness that coincided with Abbasid decline. Yet drawing and redrawing political boundaries did not result in the rigid division of the Islamic world into kingdoms.

The Alhambra of Granada A palace built in the mid-fourteenth century by the kings of Granada, the Alhambra is considered the purest example of Hispano-Moorish architecture. Carefully restored, it is now a UNESCO World Heritage Site.

Bill Heinsohn/Alamy

Religious and cultural developments, particularly the rise in cities of a social group of religious scholars known as the **ulama** (oo-leh-MAH)—Arabic for "people with (religious) knowledge"—worked against any permanent division of the Islamic umma.

Assault from Within and Without, 1050–1258

The role played by Turkish mamluks in the decline of Abbasid power established an enduring stereotype of the Turk as a ferocious, unsophisticated warrior. This image gained strength in the 1030s when the Seljuk (sel-JOOK) family established a Turkish Muslim state based on nomadic power. Taking the Arabic title *Sultan*, meaning "power," and the revived Persian title *Shahan-shah*, or King of Kings, the Seljuk ruler Tughril (TUUG-ruhl) Beg created a kingdom that stretched from northern Afghanistan to Baghdad, which he occupied in 1055. After a century under the thumb of the Shi'ite Buyids, the Abbasid caliph breathed easier under the slightly lighter thumb of the Sunni Turks. The Seljuks pressed on into Syria and Anatolia, administering a lethal blow to Byzantine power at the Battle of Manzikert (MANZ-ih-kuhrt) in 1071. The Byzantine army fell back on Constantinople, leaving Anatolia open to Turkish occupation.

Under Turkish rule, cities shrank as pastoralists overran their agricultural hinterlands. Irrigation works suffered from lack of maintenance in the unsettled countryside, and tax revenues fell. Quarreling twelfth-century princes fought over cities, but few Turks participated in urban cultural and religious life. The gulf between a religiously based urban society and the culture and personnel of the government deepened. When factional riots broke out between Sunnis and Shi'ites, or between rival schools of Sunni law, rulers generally remained aloof, even as destruction and loss of life mounted.

By the early twelfth century, unrepaired damage from floods, fires, and civil disorder had reduced old Baghdad on the west side of the Tigris to ruins. The withering of Baghdad reflected a broader environmental problem: the collapse of the canal system on which agriculture in the Tigris and Euphrates Valley depended. For millennia a center of world

ulama Muslim religious scholars. From the ninth century onward, the primary interpreters of Islamic law and the social core of Muslim urban societies.

civilization, Mesopotamia underwent substantial population loss and never again regained its geographical importance.

The Turks alone cannot be blamed for the demographic and economic misfortunes of Iran and Iraq. Too-robust urbanization and an apparent chilling of the climate after 1000 had strained food resources. The growing practice of paying soldiers and courtiers with land grants led to absentee landlords using agents to collect taxes. These agents gouged villagers and took little interest in improving production, thus intensifying the agricultural crisis.

Internecine feuding was preoccupying the Seljuk family when the first Christian crusaders reached the Holy Land and captured Jerusalem in 1099 (see Chapter 10). Though charged with the stuff of romance, the Crusades had little lasting impact on the Islamic lands. The four crusader principalities of Edessa, Antioch, Tripoli, and Jerusalem simply became pawns in the shifting pattern of politics already in place. Newly arrived knights eagerly attacked the Muslim enemy, whom they called "Saracens" (SAR-uh-suhn), but veteran crusaders recognized that practicing diplomacy and seeking partners of convenience among rival Muslim princes offered a sounder strategy.

The Muslims finally unified to face the European enemy in the mid-twelfth century. Nur al-Din ibn Zangi (NOOR al-DEEN ib-uhn ZAN-gee) established a strong state based in Damascus and sent an army to terminate the Fatimid Caliphate in Egypt. A nephew of the Kurdish commander of that expedition, Salah-al-Din, known in the West as Saladin, took advantage of Nur al-Din's timely death to seize power and unify Egypt and Syria. The Fatimid dynasty fell in 1171. In 1187 Saladin recaptured Jerusalem from Europeans.

Saladin's descendants fought off subsequent Crusades. After one such battle, however, in 1250, Turkish mamluk troops seized control of the government in Cairo, ending Saladin's dynasty. In 1260 these mamluks rode east to confront a new invading force. At the Battle of Ain Jalut (ine jah-LOOT) (Spring of Goliath) in Syria, they met and defeated an army of Mongols from Central Asia (see Chapter 12), thus stemming an invasion that had begun several decades before and legitimizing their claim to dominion over Egypt and Syria.

SECTION REVIEW

- By 711, Arab armies had conquered an empire stretching from Sind in the east to Spain in the west.
- The Umayyad caliphs ruled an ethnic empire; they governed from Damascus using Sasanid and Byzantine administrative methods.
- The Umayyads fell to rebels who established the Abbasid Caliphate at Baghdad, while surviving Umayyads fled to Spain.
- Influenced by Persian culture, the Abbasids presided over significant spiritual, intellectual, and artistic activity.
- Abbasid decline led to fragmentation of the caliphate into independent states, but the Islamic umma remained intact.
- Political divisions continued as successor states to the former caliphate fell, replaced by Seljuk Turk, Crusader, mamluk, and Mongol states.

During the ensuing Mamluk period a succession of slave-soldier sultans ruled Egypt and Syria until 1517. Fear of new Mongol attacks receded after 1300, but by then the new ruling system had become fixed. Young Turkish or Circassian slaves, the latter from the eastern end of the Black Sea, were imported from non-Muslim lands, raised in training barracks, and converted to Islam. Owing loyalty to the mamluk officers who purchased them, they formed a military class that was socially disconnected from the Arabic-speaking native population.

The Mongol invasions, especially their destruction of the Abbasid Caliphate in Baghdad in 1258, shocked the world of Islam. The mamluk sultan enthroned a relative of the last Baghdad caliph in Cairo, but the Egyptian Abbasids were mere puppets serving mamluk interests. From Iraq eastward, non-Muslim rule lasted for much of the thirteenth century. Although the Mongols left few ethnic or linguistic traces in these lands, their initial destruction of cities and slaughter of civilian populations, their diversion of Silk Road trade from Baghdad to more northerly routes ending at Black Sea ports, and their casual disregard, even after conversion to Islam, for Muslim religious life and urban culture hastened currents of change already under way.

Islamic Civilization

How did regional diversity affect the development of Islamic civilization?

Though increasingly unsettled in its political dimension and subject to economic disruptions caused by war, the ever-expanding Islamic world underwent a fruitful evolution in law, social structure, and religious expression. Religious conversion and urbanization reinforced each other to create a distinct Islamic civilization. The immense geographical and human diversity of the Muslim lands allowed many "small traditions" to coexist with the developing "great tradition" of Islam.

Law and Dogma

The Shari'a, the law of Islam, provides the foundation of Islamic civilization. Yet aside from certain Quranic verses conveying specific divine ordinances—most pertaining to personal and family matters—Islam had no legal system in the time of Muhammad. Arab custom and the Prophet's own authority offered the only guidance. After Muhammad died, the umma tried to follow his example. This became harder and harder to do, however, as those who knew Muhammad best passed away and many Arabs found themselves living in far-off lands. Non-Arab converts to Islam, who at first tried to follow Arab customs they had little familiarity with, had an even harder time.

Islam slowly developed laws to govern social and religious life. The full sense of Islamic civilization, however, goes well beyond the basic Five Pillars mentioned earlier. Some Muslim thinkers felt that the reasoned consideration of a mature man offered the best resolution of issues not covered by Quranic revelation. Others argued for the sunna, or tradition, of the Prophet as the best guide. To understand that sunna they collected and studied thousands of reports, called **hadith** (hah-DEETH), purporting to convey the precise words or deeds of Muhammad. It became customary to precede each hadith with a chain of oral authorities leading back to the person who had direct acquaintance with the Prophet.

Many hadith dealt with ritual matters, such as how to wash before prayer. Others provided answers to legal questions not covered by Quranic revelation or suggested principles for deciding such matters. By the eleventh century most legal thinkers had accepted the idea that Muhammad's personal behavior provided the best role model and that the hadith constituted the most authoritative basis for law after the Quran itself.

Yet the hadith posed a problem because the tens of thousands of anecdotes included both genuine and invented reports, the latter sometimes politically motivated, as well as stories derived from non-Muslim religious traditions. Only a specialist could hope to separate a sound from a weak tradition. As the hadith grew in importance, so did the branch of learning devoted to their analysis. Scholars discarded thousands for having faulty chains of authority. The most reliable they collected into books that gradually achieved authoritative status. Sunnis placed six books in this category; Shi'ites, four.

As it gradually evolved, the Shari'a embodied a vision of an umma in which all subscribed to the same moral values and political and ethnic distinctions lost importance. Every Muslim ruler was expected to abide by and enforce the religious law. In practice, this expectation often lost out in the hurly-burly of political life. But the Shari'a proved an important basis for an urban lifestyle that varied surprisingly little from Morocco to India.

Converts and Cities

Conversion to Islam, more the outcome of people's learning about the new rulers' religion than an escape from the tax on non-Muslims, as some scholars have suggested, helped spur urbanization. Conversion did not require extensive knowledge of the faith. To become a Muslim, a person simply stated, in the presence of a Muslim: "There is no God but God, and Muhammad is the Messenger of God."

Few converts spoke Arabic, and fewer could read the Quran. Many converts knew no more of the Quran than the verses they memorized for daily prayers. Muhammad had established no priesthood to define and spread the faith. Thus new converts, whether Arab or non-Arab, faced the problem of finding out

---

hadith A tradition relating the words or deeds of the Prophet Muhammad; next to the Quran, the most important basis for Islamic law.

for themselves what Islam was about and how they should act as Muslims. This meant spending time with Muslims, learning their language, and imitating their practices.

In many areas, conversion involved migrating to an Arab governing center. The alternative, converting to Islam but remaining in one's home community, was difficult because religion had become the main component of social identity in Byzantine and Sasanid times. Converts to Islam thus encountered discrimination if they stayed in their Christian, Jewish, or Zoroastrian communities. Migration both averted discrimination and took advantage of the economic opportunities opened up by tax revenues flowing into the Arab governing centers.

The Arab military settlements of Kufa and Basra in Iraq blossomed into cities and became important centers for Muslim cultural activities. As conversion rapidly spread in the mid-ninth century, urbanization accelerated in other regions, most visibly in Iran, where most cities previously had been quite small. Nishapur in the northeast grew from fewer than 10,000 pre-Islamic inhabitants to between 100,000 and 200,000 by the year 1000. Other Iranian cities experienced similar growth. In Iraq, Baghdad and Mosul joined Kufa and Basra as major cities. In Syria, Aleppo and Damascus flourished under Muslim rule. Fustat in Egypt developed into Cairo, one of the largest and greatest Islamic cities. The primarily Christian patriarchal cities of Jerusalem, Antioch, and Alexandria, not being Muslim governing centers, shrank and stagnated.

Conversion-related migration meant that cities became heavily Muslim before the countryside did. This reinforced the urban orientation deriving from the fact that Muhammad and his first followers came from the commercial city of Mecca. Mosques in large cities served both as ritual centers and as places for learning and social activities.

Islam colored all aspects of urban social life. Initially the new Muslims imitated Arab dress and customs and emulated people they regarded as particularly pious. In the absence of a central religious authority, local variations developed in the way people practiced Islam and in the hadith they attributed to the Prophet. This gave the rapidly growing religion the flexibility to accommodate many different social situations.

By the tenth century, urban growth was affecting the countryside by expanding the consumer market. Citrus fruits, rice, and sugar cane, introduced by the Sasanids, increased in acreage and spread to new areas. Cotton became a major crop in Iran and elsewhere and stimulated textile production. Irrigation works expanded. Abundant coinage facilitated a flourishing intercity and long-distance trade that provided regular links between isolated districts and integrated the pastoral nomads, who provided pack animals, into the region's economy. Trade encouraged the manufacture of cloth, metal goods, and pottery.

Science and technology also flourished. Building on Hellenistic traditions and their own observations and experience, Muslim doctors and astronomers developed skills and theories far in advance of their European counterparts. Working in Egypt in the eleventh century, the mathematician and physicist Ibn al-Haytham (IB-uhn al-HY-tham) wrote more than a hundred works. Among other things, he determined that the Milky Way lies far beyond earth's atmosphere, proved that light travels from a seen object to the eye and not the reverse, and explained why the sun and moon appear larger on the horizon than overhead.

Women and Islam

Women seldom traveled. Those living in rural areas worked in the fields and tended animals. Urban women, particularly members of the elite, lived in seclusion and did not leave their homes without covering themselves (see Material Culture: Head Coverings). Seclusion of women and veiling in public already existed in Byzantine and Sasanid times. Through interpretation of specific verses from the Quran, these practices now became fixtures of Muslim social life. Although women sometimes became literate and studied with relatives, they did so away from the gaze of unrelated men, and while they played influential roles within the family, public roles were generally barred. Only slave women could perform before unrelated men as musicians and dancers. A man could have sexual relations with as many slave concubines as he pleased, in addition to marrying as many as four wives.

Muslim women fared better legally under Islamic law than did Christian and Jewish women under their

Material Culture

Head Coverings

Covering the head is one of the most universal of human cultural characteristics. It is also one of the most common ways of signaling social status. Examples can be drawn from every part of the world, from earliest times down to the modern era. In premodern Chinese society the color and design of a man's cap indicated his rank as clearly as the insignia on military head coverings does today. In most European societies in the seventeenth and eighteenth centuries, men and frequently women of the higher social orders wore wigs, a practice that still survives in the costume of British judges. Head coverings were particularly important for royalty. From ancient Egypt, where the earliest Pharaonic crowns symbolized the union of the northern and southern parts of the Nile Valley, down to the twentieth century and the jewel-studded crown of the shah of Iran, each land developed its own distinctive royal headdress. This also held true for Native American societies in pre-Columbian times and for African and Polynesian societies. In some societies, such as Sasanid Iran and the Ottoman Empire in what is today Turkey, each ruler's crown or turban had a distinctive design that signaled his rule.

Head coverings have also played significant roles in religion. In orthodox Judaism, for example, men wear hats or skullcaps, and married women wear wigs, as signs of acceptance of God's laws. In Islam, head coverings for women, borrowed from pre-Islamic practice in the Middle East, have become politically controversial in recent years; but prior to the twentieth century it was considered equally improper for a Muslim man to go bareheaded.

Wearing no hat at all was usually a characteristic of slaves or of the poorest elements in society. But it could also signify a deliberate desire to be regarded as humble. Sumerian priests, Buddhist monks and nuns, and certain Sufis in the Muslim world shaved their heads clean. In Europe, early Christian monks and priests shaved the crown of their heads in the Roman Catholic tradition. This form of tonsure competed with and eventually superseded an Irish Catholic practice of shaving the front of the head. Yet head shaving did not always signify humility. Japanese samurai, or warriors, also shaved the front of their heads.

Head coverings for women, as well as wigs and hairdressing styles, sometimes show greater diversity than those for men. This has been particularly true in societies where women of high status mix with men on public occasions. A magnificent wig, hat, or coiffure under these circumstances might speak as much for the social rank of the woman's husband as for her own.

Given this long history of distinctive head coverings, the abandonment of both men's and women's hats in the second half of the twentieth century marked a major turning point in the history of symbolism. Around the world, the hat-making industry has greatly contracted. Whether one visits China, Egypt, India, France, or Brazil, one finds it difficult to determine the rank or status of most people by looking at what they have on their heads. Heads of government typically pose for group photographs with no hats on at all. Aside from conservative religious groups, the head coverings that remain most often indicate occupations: military, police, construction, athletics, and so on.

The reasons for this change are unclear. The spread of democracy and decline of aristocracy may have contributed to it, but hats have become equally uncommon in dictatorships. A more likely cause is the worldwide role of news photographs, movies, and other pictorial media. The media developed in Europe and the United States tend to take Western customs as normal and exoticize non-Western styles as "native costumes." People everywhere have thus felt pressure to switch to Western styles, including bareheadedness, to fit into the image of the modern world.

Christ Before Caiphas

Though distinctive hair and hat customs were a hallmark of the Christian churches, Jesus stands out for his untrimmed hair and lack of a head cover, except for a crown of thorns.

Institute Amatiler d'Art Hispanic. © Patrimonio Nacional, Madrid

Women Playing Chess in Muslim Spain As shown in this thirteenth-century miniature, women in their own quarters, without men present, wore whatever clothes and jewels they liked. Notice the henna decorating the hands of the woman in the middle. The woman on the left, probably a slave, plays an oud.

respective religious codes. Because Islamic law guaranteed daughters a share in inheritance equal to half that of a son, the majority of women inherited some amount of money or real estate. This remained their private property to keep or sell. Muslim law put the financial burden of supporting a family exclusively on the husband, who could not legally compel his wife to help out.

Women could also remarry if their husbands divorced them, and they received a cash payment upon divorce. Although a man could divorce his wife without stating a cause, a woman could initiate divorce under specified conditions. Women could also practice birth control. They could testify in court, although their testimony counted as half that of a man. They could also go on pilgrimage. Nevertheless, a misogynistic tone sometimes appears in Islamic writings. One saying attributed to the Prophet observed: "I was raised up to heaven and saw that most of its denizens were poor people; I was raised into the hellfire and saw that most of its denizens were women."[3]

In the absence of writings by women about women from this period, the status of women must be deduced from the writings of men. Two episodes involving the Prophet's wife A'isha, the daughter of Abu Bakr, provide examples of how Muslim men appraised women in society. Only eighteen when Muhammad died, A'isha lived for another fifty years. Early reports stress her status as Muhammad's favorite, the only virgin he married and the only wife to see the angel Gabriel. These reports emanate from A'isha herself, who was an abundant source of hadith. As a fourteen-year-old she had become separated from a caravan and rejoined it only after traveling through the night with a man who found her alone in the desert. Gossips accused her of being untrue to the Prophet, but a revelation from God proved her innocence. The second event was her participation in the Battle of the Camel, fought to derail Ali's caliphate. These two episodes came to epitomize what Muslim men feared most about women: sexual infidelity and meddling in politics. Even though the earliest literature dealing with A'isha stresses her position as Muhammad's favorite, his first wife, Khadija, and his daughter, Ali's wife Fatima, eventually surpassed A'isha as ideal women. Both appear as model wives and mothers with no suspicion of sexual irregularity or political manipulation.

As the seclusion of women became commonplace in urban Muslim society, some writers extolled homosexual relationships, partly because a male lover could appear in public or go on a journey. Although Islam deplored homosexuality, one ruler wrote a book advising his son to follow moderation in all things and thus share his affections equally between men and women. Another ruler and his slave-boy became models of perfect love in the verses of mystic poets.

Islam allowed slavery but forbade Muslims from enslaving other Muslims or so-called People of the Book—Jews, Christians, and Zoroastrians, who revered holy books respected by the Muslims. Being enslaved as a prisoner of war constituted an exception. Later centuries saw a constant flow of slaves into Islamic territory from Africa and Central Asia. A hereditary slave society, however, did not develop. Usually slaves converted to Islam, and many masters then freed them as an act of piety. The offspring of slave women and Muslim men were born free.

The Recentering of Islam

Early Islam centered on the caliphate, the political expression of the unity of the umma. No formal organization or hierarchy, however, directed the process of conversion. Thus there emerged a multitude of local Islamic communities so disconnected from each other that numerous competing interpretations of the developing religion arose. Inevitably, the centrality of the caliphate diminished (see Map 9.1). The appearance of rival caliphates in Tunisia and Cordoba accentuated the problem of decentralization. The rise of the ulama as community leaders did not prevent growing fragmentation because the ulama themselves divided into contentious factions. During the twelfth century factionalism began to abate, and new socioreligious institutions emerged to provide the umma with a different sort of religious center. These new developments stemmed in part from an exodus of religious scholars from Iran in response to economic and political disintegration during the late eleventh and twelfth centuries. The flow of Iranians to the

Arab lands and to newly conquered territories in India and Anatolia increased after the Mongol invasion. Fully versed in Arabic as well as their native Persian, immigrant scholars were warmly received. They brought with them a view of religion developed in Iran's urban centers. A type of religious college, the *madrasa* (MAH-dras-uh), gained sudden popularity outside Iran, where madrasas had been known since the tenth century. Scores of madrasas, many founded by local rulers, appeared throughout the Islamic world.

Iranians also contributed to the growth of mystic groups known as *Sufi* brotherhoods in the twelfth and thirteenth centuries. The doctrines and rituals of certain Sufis spread from city to city, giving rise to the first geographically extensive Islamic religious organizations. Sufi doctrines varied, but a quest for a sense of union with God through rituals and training was a common denominator. Sufism had begun in early Islamic times and had doubtless benefited from the ideas and beliefs of people from religions with mystic traditions who converted to Islam.

The early Sufis had been saintly individuals given to ecstatic and poetic utterances and wonder-working. They attracted disciples but did not try to organize them. The growth of brotherhoods, a less ecstatic form of Sufism, set a tone for society in general. It soon became common for most Muslim men, particularly in the cities, to belong to at least one brotherhood.

A sense of the social climate the Sufi brotherhoods fostered can be gained from a twelfth-century manual:

> Every limb has its own special ethics. . . . The ethics of the tongue. The tongue should always be busy in reciting God's names (*dbikr*) and in saying good things of the brethren, praying for them, and giving them counsel. . . . The ethics of hearing. One should not listen to indecencies and slander. . . . The ethics of sight. One should lower one's eyes in order not to see forbidden things.[4]

Special dispensations allowed people who merely wanted to emulate the Sufis and enjoy their company to follow less demanding rules:

> It is allowed by way of dispensation to possess an estate or to rely on a regular income. The Sufis' rule in this matter is that one should not use all of it for himself, but should dedicate this to public

charities and should take from it only enough for one year for himself and his family. . . .

There is a dispensation allowing one to watch all kinds of amusement. This is, however, limited by the rule: What you are forbidden from doing, you are also forbidden from watching.[5]

Some Sufi brotherhoods spread in the countryside. Local shrines and pilgrimages to the tombs of Muhammad's descendants and saintly Sufis became popular. The end of the Abbasid Caliphate enhanced the religious centrality of Mecca, which eventually became an important center of madrasa education, and gave renewed importance to the annual pilgrimage.

Conclusion

Islam began as a religious movement that united the peoples of Arabia. So powerful was its message, however, that it inspired Arabian warriors to spread out from Arabia to neighboring countries, which rapidly succumbed to the new conquerors. For many years, in the lands that Arabians had conquered they kept themselves separate from their subjects, imposing taxes and laws but tolerating the practice of Judaism and Christianity. The appeal of Islam and the practical advantages offered to Muslims in the Arab Empire were so strong that many of the subject peoples converted to Islam and joined the umma. In the process, Islam was influenced by the cultural traditions of the newly converted, especially Iranian, Egyptian, and Spanish Muslims. Even as the Abbasid Caliphate became weaker from the ninth century onward, the number of Muslims grew and the religion of Islam gained new converts far from the original centers of Islamic life in Arabia and the Middle East. Muslim states arose in West Africa, in Southeast Asia and Indonesia, and in Central Asia. The Arabic language, an important aspect of Islam because it is the language of the Quran, replaced the common languages of the Middle East and North Africa, but it did not spread to Iran or beyond, nor to sub-Saharan Africa. As Islam distanced itself from its original identification with Arabians, it became a universal world religion.

CHAPTER REVIEW

Download the MP3 audio file of the Chapter Review to listen to on the go.

How did the traditions and religious views of pre-Islamic peoples become integrated into the culture shaped by Islam? (page 214)

During Muhammad's lifetime, virtually all Muslims were Arabs from central or southern Arabia. Their cultural traditions underlie many verses of the Quran. But the conquests brought many other peoples under the rule of the caliphate. Non-Arabs who converted to Islam, as well as Arabs from previously Christian groups in Syria and Iraq, brought with them some of the traditions and religious views of their former faith communities. Bits of this cultural heritage sometimes became incorporated into the body of lore accepted as the sayings of Muhammad. Other materials, notably in science and philosophy, were translated in book form into Arabic. And still more seeped into the rich store of legend and customary knowledge in different parts of the caliphate.

Was the Baghdad caliphate really the high point of Muslim civilization? (page 218)

A division of the caliphate into smaller political units accompanied this growth in ethnic diversity. The glittering cosmopolitan Baghdad of the early Abbasid Caliphate lost its luster as the conversion of non-Arabs to Islam increased and other cities from Spain to Pakistan evolved into regional Muslim centers. Despite Baghdad's reputation, these later centers, looked at collectively, contributed more to the distinctiveness of medieval Islamic culture than did Baghdad.

How did regional diversity affect the development of Islamic civilization? (page 226)

Spain, Egypt, and Iran were three regions that flourished as Baghdad declined. Each developed a particular intellectual, religious, and artistic character within the overall unity of Islam. Politically as well, regional variation was important. The coming of the Turks and Mongols left North Africa and Spain mostly untouched, the Crusades were of negligible importance for Iran, and the confrontation of the Muslims of Spain with the Christians to their north meant little to the Egyptians. Yet all of these events contributed to the shaping of medieval Islamic civilization as a whole.

Key Terms

Mecca *(p. 214)*	Shi'ites *(p. 217)*
Muhammad *(p. 215)*	Umayyad Caliphate *(p. 218)*
Muslim *(p. 216)*	Sunnis *(p. 218)*
Islam *(p. 216)*	Abbasid Caliphate *(p. 219)*
Medina *(p. 216)*	mamluks *(p. 220)*
umma *(p. 216)*	Ghana *(p. 222)*
caliphate *(p. 217)*	ulama *(p. 224)*
Quran *(p. 217)*	hadith *(p. 226)*

Web Resources

Pronunciation Guide

Interactive Map
- MAP 9.1 Rise and Fall of the Abbasid Caliphate

Primary Sources
- The Constitution of Medina: Muslims and Jews at the Dawn of Islam
- The Quran: Muslim Devotion to God
- The Book of Routes and Realms

Answer to the History in Focus Question
See photo on page 213, "Scholarly Life in Medieval Islam."

CourseMate Visit the CourseMate website at www.cengagebrain.com for additional study tools and review materials for this chapter.

Christian Europe Emerges

© Cengage Learning

Visit the CourseMate website at **www.cengagebrain.com** for additional study tools and review materials for this chapter.

In 800, **Charlemagne** (SHAHR-leh-mane) (from Latin *Carolus magnus*, "Charles the Great") became the first man in western Europe to bear the title *emperor* in over three hundred years. Rome's decline and Charlemagne's rise marked a shift of focus for Europe—away from the Mediterranean and toward the north and west. German custom and Christian piety transformed the Roman heritage to create a new civilization. Irish monks preaching in Latin became intellectual leaders in Germanic lands, while the memory of Greek and Roman philosophy faded. Urban life continued the decline begun in the later days of the Roman Empire. Historians originally called this era "**medieval**," literally "middle age," because it comes between the era of Greco-Roman civilization and the intellectual, artistic, and economic changes of the Renaissance in the fourteenth century. In fact, many aspects of medieval culture were as rich and creative as those that came earlier and later.

Charlemagne was not the only ruler in Europe to claim the imperial title. Another emperor held sway in the Greek-speaking east, where Rome's political and legal heritage continued in the Eastern Roman or **Byzantine Empire**. While western Europeans lived amid the ruins of empire, the Byzantines maintained and reinterpreted Roman traditions. The authority of the Byzantine emperors blended with the influence of the Christian church in a cultural synthesis that helped shape the emerging kingdom of **Kievan Russia**. Byzantium's centuries-long conflict with Islam helped spur the crusading passion that overtook western Europe in the eleventh century.

The comparison between western and eastern Europe appears paradoxical. Byzantium inherited a robust and self-confident late Roman society and economy, while western Europe could not achieve political unity and suffered severe economic decline. Yet by 1200 western Europe was showing renewed vitality and flexing its military muscles, while Byzantium was showing signs of decline and military weakness. As we explore these different historical paths, we must remember that the emergence of Christian Europe included both developments.

The Byzantine Empire, 600–1200

How did the Byzantine Empire maintain Roman imperial traditions in the east?

The Byzantine emperors established Christianity as their official religion (see Chapter 6). They also represented a continuation of Roman imperial rule and tradition. Whereas only provincial forms of Roman law survived in the west, Byzantium inherited imperial law intact. Combining the imperial role with political oversight of the Christian church, the emperors made a comfortable transition into the role of all-powerful Christian monarchs. The Byzantine drama, however, played on a steadily shrinking stage. Territorial losses and almost constant military pressure from north and south deprived the empire of long periods of peace.

Church and State

In 324, in the nineteenth year of his reign, the emperor Constantine (r. 306–337) led a procession marking the expanded limits of his new capital: the millennium-old Greek city of Byzantium, located on a long, narrow inlet at the entrance to the Bosporus strait. In the forum of the new Constantinople (cahn-stan-tih-NO-pul), he erected a 120-foot-tall (36-meter) column topped with a statue of Apollo, and he retained the old Roman title *pontifex maximus* (PAHN-tih-fex

Charlemagne (742–814) King of the Franks (r. 768–814); emperor (r. 800–814). Through a series of military conquests he established the Carolingian Empire, which encompassed all of Gaul and parts of Germany and Italy. Though illiterate himself, he sponsored a brief intellectual revival.

medieval Literally "middle age," a term that historians of Europe use for the period ca. 500 to ca. 1500, signifying its intermediate point between Greco-Roman antiquity and the Renaissance.

Byzantine Empire Historians' name for the eastern portion of the Roman Empire from the fourth century onward, taken from "Byzantion," an early name for Constantinople, the Byzantine capital city.

Kievan Russia State established at Kiev in Ukraine ca. 879 by Scandinavian adventurers asserting authority over a mostly Slavic farming population.

Chronology

	Western Europe	Eastern Europe
600		**634–650** Muslims conquer Byzantine provinces of Syria, Egypt, and Tunisia
800	**711** Muslim conquest of Spain **732** Charles Martel stops Muslim advance into France at the Battle of Tours **800** Coronation of Charlemagne **843** Treaty of Verdun divides Carolingian Empire among Charlemagne's grandsons **910** Monastery of Cluny founded **962** Beginning of Holy Roman Empire	**882** Varangians take control of Kiev
1000	**1054** Formal schism between Latin and Orthodox Churches **1066** Normans under William the Conqueror invade England **1076–1078** Climax of investiture controversy **1095** Pope Urban II preaches First Crusade	**980** Vladimir becomes grand prince of Kievan Russia
1200		**1081–1118** Alexius Comnenus rules Byzantine Empire, calls for western military aid against Muslims **1204** Western knights sack Constantinople in Fourth Crusade

MAX-ih-muhs) (chief priest). Nevertheless, he leaned toward Christianity—historians disagree on when he embraced it fully—and he and his mother studded both his capital and the Christian centers of Jerusalem and Rome with important churches.

Constantine appointed the patriarch of Constantinople and involved himself in doctrinal disputes over which beliefs constituted heresy. In 325 he called hundreds of bishops to a council at the city of Nicaea (nye-SEE-uh) (modern Iznik in northwestern Turkey) to resolve disputes over religious doctrine. The bishops rejected the views of a priest from Alexandria named Arius, who maintained that Jesus was of lesser importance than God the Father. The Arian doctrine enjoyed greatest popularity among the Germanic peoples then migrating along the Danube frontier and into the western Roman lands. An Arian bishop named Ulfilas (ca. 311–383), himself belonging to the Germanic people known as Goths, translated the Bible into Gothic, reportedly using an alphabet of his own devising. This set the Arians apart from Christians who relied on scriptures written in Latin or Greek. Following the Arian controversy, disputes

over theology and quarrels among the patriarchs of Constantinople, Alexandria, and Antioch continued to tear at the Byzantine Empire. Literature of the period shows widespread concern for religious affairs, which deeply permeated society. A fourth-century bishop reported: "Everything is full of those who are speaking of unintelligible things. . . . I wish to know the price of bread; one answers, 'The Father is greater than the Son.' I inquire whether my bath is ready; one says, 'The Son has been made out of nothing.'"[1] Early Christians had established communities in many cities (see Map 10.1 on page 237). The most prominent were in Jerusalem, Antioch, Alexandria, and Rome, and their bishops became recognized as patriarchs, or paramount leaders. Other important theologians, like St. Augustine (354–430), the bishop of Hippo in North Africa, were not patriarchs. Constantine made Constantinople a fifth patriarchate (PAY-tree-ar-kayt). The patriarchs appointed bishops throughout their regions, and each bishop consecrated priests within his area of jurisdiction, called a diocese or see. Church rules set by the patriarch or by councils of bishops guided priests in serving ordinary believers.

Priests commemorated Christ's sacrifice on the cross in the consumption of wine and a wafer of bread in the Mass, or church service. Church leaders differed on the precise form of other rituals and on which should be considered sacred mysteries, or sacraments. Before baptism became standardized as a ritual for newborns, for example, it was sometimes postponed until late in life so that the person could benefit from the forgiveness of sin that it conveyed.

Byzantine Church from a Twelfth-Century Manuscript The upper portion shows the church façade and domes. The lower portion shows the interior with a mosaic of Christ enthroned at the altar end.   Bibliothèque nationale de France

History in Focus *Examine the figures carefully; notice how they appear and the space they occupy. What does this image suggest about the major goals of Byzantine religious artists? Find the answer online.*

One area of disagreement within the church hierarchy centered on Jesus's relationship to God the Father and to the Holy Spirit. The bishops gathered for the Council of Nicaea agreed that, contrary to the Arian view, the three formed a divine Trinity in which three aspects or manifestations of God somehow came together. But they did not all understand the Trinity in the same way. They also disagreed on whether Mary was the mother of God or the mother of a human named Jesus. Some Christians thought that images of God or Jesus or Mary, called icons, were proper objects to pray before because they stimulated pious thoughts; others, known as iconoclasts, or image-breakers, condemned the practice as too much like praying to pagan statues.

For some four centuries after 300, disagreements like these led to charges and countercharges of heresy. A heresy was a belief or practice so unacceptable as to be un-Christian. The most severe disagreements arose in North Africa and the lands of the eastern Mediterranean and resulted in **schism** (SKIZ-uhm) or formal theological break. Monophysite (muh-NAH-fi-site) (Greek for "one nature") doctrine, for example, emphasized the divinity of Jesus Christ and minimized his human characteristics. Finding abhorrent the idea that Christ suffered like an ordinary human on the cross, some Monophysites maintained that another man had been substituted for him. Versions of Monophysitism persist to this day in Egyptian, Ethiopian, and Armenian churches.

Christianity progressed most rapidly in urban centers. Though the country folk (Latin *pagani*, whence the word *pagan* used as a negative label for polytheists) long retained customs deriving from worship of the old gods, the emperor Julian (r. 361–363) tried in vain to restore the old polytheism as the state cult. When a blind Christian addressed Julian by the pejorative term "apostate" (renegade from Christianity)—historians commonly call him Julian the Apostate—the emperor said, "You are blind, and your God will not cure you." To this the Christian

---

schism A formal split within a religious community.

replied, "I thank God for my blindness, since it prevents me from beholding your impiety."[2] In 392 the emperor Theodosius banned all pagan ceremonies. The following year he terminated the eleven-hundred-year-old tradition of the Olympic Games, which had originated as religious rites but had become increasingly professionalized in Roman times.

Having a single ruler endowed with supreme legal and religious authority prevented the breakup of the Eastern Empire into petty principalities, but a series of territorial losses sapped the empire's strength. A strong emperor might temporarily recover lost ground, as Justinian (r. 527–565) did in seizing Tunisia from Germanic Vandal rulers and reasserting Byzantine control along the east coast of Italy, but military pressures seldom abated. A new Iranian empire ruled by the Sasanid family (see Chapter 8) threatened from the east in the fourth century. Various enemies, including the Germanic Goths and the nomadic Huns of Central Asia, threatened from the north at different periods. Bribes, diplomacy, and occasional military victories usually persuaded the Goths and Huns to settle peacefully or move on and attack western Europe. War with the Sasanids, however, flared up repeatedly for almost three hundred years. Finally, a new enemy appeared from the Arabian peninsula:

Map 10.1   The Spread of Christianity By the early eighth century, Christian areas around the southern Mediterranean from northern Syria to northern Spain, accounting for most of the Christian population, had fallen under Muslim rule; the slow process of conversion to Islam had begun. This accentuated the importance of the patriarchs of Constantinople, the popes in Rome, and the later converting regions of northern and eastern Europe. © Cengage Learning

Interactive Map

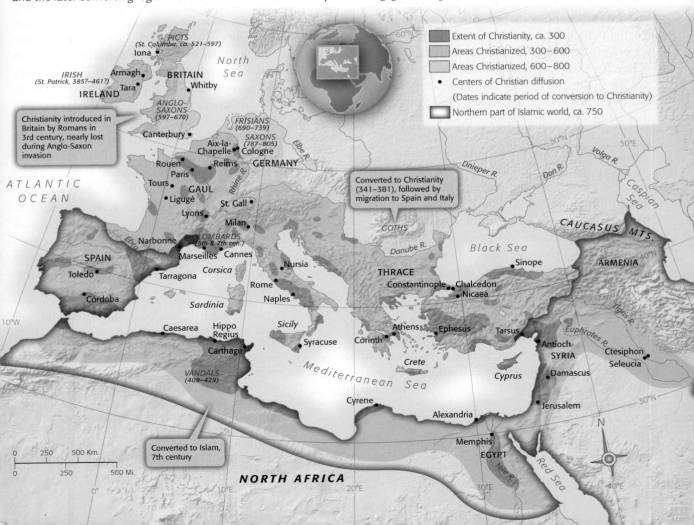

followers of the Arab prophet Muhammad (see Chapter 9). Between 634 and 650, Arab armies destroyed the Sasanid Empire and captured Byzantine Egypt, Syria, and Tunisia. By the end of the twelfth century, at least two-thirds of the Christians in these former Byzantine territories had adopted the Muslim faith.

The loss of such populous and prosperous provinces shook the empire and reduced its power. Although the empire had largely recovered and reorganized militarily by the tenth century, it never regained the lost lands and eventually succumbed to Muslim conquest in 1453. The later Byzantine emperors faced new enemies in the north and south. Following the wave of Germanic migrations, Slavic and Turkic peoples appeared on the northern frontiers as part of centuries-long population migrations in Eurasian steppe lands. Other Turks led by the Seljuk family became the primary foe in the south.

At the same time, relations with the popes and princes of western Europe steadily worsened. In the mid-ninth century the patriarchs of Constantinople had challenged the territorial jurisdiction of the popes of Rome and some of the practices of the Latin Church. These arguments worsened over time and in 1054 culminated in a formal schism between the Latin Church and the Orthodox Church—a break that has been only partially mended.

Society and Urban Life

Imperial authority and urban prosperity in the eastern provinces of the old Roman Empire initially sheltered Byzantium from the economic reverses and population losses western Europe suffered from the third century on. However, the territorial losses to Arab invaders coming on the heels of a devastating sixth-century epidemic of bubonic plague, known as "the plague of Justinian," gave Byzantium a taste of decline. Popular narratives of saints' lives show a transition from stories about educated saints hailing from cities to stories about saints who originated as peasants. In many areas, barter replaced money transactions; some cities declined in population and wealth; and the traditional class of local urban notables nearly disappeared.

As the urban elite shrank, high-ranking aristocrats at the imperial court and rural landowners gained importance. Power organized by family began

to rival power from class-based officeholding. By the end of the eleventh century, a family-based military aristocracy had emerged. Of Byzantine emperor Alexius Comnenus (uh-LEX-see-uhs kom-NAY-nuhs) (r. 1081–1118) it was said: "He considered himself not a ruler, but a lord, conceiving and calling the empire his own house."[3]

The situation of women changed, too. Although earlier Roman family life was centered on a legally all-powerful father, women enjoyed comparative freedom in public. After the seventh century women increasingly found themselves confined to the home. Some sources indicate that when they went out, they concealed their faces behind veils. Paradoxically, however, from 1028 to 1056 women ruled the Byzantine Empire alongside their husbands. The apparent increase in the seclusion of women resembles simultaneous developments in neighboring Islamic countries, but a firm linkage between them has yet to be found.

Economically, the Byzantine emperors continued the Late Roman inclination to set prices, organize grain shipments to the capital, and monopolize luxury goods like Tyrian purple cloth. Such government intervention may have slowed technological development and economic innovation. In the countryside, Byzantine farmers continued to use slow oxcarts and light scratch plows, which were efficient for many, but not all, soil types, long after farmers in western Europe had begun to adopt more efficient techniques.

Because Byzantium's Roman inheritance remained so much more intact than western Europe's, few people recognized the slow deterioration. Gradually, however, pilgrims and visitors from the west saw the reality beyond the awe-inspiring, incense-filled domes of cathedrals and beneath the glitter and silken garments of the royal court. An eleventh-century French visitor wrote:

> The city itself [Constantinople] is squalid and fetid and in many places harmed by permanent darkness, for the wealthy overshadow the streets with buildings and leave these dirty, dark places to the poor and to travelers; there murders and robberies and other crimes which love the darkness are committed. Moreover, since people live lawlessly in this city, which has ... almost as many thieves as poor men, a criminal knows neither fear nor shame, because crime is not punished by law and never entirely comes to light. In

every respect she exceeds moderation; for, just as she surpasses other cities in wealth, so too, does she surpass them in vice.[4]

A Byzantine contemporary, Anna Comnena, the brilliant daughter of Emperor Alexius Comnenus, expressed the view from the other side. She scornfully described a prominent churchman and philosopher who happened to be from Italy: "Italos . . . was unable with his barbaric, stupid temperament to grasp the profound truths of philosophy; even in the act of learning he utterly rejected the teacher's guiding hand, and full of temerity and barbaric folly, [believed] even before study that he excelled all others."[5]

Cultural Achievements

Justinian's collection of Roman laws endured far longer than his restoration of Byzantine rule in Italy and North Africa. At his command a team of seventeen legal scholars made a systematic compilation, in Latin, of a thousand years of Roman legal tradition. The *Corpus Juris Civilis* (*Body of Civil Law*), as it has been called since the sixteenth century, consisted of four sections: a general introduction and survey, a digest for lawyers and judges containing specific laws and quotations from well-known commentaries, a collection of imperial decrees since the time of the emperor Hadrian (r. 117–138), and another collection of recent decrees not previously collected. In the eleventh century a legal scholar named Irnerius (ca. 1055–ca. 1130) revived the study of this code (see below) at the University of Bologna (boe-LOAN-yuh) in Italy, and it subsequently became the basis of most modern European legal systems.

Constantinople's cathedral, the Hagia Sophia (AH-yah SOH-fee-uh) ("Sacred Wisdom"), also dates in its present form to the reign of Justinian and his influential wife, the empress Theodora. Its great dome became a hallmark of Byzantine architecture. Artistic creativity appeared in the design and ornamentation of other churches and monasteries as well. Byzantine religious art, featuring stiff but arresting images of holy figures against gold backgrounds, strongly influenced painting in western Europe down to the thirteenth century, and Byzantine musical traditions strongly affected the chanting employed in medieval Latin churches.

Other important Byzantine achievements date to the empire's long period of political decline. In the

SECTION REVIEW

- With Christianity as the state religion, the Byzantine Empire continued Roman imperial and legal traditions in the east.

- The empire faced political threats from the Arabs, crusaders, Slavs, and Turks and religious challenges from Islam and the Western Church.

- Plagues and invasions caused significant cultural and political shifts.

- Emperors continued Late Roman economic policies, and even Constantinople declined as a result.

- Byzantine civilization included notable achievements in art, architecture, music, and missionary work among the Slavs.

ninth century, two brothers named Cyril and Methodius embarked on a highly successful mission to the Slavs of Moravia (part of the modern Czech Republic). Like the Gothic bishop Ulfilas in the fourth century, they preached in the local language, and their followers perfected a writing system, called Cyrillic (sih-RIL-ik), that came to be used by Slavic Christians adhering to the Orthodox—that is, Byzantine—rite. Their careers also mark the beginning of a competition between the Greek and Latin forms of Christianity for the allegiance of the Slavs. The use today of the Cyrillic alphabet among the Russians and other Slavic peoples of Orthodox Christian faith, and of the Roman alphabet among the Poles, Czechs, and Croatians, testifies to this competition.

Early Medieval Europe, 600–1000

How did the culture of early medieval Europe develop in the absence of imperial rule?

The disappearance of the imperial legal framework that had persisted to the final days of the Western Roman Empire (see Chapter 6) and the rise of various kings, nobles, and chieftains changed the legal and political landscape of western Europe. In region after region, the family-based traditions of the Germanic peoples, which often fit local conditions better than previous practices, supplanted the edicts of the Roman emperors (see Map 10.2).

Map 10.2 Germanic Kingdoms Though German kings asserted authority over most of western Europe, German-speaking peoples were most numerous east of the Rhine River. In most other areas, Celtic languages such as Breton or languages derived from Latin predominated. Though the absolute number of Germanic settlers seems to have been fairly limited, the Germanic Anglo-Saxon tongue increasingly supplanted the Celtic Welsh and Scottish in Britain.

© Cengage Learning

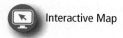 Interactive Map

Fear and physical insecurity led communities to seek the protection of local strongmen. In places where looters and pillagers might appear at any moment, a local lord with a castle in which peasants could take refuge counted for more than a distant king. Dependency of weak people on strong people became a hallmark of the post-Roman period in western Europe.

The Time of Insecurity

By 530 the Western Roman Empire had fragmented into a handful of dissimilar kingdoms under Germanic rulers. The Franks held much of Gaul, the Visigoths ruled in Spain, and the Ostrogoths ruled in Italy and present-day Austria and Hungary. By 600 the Lombards had replaced the Ostrogoths in northern Italy, and the Byzantine Empire had regained footholds in the south and around Ravenna along the east coast. The city of Rome lost most of its population and its political importance but retained prominence as the seat of the bishop of Rome. Local noble families competed for control of this position, which over several centuries acquired the title *pope* along with supreme power in the Latin-speaking church.

The educated few, most of them Christian priests and monks, spoke and wrote a simplified form of Latin, but the uneducated masses who had lived under Roman rule spoke Romance dialects that eventually became modern Portuguese, Spanish, French, Italian, and Romanian. In the north and east of the Rhine River, where Roman culture had scarcely penetrated, people spoke Germanic and related Scandinavian languages. East of the Elbe River, Slavic speakers formed a third major group. Whatever sense of unity Europe may have experienced under Roman rule gave way to strongly localized identities.

In 711 a frontier raiding party of Muslim Arabs and Berbers crossed the Strait of Gibraltar and defeated the Visigoths in Spain (see Chapter 9). After pushing the remaining Christian chieftains into the northern mountains, the Muslims moved on to France. They occupied much of the southern coast

Boatbuilding Scene from the Bayeux Tapestry Eleventh-century shipwrights prepare vessels for William of Norman-dy's invasion of England in 1066.

and penetrated as far north as Tours, less than 150 miles (240 kilometers) from the English Channel, before the Frankish leader Charles Martel, Charlemagne's grandfather, stopped their most advanced raiding party in 732 at the Battle of Tours.

Military effectiveness was key to the rise of the Carolingian (kah-roe-LIN-gee-uhn) family (from Latin *Carolus*, "Charles"), first as protectors of the Frankish kings, then as kings themselves under Charlemagne's father Pépin (r. 751–768), and finally with Charlemagne as emperors. Charlemagne's Carolingian Empire encompassed all of Gaul and parts of Germany and Italy. When Charlemagne's son Louis the Pious died, the Germanic tradition of splitting property among sons led to the Treaty of Verdun (843), which divided the empire into three parts. French-speaking in the west (France) and middle (Burgundy), and German-speaking in the east (Germany), the three regions never reunited (see Map 10.2). Nevertheless, the Carolingian economic system

based on landed wealth and a brief intellectual revival sponsored personally by Charlemagne—himself illiterate—provided a common heritage.

In 793, Viking sea raiders from Scandinavia attacked and plundered an English coastal monastery, the first of hundreds of similar raids. Local sources from France, the British Isles, and Muslim Spain reflect widespread dread of Viking warriors descending from multi-oared, dragon-prowed boats to pillage monasteries, villages, and towns. Versatile Vikings could both brave the stormy North Atlantic and maneuver up rivers. By the ninth century raiders from Denmark and Norway were harrying the British and French coasts while Varangians (va-RAN-gee-anz) (Swedes) pursued raiding and trading interests along the rivers of eastern Europe and Russia. In the 800s and 900s Viking captains organized the settlement of Iceland and Greenland, and, around the year 1000, they reached the northern tip of Newfoundland, which they called Vinland ("the land of grapevines").

Vikings long settled on lands they had seized in Normandy (in northwestern France) organized the most important and ambitious expeditions in terms of numbers of men and horses and long-lasting impact. William the Conqueror, the duke of Normandy, invaded England in 1066 and brought Anglo-Saxon

Primary Source: The Life of Charlemagne: The Emperor Himself Would you know Charlemagne if you saw him? Check out this description of the great man's appearance and habits.

domination of the island to an end. Other Normans (from "north men") attacked Muslim Sicily in the 1060s and, after thirty years of fighting, permanently severed it from the Muslim world.

A Self-Sufficient Economy

Archaeology and monastic records reveal a profound economic transformation that accompanied the Germanic political order. The new rulers cared little for the Romans' urban-based culture, which accordingly shrank in importance. Change was more rapid in some regions than others, but most cities lost population, or even became villages. Roman roads fell into disuse and disrepair. Small thatched houses sprang up beside abandoned villas, and marble public buildings became dilapidated. Paying for purchases in coin gave way to bartering goods and services. Trade across the Mediterranean largely dried up before the Arab conquests, but occasional shipments from North Africa and Syria continued to reach western ports.

Roman centralization had channeled the wealth and production of the empire to the capital, which in turn radiated Roman cultural styles and tastes to the provinces. As the new Germanic territorial lords found the riches of their own culture more appealing than those of Rome, local self-sufficiency became more important. The decline of literacy and other aspects of Roman life made room for the growth of Celtic and Germanic cultural traditions.

The northern diet featured beer, lard or butter, and bread made of barley, rye, or wheat, all supplemented by pork from herds of swine fed on forest acorns and beechnuts, and by game from the same forests. Nobles ate better than peasants, but even the peasant diet was reasonably balanced. The Roman diet based on wheat, wine, and olive oil persisted in the south. The average western European of the ninth century was probably better nourished than his or her descendants three hundred years later, when population increased and the nobles monopolized the resources of the forests.

In both north and south, self-sufficient farming estates known as **manors** became centers of agricultural production. Fearful farmers in the most vulnerable regions gave their lands to large landowners in return for political and physical protection. The warfare and instability of the post-Roman centuries made

unprotected country houses especially vulnerable to pillaging. Isolated by poor communications and lack of organized government, landowners depended on their own resources for survival. Many became warriors, maintained a force of armed men, or swore allegiance to landowners who had such a force.

A well-appointed manor possessed fields, gardens, grazing lands, fishponds, a mill, a church, workshops for making farm and household implements, and a village where the farmers dependent on the lord of the manor lived. Protection ranged from a ditch and wooden stockade to a stone wall surrounding a fortified keep (a stone building).

Manor life reflected personal status. Nobles and their families exercised almost unlimited power over their **serfs**—agricultural workers who belonged to the manor, tilled its fields, and owed other dues and obligations. Serfs could not leave the manor where they were born and attach themselves to another lord. Most peasants in England, France, and western Germany were unfree serfs in the tenth and eleventh centuries. In Bordeaux (bore-DOE), Saxony, and a few other regions, free peasantry survived based on the egalitarian social structure of the Germanic peoples during their period of migration. Outright slavery, the mainstay of the Roman economy (see Chapter 6), diminished as more and more peasants became serfs in return for a lord's protection. At the same time, taking prisoners to serve as slaves became less important as an object of warfare.

Early Medieval Society

Reversion to a self-sufficient economy limited the freedom and potential for personal achievement of most people, but an emerging class of nobles reaped great benefits. During the Germanic migrations and later among the Vikings of Scandinavia, men regularly answered the call to arms issued by war chiefs, to whom they swore allegiance. All

manor In medieval Europe, a large, self-sufficient landholding consisting of the lord's residence (manor house), outbuildings, peasant village, and surrounding land.
serf In medieval Europe, an agricultural laborer legally bound to a lord's property and obligated to perform set services for the lord.

Armored Knights in Battle This painting from around 1135 shows the armament of knights at the time of the Crusades. Chain mail, a helmet, and a shield carried on the left side protect the rider. The lance carried underarm and the sword are the primary weapons. Notice that riders about to make contact with lances have their legs straight and braced in the stirrups.   Pierpont Morgan Library/Art Resource, NY

Starting in the sixteenth century, it became common to refer to medieval Europe as a "feudal society" in which kings and lords gave land to "vassals" in return for sworn military support. By analyzing original records, more recent historians have discovered this to be an oversimplification. Relations between landholders and serfs and between lords and vassals differed too much from one place to another, and from one time to another, to fit together in anything resembling a system.

The German foes of the Roman legions had equipped themselves with helmets, shields, and swords, spears, or throwing axes. Most fought on foot. Horsemen, using stirrups first invented by Central Asian pastoralists around the first century C.E., were able to stand in the saddle and absorb the impact when their lances struck the enemy at full gallop. This type of warfare required grain-fed horses that were larger and heavier than the small, grass-fed animals of the Central Asian nomads. Thus agricultural Europe rather than the Eurasian steppelands produced the charges of armored knights that came to dominate the battlefield.

By the eleventh century, knights had come to dominate the battlefield. They wore an open-faced helmet and a long linen shirt, or hauberk (HAW-berk), studded with small metal disks (see Environment and Technology: Iron Production). A century later, knightly equipment commonly included a visored helmet that covered the head and neck and a hauberk of chain mail.

warriors shared in the booty gained from raiding. As settlement enhanced the importance of agricultural tasks, laying down the plow and picking up the sword at the chieftain's call became harder.

Those who continued to join the war parties included a growing number of horsemen. Mounted warriors became the central force of the Carolingian army. At first, fighting from horseback did not make a person either a nobleman or a landowner. By the tenth century, however, nearly constant warfare to protect land rights or support the claims of a lord brought about a gradual transformation in the status of the mounted warrior. At different rates in different areas, landholding became almost inseparable from military service.

Iron Production

Despite the collapse of the Roman economy, iron-working expanded throughout Europe. The iron swords of the Germans outperformed traditional Roman weapons, which became obsolete. The spreading use of armor also increased the demand for iron. Archaeologists have found extensive evidence of iron smelting well beyond the frontiers of the Roman Empire. Helg Island in a lake near Stockholm, Sweden, had a large walled settlement that relied entirely on iron trading. Discoveries of a Buddha from India and a christening spoon from Egypt, both datable to the sixth century C.E., indicate the range of these trade contacts. At Zelechovice in the Czech Republic remains of fifty "slag-pit" furnaces have been dated to the ninth century.

Most iron smelting was done on a small scale. Ore containing iron oxide was shoveled onto a charcoal fire in an open-air hearth pit. The carbon in the charcoal combined with the oxygen in the ore to form carbon dioxide gas. This left behind a soft glowing lump of iron called a "bloom." This bloom was then pounded on a stone to remove the remaining impurities, like sand and clay, before being turned over to the blacksmith for fabricating into swords or armor.

During the post-Roman centuries, smelters learned to build walls around the hearth pits and then to put domes and chimneys on them. The resulting "slag-pit" furnaces produced greater amounts of iron. They also consumed great amounts of wood. Twelve pounds of charcoal, made from about 25 pounds of wood, were needed to produce 1 pound of bloom iron, and about 3 pounds of useless slag. Though bellows were developed to force oxygen into the fire, temperatures in slag-pit furnaces never became high enough to produce molten metal.

Iron Smelting Two bellows blowing alternately provide a constant stream of air to the furnace. The man on the right pounds the bloom into bars or plates that a blacksmith will reheat and shape.

Noblewoman Directing Construction of a Church This picture of Berthe, wife of Girat de Rouissillion, acting as mistress of the works comes from a tenth-century manuscript that shows a scene from the ninth century. Wheelbarrows rarely appear in medieval building scenes.

More armor for knight and horse meant a greater financial outlay. Since land was the basis of wealth, a knight needed financial support from land revenues. Accordingly, kings began to reward armed service with grants of land from their own property. Lesser nobles with extensive properties built their own military retinues the same way. A grant of land in return for a pledge to provide military service was often called a **fief**. At first, kings granted fiefs to their noble followers, known as **vassals**, on a temporary basis. By the tenth century, most fiefs could be inherited as long as the specified military service continued to be provided. Kings and lords commanded the service of their vassals for only part of the year. Vassals could hold land from several different lords and owe loyalty to each one. Moreover, the allegiance that a vassal owed to one lord could entail military service to that lord's master in time of need.

A typical medieval realm—actual practices varied widely—consisted of lands directly owned by a king or a count and administered by royal officers. The king's or count's major vassals held and administered other lands, often the greater portion, in return for military service. These vassals, in turn, granted land to their own vassals. The lord of a manor rather than the king provided governance and justice locally. Members of the clergy, along with the extensive agricultural lands owned by monasteries and convents, fell under the jurisdiction of the church, which further limited the reach and authority of the monarch.

Noblewomen became enmeshed in this tangle of obligations as heiresses and as candidates for marriage. A man who married the widow or daughter of a lord with no sons could gain control of that lord's property. Marriage alliances affected entire kingdoms. Noble daughters and sons had little say in marriage matters; issues of land, power, and military service took precedence.

Nevertheless, a noblewoman could own land or administer her husband's estates when he was away at war. Nonnoble women usually worked alongside their menfolk, performing agricultural tasks such as

---

fief In medieval Europe, land granted in return for a sworn oath to provide specified military service.
vassal In medieval Europe, a sworn supporter of a king or lord committed to rendering specified military service to that king or lord.

SECTION REVIEW

- Post-Roman European society was marked by the prevalence of Germanic traditions and the dependency of the weak on the strong.

- The eighth century through the mid-eleventh was a period of great insecurity, with Charlemagne's empire providing short-lived stability.

- After the fall of the empire, technological sophistication and urban life declined, and self-sufficient manorialism dominated agriculture.

- The mounted warrior elite came to dominate a society shaped by the exchange of rights and obligations.

- Noblewomen were part of this exchange system, while nonnoble women worked alongside men.

communications, and political disorder posed formidable obstacles to unifying church standards and practices. Clerics in some parts of western Europe were still issuing prohibitions against the worship of rivers, trees, and mountains as late as the eleventh century. Church problems included lingering polytheism, lax enforcement of prohibitions against priests marrying, nepotism (giving preferment to close kin), and simony (selling ecclesiastical appointments, often to laymen). The persistence of the papacy in asserting its legal jurisdiction over clergy, combating polytheism and heretical beliefs, and calling on secular rulers to recognize the pope's authority constituted a rare force for unity and order in a time of disunity and chaos.

raking and stacking hay, shearing sheep, and picking vegetables. As artisans, women spun, wove, and sewed clothing. The Bayeux (bay-YUH) Tapestry, a piece of embroidery 230 feet (70 meters) long and 20 inches (51 centimeters) wide depicting William the Conqueror's invasion of England in 1066, was designed and executed entirely by women, though historians do not agree on who those women were.

The Western Church

What role did the Western Church play in the politics and culture of Europe?

Just as eastern European Christians followed the religious guidance of the patriarch of Constantinople, so did the pope wield authority over church affairs in western Europe. And while Orthodox missionaries spread Christianity among the Slavs, Catholic missionaries added territory to Christendom in the British Isles and the lands of the Germans.

In the west, when Roman nobles lost control of the **papacy**—the office of the pope—after the tenth century, it became a more powerful international office. Councils of bishops—which normally set rules called canons to regulate the priests and laypeople under their jurisdiction—became increasingly responsive to papal direction.

Nevertheless, regional disagreements over church regulations, shortages of educated clergy, difficult

Politics and the Church

The pope needed allies. Charlemagne's father Pepin was a strong supporter of the papacy. The relationship between kings and popes was tense, however, since both considered themselves ultimate authorities. In 962 the pope crowned the first "Holy Roman Emperor" (Charlemagne never held this full title). This designation of a secular political authority as the guardian of collective Christian interests proved more apparent than real. Essentially a loose confederation of German princes who named one of their own as emperor, the **Holy Roman Empire** had little influence west of the Rhine River.

Although the pope crowned the early Holy Roman Emperors, this did not signify political superiority. The law of the church (known as canon law because each law was called a canon) gave the pope exclusive legal jurisdiction over clergy and church property wherever located. But bishops who held land as vassals owed military support or other services and dues to kings and princes. The secular rulers demanded the power to appoint those bishops because that was the only way to guarantee fulfillment of their duties as vassals. The popes disagreed.

---

papacy The central administration of the Roman Catholic Church, of which the pope is the head.
Holy Roman Empire Loose federation of mostly German states and principalities, headed by an emperor elected by the princes. It lasted from 962 to 1806.

In the eleventh century, this conflict over the control of ecclesiastical appointments came to a head. Hildebrand (HILL-de-brand), an Italian monk, capped a career of reorganizing church finances when the cardinals (a group of senior bishops) meeting in Rome selected him to be Pope Gregory VII in 1073. His personal notion of the papacy (preserved among his letters) represented an extreme position, stating among other claims, that

§ The pope can be judged by no one;
§ The Roman church has never erred and never will err till the end of time;
§ The pope alone can depose and restore bishops;
§ He alone can call general councils and authorize canon law;
§ He can depose emperors;
§ He can absolve subjects from their allegiance;
§ All princes should kiss his feet.[6]

Such claims antagonized lords and monarchs, who had become accustomed to *investing*—that is, conferring a ring and a staff as symbols of authority on bishops and abbots in their domains. Historians apply the term **investiture controversy** to the medieval struggle between the church and the lay lords to control ecclesiastical appointments; the term also refers to the broader conflict of popes versus monarchs. When Holy Roman Emperor Henry IV defied Gregory's reforms, Gregory excommunicated him in 1076, thereby cutting him off from church rituals. Stung by the resulting decline in his influence, Henry stood barefoot in the snow for three days outside a castle in northern Italy waiting for Gregory, a guest there, to receive him. Henry's formal act of penance induced Gregory to forgive him and restore him to the church; but the reconciliation, an apparent victory for the pope, proved hollow. In 1078 Gregory deposed Henry but then had to flee from Rome to Salerno, where he died two years later.

A compromise was reached in 1122 at Worms, a town in Germany. In the Concordat of Worms, Emperor Henry V renounced his right to choose bishops and abbots or bestow spiritual symbols upon them. In return, Pope Calixtus II permitted the emperor to invest papally appointed bishops and abbots with any lay rights or obligations before their spiritual consecration. Such compromises did not fully solve the problem, but they reduced tensions between the two sides.

Assertions of royal authority triggered other conflicts as well. Though barely twenty when he became king of England in 1154, Henry II, a great-grandson of William the Conqueror, acted to strengthen the power of the Crown and weaken the nobility. He appointed traveling justices to enforce his laws and made juries, a holdover from traditional Germanic law, into powerful legal instruments. He also established the principle that criminal acts violated the "king's peace" and should be tried and punished in accordance with charges brought by the Crown instead of in response to charges brought by victims.

Henry had a harder time controlling the church. His closest friend and chancellor, or chief administrator, Thomas à Becket (ca. 1118–1170), lived the grand life of a courtier. In 1162 Henry persuaded Becket to become a priest and assume the position of archbishop of Canterbury, the highest church office in England. Becket agreed but cautioned that from then on he would act solely in the interest of the church. When Henry sought to try clerics accused of crimes in royal instead of ecclesiastical courts, Archbishop Thomas, now leading an austere and pious life, resisted. In 1170 four of Henry's knights, knowing that the king desired Becket's death, murdered the archbishop in Canterbury Cathedral. Their crime backfired, and an outpouring of sympathy caused Canterbury to become a major pilgrimage center. In 1173 the pope declared the martyred Becket a saint. Henry allowed himself to be publicly whipped twice in penance for the crime, his authority badly damaged.

Henry II's conflict with Thomas à Becket, like the Concordat of Worms, yielded no clear victor. The problem of competing legal traditions made political life in western Europe more complicated than in Byzantium. So-called feudal law, rooted in Germanic custom, gave supreme power to the king. Canon law, based on Roman precedent, visualized a single church

---

investiture controversy Dispute between the popes and the Holy Roman Emperors over who held ultimate authority over bishops in imperial lands.

with jurisdiction over all of western Christendom. In the eleventh century Roman civil law, contained in the *Corpus Juris Civilis*, added a third tradition.

Monasticism

Monasticism featured prominently in the religious life of almost all Christian lands. The origins of group monasticism lay in the eastern lands of the Roman Empire. Pre-Christian practices such as celibacy, continual devotion to prayer, and living apart from society (alone or in small groups) came together in Christian form in Egypt.

Monasticism in western Europe, however, normally involved groups of monks or nuns living together in organized communities. The person most responsible for introducing this practice to the Latin west was Benedict of Nursia (ca. 480–547) in Italy. Benedict began his pious career as a hermit in a cave but eventually organized several monasteries, each headed by an abbot. In the seventh century monasteries based on his model spread far beyond Italy. The Rule of Benedict, written to govern the monks' behavior, envisions a balance between devotion and work, along with obligations of celibacy, poverty, and obedience to the abbot. Those who lived by this or other monastic rules became *regular clergy*, in contrast to *secular clergy*, priests who lived in society instead of in seclusion. The Rule of Benedict was the starting point for most forms of western European monastic life and remains in force today in Benedictine monasteries.

Though monks and nuns (women who lived by monastic rules in convents) constituted a small percentage of the total population, their secluded way of life reinforced the separation of religious affairs from ordinary politics and economics. Monasteries followed Jesus's axiom to "render unto Caesar what is Caesar's and unto God what is God's" better than the many town-based bishops who behaved like lords.

SECTION REVIEW

- In western Europe, the papacy became the most powerful international institution and thus a source of cultural unity.
- Popes sought secular allies by engaging the support of kings and conferring the title "Holy Roman Emperor."
- Pope Gregory VII asserted papal primacy and touched off the investiture controversy with the Holy Roman Empire.
- Although the Concordat of Worms resolved the controversy, conflicts between secular and papal authority continued.
- Western monasticism originated with Benedict of Nursia, and monasteries and convents became important cultural centers.
- Failing monastic discipline led to the Cluniac and Cistercian reform movements.

Monasteries preserved literacy and learning in the early medieval period, although some rulers, like Charlemagne, encouraged scholarship at court. Regular clergy saw copying manuscripts and even writing books as a religious calling, thereby preserving many Roman works that would otherwise have disappeared. The survival of Greek works depended more on Byzantine and Muslim scribes in the east.

Monasteries could plant Christianity in new lands, as Irish monks did in parts of Germany, service the needs of travelers, organize agricultural production on their lands, and raise abandoned infants. Convents provided refuge for widows and other women who lacked male protection or desired a spiritual life. Yet oversight was a problem. A bishop might have authority over an abbot or abbess (head of a convent), but he could not exercise constant vigilance over what went on behind monastery walls.

monasticism Living in a religious community apart from secular society and adhering to a rule stipulating chastity, obedience, and poverty. It was a prominent element of medieval Christianity and Buddhism. Monasteries were the primary centers of learning and literacy in early medieval Europe.

A reform movement focused on monastic discipline took shape in the Benedictine abbey of Cluny (KLOO-nee) in eastern France. William the Pious, the first duke of Aquitaine, founded Cluny in 910 and freed it of lay authority. A century later the local bishop conferred similar freedom. Cluny's abbots pursued a vigorous campaign, eventually allying with reforming popes like Gregory VII to improve monastic discipline and administration. A magnificent new abbey church—with later additions, the largest in the world—symbolized Cluny's preeminence.

At the peak of Cluny's influence, nearly a thousand Benedictine abbeys and priories (lower-level monastic houses) in various countries accepted the authority of its abbot. The Benedictine Rule made each monastery independent; but the Cluniac reformers stipulated that every abbot and prior (head of a priory) be appointed by the abbot of Cluny and have personal experience of the religious life of Cluny. Monastic reform gained new impetus in the second half of the twelfth century with the rapid rise of the Cistercian order, which emphasized a life of asceticism and poverty.

Kievan Russia, 900–1200

What was the significance of the adoption of Orthodox Christianity by Kievan Russia?

Though Latin and Orthodox Christendom later followed different paths, which would flourish more was not apparent in 900. Many Slavs living in the north eventually accepted the Catholicism of Rome as taught by German missionaries. The Serbs and other southern Slavs took their faith from Constantinople.

The conversion of Kievan Russia, farther to the east, shows how economics, politics, and religious life were closely intertwined. The choice of Orthodoxy over Catholicism had important consequences for later European history.

The Rise of the Kievan Empire

The territory between the Black and Caspian Seas in the south and the Baltic and White Seas in the north divides into a series of east-west zones. Frozen tundra in the far north gives way to a cold forest zone, then to a more temperate forest, then to a mix of forest and steppe grasslands, and finally to grassland only. Several navigable rivers, including the Volga, the Dnieper (d-NYEP-er), and the Don, run from north to south across these zones.

Early historical sources reflect repeated linguistic and territorial changes, seemingly under pressure from population migrations. Most of the Germanic peoples, along with some Iranian and west Slavic peoples, migrated into eastern Europe from Ukraine and Russia in Roman times. The peoples who remained behind spoke eastern Slavic languages, except in the far north and south: Finns and related peoples lived in the former region, Turkic-speakers in the latter.

Forest dwellers, farmers, and steppe nomads complemented each other economically. Nomads traded animals for the farmers' grain; and honey, wax, and furs from the forest became important exchange items. Traders could travel east and west by steppe caravan (see Chapter 8), or they could use boats on the rivers to move north and south.

Hoards containing thousands of Byzantine and Islamic coins buried in Poland and on islands in the Baltic Sea where fairs were held attest to the trading activity of Varangians (Swedish Vikings) who sailed across the Baltic and down Russia's rivers. They exchanged forest products and slaves for manufactured goods and coins, which they may have used as jewelry rather than as money, at markets controlled by the Khazar Turks, whose powerful kingdom centered around the mouth of the Volga River.

Historians debate the early meaning of the word *Rus* (from which *Russia* is derived), but at some point it came to refer to Slavic-speaking peoples ruled by Varangians. Unlike western European lords, the Varangian princes and their *druzhina* (military retainers) lived in cities, while the Slavs farmed. The princes occupied themselves with trade and fending off enemies. The Rus of the city of Kiev (KEE-yev), which was taken over by Varangians in 882, controlled trade on the Dnieper River and dealt more with Byzantium than with the Muslim world because the Dnieper flows into the Black Sea. The Rus of Novgorod (NOHV-goh-rod) played the same role on the Volga. The semilegendary account of the Kievan Rus conversion to Christianity must be seen against this background.

Baptism of Vladimir I In 988 Vladimir I, the ruler of Kiev, opted to convert to the Greek Orthodox form of Christianity. This portrayal of the event in a Greek manuscript may be largely invented, but it is probably realistic in showing the full immersion of the king in the baptismal font.

In 980 Vladimir (VLAD-ih-mir) I, a ruler of Novgorod who had fallen from power, returned to Kiev with a band of Varangians and made himself the grand prince of Kievan Russia (see Map 10.3). Though his grandmother Olga had been a Christian, Vladimir built a temple on Kiev's heights and placed there the statues of the six gods his Slavic subjects worshiped. The earliest Russian chronicle reports that Vladimir and his advisers decided against Islam as the official religion because of its ban on alcohol, rejected Judaism (the religion to which the Khazars had converted) because they thought that a truly powerful god would not have let the ancient Jewish kingdom be destroyed, and even spoke with German emissaries advocating Latin Christianity. Why Vladimir chose Orthodox Christianity over the Latin version is not precisely known. The magnificence of Constantinople seems to have been a consideration. After visiting Byzantine churches, his agents reported: "We knew not whether we were in heaven or on earth, for on earth there is no such splendor of [sic] such beauty, and we are at a loss how to describe it. We know only that God dwells there among men, and their service is finer than the ceremonies of other nations."[7]

After choosing a reluctant bride from the Byzantine imperial family, Vladimir converted to Orthodox Christianity, probably in 988, and opened his lands to Orthodox clerics and missionaries. The patriarch of Constantinople appointed a metropolitan (chief bishop) at Kiev to govern ecclesiastical affairs. Churches arose in Kiev, one of them on the ruins of Vladimir's earlier hilltop temple. Writing was introduced, using the Cyrillic alphabet devised earlier for the western Slavs. This extension of Orthodox Christendom northward provided a barrier against the eastward expansion of Latin Christianity. Kiev became firmly oriented toward trade with Byzantium and turned its back on the Muslim world, though the Volga trade continued through Novgorod.

Struggles within the ruling family and with other enemies, most notably the steppe peoples of the south, marked the later political history of Kievan Russia. But down to the time of the Mongols in the thirteenth century (see Chapter 11), the state remained and served as an instrument for the Christianization of the eastern Slavs.

Society and Culture

In Kievan Russia political power derived from trade rather than from landholding, so the manorial agricultural system of western Europe never developed. Farmers practiced shifting cultivation of their own lands. They would burn a section of forest, then lightly scratch the ash-strewn surface with a plow. When fertility waned, they would move to another section of forest. Poor land and a short growing season in the most northerly latitudes made food scarce. Living on their own estates, the druzhina evolved from infantry into cavalry and focused their efforts more on horse breeding than on agriculture.

Large cities like Kiev and Novgorod may have reached 30,000 or 50,000 people—roughly the size of contemporary London or Paris, but far smaller than Constantinople or major Muslim metropolises like Baghdad and Nishapur. Many cities amounted to little more than fortified trading posts. Yet they served as centers for the development of crafts, some, such as glassmaking, based on skills imported from Byzantium. Artisans enjoyed higher status in society than peasant farmers. Construction relied on wood from

Map 10.3   Kievan Russia and the Byzantine Empire in the Eleventh Century
By the mid-eleventh century, the princes of Kievan Russia had brought all the eastern Slavs under their rule. The loss of Egypt, Syria, and Tunisia to Arab invaders in the seventh to eighth century had turned Byzantium from a far-flung empire into a fairly compact state. From then on the Byzantine rulers looked to the Balkans and Kievan Russia as the primary arena for extending their political and religious influence.   © Cengage Learning

 Interactive Map

the forests, although Christianity brought the building of stone cathedrals and churches on the Byzantine model.

Christianity penetrated the general population slowly. Several polytheist uprisings occurred in the eleventh century, particularly in times of famine. Passive resistance led some groups to reject Christian burial and persist in cremating the dead and keeping the bones of the deceased in urns. Women continued to use polytheist designs on their clothing and bracelets, and as late as the twelfth century they were still turning to polytheist priests for charms to cure sick children. Traditional Slavic marriage practices involving casual and polygamous relations particularly scandalized the clergy.

Christianity eventually triumphed, and its success led to increasing church engagement in political and economic affairs. In the twelfth century, Christian clergy became involved in government administration, some of them collecting fees and taxes related to trade. Direct and indirect revenue from trade provided the rulers with the money they needed to pay their soldiers. The rule of law also spread as Kievan Russia experienced its peak of culture and prosperity in the century before the Mongol invasion of 1237.

Western Europe Revives, 1000–1200

How did Mediterranean trade help revive western Europe?

Between 1000 and 1200 western Europe slowly emerged from nearly seven centuries of subsistence economy. Population and agricultural production climbed, and a growing food surplus found its way to town markets, speeding the return of a money-based economy and providing support for larger numbers of craftspeople, construction workers, and traders.

Historians have attributed western Europe's revival to population growth spurred by new technologies and to the appearance in Italy and Flanders, on the coast of the North Sea, of self-governing cities devoted primarily to seaborne trade. For monarchs, the changes facilitated improvements in central administration, greater control over vassals, and consolidation of realms on the way to becoming stronger kingdoms.

The Role of Technology

A lack of concrete evidence confirming the spread of technological innovations frustrates efforts to relate revival to technological change. Nevertheless, most historians agree that technology played a significant role in the near doubling of the population of western Europe between 1000 and 1200. The population of England seems to have risen from 1.1 million in 1086 to 1.9 million in 1200, and the population of the territory of modern France seems to have risen from 5.2 million to 9.2 million over the same period.

The history of plows and draft harnesses illustrates the difficulty of drawing historical conclusions from scattered evidence. Farmers in southern Europe and Byzantium continued to use the Roman plow, which scratched shallow grooves into loose, dry Mediterranean soils. But a new plow cut deep into the soil with a knifelike blade, while a curved board mounted behind the blade lifted the cut layer and turned it over, making it possible to farm the heavy, wet clays of the northern river valleys. This required more energy, which meant harnessing several teams of oxen or horses.

Horses plowed faster than oxen but were more demanding. Iron horseshoes, which were widely adopted in this period, helped protect their hooves, but like the plow itself, they added to the farmer's expenses. Roman horse harnesses put such pressure on the animal's throat that a horse pulling a heavy load risked strangulation. A mystery surrounds the adoption of more efficient designs. The **horse collar**, which moves the point of traction from the animal's throat to its shoulders, first appeared around 800 in a miniature painting, and it is shown clearly as a harness for plow horses in the Bayeux Tapestry, embroidered after 1066. The simpler breast-strap harness, appearing around 500, was not as suitable for the heaviest work but was preferred in southern Europe.

horse collar Harnessing method that increased the efficiency of horses by shifting the point of traction from the animal's neck to the shoulders; its adoption favors the spread of horse-drawn plows and vehicles.

In both cases, linguists have traced key technical terms to Chinese or Turko-Mongol words and have argued for an eastern origin. Yet third-century Roman farmers in Tunisia and Libya used both types of harness to hitch horses and camels to plows and carts. This technology, which is still employed in Tunisia, appears clearly on Roman bas-reliefs and lamps; but there is no more evidence of its movement northward into Europe than there is of similar harnessing moving across Asia. Thus the question of where efficient harnessing came from and whether it began in 500 or in 800 or was known even earlier but not extensively used, cannot be easily resolved.

Hinging on this problem is the question of when and why landowners in northern Europe began to use teams of horses to pull plows through soils that were too heavy for teams of oxen. Horses increased productivity by reducing the time needed for plowing, but they cost more to feed and equip. Thus, it is difficult to say that one technology was always better. Agricultural surpluses did grow and better plowing did play a role in this growth, but areas that continued to use oxen and even old-style plows shared in the general population growth of the period.

Cities and the Rebirth of Trade

Independent cities governed and defended by communes appeared first in Italy and Flanders and then elsewhere. Communes were groups of leading citizens who banded together to defend their cities and demand the privilege of self-government from their lay or ecclesiastical lord. Lords who granted such privileges benefited from the commune's economic dynamism. Lacking extensive farmlands, these cities enacted laws to encourage manufacturing and trade. Cities in Italy that had shrunk within walls built by the Romans now pressed against those walls, forcing the construction of new ones. Pisa, for example, built a new wall in 1000 and expanded it in 1156.

Islands at the northern end of the Adriatic Sea had been largely uninhabited in Roman times. Now settlers organized themselves into the city of Venice. In the eleventh century it became the dominant sea power in the Adriatic, competing with Pisa and Genoa, on the western side of Italy, for leadership in

SECTION REVIEW

- Between 1000 and 1200, western Europe experienced economic and political revivals.
- Populations grew throughout Europe, stimulated in part by new agricultural methods and technologies.
- Independent cities emerged and grew into trade and manufacturing centers.
- Long-distance trade, dominated by Italian cities, resumed throughout the Mediterranean area.
- Flemish cities dominated the fishing and wool trades of the North Sea region.
- Extensive coinage signaled the return of a money-based economy.

trade with Muslim ports. One merchant's list mentions trade in some three thousand "spices" (including dyestuffs, textile fibers, and raw materials), some of them products of Muslim lands and some coming via the Silk Road or the Indian Ocean trading system (see Chapter 8). Among them were eleven types of alum (for dyeing), eleven types of wax, eight types of cotton, four types of indigo, five types of ginger, four types of paper, and fifteen types of sugar. By the time of the Crusades (see below), European commerce depended heavily on Italian ships.

Ghent, Bruges (broozh), and Ypres (EEP-r) in Flanders rivaled the Italian cities in prosperity and trade. Granted privileges by the counts of Flanders, these cities dominated the fishing and wool industries of the North Sea region. Around 1200 raw wool from England began to be woven into cloth for a very large market.

Coinage also signaled the upturn in economic activity. In the ninth and tenth centuries most gold coins had come from Muslim lands and the Byzantine Empire. Worth too much for most trading purposes, they seldom reached Germany, France, and England. The widely imitated Carolingian silver penny sufficed. With economic revival in the twelfth century came the minting of silver coins in Scandinavia, Poland, and other outlying regions. In the following century the Italian cities followed with a new and abundant gold coinage.

Courtesy, Master and Fellows of Trinity College, Cambridge, Ms. R17.I.f.260 (detail)

Vertical Two-Beam Loom These women weavers set up their loom out of doors. The vertical strands are the warp threads around which the weft is interwoven. The pole across the bottom of the loom holds the warp threads taut. The kneeling weaver holds a beater to compact the weft at the loom's bottom. In Europe, horizontal looms were more common and paved the way for the mechanization of weaving.

The Crusades, 1095–1204

What were the origins and impact of the Crusades?

Revival coincided with and contributed to the **Crusades**, a series of religiously inspired Christian military campaigns against Muslims in the eastern Mediterranean. Four great expeditions between 1095 and 1204 (see Chapter 9), the last redirected against Constantinople, which the Catholic knights looted, constituted the region's largest military undertakings since the fall of Rome. As a result of the Crusades, noble courts and burgeoning cities in western Europe consumed more goods from the east and later adopted ideas, artistic styles, and industrial processes from the lands of Islam.

The Roots of the Crusades

Several social and economic currents of the eleventh century contributed to the Crusades. First, church reformers seeking to soften warlike habits popularized the Truce of God, a movement to limit

Crusades (1095–1204) Armed pilgrimages to the Holy Land by Christians determined to recover Jerusalem from Muslim rule. The Crusades brought an end to western Europe's centuries of intellectual and cultural isolation.

fighting between Christian lords by specifying times of truce, such as during Lent (the forty days before Easter) and on Sundays. Many knights welcomed a religiously approved alternative to fighting other Christians. Second, ambitious rulers, like the Norman chieftains who invaded Sicily, were looking for new lands to conquer. Nobles, particularly younger sons in areas where the oldest son inherited everything, were hungry for land and titles. Third, Italian merchants wanted trading posts in Muslim territory. Without the rivalry between popes and kings and without the desire of the church to demonstrate its political authority, the Crusades might never have occurred.

Several factors focused attention on the Holy Land, which had been under Muslim rule for four centuries. **Pilgrimages** played an important role in European religious life. In western Europe, pilgrims traveled under royal protection. Some were actually thieves, beggars, and peddlers, but genuinely pious pilgrims thronged to visit old churches and sacred relics. Rome and Constantinople were favored destinations, but the most intrepid went on to Jerusalem and Antioch to fulfill a vow or atone for a sin.

Pilgrims who crossed northern Spain to pray at the shrine of Santiago de Compostela learned of exploits of Christian kings fighting the Muslims to the south. The Umayyad Caliphate in al-Andalus had broken up in the eleventh century, leaving its smaller successor states prey to Christian attacks from the north (see Chapter 9). The word *crusade*, taken from Latin *crux* for "cross," was first used in Spain. Pilgrims returning from Palestine urged both churchmen and nobles to consider the Muslims a proper target for Christian arms. Muslim rulers generally tolerated and protected Christian pilgrims, but after 1071, when the Seljuks defeated the Byzantines at Manzikert (see Chapter 9), security along the pilgrimage route through Anatolia, already none too good, deteriorated further.

Despite the theological differences between the Orthodox and Catholic churches, the Byzantine emperor Alexius Comnenus asked the pope and western European rulers for help against the Muslims. Pope Urban II responded at the Council of Clermont in 1095. He addressed a huge crowd of people gathered in a field and called on them, as Christians, to stop fighting one another and go to the Holy Land to fight Muslims.

"God wills it!" exclaimed voices in the crowd. People cut cloth into crosses and sewed them on their shirts to symbolize their willingness to march on Jerusalem. Thus began the First Crusade, though people at the time more often used the word *peregrinatio*, "pilgrimage." Urban promised to free crusaders who had committed sins from their normal penance, or acts of atonement, the usual reward for peaceful pilgrims to Jerusalem.

The First Crusade captured Jerusalem in 1099 and established four crusader principalities, the most important being the Latin Kingdom of Jerusalem. The next two expeditions strove with diminishing success to protect these gains. Muslim forces retook Jerusalem in 1187. By the time of the Fourth Crusade in 1204, the original religious ardor had so diminished that the commanders agreed, at the urging of the Venetians, to sack Constantinople first to defray the cost of transporting the army by ship.

The Impact of the Crusades

Exposure to Muslim culture in Spain, Sicily, and the crusader principalities awakened Europeans to things that were lacking in their own lives. Borrowings from Muslim society occurred gradually and are not always easy to date, but Europeans began to produce pasta, paper, refined sugar, colored glass, and many other formerly exotic items.

Primary Source: Nicetas Choniates: *Annales*
Read a strange tale of heartlessness in battle.

pilgrimage Journey to a sacred shrine by Christians seeking to show their piety, fulfill vows, or gain absolution for sins. Other religions also have pilgrimage traditions, such as the Muslim pilgrimage to Mecca and the pilgrimages made by early Chinese Buddhists to India in search of sacred Buddhist writings.

SECTION REVIEW

- The Crusades coincided with and fueled the western European revival.

- Several religious, political, and economic factors prompted the Crusades, the most immediate of which was the decline of Byzantine power under Seljuk pressure.

- Responding to Byzantine calls for aid, Pope Urban II proclaimed the First Crusade in 1095.

- As a result of the Crusades, western Europeans gradually absorbed Muslim technological and intellectual achievements.

- Contact with Muslim culture affected the elite most immediately by shaping court life and the troubadour tradition of courtly love.

Greek philosophical and scientific writings and equally important works by Arabs and Iranians were translated into Latin with powerful effect. Some manuscripts came from conquered territory: Sicily, Spain, the Holy Land, and Constantinople. For others, translators worked in parts of Spain still under Muslim rule. Generations passed before all these works were studied and understood, but they eventually transformed the intellectual world of the western Europeans.

Changes in noble lifestyle took place more quickly. Eleanor of Aquitaine (1122–1204), the most influential woman of the crusading era, accompanied her husband, King Louis VII of France, on the Second Crusade (1147–1149). The court life of her uncle Raymond, who ruled the crusader principality of Antioch, particularly appealed to her. Once back in France, a lack of male offspring led to an annulment of her royal marriage, and she married Henry of Anjou instead. Three years later in 1154 he inherited the throne of England as Henry II. Eleanor's sons Richard Lion-Heart, famed as the chivalrous foe of Saladin during the Third Crusade (1189–1192), and John rebelled against their father but eventually succeeded him as kings of England. In Aquitaine, a powerful duchy in southern France, Eleanor maintained her own court for a time. Poet-singers called troubadours enjoyed her favor and made her court a center

for music based on the idea of "courtly love," an idealization of feminine beauty and grace that influenced later European ideas of romance. Surviving troubadour melodies show the influence of poetry styles then current in Muslim Spain. The favorite troubadour instrument, moreover, was the lute, a guitarlike instrument with a bulging shape whose design and name (Arabic *al-ud*) come from Muslim Spain.

Conclusion

The division of the Roman Empire by Constantine into an eastern and a western branch marked Europe from that time on. When the Western Roman Empire collapsed, the Germanic tribes that settled on its territory formed numerous competing kingdoms and principalities. For several centuries, the only unifying factor was the Catholic Church, which provided intellectual and some administrative continuity with the vanished Roman Empire. Secular authorities, however, arose to contest the political authority of the church. Thus, western Europe remained divided among competing states and power centers. After the Viking invasions tapered off in the late tenth century, the economy, culture, and population of western Europe showed a new dynamism that spread to areas of northern Europe that the Romans had never reached. It also carried over into expansionism overseas, against the Muslims of the Levant and against Constantinople itself.

Eastern Europe evolved very differently, under the influence of Constantinople. Though it lost many provinces, the Eastern Roman Empire was not overrun by barbarians as the west had been, but retained its imperial structure for another thousand years. Though Christianity replaced all earlier religions as it did in the west, it was in the form of the Orthodox Church, a subordinate branch of the imperial Byzantine government, rather than an independent and competing organization like the Catholic Church in the west. As northeastern Europe filled in after the Viking raiders settled down to trade and build cities, its peoples adopted the Orthodox form of Christianity and with it the subordination of church to state that prevailed in the Byzantine Empire.

CHAPTER REVIEW

 Download the MP3 audio file of the Chapter Review to listen to on the go.

How did the Byzantine Empire maintain Roman imperial traditions in the east? (page 234)

Divergent ecclesiastical practices paralleled a political separation that dated from the fourth-century division of the Roman Empire into an eastern portion, the Byzantine Empire ruled from Constantinople, and a western portion that became increasingly fragmented as warlike Germanic peoples assumed more and more control. For the east, the collection and analysis of imperial laws symbolized continuing imperial rule. The emperor also assumed control over the Christian church.

How did the culture of early medieval Europe develop in the absence of imperial rule? (page 239)

In the west, the heritage of Rome consisted more in the elite use of Latin and the popular rise of Romance languages. The Roman Empire became more and more a shared memory as great buildings decayed into ruins. This memory, however, could be used as a basis of political power, as the rule of Charlemagne demonstrates. After Charlemagne's death, Viking invasions continued to disrupt European life, but their migrations laid the foundations of powerful states in Russia and Normandy. Although some long-distance trade continued, poor infrastructure and the absence of centralized authority led to the rise of a self-sufficient economy based on the manor. The lords and warriors who protected serfs became a mounted military elite that dominated the system of rights and obligations loosely termed "feudalism."

What role did the Western Church play in the politics and culture of Europe? (p. 246)

Unlike the Eastern Church, where the emperor played a dominating role, the bishops and abbots who spoke for western Christendom sought complete control of both the political and the social realm. They ultimately came into conflict with kings and dukes who resented these claims to power, but the lower ranks of society became increasingly immersed in a Christian culture based on respect for the clergy.

What was the significance of the adoption of Orthodox Christianity by Kievan Russia? (page 249)

The Eastern and Western Churches competed in converting the Slavic peoples. The Poles became Roman Catholics, while the Russians established their own Orthodox Church on the Byzantine pattern. Since the rulers of Kiev were of Scandinavian origin like the Norman rulers of northern France, England, and Sicily, there was potentially a basis for continuing interconnections across northern Europe. The decision to follow the Byzantine form of Christianity eliminated that possibility and raised a barrier between Russia and western Europe that lasted for centuries.

How did Mediterranean trade help revive western Europe? (p. 252)

Byzantium and Russia did not share in the revival of western Europe that began during a period of unprecedented borrowing from the Islamic world. During the twelfth and thirteenth centuries European intellectual life enjoyed the stimulus of scientific and philosophical ideas translated from Arabic into Latin. Shortly thereafter, Muslim manufacturing practices, such as glassmaking and papermaking, and popular pastimes, such as chess and lute playing, began to change European culture. Improved communications provided by Italian seafarers played a crucial role in spreading these new ideas into western Europe.

What were the origins and impact of the Crusades?
(page 254)

The Crusades originated as armed pilgrimages aimed at restoring Christian control in the Holy Land. Though the states the crusaders created were short-lived, the experiences of the crusaders living in the Middle East fostered a wider knowledge of the world and a taste for a more refined style of life. Thus the Crusades, in addition to creating a military confrontation with Islam, also contributed to the reinvigoration of culture in western Europe.

Key Terms

Charlemagne *(p. 234)*

medieval *(p. 234)*

Byzantine Empire *(p. 234)*

Kievan Russia *(p. 234)*

schism *(p. 236)*

manor *(p. 242)*

serf *(p. 242)*

fief *(p. 245)*

vassal *(p. 245)*

papacy *(p. 246)*

Holy Roman Empire *(p. 246)*

investiture controversy
    (p. 247)

monasticism *(p. 248)*

horse collar *(p. 252)*

Crusades *(p. 254)*

pilgrimage *(p. 255)*

Web Resources

Pronunciation Guide
Interactive Maps
- MAP 10.1 The Spread of Christianity
- MAP 10.2 Germanic Kingdoms
- MAP 10.3 Kievan Russia and the Byzantine Empire in the Eleventh Century

Primary Sources
- The Life of Charlemagne: The Emperor Himself
- The Rule of Saint Benedict: Work and Pray
- Nicetas Choniates: *Annales*

Answer to the History in Focus Question
See photo on page 236, "Byzantine Church from a Twelfth-Century Manuscript."

Visit the CourseMate website at www.cengagebrain.com for additional study tools and review materials for this chapter.

Inner and East Asia

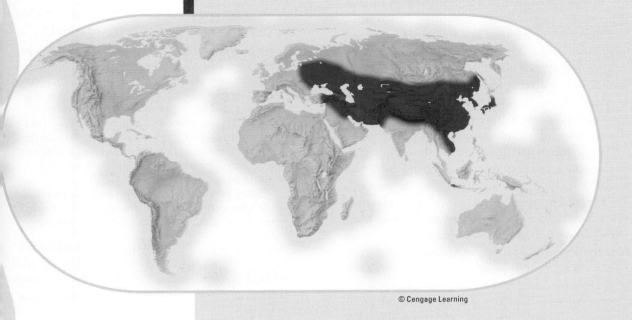

© Cengage Learning

Visit the CourseMate website at **www.cengagebrain.com** for additional study tools and review materials for this chapter.

The powerful and expansive Tang Empire (618–907) ended four centuries of rule by short-lived and competing states that had left China in turmoil after the fall of the Han Empire in 220 C.E. (see Chapter 6). Tang rule also encouraged the spread of Buddhism, brought by missionaries from India and by Chinese pilgrims returning with sacred Sanskrit texts. The Tang left an indelible mark on the Chinese imagination long after it too fell. In southern China, it was succeeded by the Song (soong) Empire.

According to surviving memoirs, Song people watched shadow plays and puppet shows, listened to music and scholarly lectures, or took in less edifying spectacles like wrestling and bear baiting in urban entertainment quarters. From the 1170s onward, singer-storytellers spun long romantic narratives that alternated prose passages with sung verse. Master Tung's *Western Chamber Romance* stood out for its literary quality. In 184 prose passages and 5,263 lines of verse the narrator tells of a love affair between Chang, a young Confucian scholar, and Ying-ying, a ravishing damsel. Secondary characters include Ying-ying's shrewd and worldly mother, a general who practices just and efficient administration, and a fighting monk named Fa-ts'ung (fa-soong). The romance is based on *The Story of Ying-ying* by the Tang period author Yuan Chen (you-ahn shen) (779–831).

As the tale begins, the abbot of a Buddhist monastery responds to Chang's request to rent him a study, singing:

> Sir, you're wrong to offer me rent.
> We Buddhists and Confucians are of one family.
> As things stand, I can't give you
> A place in our dormitory,
> But you're welcome to stay
> In one of the guest apartments.

As soon as Chang spies Ying-ying, who lives there with her mother, thoughts of studying flee his mind. Romance takes a detour, however, when bandits attack the monastery, frightening the monks. A prose passage explains:

> During the T'ang dynasty, troops were stationed in the P'u prefecture. The year of our story, the commander of the garrison, Marshal Hun, died.

Because the second-in-command, Ting Wen-ya, did not have firm control of the troops, Flying Tiger Sun, a subordinate general, rebelled with five thousand soldiers. They pillaged and plundered the P'u area. How do I know this to be true? It is corroborated by *The Ballad of the True Story of Ying-ying*.

As the frightened monks dither, one of them lifts his robe to reveal his "three-foot consecrated sword."

> [Prose] Who was this monk? He was none other than Fa-ts'ung. Fa-ts'ung was a descendant of a tribesman from western Shensi. When he was young he took great pleasure in archery, fencing, hunting, and often sneaked into foreign states to steal. He was fierce and courageous. When his parents died, it suddenly became clear to him that the way of the world was frivolous and trivial, so he became a monk in the Temple of Universal Salvation. . . .
>
> [Song] He didn't know how to read sutras; He didn't know how to follow rituals; He was neither pure nor chaste but indomitably courageous . . . [1]

Amidst the love story, the ribaldry, and the derring-do, the author implants historical vignettes that mingle fact and fiction. Sophisticates of the Song era, living a life of ease, enjoyed these romanticized portrayals of Tang society.

The Sui and Tang Empires, 581–755

What was the importance of Inner and Central Asia as a region of interchange during the Tang period?

The reunification of China took place under the Sui (sway) dynasty, father and son rulers who held sway from 581 until Turks from Inner Asia (the part of the Eurasian steppe east of the Pamir Mountains) defeated the son in 615. He was assassinated three years later, and the Tang filled the political vacuum.

The small kingdoms of northern China and Inner Asia that had come and gone during the centuries

---

1. From *Master Tung's Western Chamber Romance*, translated by Li-li Ch'en. Copyright © 1994 Columbia University Press. Reprinted with permission of the publisher.

Chronology

	Inner Asia	China	Northeast Asia	Japan
200		220–589 China disunited		
	552 Turks control Tarim Basin	581–618 Sui unification		
600		618 Tang Empire founded	668 Silla victory in Korea	645–655 Taika era
	751 Battle of Talas River	626–649 Li Shimin reign		710–784 Nara as capital
		690–705 Wu Zhao reign		
		755–763 An Lushan rebellion		752 "Eye-Opening" ceremony
800		840 Suppression of Buddhism		794 Heian era
	ca. 850 Buddhist political power secured in Tibet	879–881 Huang Chao rebellion		866–1180 Fujiwara influence
		907 End of Tang Empire		
			916 Liao Empire founded	
			918 Koryo founded	
1000		960 Song Empire founded		ca. 1000 The Tale of Genji
			1115 Jin Empire founded	
1200		1127–1279 Southern Song period		1185 Kamakura Shogunate founded

following the fall of the Han Empire had structured themselves around a variety of political ideas and institutions. Some favored the Chinese tradition, with an emperor, a bureaucracy using exclusively the Chinese language, and a Confucian state philosophy (see Chapter 6). Others reflected Tibetan, Turkic, or other regional cultures and depended on Buddhism to legitimate their rule. Throughout the period the relationship between northern China and the deserts and steppe of Inner Asia remained a central focus of political life, a key commercial linkage, and a source of new ideas and practices.

The Sui rulers called their new capital Chang'an (chahng-ahn) in honor of the old Han capital nearby in the Wei (way) River Valley (modern Shaanxi province). Though northern China constituted the Sui heartland, population centers along the Yangzi (yahng-zeh) River in the south grew steadily and pointed to what would be the future direction of Chinese expansion. To facilitate communication and trade with the south, the Sui built the 1,100-mile (1,771-kilometer) **Grand Canal** linking the Yellow River with the Yangzi, and they also constructed irrigation systems in the Yangzi Valley. On their northern frontier, the Sui also improved the Great Wall, the barrier against nomadic incursions that had been gradually constructed by several earlier states.

Sui military ambition, which extended to Korea and Vietnam as well as Inner Asia, required high levels of organization and mustering of resources—manpower, livestock, wood, iron, and food supplies. The same was true of their massive public works projects. These burdens proved more than the Sui could sustain. Overextension compounded the political dilemma stemming from the military defeat and subsequent assassination of the second Sui emperor. These circumstances opened the way for another strong leader to establish a new state.

Grand Canal The 1,100-mile (1,771-kilometer) waterway linking the Yellow and the Yangzi Rivers. It was begun in the Han period and completed during the Sui Empire.

Iron Stirrups This bas-relief from the tomb of Li Shimin depicts the type of horse on which the Tang armies conquered China and Inner Asia. Saddles with high supports in front and back, breast-plates, and straps beneath the tail to keep the saddle in place point to the importance of high speeds and quick maneuvering. Iron stirrups, available to Central and East Asian horsemen since the fifth century, could support the weight of shielded and well-armed soldiers rising in the saddle to shoot arrows or use lances.

In 618 the powerful Li family took advantage of Sui disorder to carve out an empire of similar scale and ambition. They adopted the dynastic name Tang (Map 11.1). The brilliant emperor **Li Shimin** (lee shir-meen) (r. 626–649) extended his power primarily westward into Inner Asia. Though he and succeeding rulers of the **Tang Empire** retained many Sui governing practices, they avoided overcentralization by allowing local nobles, gentry, officials, and religious establishments to exercise significant power.

The Tang emperors and nobility descended from the Turkic elites that built small states in northern China after the Han, as well as from Chinese officials and settlers who had moved there. They appreciated the pastoral nomadic culture of Inner Asia (see Chapter 8) as well as Chinese traditions. Some of the most impressive works of Tang art, for example, are large

pottery figurines of the horses and two-humped camels used along the Silk Road, brilliantly colored with glazes devised by Chinese potters. In warfare, the Tang combined Chinese weapons—the crossbow and armored infantrymen—with Inner Asian expertise in horsemanship and the use of iron stirrups. At their peak, from about 650 to 751, the Tang armies were a formidable force.

Li Shimin (599–649) One of the founders of the Tang Empire and its second emperor (r. 626–649). He led the expansion of the empire into Central Asia.

Tang Empire Empire unifying China and part of Central Asia, founded 618 and ended 907. The Tang emperors presided over a magnificent court at their capital, Chang'an.

Buddhism and the Tang Empire

The Tang rulers followed Inner Asian precedents in their political use of Buddhism. State cults based on Buddhism had flourished in Inner Asia and north China since the fall of the Han. Some interpretations of Buddhist doctrine accorded kings and emperors the spiritual function of welding humankind into a harmonious Buddhist society. Protecting spirits were to help the ruler govern and prevent harm from coming to his people.

Mahayana (mah-huh-YAH-nah), or "Great Vehicle," Buddhism predominated. Mahayana fostered faith in enlightened beings—bodhisattvas—who postpone nirvana (see Chapter 5) to help others achieve enlightenment. This permitted the absorption of local gods and goddesses into Mahayana sainthood and thereby made conversion more attractive to the common people. Mahayana also encouraged translating Buddhist scripture into local languages, and it accepted religious practices not based on written texts. The tremendous reach of Mahayana views proved adaptable to different societies and classes of people, invigorating travel, language learning, and cultural exchange.

Early Tang princes competing for political influence enlisted monastic leaders to pray for them, preach on their behalf, counsel aristocrats to support them, and—perhaps most important—contribute monastic wealth to their war chests. In return, the monasteries received tax exemptions, land privileges, and gifts.

To Chang'an by Land and Sea

As the Tang Empire expanded westward, contacts with Central Asia and India increased, and so did the complexity of Buddhist influence throughout

Map 11.1 The Tang Empire in Inner and Eastern Asia, 750 For over a century the Tang Empire controlled China and a very large part of Inner Asia. The defeat of Tang armies in 751 by a force of Arabs, Turks, and Tibetans at the Talas River in present-day Kyrgyzstan ended Tang westward expansion. To the east the Tang dominated Annam. Japan and the Silla kingdom in Korea were leading tributary states of the Tang.   © Cengage Learning

Interactive Map

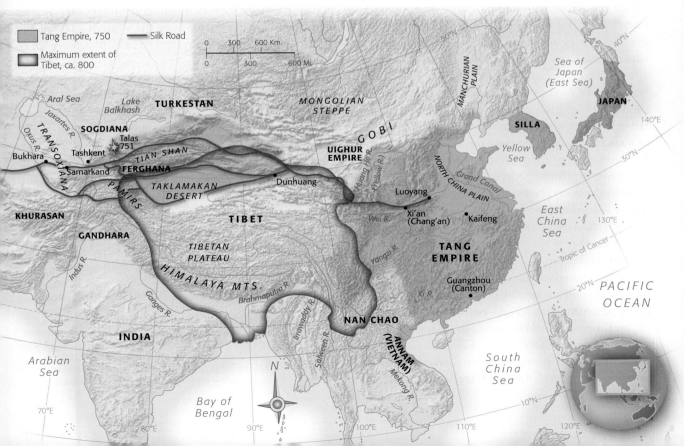

China. Chang'an, the Tang capital, became the center of a continent-wide system of communication. Central Asians, Tibetans, Vietnamese, Japanese, and Koreans regularly visited the capital and took away with them the most recent ideas and styles. Thus the Mahayana network connecting Inner Asia and China intersected a vigorous commercial world in which material goods and cultural influences mixed. Though Buddhism and Confucianism proved attractive to many different peoples, regional cultures and identities remained strong, just as regional commitments to Tibetan, Uighur, and other languages and writing systems coexisted with the widespread use of written Chinese. Textiles reflected Persian, Korean, and Vietnamese styles, while influences from every part of Asia appeared in sports, music, and painting. Many historians characterize the Tang Empire as "cosmopolitan" because of its breadth and diversity.

Well-maintained roads and water transport connected Chang'an to the coastal towns of south China, most importantly Guangzhou (gwahng-jo) (Canton). Though the Grand Canal did not reach Chang'an, it was the key component of this transportation network. Chang'an became the center of what is often called the **tributary system**, a type of political relationship dating from Han times by which independent countries acknowledged the Chinese emperor's supremacy. Each tributary state sent regular embassies to the capital to pay tribute (see Chapter 6). As symbols of China's political supremacy, these embassies sometimes meant more to the Chinese than to the tribute-payers, who might have seen them primarily as a means of accessing the Chinese trading system.

During the Tang period, Chang'an had something over a million people, only a minority of whom lived in the central city. Most people lived in suburbs that extended beyond the main gates. Many also dwelt in outlying towns that had special responsibilities like maintaining nearby imperial tombs or operating the imperial resort. In Chang'an and other entrepôts, foreigners, whether merchants, students, or ambassadors, resided in special compounds that included living accommodations and general stores. By the end of the Tang period, West Asians in Chang'an probably numbered over 100,000.

In the main parts of the city, restaurants, inns, temples, mosques, and street stalls along the main thoroughfares were busy every evening. At curfew, generally between eight and ten o'clock, commoners returned to their neighborhoods, which were enclosed by brick walls and wooden gates that guards locked until dawn to control crime.

Of the many routes converging on Chang'an, the Grand Canal commanded special importance with its own army patrols, boat design, canal towns, and maintenance budget. It conveyed vital supplies and contributed to the economic and cultural development of eastern China, where later capitals were built within easier reach.

The Tang consolidated Chinese control of the southern coastal region, increasing access to the Indian Ocean and facilitating the spread of Islamic and Jewish influences. A legend credits an uncle of Muhammad with erecting the Red Mosque at Canton in the mid-seventh century. Chinese mariners and shipwrights excelled in compass design and the construction of very large oceangoing vessels. The government took direct responsibility for outfitting grain transport vessels for the Chinese coastal cities and the Grand Canal. Commercial ships, built to sail from south China to the Philippines and Southeast Asia, carried twice as much as contemporary vessels in the Mediterranean Sea or the western parts of the Indian Ocean trading system (see Chapter 8).

Trade and Cultural Exchange

Influences from Central Asia and the Islamic world, largely transmitted by Turkic peoples, introduced lively new motifs to ceramics, painting, and silk designs. At the other end of the Silk Road, Iranian potters imitated the glazes of Tang vessels. Clothing styles changed in north China; working people switched from robes to the pants favored by horse-riding Turks from Central Asia. Inexpensive cotton imported from Central Asia, where cotton production boomed in the early Islamic centuries, gradually

tributary system A system in which, from the time of the Han Empire, countries in East and Southeast Asia not under the direct control of empires based in China nevertheless enrolled as tributary states, acknowledging the superiority of the emperors in China in exchange for trading rights or strategic alliances.

replaced hemp in clothes worn by commoners. The Tang court promoted polo, a pastime from the steppes, and followed the Inner Asian tradition of allowing noblewomen to compete. Various stringed instruments reached China across the Silk Road, along with Turkic folk melodies. Grape wine from West Asia and tea, sugar, and spices from India and Southeast Asia transformed the Chinese diet.

Such changes reflected new economic and trade relationships (see Material Culture: Salt). Silk had dominated the caravan trade across Central Asia in Han times (see Chapter 8). Though China's monopoly on silk disappeared as centers in West Asia learned to compete, China remained the source of superior silks. Tang factories created more and more complex styles, partly to counter foreign competition.

By about the year 1000 the magnitude of exports from Tang territories, facilitated by China's excellent transportation systems, dwarfed Chinese imports from Europe, West Asia, and South Asia. Tang exports tilted the trade balance with both the Central Asia caravan cities and the lands of the Indian Ocean, causing precious metal to flow into China in return

for export goods. As travel along the Silk Road and to the various ports of the Indian Ocean trading system increased, the economies of seaports and entrepôts involved in the trade—even distant ones—became increasingly commercialized, leading to networks of private traders devising new instruments of credit and finance.

SECTION REVIEW

- The Sui reunified China, reestablished Confucianism, and undertook programs of military expansion and public works.
- The Sui fell to the Tang, who built a less centralized empire and adopted Central Asian cultural practices.
- Under Central Asian influence, Mahayana Buddhism was firmly rooted in China and became part of a larger cosmopolitan culture.
- The Tang capital of Chang'an became the center of the tributary system, and transportation technology flourished.
- The Tang presided over an integration of cultures, and Chinese commercial activity shaped the larger international economy.

Xinjiang Uighur Autonomous District Museum

Women of Turfan Grinding Flour Women throughout Inner and East Asia were critical to all facets of economic life. In the Turkic areas of Central and Inner Asia, women commonly headed households, owned property, and managed businesses. These small figurines, made to be placed in tombs, portray women of Turfan—an Inner Asian area crossed by the Silk Road—performing tasks in the preparation of wheat flour.

Material Culture

Salt

Though sodium chloride, or table salt, is one of the world's most abundant chemicals, its abundance in some areas and scarcity in others has frequently given it an important role in economic history. Here are some examples.

Outcroppings of rock salt known as salt licks play a nutritional role in the lives of many wild mammals. Prehistoric human hunters sought game at these natural animal gathering places, and some scholars believe that human provision of salt played an important role in domesticating some species.

Trade in salt from the southern regions of the Sahara Desert is described as early as the ninth century C.E., but it is probably much older because the Saharan deposits formed an important nutritional source for salt-poor sub-Saharan Africa. The legendary exchange of salt for equivalent quantities of gold symbolizes this commercial importance. Bilma, an oasis town in eastern Niger, still produces salt that is distributed by means of camel caravans trekking across the sand dunes of the Ténéré Desert.

In ancient Rome, a strong-smelling sauce known as *garum* became a cooking staple and an important export item. *Garum* was made by crushing cut up fish, with their entrails, in a small amount of brine. The salt prevented the sauce from spoiling. For common people, using *garum* was a way of avoiding the tax on salt.

Early in the fourteenth century C.E. a Flemish fisherman devised a method of preserving herring, a small fish. After the head and certain internal organs were removed, enzymes from the pancreas began to digest the flesh and make it tender. Then the fish were packed with salt in casks. Salted herring and its raw materials, salt and herring, became mainstays of the commerce of Scotland, northern Germany, and in particular the Netherlands. A Dutch proverb maintains that the city of Amsterdam was built on herring casks.

In France, a salt tax known as the *gabelle* became a permanent part of royal revenues in the late fourteenth century C.E. Everyone over the age of eight was forced to buy a minimum amount of salt every week at a price fixed by the government. Most of the salt was produced by evaporating seawater, but inland provinces in the east exploited salt marshes. Popular resentment against the tax contributed to the French Revolution in 1789. A year later the *gabelle* was canceled.

In nineteenth-century China, where the salt tax had been a mainstay of government revenues since the Tang dynasty, brine (saltwater) wells around the western city of Zigong became the basis for one of the country's most prosperous industries. The family-based trusts that extracted the salt from as deep as 3,000 feet were

Rivals for Power in Inner Asia and China, 600–907

What were the effects of the fracturing of power in Central Asia and China?

Li Bo, the most renowned Tang poet and one of the greatest ever to write in the Chinese language, wrote in 751 of the seemingly endless succession of wars:

> The beacons are always alight, fighting and
>   marching never stop.
> Men die in the field, slashing sword to sword;
> The horses of the conquered neigh piteously to
>   Heaven.
> Crows and hawks peck for human guts,
> Carry them in their beaks and hang them on the
>   branches of withered trees.
> Captains and soldiers are smeared on the bushes
>   and grass;
> The General schemed in vain.
> Know therefore that the sword is a cursed thing
> which the wise man uses only if he must.[2]

Between 600 and 751, when the Tang Empire was at its height, the Turkic-speaking **Uighurs** (WEE-ger) and the Tibetans built large rival states astride the caravan routes of Inner Asia. The Tibetan Empire at its

2. From Arthur Waley, *Poetry and Career of Li Po* (London: Unwin Hyman, 1954), 35. © copyright by permission of The Arthur Waley Estate. Reprinted by permission of The Arthur Waley Estate.

comparable in capital accumulation, management skill, and technological innovation to contemporary European corporations.

In 1930 the British monopoly on salt production in India became the center of a peaceful protest led by Mahatma Gandhi. With seventy-eight followers he marched 240 miles to the seacoast, where the protestors picked up a small lump of salt, thereby breaking the law against private harvesting of salt. Though many were imprisoned, the Salt March became an important model of civil disobedience.

Though salt naturally brings a taste to mind, its historic role relates more to its chemical properties. Salt in water passes easily through the membranes that surround the cells of plants and animals. After a period of time, the moisture within the cell acquires the chemical properties of the salty moisture on the outside. Pieces of pork transform into ham, cucumbers and other vegetables become pickles, and sturgeon eggs become caviar. Since high concentrations of salt kill bacteria, salted foods can be transported and stored for long periods without spoiling or becoming dangerous to eat.

Producing salt from seawater and other sources of brine requires evaporation or boiling. But salt is also available in solid form and can be mined. Cities like Salzburg (literally "Salt Town") in Austria may grow up around salt mines. Underground layers of salt, sometimes hundreds of feet thick, are the residue of dried-up prehistoric seas or oceans. In addition to being processed for consumption, rock salt is used on icy roads. Since saltwater freezes at a lower temperature than fresh water, salt deposited on snow or ice causes melting.

VOLKMAR K. WENTZEL/National Geographic Stock/Getty Images

Camel Caravan Carrying Salt in West Africa Natural salt deposits, such as those at Bilma in the southern Sahara desert in Niger, have time and again become the bases for extensive regional and international trade. Transporting the salt can be a challenge, however. Camel transport made salt trading an integral part of the trade between the Saharan region and the agricultural countries of west Africa. In northern Europe the salt springs at Lüneburg near Hamburg, Germany fed into a maritime trading network throughout the Baltic and North Sea region. Coastal lands could extract salt from seawater by evaporation, though in colder climates, such as Japan, boiling was needed to supplement the power of natural sunlight and heat.

QUESTIONS FOR ANALYSIS

1. Why did salt become such an important trade product?
2. Why would a tax on salt be easy to administer?
3. How many uses of salt can you think of?

---

peak stretched well beyond modern Tibet into northeastern India and southwestern China, as well as the Tarim Basin. The contest between these states and the Tang for control of the land routes and nomadic peoples west of China reached a standoff by the end of the period. By the mid-800s all three empires were experiencing political decay and military decline, allowing soldiers, criminals, and freebooters to roam into neighboring territories.

Centralization and integration being most extensively developed in Tang territory, the impact fell most heavily there. By the early 800s, the period reflected in the original romance of Ying-ying described at the start of this chapter, nothing remained of Tang power

but pretense. In the provinces military governors suppressed the rebellion of General An Lushan (ahn loo-shahn), a commander of Central Asian and Turkic origin, which raged from 755 to 763, and then seized power for themselves.

The Uighur and Tibetan Empires

The original homeland of the Turks lay in the northern part of modern Mongolia. After the fall of the Han Empire, Turkic peoples began moving

Uighurs A group of Turkic-speakers who controlled their own centralized empire from 744 to 840 in Mongolia and Central Asia.

south and west, through Mongolia, then west to Central Asia, on the long migration that brought them, after many centuries, to what is today modern Turkey (see Chapter 8). In 552 the Tang established control over the basin of the Tarim River, a largely desert area north of Tibet that formed a vital link on the Silk Road. Yet within a century, a new Turkic group, the Uighurs, had supplanted them.

Under the Uighurs, caravan cities like Kashgar and Khotan (see Map 11.1) enjoyed commercial ties with both the Islamic world and China and showed enthusiasm for Buddhist teachings and religious art derived from northern India. The Uighurs excelled as merchants and as scribes able to transact business in many languages. They adapted the syllabic script of the Sogdians, an Iranian people who lived west of them in Central Asia, to writing Turkic.

Unified Uighur power collapsed after half a century, leaving Tibet as the lone rival to the Tang in Inner Asia. A large, stable empire critically positioned where China, Southeast Asia, South Asia, and Central Asia meet, **Tibet** experienced a variety of cultural influences. In the seventh century Chinese Buddhists on pilgrimage to India advanced contacts between India and Tibet. The Tibetans derived their alphabet from India, as well as a variety of artistic and architectural styles, and India and China both contributed to Tibetan knowledge of mathematics, astronomy, divination, farming, and milling of grain. Islam and the monarchical traditions of Iran and Rome became familiar through Central Asian trading connections. For example, the Tibetan royal family favored Greek medicine transmitted through Iran.

In 634 a Tang princess, called Kongjo by the Tibetans, came to Tibet to marry the Tibetan king and cement an alliance. She brought with her Mahayana Buddhism, which combined with the native religion to create a distinctive form of Buddhism. Tibet also sent ambassadors and students to the Tang imperial capital, and for a time regular contact and Buddhist influences consolidated the Tang-Tibet relationship. The Tibetan kings encouraged Buddhist religious establishments and prided themselves on being cultural intermediaries between India and China.

Horses and armor, techniques borrowed from the Turks, raised Tibetan forces to a level that startled even the Tang. By the late 600s the Tang emperor and the Tibetan king were rivals for religious leadership and political dominance in Inner Asia. War weariness affected both empires after 751, however.

In the 800s a new king in Tibet decided to follow the Tang lead and eliminate the political and social influence of the monasteries (see below). He was assassinated by Buddhist monks, and control of the Tibetan royal family passed into the hands of religious leaders. In the centuries that followed down to modern times, monastic domination isolated Tibet from surrounding regions.

Upheavals and Repression, 750–879

The later years of the Tang Empire saw increasing turmoil. The Confucian elites came to see Buddhism as undermining the idea of the family as the model for the state. In their backlash against "foreigners," they included Buddhists. The Confucian scholar Han Yu (768–824) spoke powerfully for a return to traditional Confucian practices. In "Memorial on the Bone of Buddha" written to the emperor in 819 on the occasion of ceremonies to receive a bone of the Buddha in the imperial palace, he scornfully disparages the Buddha and his followers.

> Now Buddha was a man of the barbarians who did not speak the language of China and wore clothes of a different fashion. His sayings did not concern the ways of our ancient kings, nor did his manner of dress conform to their laws. He understood neither the duties that bind sovereign and subject nor the affections of father and son. If

Primary Source: Memorial on Buddhism Find out what it is about the practice of Buddhism in China that causes Han Yu to report that he is "truly alarmed, truly afraid."

Tibet Country centered on the high, mountain-bounded plateau north of India. Tibetan political power occasionally extended farther to the north and west between the seventh and thirteenth centuries.

he were still alive today and came to our court by order of his ruler, Your Majesty might condescend to receive him, but . . . he would then be escorted to the borders of the state, dismissed, and not allowed to delude the masses. How then, when he has long been dead, could his rotten bones, the foul and unlucky remains of his body, be rightly admitted to the palace? Confucius said, "Respect spiritual beings, while keeping at a distance from them."[3]

Buddhism was also attacked for encouraging women in politics. In 690 Wu Zhao (woo jow), a woman who had married into the imperial family, seized control of the government and declared herself emperor. She based her legitimacy on claiming to be a bodhisattva, an enlightened soul who had chosen to remain on earth to lead others to salvation. She also favored Buddhists and Daoists over Confucianists in her court and government.

Later Confucian writers expressed contempt for Wu Zhao and other powerful women, such as the concubine Yang Guifei (yahng gway-fay). Bo Zhuyi (baw joo-ee), in his poem "Everlasting Remorse," lamented the influence of women at the Tang court, which had caused "the hearts of fathers and mothers everywhere not to value the birth of boys, but the birth of girls."[4] Confucian elites heaped every possible charge on prominent women who offended them, accusing Emperor Wu of grotesque tortures and murders, including tossing the dismembered but still living bodies of enemies into wine vats and cauldrons. They blamed Yang Guifei for the outbreak of the An Lushan rebellion in 755.

Serious historians dismiss the stories about Wu Zhao as stereotypical characterizations of "evil" rulers. Eunuchs (castrated palace servants) charged by historians with controlling Chang'an and the Tang court and publicly executing rival bureaucrats represent a similar stereotype. In fact Wu seems to have ruled effectively and was not deposed until 705, when extreme old age (eighty-plus) incapacitated her. Nevertheless, traditional Chinese historians commonly describe unorthodox rulers and all-powerful women as evil, and the truth about Wu will never be known.

Even Chinese gentry living in safe and prosperous localities associated Buddhism with social ills. People who worried about "barbarians" ruining their society

SECTION REVIEW

- Uighur rule in Central Asia prompted the development of a literate urban culture in which Buddhism flourished.

- Tibet combined a variety of cultural influences and checked Tang imperial designs until it fell under Buddhist religious rule.

- The Tang Empire, along with the rival Uighur and Tibetan states, experienced political problems that steadily weakened it.

- In China, this turmoil resulted in a backlash against foreign cultural influences and especially Buddhism, as Tang elites led a neo-Confucian reaction.

- The Tang fell due to a combination of destabilizing forces.

pointed to Buddhism as evidence of the foreign evil since it had such strong roots in Inner Asia and Tibet. Because Buddhism shunned earthly ties, monks and nuns severed relations with the secular world in search of enlightenment. By the ninth century, hundreds of thousands of people had entered tax-exempt Buddhist institutions. They paid no taxes, served in no army. They deprived their families of advantageous marriage alliances and denied descendants to their ancestors. The Confucian elites saw all this as threatening to the family and to the family estates that underlay the Tang economic and political structure. In 840 the government moved to crush the monasteries whose tax exemption had allowed them to accumulate land, serfs, and precious objects, often as gifts. Within five years 4,600 temples had been destroyed. Now an enormous amount of land and 150,000 workers were returned to the tax rolls.

Buddhist centers like the cave monasteries at Dunhuang were protected by local warlords loyal to Buddhist rulers in Inner Asia. Nevertheless, China's cultural heritage suffered a great loss in the dissolution of the monasteries. Some sculptures and grottoes survived only in defaced form. Wooden temples and façades sheltering great stone carvings burned to the ground. Monasteries became legal again in later times, but Buddhism never recovered the influence of early Tang times.

Buddhist Cave Painting at Dunhuang Hundreds of caves dating to the period when Buddhism enjoyed popularity and government favor in China survive in Gansu province, which was beyond the reach of the Tang rulers when they turned against Buddhism. This cave, dated to the year 538/9, contains elaborate wall decorations narrating the life of the Buddha and depicting scenes from the Western Paradise, where devotees of the Pure Land sect of Buddhism hoped to be reborn.

Pierre Colombel/Corbis

The End of the Tang Empire, 879–907

The campaigns of expansion in the seventh century had left the empire dependent on local military commanders and a complex tax collection system. Reverses like the Battle of the Talas River in 751, where Arabs halted Chinese expansion into Central Asia, led to military demoralization and underfunding. In 755 An Lushan, a Tang general on the northeast frontier, led about 200,000 soldiers in rebellion. The emperor fled Chang'an and executed his favorite concubine, Yang Guifei, who was rumored to be An Lushan's lover. The rebellion lasted for eight years and resulted in new powers for the provincial military governors who helped suppress it.

A disgruntled member of the gentry, Huang Chao (wang show), led the most devastating uprising between 879 and 881. Despite his ruthless treatment of the villages he controlled, his rebellion attracted poor farmers and tenants who could not protect themselves from local bosses and oppressive landlords, or who simply did not know where else to turn in the deepening chaos. The new hatred of "barbarians" spurred the rebels to murder thousands of foreign residents in Canton and Beijing (bay-jeeng).

Local warlords finally wiped out the rebels, but Tang society did not find peace. Refugees, migrant workers, and homeless people became common sights. Residents of northern China fled to the southern frontiers as groups from Inner Asia moved into localities in the north. Though Tang emperors continued in Chang'an until a warlord terminated their line in 907, they never regained power after Huang Chao's rebellion.

The Emergence of East Asia, to 1200

How did East Asia develop between the fall of the Tang and 1200?

In the aftermath of the Tang, three new states emerged and competed to inherit its legacy. The Liao (lee-OW) Empire of the Khitan (kee-THAN) people, pastoral nomads related to the Mongols living on the northeastern frontier, established their rule in the north. They centered their government on several cities, but their emperors preferred life in nomad encampments. In western China, the Minyak people (cousins of the Tibetans) established a state they called "Tanggut" (TAHNG-gut) to show their connection with the fallen empire. The third state, the Chinese-speaking **Song Empire**, came into being in 960 in central China.

These states embodied the political ambitions of peoples with different religious and philosophical systems—Mahayana Buddhism among the Liao, Tibetan Buddhism among the Tangguts, and Confucianism among the Song. Cut off from Inner Asia, the Song used advanced seafaring and sailing technologies to forge maritime connections with other states in East, West, and Southeast Asia. The Song elite shared the late Tang dislike of "barbaric" or "foreign" influences as they tried to cope with multiple enemies that heavily taxed their military capacities. Meanwhile, Korea, Japan, and some Southeast Asian states strengthened political and cultural ties with China.

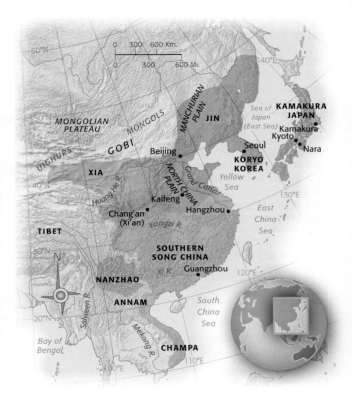

Interactive Map

Map 11.2 Jin and Southern Song Empires, ca. 1200 After 1127 the Song abandoned its northern territories to Jin. The Southern Song continued the policy of annual payments—to Jin rather than Liao—and maintained high military preparedness to prevent further invasions. © Cengage Learning

The Liao and Jin Challenge

The Liao Empire of the Khitan people extended from Siberia to Inner Asia. Variations on the Khitan name became the name for China in these distant regions: "Kitai" for the Mongols, "Khitai" for the Russians, and "Cathay" for Italian merchants like Marco Polo who reported on China in Europe.

The Liao rulers prided themselves on their pastoral traditions as horse and cattle breeders, the continuing source of their military might, and they made no attempt to create a single elite culture. They encouraged Chinese elites to use their own language, study their own classics, and see the emperor through Confucian eyes; and they encouraged other peoples to use their own languages and see the emperor as a champion of Buddhism or as a nomadic chieftain. On balance, Buddhism far outweighed Confucianism in this and other northern states, where rulers depended on their roles as bodhisattvas or as Buddhist kings to legitimate power. Liao rule lasted from 916 to 1121.

> **Song Empire** Empire in central and southern China (960–1126) while the Liao people controlled the north. Empire in southern China (1127–1279; the "Southern Song") while the Jin people controlled the north. Distinguished for its advances in technology, medicine, astronomy, and mathematics.

Su Song's Astronomical Clock This gigantic clock built at Kaifeng between 1088 and 1092 combined mathematics, astronomy, and calendar-making with skillful engineering. The team overseen by Su Song placed an armillary sphere on the observation platform and linked it with chains to the water-driven central mechanism shown in the cutaway view. The water wheel also rotated the Buddha statues in the multistory pagoda the spectators are looking at. Other devices displayed the time of the day, the month, and the year.   From Joseph Needham, ed., *Science and Civilization in China*, after a drawing of Su Song's book of 1090.

Superb horsemen and archers, the Khitans also challenged the Song with siege machines from China and Central Asia. A truce concluded in 1005 required the Song emperor to pay the Liao great quantities of cash and silk annually. A century later, the Song tired of paying tribute and secretly allied with the Jurchens of northeastern Asia, who also resented Liao rule. In 1115 the Jurchens first destroyed the Liao capital in Mongolia and proclaimed their own empire, the Jin (see Map 11.2), and then turned on the Song.

The Jurchens grew rice, millet, and wheat, but they also spent a good deal of time hunting, fishing, and tending livestock. Using Khitan military arts and political organization, they became formidable enemies in an all-out campaign against the Song in 1127. They laid siege to the Song capital, Kaifeng (kie-fuhng), and captured the Song emperor. Within a few years the Song withdrew south of the Yellow River and established a new capital at Hangzhou (hahng-jo), leaving central as well as northern China in Jurchen

control. Annual payments to the Jin Empire staved off further warfare. Historians generally refer to this period as the "Southern Song" (1127–1279).

Song Industries

The Southern Song came closer to initiating an industrial revolution than any other premodern state. Many Song advances in technology, medicine, astronomy, and mathematics had come to China in Tang times, sometimes from very distant places. Song officials, scholars, and businessmen had the motivation and resources to adapt this Tang lore to meet their military, agricultural, and administrative needs.

Song mathematicians introduced the use of fractions, first employing them to describe the phases of the moon. From lunar observations, Song astronomers constructed a very precise calendar and, alone among the world's astronomers, noted the explosion of the Crab Nebula in 1054. Song inventors drew on their knowledge of celestial coordinates, particularly the Pole Star, to refine compass design. The magnetic compass, an earlier Chinese invention, shrank in size and gained a fixed pivot point for the needle. With a protective glass cover, the compass now became suitable for seafaring, a use first attested in 1090.

Development of the seaworthy compass coincided with new techniques in building China's main oceangoing ship, the **junk**. A stern-mounted rudder improved the steering of the large ship in rough seas, and watertight bulkheads helped keep it afloat in emergencies. The shipwrights of the Persian Gulf soon copied these features in their ship designs.

Because they needed iron and steel to make weapons for their army of 1.25 million men, the Song rulers fought their northern rivals for control of mines in north China. Production of coal and iron soared. By the end of the eleventh century cast iron production reached about 125,000 tons (113,700 metric tons) annually, putting it on a par with the output of eighteenth-century Britain. Engineers became skilled at high-temperature metallurgy using enormous bellows, often driven by water wheels, to superheat the molten ore. Military engineers used iron to buttress defensive works because it was impervious to fire or concussion, and armorers mass-produced body armor. Iron construction also appeared in bridges and small buildings. Mass-production techniques for bronze and ceramics in use in China for nearly two thousand years were adapted to iron casting and assembly.

To counter cavalry assaults, the Song experimented with **gunpowder**, which they initially used to propel clusters of flaming arrows. During the wars against the Jurchens in the 1100s the Song introduced a new and terrifying weapon. Shells launched from Song fortifications exploded in the midst of the enemy, blowing out iron shrapnel and dismembering men and horses. However, the short range of these shells limited them to defensive uses.

Economy and Society in Song China

In a warlike era, Song elite culture idealized civil pursuits, and civilians outranked military men socially. Private academies, designed to train young men for the official examinations, became influential in culture and politics. New interpretations of Confucian teachings became so important and influential that the term **neo-Confucianism** is used for Song and later versions of Confucian thought.

Zhu Xi (jew she) (1130–1200), the most important early neo-Confucian thinker, reacted to the many centuries during which Buddhism and Daoism had overshadowed the precepts of Confucius. He and others worked out a systematic approach to cosmology that focused on the central conception that human nature is moral, rational, and essentially good. To combat the Buddhist dismissal of worldly affairs as a transitory distraction, they reemphasized individual moral and social responsibility. Their human ideal was the sage, a person who could preserve mental stability and serenity while dealing conscientiously with troubling social problems. Whereas earlier Confucian thinkers had written about sage kings and political leaders, the neo-Confucians espoused the spiritual idea of universal sagehood, a state that could be achieved through proper study of the new Confucian principles and cosmology.

Popular Buddhist sects also persisted during the Song, as indicated by the song-story line quoted at the beginning of this chapter: "We Buddhists and Confucians are of one family." While historically suitable for the time before the Tang abolition of Buddhist monasteries when the original story of Ying-ying was written, it is unlikely that the line would have pleased a Song audience if anti-Buddhist feelings had remained so ferocious. Some Buddhists elaborated on Tang-era folk practices derived from India and Tibet. The best known, Chan Buddhism (known as **Zen** in Japan and

junk A very large flatbottom sailing ship produced in the Tang, Ming, and Song Empires, specially designed for long-distance commercial travel.
gunpowder A mixture of saltpeter, sulfur, and charcoal, in various proportions. The formula, brought to China in the 400s or 500s, was first used to make fumigators to keep away insect pests and evil spirits. In later centuries it was used to make explosives and grenades and to propel cannonballs, shot, and bullets.
neo-Confucianism Term used to describe new approaches to understanding classic Confucian texts that became the basic ruling philosophy of China from the Song period to the twentieth century.
Zen The Japanese word for a branch of Mahayana Buddhism based on highly disciplined meditation. It is known in Sanskrit as *dhyana*, in Chinese as *chan*, and in Korean as *son*.

as Son in Korea), asserted that mental discipline alone could win salvation.

Meditation, a key Chan practice, was employed by Confucians as well as Buddhists. It afforded prospective officials relief from studying for civil service examinations, which continued into the Song from the Tang period. Unlike the ancient Han policy of hiring and promoting on the basis of recommendations, Song-style examinations involved a large bureaucracy. Test questions, which changed each time the examinations were given, often related to economic management or foreign policy even though they were always based on Confucian classics.

Hereditary class distinctions meant less than they had in Tang times, when noble lineages played a greater role in the structure of power. The new system recruited the most talented men, whatever their origin. Yet men from wealthy families enjoyed an advantage, for preparation for the tests consumed so much time that peasant boys could rarely compete. Success in the examinations brought good marriage prospects, the chance for a high salary, and enormous prestige. Failure could bankrupt a family and ruin a man both socially and psychologically. This put great pressure on candidates, who spent days writing essays in tiny, dim, airless examination cells.

For some, preparation became easier thanks to a technical change from woodblock to an early form of **movable type**, which made printing cheaper. To promote its ideological goals, the Song government authorized the mass production of test preparation books in the years before 1000. Although a man had to be literate to read the preparation books and basic education was still rare, a growing number of candidates without noble, gentry, or elite backgrounds entered the Song bureaucracy.

The availability of printed books changed country life as well, since landlords gained access to expert advice on planting and irrigation techniques, harvesting, tree cultivation, threshing, and weaving. Landlords frequently gathered their tenants and workers

to show them illustrated texts on the craft of farming and explain their meaning. New agricultural land was developed south of the Yangzi River, and iron implements such as plows and rakes, first used in the Tang era, were adapted to southern wet-rice cultivation. The growing profitability of agriculture interested ambitious members of the gentry. Still a frontier for Chinese settlers under the Tang, the south saw increasing concentration of land in the hands of a few wealthy families. In the process, the indigenous inhabitants of the region retreated into the mountains or southward toward Vietnam.

During the 1100s the total population of the Chinese territories, spurred by prosperity, rose above 100 million. The leading Song cities were still among the largest cities in the world. Health and crowding posed problems in the Song capitals. Multistory wooden apartment houses fronted on narrow streets—sometimes only 4 or 5 feet (1.2 to 1.5 meters) wide—that were clogged by peddlers or families spending time outdoors. The crush of people called for new techniques in waste management, water supply, and firefighting. In Hangzhou engineers diverted the nearby river to flow through the city, flushing away waste and disease. Arab and European travelers who had firsthand experience with the Song capital and who were sensitive to urban conditions in their own societies expressed amazement at Hangzhou's amenities: restaurants, parks, bookstores, wine shops, tea houses, theaters, and the entertainments mentioned at the start of this chapter.

The idea of credit, originating in the robust long-distance trade of the Tang period, spread widely under the Song. Intercity or interregional credit—what the Song called "flying money"—depended on the acceptance of guarantees that the paper could be redeemed for coinage at another location. The public accepted the practice because credit networks tended to be managed by families, so that brothers and cousins were usually honoring each other's certificates.

Primary Source: Craft of Farming Examine the kind of practical advice that helped farmers prosper during the Song period.

movable type Type in which each individual character is cast on a separate piece of metal. It replaced woodblock printing, allowing for the arrangement of individual letters and other characters on a page, rather than requiring the carving of entire pages at a time. It may have been invented in Korea in the thirteenth century.

The Palace Museum, Beijing

The Players Women, often enslaved, entertained at Chinese courts from early times. Tang art often depicts women with slender figures, but Tang taste also admired more robust physiques. Song women, usually pale with willowy figures, appear as here with bound feet. The practice appeared in Tang times but was not widespread until the Song, when the image of weak, housebound women unable to work became a status symbol and pushed aside the earlier enthusiasm for healthy women who participated in family businesses.

History in Focus *Clothing is a marker of social status, a clue to the values of the day. What do the clothes of these two women emphasize about them and suggest about the priorities of their culture? Find the answer online.*

"Flying money" certificates differed from government-issued paper money, which the Song pioneered. In some years, military expenditures consumed 80 percent of the government budget. The state responded to this financial pressure by distributing paper money. But this made inflation so severe that by the beginning of the 1100s paper money was trading for only 1 percent of its face value. Eventually the government withdrew paper money and instead imposed new taxes, sold monopolies, and offered financial incentives to merchants.

Hard-pressed for the revenue needed to maintain the army, canals, roads, waterworks, and other state functions, the government finally resorted to tax farming, selling the rights to tax collection to private individuals. Tax farmers made their profit by collecting the maximum amount and sending an agreed-upon smaller sum to the government. This meant exorbitant rates for taxable services, such as tolls, and much heavier tax burdens on the common people.

Rapid economic growth undermined the remaining government monopolies and the traditional strict regulation of business. Now merchants and artisans as well as gentry and officials could make fortunes. With land no longer the only source of wealth, the traditional social hierarchy common to an agricultural economy weakened, while cities, commerce, consumption, and the use of money and credit boomed. Urban life reflected the elite's growing taste for fine fabrics, porcelain, exotic foods, large houses, and exquisite paintings and books.

Along with the revival of Confucianism that began under the Tang and intensified under the Song, women were increasingly subordinated, legally disenfranchised, and socially restricted. Merchants spent long periods away from home, and many maintained several wives in different locations. They often depended on wives to manage their homes and even their businesses in their absence. But though women took on responsibility for the management of their husbands' property, their own property rights suffered legal erosion. Under Song law, a woman's property automatically passed to her husband, and she could not remarry if her husband divorced her or died.

As the subordination of women proved compatible with Confucianism, it became fashionable to educate girls just enough to read simplified versions of Confucian philosophy that emphasized the lowly role of women. Literacy made these young women more desirable as companions for the sons of gentry or noble families and as mothers in lower-ranking families aspiring to improve their status. The poet Li Qingzhao (lee CHING-jow) (1083–1141) made fun of her unusual status as a highly celebrated female writer:

> Although I've studied poetry for thirty years
> I try to keep my mouth shut and avoid reputation.
> Now who is this nosy gentleman talking about my poetry
> Like Yang Ching-chih (yahng SHING-she)
> Who spoke of Hsiang Ssu (sang sue) everywhere he went.[5]

(Her reference is to Yang Ching-chih, a hermit poet of the ninth century who was continually and extravagantly praised by a court official.)

Female footbinding first appeared among slave dancers at the Tang court, but it did not become widespread until the Song period. The bindings forced the toes under and toward the heel, so that the bones eventually broke and the woman could not walk on her own. In noble and gentry families, footbinding began between ages five and seven. In less wealthy families, girls worked until they were older, so footbinding began only in a girl's teens.

Many literate men condemned the maiming of innocent girls and the general uselessness of footbinding. Nevertheless, bound feet became a status symbol. By 1200 a woman with unbound feet had become undesirable in elite circles, and mothers of elite status, or aspiring to such status, almost without exception bound their daughters' feet. They knew that girls with unbound feet faced rejection. Working women and the indigenous peoples of the south, where northern practices took a longer time to penetrate, did not practice footbinding. Consequently they enjoyed considerably more mobility and economic independence than did elite Chinese women.

SECTION REVIEW

- Several rival states replaced the fallen Tang Empire, and the close relations between Central Asia and East Asia ended.
- The Liao and Jin Empires encouraged culturally diverse societies and confronted Song China with formidable military threats.
- The Song Empire of central and southern China built upon Tang achievements in technology and science and promoted civil ideals.
- Under the Song, print culture developed, urban populations rose, commercial activity grew through innovation, and women were subordinated to men.

New Kingdoms in East Asia

To what extent do shared practices justify thinking of East Asia as a unified cultural region in the post-Tang era?

The best possibilities for expanding the Confucian world-view of the Song lay with newly emerging kingdoms to the east and south. Korea, Japan, and Vietnam, like Song China, devoted great effort to the cultivation of rice. This fit well with Confucian social ideas. Tending the young rice plants, irrigating the rice paddies, and managing the harvest required coordination among many village and kin groups and rewarded hierarchy, obedience, and self-discipline. Confucianism also justified using agricultural profits to support the education, safety, and comfort of the literate elite. In each of these new kingdoms Song civilization melded with indigenous cultural and historical traditions to create a distinctive synthesis.

Chinese Influences

Korea, Japan, and Vietnam had first centralized power under ruling houses in the early Tang period, and their state ideologies continued to resemble that of the early Tang, when Buddhism and Confucianism seemed compatible. Government offices went to noble families and did not depend on passing examinations on Confucian texts. Landowning and agriculture remained the major sources of income, and landowners faced no challenges from a merchant class or urban elite.

Nevertheless, learned men prized literacy in classical Chinese and knowledge of Confucian texts.

Korean Wall Painting This depiction of women dancing before an audience comes from a sixth-century tomb near an early Korean capital north of the Yalu River.

Kim Wonyong, ed., *The Complete Collection of Korean Art*, vol. 4 (Seoul: Tonghwa ch'ulp'an kongsa, 1974), plate 55, p. 76.

Though formal education was available to only a small number of people, the ruling and landholding elites sought to instill Confucian ideals of hierarchy and harmony among the general population.

Korea Our first knowledge of Korea, Japan, and Vietnam comes from early Chinese officials and travelers. When the Qin Empire established its first colony in the Korean peninsula in the third century B.C.E., Chinese bureaucrats began documenting Korean history and customs. Han writers noted the horse breeding, strong hereditary elites, and **shamanism** (belief in the ability of certain individuals to contact ancestors and the invisible spirit world) of Korea's small kingdoms. But Korea quickly absorbed Confucianism and Buddhism.

Mountainous in the east and north, Korea was heavily forested until modern times. The land that can be cultivated (less than 20 percent) lies mostly in the south, where a warm climate and monsoon rains support two crops per year. Population movements from Manchuria, Mongolia, and Siberia to the north and to Japan in the east promoted the spread of languages that were very different from Chinese but distantly related to the Turkic tongues of Inner Asia.

In the early 500s the dominant landholding families made inherited status—the "bone ranks"—permanent in Silla (SILL-ah or SHILL-ah), a kingdom in the southeast of the peninsula. In 668 the northern Koguryo kingdom came to an end after prolonged conflict with the Sui and Tang. Supported by the Tang, Silla took control of much of the Korean peninsula. The Silla rulers imitated Tang government and examined officials on the Confucian classics. The fall of the Tang in the early 900s coincided with Silla's collapse and enabled the ruling house of **Koryo** (KAW-ree-oh), from which the modern name "Korea" derives, to rule a united peninsula for the next three centuries. Threatened constantly by the Liao and then the Jin in northern China, Koryo maintained amicable relations with Song China in the south. The Koryo kings supported Buddhism and made superb printed editions of Buddhist texts.

The oldest surviving woodblock print in Chinese characters comes from Korea in the middle 700s. Commonly used during the Tang period, woodblock printing required great technical skill. A calligrapher would write the text on thin paper, which would then

shamanism The practice of identifying special individuals (shamans) who will interact with spirits for the benefit of the community. Characteristic of the Korean kingdoms of the early medieval period and of early societies of Central Asia.

Koryo Korean kingdom founded in 918 and destroyed by a Mongol invasion in 1259.

be pasted upside down on a block of wood. Once wetted, the characters showed through from the back, and an artisan would carve away the wooden surface surrounding each character. A fresh block had to be carved for each printed page. Korean artisans developed their own advances in printing. By Song times, Korean experiments with movable type reached China, where further improvements led to metal or porcelain type from which texts could be cheaply printed.

Japan

Japan consists of four main islands and many smaller ones stretching in an arc from as far south as Georgia to as far north as Maine. The nearest point of contact with the Asian mainland lies 100 miles away in southern Korea. In early times Japan was even more heavily forested than Korea, with only 11 percent of its land area suitable for cultivation. Mild winters and monsoon rains supported the earliest population centers on the coastlands of the Inland Sea between Honshu and Shikoku Islands. The first rulers to extend their power broadly in the fourth and fifth centuries C.E. were based in the Yamato River Basin on the Kinai Plain at the eastern end of the sea.

The first Chinese description of Japan, dating from the fourth century, tells of an island at the eastern edge of the world, divided into hundreds of small countries and ruled over by a shamaness named Himiko or Pimiko. How Japan became unified remains a question, but horse-riding warriors from Korea may have played a central role in uniting these small countries under the Yamato-based rulers. In the mid-600s these rulers implemented the Taika (TIE-kah) and other reforms, giving the Yamato regime the key features of Tang government, which they knew of from Korean contacts and embassies to Chang'an sent by five different kings. A legal code, an official variety of Confucianism, and an official reverence for Buddhism blended with the local recognition of indigenous and immigrant chieftains as territorial administrators. Within a century a centralized government with a complex system of law had emerged, as attested by a massive history in the Confucian style.

Women from the aristocracy became royal consorts and thereby linked their kinsmen with the royal court. At the death of her husband in 592, Suiko, a woman from the aristocratic family of Soga, became empress. She occupied the throne until 628, enjoying a longer reign than any other ruler down to the nineteenth century. Asuka, her capital, saw a flowering of Buddhist art, and her nephew Shotoku opened relations with Sui China and promulgated in 604 a "Constitution" that had lasting influence on Japan's governing philosophy.

The Japanese mastered Chinese building techniques so well that Nara (NAH-rah) and Kyoto, Japan's early capitals, provide invaluable evidence of the wooden architecture long since vanished from China. During the eighth century Japan in some ways surpassed China in Buddhist studies. In 752 dignitaries from all over Mahayana Buddhist Asia gathered at the enormous Todaiji temple, near Nara, to celebrate the "eye-opening" of the "Great Buddha" statue.

Though the Japanese adopted Chinese building styles and some street plans, Japanese cities were built without walls. Central Japan was not plagued by constant warfare. Also, the Confucian Mandate of Heaven, which justified dynastic changes, played no role in legitimating Japanese government. The tenno—often called "emperor" in English—belonged to a family believed to have ruled Japan since the beginning of history. The dynasty never changed. A prime minister and the leaders of the native religion, in later times called Shinto, or "way of the gods," exercised real control.

By 750 the government in Nara had reached its zenith, employing seven thousand men in its central bureaucracy. The rulers encouraged an extension of Japanese rice-growing culture into the territory of the Hayato people of southern Kyushu and into northeastern Honshu, where the Emishi, a non-Japanese indigenous population, practiced slash-and-burn agriculture.

In 794 the central government moved to Kyoto, usually called by its ancient name, Heian. Though power became decentralized toward the end, legally centralized government lasted there until 1185. During this time members of the **Fujiwara** (foo-jee-WAH-rah) clan—a family of priests, bureaucrats, and warriors who had succeeded the Soga clan in influence—controlled power and protected the emperor. Fujiwara dominance favored men of Confucian learning over the generally illiterate warriors. Noblemen

Scene from the Tale of Genji Written around 1000 by Murasaki Shikibu, a highly educated woman belonging to the aristocratic Fujiwara family, the *Tale of Genji* has supplied subject matter for Japanese painters for centuries. This early scroll painting is in a typical style with the roof of a house removed to reveal the interior and the figures garbed in the elaborate court dress of the time. The story concerns the life and love affairs of Prince Genji, the favorite son of a Japanese emperor. Tokugawa Reimeikai Foundation, Tokyo, Japan. Photo © AISA/The Bridgeman Art Library International

of the Fujiwara period read the Chinese classics and appreciated painting and poetry.

Pursuit of an aesthetic way of life prompted the Fujiwara nobles to entrust responsibility for local government, policing, and tax collection to their warriors. Though often of humble origins, a small number of warriors had achieved wealth and power by the late 1000s. By the middle 1100s the nobility had lost control, and civil war between rival warrior clans engulfed the capital.

Like other East Asian states influenced by Confucianism, the elite families of Fujiwara Japan did not encourage education for women. However, this did not prevent exceptional women from having a strong cultural impact. The hero of the celebrated Japanese novel about Fujiwara court culture, *The Tale of Genji*, written around the year 1000 by the noblewoman Murasaki Shikibu, remarks: "Women should have a

general knowledge of several subjects, but it gives a bad impression if they show themselves to be attached to a particular branch of learning."[6]

Fujiwara noblewomen lived in near-total isolation, generally spending their time on cultural pursuits and the study of Buddhism. To communicate with their families or among themselves, they depended on writing. The simplified syllabic script that they used represented the Japanese language in its fully inflected form (the Chinese classical script used by Fujiwara men could not do so). Loneliness, free time, and a ready instrument for expression produced an outpouring of poetry, diaries, and storytelling by women of the Fujiwara era. Sei Shonagon (SAY SHON-nah-gohn), a lady attending one of the royal consorts, composed her *Pillow Book* between 996 and 1021. Most likely named for being kept by the author's pillow so she could jot down occasional thoughts, this famous work begins:

> In spring it is the dawn that is most beautiful. As the light creeps over the hills, their outlines are dyed a faint red and wisps of purplish cloud trail over them.
>
> In summer the nights. Not only when the moon shines, but on dark nights too, as the fireflies flit to and fro, and even when it rains, how beautiful it is![7]

Military values acquired increasing importance during the period 1156–1185, and warfare between rival clans culminated in the establishment of the **Kamakura** (kah-mah-KOO-rah) **Shogunate** in eastern Honshu, far from the old religious and political center at Kyoto. The standing of the Fujiwara family fell as nobles and the emperor hurried to accommodate the new warlords. *The Tale of the Heike*, an anonymously composed thirteenth-century epic account of the clan war, reflects a Buddhist appreciation of the impermanence of worldly things, a view that became common among the new warrior class. This class, in later times called samurai, eventually absorbed some of the Fujiwara aristocratic values,

---

7. From *The Pillow Book of Sei Shonagon*, translated by Ivan Morris. Copyright © 1967 by Ivan Morris, © 1991 Columbia University Press. Reprinted with permission of the publishers, Columbia University Press and Oxford University Press.

Fujiwara Aristocratic family that dominated the Japanese imperial court between the ninth and twelfth centuries.
Kamakura Shogunate The first of Japan's decentralized military governments (1185–1333).

but the ascendancy of the nonmilitary civil elite had come to an end.

Vietnam

Not until Tang times did the relationship between Vietnam and China become close enough for economic and cultural interchange to play an important role. Occupying the coastal regions east of the mountainous spine of mainland Southeast Asia, Vietnam's economic and political life centered on two fertile river valleys, the Red River in the north and the Mekong (may-KONG) in the south. The rice-based agriculture of Vietnam made the region well suited for integration with southern China. In both regions the wet climate and hilly terrain demanded expertise in irrigation.

Early Vietnamese peoples may have preceded the Chinese in using draft animals in farming and working with metal. But in Tang and Song times the elites of "Annam" (ahn-nahm)—as the Chinese called early Vietnam—adopted Confucian bureaucratic training, Mahayana Buddhism, and other aspects of Chinese culture. Annamese elites continued to rule in the Tang style after that dynasty's fall. Annam assumed the name Dai Viet (die vee-yet) in 936 and maintained good relations with Song China as an independent country.

Champa, located in what is now southern Vietnam, rivaled the Dai Viet state. The cultures of India and the Malay Peninsula strongly influenced Champa through maritime networks of trade and communication. During the Tang period, Champa fought with Dai Viet, but both kingdoms cooperated with the less threatening Song. Among the tribute gifts brought to the Song court by Champa emissaries was **Champa rice** (originally from India). Chinese farmers soon made use of this fast-maturing variety to improve their yields of the essential crop.

Vietnam shared the general Confucian interest in hierarchy, but attitudes toward women, like those in Korea and Japan, differed from the Chinese model. None of the societies adopted footbinding. In Korea strong family alliances that functioned like political and economic organizations allowed women a role in negotiating and disposing of property. Before the adoption of Confucianism, Annamese women had enjoyed higher status than women in China, perhaps because both women and men participated in wet-rice cultivation. The Trung sisters of Vietnam, who lived in the

SECTION REVIEW

- Korea, Japan, and Vietnam adapted Chinese cultural and political models, including the Tang blend of Confucianism and Buddhism.
- In all three cultures, landowning and agriculture remained the principal source of wealth.

second century C.E. and led local farmers in resistance against the Han Empire, still serve as national symbols in Vietnam and as local heroes in southern China.

Conclusion

Under the Sui and Tang dynasties, China became a unified state for the first time since the end of the Han in 220 C.E. The Tang rulers were of Turkic origin and expanded the territory under their control to Central Asia, far beyond the lands inhabited by Chinese people. Their empire became cosmopolitan and open to foreign trade and influences, in particular the spread of Buddhism. Meanwhile, people from northern China migrated in ever-larger numbers to the Yangzi Valley and beyond, into tropical southern China. Like the Assyrian, the Roman, and other empires that expanded far from their homeland, maintaining a large army at a great distance eventually weakened the Tang and left them vulnerable to invasion by nomadic herdsmen—whom the Chinese termed *barbarians*—from the northern steppes.

After the fall of the Tang in 907, northern China remained divided for many centuries between competing states and dynasties of Mongolian or Central Asian origin. But southern China, to which the Song dynasty retreated in 1127, attracted immigrants from the north and prospered thanks to a flourishing agriculture and maritime trade with Southeast Asia and the Indian Ocean. As a result of China's great size, ancient culture, and advanced technology, smaller states of East Asia such as Vietnam, Korea, and Japan modeled their political and cultural life on China.

Champa rice Quick-maturing rice that can allow two harvests in one growing season. Originally introduced into Champa from India, it was later sent to China as a tribute gift by the Champa state.

CHAPTER REVIEW

 Download the MP3 audio file of the Chapter Review to listen to on the go.

What was the importance of Inner and Central Asia as a region of interchange during the Tang period? (page 260)

Though the Tang emperors presided over one of the most celebrated periods in Chinese history, they were of Turkic descent and made extensive use of the military and cultural practices of Inner Asian nomads. Silk Road trade flourished under the Tang, and the new popularity of Buddhism entering China from the northwest greatly affected Chinese culture. Nevertheless, most Tang officials came from long-established aristocratic Chinese families.

What were the effects of the fracturing of power in Central Asia and China? (page 266)

After the Tang fell, warlords of different ethnic identities fought for control of northern China. Connections with nomad country remained important, but a simultaneous southward flight of people across the Yangzi River led to the formation of power centers well removed from the northwest frontier. The Song dynasty brought political and economic prominence to southern China for the first time.

How did East Asia develop between the fall of the Tang and 1200? (page 271)

Elsewhere in East Asia, the Tang remained the model of empire. But in Korea and Vietnam, the collapse of the Tang encouraged local independence. Chinese culture continued to be admired and imitated, but the new ruling families rejected Chinese political influence even while recognizing that China provided the greatest market for their trade, particularly under the robust economic conditions of the southern Song.

To what extent do shared practices justify thinking of East Asia as a unified cultural region in the post-Tang era? (page 276)

A reverence for Confucian classics spread from China to all neighboring lands and formed the core of elite education. Buddhism also spread at both the elite and popular levels. However, neither played as strong a political role as Islam did in the Middle East or Christianity in Europe. As a consequence, East Asia emerged during this period as a region with strong cultural links but without a common philosophical or religious tradition of rulership.

Key Terms

Grand Canal (p. 261)

Li Shimin (p. 262)

Tang Empire (p. 262)

tributary system (p. 264)

Uighurs (p. 266)

Tibet (p. 268)

Song Empire (p. 271)

junk (p. 273)

gunpowder (p. 273)

neo-Confucianism (p. 273)

Zen (p. 273)

movable type (p. 274)

shamanism (p. 277)

Koryo (p. 277)

Fujiwara (p. 279)

Kamakura Shogunate (p. 279)

Champa rice (p. 280)

Web Resources

Pronunciation Guide
Interactive Maps
- MAP 11.1 The Tang Empire in Inner and Eastern Asia, 750
- MAP 11.2 Jin and Southern Song Empires, ca. 1200

Primary Sources
- Memorial on Buddhism
- Craft of Farming

Answer to the History in Focus Question
See photo on page 275, "The Players."

 **CourseMate** Visit the CourseMate website at www.cengagebrain.com for additional study tools and review materials for this chapter.

Religious Conversion

Religious conversion has two meanings that often get confused. The term can refer to the inner transformation an individual may feel on joining a new religious community or becoming revitalized in his or her religious belief. Conversions of this sort are often sudden and deeply emotional. In historical terms, they may be important when they transform the lives of prominent individuals.

In its other meaning, religious conversion refers to a change in the religious identity of an entire population, or a large portion of a population. This generally occurs slowly and is hard to trace in historical documents. As a result, historians have sometimes used superficial indicators to trace the spread of a religion. Doing so can result in misleading conclusions, such as considering the spread of the Islamic faith to be the result of forced conversion by Arab conquerors, or taking the routes traveled by Christian or Buddhist missionaries as evidence that the people they encountered adopted their spiritual message, or assuming that a king or chieftain's adherence to a new religion immediately resulted in a religious change among subjects or followers.

In addition to being difficult to document, religious conversion in the broad societal sense has followed different patterns according to changing circumstances of time and place. Historians have devised several models to explain the different conversion patterns. According to one model, religious labels in a society change quickly, through mass baptism, for example, but devotional practices remain largely the same. Evidence for this can be found in the continuation of old religious customs among people who identify themselves as belonging to a new religion. Another model sees religious change as primarily a function of economic benefit or escape from persecution. Taking this approach makes it difficult to explain the endurance of certain religious communities in the face of hardship

and discrimination. Nevertheless, most historians pay attention to economic advantage in their assessments of mass conversion. A third model associates a society's religious conversion with its desire to adopt a more sophisticated way of life, by shifting, for example, from a religion that does not use written texts to one that does.

One final conceptual approach to explaining the process of mass religious change draws on the quantitative models of innovation diffusion that were originally developed to analyze the spread of new technologies in the twentieth century. According to this approach, new ideas, whether in the material or religious realm, depend on the spread of information. A few early adopters—missionaries, pilgrims, or conquerors, perhaps—spread word of the new faith to the people they come in contact with, some of whom follow their example and convert. Those converts in turn spread the word to others, and a chain reaction picks up speed in what might be called a bandwagon effect. The period of bandwagon conversion tapers off when the number of people who have not yet been offered an opportunity to convert diminishes. The entire process can be graphed as a logistic or S-shaped curve. Figure 1, the graph of conversion to Islam in Iran based on changes from Persian (non-Islamic) to Arabic (Islamic) names in family genealogies, shows such a curve over a period of almost four centuries.

In societies that were largely illiterate, like those in which Buddhism, Christianity, and Islam slowly achieved spiritual dominance, information spread primarily by word of mouth. The proponents of the new religious views did not always speak the same language as the people they hoped to bring into the faith. Under these circumstances, significant conversion, that is, conversion that involved some understanding of the new religion, as opposed to forced baptism or imposed mouthing of a profession of faith, must surely have started with fairly small numbers.

Language was crucial. Chinese pilgrims undertook lengthy travels to visit early Buddhist sites in India. There they acquired Sanskrit texts, which they translated into Chinese. These translations became the core texts of Chinese Buddhism. In early Christendom, the presence of bilingual (Greek-Aramaic) Jewish communities in the eastern parts of the Roman Empire facilitated the early spread of the religion beyond its Aramaic-speaking homeland. By contrast, Arabic, the language of Islam, was spoken only in the Arabian peninsula and the desert borderlands that extended northwards from Arabia between Syria, Jordan, and Iraq. This initial impediment to the spread of knowledge about Islam dissolved only when intermarriage with non-Muslim, non-Arab women, many of them taken captive and distributed as booty during the conquests, produced bilingual offspring. Bilingual preachers of the Christian faith were similarly needed in the Celtic, Germanic, and Slavic language areas of western and eastern Europe.

This slow process of information diffusion, which varied from region to region, made changing demands on religious leaders and institutions. When a faith was professed primarily by a ruler, his army, and his dependents, religious leaders gave the highest priority to servicing the needs of the ruling minority and perhaps discrediting, denigrating, or exterminating the practices of the majority. Once a few centuries had passed and the new faith had become the religion of the great majority of the population, religious leaders turned to establishing popular institutions and reaching out to the common people. Historical interpretation can benefit from knowing where a society is in a long-term process of conversion.

These various models reinforce the importance of distinguishing between emotional individual conversion experiences and broad changes in a society's religious identity. New converts are commonly thought of as especially zealous in their faith, and that description is often apt in instances of individual conversion experiences. It is less appropriate, however, to broader episodes of conversion. In a conversion wave that starts slowly, builds momentum in the bandwagon phase, and then tapers off, the first individuals to convert are likely to be more spiritually motivated than those who join the movement toward its end. Religious growth depends as much on making the faith attractive to late converts as to ecstatic early converts.

Figure 1 Conversion to Islam in Iran

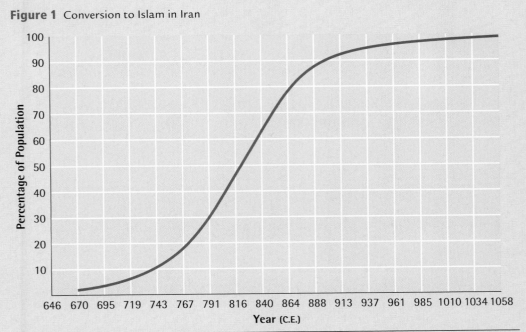

Source: Richard W. Bulliet, *Conversion to Islam in the Medieval Period*, Cambridge, MA: Harvard University Press, 1979, 23. Copyright © by the President and Fellows of Harvard College.

283

Part Four

Interregional Patterns of Culture and Contact, 1200–1550

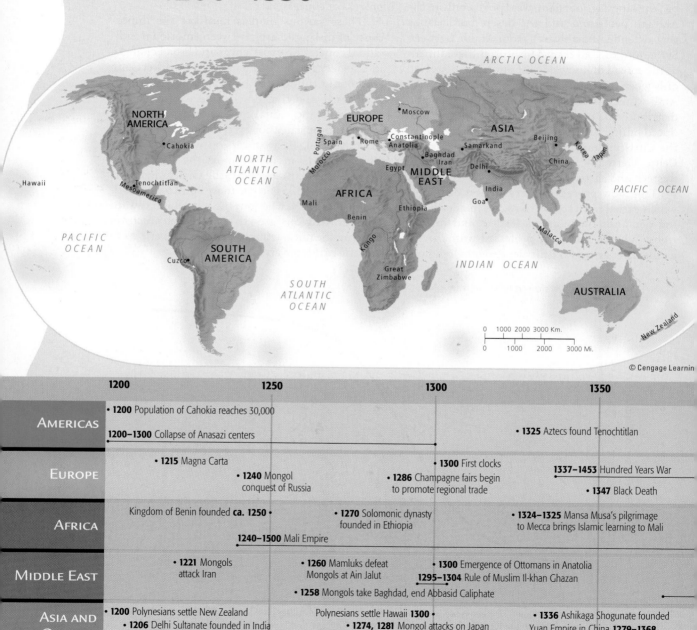

ARCTIC OCEAN

NORTH AMERICA

EUROPE

ASIA

Moscow

Cahokia

Portugal

Spain · Rome

Constantinople
Anatolia

Samarkand

Beijing

Korea

Japan

NORTH ATLANTIC OCEAN

Morocco

Baghdad
Iran

China

Hawaii

Tenochtitlan

Mesoamerica

Egypt

MIDDLE EAST

Delhi

AFRICA

India

Goa

PACIFIC OCEAN

Mali

PACIFIC OCEAN

Benin

Ethiopia

SOUTH AMERICA

Cuzco

Kongo

Malacca

INDIAN OCEAN

SOUTH ATLANTIC OCEAN

Great Zimbabwe

AUSTRALIA

New Zealand

0   1000 2000 3000 Km.

0   1000   2000   3000 Mi.

© Cengage Learnin

	1200	1250	1300	1350
AMERICAS	• **1200** Population of Cahokia reaches 30,000			• **1325** Aztecs found Tenochtitlan
	1200–1300 Collapse of Anasazi centers			
EUROPE	• **1215** Magna Carta		• **1300** First clocks	**1337–1453** Hundred Years War
		• **1240** Mongol conquest of Russia	• **1286** Champagne fairs begin to promote regional trade	• **1347** Black Death
AFRICA	Kingdom of Benin founded **ca. 1250** •	• **1270** Solomonic dynasty founded in Ethiopia		• **1324–1325** Mansa Musa's pilgrimage to Mecca brings Islamic learning to Mali
		1240–1500 Mali Empire		
MIDDLE EAST	• **1221** Mongols attack Iran	• **1260** Mamluks defeat Mongols at Ain Jalut	• **1300** Emergence of Ottomans in Anatolia	
			1295–1304 Rule of Muslim Il-khan Ghazan	
		• **1258** Mongols take Baghdad, end Abbasid Caliphate		
ASIA AND OCEANIA	• **1200** Polynesians settle New Zealand	Polynesians settle Hawaii **1300** •		• **1336** Ashikaga Shogunate founded
	• **1206** Delhi Sultanate founded in India	• **1274, 1281** Mongol attacks on Japan		Yuan Empire in China **1279–1368**
	1206–1227 Reign of Genghis Khan	**1265–1294** Reign of Khubilai Khan		Ming Empire founded in China **1368** •

CHAPTER 12
Mongol Eurasia and Its Aftermath, 1200–1500
CHAPTER 13
Tropical Africa and Asia, 1200–1500
CHAPTER 14
The Latin West, 1200–1500
CHAPTER 15
The Maritime Revolution, to 1550

Overland trade along the Silk Road peaked under the Mongols. The empire formed by Genghis Khan's conquests made Mongolia the center of an administrative and trading system linking Europe, the Middle East, Russia, and East Asia. Some lands flourished; others suffered physical devastation or groaned under tax burdens.

Societies that escaped conquest also felt the Mongol impact. Around the eastern Mediterranean coast and in eastern Europe, Southeast Asia, and Japan, fear of Mongol attack stimulated defense planning and accelerated processes of urbanization, technological development, and political centralization.

By 1500, Mongol dominance had waned, and a new Chinese dynasty, the Ming, was expanding its influence in Southeast Asia. The Ottomans had overthrown the Byzantine Empire, and Christian monarchs in Spain and Portugal, victorious over Muslim enemies, were laying the foundations of new overseas empires.

As Eurasia's overland trade faded, merchants, soldiers, and explorers took to the seas. The Chinese state sponsored admiral Zheng He's long-distance voyages, which were spectacular but without long-term results. In the 1300s and 1400s, Africans explored the Atlantic, and Polynesians colonized the central and eastern Pacific. And by 1500 Christopher Columbus had reached the Americas; within twenty-five years a Portuguese ship would sail around the world.

The overland routes of Eurasia had generated massive wealth in East Asia and a growing hunger for commerce in Europe. These factors similarly spurred the development of maritime trade. Exposure to the achievements, wealth, and resources of the Americas, sub-Saharan Africa, and Asia guaranteed the further expansion of European exploration and maritime power.

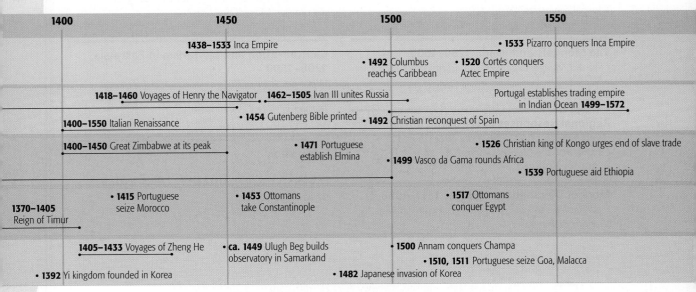

1400	1450	1500	1550
	1438–1533 Inca Empire		• **1533** Pizarro conquers Inca Empire
		• **1492** Columbus reaches Caribbean	• **1520** Cortés conquers Aztec Empire
	1418–1460 Voyages of Henry the Navigator	**1462–1505** Ivan III unites Russia	Portugal establishes trading empire in Indian Ocean **1499–1572**
1400–1550 Italian Renaissance	• **1454** Gutenberg Bible printed	• **1492** Christian reconquest of Spain	
1400–1450 Great Zimbabwe at its peak	• **1471** Portuguese establish Elmina		• **1526** Christian king of Kongo urges end of slave trade
		• **1499** Vasco da Gama rounds Africa	• **1539** Portuguese aid Ethiopia
1370–1405 Reign of Timur	• **1415** Portuguese seize Morocco	• **1453** Ottomans take Constantinople	• **1517** Ottomans conquer Egypt
	1405–1433 Voyages of Zheng He	• **ca. 1449** Ulugh Beg builds observatory in Samarkand	• **1500** Annam conquers Champa
• **1392** Yi kingdom founded in Korea		• **1482** Japanese invasion of Korea	• **1510, 1511** Portuguese seize Goa, Malacca

Mongol Eurasia and Its Aftermath

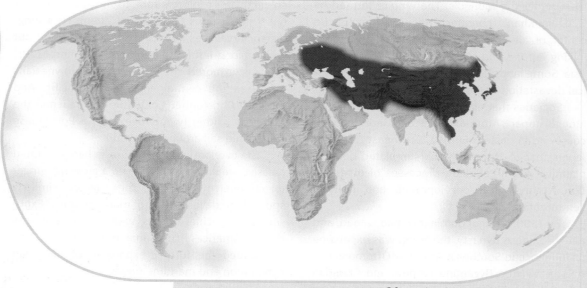

© Cengage Learning

CHAPTER PREVIEW

The Rise of the Mongols, 1200–1260

What accounts for the magnitude and speed of the Mongol conquests?

The Mongols and Islam, 1260–1500

How did Mongol expansion and Islam affect each other?

Regional Responses in Western Eurasia

What benefits resulted from the integration of Eurasia into the Mongol Empire?

Mongol Domination in China, 1271–1368

How did Mongol rule in China foster cultural and scientific exchange?

The Early Ming Empire, 1368–1500

In what ways did the Ming Empire continue or discontinue Mongol practices?

Centralization and Militarism in East Asia, 1200–1500

What are some of the similarities and differences in how Korea and Japan responded to the Mongol threat?

Conclusion

DIVERSITY & DOMINANCE: Observations of Mongol Life

Visit the CourseMate website at **www.cengagebrain.com** for additional study tools and review materials for this chapter.

When the Mongol Temüjin (TEM-uh-jin) was a boy, a rival group murdered his father. Temujin's mother tried to shelter him, but she could not find a safe haven, so at fifteen Temüjin sought refuge with the leader of the Keraits (keh-rates), a warring confederation whose people spoke Turkic and respected both Christianity and Buddhism. Temüjin learned the importance of religious tolerance, the necessity of dealing harshly with enemies, and the variety of Inner Asia's cultural and economic traditions.

In 1206 the **Mongols** and their allies acknowledged Temüjin as **Genghis Khan** (GENG-iz KAHN), or supreme leader. His advisers spoke many languages and belonged to different religions. His deathbed speech, which cannot be literally true even though a contemporary recorded it, captures the strategy behind Mongol success: "If you want to retain your possessions and conquer your enemies, you must make your subjects submit willingly and unite your diverse energies to a single end."[1] By implementing this strategy, Genghis Khan became the most famous conqueror in history, initiating an expansion of Mongol dominion that by 1250 stretched from Poland to northern China.

European and Asian sources of the time vilified the Mongols as agents of death, suffering, and conflagration, a still-common viewpoint based on reliable accounts of horrible massacres. Scholars today, however, stress the positive developments that transpired under Mongol rule. The tremendous extent of the Mongol Empire promoted the movement of people and ideas from one end of Eurasia to the other. Trade routes improved, markets expanded, and the demand for products grew. Trade on the Silk Road, which had declined with the fall of the Tang Empire (see Chapter 11), revived.

Between 1218 and about 1350 in western Eurasia and down to 1368 in China, the Mongols focused on specific economic and strategic interests, usually permitting local cultures to survive and develop. In some regions, local reactions to Mongol domination sowed seeds of regional and ethnic identity that blossomed in the period of Mongol decline. Regions as widely separated as Russia, Iran, China, Korea, and Japan benefited from the Mongol stimulation of economic and cultural exchange and also found in their opposition to the Mongols new bases for political consolidation and affirmation of cultural difference.

The Rise of the Mongols, 1200–1260

What accounts for the magnitude and speed of the Mongol conquests?

The Mongol Empire owed much of its success to the cultural institutions and political traditions of the Eurasian steppes (prairies) and deserts. The pastoral way of life known as **nomadism** only occasionally gives rise to imperial expansion, and historians disagree about what triggers these episodes. In the case of the Mongols, a precise assessment of the personal contributions of Genghis Khan and his successors remains uncertain.

Nomadism in Central and Inner Asia

The pastoral nomads of the Eurasian steppes played an on-again, off-again role in European, Middle Eastern, and Chinese history for hundreds of years before the rise of the Mongols (see Chapter 8). The Mongol way of life probably did not differ materially from that of those earlier peoples (see Diversity and Dominance: Observations of Mongol Life). Moving regularly and efficiently with flocks and herds required firm decision making, with many voices being heard. A council with representatives from powerful families ratified the decisions of the

---

Mongols As early as the Tang Empire, Chinese records mention a people of this name living as nomads in northern Eurasia. After 1206, under Genghis Khan, they established an enormous empire linking western and eastern Eurasia.

Genghis Khan (ca. 1167–1227) The title of Temüjin when he ruled the Mongols (1206–1227). It means the "oceanic" or "universal" leader. Genghis Khan was the founder of the Mongol Empire.

nomadism A way of life in which groups of people and their herds of animals continually migrate to find pastures and water.

Mongolian Landscape The essentials of Inner Asian pastoral life still persist in Mongolia. Here a party of Mongol horsemen carrying their equivalent of lassos ride past a group of yurts. These dwellings made of pieces of felt covering a wooden lattice framework are easily disassembled and moved when the nomads change campsite. Arid plains and bare mountains are typical of Inner Asia.

Claro Cortes IV/Reuters/Corbis

leader, the khan. Yet people who disagreed with a decision could strike off on their own. Even during military campaigns, warriors moved with their families and possessions.

Menial work in camps fell to slaves—people who were either captured during warfare or who sought refuge in slavery to escape starvation. Weak groups secured land rights and protection from strong groups by providing them with slaves, livestock, weapons, silk, or cash. More powerful groups, such as Genghis Khan's extended family and descendants, lived almost entirely off tribute, so they spent less time and fewer resources on herding and more on warfare designed to secure greater tribute.

Leading families combined resources and solidified intergroup alliances through arranged marriages and other acts, a process that helped generate political federations. Marriages were arranged in childhood—in Temujin's case, at the age of eight—and children thus became pawns of diplomacy. Women from prestigious families could wield power in negotiation and management, though they ran the risk of assassination or execution just like men.

The wives and mothers of Mongol rulers traditionally managed state affairs during the interregnum between a ruler's death and the selection of a successor. Princes and heads of ministries treated such regents with great deference and obeyed their commands without question. Since a female regent could not herself succeed to the position of khan, her political machinations usually focused on gaining the succession for a son or other male relative. Families often included believers in two or more religions, most commonly Buddhism, Christianity, or Islam. Virtually all Mongols observed the practices of traditional shamanism, rituals in which special individuals visited and influenced the supernatural world. Whatever their faith, the Mongols believed in world rulership by a khan who, with the aid of his shamans, could speak to and for an ultimate god, represented as Sky or Heaven. This universal ruler transcended particular cultures and dominated them all.

The Mongol Conquests, 1215–1283

Shortly after his acclamation in 1206, Genghis initiated two decades of Mongol aggression. By 1209 he had cowed the Tanggut rulers of northwest China, and in 1215 he captured the Jin capital of Yanjing, today known as Beijing. He turned westward in 1219 with an invasion of Khwarezm, a state east of the Caspian Sea that included much of

Chronology

	Mongolia and China	Central Asia and Middle East	Russia	Korea, Japan, and Southeast Asia
1200	1206 Temüjin becomes Genghis Khan			
		1219–1221 Invasion of Iran	1237–1240 Russia invaded	1258 Mongols conquer Koryo
	1234 North China seized	1258 Mongols sack Baghdad		
	1271 Founding of Yuan Empire			1274, 1281 Mongols attack Japan
	1279 Southern Song attacked			
1300				1333–1338 End of Kamakura Shogunate
		ca. 1350 Plague in Egypt	1346 Plague in Kaffa	
	1368 Ming Empire founded			1392 Korean Yi kingdom
1400		1453 Ottomans capture Constantinople		
			1462–1505 Ivan III tsar	

Iran. After 1221, when most of Iran had fallen, Genghis left the command of most campaigns to subordinate generals.

Ögödei (ERG-uh-day), Genghis's son, became the Great Khan in 1227 after his father's death. He completed the destruction of the Tanggut and the Jin and put their territories under Mongol governors. By 1234 he controlled most of northern China and was threatening the Southern Song (see Chapter 11). Three years later Genghis's grandson Batu (BAH-too) (d. 1255) attacked Russian territories, took control of the towns along the Volga (VOHL-gah) River, and conquered Kievan Russia, Moscow, Poland, and Hungary in a five-year campaign. Only the death of Ögödei in 1241, which caused a suspension of campaigning, saved western Europe from invasion. With Genghis's grandson Güyük (gi-yik) installed as the new Great

Khan, the conquests resumed. In the Middle East a Mongol army sacked Baghdad in 1258 and executed the last Abbasid caliph (see Chapter 9).

Genghis Khan's original objective had probably been collecting tribute, but the success of the Mongol conquests created a new situation. Ögödei unquestionably sought to rule a united empire based at his capital, Karakorum (kah-rah-KOR-um), but after his death family unity began to unravel. The Golden Horde in Russia, the Jagadai domains in Central Asia, and the Il-khans in Iran were subordinate domains (see Map 12.1 on page 292); but when Khubilai (KOO-bih-lie) declared himself Great Khan in 1265, the descendants of Genghis's son Jagadai (d. 1242) and other branches of the family refused to accept him. Since Karakorum was destroyed in the ensuing fighting, Khubilai transferred his court to the old Jin capital now renamed

Diversity & Dominance

Observations of Mongol Life

The Mongols, despite the power, geographical extent, and durability of their empire, are known mainly from the observations made by non-Mongols who either traveled in their territory or worked for them. The following passages come from three such authors.

William of Rubruck, a Franciscan friar, journeyed to the court of the Great Khan Mönke in 1253–1255 after living for some period of time in crusader territory in the Middle East. He carried a letter from the French king, Louis IX (ruled 1226–1270), asking that the friar and a companion be allowed to stay with the Mongols, preach Christianity, and comfort German prisoners. William never made contact with the Germans, but his highly personal observations on Mongol life fascinated European readers.

The dwelling in which they sleep is based on a hoop of interlaced branches, and its supports are made of branches, converging at the top around a smaller hoop, from which projects a neck like a chimney. They cover it with white felt: quite often they also smear the felt with chalk or white clay and ground bones to make it gleam whiter, or sometimes they blacken it. . . . These dwellings are constructed to such a size as to be on occasion thirty feet across: I myself once measured a breadth of twenty feet between the wheeltracks of a wagon, and when the dwelling was on the wagon it protruded beyond the wheels by at least five feet on either side. . . .

The married women make themselves very fine wagons. . . . One rich Mo'al [i.e., Mongol] or Tartar has easily a hundred or two hundred such wagons with chests. Baatu has twenty-six wives, each of whom has a large dwelling, not counting the other, smaller ones placed behind the large one, which are chambers, as it were, where the maids live: to each of these dwellings belong a good two hundred wagons. When they unload the dwellings, the chief wife pitches her residence at the westernmost end, and the others follow according to rank. . . . Hence the court of one wealthy Mo'al will have the appearance of a large town, though there will be very few males in it. . . .

The History of the World-Conqueror by the Iranian historian 'Ata-Malik Juvaini, who worked for the Mongols in Iran, was written in elegant Persian during the 1250s. It combines a glorification of the Mongol rulers with an unflinching picture of the cruelties and devastation inflicted by their conquests.

He [i.e., Chingiz-Khan] paid great attention to the chase and used to say that the hunting of wild beasts was a proper occupation for the commanders of armies; and that instruction and training therein was incumbent on warriors and men-at-arms. . . . Whenever the Khan sets out on the great hunt (which takes place at the beginning of the winter season), he issues orders that the troops stationed around his headquarters and in the neighborhood . . . shall make preparation for the chase. . . .

The right wing, left wing and center of the army are drawn up and entrusted to the great emirs; and they set out together with the Royal Ladies and the concubines, as well as provisions of food and drink. For a month, or two, or three they form a hunting ring and drive the game slowly and gradually before them, taking care lest any escape from the ring. . . . Finally . . . the troops come to a halt all around the ring, standing shoulder to shoulder. The ring is now filled with the cries and commotion of every manner of game and the roaring and tumult of every kind of ferocious beast. . . .

When the ring has been so much contracted that the wild beasts are unable to stir, first the Khan rides in together with some of his retinue; then after he has wearied of the sport, they dismount upon high ground in the center . . . to watch the princes likewise entering the ring, and after them, in due order, the noyons [chiefs], the commanders and the troops. Several days pass in this manner; then, when nothing is left of the game but a few wounded and emaciated stragglers, old men and greybeards humbly approach the Khan, offer up prayers for his well-being and intercede for the lives of the remaining animals asking that they be suffered to depart to someplace nearer to grass and water. . . .

Now war—with its killing, counting of the slain and sparing of the survivors—is after the same fashion, and indeed analogous in every detail, because all that is left in the neighborhood of the battlefield are a few broken-down wretches.

In 1330 Hu Szu-hui, a physician of Chinese-Turkic family background, presented the Yuan emperor with a manual entitled *Proper and Essential Things for the Emperor's Food and Drink*. His work reflects both the meat-heavy diet of the steppes and traditional Chinese concern with good nutrition.

Foods That Cure Various Illnesses [60 entries]

Donkey's Head Gruel

It cures apoplexy-vertigo, debility of hand and foot, annoying pain of extremities, and trouble in speaking:

Black donkey's head (one; remove hair and wash clean), black pepper (two measures), tsaoko cardamom (two measures). Cook ingredients until overcooked. Add the five spices in fermented black bean juice. Flavor with the spices. Flavor evenly. Eat on an empty stomach.

Bear Meat Gruel

It cures the various winds, foot numbness–insensitivity and five flaccidities tendon and muscle spasms:

Bear meat (one measure). [To] ingredient add the five spices in fermented black beans. [Add] onions and sauce. Cook. When done eat on an empty stomach.

Sheep's Stomach Gruel

It cures the various apoplexies:

Sheep's stomach (one; wash clean), non-glutinous rice (two measures), green onions (several), salted fruits, Chinese flower pepper (remove the closed up corns, roast to bring out the juice; 30 corns), sprouting ginger (two measures and a half cut up finely). Combine the six ingredients evenly and put inside the sheep's stomach. Cook until overcooked. When done, flavor with the five spices. Eat on an empty stomach.

Foodstuffs That Mutually Conflict [55 entries]

Horse meat cannot be eaten together with granary rice.

Sheep's liver cannot be eaten together with pepper. It wounds the heart.

Hare meat cannot be eaten together with ginger.

Beef cannot be eaten together with chestnuts.

Mare's milk cannot be eaten together with fish hash. It produces obstruction of the bowels.

Venison cannot be eaten together with catfish.

Beef stomach cannot be eaten together with dog meat. Quail meat cannot be eaten together with pork. The face will turn black.

Pheasant eggs cannot be eaten together with onions. It produces vermin.

Meat of sparrows cannot be eaten together with plums. Eggs cannot be eaten together with turtle meat.

Lettuce cannot be eaten together with cream.

Ground mustard cannot be eaten together with hare meat. It produces sores.

QUESTIONS FOR ANALYSIS

1. Can you determine from the subject matter of these passages the different viewpoints of a European, an Iranian, and a Chinese?
2. Is there anything in these passages to indicate that the Mongols were Muslims, Christians, Buddhists, or Confucians?
3. Do you expect the observations of a traveler to be more or less valuable as historical sources than those of someone who served a Mongol ruler?

Source: From Peter Jackson, tr., *The Mission of Friar William of Rubruck. His Journey to the Court of the Great Khan Mönke 1253–1255*, pp. 73–74. Copyright © 1990. Reprinted by permission of David Higham Associates Limited; From Ata-Malik Juvaini's *The History of the World Conqueror*, vol. 2, translated by Andrew Boyle, pp. 27–29, Collection of Representative works: Persian series, © 1958 by UNESCO. Cambridge, Mass.: Harvard University Press, Copyright © 1958 by Manchester University Press. Reprinted by permission of the publishers, Harvard University Press and UNESCO; Paul D. Buell and Eugene N. Anderson, *A Soup for the Qan* (London: Kegan Paul International, 2000), 428–429, 438–440. Reprinted by permission of Koninklijke BRILL NV.

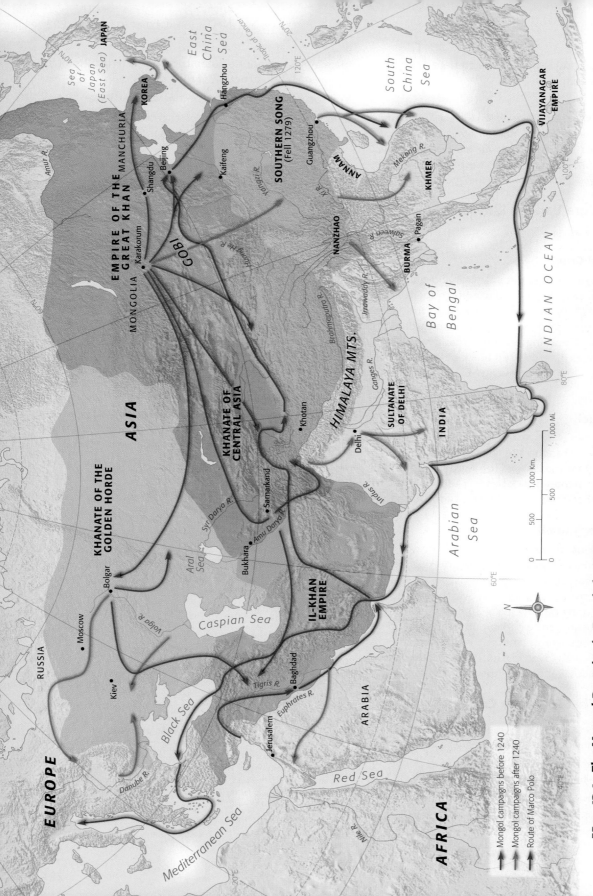

Interactive Map

Map 12.1 The Mongol Domains in Eurasia in 1300 After the death of Genghis Khan in 1227, his empire was divided among his sons and grandsons. Son Ögödei succeeded Genghis as Great Khan. Grandson Khubilai expanded the domain of the Great Khan into southern China by 1279. Grandson Hülegü was the first Il-khan in the Middle East. Grandson Batu founded the Khanate of the Golden Horde in southern Russia. Son Jagadai ruled the Jagadai Khanate in Central Asia. © Cengage Learning

Mongol campaigns before 1240
Mongol campaigns after 1240
Route of Marco Polo

Beijing, and in 1271 he declared himself founder of the **Yuan Empire**.

Jagadai's descendants continued to dominate Central Asia and enjoyed close relations with the region's Turkic-speaking nomads. This, plus a continuing hatred of Khubilai, contributed to Central Asia becoming an independent Mongol center and to the spread of Islam there.

After the Yuan destroyed the Southern Song (see Chapter 11) in 1279, Mongol troops attacked Annam—now northern Vietnam. They occupied Hanoi three times and then withdrew after arranging for tribute. In 1283 Khubilai's forces invaded Champa—now southern Vietnam—and made it a tribute nation as well. A plan to invade Java by sea failed, as did two invasions of Japan in 1274 and 1281.

The Mongols seldom outnumbered their enemies, but they were extraordinary riders and utilized superior bows. The Central Asian bow, made by laminating layers of wood, leather, and bone, could shoot one-third farther (and was correspondingly more difficult to pull) than the bows used by sedentary enemies. Rarely did an archer expend all of the five dozen arrows in his quiver. As the battle opened, arrows shot from a distance decimated enemy marksmen. Then the Mongols charged the enemy's infantry to fight with sword, lance, javelin, and mace. The Mongol cavalry met its match only at the Battle of Ain Jalut (ine jah-LOOT) in Palestine, where an under-strength force of Mongols confronted Turkic-speaking mamluks whose war techniques matched their own (see Chapter 9).

The Mongols also fired flaming arrows and hurled enormous projectiles—sometimes flaming—from catapults. The first Mongol catapults, built on Chinese models, transported easily but had short range and poor accuracy. During western campaigns in Central Asia, however, the Mongols encountered a design that was half again as powerful and used it to hammer the cities of Iran and Iraq. Cities that resisted faced siege and annihilation, leaving surrender as the only option. The slaughter the Mongols inflicted on Balkh (bahlk) (in present-day northern Afghanistan) spread terror and caused other cities to surrender. Each conquered area contributed men to the "Mongol" armies; in the Middle East, a few Mongol officers commanded armies of recently recruited Turks and Iranians.

Overland Trade and the Plague

Commercial integration under Mongol rule affected all parts of the empire. Like earlier nomad elites, Mongol nobles had the exclusive right to wear silk, almost all of which came from China. Trade brought new styles and huge quantities of silk westward to feed the luxury trade in the Middle East and Europe, and artistic motifs from Japan and Tibet reached as far as England and Morocco. Porcelain, another eastern luxury, became important in trade and strongly influenced later tastes in the Islamic world.

Merchants encountered ambassadors, scholars, and missionaries over the long routes to the Mongol courts. Some of the resulting travel literature, like the account of the Venetian Marco Polo (1254–1324), freely mixed the fantastic with the factual. Stories of fantastic wealth stimulated a European ambition to find easier routes to Asia.

Exchange also spread disease. In southwestern China **bubonic plague** had festered since the early Tang period. In the mid-thirteenth century, supply trains servicing the Mongol garrison in Yunnan (YOON-nahn) province facilitated the spread of rats carrying infected fleas. Marmots and other rodents along the caravan routes became infected and passed the disease to dogs and people. In 1346 plague incapacitated the Mongol army during their assault on the city of Kaffa (KAH-fah) in Crimea (cry-MEE-ah). They withdrew, but the plague remained. From Kaffa flea-infested rats reached Europe and Egypt by ship (see Chapter 14).

Primary Source: Description of the World
Melons over 6 feet around and big enough to feed twenty or thirty men, dirt from a tomb that can restore a dying person to life, days only six hours long—learn about the strange and interesting countries of the Mongol world.

Yuan Empire (1271–1368) Empire created in China and Siberia by Khubilai Khan.
bubonic plague A bacterial disease that can be transmitted by flea bites to rodents and humans; humans in late stages of the illness can spread the bacteria by coughing. Because of its very high mortality rate and the difficulty of preventing its spread, major outbreaks have created epidemics in many parts of the world.

SECTION REVIEW

- The society of the nomadic Mongols functioned through kinship and tribute ties, in which women often played important roles.

- Genghis Khan began the Mongol conquests to win tribute from Eurasian kingdoms.

- His successors turned to territorial rule, yet internal politics split the empire into smaller ones in China and Central Asia.

- The Mongols won territory through superior battle tactics and integrated it into a vast overland commercial network.

- That network allowed the bubonic plague and other diseases to spread across Asia into Europe.

Typhus, influenza, and smallpox traveled the same route. The combination of these and other diseases created what is called the "great pandemic" of 1347–1352 and spread devastation far in excess of what the Mongol armies inflicted. Peaceful trade, not conquest, ended up taking the greatest toll in lives.

The Mongols and Islam, 1260–1500

How did Mongol expansion and Islam affect each other?

From the perspective of Mongol imperial history, political rivalries determined which branches of the family adopted Islam and which did not. From the standpoint of Islamic history, however, recovery from the devastation that culminated in the destruction of the Abbasid Caliphate in Baghdad in 1258 attests to the vitality of the faith and the ability of Muslims to overcome adversity. Within fifty years of its darkest hour, Islam reemerged as a potent ideological and political force.

Mongol Rivalry By 1260 the **Il-khan** (IL-con) state, established by Genghis's grandson Hülegü, controlled Iran, Azerbaijan, Mesopotamia, and parts of Armenia. North of the Caspian Sea the Mongols who had conquered southern Russia established the capital of their Khanate of the **Golden Horde** (also called the Kipchak [KIP-chahk] Khanate) at Sarai (sah-RYE) on the Volga River. Like the

Passport The Mongol Empire facilitated the movement of products, merchants, and diplomats over long distances. The *paisa* (from a Chinese word for "card" or "sign"), with its inscription in Mongolian, proclaimed that the traveler had the ruler's permission to travel throughout the region. Europeans later adopted the practice, thus making the *paisa* the ancestor of modern passports and visas.   Image copyright © The Metropolitan Museum of Art/Art Resource, NY

History in Focus *Why do governments insist that foreigners traveling through their lands have passports (and often visas as well)? Do you think that the Mongols issuing* paisas *encouraged or discouraged travelers? Find the answer online.*

Il-khans, they ruled an indigenous Muslim population, mostly Turkic-speaking.

Some members of the Mongol imperial family professed Islam before the Mongol assault on the Middle East, and Turkic Muslims served the family

Il-khan A "secondary" or "peripheral" khan based in Persia. The Il-khans' khanate was founded by Hülegü, a grandson of Genghis Khan, and was based at Tabriz in modern Azerbaijan. It controlled much of Iran and Iraq.

Golden Horde Mongol khanate founded by Genghis Khan's grandson Batu. It was based in southern Russia and quickly adopted both the Turkic language and Islam. Also known as the Kipchak Khanate.

in various capacities. Hülegü himself, though a Buddhist, had a trusted Shi'ite adviser and granted privileges to the Shi'ites. However, the Mongols under Hülegü's command came only slowly to Islam.

Islamic doctrines clashed with Mongol ways. Muslims abhorred the Mongols' worship of Buddhist and shamanist idols. Furthermore, Mongol law specified slaughtering animals without spilling blood, which involved opening the chest and stopping the heart. This horrified Muslims, who were forbidden to consume blood and slaughtered animals by slitting their throats and draining the blood.

Islam became a point of inter-Mongol tension when Batu's successor as leader of the Golden Horde declared himself a Muslim. He swore to avenge the murder of the Abbasid caliph and laid claim to the Caucasus—the mountains between the Black and Caspian Seas—which the Il-khans also claimed.

Some European leaders believed that if they helped the non-Muslim Il-khans repel the Golden Horde from the Caucasus, the Il-khans would help them relieve Muslim pressure on the Crusader principalities in Syria, Lebanon, and Palestine (see Chapter 9). This resulted in a brief correspondence between the Il-khan court and Pope Nicholas IV (r. 1288–1292) and a diplomatic mission that sent two Christian Turks to western Europe as Il-khan ambassadors in the late 1200s. The Golden Horde responded by seeking an alliance with the Muslim mamluks in Egypt (see Chapter 9) against both the Crusaders and the Il-khans. Before the Europeans' diplomatic efforts could bear fruit, a new Il-khan ruler, Ghazan (haz-ZAHN) (1271–1304), declared himself a Muslim in 1295. Conflicting indications of Sunni and Shi'ite affiliation, such as coin inscriptions, indicate that Ghazan had a casual attitude toward theological matters. It is similarly unclear whether the Muslim Turkic nomads who served in the army were Shi'ite or Sunni.

Islam and the State

The Il-khans gradually came to appreciate the traditional urban culture of the Muslim territories they ruled. Nevertheless, they used tax farming to extract maximum wealth from their subjects. The government sold tax-collecting contracts to small partnerships, mostly consisting of merchants who might also finance caravans, small industries, or military expeditions. Whoever offered to collect the most revenue for the government won the contracts. They could use whatever methods they chose and could keep anything over the contracted amount.

Contracting tax collection initially lowered administrative costs; but over the long term, the extortions of the tax farmers drove many landowners into debt and servitude. Agricultural productivity declined, making it hard to supply the army. So the government resorted to taking land to grow its own grain. Like land held by religious trusts, this land paid no taxes. Thus the tax base shrank even as the demands of the army and the Mongol nobility continued to grow.

Ghazan faced many economic problems. Citing Islam's humane values, he promised to reduce taxes, but the need for revenue kept the decrease from becoming permanent. The Chinese practice of printing paper money had been tried unsuccessfully by a predecessor. Having no previous exposure to paper money, the Il-khan's subjects pushed the economy into a depression that lasted beyond the end of the Il-khan state in 1349. Mongol nobles competed among themselves for the decreasing revenues, and fighting among Mongol factions destabilized the government.

In the mid-fourteenth century the Golden Horde moved through the Caucasus into the western regions of the Il-khan Empire and then into the Il-khan's central territory, Azerbaijan, briefly occupying its major cities. At the same time a new power was emerging in the Central Asian Khanate of Jagadai (see Map 12.1). The leader **Timur** (TEE-moor), known to Europeans as Tamerlane, maneuvered himself into command of the Jagadai forces and launched campaigns into western Eurasia, apparently seeing himself as a new Genghis Khan. By ethnic background he was a Turk with only an in-law relationship to the family of the Mongol conqueror. This prevented him from assuming the title *khan*, but not from sacking the Muslim sultanate of Delhi in northern India in 1398 or defeating the sultan of the rising Ottoman Empire in Anatolia in 1402. He was reportedly preparing to march on China when he died in 1405. Timur's descendants could not

---

Timur (1336–1405) Member of a prominent family of the Mongols' Jagadai Khanate, Timur conquered much of Central Asia and Iran. He consolidated the status of Sunni Islam as the orthodox religion, and his descendants, the Timurids, maintained his empire for nearly a century and founded the Mughal Empire in India.

hold the empire together, but they laid the ground-work for the establishment in India of a Muslim regime, the Mughals, in the sixteenth century.

Culture and Science in Islamic Eurasia

The Il-khans and Timurids (descendants of Timur) presided over a brilliant cultural flower-ing in Iran, Afghanistan, and Central Asia based on blending Iranian and Chinese artistic trends and cultural prac-tices. The dominant cultural tendencies were Muslim, however. Timur died before he could reunite Iran and China, but by transplanting Middle Eastern scholars, artists, and craftsmen to his capital, Samarkand, he fostered the cultural achievements of his descendants.

The historian Juvaini (joo-VINE-nee) (d. 1283), who recorded Genghis Khan's deathbed speech cited at the beginning of this chapter, came from the city of Balkh, which the Mongols had devastated in 1221. His family switched their allegiance to the Mongols, and both Juvaini and his older brother assumed high government posts. The Il-khan Hülegü, seeking to immortalize and justify his conquests, enthusiasti-cally supported Juvaini's writing of the first compre-hensive narrative of Genghis Khan's empire.

Juvaini combined a florid style with historical objectivity, often criticizing the Mongols. This approach served as an inspiration to **Rashid al-Din** (ra-SHEED al-DEEN), Ghazan's prime minister, when he attempted the first history of the world. Rashid al-Din's work included the earliest known general history of Europe, derived from conversations with European monks, and a detailed description of China based on information from an important Chinese Muslim official stationed in Iran. The miniature paintings that accompanied some copies of Rashid al-Din's work included depic-tions of European and Chinese people and events and reflected the artistic traditions of both cultures. Rashid al-Din traveled widely and collaborated with administrators from other parts of the far-flung Mon-gol dominions. His idea that government should be in accord with the moral principles of the majority of the population buttressed Ghazan's adherence to Islam.

Under the Timurids, the tradition of the Il-khan historians continued. After conquering Damascus, Timur himself met there with the greatest historian of the age, Ibn Khaldun (ee-bin hal-DOON) (1332–1406), a Tunisian. In a scene reminiscent of Ghazan's

(vertical credit line) Sassoon/Robert Harding Picture Library

Tomb of Timur in Samarkand The turquoise tiles that cover the dome are typical of Timurid architectural decoration. Timur's family ornamented his capital with an enormous mosque, three large religious colleges facing one another on three sides of an open plaza, and a lane of brilliantly tiled family tombs in the midst of a cemetery. Timur brought craftsmen to Samarkand from the lands he conquered to build these magnificent structures.

answering Rashid al-Din's questions on the history of the Mongols, Timur and Ibn Khaldun exchanged his-torical, philosophical, and geographical viewpoints. Like Genghis, Timur saw himself as a world con-queror. At their capitals of Samarkand and Herat (in western Afghanistan), later Timurid rulers sponsored historical writing in both Persian and Turkish.

A Shi'ite scholar named **Nasir al-Din Tusi** (nah-SEER al-DEEN TOO-si) represents the beginning

Rashid al-Din (d. 1318) Adviser to the Il-khan ruler Ghazan, who converted to Islam on Rashid's advice.
Nasir al-Din Tusi (1201–1274) Persian mathemati-cian and cosmologist whose academy near Tabriz provided the model for the movement of the planets that helped to inspire the Copernican model of the solar system.

of Mongol interest in the scientific traditions of the Muslim lands. Nasir al-Din may have joined the entourage of Hülegü during a campaign in 1256 against the Assassins, a Shi'ite religious sect derived from the Fatimid dynasty in Egypt and at odds with his more mainstream Shi'ite views (see Chapter 9). Nasir al-Din wrote on history, poetry, ethics, and religion, but he made his most outstanding contributions in mathematics and cosmology. Following Omar Khayyam (oh-mar kie-YAM) (1038?–1131), a poet and mathematician of the Seljuk (SEL-jook) period, he laid new foundations for algebra and trigonometry.

Some followers working at an observatory built for Nasir al-Din at Maragheh (mah-RAH-gah), near the Il-khan capital of Tabriz, used the new mathematical techniques to reach a better understanding of celestial orbits. The mathematical tables and geometric models of lunar motion devised by one of his students somehow became known to Nicholas Copernicus (1473–1543), a Polish monk and astronomer. Copernicus adopted this lunar model as his own, virtually without revision, and then proposed the model of lunar movement developed under the Il-khans as the proper model for planetary movement as well—but with the planets circling the sun.

Observational astronomy and calendar-making had engaged the interest of earlier Central Asian rulers, particularly the Uighurs (WEE-ger) and the Seljuks. Under the Il-khans, the astronomers of Maragheh excelled in predicting eclipses, and astrolabes, armillary spheres, three-dimensional quadrants, and other instruments acquired new precision.

The remarkably accurate eclipse predictions and tables prepared by Il-khan and Timurid astronomers reached the mamluk lands in Arabic translation. Byzantine monks took them to Constantinople and translated them into Greek, Christian scholars working in Muslim Spain translated them into Latin, and in India the sultan of Delhi ordered them translated into Sanskrit. The Great Khan Khubilai (see below) summoned a team of Iranians to Beijing to build an observatory for him. Timur's grandson Ulugh Beg (oo-loog bek) (1394–1449), whose avocation was astronomy, constructed a great observatory in Samarkand and actively participated in compiling observational tables that were later translated into Latin and used by European astronomers.

SECTION REVIEW

- For the Mongols of the Il-khan and Golden Horde states, Islam became a matter of political rivalry.
- In the Il-khan state Islamic values struggled with economic needs, and the resulting unrest left it open to invasions by Golden Horde Mongols.
- At the same time, Timur took control of Jagadai and began his own imperial conquests.
- Under the Il-khans and Timurids, Iran and Central Asia experienced a flowering of Islamic culture.
- These rulers fostered great achievements in historical writing, literature, art, mathematics, and science.

A further advance made under Ulugh Beg came from the mathematician Ghiyas al-Din Jamshid al-Kashi (gee-YASS al-DIN jam-SHEED al-KAH-shee), who noted that Chinese astronomers had long used one ten-thousandth of a day as a unit in calculating the occurrence of a new moon. This seems to have inspired him to employ decimal notation, by which quantities less than one could be represented by a marker to show place. Al-Kashi's proposed value for pi (π) was far more precise than any previously calculated. This innovation arrived in Europe by way of Constantinople, where a Greek translation of al-Kashi's work appeared in the fifteenth century.

Regional Responses in Western Eurasia

What benefits resulted from the integration of Eurasia into the Mongol Empire?

Safe, reliable overland trade benefited Mongol ruling centers and commercial cities along the Silk Road. But the countryside, ravaged by conquest, sporadic violence, and heavy taxes, suffered terribly. As Mongol control weakened, regional forces in Russia, eastern Europe, and Anatolia reasserted themselves. Sometimes this meant collaborating with the Mongols; at other times it meant using local ethnic or religious traditions to resist or roll back Mongol influence.

Russia and Rule from Afar

The Golden Horde, established after Genghis's grandson Batu defeated a combined Russian and Kipchak (a Turkic people) army in 1223, started as a unified state but gradually lost unity as some districts crystallized into smaller khanates. The White Horde, for instance, ruled much of southeastern Russia in the fifteenth century, and the Crimean khanate on the northern shore of the Black Sea succumbed to Russian power only in 1783.

East-west routes across the steppe and north-south routes along the rivers of Russia and Ukraine (you-CRANE) conferred importance on certain trading entrepôts (places where goods are stored and from which they are distributed), as they had under Kievan Russia (see Chapter 10). The Golden Horde capital was (Old) Sarai, just north of where the Volga flows into the Caspian Sea (see Map 12.1). The Mongols ruled their Russian domains to the north and east from afar. To facilitate control, they granted privileges to the Orthodox Church, a practice that helped reconcile the Russian people to their distant masters.

The politics of language played a role in subsequent history. Old Church Slavonic, an ecclesiastical language, revived; but Russian steadily acquired greater importance and eventually became the dominant written language. Russian scholars shunned Byzantine Greek, previously the main written tongue, even after the Golden Horde permitted renewed contacts with Constantinople. The Golden Horde enlisted Russian princes to act as their agents, primarily as tax collectors and census takers.

The flow of silver and gold into Mongol hands starved the local economy of precious metal. Like the Il-khans, the khans of the Golden Horde attempted to introduce paper money as a response to the currency shortage. The unsuccessful experiment left such a vivid memory that the Russian word for money (*denga* [DENG-ah]) comes from the Mongolian word for the stamp (*tamga* [TAHM-gah]) used to create paper currency. In fact, commerce depended more on barter than on currency transactions.

Alexander Nevskii (nih-EFF-skee) (ca. 1220–1263), the prince of Novgorod, persuaded some fellow princes to submit to the Mongols. In return, the Mongols favored both Novgorod and the emerging town of Moscow, ruled by Alexander's son Daniel. As these towns eclipsed devastated Kiev as political, cultural, and economic centers, they drew people northward to open new agricultural land far from the Mongol steppe lands. Decentralization continued in

Transformation of the Kremlin Like other northern Europeans, the Russians preferred to build in wood, which was easy to handle and comfortable to live in. But they fortified important political centers with stone ramparts. In the 1300s, the city of Moscow emerged as a new capital, and its old wooden palace, the Kremlin, was gradually transformed into a stone structure.

the 1300s, with Moscow only very gradually becoming Russia's dominant political center.

In appraising the Mongol era, some historians stress Mongol destructiveness and brutal tax collection methods. Ukraine, a fertile and well-populated region in the late Kievan period (1000–1230), suffered severe population loss from these sources. Isolated from developments to the west, Russia and parts of eastern Europe are portrayed as suffering under the "Mongol yoke."

Alexander Nevskii (ca. 1220–1263) Prince of Novgorod (r. 1236–1263). He submitted to the invading Mongols in 1240 and received recognition as the leader of the Russian princes under the Golden Horde.

Other historians point out that even before the Mongols struck, Kiev had declined economically and ceased to mint coins. Yet the Russian territories regularly paid the heavy Mongol taxes in silver, indicating both economic surpluses and an ability to convert goods into cash. The burdensome taxes stemmed less from the Mongols than from their tax collectors, Russian princes who often exempted their own lands and shifted the load to the peasants.

As for Russia's cultural isolation, skeptics observe that before the Mongol invasion, the powerful and constructive role played by the Orthodox Church oriented Russia primarily toward Byzantium (see Chapter 10). This situation discouraged but did not eliminate contacts with western Europe, which probably would have become stronger after the fall of Constantinople to the Ottomans in 1453 regardless of Mongol influence.

The traditional structure of local government survived Mongol rule, as did the Russian princely families, who continued to battle among themselves for dominance. The Mongols merely added a new player to those struggles. Ivan (ee-VAHN) III, the prince of Moscow (r. 1462–1505), established himself as an autocratic ruler in the late 1400s. Before Ivan, the title **tsar** (from *caesar*), of Byzantine origin, applied only to foreign rulers, whether the emperors of Byzantium or the Turkic khans of the steppe. Ivan's use of the title probably represents an effort to establish a basis for legitimate rule with the decline of the Golden Horde and the disappearance of the Byzantine Empire.

New States in Eastern Europe and Anatolia

Anatolia and parts of Europe responded dynamically to the Mongol challenges. Raised in Sicily, the Holy Roman Emperor Frederick II (r. 1212–1250) appreciated Muslim culture and did not recoil from negotiating with Muslims. When the pope threatened to excommunicate him unless he waged a crusade, Frederick nominally regained Jerusalem through a flimsy treaty with the mamluk sultan in Egypt. Dissatisfied, the pope continued to quarrel with the emperor, leaving Hungary, Poland, and Lithuania to deal with the Mongol onslaught on their own. Many princes capitulated and went to (Old) Sarai to offer their submission to Batu.

However, the Teutonic (two-TOHN-ik) Knights resisted. These German-speaking warriors were dedicated to Christianizing the Slavic and Kipchak populations of northern Europe and to colonizing their territories with German settlers. To protect Slav territory, Alexander Nevskii joined the Mongols in fighting the Teutonic Knights and their Finnish allies. The latter suffered a catastrophe in 1242, when many broke through an icy northern lake and drowned. This event destroyed the power of the Knights, and the northern Crusades virtually ceased.

The "Mongol" armies encountered by the Europeans consisted mostly of Turks, Chinese, Iranians, a few Europeans, and at least one Englishman, who went to crusade in the Middle East but joined the Mongols and served in Hungary. But most commanders were Mongol.

Initial wild theories describing the Mongols as coming from Hell or from caves where Alexander the Great had confined monsters gradually yielded to a more sophisticated understanding as European embassies to Mongol courts returned with reliable intelligence. In some quarters terror gave way to appreciation. Europeans learned about diplomatic passports, coal mining, movable type, high-temperature metallurgy, higher mathematics, gunpowder, and, in the fourteenth century, the casting and use of bronze cannon. Yet with the outbreak of bubonic plague in the late 1340s (see Chapter 14), the memory of Mongol terror helped ignite religious speculation that God might again be punishing the Christians.

In the fourteenth century several regions, most notably Lithuania, escaped the Mongol grip. When Russia fell to the Mongols, Lithuania had experienced an unprecedented centralization and military strengthening. Like Alexander Nevskii, the Lithuanian leaders maintained their independence by cooperating with the Mongols. In the late 1300s Lithuania capitalized on its privileged position to dominate Poland and ended the Teutonic Knights' hope of regaining power.

In the Balkans independent kingdoms separated themselves from the chaos of the Byzantine Empire

tsar From Latin *caesar*, this Russian title for a monarch was first used in reference to a Russian ruler by Ivan III (r. 1462–1505).

SECTION REVIEW

- Mongol conquest devastated Kievan Russia, but the Russian language achieved greater importance, and many Russian traditions survived.

- Mongol conquest prompted decentralization of Russian power away from Kiev, but the Golden Horde's decline set the stage for the rise of Russian autocracy.

- The decline of Mongol power and Byzantine weakness enabled the rise of Lithuania and Serbia in eastern Europe and of the Ottoman Empire in Anatolia.

and thrived amidst the political uncertainties of the Mongol period. The Serbian king Stephen Dushan (ca. 1308–1355) proved the most effective leader. Seizing power from his father in 1331, he took advantage of Byzantine weakness to turn the archbishop of Serbia into an independent patriarch. In 1346 the patriarch crowned him "tsar and autocrat of the Serbs, Greeks, Bulgarians, and Albanians," a title that fairly represents the wide extent of his rule. As in the case of Timur, however, his kingdom declined after his death in 1355 and disappeared entirely after a defeat by the Ottomans at the battle of Kosovo in 1389.

The Turkic nomads whose descendants established the **Ottoman Empire** came to Anatolia in the same wave of Turkic migrations as the Seljuks (see Chapter 9). Though Il-khan influence was strong in eastern Anatolia, a number of small Turkic principalities emerged in the west. The Ottoman principality was situated in the northwest, close to the Sea of Marmara. This not only put them in a position to cross into Europe and take part in the dynastic struggles of the declining Byzantine state, but it also attracted Muslim religious warriors who wished to do battle with Christians on the frontiers. The defeat of the Ottoman sultan by Timur in 1402 was only a temporary setback. In 1453 Sultan Mehmet II captured Constantinople and brought the Byzantine Empire to an end.

The Ottoman sultans, like the rulers of Russia, Lithuania, and Serbia, seized opportunities that arose with the decay of Mongol power. The powerful states they created put strong emphasis on religious and linguistic identity, factors that the Mongols themselves did not stress. As we shall see, Mongol rule stimulated similar reactions in the lands of East and Southeast Asia.

Mongol Domination in China, 1271–1368

How did Mongol rule in China foster cultural and scientific exchange?

After conquering northern China in the 1230s, Great Khan Ögödei told a Confucian adviser that he planned to turn the heavily populated North China Plain into a pasture for livestock. The adviser reacted calmly but argued that taxing the cities and villages would bring greater wealth. The Great Khan agreed, but he imposed an oppressive tax-farming system instead of the fixed-rate method traditional to China.

The Chinese suffered under this system during the early years, but the Yuan Empire, established by Genghis Khan's grandson Khubilai in 1271, also brought benefits: secure trade routes, exchange of experts between eastern and western Eurasia, and transmission of information, ideas, and skills.

The Yuan Empire, 1271–1368

The Yuan sought a fruitful synthesis of the Mongol and Chinese traditions. **Khubilai Khan** gave his oldest son a Chinese name and had Confucianists participate in the boy's education. In public announcements and the crafting of laws, he took Confucian conventions into consideration. Buddhist and Daoist leaders who visited the Great Khan came away believing that they had all but convinced him of their beliefs.

Buddhist priests from Tibet called **lamas** became popular with some Mongol rulers. Their idea of a militant universal ruler bringing the whole world under control of the Buddha and thus pushing it nearer to salvation mirrored an ancient Inner Asian idea of universal rulership.

Ottoman Empire Islamic state founded by Osman in northwestern Anatolia ca. 1300. After the fall of the Byzantine Empire, the Ottoman Empire was based at Istanbul (formerly Constantinople) from 1453 to 1922. It encompassed lands in the Middle East, North Africa, the Caucasus, and eastern Europe.
Khubilai Khan (1215–1294) Last of the Mongol Great Khans (r. 1260–1294) and founder of the Yuan Empire. Original architect of the Forbidden City.
lama In Tibetan Buddhism, a teacher.

Beijing, the Yuan capital, became the center of cultural and economic life. Karakorum had been geographically remote, but Beijing served as the eastern terminus of caravan routes that began near Tabriz, the Il-khan capital, and (Old) Sarai, the Golden Horde capital. A horseback courier system utilizing hundreds of stations maintained communications along routes that were generally safe for travelers. Ambassadors and merchants arriving in Beijing found a city that was much more Chinese in character than Karakorum had been.

Called Great Capital (Dadu) or City of the Khan (khan-balikh [kahn-BAL-ik], Marco Polo's "Cambaluc"), Khubilai's capital included the Forbidden City, a closed imperial complex with wide streets and a network of linked lakes and artificial islands. In summer, Khubilai practiced riding and shooting at a palace and park in Inner Mongolia. This was Shangdu (shahng-DOO), the "Xanadu" (ZAH-nah-doo) with its "stately pleasure dome" celebrated by the English poet Samuel Taylor Coleridge.

Three separate states competed in China before the Mongols reunified the country (see Chapter 11). The Tanggut and Jin Empires controlled the north, the Southern Song most of the area south of the Yellow River. They had different languages, writing systems, forms of government, and elite cultures. The Great Khans destroyed all three and encouraged the restoration or preservation of many features of Chinese government and society.

By law, Mongols ranked highest. Below them came Central Asians and Middle Easterners, then northern Chinese, and finally southern Chinese. This reflected a hierarchy of functions. The Mongols were the empire's warriors, the Central Asians and Middle Easterners its census takers and tax collectors. The northern Chinese outranked the southern Chinese because they came under Mongol control almost two generations earlier.

Though Khubilai included some "Confucians" (under the Yuan, a formal and hereditary status) in government, their position compared poorly with pre-Mongol times. The Confucians disparaged merchants, many of whom were from the Middle East or Central Asia, and physicians. Whereas they regarded doctors as mere technicians or Daoist mystics, the Yuan encouraged doctors and began the process of integrating Chinese medical approaches with those contained in Muslim and Hellenistic sources.

Like the Il-khans, the Yuan rulers stressed census taking and tax collecting. Persian, Arab, and Uighur administrators staffed the offices of taxation and finance, and Muslim scholars worked at calendar-making and astronomy. The Mongols organized all of China into provinces. Central appointment of provincial governors, tax collectors, and garrison commanders marked a radical change by systematizing control in all parts of the country.

Many cities prospered: in north China by being on the caravan routes, in the interior by being on the Grand Canal, and along the coast by participating in maritime grain shipments from south China. The reintegration of East Asia (though not Japan) with the overland Eurasian trade, which had lapsed with the fall of the Tang (see Chapter 11), stimulated the urban economies.

With merchants a privileged group, life in the cities changed. So few government posts were open to the old Chinese elite that families that had previously spent fortunes on educating their sons for government service sought other opportunities. Many gentry families chose commerce. Corporations—investor groups that behaved as single commercial and legal units and shared the risk of doing business—handled most economic activities, starting with financing caravans and expanding into tax farming and lending money to the Mongol aristocracy. Central Asians and Middle Easterners headed most corporations in the early Yuan period; but as Chinese bought shares, many acquired mixed membership, or even complete Chinese ownership.

The agricultural base, damaged by war, overtaxation, and the passage of armies, could not satisfy the financial needs of the Mongol aristocracy. Following earlier precedent, the imperial government made up the shortfall with paper money. But people doubted the value of the notes, which were unsecured. Copper coinage partially offset the failure of the paper currency. During the Song, exports of copper to Japan, where the metal was scarce, had caused a severe shortage in China, leading to a rise in the value of copper in relation to silver. By cutting off trade with Japan, the Mongols stabilized the value of copper coins.

Many gentry families moved from their traditional homes in the countryside to engage in urban

Beijing China's northern capital, first used as an imperial capital in 906.

commerce as city life began to cater to the tastes of merchants instead of scholars. Specialized shops selling clothing, grape wine, furniture, and religiously butchered meats became common. Teahouses offered sing-song girls, drum singers, operas, and other entertainments previously considered coarse. Writers published works in the style of everyday speech. And the increasing influence of the northern, Mongolian-influenced Chinese language, often called Mandarin in the West, resulted in lasting linguistic change.

Cottage industries linked to the urban economies dotted the countryside, where 90 percent of the people lived. Some villages cultivated mulberry trees and cotton using dams, water wheels, and irrigation systems patterned in part on Middle Eastern models. Treatises on planting, harvesting, threshing, and butchering were published. One technological innovator, Huang Dao Po (hwahng DOW poh), brought knowledge of cotton growing, spinning, and weaving from her native Hainan Island to the fertile Yangzi Delta.

Yet on the whole, the countryside did poorly during the Yuan period. Initially, the Mongol princes evicted many farmers and subjected the rest to brutal tax collection. By the time the Yuan shifted to lighter taxes and encouragement of farming at the end of the 1200s, it was too late. Servitude or homelessness had overtaken many farmers. Neglect of dams and dikes caused disastrous flooding, particularly on the Yellow River.

According to Song records from before the Mongol conquest and the Ming census taken after their overthrow—each, of course, subject to inaccuracy or exaggeration—China's population may have shrunk by 40 percent during eighty years of Mongol rule, with many localities in northern China losing up to five-sixths of their inhabitants. Scholars have suggested several causes: prolonged warfare, rural distress causing people to resort to female infanticide, bubonic plague, a southward flight of refugees, and flooding of the Yellow River. The last helps explain why losses in the north exceeded those in the south and why the population along the Yangzi River markedly increased.

The Fall of the Yuan Empire

In the 1340s strife broke out among the Mongol princes, and within twenty years farmer rebellions and inter-Mongol feuds engulfed the land. Amidst the chaos, a charismatic Chinese leader, Zhu Yuanzhang (JOO yuwen-JAHNG), mounted a campaign that destroyed the Yuan Empire and brought China under control of his new dynasty, the Ming, in 1368. Many Mongols—as well as the Muslims, Jews, and Christians who had come with them—remained in China. Most of their descendants took Chinese names and became part of the diverse cultural world of China.

Many other Mongols, however, who had never moved out of their home territories in Mongolia, now welcomed back refugees from the Yuan collapse. Though Turkic peoples were becoming predominant in the steppe regions in the west, including territories still ruled by descendants of Genghis Khan, Mongols continued to predominate in Inner Asia, the steppe regions bordering on Mongolia. Some Mongol groups adopted Islam; others favored Tibetan Buddhism. But religious affiliation proved less important than Mongol identity in fostering a renewed sense of unity.

The Ming thus fell short of dominating all the Mongols. The Mongols of Inner Asia paid tribute to the extent that doing so facilitated their trade. Other Mongols, however, remained a continuing threat on the northern Ming frontier.

The Early Ming Empire, 1368–1500

In what ways did the Ming Empire continue or discontinue Mongol practices?

Historians of China, like historians of Russia and Iran, divide over the overall impact of the Mongol

SECTION REVIEW

- The Great Khans reunified China and fostered a synthesis of ideas and cultural traditions.
- Khubilai Khan made Beijing the capital of the Yuan Empire and presided over a social hierarchy with Mongols at the top and southern Chinese at the bottom.
- Mongol rule systematized government, but cities benefited more from Mongol policies than did the countryside.
- China's population shrank as a result of Mongol conquest and rule.
- Mongol-protected trade routes encouraged a steady exchange of scientific and cultural ideas.
- Internal strife weakened the Yuan Empire, which fell to the Ming in 1368, but many Mongols remained in China.

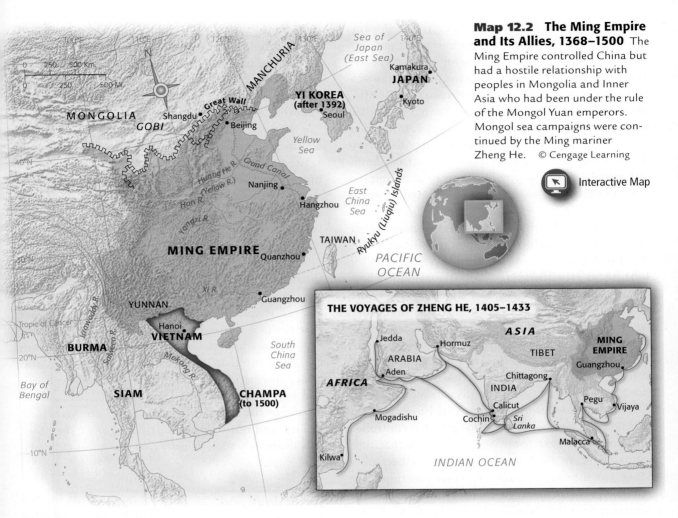

Map 12.2 The Ming Empire and Its Allies, 1368–1500 The Ming Empire controlled China but had a hostile relationship with peoples in Mongolia and Inner Asia who had been under the rule of the Mongol Yuan emperors. Mongol sea campaigns were continued by the Ming mariner Zheng He.   © Cengage Learning

Interactive Map

era. Since the **Ming Empire** reestablished many practices that are seen as purely Chinese, they receive praise from people who ascribe central importance to Chinese traditions. On the other hand, historians who look upon the Mongol era as a pivotal historical moment when communication across the vast interior of Eurasia served to bring east and west together sometimes see the inward-looking Ming as less productive than the Yuan.

Ming China on a Mongol Foundation

Zhu Yuanzhang, a former monk, soldier, and bandit, had watched his parents and other family members die of famine and disease, conditions he blamed on Mongol misrule. During the Yuan Empire's chaotic last decades, he vanquished rival rebels and assumed imperial power under the name Hongwu (r. 1368–1398).

Hongwu moved the capital to Nanjing (nahn-JING) ("southern capital") on the Yangzi River, turning away from the Mongol's Beijing ("northern capital"; see Map 12.2). Though Zhu Yuanzhang the rebel had espoused a radical Buddhist belief in a coming age of salvation, once in power he used Confucianism to depict the emperor as the champion of civilization and virtue.

Hongwu choked off relations with Central Asia and the Middle East and imposed strict limits on

Ming Empire (1368–1644) Empire based in China that Zhu Yuanzhang established after the overthrow of the Yuan Empire. The Ming emperor Yongle sponsored additions to the Forbidden City and the voyages of Zheng He. The later years of the Ming saw a slowdown in technological development and economic decline.

imports and foreign visitors. Silver replaced paper money for tax payments and commerce. These practices, illustrative of an anti-Mongol ideology, proved as economically unhealthy as some of the Yuan economic policies and did not last. Eventually, the Ming government came to resemble the Yuan. Ming rulers retained the provincial structure and continued to observe the hereditary professional categories of the Yuan period. Muslims made calendars and astronomical calculations at a new observatory at Nanjing, a replica of Khubilai's at Beijing. The Mongol calendar continued in use.

Continuities with the Yuan became more evident after an imperial prince seized power through a coup d'état to rule as the emperor **Yongle** (yoong-LAW) (r. 1403–1424). He returned the capital to Beijing, enlarging and improving Khubilai's Forbidden City, which now acquired its present features: moats, orange-red outer walls, golden roofs, and marble bridges. Yongle intended this combination fortress, religious site, bureaucratic center, and imperial residential park to overshadow Nanjing, and it survives today as China's most imposing traditional architectural complex.

Yongle also restored commercial links with the Middle East. Because hostile Mongols still controlled much of the caravan route, Yongle explored maritime connections. In Southeast Asia, Annam became a Ming province as the early emperors continued the Mongol program of aggression. This focus on the southern frontier helped inspire the naval expeditions of the trusted imperial eunuch **Zheng He** (jehng huh) from 1405 to 1433.

A Muslim whose father and grandfather had made the pilgrimage to Mecca, Zheng He had a good knowledge of the Middle East, and his religion eased relations with the states of the Indian subcontinent, to which he directed his first three voyages. Subsequent expeditions reached Hormuz on the Persian Gulf, sailed the southern coast of Arabia and the Horn of Africa (modern Somalia), and possibly reached as far south as the Strait of Madagascar.

On early voyages Zheng He visited long-established Chinese merchant communities in Southeast Asia to cement their allegiance to the Ming Empire and to collect taxes. When a community on the island of Sumatra resisted, he slaughtered the men to set an example. The expeditions added some fifty new tributary states to the Ming imperial universe, but trade did not increase as dramatically. Sporadic embassies reached Beijing from rulers in India, the Middle East, Africa, and Southeast Asia. During one visit the ruler of Brunei (broo-NIE) died and received a grand burial at the Chinese capital. The expeditions stopped in the 1430s after the deaths of Yongle and Zheng He.

Why did the Chinese not develop seafaring for commercial and military gain? Contemporaries considered the voyages a personal project of Yongle, an upstart ruler who had always sought to prove his worthiness. Building the Forbidden City in Beijing and sponsoring gigantic encyclopedia projects might be taken to reflect a similar character. Yongle may also have been emulating Khubilai Khan's sea expeditions against Japan and Southeast Asia. This would fit with the rumor spread by Yongle's political enemies that he was actually a Mongol.

A less speculative approach starts with the fact that the new commercial opportunities fell short of expectations, despite bringing foreign nations into the Ming orbit. In the meantime, Japanese coastal piracy intensified, and Mongol threats in the north and west grew. The human and financial demands of fortifying the north, redesigning and strengthening Beijing, and outfitting campaigns against the Mongols ultimately took priority over the quest for maritime empire.

Technology and Population

The Ming government limited mining, partly to keep the value of metal coins and partly to tax the industry. As a consequence, metal implements became more expensive for farmers. Techniques for making the high-quality bronze and steel used for weapons also declined. Japan quickly surpassed China in the production of extremely high-quality swords.

After the death of Emperor Yongle in 1424, shipbuilding skills deteriorated, and few advances

---

Yongle Reign of Zhu Di (1360–1424), the third emperor of the Ming Empire (r. 1403–1424). He sponsored further work on the Forbidden City, the expeditions of Zheng He, and the reopening of China's borders to trade and travel.

Zheng He (1371–1433) An imperial eunuch and Muslim who was entrusted by the Ming emperor Yongle with a series of state voyages that took his ships through the Indian Ocean, from Southeast Asia to Africa.

occurred in printing, timekeeping, and agricultural technology. Agricultural production peaked around the mid-1400s and remained level for more than a century. New weaving techniques did appear, but technological development in this field had peaked by 1500.

Reactivation of the examination system for recruiting government officials (see Chapter 11) drew large numbers of ambitious men into a renewed study of the Confucian classics. This reduced the vitality of commerce, where they had previously been employed, just as population growth was creating a labor surplus. Records indicating a growth from 60 million at the end of the Yuan period in 1368 to nearly 100 million by 1400 may not be entirely reliable, but rapid population growth encouraged the production of staples—wheat, millet, and barley in the north and rice in the south—at the expense of commercial crops such as cotton that had stimulated many technological innovations under the Song. Staple crops yielded lower profits, which further discouraged capital improvements. New foods, such as sweet potatoes, became available but were little adopted. Population growth in southern and central China caused deforestation and raised the price of wood.

Against the Mongol horsemen in the north the Ming used scattershot mortars and explosive canisters. They even used a few cannon, which they knew about from contacts with the Middle East and later with Europeans. Fearing a loss of technological secrets, the government censored the chapters on gunpowder and guns in early Ming encyclopedias. Shipyards and ports shut down to avoid contact with Japanese pirates and to prevent Chinese from migrating to Southeast Asia.

A technology gap with Korea and Japan opened up nevertheless. When superior steel was needed, supplies came from Japan. Korea moved ahead of China in the design and production of firearms and ships, in printing techniques, and in the sciences of weather prediction and calendar-making. The desire to tap the wealthy Ming market spurred some of these advances.

The Ming Achievement

In the late 1300s and the 1400s the wealth and consumerism of the early Ming stimulated high achievement in literature, the decorative arts, and painting. The plain writing of the Yuan period had produced some of the world's earliest novels: *Water Margin*, which

SECTION REVIEW

- The first Ming emperor, Hongwu, based his policies on an anti-Mongol ideology, but the Ming government came to adopt Yuan practices.
- Yongle reestablished international commerce and sent Zheng He to explore maritime connections to the Middle East.
- Technological innovation continued, but with less frequent advances and reduced output, and some techniques became guarded secrets.
- The Ming reestablished the Confucian examination system, reducing the vitality of commerce.
- The greatest Ming achievements were in literature, the arts, and porcelain production.

originated in the raucous drum-song performances loosely related to Chinese opera, and *Romance of the Three Kingdoms*, which describes the attempts of an upright but doomed war leader and his followers to restore the Han Empire of ancient times and resist the power of the cynical but brilliant villain. *Romance of the Three Kingdoms* and *Water Margin* express the militant but joyous pro-China sentiment of the early Ming era and remain among the most appreciated Chinese fictional works.

Probably the best-known product of Ming technological advance was porcelain. The imperial ceramic works at Jingdezhen (JING-deh-JUHN) experimented with new production techniques and new ways of organizing workers. "Ming ware," a blue-on-white style developed in the 1400s from Indian, Central Asian, and Middle Eastern motifs, became especially prized. Other Ming goods in high demand included furniture, lacquered screens, and silk, all of which found ready markets in Southeast Asia and the Pacific, India, the Middle East, and East Africa.

Centralization and Militarism in East Asia, 1200–1500

What are some of the similarities and differences in how Korea and Japan responded to the Mongol threat?

Korea, Japan, and Annam, the other major states of East Asia, were all affected by confrontation with the Mongols, but with differing results. Japan and Annam escaped Mongol conquest but changed in response to the Mongol threat, becoming more effective and expansive regimes with enhanced commitments to independence.

As for Korea, just as the Ming stressed Chinese traditions and identity in the aftermath of Yuan rule, so Mongol domination contributed to revitalized interest in Korea's own language and history. The Mongols conquered Korea after a difficult war, and though Korea suffered socially and economically under Mongol rule, members of the elite associated closely with the Yuan Empire. After the fall of the Yuan, merchants continued the international connections established in the Mongol period, while Korean armies consolidated a new kingdom and fended off pirates.

Korea from the Mongols to the Yi, 1231–1500

Korea was the answer to the Mongols' search for coastal areas from which to launch naval expeditions and choke off the sea trade of their adversaries. When the Mongols attacked in 1231, the leader of a prominent Korean family assumed the role of military commander and protector of the king (not unlike the shoguns of Japan). Twenty years of defensive war left a ravaged countryside, exhausted armies, and burned treasures, including the renowned nine-story pagoda at Hwang-nyong-sa (hwahng-NEEYAHNG-sah) and the wooden printing blocks of the Tripitaka (tri-PIH-tah-kah), a ninth-century masterpiece of printing art. The commander's underlings killed him in 1258. Soon afterward the Koryo (KAW-ree-oh) king surrendered to the Mongols and became a subject monarch by linking his family to the Great Khan by marriage.

By the mid-1300s the Koryo kings were of mostly Mongol descent and favored Mongol dress, customs, and language. The kings, their families, and their entourages often traveled between China and Korea, thus exposing Korea to the philosophical and artistic styles of Yuan China: neo-Confucianism, Chan Buddhism (called Soøn in Korea), and celadon (light green) pottery.

Mongol control broke down centuries of comparative isolation. Cotton was introduced in southern Korea; gunpowder came into use; and the art of calendar-making stimulated astronomical observation and mathematics. Avenues of advancement opened for

Korean scholars willing to learn Mongolian, landowners willing to open their lands to falconry and grazing, and merchants servicing the new royal exchanges with Beijing. These developments contributed to the rise of a new landed and educated class.

When the Yuan Empire fell in 1368, the Koryo ruling family remained loyal to the Mongols and had to be forced to recognize the new Ming Empire. In 1392 the **Yi** (YEE) established a new kingdom with a capital in Seoul and sought to reestablish a distinctive Korean identity. Like Russia and Ming China, the Yi regime publicly rejected the period of Mongol domination. Yet the Yi government continued to employ Mongol-style land surveys, taxation in kind, and military garrison techniques.

Like the Ming emperors, the Yi kings revived the study of the Confucian classics, an activity that required knowledge of Chinese and showed the dedication of the state to learning. This revival may have led to a key technological breakthrough in printing technology. Koreans had begun using Chinese woodblock printing in the 700s. This technology worked well in China, where a large number of buyers wanted copies of a comparatively small number of texts. But in Korea, the comparatively few literate men had interests in a wide range of texts. Movable wooden or ceramic type appeared in Korea in the early thirteenth century and may have been invented there. But the texts were frequently inaccurate and difficult to read. In the 1400s Yi printers, working directly with the king, developed a reliable device to anchor the pieces of type to the printing plate: they replaced the old beeswax adhesive with solid copper frames. This improved the legibility of the printed page, and high-volume, accurate production became possible. Combined with the phonetic han'gul (HAHN-goor) writing system, this printing technology laid the foundation for a high literacy rate in Korea.

Yi publications told readers how to produce and use fertilizer, transplant rice seedlings, and engineer reservoirs. Building on Eurasian knowledge imported by the Mongols and introduced under the Koryo, Yi scholars developed a meteorological science of their own. They invented or redesigned instruments to

Yi (1392–1910) The Yi dynasty ruled Korea after the fall of the Koryo kingdom.

Movable Type The improvement of cast bronze tiles, each showing a single character, eliminated the need to cast or carve whole pages. Individual tiles—the ones shown are Korean—could be moved from page frame to page frame and gave an even and pleasing appearance. All parts of East Asia eventually adopted this form of printing for cheap, popular books. In the mid-1400s Korea also experimented with a fully phonetic form of writing, which in combination with movable type allowed Koreans unprecedented levels of literacy and access to printed works.   Courtesy, Yushin Yoo

measure wind speed and rainfall and perfected a calendar based on minute comparisons of the Chinese and Islamic systems.

In agriculture, farmers expanded the cultivation of cash crops, the reverse of what was happening in Ming China. Cotton, the primary crop, enjoyed such high value that the state accepted it for tax payments. The Yi army used cotton uniforms, and cotton became the favored fabric of the Korean elite. With cotton gins and spinning wheels powered by water, Korea advanced more rapidly than China in mechanization and began to export considerable amounts of cotton to China and Japan.

Although both the Yuan and the Ming withheld the formula for gunpowder from the Korean government, Korean officials acquired the information by subterfuge. By the later 1300s they had mounted cannon on ships that patrolled against pirates and used gunpowder-driven arrow launchers against enemy personnel and the rigging of enemy ships. Combined with skills in armoring ships, these techniques made the small Yi navy a formidable defense force.

Political Transformation in Japan, 1274–1500

Having secured Korea, the Mongols looked toward Japan, a target they could easily reach from Korea. Their first thirty-thousand-man invasion force in 1274 included Mongol cavalry and archers and sailors from Korea and northeastern Asia. Its weaponry included light catapults and incendiary and explosive projectiles of Chinese manufacture. The Mongol forces landed successfully and decimated the Japanese cavalry, but a great storm on Hakata (HAH-kah-tah) Bay on the north side of Kyushu (KYOO-shoo) Island prevented the establishment of a beachhead and forced the Mongols to sail back to Korea.

The invasion hastened social and political changes that were already under way. Under the Kamakura (kah-mah-KOO-rah) Shogunate established in 1185—another powerful family actually exercised control—the shogun, or military leader, distributed land and privileges to his followers. In return they paid him tribute and supplied him with soldiers. This stable, but decentralized, system depended on balancing the power of regional warlords. Lords in the north and east of Japan's main island were remote from those in the south and west. Beyond devotion to the emperor and the shogun, little united them until the terrifying Mongol threat materialized.

After the return of his fleet, Khubilai sent envoys to Japan demanding submission. Japanese leaders executed them and prepared for war. The shogun took steps to centralize his military government. The effect was to increase the influence of warlords from the south and west of Honshu (Japan's main island) and from the island of Kyushu acting under the shogun's orders, because this was where invasion seemed most likely.

Military planners studied Mongol tactics and retrained and outfitted Japanese warriors for defense against advanced weaponry. Farm laborers drafted from all over the country constructed defensive fortifications. This effort demanded, for the first time, a national system to move resources toward western points rather than toward the imperial or shogunal centers to the east.

The Mongols attacked in 1281. They brought 140,000 warriors, including many non-Mongols, as well as thousands of horses, in hundreds of ships. However, the wall the Japanese had built to cut off Hakata Bay from the mainland deprived the Mongol forces of a reliable landing point. Japanese swordsmen

Tokyo National Museum. Image: TNM Image Archives. http://TnmArchives.jp

Defending Japan Japanese warriors board Mongol warships with swords to prevent the landing of the invasion force in 1281.

rowed out and boarded the Mongol ships lingering offshore. Their superb steel swords shocked the invaders. After a prolonged standoff, a typhoon struck and sank perhaps half of the Mongol ships. The remainder sailed away, never again to harass Japan. The Japanese gave thanks to the "wind of the Gods"—*kamikaze* (KUM-i-kuh-zee)—for driving away the Mongols.

Nevertheless, the Mongol threat continued to influence Japanese development. Prior to his death in 1294, Khubilai had in mind a third invasion. His successors did not carry through with it, but the shoguns did not know that the Mongols had given up the idea. They rebuilt coastal defenses well into the fourteenth century, helping to consolidate the social position of Japan's warrior elite and stimulating the development of a national infrastructure for trade and communication. But the Kamakura Shogunate, based on regionally collected and regionally dispersed revenues, suffered financial strain in trying to pay for centralized road and defense systems.

Between 1333 and 1338 the emperor Go-Daigo broke the centuries-old tradition of imperial seclusion and aloofness from government and tried to reclaim power from the shoguns. This ignited a civil war that destroyed the Kamakura system. In 1338, with the Mongol threat waning, the **Ashikaga** (ah-shee-KAH-gah) **Shogunate** took control at the imperial center of Kyoto.

Provincial warlords enjoyed renewed independence. Around their imposing castles, they sponsored the development of market towns, religious institutions, and schools. The application of technologies imported in earlier periods, including water wheels, improved plows, and Champa rice, increased agricultural productivity. Growing wealth and relative peace stimulated artistic creativity, mostly reflecting Zen Buddhist beliefs held by the warrior elite. In the simple elegance of architecture and gardens, in the contemplative landscapes of artists, and in the eerie, stylized performances of the Noh theater, the aesthetic code of Zen became established in the Ashikaga era.

Despite the technological advancement, artistic productivity, and rapid urbanization of this period, competition among warlords and their followers led to regional wars. By the later 1400s these conflicts resulted in the near destruction of the warlords. The great Onin War in 1477 left Kyoto devastated and the Ashikaga Shogunate a central government in name

kamikaze The "divine wind" that the Japanese credited with blowing Mongol invaders away from their shores in 1281.
Ashikaga Shogunate (1338–1573) The second of Japan's military governments headed by a shogun (a military ruler). Sometimes called the Muromachi Shogunate.

Noh Drama Performance This slow, rhythmic, chanted form of drama appealed to the military elite with its stories of warriors, women, gods, and demons. The minimal stage is normally bare except for a painting at the rear of a pine tree, symbolizing the means by which deities descend to earth, and a narrow bridge to the left by which major actors enter the stage. The actors wear masks and lavish costumes. Four instrumentalists playing a flute and three types of drum punctuate the chanting.

only. Ambitious but low-ranking warriors, some with links to trade with the continent, began to scramble for control of the provinces.

After the fall of the Yuan in 1368 Japan resumed overseas trade, exporting raw materials and swords, as well as folding fans, invented in Japan during the period of isolation. Japan's primary imports from China were books and porcelain. The volatile political environment in Japan gave rise to partnerships between warlords and local merchants. All worked to strengthen their own towns and treasuries through overseas commerce or, sometimes, through piracy.

The Emergence of Vietnam, 1200–1500

Before the first Mongol attack in 1257, the states of Annam (northern Vietnam) and Champa (southern Vietnam) had clashed frequently. Annam (once called Dai Viet) looked toward China and had once been subject to the Tang. Chinese political ideas, social philosophies, dress, religion, and language heavily influenced its official culture. Champa related more closely to the trading

SECTION REVIEW

- Mongol conquest devastated Korea, but Mongol rule opened it to new ideas and technologies.
- The Yi dynasty succeeded the Koryo and fostered local identity while encouraging economic expansion and technological innovation.
- In Japan, the Mongol threat forced military and organizational innovations, but the expense of these defenses weakened the Kamakura Shogunate.
- Go-Daigo's failed attempt to reassert imperial power resulted in the rise of the Ashikaga Shogunate.
- The warring states of Vietnam avoided Mongol conquest but paid tribute to the Yuan Empire.
- After the Ming withdrawal, Annam conquered Champa, establishing a unified state on both Confucian and local practices.

networks of the Indian Ocean; its official culture was strongly influenced by Indian religion, language, architecture, and dress.

Champa's relationship with China depended in part on how close its enemy Annam was to China at any particular time. During the Song period Annam was neither formally subject to China nor particularly threatening to Champa militarily, so Champa inaugurated a trade and tribute relationship with China that spread fast-ripening Champa rice throughout East Asia.

The Mongols exacted tribute from both Annam and Champa until the fall of the Yuan Empire in 1368. Mongol political and military ambitions were mostly focused elsewhere, however, which minimized their impact on politics and culture. The two Vietnamese kingdoms soon resumed their warfare. When Annam moved its army to reinforce its southern border, Ming troops occupied the capital, Hanoi, and installed a puppet government. Almost thirty years elapsed before Annam regained independence and resumed a tributary status. By then the Ming were turning to meet Mongol challenges to their north. In a series of ruthless campaigns, Annam terminated Champa's independence, and by 1500 the ancestor of the modern state of Vietnam, still called Annam, had been born.

The new state still relied on Confucian bureaucratic government and an examination system, but some practices differed from those in China. The Vietnamese legal code, for example, preserved group landowning and decision making within the villages, as

National Museum of Japanese History/DNP

well as women's property rights. Both developments probably had roots in an early rural culture based on the growing of rice in wet paddies; by this time the Annamese considered them distinctive features of their own culture.

Conclusion

The Mongols were the most successful warriors the world had ever seen. In less than a hundred years, they had conquered an empire that covered half of Eurasia and reached from Poland to Vietnam. And yet half a century later, their empire had broken apart and they had lost most of what they had gained. Why were their conquests so short-lived compared with those of the Romans or the Arabs?

The Mongols, though ferocious warriors, were too few in number to manage a huge empire, and so they turned to the peoples they had conquered—Chinese, Persians, Turks, and Arabs—to carry out the tasks of administration. They were famous for tolerating many religions and cultures among the people who accepted their rule, but they had no common religion or ideology upon which to build a lasting political culture. Some Mongols converted to Islam, others to Buddhism, and yet others became Chinese in language and culture. As the Mongol armies were widely scattered, subject peoples whose culture had never been erased by the Mongols reasserted themselves politically and militarily.

Once Mongol rule was in place, travel across the breadth of Eurasia became safer and easier than it had ever been before or was to be for centuries thereafter. Trade flourished, as did the spread of ideas and technologies. Yet with trade came the plague, which decimated all the regions that they occupied. When the subject peoples reasserted themselves, they remembered the Mongols for the violence and brutality of their conquest and for the disease they carried. Unlike the Roman or the Arabs, the Mongols did not leave a legacy of culture, administration, or religion, only memories of death and destruction.

CHAPTER REVIEW

 Download the MP3 audio file of the Chapter Review to listen to on the go.

What accounts for the magnitude and speed of the Mongol conquests? (page 287)

Nomadic mobility and endurance, expertise in military technology, and systematic army organization made the armies of Genghis Khan all but invincible. While the Mongols did not usually outnumber their enemies, they were experts on horseback and used superior bows. Turkic pastoral peoples who suffered defeat often enrolled in the Mongol ranks, thus magnifying the power of the Mongols themselves.

How did Mongol expansion and Islam affect each other? (page 294)

As rivalries mounted between the Il-khan and Golden Horde states, Islam became a point of contention. Rulers who converted to Islam were initially lax in their observance and affiliations. The Il-khans came to value urban Muslim culture, but they taxed farmers mercilessly.

This contributed to a weakness that allowed the Golden Horde to make inroads on Il-khan territory. Meanwhile, Timur rose to power in Jagadai territory and undertook wide-ranging conquests. The Il-khans, Timur, and his successors presided over a flowering of Islamic culture that drew upon Iranian and Chinese cultural elements to contribute notable achievements in historical writing, art, mathematics, and astronomy.

What benefits resulted from the integration of Eurasia into the Mongol Empire? (page 297)

The Great Khans attracted emissaries and traders from all over Eurasia to their court, revitalizing the Silk Road. Cultural contact between east and west had greater long-term impact than the Mongols' political power. Muslim astronomers and calendar makers found a welcome reception in China, and Chinese artistic styles became popular in Iran. Mongol occupation, or the threat of Mongol conquest, also helped non-Mongol political leaders galvanize popular support for local state building.

How did Mongol rule in China foster cultural and scientific exchange? (page 300)

In China, Yuan rule reestablished connections with Inner Asia that had earlier benefited Tang rule (see Chapter 11). The empire rewarded skills more than ethnic or linguistic identity. Beijing, the Yuan capital, developed a dynamic cultural scene, even though the turmoil of the period also produced war casualties, spread of disease, and migration to southern China.

In what ways did the Ming Empire continue or discontinue Mongol practices? (page 302)

The Ming overthrew the Yuan and reaffirmed Chinese ethnicity as a basis for rule. Leaving Beijing, they located their capital in the south and relied on study of the Confucian classics and the examination system for choosing imperial officials. Nevertheless, Mongols still served in the army, and after a time Beijing again became the capital. Though some Yuan administrative practices continued, contact and trade with Inner Asia dwindled because of political disunity in the old Mongol core area.

What are some of the similarities and differences in how Korea and Japan responded to the Mongol threat? (page 305)

The conquered Korean rulers remained loyal to the Yuan and benefited from new technologies and administrative

techniques. When the Yuan fell, however, a Korean dynasty emerged that stressed non-Mongol ethnicity and reviled the earlier Mongol domination, even while retaining many of the innovations of that period.

After twice repelling Mongol invasions, Japan remained highly militarized. Paradoxically, regional warlords embraced cultural innovations, many of Chinese inspiration, that subsequently became central to Japanese identity. Zen Buddhism, Noh drama, and the ritual of the tea ceremony united the Japanese elite even as the warlords, with their samurai armies, seized control from the ineffective imperial government.

Key Terms

Mongols (p. 287)
Genghis Khan (p. 287)
nomadism (p. 287)
Yuan Empire (p. 293)
bubonic plague (p. 293)
Il-khan (p. 294)
Golden Horde (p. 294)
Timur (p. 295)
Rashid al-Din (p. 296)
Nasir al-Din Tusi (p. 296)
Alexander Nevskii (p. 298)

tsar (p. 299)
Ottoman Empire (p. 300)
Khubilai Khan (p. 300)
lama (p. 300)
Beijing (p. 301)
Ming Empire (p. 303)
Yongle (p. 304)
Zheng He (p. 304)
Yi (p. 306)
kamikaze (p. 308)
Ashikaga Shogunate (p. 308)

Web Resources

Pronunciation Guide
Interactive Maps
• MAP 12.1 The Mongol Domains in Eurasia in 1300
• MAP 12.2 The Ming Empire and Its Allies, 1368–1500

Primary Source
• Description of the World
Answer to the History in Focus Question
See photo on page 294, "Passport."

 Visit the CourseMate website at www.cengagebrain.com for additional study tools and review materials for this chapter.

Tropical Africa and Asia

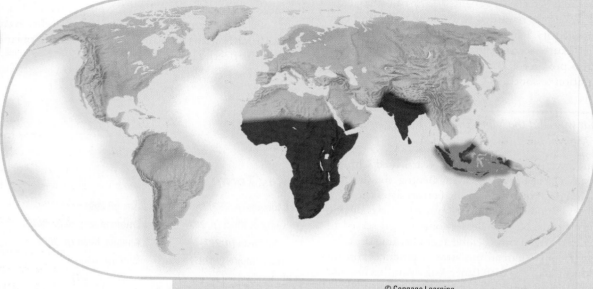

© Cengage Learning

CHAPTER PREVIEW

Tropical Lands and Peoples
How did environmental differences shape cultural differences in tropical Africa and Asia?

New Islamic Empires
Under what circumstances did the first Islamic empires arise in Africa and India?

Indian Ocean Trade
How did cultural and ecological differences promote trade, and in turn how did trade and other contacts promote state growth and the spread of Islam?

Social and Cultural Change
What social and cultural changes are reflected in the history of peoples living in tropical Africa and Asia during this period?

Conclusion

ENVIRONMENT & TECHNOLOGY:
The Indian Ocean Dhow

Visit the CourseMate website at **www.cengagebrain.com** for additional study tools and review materials for this chapter.

ultan Abu Bakr (a-BOO BAK-uhr) customarily offered hospitality to distinguished visitors to his city of Mogadishu, an Indian Ocean port on the northeast coast of Africa. In 1331, he provided food and lodging for Muhammad ibn Abdullah **Ibn Battuta** (IB-uhn ba-TOO-tuh) (1304–1369), a young Muslim scholar from Morocco who had set out to explore the Islamic world. Having already made a pilgrimage to Mecca and traveled throughout the Middle East, Ibn Battuta was touring the trading cities of the Red Sea and East Africa. Subsequent travels took him to Central Asia and India, China and Southeast Asia, Muslim Spain, and sub-Saharan West Africa. Recounting some 75,000 miles (120,000 kilometers) of travel over twenty-nine years, Ibn Battuta's journal provides invaluable information on these lands.

Hospitality being considered a noble virtue among Muslims, regardless of physical and cultural differences, his reception at Mogadishu mirrored that at other cities. Ibn Battuta noted that Sultan Abu Bakr had skin darker than his own and spoke a different native language (Somali), but as brothers in faith, they prayed together at Friday services, where the sultan greeted his foreign guest in Arabic, the common language of the Islamic world: "You are heartily welcome, and you have honored our land and given us pleasure." When Sultan Abu Bakr and his jurists heard and decided cases after the mosque service, they used the religious law familiar in all Muslim lands.

In addition to the religion of Islam, the diverse peoples of Africa and southern Asia whom Ibn Battuta visited were also linked by the tropical environment itself. A network of overland and maritime routes joined their lands (see Chapter 8), providing avenues for the spread of beliefs and technologies, as well as goods. Ibn Battuta traveled with merchants who regularly sailed down the coast of East Africa. He joined trading caravans across the Sahara to West Africa. His path to India followed overland trade routes, and a merchant ship carried him on to China. This chapter discusses the lands that Ibn Battuta visited in his long voyages, the natural geographic features they shared, and the commercial, cultural, and religious links that tied them together.

Tropical Lands and Peoples

How did environmental differences shape cultural differences in tropical Africa and Asia?

To obtain food, the people who inhabited the tropical regions of Africa and Asia used methods that generations of experimentation had proved successful, whether at the desert's edge, in grasslands, or in tropical rain forests. Much of their success lay in learning how to blend human activities with the natural order, but they also modified the environment to suit their needs with irrigation works and mining.

The Tropical Environment

Because of the angle of earth's axis, the sun's rays warm the **tropics** year-round. The equator marks the center of the tropical zone, and the Tropic of Cancer and Tropic of Capricorn mark its outer limits. Africa lies almost entirely within the tropics, as do southern Arabia, most of India, and all of the Southeast Asian mainland and islands.

Lacking the hot and cold seasons of temperate lands, the rainy and dry seasons of the Afro-Asian tropics derive from wind patterns across the surrounding oceans. Winds from a permanent high-pressure air mass over the South Atlantic deliver heavy rainfall to the western coast of Africa during much of the year. However, in December and January, large high-pressure zones over northern Africa and Arabia produce a southward movement of dry air that limits the inland penetration of the moist ocean winds.

In the lands around the Indian Ocean, the rainy and dry seasons reflect the influence of alternating

Ibn Battuta (1304–1369) Moroccan Muslim scholar, the most widely traveled individual of his time. He wrote a detailed account of his visits to Islamic lands from China to Spain and the western Sudan.
tropics Equatorial region between the Tropic of Cancer and the Tropic of Capricorn. It is characterized by generally warm or hot temperatures year-round, though much variation exists due to altitude and other factors. Temperate zones north and south of the tropics usually have a winter season.

East African Pastoralists Herding large and small livestock has long been a way of life in the drier parts of the tropics. These herders, perhaps Massai, bring their cattle, goats, and sheep to a river to drink.

© Victor Englebert

History in Focus *What vegetation do you see in the picture? What do you think herds of animals do to the vegetation near watering places? How can herders in dry places balance their animals' need for both water and food? Find the answer online.*

winds known as **monsoons**. Between April and August, as the continent of Asia heats up more than the surrounding seas, it forms a low-pressure zone that creates a northward movement of air from the Indian Ocean (the southwest monsoon) and brings southern Asia the heavy rains of its wet season. From December to March, as the continent cools off, a high pressure zone develops over Tibet and the Himalaya (him-AH-LAY-uh) Mountains that forces air to flow outward toward the ocean: the dry northeast monsoon.

Areas with the heaviest rainfall—the broad belt along the equator in coastal West Africa and West-Central Africa, parts of coastal India, and Southeast Asia—have dense rain forests. Lighter rains produce other forest patterns. The English word *jungle* comes from an Indian word for the tangled undergrowth in the forests that once covered most of India.

Some other parts of the tropics rarely see rain at all. The world's largest desert, the Sahara, stretches across northern Africa and continues eastward across Arabia, southern Iran, Pakistan, and northwest India. Another desert occupies southwestern Africa. Most of tropical India and Africa falls between the deserts and rain forests and experiences moderate rainy seasons. These lands range from fairly wet woodlands to the

much drier grasslands characteristic of much of East Africa.

Altitude produces other climatic variations. Thin atmospheres at high altitudes hold less heat than atmospheres at lower elevations. Snow covers some of the volcanic mountains of eastern Africa all or part of the year. The snowcapped Himalayas that form India's northern frontier rise so high that they block cold air from moving south and thus give northern India a more tropical climate than its latitude would suggest. The plateaus of inland Africa and the Deccan (DEK-ahn) Plateau of central India also enjoy cooler temperatures than the coastal plains.

Human Ecosystems

Thinkers in temperate lands once imagined that surviving in the tropics was simply a matter of picking wild fruit off trees. A careful observer touring the tropics in 1200 would have noticed, however, many differences in societies deriving from their particular ecosystems—that is, from how human groups used the

---

monsoons Seasonal winds in the Indian Ocean caused by the differences in temperature between the rapidly heating and cooling landmasses of Africa and Asia and the slowly changing ocean waters. These strong and predictable winds have long been ridden across the open sea by sailors, and the large amounts of rainfall that they deposit on parts of India, Southeast Asia, and China permit the cultivation of several crops a year.

Chronology

	The Arab Lands	Iran and Central Asia
1200		1206 Delhi Sultanate founded in India
	1230s Mali Empire founded	
	1270 Solomonic dynasty in Ethiopia founded	
1300		1298 Delhi Sultanate annexes Gujarat
	1324–1325 Mansa Musa's pilgrimage to Mecca	
1400		1398 Timur sacks Delhi; Delhi Sultanate declines
	1400s Great Zimbabwe at its peak	
	1433 Tuareg retake Timbuktu; Mali declines	
1500		1500 Port of Malacca at its peak

plants, animals, and other resources of their physical environments.

Domesticated plants and animals had become commonplace long before 1200, but people in some environments continued to rely primarily on hunting, fishing, and gathering. For Pygmy (PIG-mee) hunters in the dense forests of Central Africa, small size permitted pursuit of prey through dense undergrowth. Hunting also prevailed in the upper altitudes of the Himalayas and in some desert environments. A Portuguese expedition led by Vasco da Gama visited the arid coast of southwestern Africa in 1497 and saw there healthy people feeding themselves on "the flesh of seals, whales, and gazelles, and the roots of wild plants." Fishing, which was common along all the major lakes and rivers as well as in the oceans, might be combined with farming. The ocean fishermen of East Africa, Southeast Asia, and coastal India had boating skills that often led to engagement in ocean trade.

Herding provided sustenance in areas too arid for agriculture. Pastoralists consumed milk from their herds and traded hides and meat to farmers in return for grain and vegetables. The world's largest concentration of pastoralists inhabited the arid and semi-arid lands of northeastern Africa and Arabia. Like Ibn Battuta's host at Mogadishu, some Somalis lived in towns, but most grazed goats and camels in the desert hinterland of the Horn of Africa. The western Sahara sustained herds of sheep and camels belonging to the Tuareg (TWAH-reg), whose intimate knowledge of the desert made them invaluable as guides to caravans. Along the Sahara's southern edge the cattle-herding Fulani (foo-LAH-nee) people gradually extended their

range, and by 1500 they had spread throughout the western and central Sudan.

The density of agricultural populations reflected the adequacy of rainfall and soils. South and Southeast Asia were generally wetter than tropical Africa, making intensive cultivation possible. High yields supported dense populations. In 1200, over 100 million people lived in South and Southeast Asia, more than four-fifths of them on the fertile Indian mainland. Though a little less than the population of China, this was triple the number of people living in all of Africa and nearly double the number in Europe.

India's lush vegetation led one Middle Eastern writer to call it "the most agreeable abode on earth. Its delightful plains resemble the garden of Paradise."[1] Rice cultivation dominated in the fertile Ganges plain of northeast India, mainland Southeast Asia, and southern China. In drier areas, farmers grew grains—wheat, sorghum, and millet, and legumes such as peas and beans whose ripening cycles matched the pattern of the rainy and dry seasons. Tubers and tree crops characterized farming in rain-forest clearings.

The spread of farming, including the movement to Africa of Asian crops like yams, cocoyams, and bananas, did not necessarily change the natural environment. In most of sub-Saharan Africa and much of Southeast Asia, extensive rather than intensive cultivation prevailed. Instead of enriching fields with manure and vegetable compost so they could be cultivated year after year, farmers abandoned fields when the natural fertility of the soil fell and cleared new fields—a type of agriculture called swidden. Ashes from the brush, grasses, and tree limbs they cut down and burned boosted the new fields' fertility. Shifting to new land every few years made efficient use of labor in areas with comparatively poor soils.

Water Systems and Irrigation

The inland delta of the Niger River received naturally fertilizing annual floods with which farmers could grow rice for sale to the trading cities along the Niger bend. Elsewhere, tropical farmers had to move the water to their crops. In Vietnam, Java, Malaya, and Burma, farmers had built terraces on hillsides to conserve some of the monsoon rainfall for growing rice during the dry season. North and south India also had water-storage dams and irrigation canals. Villagers in southeast India built stone and earthen dams across rivers to store water for gradual release through elaborate irrigation canals. Extended over many generations, these canals irrigated a wide area.

As had been true since the days of the first river-valley civilizations (see Chapter 1), governments built and controlled the largest irrigation systems. The **Delhi** (DEL-ee) **Sultanate** (1206–1526) in northern India acquired extensive new water-control systems. Ibn Battuta admired a large reservoir constructed in the first quarter of the thirteenth century that supplied the city of Delhi with water. As the water level fell during the dry season, farmers planted sugar cane, cucumbers, and melons along the reservoir's rim. In the fourteenth century, the Delhi sultan built in the Ganges plain a network of irrigation canals that remained unsurpassed until the nineteenth century. Such systems made it possible to grow crops throughout the year.

Since the tenth century, the Indian Ocean island of Ceylon (modern Sri Lanka [shree LAHNG-kuh]) had been home to the world's greatest concentration of irrigation reservoirs and canals. These facilities supported the large population of the Sinhalese (sin-huh-LEEZ) kingdom in arid northern Ceylon. In Southeast Asia, another impressive system of reservoirs and canals served Cambodia's capital city, Angkor (ANG-kor).

Between 1250 and 1400, however, the irrigation complex in Ceylon fell into ruin when invaders from south India disrupted the Sinhalese government. As a result, malaria spread by mosquitoes breeding in the irrigation canals ravaged the population. In the fifteenth century, the great Cambodian system fell into ruin when the government that maintained it collapsed. Neither system was ever rebuilt. The vulnerability of complex irrigation systems built by powerful governments contrasts with village-based irrigation systems. Though invasion and natural calamity might damage the latter, they usually bounced back because they depended on local initiative and simpler technologies.

Mineral Resources

The most productive metal trade in the tropics, iron-working, provided the hoes, axes, and knives farmers used to clear and cultivate their fields. Between 1200 and 1500, the rain forests of coastal West Africa and Southeast Asia opened up for farming. Iron also supplied spear and arrow points, needles, and nails. Indian metalsmiths became known for forging strong and beautiful swords. In Africa, many people attributed magical powers to iron smelters and blacksmiths.

Copper and its alloys had special importance in the Copperbelt of southeastern Africa during the fourteenth and fifteenth centuries. Smelters cast the metal into large X-shaped ingots (metal castings), and local coppersmiths worked these into wire and decorative objects. In the western Sudan, Ibn Battuta described a mining town that produced two sizes of copper bars that served as currency in place of coins. Some coppersmiths in West Africa cast copper and brass (an alloy of copper and zinc) statues and heads that now rank as masterpieces of world art. They utilized the "lost-wax" method, in which molten metal melts a thin layer of wax sandwiched between clay forms, replacing the "lost" wax with hard metal.

African gold moved in quantity across the Sahara and into the Indian Ocean and Red Sea trades. Some came from streambeds along the upper Niger River and farther south in modern Ghana (GAH-nuh). In the hills south of the Zambezi (zam-BEE-zee) River, archaeologists have discovered thousands of mineshafts, dating from 1200, that were sunk up to 100

Delhi Sultanate (1206–1526) Centralized Indian empire, created by Muslim invaders.

feet (30 meters) into the ground to get at gold ores. Although panning for gold remained important in the streams descending from the mountains of northern India, the gold and silver mines in India seem to have been exhausted by this period. Thus, Indians imported from Southeast Asia and Africa considerable quantities of gold for jewelry and temple decoration.

New Islamic Empires

Under what circumstances did the first Islamic empires arise in Africa and India?

The empires of Mali in West Africa and Delhi in northern India, the largest and richest tropical states of the period between 1200 and 1500, both utilized administrative and military systems introduced from the Islamic heartland. Yet **Mali**, an indigenous African dynasty that had earlier adopted Islam through the peaceful influence of Muslim merchants and scholars, differed in many ways from the Delhi Sultanate founded and ruled by invading Turkish and Afghan Muslims. The wealth of Mali depended on trans-Saharan trade, but long-distance trade played only a minor role in Delhi.

Mali in the Western Sudan

Muslim rule beginning in the seventh century (see Chapter 9) greatly stimulated increased trade along the routes that crossed the Sahara. In the centuries that followed, the faith of Muhammad gradually spread to the lands south of the desert, which the Arabs called the *bilad al-sudan* (bih-LAD uhs-soo-DAN), "land of the blacks."

Muslim Berbers invading out of the desert in 1076 caused the collapse of Ghana, the empire that preceded Mali in the western Sudan (see Chapter 9), but their conquest did little to spread Islam. To the east, the Muslim attacks that destroyed the Christian Nubian kingdoms on the upper Nile in the late thirteenth century opened that area to Muslim influences, but Christian Ethiopia successfully withstood Muslim advances. Instead, Islam's spread south of the Sahara usually followed a pattern of gradual and peaceful conversion. The expansion of commercial contacts in the western Sudan and on the East African coast greatly promoted the conversion process. Most Africans found meaning and benefit in the teachings of Islam. Takrur (TAHK-roor) in the far western Sudan became the first sub-Saharan African state to adopt the new faith around 1030.

Shortly after 1200, Takrur expanded under King Sumanguru (soo-muhn-GOO-roo), only to suffer a major defeat some thirty years later at the hands of Sundiata (soon-JAH-tuh), the upstart leader of the Malinke (muh-LING-kay) people. Though both leaders professed Islam, Malinke legends recall their battles as clashes between powerful magicians, suggesting how much old and new beliefs mingled. Sumanguru could reportedly appear and disappear at will, assume dozens of shapes, and catch arrows in midflight. Sundiata defeated Sumanguru's much larger forces through superior military maneuvers and by successfully wounding his adversary with a special arrow that robbed him of his magical powers. This victory was followed by others that created Sundiata's Mali Empire (see Map 13.1).

Mali, the empire that grew from Sundiata's victories, depended on a well-developed agricultural base and control of the regional and trans-Saharan trade routes, as had Ghana before it. Mali, however, controlled a greater area than Ghana, including not

Mali Empire created by indigenous Muslims in western Sudan of West Africa from the thirteenth to fifteenth century. It was famous for its role in the trans-Saharan gold trade.

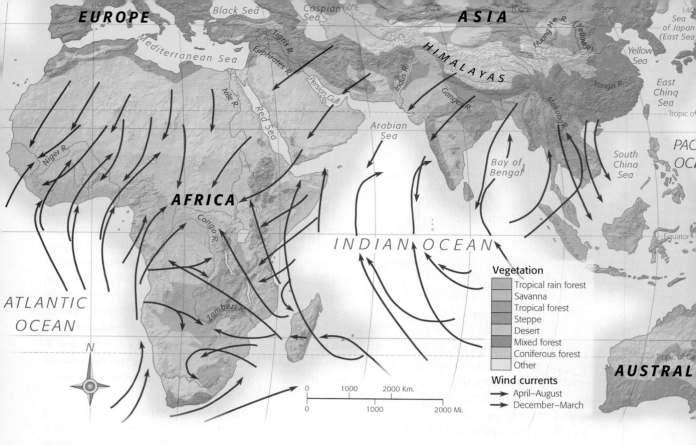

Map 13.1 Africa, 1200–1500 Many African states had beneficial links to the trade that crossed the Sahara and the Indian Ocean. Before 1500, sub-Saharan Africa's external ties were primarily with the Islamic world. © Cengage Learning

 Interactive Map

only the core trading area of the upper Niger but also the gold fields of the Niger headwaters to the southwest. Moreover, its rulers fostered the spread of Islam among the empire's political and trading elites. Control of the gold and copper trades and contacts with North African Muslim traders gave Mali unprecedented prosperity.

Under the ruler **Mansa Kankan Musa** (MAHN-suh KAHN-kahn MOO-suh) (r. 1312–1337), the empire's reputation for wealth spread far and wide. Mansa Musa's pilgrimage to Mecca in 1324–1325 fulfilled his personal duty as a Muslim and at the same time put on display his exceptional wealth. He traveled with a large entourage. Besides his senior wife and five hundred of her ladies in waiting and their slaves, one account says there were also sixty thousand porters and a vast caravan of camels carrying supplies and provisions. For purchases and gifts, he

brought along eighty packages of gold, each weighing 122 ounces (3.8 kilograms). In addition, five hundred slaves each carried a golden staff. Mansa Musa dispersed so many gifts when he passed through Cairo that the value of gold was depressed for years.

On his return from this pilgrimage, Mansa Musa built new mosques and opened Quran schools in the cities along the Niger bend. Ibn Battuta, who visited Mali from 1352 to 1354 during the reign of Mansa Musa's successor, Mansa Suleiman (MAHN-suh SOO-lay-mahn) (r. 1341–1360), lauded the Malians for their faithful recitation of prayers and their zeal in teaching

Mansa Kankan Musa Ruler of Mali (r. 1312–1337). His pilgrimage through Egypt to Mecca in 1324–1325 established the empire's reputation for wealth in the Mediterranean world.

King and Queen of Ife This copper-alloy work shows the royal couple of the Yoruba kingdom of Ife, the oldest and most sacred of the Yoruba kingdoms of southwestern Nigeria. The casting dates to the period between 1100 and 1500, except for the reconstruction of the male's face, the original of which shattered in 1957 when the road builder who found it accidentally struck it with his pick.   Andre Held Collection/The Bridgeman Art Library

leatherworking. The central Sudanic state of Kanem-Bornu (KAH-nuhm-BOR-noo) also expanded in the late fifteenth century from the ancient kingdom of Kanem, whose rulers had accepted Islam in about 1085. At its peak around 1250, Kanem had absorbed the state of Bornu south and west of Lake Chad and gained control of routes crossing the central Sahara. As Kanem-Bornu's armies conquered new territories, they also spread the rule of Islam.

The Delhi Sultanate in India

Having long ago lost the defensive unity of the Gupta Empire (see Chapter 5), the divided states of northwest India fell prey to raids by Afghan warlords beginning in the early eleventh century. In the last decades of the twelfth century, a Turkish dynasty armed with powerful crossbows captured the northern Indian cities of Lahore and Delhi. One partisan Muslim chronicler wrote: "The city [Delhi] and its vicinity was freed from idols and idol-worship, and in the sanctuaries of the images of the [Hindu] Gods, mosques were raised by the worshippers of one God."[2] Turkish adventurers from Central Asia flocked to join the invading armies, overwhelming the small Indian states, which were often at war with one another.

Between 1206 and 1236, the Muslim invaders extended their rule over the Hindu princes and chiefs in much of northern India. Sultan Iltutmish (il-TOOT-mish) (r. 1211–1236) consolidated the conquest in a series of military expeditions that made his realm the largest in India (see Map 13.2). He also secured official recognition of the Delhi Sultanate as a Muslim state by the caliph of Baghdad. Although pillaging continued, especially on the frontiers, the incorporation of

children the Quran. He also reported that "complete and general safety" prevailed in the vast territories ruled by Suleiman and that foreign travelers had no reason to fear being robbed or having their goods confiscated if they died. Two centuries after its founding, Mali began to disintegrate. Mansa Suleiman's successors could not prevent rebellions breaking out among the diverse peoples subjected to Malinke rule, while other groups attacked from without. In 1433 the desert Tuareg retook their city of Timbuktu (tim-buk-TOO), and by 1500 the rulers of Mali had dominion over little more than the Malinke heartland.

The cities of the upper Niger survived Mali's collapse, but some trade and intellectual life moved east to the central Sudan. Shortly after 1450, several Hausa city-states officially adopted Islam and took on importance as manufacturing and trading centers, becoming famous for cotton textiles and

Dijinguere Ber Mosque in Timbuktu Built almost entirely of earth and organic materials, this fourteenth-century mosque can accommodate 2,000 worshippers. Mansa Kankan Musa, the most famous ruler of the Empire of Mali, is said to have paid Abu Ishaq al-Sahili, a native of Granada in Muslim Spain, 200 kilograms of gold for designing this masterful combination of Islamic and African traditions.

north India into the Islamic world marked the beginning of the invaders' transformation from brutal conquerors to somewhat more benign rulers. Muslim commanders extended protection to the conquered, freeing them from persecution in return for payment of a special tax. Yet Hindus never forgot the intolerance and destruction of their first contacts with the invaders.

Iltutmish astonished his ministers by passing over his weak and pleasure-seeking sons and designating as his heir his beloved and talented daughter Raziya (rah-ZEE-uh). When they questioned the unprecedented idea of a woman ruling a Muslim state, he said, "My sons are devoted to the pleasures of youth: no one of them is qualified to be king. . . . There is no one more competent to guide the State than my daughter." Her brother—who delighted in riding his elephant through the bazaar, showering the crowds with coins—ruled ineptly for seven months before the ministers relented and put Raziya on the throne. A chronicler who knew her explained why this able ruler lasted less than four years (r. 1236–1240):

Sultan Raziya was a great monarch. She was wise, just, and generous, a benefactor to her kingdom, a dispenser of justice, the protector of her subjects, and the leader of her armies. She was endowed with all the qualities befitting a king, but she was not born of the right sex, and so in the estimation of men all these virtues were worthless. May God have mercy upon her![3]

Doing her best to prove herself a proper king, Raziya dressed like a man and led her troops atop an elephant. In the end, however, the Turkish chiefs imprisoned her. She escaped, but she was killed by a robber soon after.

After a half-century of stagnation and rebellion, the ruthless but efficient policies of Sultan Ala-ud-din Khalji (uh-LAH-uh-DEEN KAL-jee) (r. 1296–1316) increased control over the empire's outlying provinces. Successful frontier raids and high taxes kept his treasury full, wage and price controls in Delhi kept down the cost of maintaining a large army, and a network of spies stifled intrigue. When a Mongol threat from Central Asia eased, Ala-ud-din's forces extended

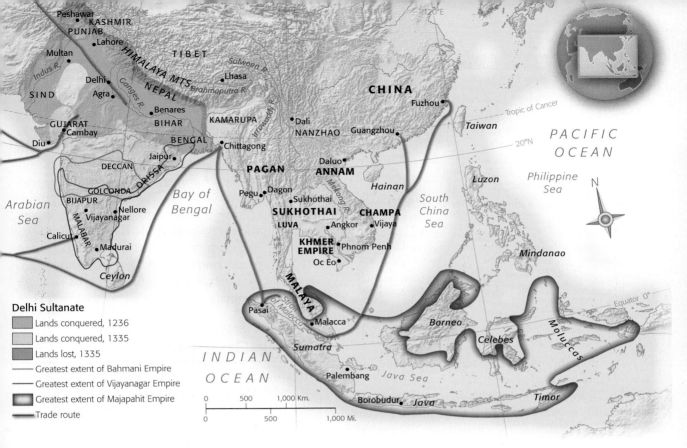

Map 13.2 South and Southeast Asia, 1200–1500

Delhi Sultanate

- Lands conquered, 1236
- Lands conquered, 1335
- Lands lost, 1335
- Greatest extent of Bahmani Empire
- Greatest extent of Vijayanagar Empire
- Greatest extent of Majapahit Empire
- Trade route

Map 13.2 South and Southeast Asia, 1200–1500 The rise of new empires and the expansion of maritime trade reshaped the lives of many tropical Asians.   © Cengage Learning

 Interactive Map

the sultanate's southern flank, seizing the rich trading state of **Gujarat** (goo-juh-RAHT) in 1298, and then drove southward, briefly seizing the southern tip of the Indian peninsula.

When Ibn Battuta visited Delhi, Sultan Muhammad ibn Tughluq (TOOG-look) (r. 1325–1351) received him in his celebrated Hall of a Thousand Pillars. The world traveler praised the sultan's piety and generosity, but he also recounted his cruelties. The sultan enlarged the sultanate to its greatest extent at the expense of the independent Indian states but balanced his aggressive policy with religious toleration. He even attended Hindu religious festivals. However, his successor, Firuz Shah (fuh-ROOZ shah) (r. 1351–1388), alienated powerful Hindus by taxing the Brahmins, preferring to cultivate good relations with the Muslim elite. Muslim chroniclers praised him for constructing forty mosques, thirty colleges, and a hundred hospitals.

A small minority in a giant land, the Turkish rulers relied on terror to keep their subjects submissive, on harsh military reprisals to put down rebellion, and on pillage and high taxes to sustain the ruling elite in luxury and power. Though little different from most other large states of this time (including Mali) in being more a burden than a benefit to most of its subjects, the sultanate never lost the disadvantage of foreign origins and alien religious identity. Nevertheless, over time, the sultans did incorporate some Hindus into their administrations, and some members of the ruling elite also married women from prominent Hindu families, though the brides had to become Muslim.

Gujarat Region of western India famous for trade and manufacturing; the inhabitants are called Gujaratis.

321

- Islam spread into western sub-Saharan Africa usually by peaceful conversion through trading contacts.
- Founded by Sundiata, Mali depended on agriculture and control of trade routes, and Islam spread among its elites.
- Mali reached its height under Mansa Kankan Musa but declined after the death of his successor, and power shifted eastward.
- Muslim Turkish invaders conquered much of Hindu northern India to establish the Delhi Sultanate.
- The sultanate grew to encompass most of India; the sultans ruled through terror, pillage, and heavy taxation.
- Though efficient, the sultanate suffered from internal struggles and fell under pressure from rival states and invaders.

Personal and religious rivalries within the Muslim elite, along with Hindu discontent, threatened the Delhi Sultanate whenever it showed weakness and finally hastened its end. In the mid-fourteenth century, Muslim nobles challenged the sultan's dominion and established the independent Bahmani (bah-MAHN-ee) kingdom (1347–1482) on the Deccan Plateau. Defending against the southward push of Bahmani armies, the Hindu states of south India united to form the Vijayanagar (vee-juh-yah-NAH-gar) Empire (1336–1565), which at its height controlled the rich trading ports on both coasts of south India and held Ceylon as a tributary state.

The elites of Vijayanagar and the Bahmani state turned a blind eye to religious differences when doing so favored their interests. Bahmani rulers sought to balance Muslim domination with the practical policies of incorporating the Hindu leaders into the government, marrying Hindu wives, and appointing Brahmins to high offices. Vijayanagar rulers hired Muslim horsemen and archers to strengthen their military forces and formed an alliance with the Muslim-ruled state of Gujarat.

By 1351, when all of south India had cast off Delhi's rule, much of north India rose in rebellion. In the east, Bengal broke away from the sultanate in 1338, becoming a center of the mystical Sufi tradition of Islam (see Chapter 9). In the west, Gujarat regained its independence by 1390. The weakening of Delhi's

central authority tempted fresh Mongol interest in the area. In 1398, the Turko-Mongol leader Timur (see Chapter 12) captured the city of Delhi. When his armies withdrew the next year with vast quantities of loot and tens of thousands of captives, the largest city in southern Asia lay empty and in ruins. The Delhi Sultanate never recovered.

For all its shortcomings, the Delhi Sultanate triggered the development of centralized political authority in India. Prime ministers and provincial governors serving under the sultans established a bureaucracy, improved food production, promoted trade, and put in circulation a common currency. Despite the many conflicts that Muslim conquest and rule provoked, Islam gradually acquired a permanent place in South Asia.

Indian Ocean Trade

How did cultural and ecological differences promote trade, and in turn how did trade and other contacts promote state growth and the spread of Islam?

When the collapse of the Mongol Empire in the fourteenth century disrupted overland routes across Central Asia, the Indian Ocean assumed greater strategic importance in tying together the peoples of Eurasia and Africa. Between 1200 and 1500, the volume of trade in the Indian Ocean increased. The Indian Ocean routes also facilitated the spread of Islam.

Monsoon Mariners

The prosperity of Islamic and Mongol empires in Asia, cities in Europe, and new kingdoms in Africa and Southeast Asia stimulated and contributed to the vitality of the Indian Ocean network. The demand for luxuries—precious metals and jewels, rare spices, fine textiles, and other manufactures—rose. Larger ships made shipments of bulk cargoes of ordinary cotton textiles, pepper, food grains (rice, wheat, barley), timber, horses, and other goods profitable.

Some goods were transported from one end of this trading network to the other, but few ships or crews made a complete circuit. Instead, the Indian Ocean trade divided into two legs: from the Middle East across the Arabian Sea to India and from India across the Bay of Bengal to Southeast Asia (see Map 13.2).

Shipyards in ports on the Malabar Coast (southwestern India) built large numbers of dhows (dows), the characteristic cargo and passenger ships of the Arabian Sea. They grew from an average capacity of 100 tons in 1200 to 400 tons in 1500. On a typical expedition, a dhow might sail west from India to Arabia and Africa on the northeast monsoon winds (December to March) and return on the southwest monsoons (April to August). Small dhows kept the coast in sight. Relying on the stars to guide them, skilled pilots steered large vessels by the quicker route straight across the water. A large dhow could sail from the Red Sea to mainland Southeast Asia in two to four months, but few did so. Eastbound cargoes and passengers from dhows reaching India were likely to be transferred to junks, which dominated the eastern half of the Indian Ocean and the South China Sea (see Environment and Technology: The Indian Ocean Dhow).

The largest, most technologically advanced, and most seaworthy vessels of this time, junks first appeared in China and spread with Chinese influence. Enormous nails held together hulls of heavy spruce or fir planks, in contrast with dhows, whose planks were sewn together with palm fiber. Below the deck, watertight compartments minimized flooding in case of damage to the ship's hull. According to Ibn Battuta, the largest junks had twelve sails made of bamboo and carried a crew of a thousand men, including four hundred soldiers. A large junk might accommodate a hundred passenger cabins and a cargo of over 1,000 tons. Junks dominated China's foreign shipping to Southeast Asia and India, but the Chinese did not control all of the junks that plied these waters. During the fifteenth century, similar vessels came out of shipyards in Bengal and Southeast Asia to be sailed by local crews.

Decentralized and cooperative commercial interests, rather than political authorities, connected the several regions that participated in the Indian Ocean trade. The **Swahili** (swah-HEE-lee) **Coast** supplied gold from inland areas of eastern Africa, and ports around the Arabian peninsula supplied horses and goods from the northern parts of the Middle East, the Mediterranean, and eastern Europe. Merchants in the cities of coastal India received goods from east and west, sold some locally, passed others along, and added Indian goods to the trade. The Strait of Malacca (meh-LAK-eh), between the eastern end of the

Indian Ocean and the South China Sea, provided a meeting point for trade from Southeast Asia, China, and the Indian Ocean. In each region, certain ports functioned as giant emporia, consolidating goods from smaller ports and inland areas for transport across the seas.

Africa: The Swahili Coast and Zimbabwe

Trade expanded steadily along the East African coast from about 1250, giving rise to between thirty and forty separate city-states by 1500. After 1200, masonry buildings as much as four stories high replaced mud and thatch dwellings, and archaeological findings include imported glass beads, Chinese porcelain, and other exotic goods. Coastal and island peoples shared a common culture and a language built on African grammar and vocabulary but enriched with many Arabic and Persian terms and written in Arabic script. In time, these people became known as "Swahili," from the Arabic name *sawahil* (suh-WAH-hil) *al-sudan*, meaning "shores of the blacks."

Sometime after Ibn Battuta's visit to Mogadishu in 1331, the more southerly city of Kilwa surpassed it as the Swahili Coast's most important commercial center (see Map 13.1). Ibn Battuta declared Kilwa "one of the most beautiful and well-constructed towns in the world." He noted its inhabitants' dark skins and Muslim piety, and he praised their ruler for the traditional Muslim virtues of humility and generosity.

What attracted the Arab and Iranian merchants whom oral traditions associate with the Swahili Coast's commercial expansion? By the late fifteenth century, Kilwa was annually exporting a ton of gold mined by inland Africans much farther south. Much of it came from or passed through a powerful state on the plateau south of the Zambezi River. At its peak in about 1400, its capital city, now known as **Great Zimbabwe**, occupied 193 acres (78 hectares) and had some 18,000 inhabitants.

Swahili Coast East African shores of the Indian Ocean between the Horn of Africa and the Zambezi River; from the Arabic *sawahil*, meaning "shores."
Great Zimbabwe City, now in ruins (in the modern African country of Zimbabwe), whose many stone structures were built between about 1250 and 1450, when it was a trading center and the capital of a large state.

The Indian Ocean Dhow

The sailing vessels that crossed the Indian Ocean shared the diversity of that trading area. The name by which we know them, dhow, comes from the Swahili language of the East African coast. The planks of teak from which their hulls were constructed were hewn from the tropical forests of south India and Southeast Asia. Their pilots, who navigated by stars at night, used the ancient technique that Arabs had used to find their way across the desert. Some pilots used a magnetic compass, which originated in China.

Dhows came in various sizes and designs, but all shared two distinctive features. The first was hull construction. The hulls of dhows consisted of planks that were sewn together, not nailed. Cord made of fiber from the husk of coconuts or other materials was passed through rows of holes drilled in the planks. Because cord is weaker than nails, outsiders considered this shipbuilding technique strange. Marco Polo fancifully suggested that it indicated sailors' fear that large ocean magnets would pull any nails out of their ships. More probable explanations are that pliant sewn hulls were cheaper to build than rigid nailed hulls and were less likely to be damaged if the ships ran aground on coral reefs.

The second distinctive feature of dhows was their triangular (lateen) sails made of palm leaves or cotton. The sails were suspended from tall masts and could be turned to catch the wind.

The sewn hull and lateen sails were technologies developed centuries earlier, but two innovations were

Dhow This model shows the vessel's main features.

National Maritime Museum, London

made between 1200 and 1500. First, a rudder positioned at the stern (rear end) of the ship replaced the large side oar that formerly had controlled steering. Second, shipbuilders increased the size of dhows to accommodate bulkier cargoes.

Between about 1250 and 1450, local African craftsmen built stone structures for Great Zimbabwe's rulers, priests, and wealthy citizens. The largest structure, an enclosure the size and shape of a large football stadium with walls of unmortared stone 17 feet (5 meters) thick and 32 feet (10 meters) high, served as the king's court. A large conical stone tower was among the many buildings inside the walls.

As in Mali, mixed farming and cattle herding provided the economic basis of the Great Zimbabwe state, but long-distance trade brought added wealth. Trade began regionally with copper ingots from the upper Zambezi Valley, salt, and local manufactures. Gold exports to the coast expanded in the fourteenth and fifteenth centuries and brought Zimbabwe to its peak. However, historians suspect that the city's residents

Visual Connection Archive

Royal Enclosure, Great Zimbabwe
Inside these oval stone walls the rulers of the trading state of Great Zimbabwe lived. Forced to enter the enclosure through a narrow corridor between two high walls, visitors were meant to be awestruck.

depleted nearby forests for firewood while their cattle overgrazed surrounding grasslands. The resulting ecological crisis hastened the empire's decline in the fifteenth century.

Arabia: Aden and the Red Sea

The city of **Aden** (AY-den) near the southwestern tip of the Arabian peninsula had a double advantage in the Indian Ocean trade. Monsoon winds brought enough rainfall to supply drinking water to a large population and grow grain for export, and its location made it a convenient stopover for trade with India, the Persian Gulf, East Africa, and Egypt. Aden's merchants dealt in cotton cloth and beads from India; spices from Southeast Asia; horses from Arabia and Ethiopia; pearls from the Red Sea; manufactured luxuries from Cairo; slaves, gold, and ivory from Ethiopia; and grain, opium, and dyes from Aden's own hinterland.

After visiting Mecca in 1331, Ibn Battuta sailed down the Red Sea to Aden, probably wedged in among bales of trade goods. His comments on the wealth of Aden's leading merchants include a story about the slave of one merchant who bought a ram for the fabulous sum of 400 dinars in order to keep the slave of another merchant from buying it. Instead of

punishing the slave for extravagance, the master freed him as a reward for outdoing his rival. Ninety years later, a Chinese Muslim visitor, Ma Huan, found "the country . . . rich, and the people numerous," living in stone residences several stories high.

Common commercial interests generally promoted good relations among the different religions and cultures of this region. For example, in the mid-thirteenth century, a wealthy Jew from Aden named Yosef settled in Christian Ethiopia, where he acted as an adviser. South Arabia had been trading with neighboring parts of Africa since before the time of King Solomon of Israel. The dynasty that ruled Ethiopia after 1270 claimed descent from Solomon and from the South Arabian princess Sheba. Solomonic Ethiopia's consolidation accompanied a great increase in trade through the Red Sea port of Zeila (ZEYE-luh), including slaves, amber, and animal pelts, which went to Aden and on to other destinations.

Friction sometimes arose, however. In the fourteenth century, the Sunni Muslim king of Yemen sent

Aden Port city in the south Arabian country of Yemen. It has been a major trading center in the Indian Ocean since ancient times.

materials for building a large mosque in Zeila, but the local Somalis (who were Shi'ite Muslims) threw the stones into the sea. This resulted in a yearlong embargo of Zeila ships in Aden. In the late fifteenth century, Ethiopia's territorial expansion and efforts to increase control over the trade provoked conflicts with Muslims who ruled the coastal states of the Red Sea.

India: Gujarat and the Malabar Coast

The state of Gujarat in western India prospered from the expanding trade of the Arabian Sea and the rise of the Delhi Sultanate. Blessed with a rich agricultural hinterland and a long coastline, Gujarat attracted new trade after the Mongol destruction of Baghdad in 1258 disrupted the northern land routes. After the initial violence of its forced incorporation into the Delhi Sultanate in 1298, Gujarat prospered from increased trade with Delhi's ruling class, despite occasional military crackdowns. Independent again after 1390, the Muslim rulers of Gujarat extended their control over neighboring Hindu states and regained their preeminent position in the Indian Ocean trade.

Gujaratis exported cotton textiles and indigo to the Middle East and Europe, in return for gold and silver. They also shipped cotton cloth, carnelian beads, and foodstuffs to the Swahili Coast in exchange for ebony, slaves, ivory, and gold. During the fifteenth century, traders expanded eastward to the Strait of Malacca. These Gujarati merchants helped spread the Islamic faith among east Indian traders, some of whom even imported specially carved gravestones from Gujarat.

Unlike Kilwa and Aden, Gujarat manufactured goods for trade. According to the thirteenth-century Venetian traveler Marco Polo, Gujarat's leatherworkers dressed enough skins in a year to fill several ships to Arabia and other places. They made sleeping mats for export to the Middle East "in red and blue leather, exquisitely inlaid with figures of birds and beasts, and skillfully embroidered with gold and silver wire," as well as leather cushions embroidered in gold. Later observers compared the Gujarati city of Cambay with cities in Flanders and northern Italy (see Chapter 14) in the scale, artisanry, and diversity of its textile industries. Cotton, linen, and silk cloth, along with carpets and quilts, found a large market in Europe, Africa, the Middle East, and Southeast Asia. Cambay also produced polished gemstones, gold jewelry, carved ivory,

stone beads, and both natural and artificial pearls. At the height of its prosperity in the fifteenth century, its well-laid-out streets and open places boasted fine stone houses with tiled roofs. Although Muslim residents controlled most Gujarati overseas trade, its Hindu merchant caste profited so much from related commercial activities that their wealth and luxurious lives became the envy of other Indians.

More southerly cities on the Malabar Coast duplicated Gujarat's success. Calicut (KAL-ih-cut) and other coastal cities prospered from locally made cotton textiles and locally grown grains and spices, and served as clearing-houses for the long-distance trade of the Indian Ocean. The zamorin (ZAH-much-run) (ruler) of Calicut presided over a loose federation of its Hindu rulers that united the coastal region. As in eastern Africa and Arabia, rulers generally tolerated religious and ethnic groups who contributed to commercial profits. Most trading activity lay in the hands of Muslims, many originally from Iran and Arabia, who intermarried with local Indian Muslims. Jewish merchants also operated from Malabar's trading cities.

Southeast Asia: The Rise of Malacca

At the eastern end of the Indian Ocean, the Strait of Malacca between the Malay Peninsula and the island of Sumatra provided the principal passage into the South China Sea (see Map 13.2). As trade increased in the fourteenth and fifteenth centuries, this commercial choke point became the site of political rivalry. The mainland kingdom of Siam controlled most of the upper Malay Peninsula, while the Java-based kingdom of Majapahit (mah-jah-PAH-hit) extended its dominion over the lower Malay Peninsula and much of Sumatra. Majapahit, however, could not suppress Chinese pirates based at the Sumatran city of Palembang (pah-lem-BONG) who preyed on ships sailing through the strait. In 1407, a fleet sent from China smashed the pirates' power and took their chief back home for trial.

Majapahit, weakened by internal struggles, could not take advantage of China's intervention, making the chief beneficiary the newer port of **Malacca** (or Melaka), which dominated the narrowest part of the strait.

Malacca Port city in the modern Southeast Asian country of Malaysia, founded about 1400 as a trading center on the Strait of Malacca. Also spelled Melaka.

- Traversed by dhows and junks, the maritime trade network of the Indian Ocean tied together peoples of Asia, Africa, and Europe.
- Decentralized commercial interests rose throughout the network, including the Swahili city-states that exported African gold from Great Zimbabwe.
- Aden dealt in a variety of goods from Africa, Arabia, and Southeast Asia and traded with Zeila on the Red Sea.
- Despite political turmoil, the cities of Gujarat and the Malabar Coast prospered through agriculture, manufacture, and trade.
- Through astute alliances, Malacca grew into the predominant emporium of Southeast Asia.

Under a prince from Palembang, Malacca had grown from an obscure fishing village into an important port through a series of astute alliances. Nominally subject to the king of Siam, Malacca also secured an alliance with China that was sealed by the visit of the imperial fleet in 1407. The conversion of an early ruler from Hinduism to Islam helped promote trade with Muslim merchants from Gujarat and elsewhere. Merchants also appreciated Malacca's security and low taxes.

Malacca served not just as a meeting point but also as an emporium for Southeast Asian products: rubies and musk from Burma, tin from Malaya, gold from Sumatra, cloves and nutmeg from the Moluccas (or Spice Islands, as Europeans later dubbed them). Shortly after 1500, when Malacca was at its height, one resident counted eighty-four languages spoken among the merchants gathered there, who came from as far away as Turkey, Ethiopia, and the Swahili Coast. Four officials administered the foreign merchant communities: one for the Gujaratis, one for other Indians and Burmese, one for Southeast Asians, and one for the Chinese and Japanese. Malacca's wealth and its cosmopolitan residents set the standard for luxury in Malaya for centuries to come.

Social and Cultural Change

What social and cultural changes are reflected in the history of peoples living in tropical Africa and Asia during this period?

State growth, commercial expansion, and the spread of Islam between 1200 and 1500 led to many changes in the social and cultural life of tropical peoples. The political and commercial elites grew in size and power, as did the number of slaves they owned. The spread of Muslim practices and beliefs affected social and cultural life—witness words of Arabic origin like *Sahara*, *Sudan*, *Swahili*, and *monsoon*—yet local traditions remained important.

Architecture, Learning, and Religion

Social and cultural changes typically affected cities more than rural areas. As Ibn Battuta and other travelers observed, wealthy merchants and ruling elites spent lavishly on mansions, palaces, and places of worship. Most places of worship surviving from this period blend older traditions and new influences. African Muslims produced Middle Eastern mosque designs in local building materials: sun-baked clay and wood in the western Sudan and coral stone on the Swahili Coast. Hindu temple architecture influenced mosque designs in Gujarat, which sometimes incorporated pieces of older structures. The congregational mosque at Cambay, built in 1325 with the traditional Islamic courtyard, cloisters, and porches, utilized pillars, porches, and arches taken from sacked Hindu and Jain (jine) temples. The mosque erected at the Gujarati capital of Ahmadabad (AH-muhd-ah-bahd) in 1423 had the open courtyard typical of mosques everywhere, but the surrounding verandas incorporated many typical Gujarati details and architectural conventions.

In Africa, King Lalibela (LAH-lee-BEL-uh) of Ethiopia constructed his capital, Lalibela, during the first third of the thirteenth century and ordered eleven churches to be carved out of solid rock, each commemorating a sacred Christian site in Jerusalem. These structures carried on an old Ethiopian tradition of rock sculpture, though on a far grander scale.

Mosques, churches, and temples were centers of education as well as prayer. Muslims promoted literacy among their sons (and sometimes their daughters) so that they could read sacred texts. Ibn Battuta reported seeing several boys in Mali wearing chains until they completed memorizing passages of the Quran. Literacy and Islam spread together in sub-Saharan Africa, where Christian Ethiopia had previously been the only literate society. In time, scholars adapted the Arabic alphabet to write local languages.

Church of Saint George, Ethiopia King Lalibela, who ruled the Christian kingdom of Ethiopia between about 1180 and 1220, had a series of churches carved out of solid volcanic rock to adorn his kingdom's new capital (also named Lalibela). The church of Saint George, excavated to a depth of 40 feet (13 meters) and hollowed out inside, has the shape of a Greek cross.

S. Sassoon/Robert Harding World Imagery

Islam affected literacy less in India, which had a long literate heritage. Arabic served primarily for religious purposes, while Persian became the language of high culture used at court. Eventually **Urdu** (ER-doo) arose, a Persian-influenced literary form of Hindi written in Arabic characters. Muslims also introduced papermaking in India.

Advanced Muslim scholars studied Islamic law, theology, and administration, as well as works on mathematics, medicine, science, and philosophy, partly derived from ancient Greek writings. In sixteenth-century **Timbuktu** (see Map 13.1) on the Niger River, over 150 schools taught the Quran while leading clerics taught advanced classes in mosques or homes. Books imported from North Africa brought high prices. Al-Hajj Ahmed, a scholar who died in Timbuktu in 1536, possessed some seven hundred volumes, an unusually large library for that time. In Southeast Asia, Malacca became a center of Islamic learning from which scholars spread Islam throughout the region. Other important centers of learning developed in Muslim India, particularly in Delhi, the capital.

Even in lands seized by conquest, Muslim rulers seldom required conversion. Example and persuasion by merchants and Sufis proved more effective. Many Muslims worked hard to persuade others of Islam's superiority. Muslim domination of long-distance trade assisted the adoption of Islam. Commercial transactions could take place across religious boundaries, but the common code of morality and law that Islam provided encouraged trust and drew many local merchants to Islam. From the major trading centers along the Swahili Coast, in the Sudan, in coastal India, and in Southeast Asia, Islam's influence spread along regional trade routes.

Marriage also played a role. Single Muslim men traveling to and settling in tropical Africa and Asia often married local women, and their children grew up in the Islamic faith. Some wealthy men had dozens of children from up to four wives and additional slave concubines. Servants and slaves in such households normally professed Islam.

In India, Muslim invasions eliminated the last strongholds of long-declining Buddhism, including, in 1196, the great Buddhist center of study at Nalanda (nuh-LAN-duh) in Bihar (bee-HAHR). Its manuscripts were burned and thousands of monks killed or driven into exile in Nepal and Tibet. With Buddhism reduced to a minor faith in the land of its birth, Islam emerged as India's second most important religion. Hinduism still prevailed in 1500, but Islam displaced Hinduism in most of maritime Southeast Asia.

Islam also spread among rural peoples, such as the pastoral Fulani of West Africa and Somali of northeastern Africa and various pastoralists in northwest India. In Bengal, Muslim religious figures oversaw the conversion of jungle into farmland and thereby gained many converts.

The spread of Islam did not mean simply the replacement of one set of beliefs by another. Islam adapted to the cultures of the regions it penetrated, developing African, Indian, and Indonesian varieties.

Urdu A Persian-influenced form of Hindi written in Arabic characters and used as a literary language since the 1300s.

Timbuktu City on the Niger River. It was founded by the Tuareg as a seasonal camp sometime after 1000. As part of the Mali empire, Timbuktu became a major terminus of the trans-Saharan trade and a center of Islamic learning.

Social and Gender Distinctions

A growth in slavery accompanied the rising prosperity of the elites. Military campaigns in India, according to Islamic sources, reduced hundreds of thousands of Hindu "infidels" to slavery. Delhi overflowed with slaves. Sultan Ala ud-Din owned 50,000 and Firuz Shah 180,000, including 12,000 skilled artisans. Sultan Tughluq sent 100 male slaves and 100 female slaves as a gift to the emperor of China in return for a similar gift.

Mali and Bornu sent slaves across the Sahara to North Africa, including beautiful maidens and eunuchs (castrated males). The expanding Ethiopian Empire regularly sent captives for sale to Aden traders at Zeila. According to modern estimates, Saharan and Red Sea traders sold about 2.5 million enslaved Africans between 1200 and 1500. African slaves from the Swahili Coast played conspicuous roles in the navies, armies, and administrations of some Indian states, especially in the fifteenth century. A few African slaves even reached China, where a source from about 1225 says that rich families preferred gatekeepers with bodies "black as lacquer."

With "free" labor abundant and cheap, few slaves worked as farmers. In some places, hereditary castes of slaves dominated certain trades and military units. Indeed, the earliest rulers of the Delhi Sultanate rose from military slavery. A slave general in the western Sudan named Askia Muhammad seized control of the Songhai Empire (Mali's successor) in 1493. Less fortunate slaves, like the men and women who mined copper in Mali, did hard menial work.

Wealthy households used many slave servants. Eunuchs guarded the harems of wealthy Muslims, but women predominated as household slaves, serving also as entertainers and concubines. Some rich men aspired to having a concubine from every part of the world. One of Firuz Shah's nobles reportedly had two thousand harem slaves, including women from Turkey and China.

Sultan Ala ud-Din's campaigns against Gujarat at the end of the thirteenth century yielded a booty of twenty thousand maidens in addition to innumerable younger children of both sexes. The supply of captives became so great that the lowest grade of horse sold for five times as much as an ordinary female slave, although beautiful young virgins commanded far higher prices.

Hindu legal digests and commentaries suggest that the position of Hindu women may have improved somewhat compared to earlier periods. The ancient practice of sati (suh-TEE)—that is, of an upper-caste widow throwing herself on her husband's funeral pyre—remained a meritorious act strongly approved by social custom. But Ibn Battuta makes it clear that sati was strictly optional. Since the Hindu commentaries devote considerable attention to the rights of widows without sons to inherit their husbands' estates, one may even conclude that sati was exceptional.

Indian parents still gave their daughters in marriage before the age of puberty, but consummation of the marriage took place only when the young woman was ready. Wives faced far stricter rules of fidelity and chastity than their husbands and could be abandoned for any serious breach. But other offenses against law and custom usually brought lighter penalties than for men. A woman's male master—father, husband, or owner—determined her status. Women seldom played active roles in commerce, administration, or religion.

Besides child rearing, women involved themselves with food preparation and, when not prohibited by religious restrictions, brewing. In many parts of Africa, women commonly made beer from grains or bananas. These mildly alcoholic beverages played an important part in male rituals of hospitality and relaxation.

Throughout tropical Africa and Asia, women did much of the farm work. They also toted home heavy loads of food, firewood, and water balanced on their heads. Other common female activities included making clay pots for cooking and storage and making clothing. In India, the spinning wheel, introduced by the Muslim invaders, greatly reduced the cost of making thread for weaving. Women typically spun at home, leaving weaving to men. In West Africa, women often sold agricultural products, pottery, and other craftwork in the markets.

Adopting Islam did not necessarily mean accepting the social customs of the Arab world. In Mali's capital, Ibn Battuta was appalled that Muslim women both free and slave did not completely cover their bodies and veil their faces when appearing in public. He considered their nakedness an offense to women's (and men's) modesty. In another part of Mali, he berated a Muslim merchant from Morocco for permitting his wife to sit on a couch and chat with her

SECTION REVIEW

- Social and cultural life changed as a result of state formation, commercial expansion, and the spread of Islam.

- These changes mostly affected cities, where elites financed building programs, fostering hybrid styles of religious architecture.

- Islam spread mainly through peaceful adaptation and promoted education and scholarship.

- With rising prosperity came the expansion of slavery, which was endorsed by Islam.

- The position of Indian women seems to have improved, and the spread of Islam did not mean adoption of Arab gender customs.

male friend. The husband replied, "The association of women with men is agreeable to us and part of good manners, to which no suspicion attaches." Ibn Battuta refused to visit the merchant again.

Conclusion

Tropical Africa and Asia encompass a large part of the world, one in which close to half the world's people lived. That vast area possesses many similarities and also great differences. The differences are evident in the climates, from permanent rain forests to barren deserts and from easily accessible seacoasts to the interiors of continents. Yet the social and cultural differences are as important as those of climates and landscapes.

The most striking change in tropical Africa and Asia in the period 1200 to 1500 is the spread of Islam. Once limited to the Arabian peninsula, then to the Middle East and North Africa, after 1200 Islam spread widely into the Indian subcontinent, Southeast Asia, and both West and East Africa. In some areas, it spread slowly but eventually reached all but a few of the inhabitants; this was the case of sub-Saharan Africa and much of Southeast Asia. In India, however, Islam came suddenly but then encountered unexpected resistance. How can we explain the difference?

In both West and East Africa and in Southeast Asia and the Indonesian archipelago, Islam was introduced by merchants who not only traded but also preached the message of the Quran. As contacts with other parts of the world grew, a universal religion like Islam was more convincing than the animist religions and local deities that preceded it. Furthermore, the conduct of the trader-missionaries and the political advantages that local rulers saw in allying themselves with a powerful world-encompassing movement gradually overcame the older religious traditions.

In India, in contrast, Islam came first with conquering Arab armies and then with Afghan and Turkish warriors. In India, they encountered a people who had an ancient and very sophisticated religion—Hinduism—and whose indigenous elites had long benefited from the inequalities enshrined in the caste system. Islam, with its promise of equality among all Muslims, appealed to the poor and lower-caste (or outcaste) Indians but remained a threat to most others. Hence, despite initial successes, Islam did not succeed in converting the majority of Indians as it had in the Middle East and Africa, and India became a region and a civilization permanently divided along religious lines.

CHAPTER REVIEW

 Download the MP3 audio file of the Chapter Review to listen to on the go.

How did environmental differences shape cultural differences in tropical Africa and Asia? (page 313)

By 1500 tropical Africa and Asia contained nearly 40 percent of the world's population but just over a quarter of its habitable land. Living in every type of ecosystem, from lush rain forests to arid deserts, tropical peoples had become intimately familiar with their environments, learning not merely to survive but also to prosper in them. African pastoralists tended herds of domestic animals in dry regions, while in Asia the more favorable soil and rainfall enabled farmers to cultivate rice, as well as grains and legumes.

Under what circumstances did the first Islamic empires arise in Africa and India? (page 317)

The period from 1200 to 1500 saw the rise of the first powerful Islamic states outside the Middle East. Chief among these were the Delhi Sultanate, which brought South Asia its greatest political unity since the decline of the Guptas, and the Mali Empire in the western Sudan, which extended the political and trading role pioneered by Ghana. Mali was founded by an indigenous African dynasty that had earlier adopted Islam, while invading Turkish and Afghan Muslims founded the Delhi Sultanate.

How did cultural and ecological differences promote trade, and in turn how did trade and other contacts promote state growth and the spread of Islam? (page 322)

Of greatest importance to the spread of Islam throughout tropical Africa and Asia was the Indian Ocean, which directly connected lands as distant as North and East Africa, Arabia, India, and Southeast Asia. Having mastered the seasonal monsoons, merchant sailors made the Indian Ocean the world's most important and richest trading area. A host of Muslim city-states arose: Kilwa along the Swahili Coast, Aden at the entrance to the Red Sea, Gujarat in India, and Malacca at the entrance to the South China Sea.

What social and cultural changes are reflected in the history of peoples living in tropical Africa and Asia during this period? (page 327)

With the enlargement of Islam's presence in the tropical world came changes that could be brutal as well as beneficial. Slavery, common in many parts of the world at this time, was an integral part of commerce and social life. A woman's status was largely determined by her father, husband, or owner, and women were generally precluded from holding important positions in religious or political life. Muslim culture in this period also brought great benefits, however. The centrality of the Quran in much of social life contributed to a rise in literacy, first in Arabic but later in native languages as well. Centers of higher education arose in which subjects such as mathematics, medicine, and science were significantly advanced.

Key Terms

Ibn Battuta (p. 313)	Swahili Coast (p. 323)
tropics (p. 313)	Great Zimbabwe (p. 323)
monsoons (p. 314)	Aden (p. 325)
Delhi Sultanate (p. 316)	Malacca (p. 326)
Mali (p. 317)	Urdu (p. 328)
Mansa Kankan Musa (p. 318)	Timbuktu (p. 328)
Gujarat (p. 321)	

Web Resources

Pronunciation Guide

Interactive Maps
- MAP 13.1 Africa, 1200–1500
- MAP 13.2 South and Southeast Asia, 1200–1500

Answer to the History in Focus Question
See photo on page 314, "East African Pastoralists."

CourseMate Visit the CourseMate website at www.cengagebrain.com for additional study tools and review materials for this chapter.

The Latin West

© Cengage Learning

CHAPTER PREVIEW

Rural Growth and Crisis
How well did inhabitants of the Latin West, rich and poor, urban and rural, deal with their natural environment?

Urban Revival
What social and economic factors led to the growth of cities in late medieval Europe?

Learning, Literature, and the Renaissance
What factors were responsible for the promotion of learning and the arts in the Latin West?

Political and Military Transformations
What social, political, and military developments contributed to the rise of European nations in this period?

Conclusion

DIVERSITY & DOMINANCE: Persecution and Protection of Jews, 1272–1349

 Visit the CourseMate website at **www.cengagebrain.com** for additional study tools and review materials for this chapter.

In the summer of 1454, a year after the Ottoman Turks captured the Greek Christian city of Constantinople, Aeneas Sylvius Piccolomini (uh-NEE-uhs SIL-vee-uhs pee-kuh-lo-MEE-nee), destined in four years to become pope, expressed doubts as to whether anyone could persuade the rulers of Christian Europe to take up arms together against the Muslims: "Christendom has no head whom all will obey—neither the pope nor the emperor receives his due." The Christian states thought more of fighting each other. French and English armies had been battling for over a century, the German emperor presided over dozens of states but did not really control them, and the numerous kingdoms and principalities of Spain and Italy could not unite. With only slight exaggeration, Aeneas Sylvius moaned, "Every city has its own king, and there are as many princes as there are households." He attributed this lack of unity to European preoccupation with personal welfare and material gain. Both pessimism about human nature and materialism had increased during the previous century, after a devastating plague had carried off half of western Europe's population.

Yet despite all these divisions, disasters, and wars, historians now see the period from 1200 to 1500 (Europe's Late Middle Ages) as a time of unusual progress. Prosperous cities adorned with splendid architecture, institutions of higher learning, and cultural achievements counterbalanced the avarice and greed that Aeneas Sylvius lamented. Frequent wars caused havoc and destruction, but they also promoted the development of military technology and more unified monarchies.

Although their Muslim and Byzantine neighbors commonly called western Europeans "Franks," they ordinarily referred to themselves as "Latins," underscoring their allegiance to Roman Catholicism and the Latin language used in its rituals. Some common elements promoted the **Latin West**'s vigorous revival: competition, the pursuit of success, and the effective use of borrowed technology and learning.

Rural Growth and Crisis

How well did inhabitants of the Latin West, rich and poor, urban and rural, deal with their natural environment?

Between 1200 and 1500, the Latin West brought more land under cultivation using new farming techniques and made greater use of machinery and mechanical forms of energy. Yet for the nine out of ten people who lived in the countryside, hard labor brought meager returns, and famine, epidemics, and war struck often. After the devastation of the Black Death between 1347 and 1351, social changes speeded up by peasant revolts released many persons from serfdom and brought some improvements to rural life.

Peasants, Population, and Plague

In 1200, most western Europeans lived as serfs tilling the soil on large estates owned by the nobility and the church (see Chapter 10). They owed their lord both a share of their harvests and numerous labor services. As a consequence of the inefficiency of farming practices and their obligations to landowners, peasants received meager returns for their hard work. Even with numerous religious holidays, peasants labored some 54 hours a week in their fields, more than half the time in support of the local nobility. Each noble household typically lived from the labor of fifteen to thirty peasant families. The standard of living in the lord's stone castle or manor house contrasted sharply with the peasant's one-room thatched cottage containing little furniture and no luxuries.

Scenes of rural life show both men and women at work in the fields, but equality of labor did not mean equality in decision making at home. In the peasant's hut as elsewhere in medieval Europe, women were subordinate to men. The influential theologian Thomas Aquinas (uh-KWY-nuhs) (1225–1274) spoke for his age

Latin West Historians' name for the territories of Europe that adhered to the Latin rite of Christianity and used the Latin language for intellectual exchange in the period ca. 1000–1500.

when he argued that although both men and women were created in God's image, there was a sense in which "the image of God is found in man, and not in woman: for man is the beginning and end of woman; as God is the beginning and end of every creature."[1]

Rural poverty resulted from rapid population growth as well as inefficient farming methods and social inequality. In 1200, China's population may have exceeded Europe's by two to one; by 1300, the population of each was about 80 million. China's population fell because of the Mongol conquest (see Chapter 12), while Europe's more than doubled between 1100 and 1340. Some historians believe the reviving economy stimulated the increase. Others argue that severe epidemics were few, and warmer-than-usual temperatures reduced mortality from starvation and exposure.

More people required more productive farming and new agricultural settlements. One widespread new technique, the **three-field system**, replaced the custom of leaving half the land fallow (uncultivated) every year to regain its fertility. In the fall, farmers planted wheat or rye on one-third of their fields; in the spring they planted oats, barley, peas, chickpeas, lentils, or beans on a second third; and left the last third fallow. The second and third years, they repeated the process but moved each crop to the next field. The fourth year they returned to the first year's distribution. As a result, each year two-thirds of their fields were productive, instead of half: an increase of 33 percent. Furthermore, this system allowed them to grow oats, the best feed for horses. Finally, peas and beans were not only a source of proteins, but they also enriched the soil with nitrogen from the air, thereby maintaining its fertility. In much of Europe, however, farmers continued to let half of their land lie fallow and used oxen (less efficient but cheaper than horses) to pull their plows.

Population growth also encouraged new agricultural settlements. In the twelfth and thirteenth centuries, large numbers of Germans migrated into the fertile lands east of the Elbe River and into the eastern Baltic states. Knights belonging to Latin Christian religious orders slaughtered or drove away native inhabitants who had not yet adopted Christianity.

Musée Condé, Chantilly, France/Bridgeman-Giraudon/Art Resource, NY

Rural French Peasants Many scenes of peasant life in winter are visible in this small painting by the Flemish Limbourg brothers from the 1410s. Above the snow-covered beehives one man chops firewood, while another drives a donkey loaded with firewood to a little village. At the lower right a woman, blowing on her frozen fingers, heads past the huddled sheep and hungry birds to join other women warming themselves in the cottage (whose outer walls the artists have cut away).

During the thirteenth century, the Order of Teutonic Knights conquered, resettled, and administered a vast area along the Baltic that later became Prussia (see Map 14.1). Other Latin Christians founded new settlements on lands conquered from the Muslims and Byzantines in southern Europe and on Celtic lands in the British Isles.

Draining swamps and clearing forests also brought new land under cultivation. But as population continued to rise, some people had to farm lands that had poor soils or were vulnerable to flooding, frost, or drought. Average crop yields fell after 1250, and more people lived at the edge of starvation. According to one historian, "By 1300, almost every child born in western Europe faced the probability

three-field system A rotational system for agriculture in which one field grows wheat or barley, one grows oats or legumes, and one lies fallow. It gradually replaced the two-field system in medieval Europe.

Chronology

	Technology and Environment	Culture	Politics and Society
1200	**1200s** Widespread use of crossbows and windmills		**1200s** Champagne fairs flourish **1204** Fourth Crusade **1215** Magna Carta issued
		1210s Teutonic Knights, Franciscans, Dominicans **1225–1274** Philosopher-monk Thomas Aquinas **1300–1500** Rise of universities	
1300	**1315–1317** Great Famine	**1313–1375** Giovanni Boccaccio, humanist writer	**1337** Start of Hundred Years War
	1347–1351 Black Death **ca. 1350** Growing deforestation		
		ca. 1390–1441 Jan van Eyck, painter	**1381** Wat Tyler's Rebellion
1400	**1400s** Cannon and hand-held firearms in use		**1415** Portuguese take Ceuta
		1452–1519 Leonardo da Vinci, artist	**1431** Joan of Arc burned **1453** End of Hundred Years War; Ottomans take Constantinople
	1454 Gutenberg Bible	**1492** Expulsion of Jews from Spain	**1492** Fall of Muslim state of Granada

of extreme hunger at least once or twice during his expected 30 to 35 years of life."[2] One unusually cold spell produced the Great Famine of 1315–1317, which affected much of Europe.

The **Black Death** or bubonic plague reversed the population growth. This terrible plague originated in China and spread across Central Asia with the Mongol armies (see Chapter 12). In 1346, the Mongols attacked the city of Kaffa (KAH-fah) on the Black Sea; a year later, Genoese (JEN-oh-eez) traders in Kaffa carried the disease to Italy and southern France. For two years, the Black Death spread across Europe, in some places carrying off two-thirds of the population. Average losses in western Europe amounted to one in two.

Victims developed boils the size of eggs in their groins and armpits, black blotches on their skin, foul body odors, and severe pain. In most cases, death came within a few days. Town officials closed their gates to people from infected areas and burned the victims' possessions. Such measures helped to spare some communities but could not halt the advance of the disease. Bubonic plague, the primary form of the Black Death, spreads from person to person and through the bites of fleas infesting the fur of black rats. Although medieval doctors did not associate the disease with rats, eliminating the rats that thrived on urban refuse would have been difficult.

The plague left a psychological mark, bringing home to people how sudden and unexpected death could be. Some people became more religious, giving money to the church or hitting themselves with iron-tipped whips to atone for their sins. Others chose reckless enjoyment, spending their money on fancy clothes, feasts, and drinking. Whatever their mood, most people soon resumed their daily routines. Periodic returns of plague made recovery from population losses slow and uneven. Europe's population in 1400 equaled that in 1200. Not until after 1500 did it rise above its preplague level.

Black Death An outbreak of bubonic plague that spread across Asia, North Africa, and Europe in the mid-fourteenth century, carrying off vast numbers of persons.

Interactive Map

Map 14.1 Europe in 1453 This year marked the end of the Hundred Years War between France and England and the fall of the Byzantine capital city of Constantinople to the Ottoman Turks. Muslim advances into southeastern Europe were offset by the Latin Christian reconquests of Islamic holdings in southern Italy and the Iberian Peninsula and by the conversion of Lithuania.   © Cengage Learning

Spread of Roman
Christendom

In 1000 C.E.

Added 1000–1200

Lost 1000–1200
(Regained 1200–1500)

Added 1200–1500

Lost 1200–1500

English holdings, 1360

Boundary of the
Holy Roman Empire

Burying Victims of the Black Death This scene from Tournai, Flanders, captures the magnitude of the plague.   Snark/Art Resource NY

Social Rebellion

In addition to its demographic and psychological effects, the Black Death triggered social changes in western Europe. Laborers who survived demanded higher pay for their services. At first, authorities tried to freeze wages at the old levels. Seeing this as a plot by the rich, peasants rose up against wealthy nobles and churchmen. During a widespread revolt in France in 1358, known as the Jacquerie, peasants looted castles and killed dozens of persons. In a large revolt led by Wat Tyler in 1381, English peasants invaded London, calling for an end to serfdom and obligations to landowners. Demonstrators murdered the archbishop of Canterbury and many royal officials. Authorities put down these rebellions with even greater bloodshed and cruelty, but they could not stave off the higher wages and other social changes the rebels demanded.

Serfdom practically disappeared in western Europe as peasants bought their freedom or ran away. Many free persons earning higher wages saved their money and bought land. Some English landowners who could no longer afford to hire enough field-workers began pasturing sheep for their wool. Others grew crops that required less care or made greater use of draft animals and labor-saving tools. Because the plague had not killed animals, survivors had abundant meat and leather for shoes. Thus, the welfare of the rural masses generally improved after the Black Death, though the gap between rich and poor remained wide.

In urban areas, employers raised wages to attract workers. Guilds (see below) shortened the period of apprenticeship. Competition within crafts also became more common. Although the overall economy shrank with the decline in population, per capita production actually rose.

Mills and Mines

Mining, metalworking, and the use of mechanical energy expanded so greatly in the centuries before 1500 that some historians speak of an "industrial revolution" in medieval Europe. That may be too strong a term, but the landscape fairly bristled with mechanical devices. Mills powered by water or wind ground grain, sawed logs, crushed olives, tanned leather, and made paper.

In 1086, 5,600 watermills flanked England's many rivers. After 1200, mills spread rapidly across the western European mainland. By the early fourteenth century, entrepreneurs had crammed sixty-eight watermills into a 1-mile section of the Seine (sen) River in Paris. Less efficient **water wheels** depended on the flow of a river passing beneath them. Greater efficiency came from channeling water to fall over the top of the wheel so that gravity added force to the water's flow. Dams ensured a steady flow of water

water wheel A mechanism that harnesses the energy in flowing water to grind grain or to power machinery. It was used in many parts of the world but was especially common in Europe from 1200 to 1900.

throughout the year. Some watermills in France and England even harnessed the power of ocean tides.

Windmills multiplied in comparatively dry lands like Spain and in northern Europe, where ice made water wheels useless in winter. Designs for watermills dated back to Roman times, and the Islamic world, which inherited Hellenistic technologies, knew both water wheels and windmills. But people in the medieval Latin West used these devices on a much larger scale than did people elsewhere.

Owners invested heavily in building mills, but since nature furnished the energy to run them for free, they returned great profits. While individuals or monasteries constructed some mills, most were built by groups of investors. Rich millers often aroused the jealousy of their neighbors. In his *Canterbury Tales*, the English poet Geoffrey Chaucer (ca. 1340–1400) captured their unsavory reputation by portraying a miller as "a master-hand at stealing grain" by pushing down on the balance scale with his thumb.[3]

Waterpower aided the great expansion of iron making. Water powered the stamping mills that broke up the iron, the trip hammers that pounded it, and the bellows (first documented in the West in 1323) that raised temperatures to the point where the iron was liquid enough to be poured into molds. Blast furnaces producing high-quality iron are documented from 1380. Finished products ranged from armor to nails, from horseshoes to hoes.

Demand stimulated iron mining in many parts of Europe. In addition, new silver, lead, and copper mines in Austria and Hungary supplied metal for coins, church bells, cannon, and statues. Techniques of deep mining developed in central Europe spread west in the latter part of the fifteenth century. A building boom stimulated stone quarrying in France during the eleventh, twelfth, and thirteenth centuries.

Industrial growth changed the landscape. Towns grew outward and new ones were founded, dams and canals changed the flow of rivers, and quarries and mines scarred the hillsides. Human wastes and the runoff from slaughterhouses and from urban tanneries that cured and processed leather polluted streams. England's Parliament enacted the first recorded antipollution law in 1388, but enforcement proved difficult.

Deforestation accelerated. Trees provided timber for buildings and ships, and tanneries stripped bark to make acid for tanning leather. Many forests gave

SECTION REVIEW

- Population growth stimulated improved farming methods and agricultural expansion, but peasant life did not significantly improve.

- Famine and the Black Death reversed the population growth and resulted in social change throughout western Europe.

- Improved mill designs and other technology stimulated further industrial growth, which, in turn, changed the landscape.

way to farmland. The glass and iron industries used great quantities of charcoal, made by controlled burning of oak or other hardwood, to produce the high temperatures required. A single iron furnace could consume all the trees within five-eighths of a mile (1 kilometer) in just forty days. Consequently, the later Middle Ages saw the end of many of western Europe's once-dense forests, except in places where powerful landowners established hunting preserves.

Urban Revival

What social and economic factors led to the growth of cities in late medieval Europe?

In the tenth century, no town in the Latin West could compete in size, wealth, or comfort with the cities of Byzantium and Islam. Yet by the later Middle Ages, the Mediterranean, Baltic, and Atlantic coasts boasted wealthy port cities, as did some major rivers draining into these seas. Some Byzantine and Muslim cities still exceeded those of the West in size, but not in commercial, cultural, and administrative dynamism, as marked by impressive new churches, guild halls, and residences.

Trading Cities   Most urban growth after 1200 resulted from manufacturing and trade, both between cities and their hinterlands and over long distances. Northern Italy particularly benefited from maritime trade with the port cities of the eastern Mediterranean and, through them, the markets of the Indian Ocean and East Asia. In northern Europe, commercial cities in the county of Flanders (roughly today's Belgium) and around the Baltic Sea profited from regional networks and from overland and sea routes to the Mediterranean.

Flemish Weavers, Ypres The spread of textile weaving gave employment to many people in the Netherlands. The city of Ypres in Flanders (now northern Belgium) was an important textile center in the thirteenth century. This drawing from a fourteenth-century manuscript shows a man and a woman weaving cloth on a horizontal loom, while a child makes thread on a spinning wheel.

Stedelijke Openbare Bibliotheek, Ypres

A Venetian-inspired assault in 1204 against the city of Constantinople, misleadingly named the "Fourth Crusade," temporarily eliminated Byzantine control of the passage between the Mediterranean and the Black Sea and thereby allowed Venice to seize Crete and expand its trading colonies around the Black Sea. Another boon to Italian trade came from the westward expansion of the Mongol Empire, which opened trade routes from the Mediterranean to China (see Chapter 12).

In 1271 a young merchant named Marco Polo set out from Venice and reached the Mongol court in China after a long trek across Central Asia. He then served the emperor Khubilai Khan for many years as an ambassador and governor of a Chinese province. It is likely he exaggerated his account of these adventures and of his voyage through the Indian Ocean that brought him back to Venice in 1295 after an absence of twenty-four years. Similar reports of the riches of the East came from other European travelers.

When Mongol decline interrupted the caravan trade in the fourteenth century, Venetian merchants purchased eastern silks and spices brought by other middlemen to Constantinople, Damascus, and Cairo. Three times a year, Venice dispatched convoys of two or three galleys, with sixty oarsmen each, capable of bringing back 2,000 tons of goods. Other merchants explored new overland or sea routes.

The sea trade of Genoa on northern Italy's west coast probably equaled that of Venice. Genoese merchants established colonies in the western and eastern Mediterranean and around the Black Sea. In northern Europe, an association of trading cities known as the **Hanseatic** (han-see-AT-ik) **League** traded extensively in the Baltic, including the coasts of Prussia, newly conquered by German knights. Their merchants ranged eastward to Novgorod in Russia and westward across the North Sea to London.

In the late thirteenth century, Genoese galleys from the Mediterranean and Hanseatic ships from the Baltic were converging on the trading and manufacturing cities in Flanders. Artisans in the Flemish towns of Bruges (broozh), Ghent (gent [hard g as in get]), and Ypres (EE-pruh) transformed raw wool from England into a fine cloth that was softer and smoother than the coarse "homespuns" from simple village looms. Dyed in vivid hues, these Flemish textiles appealed to wealthy Europeans, who also appreciated fine textiles from Asia.

Along the overland route connecting Flanders and northern Italy, important trading fairs developed in the Champagne (sham-PAIN) region of Burgundy. The Champagne fairs began as regional markets, exchanging manufactured goods, livestock, and farm produce once or twice a year. When the king of France gained control of Champagne at the end of the twelfth century, royal guarantees of safe conduct to merchants turned these markets into international fairs

Hanseatic League An economic and defensive alliance of the free towns in northern Germany, founded about 1241 and most powerful in the fourteenth century.

that were important for currency exchange and other financial transactions. A century later, fifteen Italian cities had permanent consulates in Champagne to represent the interests of their citizens. During the fourteenth century, the large volume of trade made it cheaper to ship Flemish woolens to Italy by sea than to pack them overland on animal backs. Champagne's fairs consequently lost some international trade, but they remained important as regional markets.

In the late thirteenth century, the English monarchy raised taxes on exports of raw wool, making cloth manufacture in England more profitable than in Flanders. Flemish specialists crossed the English Channel and introduced the spinning wheel and other devices to England. Annual raw wool exports fell from 35,000 sacks of wool at the beginning of the fourteenth century to 8,000 in the mid-fifteenth century, while English wool cloth production rose from 4,000 pieces just before 1350 to 54,000 a century later.

Florence also replaced Flemish imports with its own woolens industry financed by local banking families. In 1338, Florence manufactured 80,000 pieces of cloth, while importing only 10,000. These changes in the textile industry show how competition promoted the spread of manufacturing and encouraged new specialties.

The growing textile industries used the power of wind and water channeled through gears, pulleys, and belts to drive all sorts of machinery. Flemish mills cleaned and thickened woven cloth by beating it in water, a process known as fulling. Other mills produced paper, starting in southern Europe in the thirteenth century. Unlike the Chinese and Muslim papermakers, who had pursued the craft for centuries, the Europeans introduced machines to do the heavy work.

In the fifteenth century, Venice surpassed its European rivals in the volume of its trade in the Mediterranean as well as across the Alps into central Europe. Its craftspeople manufactured luxury goods once obtainable only from eastern sources, notably silk and cotton textiles, glassware and mirrors, jewelry, and paper. Exports of Italian and northern European woolens to the eastern Mediterranean also rose. In the space of a few centuries, western European cities had used the eastern trade to increase their prosperity and then reduce their dependence on eastern goods.

Civic Life

Most northern Italian and German cities were independent states, much like the port cities of the Indian Ocean Basin (see Chapter 13). Other European cities held royal charters exempting them from the authority of local nobles. Their autonomy enabled them to adapt to changing market conditions more quickly than cities controlled by imperial authorities, as in China and the Islamic world. Since anyone who lived in a chartered city for over a year could claim freedom, urban life promoted social mobility.

Europe's Jews mostly lived in cities. Spain had the largest communities because of the tolerance of earlier Muslim rulers. Commercial cities elsewhere welcomed Jews with manufacturing and business skills. Despite official protection by certain Christian princes and kings, Jews endured violent persecutions or expulsions in times of crisis, such as during the Black Death (see Diversity and Dominance: Persecution and Protection of Jews, 1272–1349). In 1492, the Spanish monarchs expelled all Jews in the name of religious and ethnic purity. Only the papal city of Rome left its Jews undisturbed throughout the centuries before 1500.

Within most towns and cities, powerful associations known as guilds dominated civic life. **Guilds** brought together craft specialists, such as silversmiths, or merchants working in a particular trade to regulate business practices and set prices. They also trained apprentices and promoted members' interests with the city government. By denying membership to outsiders and Jews, guilds protected the interests of families that already belonged to them. They also perpetuated male dominance of most skilled jobs.

Nevertheless, in a few places, women could join guilds either on their own or as the wives, widows, or daughters of male guild members. Large numbers of poor women also toiled in nonguild jobs in urban textile industries and in the food and beverage trades, generally receiving lower wages than men.

Some women advanced socially through marriage to wealthy men. One of Chaucer's *Canterbury Tales*

guild In medieval Europe, an association of men (rarely women), such as merchants, artisans, or professors, who worked in a particular trade and banded together to promote their economic and political interests. Guilds were also important in other societies, such as the Ottoman and Safavid Empires.

Diversity & Dominance

Persecution and Protection of Jews, 1272–1349

Because they did not belong to the dominant Latin Christian faith, Jews suffered from periodic discrimination and persecution. For the most part, religious and secular authorities tried to curb such anti-Semitism. Jews, after all, were useful citizens who worshiped the same God as their Christian neighbors. Still, it was hard to know where to draw the line between justifiable and unjustifiable discrimination. The famous reviser of Catholic theology, St. Thomas Aquinas, made one such distinction in his Summa Theologica *with regard to attempts at forced conversion.*

Now, the practice of the Church never held that the children of Jews should be baptized against the will of their parents.... Therefore, it seems dangerous to bring forward this new view, that contrary to the previously established custom of the Church, the children of Jews should be baptized against the will of their parents.

There are two reasons for this position. One stems from danger to faith. For, if children without the use of reason were to receive baptism, then after reaching maturity they could easily be persuaded by their parents to relinquish what they had received in ignorance. This would tend to do harm to the faith.

The second reason is that it is opposed to natural justice ... it [is] a matter of natural right that a son, before he has the use of reason, is under the care of his father. Hence, it would be against natural justice for the boy, before he has the use of reason, to be removed from the care of his parents, or for anything to be arranged for him against the will of his parents.

The "new view" Aquinas opposed was much in the air, for in 1272 Pope Gregory X issued a decree condemning forced baptism. The pope's decree reviews the history of papal protection given to the Jews, starting with a quotation from Pope Gregory I dating from 598, and decrees two new protections of Jews' legal rights.

Even as it is not allowed to the Jews in their assemblies presumptuously to undertake for themselves more than that which is permitted them by law, even so they ought not to suffer any disadvantage in those [privileges] which have been granted them.

Although they prefer to persist in their stubbornness rather than to recognize the words of their prophets and the mysteries of the Scriptures, and thus to arrive at a knowledge of Christian faith and salvation; nevertheless, inasmuch as they have made an appeal for our protection and help, we therefore admit their petition and offer them the shield of our protection through the clemency of Christian piety. In so doing we follow in the footsteps of our predecessors of happy memory, the popes of Rome—Calixtus, Eugene, Alexander, Clement, Celestine, Innocent, and Honorius.

We decree moreover that no Christian shall compel them or any one of their group to come to baptism unwillingly. But if any one of them shall take refuge of his own accord with Christians, because of conviction, then, after his intention will have been made manifest, he shall be made a Christian without any intrigue. For indeed that person who is known to come to Christian baptism not freely, but unwillingly, is not believed to possess the Christian faith.

Moreover, no Christian shall presume to seize, imprison, wound, torture, mutilate, kill, or inflict violence on them; furthermore no one shall presume, except by judicial action of the authorities of the country, to change the good customs in the land where they live for the purpose of taking their money or goods from them or from others.

In addition, no one shall disturb them in any way during the celebration of their festivals, whether by day or by night, with clubs or stones or anything else. Also no one shall exact any compulsory service of them unless it be that which they have been accustomed to render in previous times.

Inasmuch as the Jews are not able to bear witness against the Christians, we decree furthermore that the testimony of Christians against Jews shall not be valid unless there is among these Christians some Jew who is there for the purpose of offering testimony.

Since it occasionally happens that some Christians lose their Christian children, the Jews are accused by their enemies of secretly carrying off and killing these same Christian children, and of making sacrifices of the heart and blood of these very children. It happens, too, that the parents of these children, or some other Christian enemies of these Jews, secretly hide these very children in order that they may be able to injure these Jews, and in order that they may be able to extort from them a certain amount of money by redeeming them from their straits.

And most falsely do these Christians claim that the Jews have secretly and furtively carried away these children and killed them, and that the Jews offer sacrifice from the heart and the blood of these children, since their law in this matter precisely and expressly forbids Jews to sacrifice, eat, or drink the blood, or eat the flesh of animals having claws. This has been demonstrated many times at our court by Jews converted to the Christian faith: nevertheless very many Jews are often seized and detained unjustly because of this.

We decree, therefore, that Christians need not be obeyed against Jews in such a case or situation of this type, and we order that Jews seized under such a silly pretext be freed from imprisonment, and that they shall not be arrested henceforth on such a miserable pretext, unless—which we do not believe—they be caught in the commission of the crime. We decree that no Christian shall stir up anything against them, but that they should be maintained in that status and position in which they were from the time of our predecessors, from antiquity till now.

We decree, in order to stop the wickedness and avarice of bad men, that no one shall dare to devastate or to destroy a cemetery of the Jews or to dig up human bodies for the sake of getting money [by holding them for ransom]. Moreover, if anyone, after having known the content of this decree, should—which we hope will not happen—attempt audaciously to act contrary to it, then let him suffer punishment in his rank and position, or let him be punished by the penalty of excommunication, unless he makes amends for his boldness by proper recompense. Moreover, we wish that only those Jews who have not attempted to contrive anything toward the destruction of the Christian faith be fortified by the support of such protection. . . .

Despite such decrees, violence against Jews might burst out when fears and emotions were running high. This selection is from the official chronicles of the upper-Rhineland towns.

In the year 1349 there occurred the greatest epidemic that ever happened. Death went from one end of the earth to the other, on that side and this side of the [Mediterranean] sea, and it was greater among the Saracens [Muslims] than among the Christians. In some lands everyone died so that no one was left. Ships were also found on the sea laden with wares; the crew had all died and no one guided the ship. The Bishop of Marseilles and priests and monks and more than half of all the people there died with them. In other kingdoms and cities so many people perished that it would be horrible to describe. The pope at Avignon stopped all sessions of court, locked himself in a room, allowed no one to approach him and had a fire burning before him all the time. And from what this epidemic came, all wise teachers and physicians could only say that it was God's will. And the plague was now here, so it was in other places, and lasted more than a whole year. This epidemic also came to Strasbourg in the summer of the above mentioned year, and it is estimated about sixteen thousand people died.

In the matter of this plague the Jews throughout the world were reviled and accused in all lands of having caused it through the poison which they are said to have put into the water and the wells—that is what they were accused of—and for this reason the Jews were burnt all the way from the Mediterranean into Germany, but not in Avignon, for the pope protected them there.

Nevertheless they tortured a number of Jews in Berne and Zofingen who admitted they had put poison into many wells, and they found the poison in the wells. Thereupon they burnt the Jews in many towns and wrote of this affair to Strasbourg, Freibourg, and Basel in order that they too should burn their Jews. . . . The deputies of the city of Strasbourg were asked what they were going to do with their Jews. They answered and said that they knew no evil of them. Then . . . there was a great indignation and clamor against the deputies from Strasbourg. So finally the Bishop and the lords and the Imperial Cities agreed to do away with the Jews. The result was that they were burnt in many cities, and wherever they were expelled they were caught by the peasants and stabbed to death or drowned. . . .

On Saturday—that was St. Valentine's Day—they burnt the Jews on a wooden platform in their cemetery. There were about two thousand people of them. Those who wanted to baptize themselves were spared. Many small children were taken out of the fire and baptized against the will of their fathers and mothers. And everything that was owed to the Jews was cancelled, and the Jews had to surrender all pledges and notes that they had taken for debts. The council, however, took the cash that the Jews possessed and divided it among the working-men proportionately. The money was indeed the thing that killed the Jews. If they had been poor and if the feudal lords had not been in debt to them, they would not have been burnt.

QUESTIONS FOR ANALYSIS

1. Why do Aquinas and Pope Gregory oppose prejudicial actions against Jews?
2. Why did prejudice increase at the time of the Black Death?
3. What factors account for the differences between the views of Christian leaders and the Christian masses?

Source: First selection reprinted with the permission of Pocket Books, a Division of Simon & Schuster, Inc. and Vernon and Janet Bourke Living Trust from The Pocket Aquinas, edited with translations by Vernon G. Bourke. Copyright © 1960 by Washington Square Press. Copyright renewed © 1988 by Simon & Schuster, Inc. Second and third selections from Jacob R. Marcus, ed., The Jew in the Medieval World: A Source Book, 315–1791 (Cincinnati: Union of American Hebrew Congregations, 1938), 152–154, 45–47. Copyright © 1938. Reprinted with permission of the Hebrew Union College Press, Cincinnati.

concerns a woman from Bath, a city in southern England, who became wealthy by marrying a succession of old men for their money (and then two other husbands for love), "aside from other company in youth." She was also a skilled weaver, Chaucer says: "In making cloth she showed so great a bent, / She bettered those of Ypres and of Ghent." By the fifteenth century, a new class of wealthy merchant-bankers was operating on a vast scale and specializing in money changing and loans and making investments on behalf of other parties. Merchants great and small used their services. They also handled the financial transactions of ecclesiastical and secular officials and arranged for the transmission to the pope of funds known as Peter's pence, a collection taken up annually in every church in the Latin West. Princes and kings supported their wars and lavish courts with credit. Some merchant-bankers even developed their own news services, gathering information on any topic that could affect business.

Florentine financiers invented checking accounts, organized private shareholding companies (the forerunners of modern corporations), and improved bookkeeping techniques. In the fifteenth century, the Medici (MED-ih-chee) family of Florence operated banks in Italy, Flanders, and London. Medicis also controlled the government of Florence and commissioned art works. The Fuggers (FOOG-uhrz) of Augsburg, who had ten times the Medici bank's lending capital, topped Europe's banking fraternity by 1500. Beginning as cloth merchants under Jacob "the Rich" (1459–1525), the family's many activities included the trade in Hungarian copper, essential for casting cannon.

Since Latin Christians generally considered usury (charging interest) sinful, Jews predominated in money lending. Christian bankers devised ways to profit from loans indirectly in order to get around the condemnation of usury. Some borrowers repaid loans in a different currency at a rate of exchange favorable to the lender. Others added to their repayment a "gift" in thanks to the lender. For example, in 1501, church officials agreed to repay a Fugger loan of 6,000 gold ducats in five months along with a "gift" of 400 ducats, amounting to an effective interest rate of 16 percent a year. In fact, the return was less since the church failed to repay the loan on time.

Yet most residents of western European cities lived in poverty and squalor rather than wealth.

SECTION REVIEW

- After 1200, most cities grew through manufacture and trade, particularly those of northern Italy, Flanders, and the Baltic coast.

- Expanding trade and technological innovation ultimately reduced Europe's dependence on eastern goods.

- Cities fostered social mobility, but civic life was dominated by guilds, wealthy merchants, and bankers.

- Most urban residents lived in squalor without the amenities of Islamic Middle Eastern cities.

- Gothic cathedrals became signs of special civic pride and prestige in European cities.

European cities generally lacked the civic amenities, such as public baths and water supply systems, that had existed in the cities of Western antiquity and still survived in cities of the Islamic Middle East.

Gothic Cathedrals

Master builders and associated craftsmen counted among the skilled people in greatest demand. Though cities competed with one another in the magnificence of their guild halls, town halls, and other structures, **Gothic cathedrals**, first appearing about 1140 in France, cost the most and brought the greatest prestige. The pointed, or Gothic, arch, replacing the older round, or Roman, arch, proved a hallmark of the new design. External (flying) buttresses stabilizing the high, thin, stone columns below the arches constituted another distinctive feature. This method of construction enabled master builders to push the Gothic cathedrals to great heights and fill the outside walls with giant windows depicting religious scenes in brilliantly colored stained glass. During the next four centuries, interior heights soared ever higher, towers and spires pierced the heavens, and walls became dazzling curtains of stained glass.

The men who designed and built the cathedrals had little or no formal education and limited understanding of the mathematical principles of modern civil engineering. Master masons sometimes

Gothic cathedrals Large churches originating in twelfth-century France; built in an architectural style featuring pointed arches, tall vaults and spires, flying buttresses, and large stained-glass windows.

miscalculated, causing parts of some overly ambitious cathedrals to collapse. The record-high choir vault of Beauvais Cathedral, for instance—154 feet (47 meters) in height—came tumbling down in 1284. But as builders gained experience and invented novel solutions to their problems, success rose from the rubble of their mistakes. The cathedral spire in Strasbourg reached 466 feet (142 meters) into the air—as high as a forty-story building. Such heights were unsurpassed until the twentieth century.

Learning, Literature, and the Renaissance

What factors were responsible for the promotion of learning and the arts in the Latin West?

Throughout the Middle Ages, people in the Latin West lived amid reminders of the achievements of the Romans. They wrote and worshiped in a version of their language, traveled their roads, and obeyed some of their laws. The vestments and robes of popes, kings, and emperors followed the designs of Roman officials. Yet the learning of Greco-Roman antiquity virtually disappeared with the rise of the biblical world described in the Hebrew and Christian scriptures.

A small revival of learning associated with the court of Charlemagne in the ninth century was followed by a larger renaissance (rebirth) in the twelfth century. Cities became centers of intellectual and artistic life. The universities established across the Latin West after 1200 contributed to this cultural revival. In the mid-fourteenth century, the pace of intellectual and artistic life quickened in what is often called the **Renaissance**, which began in northern Italy and later spread to northern Europe. Some Italian authors saw the Italian Renaissance as a sharp break with an age of darkness. Others see this era as the high noon of a day that had been dawning for several centuries.

Universities and Scholarship

Before 1100, Byzantine and Islamic scholarship generally surpassed scholarship in Latin Europe. When Latin Christians wrested southern Italy from the Byzantines and Sicily and Toledo, Spain, from the Muslims in the eleventh century, they acquired many manuscripts of Greek and Arabic works. These included works by Plato and Aristotle (AR-ih-staht-uhl) and Greek treatises on medicine, mathematics, and geography, as well as scientific and philosophical writings by Muslim writers. Latin translations of the Iranian philosopher Ibn Sina (IB-uhn SEE-nah) (980–1037), known in the West as Avicenna (av-uh-SEN-uh), had great influence because of their sophisticated blend of Aristotelian and Islamic philosophy. Jewish scholars contributed significantly to the translation and explication of Arabic and other manuscripts.

The thirteenth century saw the foundation of two new religious orders, the Dominicans and the Franciscans, some of whose most talented members taught in the independent colleges that arose after 1200. Some scholars believe that the colleges established in Paris and Oxford patterned themselves on similarly endowed places of study then spreading in the Islamic world—*madrasas*, which provided subsidized housing for poor students and paid the salaries of their teachers. The Latin West, however, innovated the idea of **universities**, degree-granting corporations specializing in multidisciplinary research and advanced teaching.

Between 1300 and 1500, sixty universities joined the twenty established before that time. Students banded together to start some of them; guilds of professors founded others. Teaching guilds, like the guilds overseeing manufacturing and commerce, set standards for the profession, trained apprentices and masters, and defended their professional interests.

Universities set the curriculum for each discipline and instituted final examinations for degrees. Students who passed the exams that ended their apprenticeship received a "license" to teach. Students who completed longer training and defended a masterwork of scholarship became "masters" and "doctors." The University of Paris gradually absorbed the city's various colleges,

Renaissance (European) A period of intense artistic and intellectual activity, said to be a "rebirth" of Greco-Roman culture. Usually divided into an Italian Renaissance, from roughly the mid-fourteenth to mid-fifteenth century, and a Northern Renaissance, from roughly the early fifteenth to early seventeenth century.
universities Degree-granting institutions of higher learning. Those that appeared in the Latin West from about 1200 onward became the model of all modern universities.

Dante's Divine Comedy This fifteenth-century painting by Domenico di Michelino shows Dante holding a copy of the *Divine Comedy*. Hell is depicted to the poet's left and the terraces of Purgatory behind him, surmounted by the earthly and heavenly Paradise. The city of Florence, with its recently completed cathedral, appears on the right.

but the colleges of Oxford and Cambridge remained independent, self-governing organizations.

Since all universities used Latin, students and masters could move freely across political and linguistic lines, seeking the courses they wanted and the most interesting professors. Some universities offered specialized training. Legal training centered on Bologna (buh-LOHN-yuh); Montpellier and Salerno focused on medicine; Paris and Oxford excelled in theology.

The prominence of theology stemmed from many students aspiring to ecclesiastical careers, but scholars also saw theology as "queen of the sciences"—the central discipline encompassing all knowledge. Hence, thirteenth-century theologians sought to synthesize the rediscovered philosophical works of Aristotle and the commentaries of Avicenna with the Bible's revealed truth. These efforts to synthesize reason and faith were known as **scholasticism** (skoh-LAS-tih-sizm).

Thomas Aquinas, a brilliant Dominican priest who taught theology at the University of Paris, wrote the most notable scholastic work, the *Summa Theologica* (SOOM-uh thee-uh-LOH-jih-kuh), between 1267 and 1273. Although his exposition of Christian belief organized on Aristotelian principles came to be accepted as a masterly demonstration of the reasonableness of Christianity, scholasticism upset many traditional thinkers. Some church authorities tried to ban Aristotle from the curriculum. In addition, rivalry between the leading Dominican and Franciscan theological scholars continued over the next two centuries. However, the considerable freedom of medieval universities from both secular and religious authorities enabled the new ideas to prevail over the fears of church administrators.

Humanists and Printers

Dante Alighieri (DAHN-tay ah-lee-GYEH-ree) (1265–1321) completed a long, elegant poem, the *Divine Comedy*, shortly before his death. This supreme expression of medieval preoccupations tells the allegorical story of Dante's journey through the nine circles of Hell and the seven terraces of Purgatory, followed by his entry

 Primary Source: *Summa Theologica***: On Free Will** Do humans have free will? Find out what Thomas Aquinas thinks.

scholasticism A philosophical and theological system, associated with Thomas Aquinas, that was devised to reconcile Aristotelian philosophy and Roman Catholic theology in the thirteenth century.

into Paradise. The Roman poet Virgil guides him through Hell and Purgatory; Beatrice, a woman he had loved from afar since childhood and whose death inspired the poem, guides him to Paradise.

The *Divine Comedy* foreshadows the literary fashions of the later Italian Renaissance. Dante wrote in the vernacular spoken in Tuscany (TUS-kuh-nee), the medieval version of Italian. Like Dante, later Italian writers made use of Greco-Roman classical themes and mythology and sometimes courted a broader audience by writing not in Latin but in their local language

The poet Geoffrey Chaucer, many of whose works show the influence of Dante, wrote in vernacular English. The *Canterbury Tales*, a lengthy poem written in the last dozen years of his life, contains often humorous and earthy tales told by fictional pilgrims on their way to the shrine of Thomas à Becket in Canterbury (see Chapter 10). They present a vivid cross-section of medieval people and attitudes.

Dante influenced a literary movement of **humanists** that began in his native Florence in the mid-fourteenth century. The term refers to their interest in grammar, rhetoric, poetry, history, and moral philosophy (ethics)—subjects known collectively as the humanities, an ancient discipline. With the brash exaggeration characteristic of new intellectual fashions, humanist writers like the poet Francesco Petrarch (fran-CHES-koh PAY-trahrk) (1304–1374) and the poet and storyteller Giovanni Boccaccio (jo-VAH-nee boh-KAH-chee-oh) (1313–1375) proclaimed a revival of the classical Greco-Roman tradition they felt had for centuries lain buried under the rubble of the Middle Ages.

This idea of a rebirth of learning dismisses too readily the monastic and university scholars who for centuries had been recovering all sorts of Greco-Roman learning, as well as writers like Dante (whom the humanists revered), who anticipated humanist interests by a generation. Yet the humanists had a great impact as educators, advisers, and reformers. Their greatest influence came in reforming secondary education. They introduced a curriculum centered on the languages and literature of Greco-Roman antiquity, which they felt provided intellectual discipline, moral lessons, and refined tastes. This curriculum dominated European secondary schools well into the twentieth century. The universities felt the humanist influence less, mostly after 1500. Theology, law, medicine, and

branches of philosophy other than ethics remained prominent in university education during this period.

Many humanists tried to duplicate the elegance of classical Latin and (to a lesser extent) Greek, which they revered as the pinnacle of learning, beauty, and wisdom. Boccaccio gained fame with his vernacular writings, which resemble Dante's, and especially for the *Decameron*, an earthy work that has much in common with Chaucer's boisterous tales. Under Petrarch's influence, however, Boccaccio turned to writing in classical Latin.

As humanist scholars mastered Latin and Greek, they turned their language skills to restoring the original texts of Greco-Roman writers and of the Bible. By comparing different manuscripts, they eliminated errors introduced by generations of copyists. To aid in this task, Pope Nicholas V (r. 1447–1455) created the Vatican Library, buying scrolls of Greco-Roman writings and paying to have accurate copies and translations made. Working independently, the Dutch scholar Erasmus (uh-RAZ-muhs) of Rotterdam (ca. 1466–1536) produced a critical edition of the New Testament in Greek. Erasmus corrected many errors and mistranslations in the Latin text that had been in general use throughout the Middle Ages.

The influence of the humanists grew as the new technology of printing made their critical editions of ancient texts, literary works, and moral guides more available. The Chinese and the Arabs used carved woodblocks for printing, and block-printed playing cards circulated in Europe before 1450, but after that date three European improvements revolutionized printing: (1) movable pieces of type consisting of individual letters, (2) new ink suitable for printing on paper, and (3) the **printing press**, a mechanical device that pressed inked type onto sheets of paper.

Johann Gutenberg (yoh-HAHN GOO-ten-burg) (ca. 1394–1468) of Mainz in Germany led the way. The Gutenberg Bible of 1454, the first book in the West

---

humanists (Renaissance) European scholars, writers, and teachers associated with the study of the humanities (grammar, rhetoric, poetry, history, languages, and moral philosophy), influential in the fifteenth century and later.

printing press A mechanical device for transferring text or graphics from a woodblock or type to paper using ink. Presses using movable type first appeared in Europe in about 1450.

A French Printshop, 1537 A workman operates the "press," quite literally a screw device that presses the paper to the inked type. Other employees examine the printed sheets, each of which holds four pages. When folded, the sheets make a book.

Giraudon/Art Resource, NY

History in Focus *Notice what the figures in this image are doing, how they are dressed, and the features of the space in which they work. What does this image suggest about printing as a kind of work and the position of printers in society? Find the answer online.*

printed from movable type, exhibited a beauty and craftsmanship that bore witness to the printer's years of experimentation. Humanists worked closely with the printers, who spread the new techniques to Italy and France. Erasmus did editing and proofreading for the Italian scholar-printer Aldo Manuzio (1449–1515) in Venice. Manuzio's press published many critical editions of classical Latin and Greek texts.

By 1500, at least 10 million printed volumes flowed from presses in 238 European towns, launching a revolution that affected students, scholars, and a growing literate population. These readers consumed unorthodox political and religious tracts along with ancient texts.

Renaissance Artists

Although the artists of the fourteenth and fifteenth centuries continued to depict biblical subjects, the Greco-Roman revival led some, especially in Italy, to portray ancient deities and myths. Another popular trend involved scenes of daily life.

Neither theme was entirely new, however. Renaissance art, like Renaissance scholarship, owed a debt to earlier generations. Italian painters of the fifteenth century credited the Florentine painter Giotto (JAW-toh) (ca. 1267–1337) with single-handedly reviving the "lost art of painting." In religious scenes, Giotto replaced the stiff, staring figures of the Byzantine style, which were intended to overawe viewers, with more natural and human portraits with whose emotions of grief and love viewers could identify. Rather than floating on backgrounds of gold leaf, his saints inhabit earthly landscapes. North of the Alps, the Flemish painter Jan van Eyck (yahn vahn IKE) (ca. 1390–1441) mixed his pigments with linseed oil in place of the egg yolk of earlier centuries. Oil paints dried more slowly and gave pictures a superior luster. Italian painters quickly copied van Eyck's technique, though his own masterfully realistic paintings on religious and domestic themes remained distinctive.

Leonardo da Vinci (leh-own-AHR-doh dah VIN-chee) (1452–1519) used oil paints for his *Mona Lisa.* Renaissance artists like Leonardo worked in many media, including bronze sculptures and frescos (painting on wet plaster) like *The Last Supper.* Leonardo's notebooks also contain imaginative designs for airplanes, submarines, and tanks. His younger contemporary Michelangelo (my-kuhl-AN-juh-low) (1472–1564) painted frescoes of biblical scenes on the ceiling of the Sistine Chapel in the Vatican, sculpted statues

SECTION REVIEW

- Greco-Roman learning returned to the Latin West through a series of revivals that culminated with the Renaissance.

- An infusion of Greek and Islamic scholarship during the eleventh century helped to prompt the revival of the twelfth and thirteenth centuries.

- Colleges and universities grew, with theology as the preeminent discipline.

- Foreshadowed by Dante, humanism, with its focus on classical languages, literature, ethics, and education, emerged in Italy.

- The influence of the humanists spread through the new print technology.

- Renaissance artists enlarged the thematic and technical resources of painting, sculpture, and architecture.

of David and Moses, and designed the dome for a new Saint Peter's Basilica in Rome.

The patronage of wealthy and educated merchants and prelates underlay the artistic blossoming in the cities of northern Italy and Flanders. The Florentine banker Cosimo de' Medici (1389–1464) and his grandson Lorenzo (1449–1492), known as "the Magnificent," spent immense sums on paintings, sculpture, and public buildings. In Rome, the papacy (PAY-puh-see) launched a building program that culminated in the construction of the new Saint Peter's Basilica and a residence for the pope.

These scholarly and artistic achievements exemplify the innovation and striving for excellence of the Late Middle Ages. The new literary themes and artistic styles of this period had lasting influence on Western culture. But the innovations in the organization of universities, in printing, and in oil painting had wider implications, for they were later adopted by cultures all over the world.

Political and Military Transformations

What social, political, and military developments contributed to the rise of European nations in this period?

Stronger and more unified states and armies developed in western Europe in parallel with the economic and cultural revivals (see Map 14.1). Through the prolonged struggle of the Hundred Years War, French and English monarchs forged closer ties with the nobility, the church, and the merchants. Crusades against Muslim states brought consolidation to Spain and Portugal. In Italy and Germany, however, political power remained in the hands of small states and loose alliances.

Monarchs, Nobles, and the Church

Thirteenth-century states continued early medieval state structures (see Chapter 10). Hereditary monarchs topped the political pyramid, but modest treasuries and the rights of nobles and the church limited their powers. Powerful noblemen who controlled vast estates had an important voice in matters of state, and the church guarded closely its traditional rights and independence. Towns, too, had acquired rights and privileges. Towns in Flanders, the Hanseatic League, and Italy approached independence from royal interference. In theory the ruler's noble vassals owed military service in time of war. In practice, vassals sought to limit the monarch's power.

In the year 1200, knights still formed the backbone of western European armies, but changes in weaponry brought this into question. Improved crossbows could shoot metal-tipped arrows with enough force to pierce helmets and light body armor. Professional crossbowmen, hired for wages, became increasingly common and much feared. Indeed, a church council in 1139 outlawed the crossbow—ineffectively—as being too deadly for use against Christians. The arrival in Europe of firearms based on the Chinese invention of gunpowder (see Chapter 12) further transformed the medieval army.

The church also resisted royal control. In 1302, the outraged Pope Boniface VIII (r. 1294–1303) asserted that divine law made the papacy superior to "every human creature," including monarchs. Issuing his own claim of superiority, King Philip "the Fair" of France (r. 1285–1314) sent an army to arrest the pope, a chastisement that hastened Pope Boniface's death. Philip then engineered the election of a French pope, who established a new papal residence at Avignon (ah-vee-NYON) in southern France in 1309.

A succession of French-dominated popes residing in Avignon improved church discipline but at the price of compromising their neutrality in the eyes of other rulers. The **Great Western Schism** between 1378 and 1415 saw rival papal claimants at Avignon and Rome vying for Christian loyalties. The papacy eventually regained its independence and returned to Rome, but the long crisis broke the pope's ability to challenge the rising power of monarchs like Philip, who had used the dispute to persuade his nobles to grant him a new tax.

The English monarchy wielded more centralized power as a result of consolidation that took place after the Norman conquest of 1066. The Anglo-Norman kings also extended their realm by assaults on their Celtic neighbors. Between 1200 and 1400, they incorporated Wales and reasserted control over most of Ireland. Nevertheless, under King John (r. 1199–1216), royal power suffered a severe setback. Forced to acknowledge the pope as his overlord in 1213, he lost his bid to reassert claims to Aquitaine in southern France the following year and then yielded to his nobles by signing the Magna Carta in 1215. This "Great Charter" affirmed that monarchs were subject to established law, confirmed the independence of the church and the city of London, and guaranteed the nobles' hereditary rights.

The Hundred Years War

The conflict between the king of France and his vassals known as the **Hundred Years War** (1337–1453) affords a key example of the transformation in politics and war. These vassals included the kings of England (for lands that belonged to their Norman ancestors), the counts of prosperous and independent-minded Flanders, and the dukes of Brittany and Burgundy. In typical fashion, the conflict grew out of a marriage alliance.

Marriage between Princess Isabella of France and King Edward II of England (r. 1307–1327) should have ensured the king's loyalty, as a vassal, to the French monarchy. However, when the next generation of the French ruling house produced no other sons, Isabella's son, King Edward III of England (r. 1327–1377), laid claim to the French throne in 1337. French courts instead awarded the throne to a more distant (and more French) cousin. Edward decided to fight for his rights.

The new military technology shaped the conflict. Early in the war, hired Italian cross-bowmen reinforced the French cavalry, but the English longbow proved superior. Adopted from the Welsh, the 6-foot (1.8-meter) longbow could shoot farther and more rapidly than the crossbow. Its arrows could not pierce armor, but concentrated volleys found gaps in the knights' defenses or struck their less-protected horses. Heavier and more encompassing armor provided a defense but limited a knight's movements. Once pulled off his steed by a foot soldier armed with a pike (hooked pole), he could not get up.

Later in the Hundred Years War, firearms gained prominence. The first cannon scared the horses with smoke and noise but did little damage. As they grew larger, however, they proved effective in battering the walls of castles and towns. The first artillery use against the French, at the Battle of Agincourt (1415), gave the English an important victory.

Faced with a young French peasant woman called Joan of Arc, subsequent English gains stalled. Acting, she believed, on God's instructions, she put on armor and rallied the French troops to defeat the English in 1429. Shortly afterward, she fell into English hands; she was tried by English churchmen and burned at the stake as a witch in 1431.

In the final battles, French cannon demolished the walls of once-secure castles held by the English and their allies. The truce that ended the struggle in 1453 left the French monarchy in firm control.

New Monarchies in France and England

The war proved a watershed in the rise of **new monarchies** in France and England, centralized states with fixed national boundaries and stronger representative institutions. English monarchs after 1453 consolidated control over territory within the British Isles, though the Scots defended their independence. The French monarchs

Primary Source: Magna Carta: The Great Charter of Liberties Get a feel for one of history's most important legal documents.

Great Western Schism A division in the Latin (Western) Christian Church between 1378 and 1415, when rival claimants to the papacy existed in Rome and Avignon.

Hundred Years War (1337–1453) Series of campaigns over control of the throne of France, involving English and French royal families and French noble families.

new monarchies Historians' term for the monarchies in France, England, and Spain from 1450 to 1600. The centralization of royal power was increasing within more or less fixed territorial limits.

also turned to consolidating control over powerful noble families, especially those headed by women. Mary of Burgundy (1457–1482) was forced to surrender most of her family's vast holdings to the king. Then in 1491, Anne of Brittany's forced marriage to the king led to the eventual incorporation of her duchy (DUTCH-ee) into France.

Military technology undermined the nobility. Smaller, more mobile cannon developed in the late fifteenth century pounded castle walls. Improvements in hand-held firearms, able by the late fifteenth century to pierce the heaviest armor, ended the domination of the armored knight. Armies now depended less on knights and more on bowmen, pikemen, musketeers, and artillerymen.

The new monarchies needed a way to finance their full-time armies. Some nobles agreed to money payments in place of military service and to additional taxes in time of war. For example, in 1439 and 1445, Charles VII of France (r. 1422–1461) successfully levied a new tax on his vassals' land. This not only paid the costs of the war with England but also provided the monarchy with a financial base for the next 350 years.

Merchants' taxes also provided revenues. Taxes on the English wool trade, begun by King Edward III, paid most of the costs of the Hundred Years War. Some rulers taxed Jewish merchants or extorted large contributions from wealthy towns. Individual merchants sometimes curried royal favor with loans. The fifteenth-century French merchant Jacques Coeur (cur) gained many social and financial benefits for himself and his family by lending money to French courtiers, but his debtors accused him of murder and had his fortune confiscated.

The church provided a third source of revenue through voluntary contributions to support a war. English and French monarchs won the right to appoint important church officials in their realms in the fifteenth century. They subsequently used state power to enforce religious orthodoxy more vigorously than the popes had been able to do. But reformers complained that the church's spiritual mission became subordinate to political and economic concerns.

The shift in power to the monarchs and away from the nobility and the church did not deprive nobles of their social position and roles as government officials and military officers. Moreover, the kings of England and France in 1500 had to deal with representative

SECTION REVIEW

- Between 1200 and 1500, monarchs, nobles, and the church struggled over political power.
- Tensions between the French monarchy and the papacy resulted in the Great Western Schism.
- In England, royal power was checked by the papacy and nobility, the latter imposing the Magna Carta on King John.
- The Hundred Years War between the French monarchy and its vassals introduced new military technologies.
- The war also stimulated the rise of the new centralized monarchies of England and France.
- Spain and Portugal continued the reconquest of Muslim Iberia, a process completed by Ferdinand and Isabella.

institutions that had not existed in 1200. The English Parliament proved a permanent check on royal power: the House of Lords contained the great nobles and church officials, while the House of Commons represented the towns and the leading citizens of the counties. In France, the Estates General, a similar but less effective representative body, represented the church, the nobles, and the towns.

Iberian Unification

Spain and Portugal's **reconquest of Iberia** from Muslim rule expanded the boundaries of Latin Christianity. The knights who pushed the borders of their kingdoms southward furthered both Christianity and their own interests. The spoils of victory included irrigated farmland, rich cities, and ports on the Mediterranean Sea and Atlantic Ocean. Serving God, growing rich, and living off the labor of others became a way of life for the Iberian nobility.

The reconquest proceeded over several centuries. Toledo fell and became a Christian outpost in 1085. English crusaders bound for the Holy Land helped take Lisbon in 1147. It displaced the older city of Oporto (meaning "the port"), from which Portugal took its name, as both capital and the kingdom's leading city. After a Christian victory in 1212 broke the back of

reconquest of Iberia Beginning in the eleventh century, military campaigns by various Iberian Christian states to recapture territory taken by Muslims. In 1492 the last Muslim ruler was defeated, and Spain and Portugal emerged as united kingdoms.

Muslim power, the reconquest accelerated. Within decades, Portuguese and Castilian forces captured the prosperous cities of Cordova (1236) and Seville (1248) and drove the Muslims from the southwestern region known as Algarve (ahl-GAHRV) ("the west" in Arabic). Only the small kingdom of Granada hugging the Mediterranean coast remained in Muslim hands.

By incorporating Algarve in 1249, Portugal attained its modern territorial limits. After a pause to colonize, Christianize, and consolidate this land, Portugal took the crusade to North Africa. In 1415, Portuguese knights seized the port of Ceuta (say-OO-tah) in Morocco, where they learned more about the Saharan caravan trade in gold and slaves. During the next few decades, Portuguese mariners sailed down the Atlantic coast of Africa seeking rumored African Christian allies and access to this trade (see Chapter 15).

Elsewhere in Iberia, the reconquest continued. Spain came into being when the marriage of Princess Isabella of Castile and Prince Ferdinand of Aragon in 1469 led to the union of their kingdoms when they inherited their respective thrones a decade later. Their conquest of Granada in 1492 secured the final piece of Muslim territory for the new kingdom.

Ferdinand and Isabella sponsored the first voyage of Christopher Columbus in 1492 (see Chapter 15). In a third momentous event of that year, the monarchs manifested their crusading mentality by ordering all Jews expelled from their kingdoms. Attempts to convert or expel the remaining Muslims led to a revolt at the end of 1499 that lasted until 1501. The Spanish rulers expelled the last Muslims in 1502. Portugal expelled the Jews in 1496, including 100,000 refugees from Spain.

Conclusion

For seven hundred years after the fall of Rome, western Europe was impoverished economically and culturally compared to the Roman Empire at its height, but also and more importantly, compared to the Byzantine Empire, to the Arab empires, or to China and India during that same period. Though other parts of Eurasia suffered from wars and invasions, western European towns and farmlands were devastated by repeated barbarian invasions until ca. 1100. Despite the efforts of Charlemagne and the Catholic Church to keep Roman traditions alive, life for most people remained dangerous and the towns remained small and poor. Only when the invaders settled down did towns begin to grow, trade picked up, and farmers expanded their fields and increased their harvests.

From then on, life in western Europe was gradually transformed by a series of technological innovations. Farmers increased their yields by planting more of their land and using horses in place of oxen. New wind and water mills substituted inanimate energy for human labor. Intellectual life also picked up as universities were founded and wealthy rulers, first in Italy and later in northern Europe, patronized artists, writers, and musicians and built beautiful new buildings. Though the Black Death decimated the population and set the economy back many decades, western Europe nonetheless rebounded. By the late fifteenth century, it had surpassed the Muslim world economically and was preparing to expand beyond the oceans.

CHAPTER REVIEW

Download the MP3 audio file of the Chapter Review to listen to on the go.

How well did inhabitants of the Latin West, rich and poor, urban and rural, deal with their natural environment? (page 333)

Ecologically, the peoples of Latin Europe harnessed the power of wind and water and mined and refined their mineral wealth at the cost of localized pollution and deforestation. However, food production and distribution did not keep up with population growth, and the Black Death devastated Europe in the mid-fourteenth century.

What social and economic factors led to the growth of cities in late medieval Europe? (page 338)

Politically, basic features of the modern European state began to emerge. Frequent wars caused kingdoms of moderate size to develop exceptional military strength. The ruling class saw economic strength as the twin of political power and promoted the welfare of cities specializing in trade, manufacturing, and finance, whose profits they taxed.

What factors were responsible for the promotion of learning and the arts in the Latin West? (page 344)

Culturally, autonomous universities and printing supported the advance of knowledge. Art and architecture reached unsurpassed peaks in the Renaissance. Late medieval society also displayed a fundamental fascination with tools and techniques. New inventions and improved versions of old ones underlay the new dynamism in commerce, warfare, industry, and navigation.

What social, political, and military developments contributed to the rise of European nations in this period? (page 348)

Many of the tools that the Latin West would use to challenge Eastern supremacy—printing, firearms, and navigational devices—originally came from the East. However, western European success depended as much on strong motives for expansion. From the eleventh century onward, population pressure, religious zeal, economic enterprise, and intellectual curiosity drove an expansion of territory and resources that took the crusaders to the Holy Land, merchants to the eastern Mediterranean and Black Seas, the English into Wales and Ireland, German settlers across the Elbe River, and Iberian Christians into the Muslim south. The early voyages into the Atlantic, discussed in the next chapter, extended these activities.

Key Terms

Latin West *(p. 333)*

three-field system *(p. 334)*

Black Death *(p. 335)*

water wheel *(p. 337)*

Hanseatic League *(p. 339)*

guild *(p. 340)*

Gothic cathedrals *(p. 343)*

Renaissance (European) *(p. 344)*

universities *(p. 344)*

scholasticism *(p. 345)*

humanists (Renaissance) *(p. 346)*

printing press *(p. 346)*

Great Western Schism *(p. 349)*

Hundred Years War *(p. 349)*

new monarchies *(p. 349)*

reconquest of Iberia *(p. 350)*

Web Resources

Pronunciation Guide

Interactive Maps

- MAP 14.1 Europe in 1453

Primary Sources

- *Summa Theologica*: On Free Will
- Magna Carta: The Great Charter of Liberties

Answer to the History in Focus Question

See photo on page 347, "A French Printshop, 1537."

CourseMate Visit the CourseMate website at www.cengagebrain.com for additional study tools and review materials for this chapter.

The Maritime Revolution

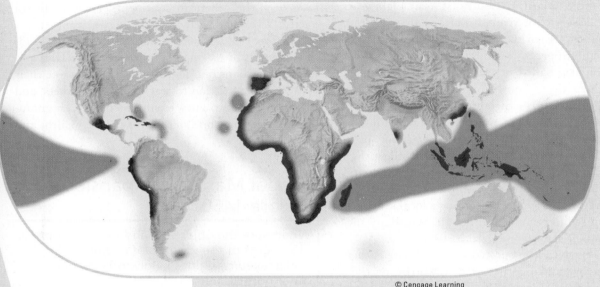

© Cengage Learning

CHAPTER PREVIEW

Visit the CourseMate website at **www.cengagebrain.com** for additional study tools and review materials for this chapter.

In 1511, the young Ferdinand Magellan sailed from Europe around the southern tip of Africa and eastward across the Indian Ocean as a member of the first Portuguese expedition to explore the East Indies (maritime Southeast Asia). Eight years later, in the service of Spain, he headed an expedition that sought to reach the East Indies by sailing westward from Europe. By the middle of 1521, Magellan's expedition had sailed across the Atlantic, rounded the southern tip of South America, and crossed the Pacific Ocean—but at a high price.

One of the five ships wrecked on a reef; the captain of another deserted and sailed back to Spain. The passage across the Pacific took much longer than anticipated. Dozens of sailors died of starvation and disease. In the Philippines, Magellan himself was killed on April 27, 1521, while aiding a local king who had promised to become a Christian. Magellan's successor met the same fate a few days later.

The expedition's survivors consolidated their resources by burning the least seaworthy of their remaining three ships and transferring the men and supplies to the smaller *Victoria*, which continued westward across the Indian Ocean, around Africa, and back to Europe. Magellan's flagship, the *Trinidad*, tried unsuccessfully to recross the Pacific to Central America. However, the *Victoria*'s return to Spain on September 8, 1522, confirmed Europe's ability and determination to master the oceans. The Portuguese crown had backed a century of daring and dangerous voyages to open routes to Africa, Brazil, and the Indian Ocean, and since 1492 Spain had opened contacts with the American continents. Now the broad Pacific Ocean had been crossed.

Before 1500, powerful states and the rich trading networks of Asia had led the way in overland and maritime expansion. The Iberians set out on their voyages of exploration to reach Eastern markets, and their success began a new era in which the West gradually became the world's center of power, wealth, and innovation.

Global Maritime Expansion Before 1450

What were the objectives and major accomplishments of the voyages of exploration undertaken by Chinese, Polynesians, and other non-Western peoples?

By 1450, mariners had discovered and settled most of the islands of the Pacific, the Atlantic, and the Indian Oceans, and a great trading system united the peoples

Polynesian Canoes Pacific Ocean mariners sailing canoes such as these, shown in an eighteenth-century painting, made epic voyages of exploration and settlement. A large platform connects two canoes at the left, providing more room for the members of the expedition, and a sail supplements the paddlers. "Tereoboo, King of Owyhee, bringing presents to Captain Cook," D. L Ref. p. xx 2f. 35. Courtesy, The Dixson Library, State Library of New South Wales

Chronology

	Pacific Ocean	Atlantic Ocean	Indian Ocean
Pre-1400	**400–1300** Polynesian settlement of Pacific islands	**700–1200** Viking voyages **1300s** Settlement of Madeira, Azores, Canaries **Early 1300s** Mali voyages	
1400 to 1500		**1418–1460** Voyages of Henry the Navigator **1440s** Slaves from West Africa **1482** Portuguese at Gold Coast and Kongo **1486** Portuguese at Benin **1492** Columbus reaches Caribbean **1493** Columbus returns to Caribbean (second voyage) **1493–1502** Spanish conquer Hispaniola **1498** Columbus reaches mainland of South America (third voyage)	**1405–1433** Voyages of Zheng He **1498** Vasco da Gama reaches India
1500 to 1550	**1518** Smallpox arrives in Caribbean **1519–1522** Magellan expedition	**1500** Cabral reaches Brazil **1513** Ponce de Léon explores Florida **1519–1521** Cortés conquers Aztec Empire **1532–1533** Pizarro conquers Inca Empire	**1505** Portuguese bombard Swahili Coast cities **1510** Portuguese take Goa **1511** Portuguese take Malacca **1515** Portuguese take Hormuz **1535** Portuguese take Diu **1538** Portuguese defeat Ottoman fleet **1539** Portuguese aid Ethiopia

around the Indian Ocean. But we know of no individual crossing the Pacific in either direction. Even the narrower Atlantic formed a barrier that kept the peoples of the Americas, Europe, and Africa in ignorance of each other's existence. The inhabitants of Australia were also completely cut off from contact with the rest of humanity. All this was about to change.

The Pacific Ocean

The vast distances that Polynesian peoples voyaged out of sight of land across the Pacific Ocean are one of the most impressive feats in maritime history before 1450 (see Map 15.1). Though they left no written records, over several thousand years mariners from the Malay (may-LAY) Peninsula of Southeast Asia explored and

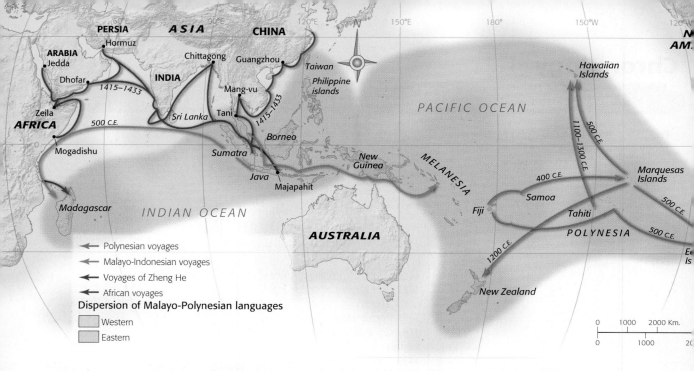

Map 15.1 **Exploration and Settlement in the Indian and Pacific Oceans Before 1500** Over many centuries, mariners originating in Southeast Asia gradually colonized the islands of the Pacific and Indian Oceans. The Chinese voyages led by Zheng He in the fifteenth century were lavish official expeditions. © Cengage Learning

Interactive Map

settled the island chains of the East Indies and continued on to New Guinea and the smaller islands of Melanesia (mel-uh-NEE-zhuh). Beginning sometime before the Common Era (C.E.), a wave of expansion from the area of Fiji brought the first humans to the islands of the central Pacific known as Polynesia. Their sailing canoes reached the easternmost Marquesas (mar-KAY-suhs) Islands about 400 C.E.; Easter Island, 2,200 miles (3,540 kilometers) off the coast of South America, a century later; and the Hawaiian Islands by 500 C.E. Settlement in New Zealand began about 1200. Between 1100 and 1300, new voyages northward from Tahiti brought more Polynesian settlers to Hawaii.

Historians once puzzled over how the Polynesians reached the eastern Pacific islands without compasses to plot their way, particularly in view of the difficulties Magellan's flagship encountered sailing eastward across the Pacific. However, there is now considerable evidence that Polynesian mariners deliberately set out to settle the islands of the eastern Pacific. The languages of the islanders relate closely to the languages of the western Pacific and ultimately to those

of Malaysia and Indonesia. In addition, accidental voyages could not have brought sufficient numbers of men and women for founding a new colony along with all the plants and domesticated animals common to other Polynesian islands.

In 1976, a Polynesian crew led by anthropologist Ben Finney used traditional navigational methods to sail the *Hokulea*, a 62-foot-long (19-meter-long) double canoe, from Hawaii south to Tahiti. Patterned after old oceangoing canoes, some of which measured 120 feet (35 meters) long, it used inverted triangular sails and was steered by paddles (not by a rudder). The *Hokulea*'s crew navigated using only their observation of the currents, stars, and evidence of land, showing that ancient Polynesians had the means and skills to cross the Pacific Ocean.

The Indian Ocean

While Polynesian mariners settled the Pacific islands, other Malayo-Indonesians sailed westward across the Indian Ocean and colonized the large island of Madagascar off the southeastern coast of Africa. These voyages continued through the fifteenth century. To this

Chinese Junk This modern drawing shows how much larger one of Zheng He's ships was than one of Vasco da Gama's vessels. Watertight interior bulkheads made junks one of the most seaworthy large ships of the fifteenth century. Sails made of pleated bamboo matting hung from the junk's masts, and a stern rudder provided steering. European ships of exploration, though smaller, were faster and more maneuverable.

Dugald Stermer

day, the inhabitants of Madagascar speak Malayo-Polynesian languages. However, part of the island's population is descended from Africans who crossed the 600 miles (1,000 kilometers) from the mainland to Madagascar, most likely in the centuries just before 1500.

The rise of Islam gave Indian Ocean trade an important boost. The great Muslim cities of the Middle East provided a demand for valuable commodities, and networks of Muslim traders tied the region together. The Indian Ocean traders operated largely independently of the empires and states that they served, but in East Asia, China's early Ming emperors took an active interest in these wealthy ports of trade, sending Admiral **Zheng He** (jung huh) on a series of expeditions (see Chapter 12).

The first Ming fleet in 1405 consisted of sixty-two specially built "treasure ships," large Chinese junks each about 300 feet long by 150 feet wide (90 by 45 meters). Most of the one hundred smaller accompanying vessels exceeded in size the flagship in which Columbus later sailed across the Atlantic. Each treasure ship had nine masts, twelve sails, many decks, and a carrying capacity of 3,000 tons (six times the capacity of Columbus's entire fleet). One expedition carried over 27,000 individuals, including infantry and cavalry troops. Although the ships carried small cannon, highly accurate crossbows dominated most Chinese sea battles.

One Chinese-Arabic interpreter kept a journal recording the customs, dress, and beliefs of the people visited, along with the trade, towns, and animals of their countries. Among his observations were these: exotic animals such as the black panther of Malaya and the tapir of Sumatra; beliefs in legendary "corpse-headed barbarians" whose heads left their bodies at night and caused infants to die; the division of coastal Indians into five classes, which correspond to the four Hindu varnas and a separate Muslim class; and the fact that traders in the Indian port of Calicut (KAL-ih-kut) could perform error-free calculations by counting on their fingers and toes rather than using the Chinese abacus. After his return, the interpreter went on tour in China, telling of these exotic places and "how far the majestic virtue of [China's] imperial dynasty extended."[1]

Interest in new contacts was not confined to the Chinese side. In 1415–1416, at least three trading cities on the Swahili (swah-HEE-lee) Coast of East Africa sent delegations to China. Although no record of African and Chinese reactions to one another survives,

---

Zheng He (1371–1433) An imperial eunuch and Muslim, entrusted by the Ming emperor Yongle with a series of state voyages that took his gigantic ships through the Indian Ocean, from Southeast Asia to Africa.

China's lavish gifts to local rulers stimulated the Swahili market for silk and porcelain.

The Atlantic Ocean

For several centuries, the Vikings, northern European raiders and pirates, used their small, open ships to attack coastal European settlements. They also discovered and settled one island after another in the North Atlantic. Like the Polynesians, the Vikings had neither maps nor navigational devices. They found their way using their knowledge of the heavens and the seas.

The Vikings first settled Iceland in 770. From there, some moved on to Greenland in 982, and one group sighted North America in 986. Fifteen years later, Leif Ericsson established a short-lived Viking settlement on the island of Newfoundland, which he called Vinland. When the climate turned colder after 1200, the northern settlements in Greenland went into decline, and Vinland became a mysterious place mentioned in Norse sagas.

Some southern Europeans also explored the Atlantic. In 1291, two Vivaldo brothers from Genoa set out to sail around Africa to India. They were never heard of again. Other Genoese and Portuguese expeditions into the Atlantic in the fourteenth century discovered (and settled) the islands of Madeira (muh-DEER-uh), the Azores (A-zorz), and the Canaries.

Mention also occurs of African voyages of exploration in the Atlantic. The Syrian geographer al-Umari (1301–1349) relates that when Mansa Kankan Musa (MAHN-suh KAHN-kahn MOO-suh), the ruler of the West African empire of Mali, passed through Egypt on his lavish pilgrimage to Mecca in 1324, he told of voyages out into the Atlantic undertaken by his predecessor, Mansa Muhammad. Muhammad had sent out four hundred vessels with men and supplies, telling them, "Do not return until you have reached the other side of the ocean or if you have exhausted your food or water." After a long time, one canoe returned, reporting the others had been swept away by a "violent current in the middle of the sea." Muhammad himself then set out at the head of a second, even larger, expedition, from which no one returned.

On the other side of the Atlantic, Amerindian voyagers from South America colonized the West Indies. By the year 1000, Amerindians known as the **Arawak**

SECTION REVIEW

- Before 1450, the Atlantic and Pacific Oceans were barriers that kept the peoples of Europe, Africa, and the Americas ignorant of each other.
- In the Pacific, Malayan seafarers settled the East Indies and Melanesia, and mariners from around Fiji colonized the Polynesian islands.
- In the Indian Ocean, Southeast Asians and Africans colonized Madagascar.
- Ming China sent expeditions to Indian Ocean ports, and the Swahili city-states dispatched delegations to China.
- Vikings colonized the islands of the North Atlantic, eventually reaching North America.
- Southern Europeans and Africans attempted to explore the Atlantic, and South American Amerindians colonized the West Indies.

(AR-uh-wahk) had moved from the small islands of the Lesser Antilles (Barbados, Martinique, Guadaloupe) into the Greater Antilles (Cuba, Hispaniola, Jamaica, and Puerto Rico), as well as into the Bahamas. Another people, the Carib, followed their route. By the late fifteenth century, they had overrun most Arawak settlements in the Lesser Antilles and were raiding parts of the Greater Antilles. From the West Indies, Arawak and Carib also undertook voyages to the North American mainland.

Iberian Expansion, 1400–1550

In this era of long-distance exploration, did Europeans have any special advantages over other cultural regions?

The preceding survey shows that maritime exploration occurred in many parts of the world before 1450. The sea voyages sponsored by the Iberian kingdoms of Portugal and Spain attract special interest because they began a maritime revolution that profoundly altered the course of world history, ending the isolation of the Americas and increasing global

Arawak Amerindian peoples who inhabited the Greater Antilles of the Caribbean at the time of Columbus.

interaction. The influence in world affairs of the Iberians and other Europeans who followed them overseas rose steadily after 1500.

Iberian overseas expansion arose from two related phenomena. First, Iberian rulers had strong economic, religious, and political motives to expand their contacts and increase their dominance. Second, improvements in maritime and military technologies gave them the means to master treacherous and unfamiliar ocean environments, seize control of existing maritime trade routes, and conquer new lands.

Background to Iberian Expansion

In many ways, these voyages continued four trends evident in the Latin West from about the year 1000: (1) the revival of urban life and trade, (2) a struggle with Islamic powers for dominance of the Mediterranean that mixed religious motives with the desire for trade with distant lands, (3) growing intellectual curiosity about the outside world, and (4) a peculiarly European alliance between merchants and rulers.

The city-states of northern Italy took the lead in all of these developments. By 1450, they had well-established trade links to northern Europe, the Indian Ocean, and the Black Sea, and their merchant princes had sponsored an intellectual and artistic Renaissance. But the Italian states did not take the lead in exploring the Atlantic, even after the expansion of the Ottoman Empire in the fourteenth and fifteenth centuries disrupted their trade to the East, because Venice and Genoa preferred to continue the lucrative alliances with Muslims that had given their merchants privileged positions and because Mediterranean ships were ill suited to the more violent weather of the Atlantic. However, many individual Italians played leading roles in Atlantic exploration.

By contrast, the Iberian kingdoms had engaged in anti-Muslim warfare since the eighth century, when Muslim forces overran most of the peninsula. By about 1250, the Iberian kingdoms of Portugal, Castile, and Aragon had conquered all the Muslim lands in Iberia except the southern kingdom of Granada. Granada finally fell to the united kingdom of Castile and Aragon in 1492, forming Spain, sixteenth-century Europe's most powerful state.

Christian militancy continued to drive Portugal and Spain in their overseas ventures. But the Iberian rulers and their adventurous subjects also sought material returns. Their small share of the Mediterranean trade made them more willing than the Italians to take risks to find new routes to Africa and Asia through the Atlantic. Moreover, both kingdoms participated in the shipbuilding changes and the gunpowder revolution under way in Atlantic Europe. Though not centers of Renaissance learning, both states had exceptional rulers who appreciated new geographical knowledge.

Portuguese Voyages

When the Muslim government of Morocco in northwestern Africa weakened in the fifteenth century, the Portuguese went on the attack, beginning with the city of Ceuta (say-OO-tuh) in 1415. This assault combined aspects of a religious crusade, a plundering expedition, and a military tournament in which young Portuguese knights displayed their bravery. Despite the capture of several more ports along Morocco's Atlantic coast, the Portuguese could not push inland and gain access to the gold trade they learned about, so they sought more direct contact with the gold producers by sailing down the African coast.

Young Prince Henry (1394–1460), third son of the king of Portugal, led the attack on Ceuta. Because he devoted the rest of his life to promoting exploration, he is known as **Henry the Navigator**. His official biographer emphasized his desire to convert Africans to Christianity, make contact with Christian rulers believed to exist in Africa, and launch joint crusades with them against the Ottomans. Profit also figured in his dreams. His initial explorations focused on Africa. His ships established permanent contact with the islands of Madeira in 1418 and the Azores in 1439. Only later did reaching India become a goal.

Henry himself never ventured farther from home than North Africa. Instead, he founded a sort of research institute at Sagres (SAH-gresh) for studying

Henry the Navigator (1394–1460) Portuguese prince who promoted the study of navigation and directed voyages of exploration down the western coast of Africa.

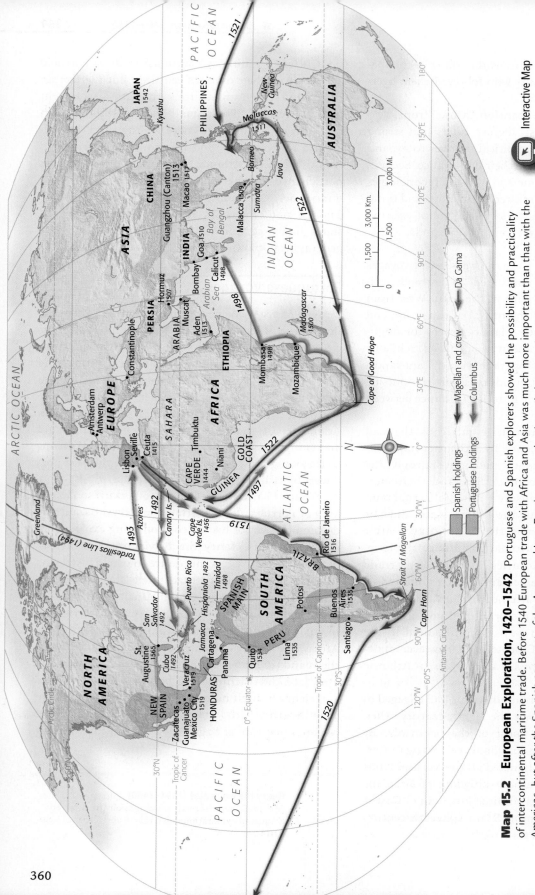

Map 15.2 European Exploration, 1420–1542 Portuguese and Spanish explorers showed the possibility and practicality of intercontinental maritime trade. Before 1540 European trade with Africa and Asia was much more important than that with the Americas, but after the Spanish conquest of the Aztec and Inca Empires transatlantic trade began to increase. Notice the Tordesillas line, which in theory separated the Spanish and Portuguese spheres of activity. © Cengage Learning

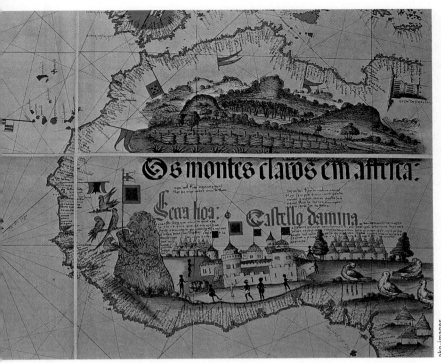

Portuguese Map of Western Africa, 1502 This map shows in great detail a section of African coastline that Portuguese explorers charted and named in the fifteenth century. The cartographer illustrated the African interior, which was almost completely unknown to Europeans, with drawings of birds and views of coastal sights: Sierra Leone (Serra lioa), named for a mountain shaped like a lion, and the Portuguese Castle of the Mine (Castello damina) on the Gold Coast.

akg-images

navigation and collecting information about new lands. His staff drew on the pioneering efforts of Italian merchants, especially the Genoese, who had learned some of the secrets of the trans-Saharan trade, and of fourteenth-century Jewish cartographers who used information from Arab and European sources to produce remarkably accurate sea charts and maps of distant places. They also studied and improved navigational instruments that had come into Europe from China and the Islamic world: the magnetic compass, first developed in China, and the astrolabe, an instrument of Arab or Greek invention that enabled mariners to determine their latitude by measuring the position of the sun or the stars.

The Portuguese developed a new type of long-distance sailing vessel, the **caravel** (KAR-uh-vel). The many-oared galleys of the Mediterranean could not carry enough food and water for long ocean voyages, and the three-masted ships of the North Atlantic, powered by square sails, could not sail against the wind. The caravel, which was only one-fifth the size of the largest European ships and the large Chinese junks, could enter shallow coastal waters and explore upriver, yet it had the strength to weather ocean storms. When equipped with lateen sails, caravels had great maneuverability and could sail deeply into the wind; when sporting square Atlantic sails, they had great speed. The addition of small cannon made them good fighting ships as well. The caravels' economy, speed, agility, and power justified a contemporary's claim that they were "the best ships that sailed the seas."[2]

Pioneering captains had to overcome their crews' fears that the South Atlantic waters were boiling hot or contained ocean currents that would prevent their ever returning home. It took Prince Henry from 1420 to 1434 to coax an expedition to venture beyond southern Morocco (see Map 15.2). The next stretch of coast, 800 miles (1,300 kilometers) of desert, offered little of interest to the explorers. Finally in 1444, the mariners reached the Senegal River and the populous, well-watered lands below the Sahara beginning at

caravel A small, highly maneuverable three-masted ship used by the Portuguese and Spanish in the exploration of the Atlantic.

what they named Cape Verde (Green Cape) because of its vegetation.

In the years that followed, Henry's explorers learned how to return speedily to Portugal. Instead of battling the prevailing northeast trade winds and currents back up the coast, they discovered that by sailing northwest into the Atlantic to the latitude of the Azores, ships could pick up prevailing westerly winds that would blow them back to Portugal. The knowledge that ocean winds tend to form large circular patterns helped explorers discover many other ocean routes.

To pay for the research, ships, and expeditions, Prince Henry drew partly on the income of the Order of Christ, a military religious order of which he was the governor. This order had been founded to inherit the Portuguese properties and the crusading tradition of the Order of Knights Templar, which had disbanded in 1314. The Order of Christ received the exclusive right to promote Christianity in all the lands that were discovered, and the Portuguese emblazoned their ships' sails with the crusaders' red cross.

The first financial returns came from selling into slavery Africans captured in raids on the northwest coast of Africa and the Canary Islands during the 1440s. By the end of the century, the Portuguese had captured or purchased 80,000 Africans. However, gold quickly became more important than slavery. By 1457, enough African gold was coming back to Portugal for the kingdom to issue a new gold coin called the *cruzado* (crusade), another reminder of how deeply the Portuguese entwined religious and secular motives. By the time Prince Henry died in 1460, his explorers had established a base of operations in the uninhabited Cape Verde Islands and explored 600 miles (950 kilometers) of coast beyond Cape Verde, as far as what they named Sierra Leone (see-ER-uh lee-OWN) (Lion Mountain). From there, they knew that the coast of Africa curved sharply toward the east. After spending four decades covering the 1,500 miles (2,400 kilometers) from Lisbon to Sierra Leone, Portuguese explorers traveled the remaining 4,000 miles (6,400 kilometers) to the continent's southern tip in only three decades.

Royal sponsorship continued, but private commercial participation sped the progress. In 1469, a Lisbon merchant named Fernão Gomes purchased from the Crown the privilege of exploring 350 miles (550 kilometers) of new coast a year for five years and

a monopoly on any resulting trade. Gomes discovered the uninhabited island of São Tomé (sow toh-MAY) on the equator; in the next century, it became a major source of sugar produced with African slave labor. He also explored what later Europeans called the **Gold Coast**, which became the headquarters of Portugal's West African trade.

The expectation of finding a passage around Africa to the Indian Ocean spurred the final thrust down the African coast. **Bartolomeu Dias** rounded the southern tip of Africa (in 1488) and entered the Indian Ocean. In 1497–1498, **Vasco da Gama** led a Portuguese expedition around Africa to India. In 1500, ships in an expedition under Pedro Alvares Cabral (kah-BRAHL), while swinging wide to the west in the South Atlantic to catch the winds that would sweep them around southern Africa and on to India, came on the eastern coast of South America, laying the basis for Portugal's later claim to Brazil.

Spanish Voyages

Spain's early discoveries owed more to haste and blind luck than to careful planning. Only in the last decade of the fifteenth century did the Spanish monarchs turn their attention from the conquest and organization of previously Muslim territories to overseas exploration. By this time, the Portuguese had already found their route to the Indian Ocean.

The leader of their overseas mission would be **Christopher Columbus** (1451–1506), a Genoese mariner. His three voyages between 1492 and 1498 would reveal the existence of vast and unexpected lands across the Atlantic. But this momentous discovery

Gold Coast (Africa) Region of the Atlantic coast of West Africa occupied by modern Ghana; named for its gold exports to Europe from the 1470s onward.
Bartolomeu Dias (1457–1500) Portuguese explorer who in 1488 led the first expedition to sail around the southern tip of Africa from the Atlantic into the Indian Ocean.
Vasco da Gama (1467–1524) Portuguese explorer. In 1497–1498 he led the first naval expedition from Europe to sail to India, opening an important commercial sea route.
Christopher Columbus (1451–1506) Genoese mariner who in the service of Spain led expeditions across the Atlantic, reestablishing contact between the peoples of the Americas and the Old World and opening the way to Spanish conquest and colonization.

Columbus Prepares to Cross the Atlantic, 1492 This later representation shows Columbus with the ships, soldiers, priests, and seaman that were part of Spain's enterprise.

G. Dagli Orti/The Art Archive

 History in Focus *Notice the figures in the foreground aboard the ships and small boat. How do they reflect attitudes and goals that drove Spanish overseas expansion? Now, look at the figures in the background. Who do you think they are? What might they suggest about the attitude of the general Spanish populace to early overseas expansion? Find the answer online.*

fell disappointingly short of Columbus's intention of finding a new route to the Indian Ocean even shorter than that of the Portuguese.

As a younger man, Columbus had gained considerable experience while participating in Portuguese explorations along the African coast, but he dreamed of a shorter way to the riches of the East. By his reckoning (based on a serious misreading of a ninth-century Arab authority), a mere 2,400 nautical miles (4,450 kilometers) separated the Canary Islands from Japan. The actual distance was five times greater.

Portuguese authorities twice rejected his plan to reach the East by sailing west, first in 1485 following a careful study and again in 1488 after Dias had established the feasibility of the African route. Columbus received more sympathy, but initially no support, from Queen Isabel of Castile. A Castilian commission appointed by Isabella studied the proposal for four years and concluded that a westward sea route to the Indies rested on questionable geographical assumptions. Nevertheless, Columbus's persistence finally won over the queen and her husband, King Ferdinand of Aragon. In 1492, elated perhaps by finally expelling the Muslims from Granada, they agreed to fund a modest expedition.

Columbus recorded in his log that the *Santa María*, the *Santa Clara* (nicknamed the *Niña*), and a vessel now known only by its nickname, the *Pinta*, with a mostly Spanish crew of ninety men "departed Friday the third day of August of the year 1492," toward "the regions of India." Their mission, the royal contract stated, was "to discover and acquire certain islands and mainland in the Ocean Sea." Columbus carried letters of introduction from the Spanish sovereigns to Eastern rulers, including one to the "Grand Khan" (meaning the Chinese emperor). An Arabic-speaking Jewish convert to Christianity had the job of communicating with the peoples of eastern Asia.

Unfavorable headwinds had discouraged other attempts to explore the Atlantic west of the Azores. But on earlier voyages along the African coast, Columbus had learned about winds blowing westward at the latitude of the Canaries. After reaching the Canaries, he replaced the *Niña*'s lateen sails with square sails, for he knew that from then on, speed would be more important than maneuverability since his supplies would last for only a fixed number of days.

In October, the expedition encountered the islands of the Caribbean. Columbus called the inhabitants "Indians" because he believed he had reached the East Indies. A second voyage in 1493 did nothing to change his mind. On a third voyage in 1498, two months after Vasco da Gama reached India, Columbus sighted the mainland of South America, which he insisted was part of Asia. But by then, other Europeans had become convinced that his discoveries were of lands previously unknown to the Old World (Europe, Asia, and Africa). Amerigo Vespucci's explorations, first on behalf of Spain and then for Portugal, led mapmakers to name the new continents "America," after him.

To prevent disputes about exploiting these new lands and spreading Christianity among their peoples, Spain and Portugal agreed to split the world between them. Modifying an earlier papal proposal, the Treaty of Tordesillas (tor-duh-SEE-yuhs), negotiated by the pope in 1494, drew an imaginary north-south line down the middle of the Atlantic Ocean. Lands east of the line in Africa and southern Asia could be claimed by Portugal; lands to the west in the Americas belonged to Spain. Cabral's discovery of Brazil, however, gave Portugal a valid claim to the part of South America that bulged east of the line.

But if the Tordesillas line were extended around the earth, where would Spain's and Portugal's spheres of influence divide in the East? Given European ignorance of the earth's true size in 1494, no one knew whether the Moluccas (muh-LOO-kuhz), the source of the valuable spices of the East Indies, belonged to Portugal or Spain. The missing information concerned the size of the Pacific Ocean, which a Spanish adventurer named Vasco Núñez de Balboa (bal-BOH-uh) had spotted in 1513 when he crossed the isthmus (a narrow neck of land) of Panama from the east. The 1519 expedition of **Ferdinand Magellan** (ca.

SECTION REVIEW

- The Portuguese and Spanish expeditions prompted a maritime revolution of global significance.

- The voyages extended from cultural trends in the Latin West since 1000, but Christian militancy and material gain were especially strong motives.

- Urged by Henry the Navigator, Portuguese explorers ventured farther into the Atlantic and colonized Madeira, the Azores, and the Canaries.

- Portuguese explorer-traders and missionaries established bases along the coast of Africa, pushed into the Indian Ocean, and crossed to South America.

- Spanish overseas expansion began with Columbus's voyages to find a western route to the Indian Ocean.

- The Treaty of Torsedillas divided the world between Spain and Portugal, a division clarified by Magellan's circumnavigation of the world.

1480–1521) sought to complete Columbus's interrupted westward voyage by sailing around the Americas and across the Pacific. The Moluccas turned out to lie well within Portugal's sphere, as Spain formally acknowledged in 1529.

Magellan's voyage laid the basis for Spanish colonization of the Philippine Islands after 1564. It also gave Magellan credit, despite his death, for being the first person to encircle the globe, for a decade earlier he had sailed from Europe to the East Indies on an expedition sponsored by his native Portugal.

Columbus and those who followed in his path laid the basis for the colonial empires of Spain and other European nations. In turn, these empires promoted, among the four Atlantic continents, a new trading network whose importance rivaled and eventually surpassed that of the Indian Ocean. Of more immediate importance, Portugal's entry into the Indian Ocean led quickly to a major European presence and profit. Both the eastward and the westward voyages of exploration marked a tremendous expansion of Europe's role in world history.

Ferdinand Magellan (1487–1521) Portuguese navigator who led the Spanish expedition of 1519–1522 that was the first to sail around the world.

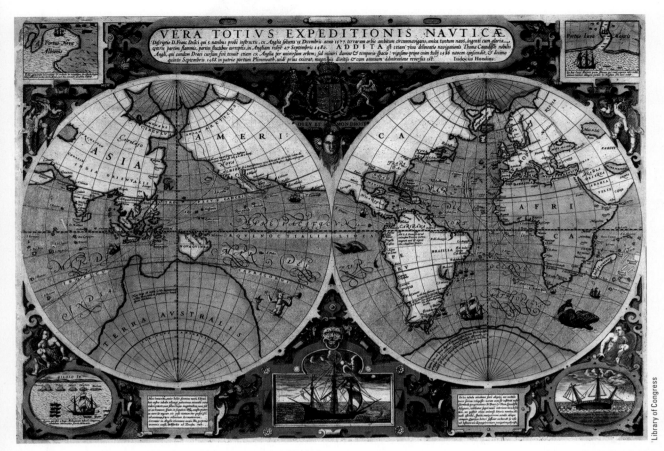

Map of the World, ca. 1595 After Ferdinand Magellan, the next explorer to circumnavigate the world was Sir Francis Drake (ca. 1540–1596). Departing with five ships in 1577, Drake completed most of his voyage in a single ship, the *Golden Hind*, returning to England in 1580. This hand-colored engraving by Jadocus Hondius shows his route. On his voyage, Drake raided Spanish ships and ports and returned with great riches. Unlike Magellan, he travelled far northward before crossing the Pacific, harboring for several weeks near San Francisco Bay and making friendly contact with native peoples there.

Encounters with Europe, 1450–1550

What were the different outcomes of European interactions with Africa, India, and the Americas?

The ways in which Africans, Asians, and Amerindians perceived their European visitors and interacted with them influenced their future relations. Some welcomed the Europeans as potential allies; others viewed them as rivals or enemies. In general, Africans and Asians readily recognized the benefits and dangers of European contact. However, the long isolation of the Amerindians added to the strangeness of their encounter with the Spanish and made them vulnerable to the unfamiliar diseases the Spanish inadvertently introduced.

Western Africa

Many Africans welcomed trade with the Portuguese, which gave them new markets for their exports and access to imports cheaper than those coming by caravan across the Sahara. Miners in the hinterland of the Gold Coast, which the Portuguese first visited in 1471, had long sold their gold to merchants from trading cities along the southern edge of the Sahara for transshipment to North Africa. Recognizing the possibility of more favorable trading terms, coastal Africans negotiated with the royal representative of Portugal, who arrived in 1482 seeking permission to erect a trading fort.

The Portuguese noble in charge and his officers (likely including the young Christopher Columbus, who had entered Portuguese service in 1476) strove to make a proper impression. They dressed in their best clothes, erected a fancy reception platform, celebrated a Catholic Mass, and signaled the start of negotiations with trumpets, tambourines, and drums. The African king, Caramansa, staged his entrance with equal ceremony, arriving with a large retinue of attendants and musicians. Through an African interpreter, the two leaders exchanged flowery speeches pledging goodwill and mutual benefit. Caramansa then gave permission for a small trading fort, assured, he said, by the appearance of these royal delegates that they were honorable persons, unlike the "few, foul, and vile" Portuguese visitors of the previous decade.

Neither side made a show of force, but Caramansa warned that if the Portuguese failed to be peaceful and honest traders, he and his people would move away and deprive their post of food and trade. Trade at the post of Saint George of the Mine (later called Elmina) enriched both sides. The Portuguese crown was soon purchasing gold amounting to one-tenth of the world's production at the time. In return, Africans received shiploads of goods brought by the Portuguese from Asia, Europe, and other parts of Africa.

Early contacts involved a mixture of commercial, military, and religious interests. Some African rulers quickly saw the value of European firearms. Coastal rulers also proved willing to test the value of Christian practices, which the Portuguese eagerly promoted. The rulers of Benin and Kongo, the largest coastal kingdoms, invited Portuguese missionaries and soldiers to accompany them into battle to test the Christians' religion along with their muskets.

The kingdom of Benin in the Niger Delta, near the peak of its power after a century of aggressive expansion, had a large capital city, also known as Benin. Its *oba* (king) responded to a Portuguese visit in 1486 by sending an ambassador to Portugal to learn more about their homeland. Then he established a royal monopoly on Portuguese trade, selling pepper and ivory tusks (to be taken back to Portugal) as well as stone beads, textiles, and prisoners of war (to be resold at Elmina). In return, Portuguese merchants provided

Bronze Figure of Benin Ruler Both this prince and his horse are protected by chainmail introduced in the fifteenth century to Benin by Portuguese merchants. Antenna Gallery Dakar Senegal/G.Dagli Orti/The Art Archive

Benin with copper and brass, fine textiles, glass beads, and a horse for the king's royal procession. In the early sixteenth century, as the demand for slaves for the Portuguese sugar plantations on the nearby island of São Tomé grew, the oba first raised the price of slaves and then imposed restrictions on their sale.

Efforts to spread Catholicism ultimately failed. Early kings showed some interest, but after 1538, the rulers declined to receive further missionaries. They also closed the market in male slaves for the rest of the sixteenth century. Both steps illustrate their power to control how much interaction they wanted.

Farther south, on the lower Congo River, the *manikongo* (mah-NEE-KONG-goh) (king) of Kongo also sent delegates to Portugal, established a royal monopoly on trade, and expressed interest in missionary teachings. But here the royal family made Catholicism the kingdom's official faith. Lacking ivory and pepper, Kongo sold more and more slaves to acquire the goods brought by the Portuguese and to pay missionary expenses.

Soon the royal trade monopoly broke down. In 1526, the Christian manikongo, Afonso I (r. 1506–ca. 1540), wrote to his royal "brother," the king of Portugal, begging for his help in stopping the slave trade because unauthorized Kongolese were kidnapping and selling people, even members of good families. Afonso asked that contacts be limited to "some priests and a few people to teach in the schools, and no other goods except wine and flour for the holy sacrament," but received no reply (see Diversity and Dominance: Kongo's Christian King). After 1540, the major part of the slave trade from this part of Africa moved farther south.

Eastern Africa

As Vasco da Gama sailed up the eastern coast of Africa in 1498, most rulers of the coastal trading states received him coolly. Visitors who painted crusader crosses on their sails raised the suspicions of their Muslim inhabitants. The ruler of Malindi, however, saw in the Portuguese an ally who could help him expand Malindi's trade, and he provided da Gama with a pilot to guide him to India. The suspicions of most rulers came to fruition seven years later when a Portuguese war fleet bombarded and looted most of the coastal cities in the name of Christ and commerce, but spared Malindi.

Christian Ethiopia also saw benefits in allying with the Portuguese. In the fourteenth and fifteenth centuries, Ethiopian conflicts with Muslim states along the Red Sea increased. After the Ottoman Turks conquered Egypt and launched a fleet in the Indian Ocean to counter the Portuguese in 1517, the warlord of the Muslim state of Adal attacked Ethiopia. A decisive victory in 1529 put the Christian kingdom in jeopardy, making Portuguese support a crucial matter.

For decades, delegations from Portugal and Ethiopia had talked of a Christian alliance. Queen Helena of Ethiopia, who acted as regent for her young sons after her husband's death in 1478, sent a letter in 1509 to "our very dear and well-beloved brother," the king of Portugal, along with a gift of two tiny crucifixes said to be made of wood from the cross on which Christ was crucified. She proposed to combine her land army and Portugal's fleet against the Turks. At her death in 1522, no alliance had come into being, but the worsening situation brought renewed Ethiopian appeals.

Finally, a small Portuguese force commanded by Vasco da Gama's son Christopher reached Ethiopia in 1539. With Portuguese help, another queen rallied the desperate Ethiopians. Muslim foes captured Christopher da Gama and tortured him to death but lost heart when their leader fell in battle. Portuguese aid helped save the Ethiopian kingdom from extinction, but Ethiopia's refusal to transfer its Christian affiliation from the patriarch of Alexandria to the pope prevented a permanent alliance.

As these examples illustrate, African encounters with the Portuguese before 1550 varied considerably. Africans and Portuguese might become royal brothers, bitter opponents, or partners in a mutually profitable trade, but Europeans were still a minor presence in most of Africa in 1550. The Indian Ocean trade by then was occupying most of their attention.

Indian Ocean States

Vasco da Gama's arrival on the Malabar Coast of India in May 1498 did not impress the citizens of Calicut. The Chinese fleets of gigantic junks that had called at Calicut sixty-five years earlier dwarfed his four small ships, which were no larger than many of the dhows (dows) already filling the harbor. The *zamorin* (ruler) of Calicut and his Muslim officials showed mild interest, but the gifts da Gama brought evoked derisive laughter: twelve pieces of striped cloth, four scarlet hoods, six hats, and six wash basins. When da Gama defended his gifts as those of an explorer, not a merchant, the zamorin cut him short, asking whether he had come to discover men or stones: "If he had come to discover men, as he said, why had he brought nothing?"

Coastal rulers soon discovered that the Portuguese had no intention of remaining poor competitors in the Indian Ocean trade. Upon da Gama's return to Portugal in 1499, the jubilant King Manuel styled himself "Lord of the Conquest, Navigation, and Commerce of Ethiopia, Arabia, Persia, and India." Previously, the Indian Ocean had been an open sea, used by merchants (and pirates) of all the surrounding coasts. Now the Portuguese crown intended to make it Portugal's sea, which others might use only on Portuguese terms.

Portugal's hope of controlling the Indian Ocean stemmed from the superiority of its ships and

Diversity & Dominance

Kongo's Christian King

The new overseas voyages brought conquest to some and opportunities for fruitful borrowings and exchanges to others. The decision of the ruler of the kingdom of Kongo to adopt Christianity in 1491 added cultural diversity to Kongolese society and in some ways strengthened the hand of the king. From then on Kongolese rulers sought to introduce Christian beliefs and rituals while at the same time Africanizing Christianity to make it more intelligible to their subjects. In addition, the kings of Kongo sought a variety of more secular aid from Portugal, including schools and medicine. Trade with the Portuguese introduced new social and political tensions, especially in the case of the export trade in slaves for the Portuguese sugar plantations on the island of São Tomé to the north.

Two letters sent to King João (zhwao) III of Portugal in 1526 illustrate how King Afonso of Kongo saw his kingdom's new relationship with Portugal and the problems that resulted from it. (Afonso adopted that name when he was baptized as a young prince.) After the death of his father in 1506, Afonso successfully claimed the throne and ruled until 1542. His son Henrique became the first Catholic bishop of the Kongo in 1521.

These letters were written in Portuguese and penned by the king's secretary João Teixera (tay-SHER-uh), a Kongo Christian who, like Afonso, had been educated by Portuguese missionaries.

6 July 1526
To the very powerful and excellent prince Dom João, our brother:

On the 20th of June just past, we received word that a trading ship from your highness had just come to our port of Sonyo. We were greatly pleased by that arrival for it had been many days since a ship had come to our kingdom, for by it we would get news of your highness, which many times we had desired to know, . . . and likewise as there was a great and dire need for wine and flour for the holy sacrament; and of this we had had no great hope for we have the same need frequently. And that, sir, arises from the great negligence of your highness's officials toward us and toward shipping us those things. . . .

Sir, your highness should know how our kingdom is being lost in so many ways that we will need to provide the needed cure, since this is caused by the excessive license given by your agents and officials to the men and merchants who come to this kingdom to set up shops with goods and many things which have been prohibited by us, and which they spread throughout our kingdoms and domains in such abundance that many of our vassals, whose submission we could once rely on, now act independently so as to get the things in greater abundance than we ourselves; whom we had formerly held content and submissive and under our vassalage and jurisdiction, so it is doing a great harm not only to the service of God, but also to the security and peace of our kingdoms and state.

And we cannot reckon how great the damage is, since every day the mentioned merchants are taking our people, sons of the land and the sons of our noblemen and vassals and our relatives, because the thieves and men of bad conscience grab them so as to have the things and wares of this kingdom that they crave; they grab them and bring them to be sold. In such a manner, sir, has been the corruption and deprivation that our land is becoming completely depopulated, and your highness should not deem this good nor in your service. And to avoid this we need from these kingdoms [of yours] no more than priests and a few people to teach in schools, and no other goods except wine and flour for the holy sacrament, which is why we beg of your highness to help and assist us in this matter. Order your agents to send here neither merchants nor wares, because it is our will that in these kingdoms there should not be any dealing in slaves nor outlet for them, for the reasons stated above. Again we beg your highness's agreement, since otherwise we cannot cure such manifest harm. May Our Lord in His mercy have your highness always under His protection and may you always do the things of His holy service. I kiss your hands many times.

From our city of Kongo. . . .

The King, Dom Afonso

18 October 1526
Very high and very powerful prince King of Portugal, our brother,

Sir, your highness has been so good as to promise us that anything we need we should ask for in our letters, and that everything will be provided. And so that there may be peace and health of our kingdoms, by God's will, in our lifetime. And as there are among us old folks and people who have lived for many days, many and different diseases happen so often that we are pushed to the ultimate extremes. And the same happens to our children, relatives, and people, because this country lacks physicians and surgeons who might know the proper cures for such diseases, as well as pharmacies and drugs to make them better. And for this reason many of those who had been already confirmed and instructed in the things of the holy faith of Our Lord Jesus Christ perish and die. And the rest of the people for the most part cure themselves with herbs and sticks and other ancient methods, so that they live putting all their faith in these herbs and ceremonies, and die believing that they are saved; and this serves God poorly.

And to avoid such a great error, I think, and inconvenience, since it is from God and from your highness that all the good and the drugs and medicines have come to us for our salvation, we ask your merciful highness to send us two physicians and two pharmacists and one surgeon, so that they may come with their pharmacies and necessary things to be in our kingdoms, for we have extreme need of each and every one of them. We will be very good and merciful to them, since sent by your highness, their work and coming should be for good. We ask your highness as a great favor to do this for us, because besides being good in itself it is in the service of God as we have said above.

Moreover, sir, in our kingdoms there is another great inconvenience which is of little service to God, and this is that many of our people, out of great desire for the wares and things of your kingdoms, which are brought here by your people, and in order to satisfy their disordered appetite, seize many of our people, freed and exempt men. And many times noblemen and the sons of noblemen, and our relatives are stolen, and they take them to be sold to the white men who are in our kingdoms and take them hidden or by night, so that they are not recognized. And as soon as they are taken by the white men, they are immediately ironed and branded with fire. And when they are carried off to be embarked, if they are caught by our guards, the whites allege that they have bought them and cannot say from whom, so that it is our duty to do justice and to restore to the free their freedom. And so they went away offended.

And to avoid such a great evil we passed a law so that every white man living in our kingdoms and wanting to purchase slaves by whatever means should first inform three of our noblemen and officials of our court on whom we rely in this matter, namely Dom Pedro Manipunzo and Dom Manuel Manissaba, our head bailiff, and Gonçalo Pires, our chief supplier, who should investigate if the said slaves are captives or free men, and, if cleared with them, there will be no further doubt nor embargo and they can be taken and embarked. And if they reach the opposite conclusion, they will lose the aforementioned slaves. Whatever favor and license we give them [the white men] for the sake of your highness in this case is because we know that it is in your service too that these slaves are taken from our kingdom; otherwise we should not consent to this for the reasons stated above that we make known completely to your highness so that no one could say the contrary, as they said in many other cases to your highness, so that the care and remembrance that we and this kingdom have should not be withdrawn. . . .

We kiss your hands of your highness many times.
From our city of Kongo, the 18th day of October,
The King, Dom Afonso

QUESTIONS FOR ANALYSIS

1. What sorts of things does King Afonso desire from the Portuguese?
2. What is he willing and unwilling to do in return?
3. What problem with his own people has the slave trade created, and what has King Afonso done about it?
4. Does King Afonso see himself as an equal to King João or his subordinate? Do you agree with that analysis?

Source: From António Brásio, ed., *Monumenta Missionaria Africana: Africa Ocidental (1471–1531)* (Lisbon: Agência Geral do Ultramar, 1952), I: 468, 470–471, 488–491. Translated by David Northrup.

weapons over the smaller and lightly armed merchant dhows. In 1505, the Portuguese fleet of 81 ships and some 7,000 men bombarded Swahili Coast cities. Goa, on the west coast of India, fell to a well-armed fleet in 1510, becoming the base from which the Portuguese menaced the trading cities of Gujarat (goo-juh-RAHT) to the north and Calicut and other Malabar Coast cities to the south. The port of Hormuz, controlling the entry to the Persian Gulf, fell in 1515. Aden, at the entrance to the Red Sea, preserved its independence, but the capture of the Gujarati port of Diu in 1535 consolidated Portuguese dominance of the western Indian Ocean.

Farther east, the independent city of Malacca (muh-LAH-kuh) on the strait separating the Malay Peninsula and Sumatra became the focus of their attention. During the fifteenth century, Malacca had become the main entrepôt (ON-truh-poh) (a place where goods are stored or deposited and from which they are distributed) for the trade from China, Japan, India, the Southeast Asian mainland, and the Moluccas. The city's 100,000 residents spoke eighty-four different languages, according to a Portuguese source, and included merchants from Cairo, Ethiopia, and the Swahili Coast. Many non-Muslim residents supported letting the Portuguese join this cosmopolitan trading community, perhaps to offset the growing

solidarity of Muslim traders. In 1511, however, the Portuguese seized Malacca with a force of a thousand fighting men, including three hundred recruited in southern India.

On the China coast, local officials and merchants persuaded the imperial government to allow the Portuguese to establish a trading post at Macao (muh-COW) in 1557. Subsequently, Portuguese ships nearly monopolized trade between China and Japan.

Control of the major port cities enabled the Portuguese to enforce their demands that all spices be carried in Portuguese ships, as well as all goods on the major ocean routes such as between Goa and Macao. The Portuguese also tried to control and tax other Indian Ocean trade. Merchant ships entering and leaving their ports had to carry a Portuguese passport and pay customs duties. Portuguese patrols seized vessels that did not comply, confiscated their cargoes, and either killed the captain and crew or sentenced them to forced labor.

Reactions to this power grab varied. Like the emperors of China, the Mughal (MOO-gahl) emperors of India largely ignored Portugal's maritime intrusions. The Ottomans confronted the Christian intruders more aggressively. They supported Egypt's defensive efforts from 1501 to 1509 and then sent their own fleet into the Indian Ocean in 1538. However,

Portuguese in India In the sixteenth century, Portuguese men moved to the Indian Ocean to work as administrators and traders. This Indo-Portuguese drawing from about 1540 shows a Portuguese man speaking to an Indian woman, perhaps to propose marriage.

Ottoman galleys proved no match for the faster, better-armed Portuguese vessels in the open ocean. They retained their advantage only in the Red Sea and Persian Gulf, where they controlled many ports.

Smaller trading states also could not challenge the Portuguese because their mutual rivalry kept them from forming a common front. Some cooperated with the Portuguese to safeguard their prosperity and security, while others engaged in evasion and resistance. When the merchants of Calicut put up sustained resistance, the Portuguese embargoed all trade with Aden, Calicut's principal trading partner, and centered their trade on the port of Cochin, which had once been a dependency of Calicut. Some Calicut merchants evaded their patrols, but Calicut's importance shrank as Cochin gradually became the major pepper-exporting port on the Malabar Coast.

Farther north, Gujarat initially resisted Portuguese attempts at monopoly and in 1509 joined Egypt's futile effort to sweep the Portuguese from the Arabian Sea. But in 1535, with his state weakened by Mughal attacks, the ruler allowed the Portuguese to build a fort at Diu in return for their support. Once established, the Portuguese gradually extended their control. By midcentury, they were licensing and taxing all Gujarati ships. Even after the Mughals took control of Gujarat in 1572, the Mughal emperor, Akbar, permitted the Portuguese to continue their maritime monopoly in return for allowing one pilgrim ship a year to sail to Mecca without paying a fee.

The Portuguese never gained complete control of the Indian Ocean trade, but their domination of key ports and trade routes brought them considerable profit in the form of spices and other luxury goods. The Portuguese broke the trading monopoly of Venice and Genoa by selling pepper for less than what they charged for shipments obtained through Egyptian middlemen.

The Americas

In the Americas, the Spanish established a vast territorial empire, in contrast to the trading empire of the Portuguese. The Spanish kingdoms drew on somewhat greater resources, but the Spanish and Portuguese monarchies had similar motives for expansion and used identical ships and weapons. The isolation of the Amerindian peoples provided a key difference. The first European settlers in the Caribbean resorted to conquest and plunder rather than trade. They later extended this practice to the more powerful Amerindian kingdoms on the American mainland. After 1518, deadly epidemics weakened the Amerindians' ability to resist.

The Arawak whom Columbus first encountered on Hispaniola (modern Haiti and the Dominican Republic) in the Greater Antilles and the Bahamas to the north cultivated maize (corn), cassava (a tuber), sweet potatoes, and hot peppers, as well as cotton and tobacco. They mined and worked gold, but they did not trade gold, nor did they have iron. They extended a cautious welcome to Columbus but told him exaggerated stories about gold in other places to persuade him to move on.

Columbus brought with him several hundred settlers from southern Iberia, as well as missionaries, on his second trip to Hispaniola in 1493. The settlers stole gold ornaments, confiscated food, and raped women, provoking the Hispaniola Arawak to war in 1495. With the advantage of horses and body armor, the Spaniards slaughtered tens of thousands of Arawak and forced the survivors to pay a heavy tax in gold, spun cotton, and food. Whoever failed to meet the quotas faced forced labor. Meanwhile, the cattle, pigs, and goats introduced by the settlers devoured the Arawak's food crops, causing deaths from famine and disease. A governor appointed by the Spanish crown in 1502 forced the Arawak on Hispaniola to become laborers under the control of Spanish settlers.

The actions of the Spanish in the Antilles reflected Spanish behavior during the wars against the Muslims in the previous centuries. They sought to serve God by defeating, controlling, and converting nonbelievers and to become rich in the process. Individual **conquistadors** (kon-KEY-stuh-dors) (conquerors) extended that pattern around the Caribbean.

Primary Source: General History of the Things of New Spain Learn the details of the horrible disaster that befell the Aztecs when the Spaniards and the plague descended upon them simultaneously.

---

conquistadors Early-sixteenth-century Spanish adventurers who conquered Mexico, Central America, and Peru.

Coronation of Emperor Moctezuma This painting by an unnamed Aztec artist depicts the Aztec ruler's coronation. Moctezuma, his nose pierced by a bone, receives the crown from a prince in the palace at Tenochtitlan.

Oronoz

Some raided the Bahamas for gold and labor as both grew scarce on Hispaniola. Arawak from the Bahamas served as slaves on Hispaniola. Juan Ponce de León (1460–1521), a veteran of the conquest of Muslim Spain and the seizure of Hispaniola, conquered the island of Borinquen (Puerto Rico) in 1508 and in 1513 explored southeastern Florida.

An ambitious and ruthless nobleman, **Hernán Cortés** (air-NAHN kor-TEZ) (1485–1547), led the most audacious expedition to the mainland. Cortés left Cuba in 1519 with six hundred fighting men and most of the island's weapons to assault the Mexican mainland in search of slaves and trade. Learning of the rich Aztec Empire in central Mexico, Cortés expanded on the American mainland the exploitation and conquest carried out in the Greater Antilles.

Many of the Amerindians whom the Aztecs had subjugated during the previous century resented the tribute, forced labor, and the large-scale human sacrifices to Aztec gods their rulers imposed on them. Consequently, some gave the Spanish their support as allies against the Aztecs. Like the Caribbean people, the mainland Amerindians had no precedent by which to judge these strangers. Later accounts suggest that some believed Cortés to be the legendary ruler Quetzalcoatl (ket-zahl-COH-ah-tal), whose return to earth had been prophesied, and treated him with great deference.

Another consequence of millennia of isolation proved even more fatal: the lack of acquired resistance to Old World diseases. Smallpox, the most deadly of the early epidemics, appeared for the first time on the island of Hispaniola in late 1518 or early 1519. An infected member of the Cortés expedition then transmitted smallpox to Mexico in 1519, where it spread with deadly efficiency.

The Aztec emperor **Moctezuma II** (mock-teh-ZOO-ma) (r. 1502–1520) sent messengers to greet Cortés and determine whether he was god or man, friend or foe. Cortés advanced steadily toward the capital, Tenochtitlan (teh-noch-TIT-lan), overcoming Aztec opposition with cavalry charges and steel swords and gaining the support of discontented tributary peoples. When the Spaniards drew near, the emperor went out in a great procession, dressed in all his finery, to welcome Cortés with gifts and flower garlands.

Despite Cortés's initial promise of friendship, Moctezuma quickly found himself a prisoner in his own palace. The Spaniards looted his treasury,

Hernán Cortés (1485–1547) Spanish explorer and conquistador who led the conquest of Aztec Mexico in 1519–1521 for Spain.
Moctezuma II (1466–1520) Last Aztec emperor, overthrown by the Spanish conquistador Hernán Cortés.

especially its gold. Soon full-scale battle broke out, during which the Aztecs and their supporters briefly gained the upper hand. They destroyed half the Spanish force and four thousand of their Amerindian allies, sacrificing fifty-three Spanish prisoners and four horses to their gods and displaying their severed heads in rows on pikes. However, reinforcements from Cuba enabled Cortés to regain the advantage. Smallpox, which weakened and killed more of the city's defenders than died in the fighting, also assisted his capture of Tenochtitlan in 1521. One source remembered that the disease "spread over the people as a great destruction."

After the capital fell, the conquistadors took over other parts of Mexico. Once they reached Panama, Spaniards began hearing of another empire in South America. This was the Inca Empire that stretched nearly 3,000 miles (5,000 kilometers) south from the equator and contained half of the population in South America. The Inca had conquered the inhabitants of the Andes Mountains and the Pacific coast of South America during the previous century, but their rule was not fully accepted by the subjugated peoples.

The Inca rulers administered a well-organized empire with highly productive agriculture, exquisite stone cities (such as the capital, Cuzco), and rich gold and silver mines. The power of the Inca emperor rested on the belief that he was descended from the sun-god and on an efficient system of roads and messengers that kept him informed about major events. Yet at the end of the 1520s, before the Spanish had even been heard of, smallpox had claimed countless lives, perhaps including the Inca emperor sometime between 1524 and 1527.

An even more devastating threat loomed: **Francisco Pizarro** (pih-SAHR-oh) (ca. 1478–1541) and his band of 180 men, 37 horses, and 2 cannon. With limited education but some military experience, Pizarro had come to the Americas in 1502 at the age of twenty-five to seek his fortune. He had participated in the conquest of Hispaniola and in Balboa's expedition across the Isthmus of Panama. By 1520 a wealthy landowner and official in Panama, he nevertheless gambled his fortune on exploring the Pacific coast to a point south of the equator, where he learned of the riches of the Inca. With a license from the king of Spain, he set out from Panama in 1531 to conquer them.

In November 1532, Pizarro arranged to meet the new Inca emperor, **Atahualpa** (ah-tuh-WAHL-puh) (r. 1531–1533), near the Andean city of Cajamarca (kah-hah-MAHR-kah). With supreme boldness and brutality, Pizarro's small band grabbed Atahualpa from a rich litter borne by eighty nobles as it passed through an enclosed courtyard. Though surrounded by an Inca army of at least 40,000, the Spaniards used their cannon to create confusion while their swords sliced the emperor's lightly armed retainers and servants to pieces.

Noting the glee with which the Spaniards seized gold, silver, and emeralds, the captive Atahualpa offered them what he thought would satisfy even the greediest among them in exchange for his freedom: a roomful of gold and silver. But after receiving 13,400 pounds (6,000 kilograms) of gold and 26,000 pounds (12,000 kilograms) of silver, the Spaniards gave Atahualpa a choice: being burned at the stake as a heathen or being strangled after a Christian baptism. He chose the latter. His death and the Spanish occupation broke the unity of the Inca Empire.

In 1533, the Spaniards took Cuzco and from there set out to conquer and loot the rest of the empire. After the defeat of a rebellion in 1536, the remaining Inca retreated to a small kingdom in the mountains that lasted until 1572. In 1541, Pizarro himself met a violent death at the hands of Spanish rivals, but the conquest of the mainland continued. Incited by the fabulous wealth of the Aztecs and Inca, conquistadors extended Spanish conquest and exploration in South and North America, dreaming of new treasuries to loot.

Patterns of Dominance

Within fifty years of Columbus's first landing, the Spanish had located and occupied the major population centers of the Americas and penetrated many of the more thinly populated areas. Why did the peoples of the Americas suffer a fate so different from that of peoples

Francisco Pizarro (ca. 1476–1541) Spanish explorer who led the conquest of the Inca Empire of Peru in 1532–1533.
Atahualpa (1497–1533) Last ruling Inca emperor of Peru. He was executed by the Spanish.

SECTION REVIEW

- Portugal and western African kingdoms forged commercial, military, and religious contacts, but missionary work and slave trading became points of tension.
- Portuguese contacts with East African states were mixed from the start, often marred by religious differences and the Portuguese focus on Indian Ocean trade.
- Naval superiority helped Portugal win control of Indian Ocean ports, and diplomacy gained it Macao in China.
- Benefiting from the Amerindians' isolation, Spain conquered a vast territorial empire in the Americas.
- Small conquistador armies subjugated island peoples and toppled the mainland Aztec and Inca Empires.
- Spain's conquest of the Americas happened as it did because of new diseases, military superiority, and precedents established by the reconquest of Spain.

1492: forced labor, forced conversion, and the incorporation of conquered lands into a new empire.

The same three factors help explain the different outcomes elsewhere. Centuries of contacts before 1500 meant that Europeans, Africans, and Asians shared the same Old World diseases and did not suffer a demographic calamity like that of the Americas. The Iberians enjoyed a military advantage at sea, but on land they lacked the advantages against more numerous armies of Africans and Asians that they had in the Americas. Everywhere, Iberian religious zeal went hand in hand with a desire for riches. In Iberia and America, conquest itself brought wealth. But in Africa and Asia, existing trading networks made wealth dependent on commercial domination rather than conquest.

in Africa and Asia? Why were the Spanish able to erect a vast land empire in the Americas so quickly?

First, unfamiliar illnesses devastated the Caribbean islands and then the mainland. Contemporaries estimated that between 25 and 50 percent of those infected with smallpox died. Repeated epidemics inhibited the Amerindians' ability to regain control. Estimates of the size of the population before Columbus's arrival, based on sparse evidence, vary widely. Yet historians agree that the Amerindian population fell sharply during the sixteenth century. The Americas became a "widowed land," open to resettlement from across the Atlantic.

A second factor was Spain's superior military technology. Steel swords, protective armor, and horses gave the Spaniards an advantage over their Amerindian opponents. Though few in number, muskets and cannon provided a psychological edge. However, the Spanish conquests also depended heavily on large numbers of Amerindian allies armed with indigenous weapons. The most decisive military advantage may have been the no-holds-barred fighting techniques the Spaniards had developed during their wars at home.

The third factor in Spain's conquest was the precedent established by the reconquest of Granada in

The Columbian Exchange

How did the Columbian Exchange alter the natural environment of the Americas?

The term **Columbian Exchange** refers to the transfer of peoples, animals, plants, diseases, and technology between the New and Old Worlds that European trade in the Atlantic opened up. We have already seen how Old World diseases devastated Amerindian peoples and led to the resettlement of the Americas by Europeans and Africans. In addition, the domesticated livestock and major agricultural crops of the Old World spread over much of the Americas, and Amerindians' staple crops enriched the agricultures of Europe, Asia, and Africa. This vast exchange of plants and animals radically altered diets and lifestyles around the world.

Transfers to the Americas

Within a century of Columbus's first voyage, new settlers in the Americas were growing all the staples of southern European agriculture—wheat,

Columbian Exchange The exchange of plants, animals, diseases, and technologies between the Americas and the rest of the world following Columbus's voyages.

E. 79

The Columbian Exchange In this painting an Amerindian woman milks a cow, suggesting how the Columbian Exchange altered native culture and environment. While livestock sometimes destroyed the fields of native peoples, cattle, sheep, pigs, and goats also provided food, leather, and wool.

Oronoz

and sugar and rice formed the basis of plantation agriculture, along with native tobacco. Other food crops arrived with slaves from Africa, including okra, black-eyed peas, yams, grains such as millet and sorghum, and mangoes. Many of these new animals and plants were useful additions to the islands, but they crowded out indigenous species, except maize, which remained a staple.

The introduction of European livestock to the mainland had a dramatic impact. Faced with few natural predators, cattle, pigs, horses, and sheep, as well as pests like rats and rabbits, multiplied rapidly in the open spaces of the Americas. On the vast plains of present-day southern Brazil, Uruguay, and Argentina, herds of wild cattle and horses exceeded 50 million by 1700. Large herds of both animals also appeared in northern Mexico and what became the Southwest of the United States.

Where Old World livestock spread most rapidly, environmental changes were most dramatic. Marauding livestock often had a destructive impact on Amerindian farmers. But on the plains of South America,

olives, grapes, and garden vegetables—along with African and Asian crops such as rice, bananas, coconuts, breadfruit, and sugar cane. Native peoples remained loyal to their traditional staples but added many Old World plants to their diet. Citrus fruits, melons, figs, and sugar, as well as onions, radishes, and salad greens, all found a place in Amerindian cuisine.

By the seventeenth century, nearly all of the domesticated animals in the Caribbean were ones that Europeans had introduced. The Spanish brought cattle, pigs, and horses, all of which multiplied rapidly. They also introduced new plants. Of these, bananas and plantain from the Canary Islands were a valuable addition to the food supply, northern Mexico, and Texas, feral cattle provided indigenous peoples with abundant supplies of meat and hides. In the present-day southwestern United States, the Navajo became sheepherders and expert weavers of woolen cloth. Individual Amerindians became muleteers, cowboys, and sheepherders.

No animal had a more striking effect on the cultures of native peoples than the horse, which increased the efficiency of hunters and the military capacity of warriors on the plains. The horse permitted the Apache, Sioux, Blackfoot, Comanche, Assiniboine, and others to hunt the vast herds of buffalo in North America more efficiently.

The most dramatic change that Europeans wrought in the Americas was the pathogens that accompanied the conquistadors and the devastating epidemics they caused. Because of their long isolation from other continents, the peoples of the New World lacked immunity to diseases introduced from the Old World by explorers and settlers. Diseases that were serious in the Old World, like smallpox, were catastrophic to the Amerindians. Old World childhood diseases like measles and mumps were fatal to adults who had never acquired any resistance to them. In many villages when disease struck, too few healthy people remained to take care of the sick, and many who might have recovered from the diseases instead died of thirst or hunger.

When smallpox arrived in the Caribbean, it killed most of the native peoples there. It was then spread to the mainland by the Spanish conquest of the Aztecs and Incas. Other diseases added to the toll: measles in the 1530s, followed by diphtheria, typhus, influenza, and perhaps pulmonary plague. Epidemic after epidemic swept through the Americas, causing the worst demographic disaster in human history, a holocaust that by 1600 had completely wiped out the indigenous populations of most of the Caribbean island and had reduced the population of Mexico by 90 to 95 percent and other parts of the Americas almost as much. When between 1520 and 1521 influenza and other ailments attacked the Cakchiquel of Guatemala, their chronicler recalled:

> Great was the stench of the dead. After our fathers and grandfathers succumbed, half the people fled to the fields. The dogs and vultures devoured the bodies. . . . So it was that we became orphans, oh my sons! . . . We were born to die![3]

Transfers from the Americas

In return for diseases and domesticated animals, the Americas offered the Old World an abundance of useful plants. The New World staples of maize and potatoes revolutionized agriculture and diet in parts of Europe because they provided more calories per acre than any of the Old World staples except rice. Beans, squash, tomatoes, sweet potatoes, peanuts, chilis, and chocolate also gained widespread acceptance in Europe and other parts of the Old World. The New World also provided the Old with plants that provided dyes, medicines, and tobacco.

Maize and cassava (a Brazilian plant cultivated for its edible roots) moved across the Atlantic to Africa. Cassava became the most important New World food in Africa. It had the highest yield of calories per acre of any staple food and thrived even in poor soils and during droughts. Both the leaves and the root could be eaten.

Cassava and maize were probably introduced accidentally into Africa by Portuguese ships from Brazil that discarded leftover supplies after reaching Angola. It did not take long for local Africans to recognize the food value of these new crops, especially in drought-prone areas. By the eighteenth century, Central African rulers hundreds of miles from the Angolan coast were actively promoting the cultivation of maize and cassava on their royal estates in order to provide a more secure food supply. Some historians believe that in the inland areas these Amerindian food crops provided the nutritional base for a population increase that partially offset losses due to the Atlantic slave trade.

Only one disease may have originated in the Americas and spread to the Eastern Hemisphere. Syphilis appeared in Spain soon after Columbus returned from the Caribbean, bringing with him an Indian who may have carried the disease; however, it is also possible that syphilis may have been a mutated form of yaws, a skin disease prevalent in Africa. Whatever its origin, a virulent form of syphilis soon spread throughout Europe. While many individuals died, it did not have the demographic impact that Old World diseases had on the New World, or that the bubonic plague had had on Europe in the fourteenth century.

Conclusion

The rapid expansion of European empires and the projection of European military power around the world, one of the most important events in world history, would have seemed unlikely in 1492. No European power matched the military and economic strength of China, and few could rival the Ottomans. Spain lacked strong national institutions and Portugal had a small population; both had limited economic resources. Because of these limitations, the monarchs of Spain and Portugal allowed their subjects greater initiative. While royal sponsorship was often crucial in the Portuguese contacts with Africa and the first voyages to Asia, many of the commercial and military expeditions were effectively organized and financed as private companies. Very often the kings of Spain and Portugal struggled to catch up with their restless and ambitious subjects, sometimes taking decades to establish royal control in new colonies.

The pace and character of European expansion were different in Africa and Asia than in the Americas. In Africa local rulers were generally able to limit European military power to coastal outposts and to control European trade. Only in the Kongo were the Portuguese able to project their power inland. When Europeans arrived in the Indian Ocean, mature markets and specialized production for distant consumers already existed. Although Portuguese naval power allowed Europeans to harvest large profits and influence local commercial patterns, most native populations continued to enjoy autonomy for centuries.

In the Americas the terrible effects of epidemic disease and the destructiveness of the conquest led to the rapid creation of European settlements and the subordination of the surviving indigenous population. As we shall see in Chapter 16, the gold, silver, and sugar that eventually produced great wealth resulted from the introduction of new technologies, the imposition of forced labor, and the development of new roads and ports.

CHAPTER REVIEW

Download the MP3 audio file of the Chapter Review to listen to on the go.

What were the objectives and major accomplishments of the voyages of exploration undertaken by Chinese, Polynesians, and other non-Western peoples? (page 354)

The voyages of exploration undertaken by the Chinese and Polynesians pursued diverse objectives. In the Chinese case, the great voyages of the early fifteenth century were made out of interest in trade, curiosity, and the projection of imperial power. The Polynesians' explorations demonstrated their seafaring expertise and opened the opportunity to settle satellite populations that would relieve population pressures on limited resources. In both cases new connections were made and societies were invigorated. The Vikings had similarly explored new lands in the North Atlantic, using their knowledge of the heavens and seas to establish settlements. There is also evidence of African voyages in the Atlantic during this same period, although their purpose is less clear.

In this era of long-distance exploration, did Europeans have any special advantages over other cultural regions? (page 358)

The projection of European influence between 1450 and 1550 was in some ways similar to that of other cultural regions in that it expanded commercial linkages, increased cross-cultural contacts, and served the ambitions of political leaders. But the result was a major turning point in world history. During those years European explorers opened new long-distance trade routes across the world's three major oceans, for the first time establishing regular contact among all the continents. As a result, a new balance of power arose in parts of Atlantic Africa, the Indian Ocean, and the Americas.

What were the different outcomes of European interactions with Africa, India, and the Americas? (page 365)

Europeans created colonial empires in the Americas quite rapidly, while their progress in Africa and Asia was much slower. Many Amerindians welcomed the Spanish settlers at first, only to have them tax their labors, steal their food, introduce disease and warfare, and eventually subjugate them. In contrast, Portuguese visitors to Africa remained a minor presence in 1550. In some regions, the Portuguese were welcomed as trading partners; in others they were regarded as potential political and military allies. The real focus of the Portuguese was to capture the rich trade of the Indian Ocean. While they never gained complete control, they used their superior military strength to dominate key ports and major trade routes.

As dramatic and momentous as these events were, they were not completely unprecedented. The riches of the Indian Ocean trade that brought a gleam to the eye of many Europeans had been developed over many centuries by the trading peoples who inhabited the surrounding lands. While rapid, the European conquest of the Americas was no more rapid or brutal than the earlier Mongol conquests of Eurasia. Even the crossing of the Pacific had been done before, though in stages, by Polynesians.

What gave this maritime revolution unprecedented importance had more to do with what happened after 1550 than with what happened earlier. The overseas empires of the Europeans would endure longer than the Mongols' and would continue to expand for three centuries after 1600. Unlike the Chinese, the Europeans did not turn their backs on the world after an initial burst of exploration. Not content with dominance in the Indian Ocean trade, Europeans opened an Atlantic maritime network that grew to rival the Indian Ocean network in the wealth of its trade; they also pioneered trade across the Pacific. The maritime expansion begun in the period from 1450 to 1550 marked the beginning of a new age of growing global interaction.

How did the Columbian Exchange alter the natural environment of the Americas? (page 374)

The arrival of Europeans dramatically changed the natural environments and peoples of the Americas. Animals brought deliberately or inadvertently from the Old World spread rapidly through the Americas, often damaging the native flora and replacing many native animals. Though Europeans brought their familiar crops, they soon found that the Americas offered many more useful plants that provided food for a growing population in the Old World. Most dramatic was the effect of the Old World diseases that accompanied the Europeans (and their African slaves) and killed nine-tenths of the Amerindian population, leaving empty lands that were taken over by herds of Old World animals or by Europeans and Africans.

Key Terms

Zheng He *(p. 357)*

Arawak *(p. 358)*

Henry the Navigator *(p. 359)*

caravel *(p. 361)*

Gold Coast (Africa) *(p. 362)*

Bartolomeu Dias *(p. 362)*

Vasco da Gama *(p. 362)*

Christopher Columbus *(p. 362)*

Ferdinand Magellan *(p. 364)*

conquistadors *(p. 371)*

Hernán Cortés *(p. 372)*

Moctezuma II *(p. 372)*

Francisco Pizarro *(p. 373)*

Atahualpa *(p. 373)*

Columbian Exchange *(p. 374)*

Web Resources

Pronunciation Guide
Interactive Maps
- MAP 15.1 Exploration and Settlement in the Indian and Pacific Oceans Before 1500
- MAP 15.2 European Exploration, 1420–1542

Visit the CourseMate website at www.cengagebrain.com for additional study tools and review materials for this chapter.

Primary Sources
- Agreement with Columbus of April 17 and April 30, 1492
- General History of the Things of New Spain

Answer to the History in Focus Question
See photo on page 363, "Columbus Prepares to Cross the Atlantic, 1492."

Periodization

Dividing history into time periods is second nature to historians. Major events like Columbus's voyages to the Western Hemisphere or the American Civil War make memorable turning points, as do the lives of well-known figures like Muhammad or Julius Caesar and the advent of major new technologies, such as printing, steam power, electrical generation, atomic energy, and the computer.

Just as common are period labels that fit the historian's interpretive scheme. European history, for example, is commonly divided into prehistoric, ancient, late ancient, early medieval, late medieval, early modern, modern, and contemporary periods. Historians of Europe do not agree precisely on the dates of these periods, but there is sufficient agreement to make them useful. Nevertheless, a historian following a Marxist interpretive framework is likely to prefer labels like *primitive communist*, *feudal*, *bourgeois*, and *socialist*.

When the study of non-European history was less common than it is today, historians specializing on other world regions adopted and adapted terms that were originally used for Europe. Terms like *medieval China*, *medieval Japan*, *medieval India*, and *medieval Islam* became commonplace even though historical writings in the native languages of those societies did not provide such labels.

Chinese writings labeled historical and cultural developments in terms of the time periods of different dynasties: Han, Tang, Song, Yuan, Ming, etc. Japanese sources named periods for capital cities—Nara, Kyoto, Edo—or dominant families—Fujiwara, Ashikaga, Tokugawa. Indian writings mention kingdoms that ruled only parts of the subcontinent, often overlapping with one another in time, and offer no time scheme for the region as a whole. Islamic histories focus on stages in the evolution of the caliphate, from Rashidun, to Umayyad, to Abbasid, and then on empires like the Ottomans and Safavids after the invading Mongols brought the Abbasid Caliphate to an end.

The study of world history poses a problem of periodization that neither indigenous historical sources nor writers in the European historical tradition had to address. Does the history of the globe as a whole fall into periods? Archaeologists answer this question positively, but they recognize that the sequence of periods, and the dates of transition from one period to the next, vary from region to region. *Paleolithic*, *Neolithic*, *Bronze Age*, and *Iron Age* are useful labels for describing the material remains of past societies, but bronze-smelting in South America, to take one example, first appeared as much as three thousand years later than the parallel craft in Mesopotamia or China.

When faced with the simplest traditional division of history, that into ancient, medieval, and modern, world historians have reached no consensus on chronological turning points. Moreover, they are reluctant to say that region X entered the modern era before or after region Y when this determination might be interpreted as a sign that region X was "more advanced" or its societies "more developed." Periodization does not necessarily imply improvement or "progress" toward some end, and most historians are careful to avoid this implication.

Some historians have sought at least a partial solution to the problem by emphasizing moments in time when different parts of the world first came to know of one another or entered into substantially closer contact. The conquests of Alexander the Great, the Arab armies inspired by the teachings of Islam, and the Mongols of Genghis Khan afford such turning points. So do the voyages of exploration that brought Europeans to the New World and the establishment of European colonial empires. Yet few of these turning points affect world history as a whole.

This does not mean that there have been no turning points affecting all or most of the planet. Some episodes of deadly disease might qualify, such as the Black Death that ravaged Europe and Asia (but not the Western Hemisphere) in the fourteenth century or the influenza epidemic of 1918, just after the end of World War I, that killed 50 million people worldwide, three times the number killed in the war. In the future, studies of climate may also suggest a sequence of periods based on hemisphere-wide or global changes in weather patterns.

Yet historians are reluctant to see history hinging on events like plagues or changes in climate over which humans have no control. They prefer to think of the watersheds that separate one period of history from another as the consequences of deliberate human action.

To put yourself in the place of a historian trying to identify historical turning points, think about the fall of the Soviet Union in 1991, the 9/11 terrorist attacks of 2001, and the global financial crisis of 2008. Do any of these qualify as turning points in history? Or as markers of the beginnings or ends of historical eras?

Abbasid Caliphate Descendants of the Prophet Muhammad's uncle, al-Abbas, the Abbasids overthrew the Umayyad Caliphate and ruled an Islamic empire from their capital in Baghdad (founded 762) from 750 to 1258. (p. 219)

abolitionists Men and women who agitated for a complete end to slavery. Abolitionist pressure ended the British transatlantic slave trade in 1808 and slavery in British colonies in 1834. In the United States the activities of abolitionists were one factor leading to the Civil War (1861–1865). (p. 500)

Acheh Sultanate Muslim kingdom in northern Sumatra. Main center of Islamic expansion in Southeast Asia in the early seventeenth century, it declined after the Dutch seized Malacca from Portugal in 1641. (p. 449)

Aden Port city in the south Arabian country of Yemen. It has been a major trading center in the Indian Ocean since ancient times. (p. 325)

Adolf Hitler (1889–1945) Born in Austria, Hitler became a radical German nationalist during World War I. He led the National Socialist German Workers' Party—the Nazis—in the 1920s and became dictator of Germany in 1933. He led Europe into World War II. (p. 660)

African National Congress An organization dedicated to obtaining equal voting and civil rights for black inhabitants of South Africa. Founded in 1912 as the South African Native National Congress, it changed its name in 1923. Though it was banned and its leaders were jailed for many years, it eventually helped bring majority rule to South Africa. (p. 686)

Afrikaners South Africans descended from Dutch and French settlers of the seventeenth century. Their Great Trek founded new settler colonies in the nineteenth century. Though a minority among South Africans, they held political power after 1910, imposing a system of racial segregation called apartheid after 1949. (p. 610)

agricultural revolution (eighteenth century) The transformation of farming that resulted in the eighteenth century from the spread of new crops, improvements in cultivation techniques and livestock breeding, and the consolidation of small holdings into large farms from which tenants and sharecroppers were forcibly expelled. (p. 508)

Agricultural Revolutions (ancient) The change from food gathering to food production that occurred between ca. 8000 and 2000 B.C.E. Also known as the Neolithic Revolution. (p. 8)

Akbar (1542–1605) Most illustrious sultan of the Mughal Empire in India (r. 1556–1605). He expanded the empire and pursued a policy of conciliation with Hindus. (p. 446)

Akhenaten Egyptian pharaoh (r. 1353–1335 B.C.E.). He built a new capital at Amarna, fostered a new style of naturalistic art, and created a religious revolution by imposing worship of the sun-disk. The Amarna letters, largely from his reign, preserve official correspondence with subjects and neighbors. (p. 59)

Albert Einstein (1879–1955) German physicist who developed the theory of relativity, which states that time, space, and mass are relative to each other and not fixed. (p. 645)

Alexander (356–323 B.C.E.) King of Macedonia in northern Greece. Between 334 and 323 B.C.E. he conquered the Persian Empire, reached the Indus Valley, founded many Greek-style cities, and spread Greek culture across the Middle East. Later known as Alexander the Great. (p. 105)

Alexander Nevskii (ca. 1220–1263) Prince of Novgorod (r. 1236–1263). He submitted to the invading Mongols in 1240 and received recognition as the leader of the Russian princes under the Golden Horde. (p. 298)

Alexandria City on the Mediterranean coast of Egypt founded by Alexander. It became the capital of the Hellenistic kingdom of the Ptolemies. It contained the famous Library and the Museum—a center for leading scientific and literary figures. Its merchants engaged in trade with areas bordering the Mediterranean and the Indian Ocean. (p. 107)

All-India Muslim League Political organization founded in India in 1906 to defend the interests of India's Muslim minority. Led by Muhammad Ali Jinnah, it attempted to negotiate with the Indian National Congress. In 1940, the League began demanding a separate state for Muslims, to be called Pakistan. (p. 679)

altepetl An ethnic state in ancient Mesoamerica, the common political building block of that region. (p. 173)

amulet Small charm meant to protect the bearer from evil. Found frequently in archaeological excavations in Mesopotamia and Egypt, amulets reflect the religious practices of the common people. (p. 20)

Amur River This river valley was a contested frontier between northern China and eastern Russia until the settlement arranged in the Treaty of Nerchinsk (1689). (p. 464)

anarchists Revolutionaries who wanted to abolish all private property and governments, usually by violence, and replace them with free associations of groups. (p. 586)

Anasazi Important culture of what is now the southwest United States (700–1200). Centered on Chaco Canyon in New Mexico and Mesa Verde in Colorado, the Anasazi culture built multistory residences and worshiped in subterranean buildings called kivas. (p. 176)

aqueduct A conduit, either elevated or underground, that used gravity to carry water from a source to a location—usually a city—that needed it. The Romans built many aqueducts in a period of substantial urbanization. (p. 147)

Arawak Amerindian peoples who inhabited the Greater Antilles of the Caribbean at the time of Columbus. (p. 358)

Armenia One of the earliest Christian kingdoms, situated in eastern Anatolia and the western Caucasus and occupied by speakers of the Armenian language. (p. 205)

Asante African kingdom on the Gold Coast that expanded rapidly after 1680. Asante participated in the Atlantic economy, trading gold, slaves, and ivory. It resisted British imperial ambitions for a quarter century before being absorbed into Britain's Gold Coast colony in 1902. (p. 614)

Ashikaga Shogunate (1338–1573) The second of Japan's military governments headed by a shogun (a military ruler). Sometimes called the Muromachi Shogunate. (p. 308)

Ashoka Third ruler of the Mauryan Empire in India (r. 269–232 B.C.E.). He converted to Buddhism and broadcast his precepts on inscribed stones and pillars, the earliest surviving Indian writing. (p. 123)

Ashurbanipal The seventh century B.C.E. Assyrian ruler who assembled a large collection of writings drawn from the ancient literary, religious, and scientific traditions of Mesopotamia. The many tablets unearthed by archaeologists constitute one of the most important sources of present-day knowledge of the long literary tradition of Mesopotamia.   (p. 68)

Asian Tigers South Korea, Taiwan, Hong Kong, and Singapore, so-called because their economies expanded so fast.   (p. 720)

Atahualpa (1497–1533) Last ruling Inca emperor of Peru. He was executed by the Spanish.   (p. 373)

Atlantic System The network of trading links after 1500 that moved goods, wealth, people, and cultures around the Atlantic Ocean Basin.   (p. 409)

Augustus (63 B.C.E.–14 C.E.) Honorific name of Octavian, founder of the Roman Principate, the military dictatorship that replaced the failing rule of the Roman Senate. After defeating all rivals, between 31 B.C.E. and 14 C.E. he laid the groundwork for several centuries of stability and prosperity in the Roman Empire.   (p. 142)

Auschwitz Nazi extermination camp in Poland, the largest center of mass murder during the Holocaust. Close to a million Jews, Gypsies, communists, and others were killed there.   (p. 671)

Ayatollah Ruhollah Khomeini Shi'ite philosopher and cleric who led the overthrow of the Shah of Iran in 1979 and created an Islamic republic.   (p. 724)

ayllu Andean lineage group or kin-based community.   (p. 179)

Aztecs Also known as Mexica, the Aztecs created a powerful empire in central Mexico (1325–1521). They forced defeated peoples to provide goods and labor.   (p. 173)

Babylon The largest and most important city in Mesopotamia. It achieved particular eminence as the capital of the Amorite king Hammurabi in the eighteenth century B.C.E. and the Neo-Babylonian king Nebuchadnezzar in the sixth century B.C.E.   (p. 13)

balance of power The policy in international relations by which, beginning in the eighteenth century, the major European states acted together to prevent any one of them from becoming too powerful.   (p. 403)

Balfour Declaration Statement issued by Britain's Foreign Secretary Arthur Balfour in 1917 favoring the establishment of a Jewish national homeland in Palestine.   (p. 633)

Bannermen Hereditary military servants of the Qing Empire, mostly descendants of various peoples who had fought for the founders of the empire.   (p. 540)

Bantu Collective name of a large group of sub-Saharan African languages and of the peoples speaking these languages.   (p. 203)

Bartolomé de Las Casas (1474–1566) First bishop of Chiapas, in southern Mexico. He devoted most of his life to protecting Amerindian peoples from exploitation. His major achievement was the New Laws of 1542, which limited the ability of Spanish settlers to compel Amerindians to labor for them.   (p. 410)

Bartolomeu Dias (1457–1500) Portuguese explorer who in 1488 led the first expedition to sail around the southern tip of Africa from the Atlantic into the Indian Ocean.   (p. 362)

Batavia Fort established ca. 1619 as headquarters of Dutch East India Company operations in Indonesia; today the city of Jakarta.   (p. 452)

Battle of Midway U.S. naval victory over the Japanese fleet in June 1942, in which the Japanese lost four of their best aircraft carriers. It marked a turning point in World War II.   (p. 667)

Battle of Omdurman British victory over the Mahdi in the Sudan in 1898. General Kitchener led a mixed force of British and Egyptian troops armed with rapid-firing rifles and machine guns.   (p. 604)

Beijing China's northern capital, first used as an imperial capital in 906.   (p. 301)

Bengal Region of northeastern India. It was the first part of India to be conquered by the British in the eighteenth century and remained the political and economic center of British India throughout the nineteenth century. The 1905 split of the province into predominantly Hindu West Bengal and predominantly Muslim East Bengal (now Bangladesh) sparked anti-British riots.   (p. 678)

Benito Mussolini (1883–1945) Fascist dictator of Italy (1922–1943). He led Italy to conquer Ethiopia (1935), joined Germany in the Axis pact (1936), and allied Italy with Germany in World War II. He was overthrown in 1943 when the Allies invaded Italy.   (p. 659)

Berlin Conference (1884–1885) Conference that German chancellor Otto von Bismarck called to set rules for the partition of Africa. It led to the creation of the Congo Free State under King Leopold II of Belgium.   (p. 609)

Bhagavad-Gita The most important work of Indian sacred literature, a dialogue between the great warrior Arjuna and the god Krishna on duty and the fate of the spirit.   (p. 124)

Black Death An outbreak of bubonic plague that spread across Asia, North Africa, and Europe in the mid-fourteenth century, carrying off vast numbers of persons.   (p. 335)

Blaise Diagne (1872–1934) Senegalese political leader, the first African elected to the French National Assembly. During World War I, in exchange for promises to give French citizenship to Senegalese, he helped recruit Africans to serve in the French army. After the war, he led a movement to abolish forced labor in Africa.   (p. 686)

Bolsheviks Radical Marxist political party founded by Vladimir Lenin in 1903. Under Lenin's leadership, the Bolsheviks seized power in November 1917 during the Russian Revolution.   (p. 634)

Borobodur A massive stone monument on the Indonesian island of Java, erected by the Sailendra kings around 800 C.E. The winding ascent through ten levels, decorated with rich relief carving, is a Buddhist allegory for the progressive stages of enlightenment.   (p. 131)

bourgeoisie In early modern Europe, the class of well-off town dwellers whose wealth came from manufacturing, finance, commerce, and allied professions.   (p. 393)

British raj The rule over much of South Asia between 1765 and 1947 by the East India Company and then by a British government.   (p. 557)

bubonic plague A bacterial disease that can be transmitted by flea bites to rodents and humans; humans in late stages of the illness can spread the bacteria by coughing. Because of its very high mortality rate and the difficulty of preventing its spread, major outbreaks have created epidemics in many parts of the world.   (p. 293)

Buddha (563–483 B.C.E.) An Indian prince named Siddhartha Gautama, who renounced his wealth and social position. After becoming "enlightened" (the meaning of *Buddha*) he enunciated the principles of Buddhism. This doctrine evolved and spread throughout India and to Southeast, East, and Central Asia.   (p. 119)

Byzantine Empire Historians' name for the eastern portion of the Roman Empire from the fourth century onward, taken from "Byzantion," an early name for Constantinople, the Byzantine capital city.   (p. 234)

caliphate Office established in succession to the Prophet Muhammad, to rule the Islamic empire; also the name of that empire.   (p. 217)

calpolli A group of up to a hundred families that served as a social building block of an altepetl in ancient Mesoamerica.   (p. 173)

capitalism The economic system of large financial institutions—banks, stock exchanges, investment companies—that first developed in early modern Europe. *Commercial capitalism,* the trading system of the early modern economy, is often distinguished from *industrial capitalism,* the system based on machine production.   (p. 424)

caravel A small, highly maneuverable three-masted ship used by the Portuguese and Spanish in the exploration of the Atlantic.   (p. 361)

Carthage City located in present-day Tunisia, founded by Phoenicians ca. 800 B.C.E. It became a major commercial center and naval power in the western Mediterranean until defeated by Rome in the third century B.C.E.   (p. 76)

Catholic Reformation Religious reform movement within the Latin Christian Church, begun in response to the Protestant Reformation. It clarified Catholic theology and reformed clerical training and discipline.   (p. 389)

Cecil Rhodes (1853–1902) British entrepreneur and politician involved in the expansion of the British Empire from South Africa into Central Africa. The colonies of Southern Rhodesia (now Zimbabwe) and Northern Rhodesia (now Zambia) were named after him.   (p. 611)

Celts Peoples sharing a common language and culture that originated in central Europe in the first half of the first millennium B.C.E. After 500 B.C.E., they spread as far as Anatolia in the east and Spain and the British Isles in the west. They were later overtaken by Roman conquest and Germanic invasions. Their descendants survive on the western fringe of Europe (Brittany, Wales, Scotland, and Ireland).   (p. 49)

Champa rice Quick-maturing rice that can allow two harvests in one growing season. Originally introduced into Champa from India, it was later sent to China as a tribute gift by the Champa state.   (p. 280)

Chang'an City in the Wei Valley in eastern China. It became the capital of the Qin and early Han Empires. Its main features were imitated in the cities and towns that sprang up throughout the Han Empire.   (p. 153)

Charlemagne (742–814) King of the Franks (r. 768–814); emperor (r. 800–814). Through a series of military conquests he established the Carolingian Empire, which encompassed all of Gaul and parts of Germany and Italy. Though illiterate himself, he sponsored a brief intellectual revival.   (p. 234)

Charles Darwin (1809–1882) He developed the theory of evolution through natural selection. Author of *On the Origin of Species* (1859).   (p. 592)

chartered companies Groups of private investors who paid an annual fee to France and England in exchange for a monopoly over trade to the West Indies colonies.   (p. 424)

Chavín The first major urban civilization in South America (900–250 B.C.E.). Its capital, Chavín de Huántar, was located high in the Andes Mountains of Peru.Chavín became politically and economically dominant in a densely populated region that included two distinct ecological zones, the Peruvian coastal plain and the Andean foothills.   (p. 165)

Chiang Kai-shek (1886–1975) Chinese military and political leader. He succeeded Sun Yat-sen as head of the Guomindang in 1925; headed the Chinese government from 1928 to 1948; and fought against the Chinese communists and Japanese invaders. After 1949 he headed the Chinese Nationalist government in Taiwan.   (p. 662)

chiefdom Form of political organization with rule by a hereditary leader who held power over a collection of villages and towns. Less powerful than kingdoms and empires, chiefdoms were based on gift giving and commercial links.   (p. 177)

Chimú Powerful Peruvian civilization based on conquest. Located in the region earlier dominated by Moche. Conquered by Inca in 1465.   (p. 180)

chinampas Raised fields constructed along lakeshores in Mesoamerica to increase agricultural yields.   (p. 169)

Christopher Columbus (1451–1506) Genoese mariner who in the service of Spain led expeditions across the Atlantic, reestablishing contact between the peoples of the Americas and the Old World and opening the way to Spanish conquest and colonization.   (p. 362)

city-state A small independent state consisting of an urban center and the surrounding agricultural territory. A characteristic political form in early Mesopotamia, archaic and classical Greece, Phoenicia, and early Italy.   (p. 15)

civilization An ambiguous term often used to denote more complex societies but sometimes used by anthropologists to describe any group of people sharing a set of cultural traits.   (p. 5)

clipper ship Large, fast, streamlined sailing vessel, often American built, of the mid-to-late nineteenth century rigged with vast canvas sails hung from tall masts.   (p. 563)

Cold War (1945–1991) The ideological struggle between communism (Soviet Union) and capitalism (United States) for world influence. The Soviet Union and the United States came to the brink of actual war during the Cuban Missile Crisis but never attacked one another. The Cold War came to an end when the Soviet Union dissolved in 1991.   (p. 703)

colonialism Policy by which a nation administers a foreign territory and develops its resources for the benefit of the colonial power.   (p. 604)

Columbian Exchange The exchange of plants, animals, diseases, and technologies between the Americas and the rest of the world following Columbus's voyages.   (p. 374)

Commodore Matthew Perry A navy commander who, on July 8, 1853, became the first foreigner to break through the barriers that had kept Japan isolated from the rest of the world for 250 years.   (p. 575)

Confucius Western name for the Chinese philosopher Kongzi (551–479 B.C.E.). His doctrine of duty and public service had a great influence on subsequent Chinese thought and served as a code of conduct for government officials.   (p. 41)

Congress of Vienna (1814–1815) Meeting of representatives of European monarchs called to reestablish the old order after the defeat of Napoleon I.   (p. 493)

conquistadors Early-sixteenth-century Spanish adventurers who conquered Mexico, Central America, and Peru.   (p. 371)

Constantine (285–337 C.E.) Roman emperor (r. 306–337). After reuniting the Roman Empire, he moved the capital to Constantinople and made Christianity a favored religion.   (p. 148)

Constitutional Convention Meeting in 1787 of the elected representatives of the thirteen original states to write the Constitution of the United States.   (p. 487)

contract of indenture A voluntary agreement binding a person to work for a specified period of years in return for free passage to an overseas destination. Before 1800 most indentured servants were Europeans; after 1800 most were Asians.   (p. 566)

Cossacks Peoples of the Russian Empire who lived outside the farming villages, often as herders, mercenaries, or outlaws. Cossacks led the conquest of Siberia in the sixteenth and seventeenth centuries.   (p. 470)

Council of the Indies The institution responsible for supervising Spain's colonies in the Americas from 1524 to the early eighteenth century, when it lost all but judicial responsibilities.   (p. 410)

creole In colonial Spanish America, the term used to describe someone of European descent born in the New World. Elsewhere in the Americas, it is used to describe all nonnative peoples. (p. 414)

Crimean War (1853–1856) Conflict between the Russian and Ottoman Empires fought primarily in the Crimean peninsula. To prevent Russian expansion, Britain and France sent troops to support the Ottomans.   (p. 533)

Crusades (1095–1204) Armed pilgrimages to the Holy Land by Christians determined to recover Jerusalem from Muslim rule. The Crusades brought an end to western Europe's centuries of intellectual and cultural isolation.   (p. 254)

Crystal Palace A gigantic greenhouse erected in Hyde Park, London, for the Great Exhibition of 1851. Made of iron and glass, it was a symbol of the industrial age.   (p. 512)

Cuban Missile Crisis (1962) Brink-of-war confrontation between the United States and the Soviet Union over the latter's placement of nuclear-armed missiles in Cuba.   (p. 707)

cultural imperialism Domination of one culture over another by a deliberate policy or by economic or technological superiority.   (p. 746)

Cultural Revolution (China) (1966–1969) Campaign in China ordered by Mao Zedong to purge the Communist Party of his opponents and instill revolutionary values in the younger generation.   (p. 720)

culture Socially transmitted patterns of action and expression. *Material culture* refers to physical objects, such as dwellings, clothing, tools, and crafts. Culture also includes arts, beliefs, knowledge, and technology.   (p. 6)

cuneiform a system of writing in which wedge-shaped symbols represented words or syllables. It originated in Mesopotamia and was used initially for Sumerian and Akkadian but later was adapted to represent other languages of western Asia. Because so many symbols had to be learned, literacy was confined to a relatively small group of administrators and scribes.   (p. 20)

Cyrus (600–530 B.C.E.) Founder of the Achaemenid Persian Empire. Between 550 and 530 B.C.E. he conquered Media, Lydia, and Babylon. Revered in the traditions of both Iran and the subject peoples, he employed Persians and Medes in his administration and respected the institutions and beliefs of subject peoples.   (p. 88)

daimyo Literally, "great name(s)." Japanese warlords and great landowners, whose armed samurai gave them control of the Japanese islands from the eighth to the later nineteenth century. Under the Tokugawa Shogunate they were subordinated to the imperial government.   (p. 456)

Daoism Chinese school of thought, originating in the Warring States Period with Laozi (604–531 B.C.E.). Daoism offered an alternative to the Confucian emphasis on hierarchy and duty. Daoists believe that the world is always changing and is devoid of absolute morality or meaning. They accept the world as they find it, avoid futile struggles, and deviate as little as possible from the Dao, or "path" of nature.   (p. 41)

Darius I (ca. 558–486 B.C.E.) Third ruler of the Persian Empire (r. 522–486 B.C.E.). He crushed the widespread initial resistance to his rule and gave all major government posts to Persians rather than to Medes. He established a system of provinces and tribute, began construction of Persepolis, and expanded Persian control in the east (Pakistan) and west (northern Greece).   (p. 89)

Decembrist revolt Abortive attempt by army officers to take control of the Russian government upon the death of Tsar Alexander I in 1825.   (p. 539)

Declaration of the Rights of Man and of the Citizen (1789) Statement of fundamental political rights adopted by the French National Assembly at the beginning of the French Revolution.   (p. 490)

deforestation The removal of trees faster than forests can replace themselves.   (p. 397)

Delhi Sultanate (1206–1526) Centralized Indian empire, created by Muslim invaders.   (p. 316)

democracy A system of government in which all "citizens" (however defined) have equal political and legal rights, privileges, and protections, as in the Greek city-state of Athens in the fifth and fourth centuries B.C.E.   (p. 94)

demographic transition A change in the rates of population growth. Before the transition, both birthrates and death rates are high, resulting in a slowly growing population; then the death rate drops but the birthrate remains high, causing a population explosion; finally the birthrate drops and the population growth slows down. This transition took place in Europe in the late nineteenth and early twentieth centuries, in North America and East Asia in the mid-twentieth century, and, most recently, in Latin America and South Asia.   (p. 736)

Deng Xiaoping (1904–1997) Communist Party leader who forced Chinese economic reforms after the death of Mao Zedong.   (p. 736)

Diaspora A Greek word meaning "dispersal," used to describe the communities of a given ethnic group living outside their homeland. Jews, for example, spread from Israel to western Asia and Mediterranean lands in antiquity and today can be found throughout the world.   (p. 72)

division of labor A manufacturing technique that breaks down a craft into many simple and repetitive tasks that can be performed by unskilled workers. Pioneered in the pottery works of Josiah Wedgwood and in other eighteenth-century factories, it greatly increased the productivity of labor and lowered the cost of manufactured goods.   (p. 510)

driver A privileged male slave whose job was to ensure that a slave gang did its work on a plantation.   (p. 422)

Druids The class of religious experts who conducted rituals and preserved sacred lore among some ancient Celtic peoples. They provided education and mediated disputes between kinship groups.   (p. 50)

Dutch West India Company (1621–1794) Trading company chartered by the Dutch government to conduct its merchants' trade in the Americas and Africa.   (p. 424)

electricity A form of energy used in telegraphy from the 1840s on and for lighting, industrial motors, and railroads beginning in the 1880s.   (p. 578)

electric telegraph A device for rapid, long-distance transmission of information over an electric wire. It was introduced in England and North America in the 1830s and 1840s.   (p. 514)

Emiliano Zapata (1879–1919) Revolutionary and leader of peasants in the Mexican Revolution. He mobilized landless peasants in south-central Mexico in an attempt to seize and divide the lands of the wealthy landowners. Though successful for a time, he was ultimately defeated and assassinated.   (p. 688)

Emilio Aguinaldo (1869–1964) Leader of the Filipino independence movement against Spain (1895–1898). He proclaimed the independence of the Philippines in 1899, but his movement was crushed and he was captured by the United States Army in 1901.   (p. 619)

Empress Dowager Cixi (1835–1908) Empress of China and mother of Emperor Guangxi. She put her son under house arrest, supported antiforeign movements, and resisted reforms of the Chinese government and armed forces.   (pp. 595, 639)

encomienda A grant of authority over a population of Amerindians in the Spanish colonies. It provided the grant holder with a supply of cheap labor and periodic payments of goods by the Amerindians and obligated the grant holder to Christianize the Amerindians.   (p. 413)

English Civil War (1642–1648)   A conflict over royal versus parliamentary rights, caused by King Charles I's arrest of his parliamentary critics and ending with his execution. Its outcome checked the growth of royal absolutism and, with the Glorious Revolution of 1688 and the English Bill of Rights of 1689, ensured that England would be a constitutional monarchy.   (p. 402)

Enlightenment   A philosophical movement in eighteenth-century Europe that fostered the belief that one could reform society by discovering rational laws that governed social behavior and were just as scientific as the laws of physics.   (pp. 392, 483)

equites   In ancient Italy, prosperous landowners second in wealth and status to the senatorial aristocracy. The Roman emperors allied with this group to counterbalance the influence of the old aristocracy and used the *equites* to staff the imperial civil service.   (p. 143)

Estates General   France's traditional national assembly with representatives of the three estates, or classes, in French society: the clergy, nobility, and commoners. The calling of the Estates General in 1789 led to the French Revolution.   (p. 489)

Ethiopia   East African highland nation lying east of the Nile River.   (p. 205)

European Community (EC)   An organization promoting economic unity in Europe, formed in 1967 by consolidation of earlier, more limited, agreements. It was replaced by the European Union (EU) in 1993.   (p. 704)

Eva Duarte Perón (1919–1952)   Wife of Juan Perón and champion of the poor in Argentina. She was a gifted speaker and popular political leader who campaigned to improve the life of the urban poor by founding schools and hospitals and providing other social benefits.   (p. 694)

extraterritoriality   The right of foreign residents in a country to live under the laws of their native country and disregard the laws of the host country. In the nineteenth and early twentieth centuries, European and American nationals living in certain areas of Chinese and Ottoman cities were granted this right.   (p. 535)

Faisal I (1885–1933)   Arab prince, leader of the Arab Revolt in World War I. The British made him king of Iraq in 1921, and he reigned under British protection until 1933.   (p. 633)

Fascist Party   Italian political party created by Benito Mussolini during World War I. It emphasized aggressive nationalism and was Mussolini's instrument for the creation of a dictatorship in Italy from 1922 to 1943.   (p. 659)

Ferdinand Magellan (1487–1521)   Portuguese navigator who led the Spanish expedition of 1519–1522 that was the first to sail around the world.   (p. 364)

fief   In medieval Europe, land granted in return for a sworn oath to provide specified military service.   (p. 245)

First Temple   A monumental sanctuary built in Jerusalem by King Solomon in the tenth century B.C.E. to be the religious center for the Israelite god Yahweh. The Temple priesthood conducted sacrifices, received a tithe or percentage of agricultural revenues, and became economically and politically powerful. The First Temple was destroyed by the Babylonians in 587 B.C.E. and was rebuilt on a modest scale in the late sixth century B.C.E. It was replaced by King Herod's Second Temple in the late first century B.C.E. and destroyed by the Romans in 70 C.E.   (p. 71)

Five-Year Plans   Plans that Joseph Stalin introduced to industrialize the Soviet Union rapidly, beginning in 1928. They set goals for the output of steel, electricity, machinery, and most other products and were enforced by the police powers of the state. They succeeded in making the Soviet Union a major industrial power before World War II.   (p. 652)

foragers   People who support themselves by hunting wild animals and gathering wild edible plants and insects.   (p. 6)

Francisco "Pancho" Villa (1877–1923)   A popular leader during the Mexican Revolution. An outlaw in his youth, when the revolution started he formed a cavalry army in the north of Mexico and fought for the rights of the landless in collaboration with Emiliano Zapata. He was assassinated in 1923.   (p. 689)

Francisco Pizarro (ca. 1476–1541)   Spanish explorer who led the conquest of the Inca Empire of Peru in 1532–1533.   (p. 373)

free-trade imperialism   Economic dominance of a weaker country by a more powerful one, while maintaining the legal independence of the weaker state. In the late nineteenth century, free-trade imperialism characterized the relations between the Latin American republics, on the one hand, and Great Britain and the United States, on the other.   (p. 620)

Fujiwara   Aristocratic family that dominated the Japanese imperial court between the ninth and twelfth centuries.   (p. 279)

Funan   An early complex society in Southeast Asia between the first and sixth centuries C.E. It was centered in the rich rice-growing region of southern Vietnam, and it controlled the passage of trade across the Malaysian isthmus.   (p. 129)

Genghis Khan (ca. 1167–1227)   The title of Temüjin when he ruled the Mongols (1206–1227). It means the "oceanic" or "universal" leader. Genghis Khan was the founder of the Mongol Empire.   (p. 287)

gens de couleur   Free mixed-race men and women in Haiti. They sought greater political rights and later supported the Haitian Revolution.   (p. 494)

gentry   In China, the class of prosperous families, next in wealth below the rural aristocrats, from which the emperors drew their administrative personnel. Respected for their education and expertise, these officials became a privileged group and made the government more efficient and responsive than in the past. In England and France, the class of landholding families below the aristocracy.   (pp. 154, 395)

George Washington (1732–1799)   Military commander of the American Revolution. He was the first elected president of the United States (1789–1799).   (p. 486)

Getulio Vargas (1883–1954)   Dictator of Brazil from 1930 to 1945 and from 1951 to 1954. Defeated in the presidential election of 1930, he overthrew the government and created a dictatorship that emphasized industrialization and helped the urban poor but did little to alleviate the problems of the peasants.   (p. 693)

Ghana   First known kingdom in sub-Saharan West Africa between the sixth and thirteenth centuries C.E. Also the modern West African country once known as the Gold Coast.   (p. 222)

Giuseppe Garibaldi (1807–1882)   Italian nationalist and revolutionary who conquered Sicily and Naples and added them to a unified Italy in 1860.   (p. 587)

global elite culture   At the beginning of the twenty-first century, the attitudes and outlook of well-educated, prosperous, Western-oriented people around the world, largely expressed in European languages, especially English.   (p. 748)

globalization   The economic, political, and cultural integration and interaction of all parts of the world brought about by increasing trade, travel, and technology.   (p. 732)

global pop culture   Popular cultural practices and institutions that have been adopted internationally, such as music, the Internet, television, food, and fashion.   (p. 748)

Gold Coast (Africa) Region of the Atlantic coast of West Africa occupied by modern Ghana; named for its gold exports to Europe from the 1470s onward. (p. 362)

Golden Horde Mongol khanate founded by Genghis Khan's grandson Batu. It was based in southern Russia and quickly adopted both the Turkic language and Islam. Also known as the Kipchak Khanate. (p. 294)

Gothic cathedrals Large churches originating in twelfth-century France; built in an architectural style featuring pointed arches, tall vaults and spires, flying buttresses, and large stained-glass windows. (p. 343)

Grand Canal The 1,100-mile (1,771-kilometer) waterway linking the Yellow and the Yangzi Rivers. It was begun in the Han period and completed during the Sui Empire. (p. 261)

"great traditions" Anthropologists' term for a literate, well-institutionalized complex of religious and social beliefs and practices adhered to by diverse societies over a broad geographical area. (p. 201)

Great Western Schism A division in the Latin (Western) Christian Church between 1378 and 1415, when rival claimants to the papacy existed in Rome and Avignon. (p. 349)

Great Zimbabwe City, now in ruins (in the modern African country of Zimbabwe), whose many stone structures were built between about 1250 and 1450, when it was a trading center and the capital of a large state. (p. 323)

guild In medieval Europe, an association of men (rarely women), such as merchants, artisans, or professors, who worked in a particular trade and banded together to promote their economic and political interests. Guilds were also important in other societies, such as the Ottoman and Safavid Empires. (p. 340)

Gujarat Region of western India famous for trade and manufacturing; the inhabitants are called Gujaratis. (p. 321)

gunpowder A mixture of saltpeter, sulfur, and charcoal, in various proportions. The formula, brought to China in the 400s or 500s, was first used to make fumigators to keep away insect pests and evil spirits. In later centuries it was used to make explosives and grenades and to propel cannonballs, shot, and bullets. (p. 273)

Guomindang Nationalist political party founded on democratic principles by Sun Yat-sen in 1912. After 1925, the party was headed by Chiang Kai-shek, who turned it into an increasingly authoritarian movement. (p. 639)

Gupta Empire A powerful Indian state based, like its Mauryan predecessor, on a capital at Pataliputra in the Ganges Valley. It controlled most of the Indian subcontinent through a combination of military force and its prestige as a center of sophisticated culture. (p. 126)

Habsburg A powerful European family that provided many Holy Roman Emperors, founded the Austrian (later Austro-Hungarian) Empire, and ruled sixteenth- and seventeenth-century Spain. (p. 400)

hadith A tradition relating the words or deeds of the Prophet Muhammad; next to the Quran, the most important basis for Islamic law. (p. 226)

Haile Selassie (1892–1975) Emperor of Ethiopia (r. 1930–1974) and symbol of African independence. He fought the Italian invasion of his country in 1935 and regained his throne during World War II, when British forces expelled the Italians. He ruled Ethiopia as a traditional autocracy until he was overthrown in 1974. (p. 686)

Hammurabi Amorite ruler of Babylon (r. 1792–1750 B.C.E.). He conquered many city-states in southern and northern Mesopotamia and is best known for a code of laws, inscribed on a black stone pillar, illustrating the principles to be used in legal cases. (p. 17)

Han A term used to designate the ethnic Chinese people who originated in the Yellow River Valley and spread throughout regions of China suitable for agriculture, as well as the dynasty of emperors who ruled from 206 B.C.E. to 220 C.E. (p. 153)

Hanseatic League An economic and defensive alliance of the free towns in northern Germany, founded about 1241 and most powerful in the fourteenth century. (p. 339)

Harappa Site of one of the great cities of the Indus Valley civilization of the third millennium B.C.E. It was located on the northwest frontier of the zone of cultivation (in modern Pakistan) and may have been a center for the acquisition of raw materials, such as metals and precious stones, from Afghanistan and Iran. (p. 113)

Hatshepsut Queen of Egypt (r. 1473–1458 B.C.E.). She dispatched a naval expedition down the Red Sea to Punt (possibly northeast Sudan or Eritria), the faraway source of myrrh. There is evidence of opposition to a woman as ruler, and after her death her name and image were frequently defaced. (p. 59)

Hebrew Bible A collection of sacred books containing diverse materials concerning the origins, experiences, beliefs, and practices of the Israelites. Most of the extant text was compiled by members of the priestly class in the fifth century B.C.E. and reflects the concerns and views of this group. (p. 69)

Hellenistic Age Historians' term for the era, usually dated 323–30 B.C.E., in which Greek culture spread across western Asia and northeastern Africa after the conquests of Alexander the Great. The period ended with the fall of the last major Hellenistic kingdom to Rome, but Greek cultural influence persisted until the seventh century C.E. (P. 105)

Henry Morton Stanley (1841–1904) British-American explorer of Africa, famous for his expeditions in search of Dr. David Livingstone. Stanley helped King Leopold II establish the Congo Free State. (p. 609)

Henry the Navigator (1394–1460) Portuguese prince who promoted the study of navigation and directed voyages of exploration down the western coast of Africa. (p. 359)

Hernán Cortés (1485–1547) Spanish explorer and conquistador who led the conquest of Aztec Mexico in 1519–1521 for Spain. (p. 372)

Herodotus (ca. 485–425 B.C.E.) Heir to the technique of historia—"investigation"—developed by Greeks in the late Archaic period. He came from a Greek community in Anatolia and traveled extensively collecting information in western Asia and the Mediterranean lands. He traced the antecedents of and chronicled the Persian Wars between the Greek city-states and the Persian Empire, thus originating the Western tradition of historical writing. (p. 96)

Hidden Imam Last in a series of twelve descendants of Muhammad's son-in-law Ali, whom Shi'ites consider divinely appointed leaders of the Muslim community. In occlusion since ca. 873, he is expected to return as a messiah at the end of time. (p. 442)

hieroglyphics A system of writing in which pictorial symbols represented sounds, syllables, or concepts. It was used for official and monumental inscriptions in ancient Egypt. Because of the long period of study required to master this system, literacy in hieroglyphics was confined to a relatively small group of scribes and administrators. Cursive symbol-forms were developed for rapid composition on other media, such as papyrus. (p. 27)

Hinduism A general term for a wide variety of beliefs and ritual practices that have developed in the Indian subcontinent since antiquity. Hinduism has roots in ancient Vedic, Buddhist, and south Indian religious concepts and practices. It spread along the trade routes to Southeast Asia.   (p. 121)

Hipólito Irigoyen (1850–1933) Argentine politician, president of Argentina from 1916 to 1922 and 1928 to 1930. The first president elected by universal male suffrage, he began his presidency as a reformer but later became conservative.   (p. 692)

Hiroshima City in Japan, the first to be destroyed by an atomic bomb, on August 6, 1945. The bombing hastened the end of World War II.   (p. 669)

history The study of past events and changes in the development, transmission, and transformation of cultural practices.   (p. 6)

Hittites A people from central Anatolia who established an empire in Anatolia and Syria in the Late Bronze Age. With wealth from the trade in metals and military power based on chariot forces, the Hittites vied with New Kingdom Egypt for control of Syria-Palestine before falling to unidentified attackers ca. 1200 B.C.E.   (p. 57)

Holocaust Nazis' program during World War II to kill people they considered undesirable. Some 6 million Jews perished during the Holocaust, along with millions of Poles, Gypsies, communists, socialists, and others.   (p. 671)

Holocene The geological era since the end of the Great Ice Age about 13,000 years ago.   (p. 10)

Holy Roman Empire Loose federation of mostly German states and principalities, headed by an emperor elected by the princes. It lasted from 962 to 1806.   (pp. 246, 400)

hoplite A heavily armored Greek infantryman of the Archaic and Classical periods who fought in the close-packed phalanx formation. Hoplite armies—militias composed of middle- and upper-class citizens supplying their own equipment—were for centuries superior to all other military forces.   (p. 93)

horse collar Harnessing method that increased the efficiency of horses by shifting the point of traction from the animal's neck to the shoulders; its adoption favors the spread of horse-drawn plows and vehicles.   (p. 252)

House of Burgesses Elected assembly in colonial Virginia, created in 1618.   (p. 417)

humanists (Renaissance) European scholars, writers, and teachers associated with the study of the humanities (grammar, rhetoric, poetry, history, languages, and moral philosophy), influential in the fifteenth century and later.   (p. 346)

Hundred Years War (1337–1453) Series of campaigns over control of the throne of France, involving English and French royal families and French noble families.   (p. 349)

Ibn Battuta (1304–1369) Moroccan Muslim scholar, the most widely traveled individual of his time. He wrote a detailed account of his visits to Islamic lands from China to Spain and the western Sudan.   (p. 313)

Il-khan A "secondary" or "peripheral" khan based in Persia. The Il-khans' khanate was founded by Hülegü, a grandson of Genghis Khan, and was based at Tabriz in modern Azerbaijan. It controlled much of Iran and Iraq.   (p. 294)

import-substitution industrialization An economic system aimed at building a country's industry by restricting foreign trade. It was especially popular in Latin American countries such as Mexico, Argentina, and Brazil in the mid-twentieth century. It proved successful for a time but could not keep up with technological advances in Europe and North America.   (p. 693)

Inca Largest and most powerful Andean empire. Controlled the Pacific coast of South America from Ecuador to Chile from its capital of Cuzco.   (p. 182)

indentured servant A migrant to British colonies in the Americas who paid for passage by agreeing to work for a set term ranging from four to seven years.   (p. 416)

Indian Civil Service The elite professional class of officials who administered the government of British India. Originally composed exclusively of well-educated British men, it gradually added qualified Indians.   (p. 559)

Indian National Congress A movement and political party founded in 1885 to demand greater Indian participation in government. Its membership was middle class, and its demands were modest until World War I. Led after 1920 by Mohandas K. Gandhi, it appealed increasingly to the poor, and it organized mass protests demanding self-government and independence.   (pp. 561, 678)

Indian Ocean Maritime System In premodern times, a network of seaports, trade routes, and maritime culture linking countries on the rim of the Indian Ocean from Africa to Indonesia.   (p. 193)

indulgence The forgiveness of the punishment due for past sins, granted by the Catholic Church authorities as a reward for a pious act. Martin Luther's protest against the sale of indulgences is often seen as touching off the Protestant Reformation.   (p. 386)

Industrial Revolution The transformation of the economy, the environment, and living conditions, occurring first in England in the eighteenth century, that resulted from the use of steam engines, the mechanization of manufacturing in factories, and innovations in transportation and communication.   (p. 507)

investiture controversy Dispute between the popes and the Holy Roman Emperors over who held ultimate authority over bishops in imperial lands.   (p. 247)

Iron Age Historians' term for the period during which iron was the primary metal for tools and weapons. The advent of iron technology began at different times in different parts of the world.   (p. 55)

Iron Curtain Winston Churchill's term for the Cold War division between the Soviet-dominated East and the U.S.-dominated West.   (p. 703)

Iroquois Confederacy An alliance of five northeastern Amerindian peoples (six after 1722) that made decisions on military and diplomatic issues through a council of representatives. Allied first with the Dutch and later with the English, the Confederacy dominated the area from western New England to the Great Lakes.   (p. 418)

Islam Religion expounded by the Prophet Muhammad (570–632 C.E.) on the basis of his reception of divine revelations, which were collected after his death into the Quran. In the tradition of Judaism and Christianity, and sharing much of their lore, Islam calls on all people to recognize one creator god—Allah—who rewards or punishes believers after death according to how they led their lives.   (p. 216)

Israel In antiquity, the land between the eastern shore of the Mediterranean and the Jordan River, occupied by the Israelites from the early second millennium B.C.E.   (p. 68)

James Watt (1736–1819) Scot who invented the condenser and other improvements that made the steam engine a practical source of power for industry and transportation. The watt, an electrical measurement, is named after him.   (p. 513)

Janissaries Infantry, originally of slave origin, armed with firearms and constituting the elite of the Ottoman army from the fifteenth century until the corps was abolished in 1826.   (pp. 437, 529)

Jawaharlal Nehru (1889–1964) Indian statesman who succeeded Mohandas K. Gandhi as leader of the Indian National Congress. He negotiated the end of British colonial rule in India and became India's first prime minister (1947–1964). (p. 681)

Jesus (ca. 5 B.C.E.–34 C.E.) A Jew from Galilee in northern Israel who sought to reform Jewish beliefs and practices. He was executed as a revolutionary by the Romans. Hailed as the Messiah and son of God by his followers, he became the central figure in Christianity, a belief system that developed in the centuries after his death. (p. 145)

joint-stock company A business, often backed by a government charter, that sold shares to individuals to raise money for its trading enterprises and to spread the risks (and profits) among many investors. (p. 395)

Joseph Stalin (1879–1953) Bolshevik revolutionary, head of the Soviet Communist Party after 1924, and dictator of the Soviet Union from 1929 to 1953. He led the Soviet Union with an iron fist, using Five-Year Plans to increase industrial production and terror to crush all opposition. (p. 652)

Josiah Wedgwood (1730–1795) English industrialist whose pottery works were the first to produce fine-quality pottery by industrial methods. (p. 510)

Juan Perón (1895–1974) President of Argentina (1946–1955, 1973–1974). As a military officer, he championed the rights of labor. Aided by his wife Eva Duarte Perón, he was elected president in 1946. He built up Argentinean industry, became very popular among the urban poor, but harmed the economy. (p. 694)

junk A very large flatbottom sailing ship produced in the Tang, Ming, and Song Empires, specially designed for long-distance commercial travel. (p. 273)

Kamakura Shogunate The first of Japan's decentralized military governments (1185–1333). (p. 279)

kamikaze The "divine wind" that the Japanese credited with blowing Mongol invaders away from their shores in 1281. (p. 308)

Kangxi (1654–1722) Qing emperor (r. 1662–1722) who oversaw the greatest expansion of the Qing Empire. (p. 464)

Karl Marx (1818–1883) German journalist and philosopher, founder of the Marxist branch of socialism. He is known for two books: *The Communist Manifesto* (1848) and *Das Kapital* (1867–1894). (p. 583)

karma In Indian tradition, the residue of deeds performed in past and present lives that adheres to a "spirit" and determines what form it will assume in its next life cycle. The doctrines of karma and reincarnation were used by the elite in ancient India to encourage people to accept their social position and do their duty. (p. 118)

keiretsu Alliances of corporations and banks that dominate the Japanese economy. (p. 719)

khipus System of knotted colored cords used by preliterate Andean peoples to transmit information. (p. 178)

Khubilai Khan (1215–1294) Last of the Mongol Great Khans (r. 1260–1294) and founder of the Yuan Empire. Original architect of the Forbidden City. (p. 300)

Kievan Russia State established at Kiev in Ukraine ca. 879 by Scandinavian adventurers asserting authority over a mostly Slavic farming population. (p. 234)

Korean War (1950–1953) Conflict that began with North Korea's invasion of South Korea and came to involve the United Nations (primarily the United States) allying with South Korea against North Korea and the People's Republic of China. (p. 706)

Koryo Korean kingdom founded in 918 and destroyed by a Mongol invasion in 1259. (p. 277)

Kush An Egyptian name for Nubia, the region alongside the Nile River south of Egypt, where an indigenous kingdom with its own distinctive institutions and cultural traditions arose in the early second millennium B.C.E. It was deeply influenced by Egyptian culture and at times under the control of Egypt, which coveted its rich deposits of gold and luxury products from sub-Saharan Africa carried up the Nile corridor. (p. 45)

labor union An organization of workers in a particular industry or trade, created to defend the interests of members through strikes or negotiations with employers. (p. 583)

laissez faire The idea that government should refrain from interfering in economic affairs. The classic exposition of laissez-faire principles is Adam Smith's *Wealth of Nations* (1776). (p. 518)

lama In Tibetan Buddhism, a teacher. (p. 300)

Latin West Historians' name for the territories of Europe that adhered to the Latin rite of Christianity and used the Latin language for intellectual exchange in the period ca. 1000–1500. (p. 333)

Lázaro Cárdenas (1895–1970) President of Mexico (1934–1940). He brought major changes to Mexican life by distributing millions of acres of land to the peasants, bringing representatives of workers and farmers into the inner circles of politics, and nationalizing the oil industry. (p. 691)

League of Nations International organization founded in 1919 to promote world peace and cooperation but greatly weakened by the refusal of the United States to join. It proved ineffectual in stopping aggression by Italy, Japan, and Germany in the 1930s, and it was superseded by the United Nations in 1945. (p. 637)

Legalism In China, a political philosophy that emphasized the unruliness of human nature and justified state coercion and control. The ruling class invoked it to validate the authoritarian nature of the regime and its profligate expenditure of subjects' lives and labor. It was later superseded by a more benevolent Confucian doctrine of governmental moderation. (p. 41)

"legitimate" trade Exports from Africa in the nineteenth century that did not include the newly outlawed slave trade. (p. 555)

Leopold II (1835–1909) King of Belgium (r. 1865–1909). He was active in encouraging the exploration of Central Africa and became the ruler of the Congo Free State (to 1908). (p. 609)

liberalism A political ideology that emphasizes the civil rights of citizens, representative government, and the protection of private property. This ideology, derived from the Enlightenment, was especially popular among the property-owning middle classes of Europe and North America. (p. 587)

Linear B A set of syllabic symbols, derived from the writing system of Minoan Crete, used in the Mycenaean palaces of the Late Bronze Age to write an early form of Greek. It was used primarily for palace records, and the surviving Linear B tablets provide substantial information about the economic organization of Mycenaean society and tantalizing clues about political, social, and religious institutions. (p. 63)

Li Shimin (599–649) One of the founders of the Tang Empire and its second emperor (r. 626–649). He led the expansion of the empire into Central Asia. (p. 262)

Little Ice Age A century-long period of cool climate that began in the 1590s. Its ill effects on agriculture in northern Europe were notable. (p. 395)

llama A hoofed animal indigenous to the Andes Mountains. It was the only domesticated beast of burden in the Americas before the arrival of Europeans. The use of llamas to transport goods made possible specialized production and trade among people living in different ecological zones and fostered the integration of these zones by Chavín and later Andean states. (p. 166)

loess A fine, light silt deposited by wind and water. It constitutes the fertile soil of the Yellow River Valley in northern China. Because loess soil is not compacted, it can be worked with a simple digging stick, but it leaves the region vulnerable to devastating floods. (p. 37)

Long March (1934–1935) The 6,000-mile (9,700-kilometer) flight of Chinese communists from southeastern to northwestern China. The communists, led by Mao Zedong, were pursued by the Chinese army under orders from Chiang Kai-shek. The four thousand survivors of the march formed the nucleus of a revived communist movement that defeated the Guomindang after World War II. (p. 663)

ma'at Egyptian term for the concept of divinely created and maintained order in the universe. Reflecting the ancient Egyptians' belief in an essentially beneficent world, the divine ruler was the earthly guarantor of this order. (p. 25)

Macartney mission The unsuccessful attempt in 1792–1793 by the British Empire to establish diplomatic relations with the Qing Empire. (p. 466)

Mahabharata A vast epic chronicling the events leading up to a cataclysmic battle between related kinship groups in early India. It includes the Bhagavad-Gita, the most important work of Indian sacred literature. (p. 124)

Mahayana Buddhism "Great Vehicle" branch of Buddhism followed in China, Japan, and Central Asia. The focus is on reverence for Buddha and for bodhisattvas, enlightened persons who have postponed nirvana to help others attain enlightenment. (p. 120)

Malacca Port city in the modern Southeast Asian country of Malaysia, founded about 1400 as a trading center on the Strait of Malacca. Also spelled Melaka. (p. 326)

Mali Empire created by indigenous Muslims in western Sudan of West Africa from the thirteenth to fifteenth century. It was famous for its role in the trans-Saharan gold trade. (p. 317)

mamluks Under the Islamic system of military slavery, Turkic military slaves who formed an important part of the armed forces of the Abbasid Caliphate of the ninth and tenth centuries. Mamluks eventually founded their own state, ruling Egypt and Syria (1250–1517). (p. 220)

Manchu Federation of Northeast Asian peoples who founded the Qing Empire. (p. 456)

Mandate of Heaven Chinese religious and political ideology developed by the Zhou, according to which it was the prerogative of Heaven, the chief deity, to grant power to the ruler of China and to take away that power if the ruler failed to conduct himself justly and in the best interests of his subjects. (p. 40)

mandate system Allocation of former German colonies and Ottoman possessions to the victorious powers after World War I, to be administered under League of Nations supervision. (p. 641)

manor In medieval Europe, a large, self-sufficient landholding consisting of the lord's residence (manor house), outbuildings, peasant village, and surrounding land. (p. 242)

mansabs In India, grants of land given in return for service by rulers of the Mughal Empire. (p. 446)

Mansa Kankan Musa Ruler of Mali (r. 1312–1337). His pilgrimage through Egypt to Mecca in 1324–1325 established the empire's reputation for wealth in the Mediterranean world. (p. 318)

Mao Zedong (1893–1976) Leader of the Chinese Communist Party (1927–1976). He led the communists on the Long March (1934–1935) and rebuilt the Communist Party and Red

Army during the Japanese occupation of China (1937–1945). After World War II, he led the communists to victory over the Guomindang. (p. 663)

Margaret Sanger (1883–1966) American nurse and author; pioneer in the movement for family planning; organized conferences and established birth control clinics. (p. 645)

maroon A slave who ran away from his or her master. Often a member of a community of runaway slaves in the West Indies and South America. (p. 423)

Marshall Plan U.S. program to support the reconstruction of western Europe after World War II. By 1961 more than $20 billion in economic aid had been disbursed. (p. 704)

mass deportation The forcible removal and relocation of large numbers of people or entire populations. The mass deportations practiced by the Assyrian and Persian Empires were meant as a terrifying warning of the consequences of rebellion. They also brought labor to the imperial center. (p. 67)

mass production The manufacture of many identical products by the division of labor into many small repetitive tasks. This method was introduced into the manufacture of pottery and into the spinning of cotton thread. (p. 510)

Mauryan Empire The first state to unify most of the Indian subcontinent. It was founded by Chandragupta Maurya in 324 B.C.E. and survived until 184 B.C.E. From its capital at Pataliputra in the Ganges Valley it grew wealthy from taxes on agriculture, iron mining, and control of trade routes. (p. 123)

Max Planck (1858–1947) German physicist who developed quantum theory and was awarded the Nobel Prize for physics in 1918. (p. 645)

Maya Mesoamerican civilization concentrated in Mexico's Yucatán Peninsula and in Guatemala and Honduras but never unified into a single empire. Major contributions were in mathematics, astronomy, and development of the calendar. (p. 170)

Mecca City in Arabia; birthplace of Muhammad; location of the Ka'ba, the holiest shrine in Islam. (p. 214)

mechanization The application of machinery to manufacturing and other activities. Among the first processes to be mechanized were the spinning of cotton thread and the weaving of cloth in late-eighteenth- and early-nineteenth-century England. (p. 511)

medieval Literally "middle age," a term that historians of Europe use for the period ca. 500 to ca. 1500, signifying its intermediate point between Greco-Roman antiquity and the Renaissance. (p. 234)

Medina City in western Arabia to which the Prophet Muhammad and his followers emigrated in 622 to escape persecution in Mecca. (p. 216)

megaliths Structures and complexes of very large stones constructed for ceremonial and religious purposes in Neolithic times. (p. 11)

Meiji Restoration The political program that followed the destruction of the Tokugawa Shogunate in 1868, in which a collection of young leaders set Japan on the path of centralization, industrialization, and imperialism. (p. 589)

Memphis The capital of Old Kingdom Egypt, near the head of the Nile Delta. Early rulers were interred in the nearby pyramids. (p. 26)

Menelik II (1844–1911) Emperor of Ethiopia (r. 1889–1911). He enlarged Ethiopia to its present dimensions and defeated an Italian invasion at Adowa (1896). (p. 614)

mercantilism European government policies of the sixteenth, seventeenth, and eighteenth centuries designed to promote overseas trade between a country and its colonies and to accumulate precious metals by requiring colonies to trade only with their motherland country. The British system was defined by the Navigation Acts, the French system by laws known as the *Exclusif*. (p. 424)

Meroë Capital of a flourishing kingdom in southern Nubia from the fourth century B.C.E. to the fourth century C.E. In this period Nubian culture shows more independence from Egypt and the influence of sub-Saharan Africa. (p. 47)

Miguel Hidalgo y Costilla (1753–1811) Mexican priest who led the first stage of the Mexican independence war in 1810. He was captured and executed in 1811. (p. 497)

Mikhail Gorbachev (b. 1931) Head of the Soviet Union from 1985 to 1991. His liberalization effort improved relations with the West, but he lost power after his reforms led to the collapse of communist governments in eastern Europe. (p. 725)

Ming Empire (1368–1644) Empire based in China that Zhu Yuanzhang established after the overthrow of the Yuan Empire. The Ming emperor Yongle sponsored additions to the Forbidden City and the voyages of Zheng He. The later years of the Ming saw a slowdown in technological development and economic decline. (pp. 303, 461)

Minoan Prosperous civilization on the Aegean island of Crete in the second millennium B.C.E. The Minoans engaged in far-flung commerce around the Mediterranean and exerted powerful cultural influences on the early Greeks. (p. 61)

mit'a Andean labor system based on shared obligations to help kinsmen and work on behalf of the ruler and religious organizations. (p. 179)

Moche Civilization of north coast of Peru (200–700 C.E.). An important Andean civilization that built extensive irrigation networks as well as impressive urban centers dominated by brick temples. (p. 179)

Moctezuma II (1466–1520) Last Aztec emperor, overthrown by the Spanish conquistador Hernán Cortés. (p. 372)

modernization The process of reforming political, military, economic, social, and cultural traditions in imitation of the early success of Western societies, often with regard for accommodating local traditions in non-Western societies. (p. 553)

Mohandas K. (Mahatma) Gandhi (1869–1948) Leader of the Indian independence movement and advocate of nonviolent resistance. After being educated as a lawyer in England, he returned to India and became leader of the Indian National Congress in 1920. He appealed to the poor, led nonviolent demonstrations against British colonial rule, and was jailed many times. Soon after independence he was assassinated for attempting to stop Hindu-Muslim rioting. (p. 680)

Mohenjo-Daro Largest of the cities of the Indus Valley civilization. It was centrally located in the extensive floodplain of the Indus River in contemporary Pakistan. Little is known about the political institutions of Indus Valley communities, but the large scale of construction at Mohenjo-Daro, the orderly grid of streets, and the standardization of building materials are evidence of central planning. (p. 113)

moksha The Hindu concept of the spirit's "liberation" from the endless cycle of rebirths. There are various avenues—such as physical discipline, meditation, and acts of devotion to the gods—by which the spirit can distance itself from desire for the things of this world and be merged with the divine force that animates the universe. (p. 119)

monasticism Living in a religious community apart from secular society and adhering to a rule stipulating chastity, obedience, and poverty. It was a prominent element of medieval Christianity and Buddhism. Monasteries were the primary centers of learning and literacy in early medieval Europe. (p. 248)

Mongols As early as the Tang Empire, Chinese records mention a people of this name living as nomads in northern Eurasia. After 1206, under Genghis Khan, they established an enormous empire linking western and eastern Eurasia. (p. 287)

monotheism Belief in the existence of a single divine entity. Some scholars cite the devotion of the Egyptian pharaoh Akhenaten to Aten (sun-disk) and his suppression of traditional gods as the earliest instance. The Israelite worship of Yahweh developed into an exclusive belief in one god, and this concept passed into Christianity and Islam. (p. 72)

monsoon Seasonal winds in the Indian Ocean caused by the differences in temperature between the rapidly heating and cooling landmasses of Africa and Asia and the slowly changing ocean waters. These strong and predictable winds have long been ridden across the open sea by sailors, and the large amounts of rainfall that they deposit on parts of India, Southeast Asia, and China allow for the cultivation of several crops a year. (pp. 116, 314)

most-favored-nation status A clause in a commercial treaty that automatically awards to the signatory all the privileges granted to the most favored of other signatories. (p. 543)

movable type Type in which each individual character is cast on a separate piece of metal. It replaced woodblock printing, allowing for the arrangement of individual letters and other characters on a page, rather than requiring the carving of entire pages at a time. It may have been invented in Korea in the thirteenth century. (p. 274)

Mughal Empire Muslim state (1526–1857) exercising dominion over most of India in the sixteenth and seventeenth centuries. (p. 446)

Muhammad (570–632 C.E.) Arab prophet; founder of religion of Islam. (p. 215)

Muhammad Ali (1769–1849) Leader of Egyptian modernization in the early nineteenth century. He ruled Egypt as an Ottoman governor but also had imperial ambitions. His descendants ruled Egypt until overthrown in 1952. (pp. 528, 553)

Muhammad Ali Jinnah (1876–1948) Indian Muslim politician who founded the state of Pakistan. A lawyer by training, he joined the All-India Muslim League in 1913. As leader of the League from the 1920s on, he negotiated with the British and the Indian National Congress for Muslim participation in Indian politics. From 1940 on, he led the movement for the independence of India's Muslims in a separate state of Pakistan, founded in 1947. (p. 683)

mummy A body preserved by chemical processes or special natural circumstances, often in the belief that the deceased will need it again in the afterlife. In ancient Egypt the bodies of people who could afford mummification underwent a complex process of removing organs, filling body cavities, dehydrating the corpse, and then wrapping the body with linen bandages and enclosing it in a wooden sarcophagus. (p. 30)

Muscovy The Russian principality that emerged gradually during the era of Mongol domination. The Muscovite dynasty ruled without interruption from 1276 to 1598. (p. 468)

Muslim An adherent of the Islamic religion; a person who "submits" (in Arabic, *Islam* means "submission") to the will of God. (p. 216)

Mycenae Site of a fortified palace complex in southern Greece that controlled a Late Bronze Age kingdom. In Homer's epic poems, Mycenae was the base of King Agamemnon, who commanded the Greeks besieging Troy. Contemporary archaeologists call the complex Greek society of the second millennium B.C.E. "Mycenaean." (p. 62)

Napoleon Bonaparte (Napoleon I) (1769–1821) The general who overthrew the French Directory in 1799 and became emperor of the French in 1804. He failed to defeat Great Britain and abdicated in 1814, then returned to power briefly in 1815 but was defeated and died in exile.   (p. 491)

Nasir al-Din Tusi (1201–1274) Persian mathematician and cosmologist whose academy near Tabriz provided the model for the movement of the planets that helped to inspire the Copernican model of the solar system.   (p. 296)

National Assembly French Revolutionary assembly (1789–1791). Called first as the Estates General, the three estates came together and demanded radical change. It passed the Declaration of the Rights of Man and of the Citizen in 1789.   (p. 489)

nationalism A political ideology that stresses people's membership in a nation—a community defined by a common culture and history as well as by territory. In the late eighteenth and early nineteenth centuries, nationalism was a force for unity in western Europe. In the late nineteenth century it hastened the disintegration of the Austro-Hungarian and Ottoman Empires. In the twentieth century it provided the ideological foundation for scores of independent countries emerging from colonialism.   (p. 586)

nawab A Muslim prince allied to British India; technically, a semi-autonomous deputy of the Mughal emperor.   (p. 556)

Nazis German political party joined by Adolf Hitler, emphasizing nationalism, racism, and war. When Hitler became chancellor of Germany in 1933, the Nazis became the only legal party and an instrument of Hitler's absolute rule. The party's formal name was National Socialist German Workers' Party.   (p. 660)

Neo-Assyrian Empire An empire extending from western Iran to Syria-Palestine, conquered by the Assyrians of northern Mesopotamia between the tenth and seventh centuries B.C.E. They used force and terror and exploited the wealth and labor of their subjects. They also preserved and continued the cultural and scientific developments of Mesopotamian civilization.   (p. 65)

neo-Confucianism Term used to describe new approaches to understanding classic Confucian texts that became the basic ruling philosophy of China from the Song period to the twentieth century.   (p. 273)

Neolithic The period of the Stone Age associated with the ancient Agricultural Revolutions. It follows the Paleolithic period.   (p. 6)

New Economic Policy Policy proclaimed by Vladimir Lenin in 1921 to encourage the revival of the Soviet economy by allowing small private enterprises.   (p. 638)

New France French colony in North America, with a capital in Quebec, founded in 1608. New France fell to the British in 1763.   (p. 418)

New Imperialism Historians' term for the late-nineteenth- and early-twentieth-century wave of conquests by European powers, the United States, and Japan, which were followed by the development and exploitation of the newly conquered territories for the benefit of the colonial powers.   (p. 600)

newly industrialized economies (NIEs) Rapidly growing new industrializing nations of the late twentieth century, including the Asian Tigers.   (p. 721)

new monarchies Historians' term for the monarchies in France, England, and Spain from 1450 to 1600. The centralization of royal power was increasing within more or less fixed territorial limits.   (p. 349)

nomadism A way of life in which groups of people and their herds of animals continually migrate to find pastures and water.   (p. 287)

nonaligned nations Developing countries that announced their neutrality in the Cold War.   (p. 709)

nongovernmental organizations (NGOs) Nonprofit international organizations devoted to investigating human rights abuses and providing humanitarian relief. Two NGOs won the Nobel Peace Prize in the 1990s: International Campaign to Ban Landmines (1997) and Doctors Without Borders (1999).   (p. 755)

North Atlantic Treaty Organization (NATO) Organization formed in 1949 as a military alliance of western European and North American states against the Soviet Union and its east European allies.   (p. 703)

Olmec The first Mesoamerican civilization. Between ca. 1200 and 400 B.C.E., the Olmec people of central Mexico created a vibrant civilization that included intensive agriculture, wide-ranging trade, ceremonial centers, and monumental construction. The Olmec had great cultural influence on later Mesoamerican societies.   (p. 162)

Oman Arab state based in Musqat, the main port in the southeastern region of the Arabian Peninsula. Oman succeeded Portugal as a power in the western Indian Ocean in the eighteenth century.   (p. 451)

Opium War (1839–1842) War between Britain and the Qing Empire that was, in the British view, occasioned by the Qing government's refusal to permit the importation of opium into its territories. The victorious British imposed the one-sided Treaty of Nanking on China.   (p. 540)

Organization of Petroleum Exporting Countries (OPEC) Organization formed in 1960 by oil-producing states to promote their collective interest in generating revenue from oil.   (p. 723)

Ottoman Empire Islamic state founded by Osman in northwestern Anatolia ca. 1300. After the fall of the Byzantine Empire, the Ottoman Empire was based at Istanbul (formerly Constantinople) from 1453 to 1922. It encompassed lands in the Middle East, North Africa, the Caucasus, and eastern Europe.   (pp. 300, 434)

Otto von Bismarck (1815–1898) Chancellor (prime minister) of Prussia from 1862 until 1871, when he became chancellor of Germany. A conservative nationalist, he led Prussia to victory against Austria (1866) and France (1870) and was responsible for the creation of the German Empire in 1871.   (p. 588)

Paleolithic The period of the Stone Age associated with the evolution of humans. It predates the Neolithic period.   (p. 6)

Panama Canal Ship canal cut across the Isthmus of Panama by U.S. Army engineers; it opened in 1914. It greatly shortened the sea voyage between the east and west coasts of North America. The United States turned the canal over to Panama on January 1, 2000.   (p. 622)

Pan-Slavism Movement among Russian intellectuals in the second half of the nineteenth century to identify culturally and politically with the Slavic peoples of eastern Europe.   (p. 537)

papacy The central administration of the Roman Catholic Church, of which the pope is the head.   (pp. 246, 386)

papyrus A reed that grows along the banks of the Nile River in Egypt. From it was produced a paper-like writing medium used by the Egyptians and many other peoples in the ancient Mediterranean and Middle East.   (p. 27)

Parthians Iranian ruling dynasty between ca. 247 B.C.E. and 224 C.E.   (p. 189)

patron/client relationship In ancient Rome, a fundamental social relationship in which the patron—a wealthy and powerful individual—provided legal and economic protection and assistance to clients, men of lesser status and means, and in return the clients supported the political careers and economic interests of their patron.   (p. 137)

Paul (ca. 5–65 C.E.) A Jew from the Greek city of Tarsus in Anatolia, he initially persecuted the followers of Jesus but became a Christian after receiving a revelation on the road to Syrian Damascus. Taking advantage of his Hellenized background and Roman citizenship, he traveled throughout Syria-Palestine, Anatolia, and Greece, preaching the new religion and establishing churches. Finding his greatest success among pagans ("gentiles"), he began the process by which Christianity separated from Judaism.   (p. 146)

pax romana Literally, "Roman peace," it connoted the stability and prosperity that Roman rule brought to the lands of the Roman Empire in the first two centuries C.E. The movement of people and trade goods along Roman roads and safe seas allowed for the spread of cultural practices, technologies, and religious ideas.   (p. 144)

Pearl Harbor Naval base in Hawaii attacked by Japanese aircraft on December 7, 1941. The sinking of much of the U.S. Pacific Fleet brought the United States into World War II.   (p. 667)

Peloponnesian War A protracted (431–404 B.C.E.) and costly conflict between the Athenian and Spartan alliance systems that convulsed most of the Greek world. The war was largely a consequence of Athenian imperialism. Possession of a naval empire allowed Athens to fight a war of attrition. Ultimately Sparta prevailed because of Athenian errors and Persian financial support.   (p. 102)

perestroika Policy of "restructuring" that was the centerpiece of Mikhail Gorbachev's efforts to liberalize communism in the Soviet Union.   (p. 725)

Pericles (ca. 495–429 B.C.E.) Aristocratic leader who guided the Athenian state through the transformation to full participatory democracy for all male citizens, supervised construction of the Acropolis, and pursued a policy of imperial expansion that led to the Peloponnesian War. He formulated a strategy of attrition but died from the plague early in the war.   (p. 98)

Persepolis A complex of palaces, reception halls, and treasury buildings erected by the Persian kings Darius I and Xerxes in the Persian homeland. It is believed that the New Year's festival was celebrated here, as well as the coronations, weddings, and funerals of the Persian kings, who were buried in cliff-tombs nearby.   (p. 90)

Persian Wars Conflicts between Greek city-states and the Persian Empire, ranging from the Ionian Revolt (499–494 B.C.E.) through Darius's punitive expedition that failed at Marathon (490 B.C.E.) and the defeat of Xerxes' massive invasion of Greece by the Spartan-led Hellenic League (480–479 B.C.E.). This first major setback for Persian arms launched the Greeks into their period of greatest cultural productivity. Herodotus chronicled these events in the first "history" in the Western tradition.   (p. 99)

Peter the Great (1672–1725) Russian tsar (r. 1689–1725). He enthusiastically introduced Western languages and technologies to the Russian elite and moved the capital from Moscow to the new city of St. Petersburg.   (p. 471)

pharaoh The central figure in the ancient Egyptian state. Believed to be an earthly manifestation of the gods, he used his absolute power to maintain the safety and prosperity of Egypt.   (p. 25)

Phoenicians Semitic-speaking Canaanites living on the coast of Lebanon and Syria in the first millennium B.C.E. From major cities such as Tyre and Sidon, Phoenician merchants and sailors explored the Mediterranean, engaged in widespread commerce, and founded Carthage and other colonies in the western Mediterranean.   (p. 73)

pilgrimage Journey to a sacred shrine by Christians seeking to show their piety, fulfill vows, or gain absolution for sins. Other religions also have pilgrimage traditions, such as the Muslim pilgrimage to Mecca and the pilgrimages made by early Chinese Buddhists to India in search of sacred Buddhist writings.   (p. 255)

Pilgrims Group of English Protestant dissenters who established Plymouth Colony in Massachusetts in 1620 to seek religious freedom after having lived briefly in the Netherlands.   (p. 417)

polis The Greek term for a city-state, an urban center and the agricultural territory under its control. It was the characteristic form of political organization in southern and central Greece in the Archaic and Classical periods. Of the hundreds of city-states in the Mediterranean and Black Sea regions settled by Greeks, some were oligarchic, others democratic, depending on the powers delegated to the Council and the Assembly.   (p. 93)

positivism A philosophy developed by the French count of Saint-Simon. Positivists believed that social and economic problems could be solved by the application of the scientific method, leading to continuous progress. Their ideas became popular in France and Latin America in the nineteenth century.   (p. 518)

Potosí Located in Bolivia, one of the richest silver mining centers and most populous cities in colonial Spanish America.   (p. 411)

printing press A mechanical device for transferring text or graphics from a woodblock or type to paper using ink. Presses using movable type first appeared in Europe in about 1450.   (p. 346)

Protestant Reformation Religious reform movement within the Latin Christian Church beginning in 1519. It resulted in the "protesters" forming several new Christian denominations, including the Lutheran and Reformed Churches and the Church of England.   (p. 386)

Ptolemies The Macedonian dynasty descended from one of Alexander the Great's officers that ruled Egypt for three centuries (323–30 B.C.E.). From their magnificent capital at Alexandria on the Mediterranean coast, the Ptolemies largely took over the system created by Egyptian pharaohs to extract the wealth of the land, rewarding Greeks and Hellenized non-Greeks serving in the military and administration.   (p. 107)

Puritans English Protestant dissenters who believed that God predestined souls to Heaven or Hell before birth. They founded Massachusetts Bay Colony in 1629.   (p. 417)

pyramid A large, triangular stone monument, used in Egypt and Nubia as a burial place for the king. The largest pyramids, erected during the Old Kingdom near Memphis with stone tools and compulsory labor, reflect the Egyptian belief that the proper and spectacular burial of the divine ruler would guarantee the continued prosperity of the land.   (p. 25)

Qin A people and state in the Wei Valley of eastern China that conquered rival states and created the first Chinese empire (221–206 B.C.E.). The Qin ruler, Shi Huangdi, standardized many features of Chinese society and ruthlessly marshaled subjects for military and construction projects, engendering hostility that led to the fall of his dynasty shortly after his death. The Qin framework was largely taken over by the succeeding Han Empire.   (p. 151)

Qing Empire Empire established in China by Manchus who overthrew the Ming Empire in 1644. At various times the Qing also controlled Manchuria, Mongolia, Turkestan, and Tibet. The last Qing emperor was overthrown in 1911.   (p. 463)

Quran Book composed of divine revelations made to the Prophet Muhammad between ca. 610 and his death in 632; the sacred text of the religion of Islam.   (p. 217)

railroads Networks of iron (later steel) rails on which steam (later electric or diesel) locomotives pulled long trains at high speeds. The first railroads were built in England in the 1830s. Their success caused a railroad-building boom throughout the world that lasted well into the twentieth century. (p. 575)

Rajputs Members of a mainly Hindu warrior caste from northwest India. The Mughal emperors drew most of their Hindu officials from this caste, and Akbar married a Rajput princess. (p. 447)

Ramesses II A long-lived ruler of New Kingdom Egypt (r. 1290–1224 B.C.E.). He reached an accommodation with the Hittites of Anatolia after a standoff in battle at Kadesh in Syria. He built on a grand scale throughout Egypt. (p. 60)

Rashid al-Din (d. 1318) Adviser to the Il-khan ruler Ghazan, who converted to Islam on Rashid's advice. (p. 296)

recaptives Africans rescued by Britain's Royal Navy from the illegal slave trade of the nineteenth century and restored to free status. (p. 555)

reconquest of Iberia Beginning in the eleventh century, military campaigns by various Iberian Christian states to recapture territory taken by Muslims. In 1492 the last Muslim ruler was defeated, and Spain and Portugal emerged as united kingdoms. (p. 350)

Renaissance (European) A period of intense artistic and intellectual activity, said to be a "rebirth" of Greco-Roman culture. Usually divided into an Italian Renaissance, from roughly the mid-fourteenth to mid-fifteenth century, and a Northern Renaissance, from roughly the early fifteenth to early seventeenth century. (pp. 344, 385)

Revolutions of 1848 Democratic and nationalist revolutions that swept across Europe. In France the monarchy was overthrown. In Germany, Austria, Italy, and Hungary the revolutions failed. (p. 493)

Romanization The process by which the Latin language and Roman culture became dominant in the western provinces of the Roman Empire. The Roman government did not actively seek to Romanize the subject peoples, but indigenous peoples in the provinces often chose to Romanize because of the political and economic advantages that it brought, as well as the allure of Roman success. (p. 145)

Roman Principate A term used to characterize Roman government in the first three centuries C.E., based on the ambiguous title *princeps* ("first citizen") adopted by Augustus to conceal his military dictatorship. (p. 142)

Roman Republic The period from 507 to 31 B.C.E., during which Rome was largely governed by the aristocratic Roman Senate. (p. 137)

Roman Senate A council whose members were the heads of wealthy, landowning families. Originally an advisory body to the early kings, in the era of the Roman Republic the Senate effectively governed the Roman state and the growing empire. Under Senate leadership, Rome conquered an empire of unprecedented extent in the lands surrounding the Mediterranean Sea. In the first century B.C.E. quarrels among powerful and ambitious senators and failure to address social and economic problems led to civil wars and the emergence of the rule of the emperors. (p. 137)

Royal African Company Trading company chartered by the English government to conduct its merchants' trade in the Americas and Africa. (p. 424)

sacrifice A gift given to a deity, often with the aim of creating a relationship, gaining favor, and obligating the god to provide some benefit to the sacrificer, sometimes in order to sustain the deity and thereby guarantee the continuing vitality of the natural world. The object devoted to the deity could be as simple as a cup of wine poured on the ground, a live animal slain on the altar, or, in the most extreme case, the ritual killing of a human being. (p. 95)

Saddam Husayn President of Iraq from 1979 until overthrown by the American invasion in 2003. Waged war on Iran from 1980 to 1988. His invasion of Kuwait was repulsed in the Persian Gulf War of 1991. (p. 724)

Safavid Empire Iranian kingdom (1502–1722) established by Ismail Safavi, who declared Iran a Shi'ite state. (p. 442)

Sahel Belt south of the Sahara; literally "the coast" in Arabic. (p. 200)

Salvador Allende Socialist president of Chile elected in 1970 and overthrown and killed by the military in 1973. (p. 718)

samurai Literally, "those who serve"; the hereditary military elite of the Tokugawa Shogunate. (p. 456)

Sandinistas Members of a leftist coalition that overthrew the Nicaraguan dictator Anastasio Somoza in 1979 and attempted to install a socialist economy. The United States financed an armed uprising against the Sandinista government. In 1990 the Sandinistas lost power after a national election. (p. 718)

Sasanid Empire Iranian empire, established ca. 224, with a capital in Ctesiphon, Mesopotamia. The Sasanid emperors established Zoroastrianism as the state religion. Islamic Arab armies overthrew the empire ca. 640. (p. 191)

satrap The governor of a province in the Achaemenid Persian Empire, often a relative of the king. He was responsible for protection of the province and for forwarding tribute to the central administration. Satraps in outlying provinces enjoyed considerable autonomy. (p. 89)

savanna Tropical or subtropical grassland, either treeless or with occasional clumps of trees. Most extensive in sub-Saharan Africa but also present in South America. (p. 201)

Savorgnan de Brazza (1852–1905) Franco-Italian explorer sent by the French government to claim part of equatorial Africa for France. Founded Brazzaville, capital of the French Congo, in 1880. (p. 609)

schism A formal split within a religious community. (p. 236)

scholasticism A philosophical and theological system, associated with Thomas Aquinas, that was devised to reconcile Aristotelian philosophy and Roman Catholic theology in the thirteenth century. (p. 345)

Scientific Revolution The intellectual movement in Europe, initially associated with planetary motion and other aspects of physics, that by the seventeenth century had laid the groundwork for modern science. (p. 391)

"scramble" for Africa Sudden wave of conquests in Africa by European powers in the 1880s and 1890s. Britain obtained most of eastern Africa, France most of northwestern Africa. Other countries (Germany, Belgium, Portugal, Italy, and Spain) acquired lesser amounts. (p. 607)

scribe In the governments of many ancient societies, a professional position reserved for men who had undergone the lengthy training required to be able to read and write using cuneiforms, hieroglyphics, or other early, cumbersome writing systems. (p. 18)

seasoning An often difficult period of adjustment to new climates, disease environments, and work routines, such as that experienced by slaves newly arrived in the Americas. (p. 422)

Semitic Family of related languages long spoken across parts of western Asia and northern Africa. In antiquity these languages included Hebrew, Aramaic, and Phoenician. The most widespread modern members of the Semitic family are Arabic and Hebrew. (p. 14)

G-14   Glossary

"separate spheres" Nineteenth-century idea in Western societies that men and women, especially of the middle class, should have clearly differentiated roles in society: women as wives, mothers, and homemakers; men as breadwinners and participants in business and politics.   (p. 581)

sepoy A soldier in South Asia, especially in the service of the British.   (p. 556)

Sepoy Rebellion The revolt of Indian soldiers in 1857 against certain practices that violated religious customs; also known as the Sepoy Mutiny.   (p. 559)

Serbia The Ottoman province in the Balkans that rose up against Janissary control in the early 1800s.   (p. 529)

serf In medieval Europe, an agricultural laborer legally bound to a lord's property and obligated to perform set services for the lord. In Russia some serfs worked as artisans and in factories; serfdom was not abolished there until 1861.   (pp. 242, 471)

shaft graves A term used for the burial sites of elite members of Mycenaean Greek society in the mid-second millennium B.C.E. At the bottom of deep shafts lined with stone slabs, the bodies were laid out along with gold and bronze jewelry, implements, weapons, and masks.   (p. 62)

Shah Abbas I (r. 1587–1629) The fifth and most renowned ruler of the Safavid dynasty in Iran. Abbas moved the royal capital to Isfahan in 1598.   (p. 443)

shamanism The practice of identifying special individuals (shamans) who will interact with spirits for the benefit of the community. Characteristic of the Korean kingdoms of the early medieval period and of early societies of Central Asia.   (p. 277)

Shang The dominant people in the earliest Chinese dynasty for which we have written records (ca. 1750–1027 B.C.E.). Ancestor worship, divination by means of oracle bones, and the use of bronze vessels for ritual purposes were major elements of Shang culture.   (p. 38)

Shi Huangdi Founder of the short-lived Qin dynasty and creator of the first Chinese Empire (r. 221–210 B.C.E.). He is remembered for his ruthless conquests of rival states, standardization of practices, and forcible organization of labor for military and engineering works. His tomb, with its army of life-size terracotta soldiers, has been partially excavated.   (p. 151)

Shi'ites Muslims belonging to the branch of Islam that believes that God vests leadership of the community in a descendant of Muhammad's son-in-law Ali. Shi'ism is the state religion of Iran.   (pp. 217, 442)

Siberia The extreme northeastern sector of Asia, including the Kamchatka Peninsula and the present Russian coast of the Arctic Ocean, the Bering Strait, and the Sea of Okhotsk.   (p. 468)

Silk Road Caravan routes connecting China and the Middle East across Central Asia and Iran.   (p. 187)

Simón Bolívar (1783–1830) The most important military leader in the struggle for independence in South America. Born in Venezuela, he led military forces there and in Colombia, Ecuador, Peru, and Bolivia.   (p. 495)

Slavophiles Russian intellectuals in the early nineteenth century who favored resisting western European influences and taking pride in the traditional peasant values and institutions of the Slavic people.   (p. 537)

"small traditions" Anthropologists' term for a localized, usually nonliterate, set of customs and beliefs adhered to by a single society, often in conjunction with a "great tradition."   (p. 201)

socialism A political ideology that originated in Europe in the 1830s. Socialists advocated government protection of workers from exploitation by property owners and government

ownership of industries. This ideology led to the founding of socialist or labor parties throughout Europe in the second half of the nineteenth century.   (p. 583)

Socrates Athenian philosopher (ca. 470–399 B.C.E.) who shifted the emphasis of philosophical investigation from questions of natural science to ethics and human behavior. He attracted young disciples from elite families but made enemies by revealing the ignorance and pretensions of others, culminating in his trial and execution by the Athenian state.   (p. 101)

Sokoto Caliphate A large Muslim state founded in 1809 in what is now northern Nigeria.   (p. 551)

Solidarity Polish trade union created in 1980 to protest working conditions and political repression. It began the nationalist opposition to communist rule that led in 1989 to the fall of communism in eastern Europe.   (p. 726)

Song Empire Empire in central and southern China (960–1126) while the Liao people controlled the north. Empire in southern China (1127–1279; the "Southern Song") while the Jin people controlled the north. Distinguished for its advances in technology, medicine, astronomy, and mathematics.   (p. 271)

Srivijaya A state based on the Indonesian island of Sumatra, between the seventh and eleventh centuries C.E. It amassed wealth and power by a combination of selective adaptation of Indian technologies and concepts, control of the lucrative trade routes between India and China, and skillful showmanship and diplomacy in holding together a disparate realm of inland and coastal territories.   (p. 130)

Stalingrad City in Russia, site of a Red Army victory over the German army in 1942–1943. The Battle of Stalingrad was the turning point in the war between Germany and the Soviet Union. Today it is known as Volgograd.   (p. 665)

steam engine A machine that turns the energy released by burning fuel into motion. Thomas Newcomen built the first crude but workable steam engine in 1712. James Watt vastly improved his device in the 1760s and 1770s. Steam power was later applied to moving machinery in factories and to powering ships and locomotives.   (p. 512)

steel A form of iron that is both durable and flexible. It was first mass-produced in the 1860s and quickly became the most widely used metal in construction, machinery, and railroad equipment.   (p. 577)

stirrup Device for securing a horseman's feet, enabling him to wield weapons more effectively. First evidence of the use of stirrups was among the Kushan people of northern Afghanistan in approximately the first century C.E.   (p. 192)

stock exchange A place where shares in a company or business enterprise are bought and sold.   (p. 395)

Stone Age The historical period characterized by the production of tools from stone and other nonmetallic substances. It was followed in some places by the Bronze Age and more generally by the Iron Age.   (p. 6)

submarine telegraph cables Insulated copper cables laid along the bottom of a sea or ocean for telegraphic communication. The first short cable was laid across the English Channel in 1851; the first successful transatlantic cable was laid in 1866.   (p. 577)

sub-Saharan Africa Portion of the African continent lying south of the Sahara.   (p. 200)

Suez Canal Ship canal dug across the Isthmus of Suez in Egypt, designed by Ferdinand de Lesseps. It opened to shipping in 1869 and shortened the sea voyage between Europe and Asia. Its strategic importance led to the British conquest of Egypt in 1882.   (p. 600)

Suleiman the Magnificent (1494–1566) The most illustrious sultan of the Ottoman Empire (r. 1520–1566); also known as Suleiman Kanuni, "The Lawgiver." He significantly expanded the empire in the Balkans and eastern Mediterranean. (p. 436)

Sumerians The people who dominated southern Mesopotamia through the end of the third millennium B.C.E. They were responsible for the creation of many fundamental elements of Mesopotamian culture—such as irrigation technology, cuneiform writing, and religious conceptions—later adopted by their Semitic successors. (p. 14)

Sunnis Muslims belonging to the branch of Islam that believes that the community should select its own leadership. The majority religion in most Islamic countries. (p. 218)

Sun Yat-sen (1867–1925) Chinese nationalist revolutionary, founder and leader of the Guomindang until his death. He attempted to create a liberal democratic political movement in China but was thwarted by military leaders. (p. 639)

Swahili Bantu language with Arabic loanwords spoken in coastal regions of East Africa. (p. 451)

Swahili Coast East African shores of the Indian Ocean between the Horn of Africa and the Zambezi River; from the Arabic *sawahil*, meaning "shores." (p. 323)

Taiping Rebellion (1850–1864) A Christian-inspired rural rebellion that threatened to topple the Qing Empire. It was the most destructive civil war before the twentieth century. (p. 543)

Tamil kingdoms The kingdoms of southern India, inhabited primarily by speakers of Dravidian languages, which developed in partial isolation, and somewhat differently, from the Aryan north. They produced epics, poetry, and performance arts. Elements of Tamil religious beliefs were merged into the Hindu synthesis. (p. 124)

Tang Empire Empire unifying China and part of Central Asia, founded 618 and ended 907. The Tang emperors presided over a magnificent court at their capital, Chang'an. (p. 262)

Tanzimat "Restructuring" reforms by the nineteenth-century Ottoman rulers intended to move civil law away from the control of religious elites and make the military and the bureaucracy more efficient. (p. 531)

Tenochtitlan Capital of the Aztec Empire, located on an island in Lake Texcoco. Its population was about 150,000 on the eve of Spanish conquest. Mexico City was constructed on its ruins. (p. 174)

Teotihuacan A powerful city-state in central Mexico (100 B.C.E.–750 C.E.). Its population was about 150,000 at its peak in 600. (p. 168)

terrorism Political belief that extreme and seemingly random violence will destabilize a government and permit the terrorists to gain political advantage. Though an old technique, terrorism gained prominence in the late twentieth century with the growth of worldwide mass media that, through their news coverage, amplified public fears of terrorist acts. (p. 750)

theater-state Historians' term for a state that acquires prestige and power by developing attractive cultural forms and staging elaborate public ceremonies (as well as redistributing valuable resources) to attract and bind subjects to the center. The Gupta Empire is an example of such a state. (p. 126)

Thebes Capital city of Egypt and home of the ruling dynasties during the Middle and New Kingdoms. Amon, patron deity of Thebes, became one of the chief gods of Egypt. Monarchs were buried across the river in the Valley of the Kings. (p. 26)

Theravada Buddhism "Way of the Elders" branch of Buddhism followed in Sri Lanka and much of Southeast Asia. Theravada remains close to the original principles set forth by the Buddha; it downplays the importance of gods and emphasizes austerity and the individual's search for enlightenment. (p. 120)

third-century crisis Historians' term for the political, military, and economic turmoil that beset the Roman Empire during much of the third century C.E.: frequent changes of ruler, civil wars, barbarian invasions, decline of urban centers, and near-destruction of long-distance commerce and the monetary economy. After 284 C.E. Diocletian restored order by making fundamental changes. (p. 147)

Third World Term applied to developing countries who professed nonalignment during the Cold War. (p. 709)

Thomas Edison (1847–1931) American inventor best known for inventing the electric light bulb, acoustic recording on wax cylinders, and motion pictures. (p. 578)

Thomas Malthus (1766–1834) Eighteenth-century English intellectual who warned that population growth threatened future generations because, in his view, population growth would always outstrip increases in agricultural production. (p. 736)

three-field system A rotational system for agriculture in which one field grows wheat or barley, one grows oats or legumes, and one lies fallow. It gradually replaced the two-field system in medieval Europe. (p. 334)

Tibet Country centered on the high, mountain-bounded plateau north of India. Tibetan political power occasionally extended farther to the north and west between the seventh and thirteenth centuries. (p. 268)

Timbuktu City on the Niger River. It was founded by the Tuareg as a seasonal camp sometime after 1000. As part of the Mali empire, Timbuktu became a major terminus of the trans-Saharan trade and a center of Islamic learning. (p. 328)

Timur (1336–1405) Member of a prominent family of the Mongols' Jagadai Khanate, Timur conquered much of Central Asia and Iran. He consolidated the status of Sunni Islam as the orthodox religion, and his descendants, the Timurids, maintained his empire for nearly a century and founded the Mughal Empire in India. (p. 295)

Tiwanaku Name of capital city and empire centered on the region near Lake Titicaca in modern Bolivia (500–1000 C.E.). (p. 180)

Tokugawa Shogunate (1603–1868) The last of the three shogunates of Japan. (p. 458)

Toltecs Powerful postclassic empire in central Mexico (900–1156) that influenced much of Mesoamerica. Aztecs claimed ties to this earlier civilization. (p. 173)

Toussaint L'Ouverture (1743–1803) Leader of the Haitian Revolution. He freed the slaves and gained effective independence for Haiti despite military interventions by the British and French. (p. 494)

trans-Saharan caravan routes Trading network linking North Africa with sub-Saharan Africa across the Sahara. (p. 197)

Treaty of Nanking (1842) The treaty that concluded the Opium War. It awarded Britain a large indemnity from the Qing Empire, denied the Qing government tariff control over some of its own borders, opened additional ports of residence to Britons, and ceded the island of Hong Kong to Britain. (p. 542)

Treaty of Versailles (1919) The treaty imposed on Germany by France, Great Britain, the United States, and other Allied Powers after World War I. It demanded that Germany dismantle its military and give up some lands to Poland. It was resented by many Germans. (p. 637)

treaty ports Cities opened to foreign residents as a result of the forced treaties between the Qing Empire and foreign signatories. In the treaty ports, foreigners enjoyed extraterritoriality. (p. 542)

tributary system A system in which, from the time of the Han Empire, countries in East and Southeast Asia not under the direct control of empires based in China nevertheless enrolled as tributary states, acknowledging the superiority of the emperors in China in exchange for trading rights or strategic alliances. (p. 264)

tribute system A system in which defeated peoples were forced to pay a tax in the form of goods and labor. This forced transfer of food, cloth, and other goods subsidized the development of large cities. An important component of the Aztec and Inca economies. (p. 174)

trireme Greek and Phoenician warship of the fifth and fourth centuries B.C.E. It was sleek and light, powered by 170 oars arranged in three vertical tiers. Manned by skilled sailors, it was capable of short bursts of speed and complex maneuvers. (p. 100)

tropical rain forest High-precipitation forest zones of the Americas, Africa, and Asia lying between the Tropic of Cancer and the Tropic of Capricorn. (p. 201)

tropics Equatorial region between the Tropic of Cancer and the Tropic of Capricorn. It is characterized by generally warm or hot temperatures year-round, though much variation exists due to altitude and other factors. Temperate zones north and south of the tropics usually have a winter season. (p. 313)

Truman Doctrine Foreign policy initiated by U.S. president Harry Truman in 1947. It offered military aid to help Turkey and Greece resist Soviet military pressure and subversion. (p. 706)

tsar (czar) From Latin *caesar*, this Russian title for a monarch was first used in reference to a Russian ruler by Ivan III (r. 1462–1505). (pp. 299, 468)

Tulip Period (1718–1730) Last years of the reign of Ottoman sultan Ahmed III, during which European styles and attitudes became briefly popular in Istanbul. (p. 441)

tyrant The term the Greeks used to describe someone who seized and held power in violation of the normal procedures and traditions of the community. Tyrants appeared in many Greek city-states in the seventh and sixth centuries B.C.E., often taking advantage of the disaffection of the emerging middle class and, by weakening the old elite, unwittingly contributing to the evolution of democracy. (p. 94)

Uighurs A group of Turkic-speakers who controlled their own centralized empire from 744 to 840 in Mongolia and Central Asia. (p. 267)

ulama Muslim religious scholars. From the ninth century onward, the primary interpreters of Islamic law and the social core of Muslim urban societies. (p. 224)

Umayyad Caliphate First hereditary dynasty of Muslim caliphs (661 to 750). From their capital at Damascus, the Umayyads ruled an empire that extended from Spain to India. Overthrown by the Abbasid Caliphate. (p. 218)

umma The community of all Muslims. A major innovation against the background of seventh-century Arabia, where traditionally kinship rather than faith had determined membership in a community. (p. 216)

United Nations International organization founded in 1945 to promote world peace and cooperation. It replaced the League of Nations. (p. 703)

Universal Declaration of Human Rights A 1948 United Nations covenant binding signatory nations to the observance of specified rights. (p. 755)

universities Degree-granting institutions of higher learning. Those that appeared in the Latin West from about 1200 onward became the model of all modern universities. (p. 344)

Ural Mountains This north-south range separates Siberia from the rest of Russia. It is commonly considered the boundary between the continents of Europe and Asia. (p. 468)

Urdu A Persian-influenced form of Hindi written in Arabic characters and used as a literary language since the 1300s. (p. 328)

Usama bin Laden Saudi-born Muslim extremist who founded the al-Qaeda organization that was responsible for several terrorist attacks, including those on the World Trade Center and the Pentagon in 2001. (p. 751)

utopian socialism A philosophy introduced by the Frenchman Charles Fourier in the early nineteenth century. Utopian socialists hoped to create humane alternatives to industrial capitalism by building self-sustaining communities whose inhabitants would work cooperatively. (p. 520)

varna/jati Two categories of social identity of great importance in Indian history. *Varna* are the four major social divisions: the *Brahmin* priest class, the *Kshatriya* warrior/administrator class, the *Vaishya* merchant/farmer class, and the *Shudra* laborer class. Within the system *varna* are many jati, regional groups of people who have a common occupational sphere, and who marry, eat, and generally interact with other members of their group. (p. 118)

Vasco da Gama (1467–1524) Portuguese explorer. In 1497–1498 he led the first naval expedition from Europe to sail to India, opening an important commercial sea route. (p. 362)

vassal In medieval Europe, a sworn supporter of a king or lord committed to rendering specified military service to that king or lord. (p. 245)

Vedas Early Indian sacred "knowledge"—the literal meaning of the term—long preserved and communicated orally by Brahmin priests and eventually written down. These religious texts, including the thousand poetic hymns to various deities contained in the Rig Veda, are our main source of information about the Vedic period (ca. 1500–500 B.C.E.). (p. 116)

Versailles The huge palace built for French King Louis XIV west of Paris. The palace symbolized the preeminence of French power and architecture in Europe and the triumph of royal authority over the French nobility. (p. 402)

Victorian Age The reign of Queen Victoria of Great Britain (r. 1837–1901). The term is also used to describe late-nineteenth-century society, with its rigid moral standards and sharply differentiated roles for men and women and for middle-class and working-class people. (p. 580)

Vietnam War (1954–1975) Conflict pitting North Vietnam and South Vietnamese communist guerrillas against the South Vietnamese government, aided after 1961 by the United States. (p. 711)

Vladimir Lenin (1870–1924) Leader of the Bolshevik (later Communist) Party. He lived in exile in Switzerland until 1917, then returned to Russia to lead the Bolsheviks to victory during the Russian Revolution and the civil war that followed. (p. 634)

Wari Andean civilization culturally linked to Tiwanaku, perhaps beginning as a colony of Tiwanaku. (p. 180)

Warsaw Pact The 1955 treaty binding the Soviet Union and countries of eastern Europe in an alliance against the North Atlantic Treaty Organization. (p. 706)

water wheel A mechanism that harnesses the energy in flowing water to grind grain or to power machinery. It was used in many parts of the world but was especially common in Europe from 1200 to 1900. (p. 337)

Western Front A line of trenches and fortifications in World War I that stretched without a break from Switzerland to the North Sea. Scene of most of the fighting between Germany, on the one hand, and France and Britain, on the other. (p. 631)

witch-hunt The pursuit of people suspected of witchcraft, especially in northern Europe in the late sixteenth and seventeenth centuries.   (p. 389)

Women's Rights Convention An 1848 gathering of women angered by their exclusion from an international antislavery meeting. They met at Seneca Falls, New York, to discuss women's rights.   (p. 501)

Woodrow Wilson (1856–1924) President of the United States (1913–1921) and the leading figure at the Paris Peace Conference of 1919. He was unable to persuade the U.S. Congress to ratify the Treaty of Versailles or join the League of Nations.   (p. 635)

World Bank A specialized agency of the United Nations that makes loans to countries for economic development, trade promotion, and debt consolidation. Its formal name is the International Bank for Reconstruction and Development.   (p. 704)

World Trade Organization (WTO) An international body established in 1995 to foster and bring order to international trade.   (p. 733)

Xiongnu A confederation of nomadic peoples living beyond the northwest frontier of ancient China. Chinese rulers tried a variety of defenses and stratagems to ward off these "barbarians," as they called them, and finally succeeded in dispersing the Xiongnu in the first century C.E.   (p. 156)

Yamagata Aritomo (1838–1922) One of the leaders of the Meiji Restoration.   (p. 595)

Yi (1392–1910) The Yi dynasty ruled Korea after the fall of the Koryo kingdom.   (p. 306)

yin/yang In Chinese belief, complementary factors that help to maintain the equilibrium of the world. Yin is associated with feminine, dark, and passive qualities; yang with masculine, light, and active qualities.   (p. 44)

Yongle Reign of Zhu Di (1360–1424), the third emperor of the Ming Empire (r. 1403–1424). He sponsored further work on the Forbidden City, the expeditions of Zheng He, and the reopening of China's borders to trade and travel.   (p. 304)

Young Ottomans Movement of young intellectuals to institute liberal reforms and build a feeling of national identity in the Ottoman Empire in the second half of the nineteenth century.   (p. 535)

Yuan Empire (1271–1368) Empire created in China and Siberia by Khubilai Khan.   (p. 293)

Yuan Shikai (1859–1916) Chinese general and first president of the Chinese Republic (1912–1916). He stood in the way of the democratic movement led by Sun Yat-sen.   (p. 639)

Zen The Japanese word for a branch of Mahayana Buddhism based on highly disciplined meditation. It is known in Sanskrit as *dhyana*, in Chinese as *chan*, and in Korean as *son*.   (p. 273)

Zheng He (1371–1433) An imperial eunuch and Muslim who was entrusted by the Ming emperor Yongle with a series of state voyages that took his ships through the Indian Ocean, from Southeast Asia to Africa.   (pp. 304, 357)

Zhou The people and dynasty that took over the dominant position in north China from the Shang and created the concept of the Mandate of Heaven to justify their rule. The Zhou era, particularly the vigorous early period (1027–771 B.C.E.), was remembered in Chinese tradition as a time of prosperity and benevolent rule. In the later Zhou period (771–221 B.C.E.), centralized control broke down, and warfare among many small states became frequent.   (p. 39)

ziggurat A massive pyramidal stepped tower made of mud bricks. It is associated with religious complexes in ancient Mesopotamian cities, but its function is unknown.   (p. 20)

Zoroastrianism A religion originating in ancient Iran with the prophet Zoroaster. It centered on a single benevolent deity—Ahuramazda—who engaged in a twelve-thousand-year struggle with demonic forces before prevailing and restoring a pristine world. Emphasizing truth-telling, purity, and reverence for nature, the religion demanded that humans choose sides in the struggle between good and evil. Those whose good conduct indicated their support for Ahuramazda would be rewarded in the afterlife. Others would be punished. The religion of the Achaemenid Persians, Zoroastrianism may have spread within their realms and influenced Judaism, Christianity, and other faiths.   (p. 91)

Zulu A people of modern South Africa whom King Shaka united in 1818.   (p. 551)

NOTES

Chapter 1

1. N. K. Sandars, *The Epic of Gilgamesh* (Baltimore: Penguin Books, 1960), 61–63.
2. Colin McEvedy and Richard Jones, *Atlas of World Population History* (New York: Penguin Books, 1978), 13–15.
3. Colin Renfrew, *Archaeology and Language: The Puzzle of Indo-European Origins* (Cambridge: Cambridge University Press, 1988), 125, 150.
4. Luigi Cavalli-Sforza, L. Luca, Paolo Menozzi, and Alberto Piazza, *The History and Geography of Human Genes* (Princeton, NJ: Princeton University Press, 1994).
5. James Mellaart, *Çatal Hüyük: A Neolithic Town in Anatolia* (New York: McGraw-Hill, 1967), 202.

Chapter 2

1. Quoted in Miriam Lichtheim, ed., *Ancient Egyptian Literature: A Book of Readings* (Berkeley: University of California Press, 1978).

Chapter 3

1. Plutarch, *Moralia,* 799 D, trans. B. H. Warmington, *Carthage* (Harmondsworth, England: Penguin 1960), 163.

Chapter 4

1. Quoted in Roland G. Kent, *Old Persian: Grammar, Texts, Lexicon,* 2nd ed. (New Haven, CT: American Oriental Society, 1953), 138, 140.
2. Richmond Lattimore, *Greek Lyrics,* 2nd ed. (Chicago: University of Chicago Press, 1960), 2.
3. G. S. Kirk and J. E. Raven, *The Presocratic Philosophers: A Critical History with a Selection of Texts* (Cambridge, England: Cambridge University Press, 1957), 169.
4. Herodotus, *The History,* trans. David Grene (Chicago: University of Chicago Press, 1988), 33 (Herodotus 1.1).
5. Plutarch, *Pericles* 12, trans. Ian Scott-Kilvert, *The Rise and Fall of Athens: Nine Greek Lives by Plutarch* (Harmondsworth: Penguin Books, 1960), 178.

Chapter 5

1. Barbara Stoler Miller, *The Bhagavad-Gita: Krishna's Counsel in Time of War* (New York: Bantam, 1986), 98–99.
2. B. G. Gokhale, *Asoka Maurya* (New York: Twayne, 1966), 152–153, 156–157, 160.
3. James Legge, *The Travels of Fa-hien: Fa-hien's Record of Buddhistic Kingdoms* (Delhi: Oriental Publishers, 1971), 77–79.

Chapter 6

1. Patricia Buckley Ebrey, ed., *Chinese Civilization and Society: A Sourcebook* (New York: Free Press, 1981), 33–34.

Chapter 7

1. Before 1492, the inhabitants of the Western Hemisphere had no single name for themselves, no sense that physical similarities created a shared identity. Identity derived from kin groups, language, cultural practices, and political structures. Conquest and the occupation by Europeans after 1492 imposed on America's original inhabitants a racial consciousness and racial identity. All collective terms for these first American peoples reflect this history. *Indians, Native Americans, Amerindians, First Peoples,* and *Indigenous Peoples* find common usage. This book uses the names of individual cultures and states wherever possible. It tries to reserve *Amerindian* and other terms that suggest transcultural identity and experience for the period after 1492.
2. From the Florentine Codex, quoted in Inga Clendinnen, *Aztecs* (Cambridge: Cambridge University Press, 1991), 213.
3. Quoted in Nigel Davies, *The Toltec Heritage: From the Fall of Tula to the Rise of Tenochtitlan* (Norman: University of Oklahoma Press, 1980), 3.
4. Bernal Díaz del Castillo, *The Conquest of New Spain,* trans. J. M. Cohen (London: Penguin Books, 1963), 217.
5. Hernando Cortés, *Five Letters, 1519–1526,* trans. J. Bayard Morris (New York: Norton, 1991), 87
6. Quoted in Irene Silverblatt, *Moon, Sun, and Witches: Gender Ideologies and Class in Inca and Colonial Peru* (Princeton, NJ: Princeton University Press, 1987), 10.

Chapter 8

1. Victor H. Mair, ed., *The Columbia Anthology of Traditional Chinese Literature* (New York: Columbia University Press, 1994), 485; translated by Victor H. Mair.

Issues in World History: Oral Societies and the Consequences of Literacy

1. D. T. Niane, *Sundiata: An Epic of Old Mali* (Harlow, U.K.: Longman, 1986), 41.

Chapter 9

1. Quran. Sura 96, verses 1–5.
2. Quran. Sura 92, verses 1–10.
3. Richard W. Bulliet, *Islam: The View from the Edge* (New York: Columbia University Press, 1994), 87.
4. Abu Najib al-Suhrawardi, *A Sufi Rule for Novices,* trans. Menahem Milson (Cambridge, MA: Harvard University Press, 1975), 45–58.
5. Ibid., 73–82.

Chapter 10

1. A. A. Vasiliev, *History of the Byzantine Empire, 324–1453,* vol. 1 (Madison: University of Wisconsin Press, 1978), 79–80.
2. Ibid., 71.
3. A. P. Kazhdan and Ann Wharton Epstein, *Change in Byzantine Culture in the Eleventh and Twelfth Centuries* (Berkeley: University of California Press, 1985), 71.
4. Ibid., 248.
5. Ibid., 255.

6. R. W. Southern, *Western Society and the Church in the Middle Ages* (Harmondsworth, England: Penguin, 1970), 102.

7. S. A. Zenkovsky, ed., *Medieval Russia's Epics, Chronicles, and Tales* (New York: New American Library, 1974), 67.

Chapter 11

1. *Master Tung's Western Chamber Romance,* trans. Li-li Ch'en (New York: Columbia University Press, 1994), 22, 42–43, 45–46.

2. Arthur Waley, *Poetry and Career of Li Po* (London: Unwin Hyman, 1954), 35.

3. Theodore de Bary, ed., *Sources of Chinese Tradition,* vol. 1, 2nd ed. (New York: Columbia University Press, 1999), 584.

4. Quoted in David Lattimore, "Allusion in T'ang Poetry," in *Perspectives on the T'ang,* ed. Arthur F. Wright and David Twitchett (New Haven, CT: Yale University Press, 1973), 436.

5. Quoted at "Women's Early Music, Art, Poetry," http://music.acu.edu/www/iawm/pages/reference/tzusongs.html.

6. Quoted in Ivan Morris, *The World of the Shining Prince: Court Life in Ancient Japan* (New York: Penguin Books, 1979), 221–222.

7. Quoted in Ivan Morris, trans., *The Pillow Book of Sei Shonagon* (New York: Columbia University Press, 1967), 1.

Chapter 12

1. Quotation adapted from Desmond Martin, *Chingis Khan and His Conquest of North China* (Baltimore: Johns Hopkins Press, 1950), 303.

Chapter 13

1. Tarikh-i-Wassaf, in Henry M. Elliot, *The History of India as Told by Its Own Historians,* ed. John Dowson (London: Trübner and Co., 1869–1871), 2:28.

2. Hasan Nizami, Taju-l Ma-asir, in ibid., 2:219.

3. Minhaju-s Siraj, Tabakat-i Nasiri, in ibid., 2:332–333.

Chapter 14

1. Quoted in Marina Warner, *Alone of All Her Sex: The Myth and Cult of the Virgin Mary* (New York: Random House, 1983), 179.

2. Harry Miskimin, *The Economy of the Early Renaissance, 1300–1460* (Englewood Cliffs, NJ: Prentice Hall, 1969), 26–27.

3. Quotations here and later in the chapter are from Geoffrey Chaucer, *The Canterbury Tales,* trans. Nevill Coghill (New York: Penguin Books, 1952), 25, 29, 32.

Chapter 15

1. Ma Huan, *Ying-yai Sheng-lan: "The Overall Survey of the Ocean's Shores,"* ed. Feng Ch'eng-Chün, trans. J. V. G. Mills (Cambridge, England: Cambridge University Press, 1970), 180.

2. Alvise da Cadamosto in *The Voyages of Cadamosto and Other Documents,* ed. and trans. G. R. Crone (London: Hakluyt Society, 1937), 2.

3. Quoted in Alfred W. Crosby, Jr., *The Columbian Exchange: Biological and Cultural Consequences of 1492* (Westport, CT: Greenwood, 1972), 58.